FAMILY LAW

TITLES IN THE DELMAR LCP SERIES

Ransford C. Pyle, *Foundations of Law for Paralegals: Cases, Commentary, and Ethics,* 1992.

Peggy N. Kerley, Paul A. Sukys, Joanne Banker Hames, *Civil Litigation for the Paralegal,* 1992.

Jonathan Lynton, Donna Masinter, Terri Mick Lyndall, *Law Office Management for Paralegals,* 1992.

Daniel Hall, *Criminal Law and Procedure,* 1992.

Daniel Hall, *Survey of Criminal Law,* 1993.

Jonathan Lynton, Terri Mick Lyndall, *Legal Ethics and Professional Responsibility,* 1994.

Michael Kearns, *The Law of Real Property,* 1994.

Angela Schneeman, *The Law of Corporations, Partnerships, and Sole Proprietorships,* 1993.

William Buckley, *Torts and Personal Injury Law,* 1993.

Gordon Brown, *Administration of Wills, Trusts, and Estates,* 1993.

Richard Stim, *Intellectual Property: Patents, Copyrights, and Trademarks,* 1994.

Ransford C. Pyle, *Family Law,* 1994.

Daniel Hall, *Administrative Law,* 1994.

Jonathan Lynton, *Ballentine's Thesaurus for Legal Research and Writing,* 1994.

Jack Handler, *Ballentine's Law Dictionary: Legal Assistant Edition,* 1994.

Angela Schneeman, *Paralegals in American Law,* 1994.

FAMILY LAW

Ransford C. Pyle

Lawyers Cooperative Publishing

Delmar
Publishers Inc.

The uniform state acts which appear in this text have been reprinted through the permission of the National Conference of Commissioners on Uniform State Laws. Copies of each act may be ordered from them at a nominal cost. They can be reached at 676 North St. Clair Street, Suite 1700, Chicago, Illinois 60611, (312) 915-0195.

Cover design by John Orozco
Cover photos: John Christopher Musco, Studio 59; Michael Upright; and
  Courtesy of Petit Format/Nestle/Photo Researchers, Inc.

Delmar Staff:

Adminstrative Editor: Jay Whitney
Developmental Editor: Christopher Anzalone
Project Editor: Andrea Edwards Myers
Production Coordinator: James Zayicek
Art & Design Coordinator: Karen Kunz Kemp

For information, address

Delmar Publishers Inc.
3 Columbia Circle
P.O. Box 15015
Albany, New York 12212-5015

COPYRIGHT © 1994 BY DELMAR PUBLISHERS INC., AND
LAWYERS COOPERATIVE PUBLISHING
A DIVISION OF THOMSON LEGAL PUBLISHING INC.

Printed in the United States of America

1 2 3 4 5 6 7 8 9 10 XXX 00 99 98 97 96 95 94

Library of Congress Cataloging-in-Publication Data

Pyle, Ransford Comstock, 1936-
    Family law / Ransford C. Pyle. — 1st ed.
      p.   cm. — (Delmar paralegal series)
    Includes index.
    ISBN 0-8273-5479-7
      1. Domestic relations—United States.   2. Legal assistants—United States—
Handbooks, manuals, etc.   I. Title.   II. Series.
KF505.P95 1994
346.7301'5—dc20
[347.30615]   93-25985
                                                           CIP

CONTENTS

Preface / xv

Acknowledgments / xix

Table of Cases / xx

PART ONE   Introduction   1

CHAPTER 1   The Family, the Law, and the Paralegal   2

1.1   Law and the Family / 3
1.2   Family Law Principally Concerned with Divorce / 4
1.3   Marriage as Contract / 5
1.4   Marriage as a Partnership / 9
1.5   Children / 9
1.6   Family Law and the Adversarial Process / 10
       "Good People at their Worst" / 10
1.7   Lawyers and Family Law / 11
1.8   Paralegals and Family Law / 11
       Pretrial Tasks / 12
       Trial Tasks / 15
       Posttrial Tasks / 15
Summary / 15
Appendix 1A   Domestic Relations Questionnaire (Massachusetts) / 17

CHAPTER 2   Ethics and Family Law   22

2.1   Confidentiality / 24
2.2   Conflict of Interest / 24
2.3   Attorneys' Fees / 32
2.4   Communication with the Opposing Side / 33
2.5   Romantic Involvement with Client / 34
2.6   The Unauthorized Practice of Law / 36
Summary / 39

CHAPTER 3   Family Law in Historical Perspective   42

3.1   Family Law: A Never-Ending Story / 43
3.2   The Making of Family Law / 44
3.3   Historical Roots of Family Law / 45
3.4   The Marriage Relationship / 46
3.5   Terminating the Marriage Relationship / 49
3.6   Children / 53
3.7   Rights of Women / 55
3.8   Changing Lifestyles / 57
Summary / 60

CHAPTER 4   Current Issues in Family Law   62

4.1   The Future of the Family and the Future of Family Law / 63
4.2   Incest and Child Abuse / 64
4.3   Mediation / 68
4.4   Marriage Counseling / 71
4.5   Definition of Family / 72
       Who Qualifies as a Parent? / 73
       Will the Real Parent Please Stand Up? / 73
       Right of the Child / 74
       Whose Child Is It Anyway? / 75
4.6   Reproductive Rights / 76
4.7   Private versus Public Control / 77
Summary / 78
Appendix 4A   Uniform Putative and Unknown Fathers Act (1988) / 80

PART TWO   Marriage as Contract   83

CHAPTER 5   Annulment   84

5.1   Annulment Defined / 85
5.2   History / 86
5.3   Annulment and Divorce Distinguished / 86
5.4   Void or Voidable? / 88
       Marriages Generally Considered Void / 88
       Examples of Marriages Merely Voidable / 94
           Fraud with Regard to Essentials of Marriage / 94
           Fraud with Regard to Inability or Unwillingness to Have
           Children / 96
           Fraud on the Court or Legal Process / 99
5.5   Consequences of Annulment / 99
5.6   Defenses / 102
Appendix 5A   Uniform Marriage and Divorce Act (1973) / 104

CHAPTER 6   Antenuptial Contracts   116

6.1   Background / 118
6.2   What Should an Antenuptial Agreement Contain? / 120
6.3   Who Should Have an Antenuptial Agreement? / 123
6.4   The Antenuptial Agreement and the Practitioner / 127
       Fairness and Conscionability / 128
       Disclosure / 131
       Voluntariness and Consent / 134
       Waiver of Rights / 135
6.5   Agreements That Encourage or Promote Divorce / 139
6.6   Support Provisions / 142
Summary / 143
Appendix 6A   Uniform Premarital Agreement Act (1983) / 145
Appendix 6B   Antenuptial Agreement (New York) / 147

CHAPTER 7   Postnuptial and Separation Agreements   152

7.1   Postnuptial Agreements Distinguished from Antenuptial
       Agreements / 153
7.2   Recital of Consideration / 156
7.3   Kinds of Postmarital Agreements / 156
7.4   Separation and Separation Agreements / 157
7.5   Merger and Incorporation: How Does the Agreement Fit
       into the Decree? / 159
7.6   Modification / 166
Summary / 167
Appendix 7A   Financial Statement for Dissolution of Marriage / 170
Appendix 7B   Settlement Agreement (Georgia) / 175

CHAPTER 8   Husband and Wife as Partners   186

8.1   Toward a Partnership Model of Marriage / 187
8.2   Public Policy / 189
8.3   The Duty to Support / 193
8.4   Heartbalm Remedies / 196
       Breach of Promise to Marry / 197
       Seduction / 197
       Criminal Conversation / 198
       Alienation of Affections / 200
8.5   Alternatives to Heartbalm Remedies / 200
8.6   The New Defendant: The Spouse / 203
8.7   The New Plaintiff: The Spouse / 206
8.8   Marriage Partners or Business Partners? / 209
Summary / 214

CHAPTER 9   Cohabitation and Marriage Alternatives   216

9.1   Introduction / 217
9.2   Common Law Marriage / 219
9.3   Conflict of Laws and Common Law Marriage / 221
9.4   Modern Equivalents to Common Law Marriage / 226
9.5   Putative Marriage / 226
9.6   Presumption of Marriage and Marriage by Estoppel / 230
9.7   Cohabitation Agreements / 237
9.8   *Marvin* and Its Progeny / 240
9.9   *Marvin*'s First Cousins / 243
9.10 Lessons from *Marvin* and Its Progeny / 244
Summary / 245

PART THREE   Breaking the Contract   249

CHAPTER 10   Property Settlements   250

10.1   Introduction / 251
10.2   Judicial Discretion / 252
10.3   The Erosion of Judicial Discretion / 255
10.4   No-Fault Divorce / 257
10.5   Community Property States and Common Law
       (or Equitable Distribution) States / 257
10.6   What Is Property and What Is Not Property? / 265
       Husband's versus Wife's Perceptions of Divorce / 266
       Title versus Partnership / 267
       If It's Property, Is It Marital Property? / 268
       Professional Licenses and Professional Degrees / 271
10.7   What Is It Worth? / 276
10.8   Dissipation Doctrine / 280
10.9   Practice / 281
Summary / 282

CHAPTER 11   Spousal Support   286

11.1   Alimony and Public Policy / 288
11.2   Terminology / 288
11.3   Alimony Is Discretionary / 289
11.4   Alimony Is Modifiable / 290
11.5   The Threshold Question: Need of the Recipient / 294
11.6   The Second Question: Ability to Pay / 296
11.7   Statutory Guidelines / 296
11.8   Permanent Alimony on the Decline / 297
11.9   Fault / 299
11.10 Termination upon Remarriage / 299
11.11 Reimbursement Alimony / 304

11.12 Tax Considerations / 307
11.13 Enforcement / 308
11.14 Modification / 308
11.15 Changed Circumstances / 309
Summary / 312

CHAPTER 12 Child Support 314

12.1 Parental Duty to Support / 316
12.2 Need and Ability to Pay / 319
12.3 Single Parents / 320
12.4 College Education / 320
12.5 Health Care / 324
12.6 Child Support and Remarriage / 324
12.7 Parents in Arrears: The Enforcement Problem / 325
12.8 Child Support Guidelines / 327
12.9 The Child "Tax" / 330
12.10 Interstate Enforcement / 335
12.11 URESA / 335
Summary / 338
Appendix 12A Revised Uniform Reciprocal Enforcement of Support Act
            1968 (RURESA) / 341

CHAPTER 13 Child Custody 348

13.1 Factors Confounding Custody Decisions / 350
13.2 Historical Overview / 351
13.3 Types of Custody / 352
13.4 Best Interests of the Child / 353
13.5 Presumptions / 359
13.6 Misconduct / 359
13.7 Modification / 361
13.8 Visitation / 363
13.9 The Natural Father / 364
13.10 Rights of Nonparents (Third Parties) to Custody / 369
13.11 Uniform Child Custody Jurisdiction Act / 370
13.12 Parental Kidnapping Prevention Act / 371
Summary / 372
Appendix 13A Uniform Child Custody Jurisdiction Act (1968) / 375

CHAPTER 14 Issues in Child Custody 380

14.1 Introduction / 381
14.2 Joint Custody / 382
     Mayer v. Mayer / 382
     Beck v. Beck / 387

14.3 Primary Caregiver Rule / 397
     David M. v. Margaret M. / 398

CHAPTER 15   Adoption and Related Matters   416

15.1 Adoption: An Overview / 417
15.2 The Parties / 418
     Blood Relatives / 419
     Foster Parents / 419
     Stepparents / 419
     Childless Strangers / 420
     Nonmarital Fathers / 420
15.3 Surrogacy / 426
15.4 Factors Influencing Adoption and Their Constitutional
     Implications / 429
     Religion / 429
     Race / 432
     Legal Bonds / 435
15.5 Equitable Adoption / 437
15.6 Dependency Proceedings / 441
Summary / 446
Appendix 15A   Uniform Adoption Act (1971) / 448
Appendix 15B   Uniform Parentage Act (1973) / 452
Appendix 15C   Uniform Status of Children of Assisted Conception Act
     (1988) / 458

PART FOUR   Dicta Ultima   461

Dicta Ultima / 462

Glossary / 464

Index / 475

DELMAR PUBLISHERS INC.

 AND

LAWYERS COOPERATIVE PUBLISHING

ARE PLEASED TO ANNOUNCE THEIR PARTNERSHIP
TO CO-PUBLISH COLLEGE TEXTBOOKS FOR
PARALEGAL EDUCATION.

DELMAR, WITH OFFICES AT ALBANY, NEW YORK, IS A PROFESSIONAL EDUCATION PUBLISHER. DELMAR PUBLISHES QUALITY EDUCATIONAL TEXT-BOOKS TO PREPARE AND SUPPORT INDIVIDUALS FOR LIFE SKILLS AND SPECIFIC OCCUPATIONS.

LAWYERS COOPERATIVE PUBLISHING (LCP), WITH OFFICES AT ROCHESTER, NEW YORK, HAS BEEN THE LEADING PUBLISHER OF ANALYTICAL LEGAL INFORMATION FOR OVER 100 YEARS. IT IS THE PUBLISHER OF SUCH RE-KNOWNED LEGAL ENCYCLOPEDIAS AS **AMERICAN LAW REPORTS, AMERICAN JURISPRUDENCE, UNITED STATES CODE SERVICE, LAWYERS EDITION,** AS WELL AS OTHER MATERIAL, AND FEDERAL- AND STATE-SPECIFIC PUBLICATIONS. THESE PUBLICATIONS HAVE BEEN DE-SIGNED TO WORK TOGETHER IN THE DAY-TO-DAY PRACTICE OF LAW AS AN INTEGRATED SYSTEM IN WHAT IS CALLED THE "TOTAL CLIENT-SERVICE LI-BRARY®" (TCSL®). EACH LCP PUBLICATION IS COMPLETE WITHIN ITSELF AS TO SUBJECT COVERAGE, YET ALL HAVE COMMON FEATURES AND EXTEN-SIVE CROSS-REFERENCING TO PROVIDE LINKAGE FOR HIGHLY EFFICIENT LEGAL RESEARCH INTO VIRTUALLY ANY MATTER AN ATTORNEY MIGHT BE CALLED UPON TO HANDLE.

INFORMATION IN ALL PUBLICATIONS IS CAREFULLY AND CONSTANTLY MON-ITORED TO KEEP PACE WITH AND REFLECT EVENTS IN THE LAW AND IN SOCIETY. UPDATING AND SUPPLEMENTAL INFORMATION IS TIMELY AND PROVIDED CONVENIENTLY.

FOR FURTHER REFERENCE, SEE:

AMERICAN JURISPRUDENCE 2D: AN ENCYCLOPEDIC TEXT COVERAGE OF THE COMPLETE BODY OF STATE AND FEDERAL LAW.

AM JUR LEGAL FORMS 2D: A COMPILATION OF BUSINESS AND LEGAL FORMS DEALING WITH A VARIETY OF SUBJECT MATTERS.

AM JUR PLEADING AND PRACTICE FORMS, REV.: MODEL PRACTICE FORMS FOR EVERY STAGE OF A LEGAL PROCEEDING.

AM JUR PROOF OF FACTS: A SERIES OF ARTICLES THAT GUIDE THE READER IN DETERMINING WHICH FACTS ARE ESSENTIAL TO A CASE AND HOW TO PROVE THEM.

AM JUR TRIALS: A SERIES OF ARTICLES DISCUSSING EVERY ASPECT OF PARTICULAR SETTLEMENTS AND TRIALS WRITTEN BY 180 CONSULTING SPECIALISTS.

UNITED STATES CODE SERVICE: A COMPLETE AND AUTHORITATIVE ANNOTATED FEDERAL CODE THAT FOLLOWS THE EXACT LANGUAGE OF THE STATUTES AT LARGE AND DIRECTS YOU TO THE COURT AND AGENCY DECISIONS CONSTRUING EACH PROVISION.

ALR AND ALR FEDERAL: SERIES OF ANNOTATIONS PROVIDING IN-DEPTH ANALYSES OF ALL THE CASE LAW ON PARTICULAR LEGAL ISSUES.

U.S. SUPREME COURT REPORTS, L ED 2D: EVERY REPORTED U.S. SUPREME COURT DECISION PLUS IN-DEPTH DISCUSSIONS OF LEADING ISSUES.

FEDERAL PROCEDURE, L ED: A COMPREHENSIVE, A–Z TREATISE ON FEDERAL PROCEDURE—CIVIL, CRIMINAL, AND ADMINISTRATIVE.

FEDERAL PROCEDURAL FORMS, L ED: STEP-BY-STEP GUIDANCE FOR DRAFTING FORMS FOR FEDERAL COURT OR FEDERAL AGENCY PROCEEDINGS.

FEDERAL RULES SERVICE, 2D AND 3D: REPORTS DECISIONS FROM ALL LEVELS OF THE FEDERAL SYSTEM INTERPRETING THE FEDERAL RULES OF CIVIL PROCEDURE AND THE FEDERAL RULES OF APPELLATE PROCEDURE.

FEDERAL RULES DIGEST, 3D: ORGANIZES HEADNOTES FOR THE DECISIONS REPORTED IN FEDERAL RULES SERVICE ACCORDING TO THE NUMBERING SYSTEMS OF THE FEDERAL RULES OF CIVIL PROCEDURE AND THE FEDERAL RULES OF APPELLATE PROCEDURE.

FEDERAL RULES OF EVIDENCE SERVICE: REPORTS DECISIONS FROM ALL LEVELS OF THE FEDERAL SYSTEM INTERPRETING THE FEDERAL RULES OF EVIDENCE.

FEDERAL RULES OF EVIDENCE NEWS

FEDERAL PROCEDURE RULES SERVICE

FEDERAL TRIAL HANDBOOK, 2D

FORM DRAFTING CHECKLISTS: AM JUR PRACTICE GUIDE

GOVERNMENT CONTRACTS: PROCEDURES AND FORMS

HOW TO GO DIRECTLY INTO YOUR OWN COMPUTERIZED SOLO PRACTICE WITHOUT MISSING A MEAL (OR A BYTE)

JONES ON EVIDENCE, CIVIL AND CRIMINAL, 7TH

LITIGATION CHECKISTS: AM JUR PRACTICE GUIDE

MEDICAL LIBRARY, LAWYERS EDITION

MEDICAL MALPRACTICE — ALR CASES AND ANNOTATIONS

MODERN APPELLATE PRACTICE: FEDERAL AND STATE CIVIL APPEALS

MODERN CONSTITUTIONAL LAW

NEGOTIATION AND SETTLEMENT

PATTERN DEPOSITION CHECKLISTS, 2D

QUALITY OF LIFE DAMAGES: CRITICAL ISSUES AND PROOFS

SHEPARD'S CITATIONS FOR ALR

SUCCESSFUL TECHNIQUES FOR CIVIL TRIALS, 2D

STORIES ET CETERA — A COUNTRY LAWYER LOOKS AT LIFE AND THE LAW

SUMMARY OF AMERICAN LAW

THE TRIAL LAWYER'S BOOK: PREPARING AND WINNING CASES

TRIAL PRACTICE CHECKLISTS

2000 CLASSIC LEGAL QUOTATIONS

WILLISTON ON CONTRACTS, 3D AND 4TH

FEDERAL RULES OF EVIDENCE DIGEST: ORGANIZES HEADNOTES FOR THE DECISIONS REPORTED IN FEDERAL RULES OF EVIDENCE SERVICE ACCORDING TO THE NUMBERING SYSTEM OF THE FEDERAL RULES OF EVIDENCE.

ADMINISTRATIVE LAW: PRACTICE AND PROCEDURE

AGE DISCRIMINATION: CRITICAL ISSUES AND PROOFS

ALR CRITICAL ISSUES: DRUNK DRIVING PROSECUTIONS

ALR CRITICAL ISSUES: FREEDOM OF INFORMATION ACTS

ALR CRITICAL ISSUES: TRADEMARKS

ALR CRITICAL ISSUES: WRONGFUL DEATH

AMERICANS WITH DISABILITIES: PRACTICE AND COMPLIANCE MANUAL

ATTORNEYS' FEES

BALLENTINE'S LAW DICTIONARY

CONSTITUTIONAL LAW DESKBOOK

CONSUMER AND BORROWER PROTECTION: AM JUR PRACTICE GUIDE

CONSUMER CREDIT: ALR ANNOTATIONS

DAMAGES: ALR ANNOTATIONS

EMPLOYEE DISMISSAL: CRITICAL ISSUES AND PROOFS

ENVIRONMENTAL LAW: ALR ANNOTATIONS

EXPERT WITNESS CHECKLISTS

EXPERT WITNESSES IN CIVIL TRIALS

FORFEITURES: ALR ANNOTATIONS

FEDERAL LOCAL COURT RULES

FEDERAL LOCAL COURT FORMS

FEDERAL CRIMINAL LAW AND PROCEDURE: ALR ANNOTATIONS

FEDERAL EVIDENCE

FEDERAL LITIGATION DESK SET: FORMS AND ANALYSIS

PREFACE

When Jay Whitney first proposed writing a text on family law for Delmar's Lawyers Co-operative Publishing Series, I was delighted because I find the subject matter of family law the most intriguing and entertaining in the legal field. I realized, however, that this project would be quite different from our previous one, *Foundations of Law. Foundations* was a general introduction for students with little or no background in law, and therefore had few restrictions other than the presentation of a clear picture of American law, leaving to other texts and other courses the job of filling in the pieces of the fabric of the law. Family law, on the other hand, was part of the quilt. Unfortunately for those who would present a clear picture of American law, the range of diversity among the states makes such a presentation difficult. This text required a series of choices about what must be included in an accurate, yet incomplete, rendition of American family law. On the one hand, the student should have a broader knowledge of family law than the law of one state, but on the other hand, those who ultimately become practitioners ordinarily concentrate on the law of the jurisdiction in which they practice. Thus, the cases chosen for the text represent a wide range of states. I have attempted to give a flavor of the American family in a national sense. No state makes law in total disregard of developments in other states, and every state experiences social change similar to other states. Lawmakers look for solutions to social problems from others who have attempted to solve similar problems. It is ironic that, of the major countries of the world, the United States has the most jurisdictionally complex legal system and the most diverse social system—yet Americans probably share a greater degree of cultural content than citizens of any other country. A premise of this book, then, is that there is something we can call American family law, which is not merely a composite of the law of each of the states, like a *Restatement of Domestic Relations,* but rather a search for common solutions to common problems. I would also argue, by the way, that our multiplicity of legal systems, like our social and cultural diversity, is more often a strength than a weakness. *E Pluribus Unum.*

Additional choices were necessary in terms of a balance between principle (some would say "theory") and practice. Although this text is aimed principally at students in paralegal programs, these programs vary greatly in their length, focus, and student background. I must assume that students in most programs, like the students in our program at the University of Central Florida, are unlikely to become specialists in family law once they enter their careers. Instructors are often torn between the desire to explore policy, principle, theory, and even blackletter law and the desire to impart detailed office skills, for the attorneys who expect the fresh paralegal graduate to "hit the ground running." In my judgment, students should get a wholesome share of both. Recognizing that, I have included materials to provide the opportunity for inquiry and assignments into specific practical problems and state-specific law. During my 17 years at the University of Central Florida, I have witnessed a dozen or so instructors teach family law. Every one of them, including myself, supplemented textual materials with state-specific materials and assignments based on state law. Each of us, however, varied considerably in the materials we chose and the assignments we gave. This text concentrates on providing an overview of family law, but I have sought also to provide materials that instructors may use for a closer examination of family law practice.

The problem of general versus applied, principle versus practice, is compounded by the multiplicity of jurisdictions in the United States. Not only do the states show major differences in law and process in the domestic arena, but they also exhibit the need to cooperate and the desire for uniformity. Thus, the movement for no-fault divorce did not end with one state, or 10, but continued until all states followed suit. Nevertheless, "no-fault" means something very different in New York than it does in Florida.

I came to the conclusion early in the process of writing this text that students ought to know about family law in general *and* about specific instances of its application in cases and disputes. If possible, they should be made to inquire into the specific law and practices of their own environments, presumably their own states. The instructors in our program who have taught family law have nearly always used national texts supplemented with state materials, principally statutes, but often cases as well.

Most family law instructors in the Legal Studies Program at the University of Central Florida require students to prepare documents for a fictitious divorce case. When I first taught the course, I required a petition for dissolution, an antenuptial agreement, and a marital separation agreement. Though it was a useful exercise, I found that the best documents turned in were copied from forms with the blanks filled in. In short, the students did precisely what I would have done in practice. I wondered whether the students did not work more on their typing skills than on family law skills! Hence, in composing the exercises for this text, I chose instead to provide questions that will force students to do simple research to answer many of the practical questions that may come up in domestic relations cases.

The instructor may want to require the students to prepare documents. If not, it may be desirable for students at least to become familiar with some of them. To this end, I have provided appendices with form antenuptial and separation agreements, a financial affidavit, and a domestic relations questionnaire. The questionnaire (appendix 1A) is useful especially for instructors who wish to give some attention to interviewing and counseling, but it is also demonstrative of the details of the information needed to pursue a divorce case. The questionnaire indicates the range of information needed to pursue a divorce case and also suggests the complexity of the marital partnership, most of which we take for granted until the prospect of divorce arises. This questionnaire applies to subsequent chapters as well, and may be used at the instructor's discretion.

I have found discussion and preparation of antenuptial agreements, financial affidavits, and separation agreements to be particularly good in helping students to address specific issues with regard to the marriage contract, the marriage partnership, and divorce. To this end, I have included samples of each. The instructor may add peculiarities not included in the samples or may require the students to compare and critique the samples with others used in any given jurisdiction. I trust that most instructors have their own ideas of how to give these issues critical attention.

I have also included several uniform acts from the National Conference of Commissioners on Uniform State Laws. These, too, may be compared with the law of specific states, but their value, in my opinion, lies in the fact that they come closest to representing a national law of family law. Even when a specific set of uniform laws is not adopted, it tends to be discussed both in judicial opinions and in professional and academic circles. I included them also because I always regretted the fact that other texts referred to the uniform acts but usually presented them in piecemeal fashion. Each appears in the chapter where it is referenced.

A.L.R. State-Specific Feature

To provide instructors with the means to investigate state law, I decided to provide in each chapter for questions aimed at state law. At the end of each chapter, there are two categories of questions. One, labeled "Questions," is designed to review the content of major substantive questions in the law covered by the chapter, as well as occasionally to raise discussion questions concerning issues related to the chapter. In addition to chapter Questions, there is a section labeled "Exercises," with the instruction to "answer the questions according to the law of your state." Many of these questions are followed by an American Law Reports (ALR) citation; the questions were modeled on the topic of the annotation. This does not mean, however, that the ALR annotations, comprehensive though they are, will necessarily answer the question for every state. The ALR annotations were used for two reasons. First, the ALR provides ready access to a source of information that can be very helpful for students relatively unfamiliar with legal materials. Directing them to the *American Law Reports,* where they can find the various annotations from volume and page numbers, can give them a headstart on answering the question, or even furnish a complete and up-to-date (via the pocket parts) answer. The second reason the ALR annotations were used comes from the simple fact that ALR annotations are practical, topical, and often controversial (in the sense that they are contemporary issues of dispute in the practice of law). Now ALR is available on compact disk as Lawdesk.

Family law offers the most challenging, provocative, personal material of any course in the legal field, offering the opportunity for the instructor to deal with problems with which every student has come in contact and about which they usually have some opinion (e.g., increasing divorce, nonpayment of child support, abortion). I have used excerpts of cases, following the pattern I used in *Foundations of Law* in the same series. I have used cases in part because of the urgent need to move the students back and forth between abstract principles and concrete events, the interplay of which perhaps provides the greatest opportunity for teaching critical thinking. To promote ease of use and application to the relevant topic, all the case excerpts have been edited to delete extraneous issues. Many footnotes and citations thus do not appear, but the case citations and Table of Cases make it easy for the curious student or researcher to locate the original, full opinions if they wish.

It is hard to imagine getting even the slightest flavor of family law without reference to the cases. I have included, inasmuch as possible, interesting, entertaining, and provocative cases that have serious instructive value.

One of the joys of teaching this area of the law is its personal and intimate nature. All students have thought about and experienced some features of family law, whether or not they have considered them in legal terms. When I want to enliven a class, I usually need look no further than today's newspaper. Daytime talkshow hosts seem to dwell particularly on family problems and family law. Many times I have been about to leave the house when my wife says, "You ought to check out the Donahue show this morning." Each year reveals a new twist on major changes in family law. I have attempted to cover the field with broad brushstrokes and to provide the materials to probe more deeply, according to the interests and needs of student and instructor alike.

I would like to express my appreciation to the reviewers whose thoughtful commentary has made this a better book:

Dr. Melody Brown
College of Great Falls (MT)

Claudia Clinton
McMurray University (TX)

Diane Dvorak
Suffolk Community College (NY)

Marjorie Fishman
Athens Area Technical College (GA)

Associate Justice Richard Huffman
University—San Diego (CA)

Nance Kriscenski
Manchester Community College (CT)

Donna Mettz
Southwestern Paralegal Institute (TX)

Dr. Kathleen Munley
Marywood College (PA)

Dr. Willard Overgaard
Boise State University (ID)

Sandy Pfaff
Denver Paralegal Institute (CO)

Susan Schulz
Southern Career Institute (FL)

Ruth Wilcox
Central Florida Community College (FL)

TABLE OF CASES

Alderson v. Alderson, 241
Anders v. Anders, 99
Arden v. State Bar of California, 29

Baby M, In re, 4, *416,* 427, 462
Back v. Back, 93
Barbara A. v. John G., 35
Bear v. Reformed Mennonite Church, 201
Beck v. Beck, 382, 387
Bell v. Bell, 302
Bennett v. Jeffreys, 380
Bilowit v. Dolitsky, 87
Booth v. Booth, 280
Boswell v. Boswell, 219, 220
Brancoveanu v. Brancoveanu, 260
Brazina v. Brazina, 158
Brooks v. Brooks, 118, 119
Brown v. Brown, 212
Butler, In re Estate of, 231
Byers v. Mount Vernon Mills, Inc., 225
Byrne, In re, 136

Catalano v. Catalano, 7, 91, 221
Conway v. Dana, 316

David M. v. Margaret M., 349, 397, 398
Dawley, In re Marriage of, 121
DeBoer v. Schmidt, 442
DeLorean v. DeLorean, 122, 127, 131
Dexter v. Dexter, 154, 156
Donohue v. Getman, 325, 328
Drummond v. Fulton County Department of Family & Childrens Services, 435

Fadgen v. Lenkner, 198
Fahrer v. Fahrer, 300
Florida Bar v. Furman, 13

Foster v. Alston, 380
Francis, In re Marriage of, 304, 305, 307
Fried v. Fried, 309
Fundermann v. Mickelson, 200

Garduno v. Garduno, 233
Garges, In re, 225
Gates v. Foley, 190, 192
Geyer, In re, 128, 136, 144
Glickman v. Collins, 157
Goldman, In re, 430
Golub v. Golub, 275
Graham v. Graham, 317
Grant v. Superior Court, 225, 226
Gregory K., 74, 75

Helms v. Franciscus, 380
Hewitt v. Hewitt, 243, 244
Hick ex rel. Feiock v. Feiock, 327
Hill v. Hill, 208

Jersey Shore Medical Center-Fitkin Hospital v. Estate of Baum, 194
Johnston v. Johnston, 163, 169
Jones v. Daly, 240
Jordan v. Jordan, 86, 94, 95

Karin T. v. Michael T., 58
Kirchberg v. Feenstra, 210

Lepis v. Lepis, 310
Levie, In re Estate of, 228
Livesay v. Hilley, 359, 362
Low v. Low, 292
Lutgert v. Lutgert, 134
Lynch v. Lynch, 263

Magruder v. Magruder, 298

Mahan v. Mahan, 93
Martin v. Farber, 130
Marvin v. Marvin, 240, 243, 244, 246, 253, 254
Mason v. Mason, 231
Mayer v. Mayer, 382
Maynard v. Hill, 9
McCarty v. McCarty, 268
McConkey v. McConkey, 100
McDowell v. McDowell, 269
McGowan v. McGowan, 274
McQuiddy v. McQiddy, 327
M.H.B. v. H.T.B., 317
Miller, In re, 212
Moye v. Moye, 354, 356

Nancy S. v. Michele G., 438
Neilson v. Neilson, 140
Noghrey, In re Marriage of, 140
Nunnally v. Trust Company Bank, 436

O'Brien v. O'Brien, 272, 275, 281, 304, 307
O'Connor Bros. Abalone Co. v. Brando, 302
Oedekoven v. Oedekoven, 160
O'Neil v. Schuckardt, 201
Orr v. Orr, 288

Painter v. Bannister, 369
Pajak v. Pajak, 124
Palmore v. Sidoti, 433, *435*
Parillo v. Parillo, 359
Parkinson v. J.&S. Tool Co., 226
People v. Liberta, 48
Pfohl v. Pfohl, 295
Piscopo v. Piscopo, 277
Ponder v. Graham, 51, 52
Posner v. Posner, 132
Powell v. Powell, 102

Quilloin v. Walcott, 421

Read v. Read, 196
Renshaw v. Heckler, 222, 223, 225, 226

Reynolds v. Reynolds, 94, 95
Riegler v. Riegler, 321, 339
Ripley v. Ewell, 192, 193
Robinson, In re Marriage of, 290
Roe v. Wade, 56
Rosenberger Estate, 219
Rumbaugh v. Rumbaugh, 323
Ruth v. Fletcher, 423, 426

S.A.V. v. K.G.V., 204
Schilling v. Bedford County Memorial Hospital, Inc., 193
Singer v. Hara, 188
Smith v. Lewis, 37
Sousa v. Freitas, 230
Stanley v. Illinois, 420, 421
State ex rel. McDonnell v. McCutcheon, 336
State v. Clark, 196
State v. Winder, 36, 37
Stewart v. Hampton, 89, 102
Stregack v. Moldofsky, 132
Strock v. Presnell, 201
Suggs v. Norris, 239, 240, 243
Suggs' Estate, In re, 219, 220
Sweeney, In re Estate of, 160, 162
Swift v. Swift, 167

T. v. M., 96
Tower, In re Marriage of, 253, 254
Vaughn v. Hufnagel, 225, 226

Warren v. State, 55
Waskin v. Waskin, 310
Watts v. Watts, 244
Womack v. Eldridge, 426
Worden v. Worden, 365

Zysk v. Zysk, 206

PART ONE
Introduction

CHAPTER 1
The Family, the Law, and the Paralegal

Celebrity Circus

In a highly publicized family court battle, actress Mia Farrow and actor/director/producer Woody Allen fought over child custody. Accusations of unfit parenting and sexual abuse, as well as conflicting psychiatric determinations, made the courtroom drama among the dirtiest in this decade. The case explored virtually all of the relevant issues involved in contemporary family law: incest, adoption, nonmarital couples, custody, and support. The trial judge ultimately found in favor of Farrow, but awarded Allen restrictive visitation rights. All this played out during the release of a 1992 film, Husbands and Wives, starring Farrow and Allen. Fiction, as usual, proved less riveting than the real-life stories of the stars as portrayed on television and in the tabloids. This chapter explores parties who are less celebrated, ordinary families, as well as the role of paralegals in family law.

— Photo courtesy of AP/Wide World Photos.

Other things may change us, but we start and end with the family.

Anthony Brandt

OUTLINE

1.1 LAW AND THE FAMILY
1.2 FAMILY LAW PRINCIPALLY CONCERNED WITH DIVORCE
1.3 MARRIAGE AS CONTRACT
1.4 MARRIAGE AS A PARTNERSHIP
1.5 CHILDREN
1.6 FAMILY LAW AND THE ADVERSARIAL PROCESS
      "Good People at their Worst"
1.7 LAWYERS AND FAMILY LAW
1.8 PARALEGALS AND FAMILY LAW
      Pretrial Tasks
      Trial Tasks
      Posttrial Tasks
      SUMMARY

1.1 LAW AND THE FAMILY

Family and *law* are two words that do not complement each other. The law, in its form of orders and commands from courts (the source of public order), approaches the family quite reluctantly. The family, traditionally a sacred and private domain, invokes the law only when things have gone terribly wrong. The history of family law in America reveals a waxing and waning of state involvement in regulating the family. It is a reflection of the nature of society's view of public intrusion into private affairs.

Every society demonstrates an awareness of the importance of the family. Families would come into being perfectly naturally through the union of man and woman and their resulting offspring. However, our society, like all societies, imposes rules on these relationships, the laws of the family. Over time, we find that our laws of the family have several primary concerns:

1. *Marriage:* Who may (or may not) marry? What constitutes a valid marriage in the eyes of the law? What rights and duties does marriage incur?
2. *Sexual relations:* What are the rules governing sexual intimacy? How do these rules relate to the legal model of the family?
3. *Parenthood:* How is procreation regulated? What rights and duties are incurred by parenthood?
4. *Dissolution of marriage:* Under what circumstances can the bonds of marriage be severed? How are former marital rights and duties distributed upon termination of the marital contract?

If these questions appear overly general and abstract, consider how many questions would be necessary to address the specific issues that arise in modern society:

1. May homosexuals marry?
2. May a single man (or woman) adopt?
3. May a Jewish couple adopt a Catholic (or Vietnamese) child?
4. Is a divorcing wife entitled to an interest in the medical license acquired by her husband, which she helped to obtain by sweeping floors while he went to medical school?
5. Should we allow **surrogate motherhood contracts**?
6. Should a child be able to sue parents for negligently raising her in such a way as to cause her emotional instability?

And so forth, for a myriad of other questions and situations. In truth, there is open debate about what exactly is denoted by the word **family**. We are somewhat confused about the part the state should play in governing the relationships within the domestic unit that is the center of our society. The dilemmas posed by these questions have provided material for talk-show hosts for many years, and their complexity and fascination show no hint of abating.

1.2 FAMILY LAW PRINCIPALLY CONCERNED WITH DIVORCE

In our society, perhaps more than any other in the world, we turn to the law and lawyers for the resolution of our social problems. The high frequency of divorce in American society makes family law practice an important area of the legal profession. **Divorce**, often called **dissolution of marriage**, is a legal matter because it involves the severing of legal bonds

LEGAL TERMS

surrogate motherhood contracts
    Contracts in which a woman agrees to carry a baby and, after birth, give it up to the contracting parties, usually a husband-and-wife couple. The baby is produced by artificial insemination with the husband's sperm or by implanting a fertilized ovum of the adopting mother. The famous *Baby M* case focused national attention on the problems with this sort of contract and led many states to enact strict laws governing them.

family
    The traditional family, defined as a husband, a wife, and their children, is under attack by those who have nontraditional relationships but want to enjoy the legal benefits of marriage and family. The ensuing debate threatens to last for many years.

created by marriage. The court ordinarily decrees or recognizes a distribution of **marital property** in the process of granting a divorce, as well as determining the relative rights and duties between parent and child. These determinations have legal consequences that powerfully affect the lives of those concerned. Although divorce is only one area of family law practice, it produces the lion's share of legal work.

As in other areas of practice, the attorney becomes involved in the family most often when things are going badly. Despite the variety of problems that family law presents, the overwhelming practical question for the law office rests in an all-important portion of the first set of questions in § 1.1: *How are former marital rights and duties distributed upon termination of the marital contract?* What happens at divorce? Oddly enough, from a legal point of view, divorce defines marriage. Divorce tells us just what the marriage was all about, because all the hidden transactions of a family must be sorted out and apportioned and assigned to the separated family members.

The principal issues of family law are in one way or another concerned with divorce: child custody, child support, spousal support (alimony), community property, equitable distribution. The second major area of concern has to do with the bonds between parent and child: paternity, legitimacy, adoption, and so on.

1.3   MARRIAGE AS CONTRACT

The fundamental unit of society is the family. Although the family may be the primary building block of society, our own society in recent decades has demonstrated that the bonds between husband and wife are often fragile and explosive. All human societies regulate and ritualize marriage and the relations created through marriage. Our society is no exception. What may be remarkable about our society is that, like so many other areas of American endeavor, we look to legal institutions to resolve family conflicts rather than to purely social or religious institutions. This means not only that courts order family rights and duties, but also that family matters are ultimately turned over to lawyers.

In their problem solving, lawyers are trained to place disputes into contexts that call for application of the law. To establish rights and duties that can be enforced—that is, recognized and ordered by courts—lawyers cast disputes in terms of property rights that are determined by mutual agreement (contract) and rights that the law imposes independent of contract (usually the area of torts). The marriage itself is traditionally viewed as a contractual arrangement because the parties voluntarily assume the relationship of husband and wife, but the most important duties are those imposed by law rather than the agreement of the parties. For example, husband and wife are obligated to provide mutual support for each other and support and nurture for their children. Individuals may avoid these duties by agreement only under special circumstances allowed by the law.

DICTA

It is ironic that marriage may be entered into by couples quite ignorant of the nature and obligations of marriage, whereas the return to single status requires an intense scrutiny of the facets of marriage.

divorce
A legal proceeding that dissolves the legal bonds of marriage. It is derived from two forms of divorce (*a mensa et thoro* and *a vinculo matrimonii*).

dissolution of marriage
Another name for divorce, which has in recent years been favored by several states.

marital property
Certain property acquired during a marriage, which is legally deemed marital property. Its principal significance concerns treatment and distribution upon divorce or death. Ownership and distribution vary from state to state.

Husband and wife today are confronted with a myriad of problems requiring outside consultation—finance and credit problems, emotional conflicts, and, much too often, marriage and divorce counseling.

In the later half of the 19th century, the English legal scholar, Sir Henry Maine, concluded his scheme of the evolution of law and society with the oft-repeated dictum that "the movement of the progressive societies has been a movement from Status to Contract." Maine considered the most primitive societies to be based principally on family ties, whereby an individual occupied a status (or several statuses) by virtue of birth, marriage, and the group of cooperative relatives that formed important ties of blood and association. Nineteenth-century society, in contrast, showed an increasing tendency to base cooperation on mutual agreement, that is, contract. *Compare* Case No. 1-1.

CASE NO. 1-1 When Is a Marriage Not a Marriage?

The following case excerpt not only illustrates the conflict between viewing marriage as status or contract (the dissent neatly argues that what starts as a contract becomes a status), but also reveals the traditional dichotomy between those who judge a contract on purely technical grounds (the majority) and those who elevate fairness over technicality (the dissent).

The overriding issue in the case is concerned with meeting the requirements of a marriage in the state of Connecticut. Fred and Maria Catalano were married in Italy in 1951. Maria remained in Italy for five years before joining her husband in Connecticut. They had one child. Fred died in 1958, and Maria is claiming the share of Fred's estate to which she would be entitled as his widow under Connecticut statutes. Unfortunately, Fred and Maria were uncle and niece and in Connecticut persons in that relationship are not allowed to marry (this was apparently also prohibited under Italian law, but Fred and Maria received a legal dispensation so that their marriage was legal in Italy).

CATALANO v. CATALANO
148 Conn. 288, 170 A.2d 726 (1961)

MURPHY, Justice.

The determination of the question propounded depends upon the interrelation and judicial interpretation of three statutes, §§ 46-1, 46-6 and 53-223. Legislation prohibiting the marriage of uncle and niece was originally enacted by the General Assembly in 1702. . . . It provided that no man should marry any woman within the degrees of kindred specified, including that of uncle and niece, and that any such marriage was null and void. . . . It has been the declared public policy of this state continuously since 1702 to prohibit marriages of uncle and niece and declare them void.

* * *

The marriage of the plaintiff and Fred Catalano, though valid in Italy under its laws, was not valid in Connecticut because it contravened the public policy of this state. The plaintiff therefore cannot qualify under § 45-250 as the surviving spouse of Fred Catalano.

In this opinion BALDWIN, C. J., and KING and SHEA, JJ., concurred.

MELLITZ, Justice (dissenting).

We are dealing here with the marriage status of a woman who was validly married at the place of her domicil and who, so far as the record discloses, was entirely innocent of any intent to evade the laws of Connecticut. . . . There is no suggestion anywhere in the record that at the time of the marriage she intended to come to America, that the parties had any intention of coming to live in Connecticut, or that the marriage was entered into in Italy for the purpose of evading the laws of Connecticut. If a

marriage status resulting from a valid marriage, such as the one here, is to be destroyed, the issue bastardized, and the relations of the parties branded as illicit, it should follow only from an explicit enactment of the legislature, giving clear expression to a public policy which compels such harsh consequences to ensue from a marriage entered into under the circumstances disclosed here.

The cases cited in the majority opinion which deal with the question we have here are all cases where the parties went to a foreign state to evade the law of the domicil and the marriage celebrated in the foreign state was refused recognition in the place of their domicil when they returned to live there after the marriage. . . .

[Section 46-1] is a validating statute and declares valid the marriage of a citizen of Connecticut celebrated in a foreign country in conformity with the law of that country, provided each party would have legal capacity to contract the marriage in Connecticut. Capacity, in the sense employed in the statute, is defined in 2 Beale, Conflict of Laws § 121.6, as follows: "By capacity to enter into a marriage is meant a quality which legally prevents the person in question marrying anyone; it does not refer to some quality which prevents the particular marriage in question, though the person may marry someone else. A typical example of capacity is nonage, or having a living spouse. A typical example of a quality which prevents the particular marriage, though the person has capacity to marry, is consanguinity."

* * *

In whatever terms "capacity," under the provisions of § 46-6, may be conceived, it relates to the capacity of the parties to enter into the contract of marriage. After the marriage, the relation between the Catalanos became a status, no longer resting merely on contract. Allen v. Allen, 73 Conn. 54, 55, 46 A. 242, 49 L.R.A. 142. A contract of marriage is sui generis. "It is simply introductory to the creation of a status, and what that status is the law determines. A contract executed in contravention of law may yet establish a status which the law will recognize, and, if one of the contracting parties were innocent of any intention to violate the law, may recognize as carrying with it in his favor the same rights and duties as if the contract had been entirely unexceptionable." Mrs. Catalano was innocent of any intent to violate our laws, and she is entitled to have recognition here of her marriage status, with all of the rights flowing from that status. The following from the opinion in Pierce v. Pierce, 58 Wash. 622, 626, 109 P. 45, aptly expresses what I conceive to be the correct view in the situation here. "We know of no public policy which will warrant a court in annulling a marriage between competent parties if there be any evidence to sustain it, and especially so where it appears that the parties have consummated the marriage, a child has been born, and the offending party has been openly acknowledged as a spouse. It will not be done unless it clearly appears that the parties willfully went beyond the jurisdiction of the courts of this state to avoid and defy our laws. It is not clear that they did so in this case."

CASE QUESTIONS

1. What are the full legal consequences of the court's refusal to recognize the Catalanos' Italian marriage?
2. Why does the dissenting opinion distinguish between consanguinity, minority (nonage), and prior undissolved marriage as impediments to a valid marriage?

Although marriage has long been described as a contract, throughout most of the history of Anglo-American law, it has not been an ordinary contract in the eyes of the law, one that could be freely made, altered, and broken. The sacred aspect of the family and procreation argued for a sacred contract. In recent decades, however, the state, which in America has assumed responsibility for domestic regulation, moved in the direction suggested by Maine, making the marriage contract much more like other contracts, in which the contracting parties controlled the relationship. Many of the features of family law can be explained by the tension between the special regard with which we view marriage and the family and the objective contractual rights and duties which the law imposes on family relationships.

It is also to be observed that, while marriage is often termed by text writers and in decisions of courts as a civil contract—generally to indicate that it might be founded upon the agreement of the parties, and does not require any religious ceremony for its solemnization—it is something more than a mere contract. The consent of the parties is of course essential to its existence; but when the contract to marry is executed by the marriage, a relation between the parties is created which they cannot change. Other contracts may be modified, restricted, or enlarged, or entirely released upon the consent of the parties. Not so with marriage. The relation once formed, the law steps in and holds the parties to various obligations and liabilities. It is an institution, in the maintenance of which in its purity the public is deeply interested, for it is the foundation of the family and of society, without which there would be neither civilization nor progress.

— *Maynard v. Hill,* 125 U.S. 190, 210 (1888).

DICTA

One economist has argued that divorce is good for the economy, because separate households require the purchase of duplicate items, such as televisions, furniture, and the like.

1.4 MARRIAGE AS A PARTNERSHIP

From an economic standpoint, the marriage contract establishes an ongoing, cooperative unit like a business partnership. In some instances the reciprocal nature of the business is clear, as when the wife works as a secretary to support her husband through law school, with the understanding that once the husband's practice is prospering, the wife will quit working and bear and raise the couple's children. The success of the partnership depends upon each spouse meeting the terms of the contract. Other marriage partners may be business partners in an objective sense, that is, they may jointly manage their own commercial enterprise. The division of profits often is not done in the way unmarried partners would ordinarily conduct a business, but in every other respect the differences may be insignificant. Perhaps a vast majority of marriages do not meet the usual characteristics of a business venture, but nearly all marriages involve important cost and savings sharing for mutual benefit, similar to a business enterprise. In fact, one of the problems of divorce and separation is that two former spouses living apart cannot enjoy the prior standard of living made possible because of the savings of living together.

Divorce may be treated like the dissolution of a business partnership. To the extent that property assets have been acquired by the joint efforts of the spouses, this model may, when used with caution, effect a fair distribution of the marital property. This is especially true when the couple is childless and both are employed.

1.5 CHILDREN

Family law, often called **domestic relations**, might more properly be titled the law of intimate relations, especially in this period in our society, in which couples exercise considerable freedom in the partners they choose and the lifestyles those partnerships express. Even though we have moved away from the expected marriage-and-children model of adult relationships, the idealized model of the family continues to be a heterosexual union having as its major motivation the creation and nurture of children. Children add a dimension to family law that distinguishes it from other areas of law. Family

LEGAL TERMS

domestic relations
  Family law as a field. Testbooks and law school courses commonly use this terminology.

law commonly deals with the welfare of human beings who have not reached the age of legal competence (majority), who are vulnerable to abuse or exploitation, and who must be protected by society through its legal institutions when the family, the primary social institution, fails. Problems in other areas of law are often neatly handled by the transfer of wealth from one pocket to another; family law involves issues that are not readily measured in dollars and cents.

1.6 FAMILY LAW AND THE ADVERSARIAL PROCESS

American legal procedure has developed around an adversarial process in which disputing parties arm themselves with legal representatives and ultimately try their cases before an impartial judge if the lawyers and the parties cannot reach an agreement. The sides are viewed as hostile and the lawyers are duty-bound to fight for the interests of their clients. This model quite naturally tends to focus and intensify the dispute, which is one of the reasons the states attempted to soften the process by adopting no-fault divorce statutes. Divorcing couples with minor children pose a serious problem for the legal system. We assume that parents will care for the interests of their children, but divorcing parents often aggravate the damage the divorce causes children by drawing them into an ongoing fight. The presence of minor children also usually means that the divorcing parents will continue to come into contact, and, unfortunately, many will continue to fight in a way that causes additional damage to the children.

In most cases the children do not have legal representation, in the sense that the attorneys are the agents of their parents. This poses an ethical problem for the attorneys and a legal problem for society. To what extent should an attorney examine the circumstances of the children? May we expect an attorney to advise a client that the opposing party would take better care of the children? To what extent should the courts and public agencies become involved with children of divorce? There are no easy answers to these questions; they will continue to haunt us as long as parents divorce each other or neglect their children.

We should also note that the disputing parties are often consumed by poorly controlled anger, jealousy, and self-reproach, which tend to intensify the warlike aspects of the underlying legal dispute. Perhaps in no other area of practice do attorneys receive the sorts of demands from clients that are common to divorce law. It is incumbent upon the attorney to maintain control over the case.

"Good People at their Worst"

There is an old saying in divorce law to the effect that divorce attorneys see "good people at their worst." Under the extreme stresses of divorce, people do and say things they would not do or say under any other circumstances. Divorce is so common today that we often fail to realize the emotional roller coaster on which divorcing couples ride. Unfortunately, law-yers all too often feel the full brunt of divorce clients' stresses. Paralegals are on an equal footing with lawyers in this regard; in fact, many are more ex-posed to clients' distress than are attorneys. Clients often regard paralegals as more approachable, less intimidating, and more responsive to personal, as opposed to strictly legal, problems. Both the lawyer and the paralegal risk burnout from the emotional problems constantly being delivered to their door-step. Clients may be pitiable one day and exasperating the next. Attor-neys and paralegals must learn to deal with this problem by mixing sympathy with objectivity. Working together, paralegal and attorney can learn to share the burden rather than putting it all on one person's shoulders.

1.7 LAWYERS AND FAMILY LAW

The lawyers are the primary participants in domestic relations cases. The facts presented to the court are dissected, framed, and presented in the form lawyers consider appropriate for judicial decision. Client spouses in the midst of divorce are often emotionally incapable of challenging the attorney's statements or advice, nor should they be expected to. With lawyers in charge, we might ask: Are matrimonial disputes settled according to the law or ac-cording to the biases of practitioners? For example, custody of children is routinely awarded to mothers, despite judicial decisions clearly indicating that fathers are not to be discriminated against under the law. Attorneys com-monly advise their clients that judges award custody to mothers, that it is generally futile for fathers to fight for custody. Is this really true? Or are at-torneys merely reflecting their perception of what judges do, or perhaps merely stating the attorneys' biases? Regardless of equality before the law, mothers are generally regarded as better nurturers of children and men are viewed with some suspicion (although not by everyone to be sure). On bal-ance, however, these traditional perceptions prevail over their alternatives.

1.8 PARALEGALS AND FAMILY LAW

The following is a short catalog of tasks that may ordinarily be per-formed by a family law paralegal. These tasks are premised upon the parale-gal's being under the direct supervision of an attorney. As long as there is attorney supervision, the scope of paralegal employment is very broad in most jurisdictions, especially where most litigation consists of brief, no-fault hearings. Although the paralegal can be active in trial preparation and the conduct of the trial, the attorney must represent the client and the case to the court. The following list describes paralegal tasks, but any and all of them may be performed by lawyers, and most were considered lawyers' tasks in the past. In short, this is a basic description of the most common tasks of family law practice.

DICTA

The dilemma of the adversarial system in this context may be stated as follows: Because our legal system is premised on an adversary contest, and because divorce requires the official adjudication of rights and duties between divorcing parties, the legal system inevitably tends away from an amicable and toward a hostile settlement of divorce.

The outline is chronological. We customarily divide procedures into pretrial, trial, and posttrial, each having its own subdivisions that tend to follow a basic chronology.

Pretrial Tasks

Initial interview   The paralegal may meet with a new client, either together with the attorney or before or after a meeting between attorney and client. There is no ideal arrangement; the way in which this is handled depends to a great extent on the nature of the relation between the attorney and the paralegal. Because the attorney has ultimate responsibility for each case, the attorney will determine the extent of paralegal involvement. Whatever their relationship, attorney and paralegal must work together in such a way as to deliver competent and efficient legal services to clients.

The attorney's meeting with a client will concentrate on developing rapport and eliciting facts that bear importantly on the nature of the dispute. The attorney should explain the paralegal's role and relationship to the case and introduce the paralegal as a valued assistant.

Many necessary facts have clerical rather than legal significance, (addresses, names, employers, etc.) and can be obtained by the paralegal. As a general rule, it is useful for the paralegal to engage in an initial interview apart from the attorney, so that paralegal and client may also develop rapport that aids subsequent communication to and through the paralegal. An important benefit of paralegal interaction with the client is the fact that paralegal time is ordinarily billed at a much lower rate than the attorney's time. Many clients are aware of this, and those who are not can be tactfully informed of the advantages of paralegal involvement in their dispute. A major advantage for the client is the recognition that two professionals are available to help in the case. It can be very reassuring for a client to know that another person is actively involved in the case. In fact, one of the most important functions of the paralegal is to maintain a cordial working relationship with the client.

The information that must be obtained in initial interviews is often reduced to checklists. These may come from commercial sources or may be tailored to individual firms and individual attorneys. Computerized checklists have made the collection of vital information easy and orderly and help in developing a routine that greatly reduces mistakes and omissions. In addition to collecting information necessary for pursuit of the case, the client may be required to sign forms necessary to proceed with the case and collection of additional information, such as income tax returns and other privileged information. Paralegals, however, should avoid making the collection of this information too mechanical. This is not a bankruptcy case. Obtaining the information is delicate, personal, and emotional, and the client must feel that the paralegal is concerned about the client's problems.

Pleadings   A paralegal may draft *initial pleadings,* that is, the documents filed with the court to begin the official legal process. In some instances, especially with no-fault divorce which does not require detailing the grounds for divorce, the initial petition or complaint may be a routine matter, essentially filling in blanks on a form. The responsible attorney is the judge of what is required, although an experienced paralegal will know what is appropriate in most cases.

The courts and bar associations are concerned over the propriety of the activities of a rising corps of legal technicians who provide assistance to the public without attorney supervision. Although divorce entails adjudication of important personal rights, there are many instances of short-term, childless marriages without accumulated marital assets that do not warrant the fees charged by most attorneys and that could be handled by competent legal assistants if permitted by law. (See Case No. 1-2.)

CASE NO. 1-2   The Limits of Legal Assistance

In the past paralegals have been excluded from giving legal help independent of attorney supervision. The following summary of a case from Florida demonstrates the perils of providing such help without membership in the Bar.

On April 26, 1984, the Florida Supreme Court, in *Florida Bar v. Furman,* 451 So. 2d 808 (Fla. 1984), sentenced Rosemary Furman to 30 days in jail for contempt of court. The contempt charge was based on her violation of a 1979 order from the same court enjoining her from engaging in the unauthorized practice of law. In her long-standing fight with the Florida Bar, Furman had become a folk hero to many. Governor Bob Graham excused her from serving the jail sentence.

Rosemary Furman is outspoken in her criticisms of the legal profession. Her primary complaint concerns the excessive fees lawyers charge people of modest means for providing routine legal services. Prior to her difficulties with the Florida Bar, she had served for more than 20 years as a court stenographer. In 1972, she assisted in creating a house for battered wives. The women who came to this house were typically without financial resources, and Ms. Furman began to help them obtain divorces. Eventually she opened her own office, offering services primarily in obtaining divorces. For her services, the charges ranged generally from $50 to $100.

Ms. Furman was not a member of the bar and was not licensed to practice law. Although she maintained that she was simply helping people to fill out forms for routine legal matters, the Florida Bar thought otherwise, contending that she was giving legal advice constituting the unauthorized practice of law. After the 1979 order of the Florida Supreme Court, Furman continued in her business and was again pursued by the Florida Bar. The matter was referred by the Florida Supreme Court to a referee, who concluded from the evidence presented by the Bar that Furman was practicing law in violation of the court order and recommended a four-month prison term. The court accepted the referee's findings, but reduced the term to 30 days on the condition that Furman comply with the original court order for 2 years. Under Florida law, Furman was not entitled to and did not receive a jury trial.

In finding her in contempt of court, the Florida Supreme Court cited evidence of several instances in which Furman advised clients to distort what they put in their petitions for divorce and how to proceed. In holding against Ms. Furman, the Florida Supreme Court emphasized its responsibility under the law to ensure that competent legal services be provided to the public.

In commuting Ms. Furman's sentence, with assurances that she would not continue her business, Governor Graham emphasized the continuing need for inexpensive public access to the courts.

CASE QUESTIONS

1. Where is the appropriate place to draw the line in a divorce case between assistance that constitutes the practice of law and assistance that does not?
2. How do we provide legal services to those in low-income economic groups who seek the resolution of family law problems?

Pretrial hearings and temporary orders   If the divorce process is at all lengthy, it may be necessary to have temporary orders approved by the court and to have temporary hearings on matters involved in the case. The paralegal will often draft such orders, submit them to the supervising attorney, and monitor their submission to the opposing attorney and the court, as well as monitoring the dates and requirement of any hearings.

Discovery   In divorce proceedings, one of the most critical issues involves ascertaining the financial assets of husband and wife, to establish a proper division of property and an appropriate level of spousal and child support. Spouses have been known to minimize the value of their assets, wages, and the like and to maximize their claims of debts and expenses. In many cases spouses will deliberately attempt to hide or disguise their assets. Attorneys and paralegals must use discovery techniques to unveil the full extent of the opposing party's assets. In some instances private investigators will be employed to ferret out hidden assets, and the paralegal may also investigate the facts. It may be necessary to arrange and prepare for depositions; much of this work is appropriate for paralegals, although the actual questioning during the deposition itself is ordinarily conducted by an attorney. Paralegals also work with the client to compose financial affidavits and prepare responses to interrogatories and depositions.

Trial Tasks

In domestic relations trials, the litigation paralegal manages the case much like other areas of litigation. The primary task is to compile, order, and index documents and all other case material in such a way that information and argument are readily accessible for the litigator. The paralegal must also keep up with deadlines and court dates. Fortunately, case handling is greatly facilitated by checklists and computer software used for litigation. Nevertheless, the paralegal is commonly responsible for keeping track of loose ends and making sure that all necessary tasks are performed.

Posttrial Tasks

Once the trial has taken place and a decree has been entered by the court, a number of clerical matters may warrant attention, such as preparing documents for the transfer of property and recording appropriate documents with the court.

The foregoing list of activities indicates the basic functions of a paralegal in a divorce case. Most divorce cases do not go to trial on contested issues because the couple, through their respective attorneys, usually completes the pretrial negotiations with a contract that spells out the division of property, specifies the nature of child custody, and provides for the payment of support. Such an agreement ordinarily leaves little for the court to do but issue a decree that conforms to or incorporates the contract into a final decree of divorce.

This does not necessarily end the legal work, however. The parties to the agreement often fail to perform their promises, and attorneys may be called in to resolve the issues that arise. For example, parents frequently fail to pay the child support promised in the marital settlement agreement and must be taken back to court to enforce the agreement.

SUMMARY

The family and family law have been in a state of change for many years, and the future does not seem to promise any greater stability. Family law is influenced on one side by changes in society and the family and on the other by the adversarial process itself. Although the legal system is often an awkward place to settle family disputes, the principal family law issue is divorce, which requires adjudication because it involves the termination of important bonds between the members of the family as well as the redistribution of marital property.

Lawyers and paralegals play important roles in family law. Most divorces are negotiated between lawyers rather than settled by the court. The outcomes may be more dependent on lawyers' values and perceptions of law and society than authoritative statements of the law by judges and legislatures.

QUESTIONS

1. What is the source of tension between the family and the law?
2. What areas of domestic relations are the primary concerns of the law?
3. Why is it appropriate to say that divorce defines marriage?
4. Why is divorce the principal area of family law practice?
5. How is a marriage contract different from a commercial contract?
6. How may a marriage be likened to a business partnership?
7. What is wrong with applying the adversarial model to family law?
8. How is the practice of family law different from other areas of the practice of law?
9. What are the major tasks the paralegal performs in family law?

EXERCISES

Answer the questions according to the law of your state.

1. What are the statutes covering marriage and divorce?
2. Do the statutes refer to divorce as "dissolution of marriage"?
3. Is there a statute governing surrogate mother contracts? If so, what does it require for a valid contract?
4. Have there been recent decisions or statutes defining the word *family*?
5. Under what circumstances does the law provide independent legal representation for children during a divorce?
6. Are there statutory restrictions on who may adopt a child?
7. Are domestic relations cases heard in equity or law?
8. Are paralegals licensed in your state? Is licensing or regulation currently being debated?
9. Who regulates paralegals in your state?
10. Does your state still have divorce based on fault (grounds)?

APPENDIX 1A

Domestic Relations Questionnaire (Massachusetts)

Source: Adapted from *Massachusetts Domestic Relations,* by Harvey, Moriarty, Hoffman, and Bryant. The Practice Systems Library, The Lawyers Co-operative Publishing Co., Rochester, NY (1989).

[The following questionnaire includes pertinent information needed for a divorce case. Much of this can be collected by the attorney or law office staff, often at the initial interview if the client agrees to retain the firm's services. Much of the information will necessarily be collected and furnished later by the client. Some of the information may be in the possession of the client's spouse or other sources and may be obtained through the discovery process. Not all items are needed for every client.]

Date of office conference:
Office conference fee:
Time spent: Asst. _____
    Atty. _____
Mailing list: Yes/No\Retainer Requested:
Hourly fees quoted:
    Partner _____
    Associate _____
    Paralegal _____
Minimum fees quoted:
Off. conf. fee pd.:   Date _____ Amt _____
    Dep _____ Initials _____

Client's name:
Preferred name:
Maiden name:
Maiden or former name to be resumed: Yes/No
Residence:
Mailing address if different:
How long at present residence:
With whom residing:
Age at marriage:
Present age:
Date of birth:
Home telephone number:
Work telephone number:
Social Security number:

Spouse's name:
Maiden name:
Maiden or former name to be resumed: Yes/No

Residence:
Mailing address if different:
How long at present residence:
With whom residing:
Age at marriage:
Present age:
Date of birth:
Social Security number:
Name of spouse's attorney:
Does spouse know client is here today: Yes/No

Date of marriage:
Where married:
Marriage certificate available: Yes/No
Any pre-nuptial agreements entered into?

Date of present separation:
Address last lived together:
Cities or towns parties lived in:
Any previous separations: Yes/No
    When   For how long   Details

Names of children
    Age   Date of birth
    Living with   Natural children
If wife presently pregnant and by whom:
Pregnancies interrupted or issue who died after birth:
Does client anticipate custody dispute: Yes/No
Client's relationship with children:
Spouse's relationship with children:
How children will react to separation:

Parties communicating about children:
Any illegitimate children:

Number of prior marriages:
   Husband   Wife
How terminated:
When terminated:
Where terminated:
To whom married:
Former married name:
Age of any children:
With whom children residing:
Cash or other support received:
Cash or other support paid:

Does husband have a criminal record:
Does wife have a criminal record:
Nature of any previous court actions:
Parties represented by counsel:
How long ago action filed:
Results:

Are parties presently in good health: Yes/No
Either party on any medication of any kind: Yes/No
Any serious illnesses, operations, diseases for either:
Any history of mental illness in parties, children,
   family:
Ever any suicide attempts by the parties:
Are the parties covered by medical insurance:
What type of medical insurance:
Who pays the premiums:

What religion are the parties:
Detail original family—who, where living, occupation,
   financial status, etc.:
   Husband   Wife

Is either party dependent upon original families:
Did the parties ever attend any marriage or other
   counseling:
Professional capacity of counselor:
Name of counselor:
How many sessions and for how long:
Who attended:
Who suggested:
Is either or both presently attending:
Reason/nature of counseling:
Dates attended/period of time:

Husband's employer:
Business address:

Job security:	Work hours:
Length of employment:	Availability of overtime:
Nature of job:	Previous annual income:
Gross wages:	Net wages:
No. of exemptions:	Pay stub available:
Promotions/raises:	

Life insurance:	Educational:
Loans:	Retirement:

Dues:	Pension:
Cost of living:	Disability:
Bonuses:	Credit union:
Commissions:	Company car:
Expense account:	Stocks:
Medical insurance:	Bonds:
Stock options:	Other:
Profit sharing:	

Previous employer:	Location:
Dates of employment:	Annual income:
Nature of job:	Why terminated:
High school education:	Graduate:
College education:	Degrees:
Other special skills or training:	
Indicate whether veteran:	Benefits derived:

Wife's employer:
Business address:

Job security:	Work hours:
Length of employment:	Availability of overtime:
Nature of job:	Previous annual income:
Gross wages:	Net wages:
No. of exemptions:	Pay stub available:
Promotions/raises:	

Life insurance:	Educational:
Loans:	Retirement:
Dues:	Pension:
Cost of living:	Disability:
Bonuses:	Credit union:
Commissions:	Company car:
Expense account:	Stocks:
Medical insurance:	Bonds:
Stock options:	Other:
Profit sharing:	

Previous employer:	Location:
Dates of employment:	Annual income:
Nature of job:	Why terminated:
High school education:	Graduate:
College education:	Degrees:
Other special skills or training:	
Indicate whether veteran:	Benefits derived:

Other income from any source: Yes/No

Jobs:	Rental income:
Interests:	Dividends:
Trust income:	Social Security:
Veterans:	Unemployment:
Welfare:	Disability:
Other:	

Joint tax returns filed for previous year: Yes/No

Can copy be obtained:	Name of accountant:
Amount of refund:	Amount of payment:
Distribution of refund:	Source of payment:

Was all income claimed on returns: Yes/No

Management of money while living together:
Management of money after separation:
Management of money presently:

Description of real estate: Location:
In whose name: Purchase price:
Form of ownership:
Amount of down payment:
Source of down payment:
Trace down payment:
Fair market value: Balance of mortgage:
Amount of equity:
Whose name on mortgage:
First mortgagee: Second mortgagee:
Amount of mortgage payments:
Occupied by whom:
Ever borrowed against:
For what purpose and whose benefit:

BANK ACCOUNTS
Location / Account / Whose funds / Balance /
   In whose name / Passbook?
   Name of bank
1. _____
2. _____
3. _____
4. _____

AUTOMOBILES
Year-Make / In whose name / Purchase price / Equity /
   Who Maintains
Driven by husband _____

_____

Driven by wife _____

_____

LIFE INSURANCE
       I.   II.   III.
Company _____
Face value _____
Type insurance _____
Insured _____
Cash surrender value _____
How long been paying _____
Beneficiary _____
Whether revokable _____
Owner _____
Who holds policy _____
Ever borrowed against _____
For what purpose _____
Who pays premiums _____

Does client have a will: Yes/No
Does spouse have a will: Yes/No
Type of wills: Executors:
Trustees: Guardians:
Terms of will:
Location of original wills:

OTHER ASSETS
Stocks: _____
Bonds: _____
Mutual funds: _____
Stock options: _____
Safety deposit box: _____
Business interests: _____
IRA accounts: _____
Credit union accounts: _____
Inheritances: _____
Jewelry: _____
Cash: _____

(include the following as appropriate: judgments,
pending suits, trademarks, copyrights, patents,
royalties, antiques, valuable personal property, coin/art
or other collections, boats, trailers, miscellaneous
vehicles or equipment, computers)
(Include in the above a description, in whose name,
who acquired the asset, what the purchase price was,
what the fair market value is, when the asset was
purchased or acquired, what the equity is, who has
possession, whether or not it was ever borrowed
against and by whom and for what purpose.)

LIABILITIES
Descrip. / Nature / When incurred / In whose name /
   Orig. debt / Balance / Payments / Who pays
1. _____
2. _____
(continue as needed)

CREDIT CARD STRUCTURE
Does spouse have authority to charge in client's
   name: Yes/No
Who has possession of credit cards:
Should creditors be notified: Yes/No

CONTRIBUTION OF PARTIES TO ASSETS
Husband: %   Wife: %
Any reason to believe spouse has undisclosed assets:
Any discussions of settlement between parties:
Terms of settlement discussions:

MARITAL PROBLEMS—CLIENT'S STATEMENTS
ABOUT SPOUSE
Cause to believe:
Alcohol
Drugs
Gambling
Physical violence
Number of occasions
Seriousness of injuries
Treatment of injuries
Dates
Places
Witnesses if any
How did it affect client

Financial
Erratic employment
Irresponsibility
Disputes about control
Extravagance

Sexual
Physiological
Psychological
Homosexuality
Dissatisfaction for whom

Infidelity
Domineering spouse
Suspicious spouse
Number of occasions
With one or more person
Name of any present ones
Financial standing

Do you consider your spouse a mature person:
Does your spouse consider him or herself to be a
  mature person:
Client's intentions, desires, direction:

MARITAL PROBLEMS—SPOUSE'S STATEMENTS ABOUT CLIENT

Cause to believe:
Alcohol
Drugs
Gambling

Physical violence
Number of occasions

Seriousness of injuries
Treatment of injuries
Dates
Places
Witnesses if any
How did it affect client

Financial
Erratic employment
Irresponsibility
Disputes about control
Extravagance

Sexual
Physiological
Psychological
Homosexuality
Dissatisfaction for whom

Infidelity
Domineering spouse
Suspicious spouse
Number of occasions
With one or more person
Name of any present ones
Financial standing

Would your spouse consider you a mature person:
Do you consider yourself to be a mature person:
Spouse's intentions, desires, direction:

Additional comments/Anything significant we ought
  to know?

Interviewer's notes

CHAPTER 2
Ethics and Family Law

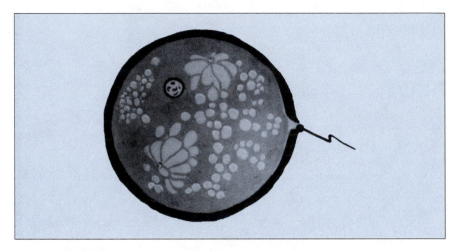

Person or Property?

Tennessee's highest court answered the unprecedented question of who has the custodial rights to seven frozen embryos claimed by Junior Lewis Davis and his ex-wife, Mary Sue. Originally, she wanted to implant and then carry the embryos to term, but he did not want to become a father against his will. Later, Mary Sue decided she wanted to donate the embryos to another couple. The court ruled that the embryos could not be protected as "persons" under state or federal law. Secondly, both parties were found to hold equal rights to the disposition of the embryos. The court ruled that the party wishing to avoid procreation (the ex-husband) was afforded greater protection than the party seeking to continue the procreation process or to donate the embryos to other individuals, and thus ruled in favor of Junior Lewis Davis. The embryos were later destroyed. Ethical dilemmas such as this one are commonplace in family law and are the subjects of this chapter.

If you have to ask yourself whether it is ethical or unethical, it's unethical.

A traditional rule of thumb for lawyers

OUTLINE

2.1 CONFIDENTIALITY
2.2 CONFLICT OF INTEREST
2.3 ATTORNEYS' FEES
2.4 COMMUNICATION WITH THE OPPOSING SIDE
2.5 ROMANTIC INVOLVEMENT WITH CLIENT
2.6 THE UNAUTHORIZED PRACTICE OF LAW
SUMMARY

The practice of family law is by its nature fraught with moral and ethical dilemmas, because it regulates the most basic human social institution and the most primal human concerns: sexuality, procreation, nurture, love, jealousy, dependence, and security. For the lawyer, the problems are complicated by the fact that immeasurables other than money are usually at stake. In contrast to a personal injury lawsuit or breach of contract, where the bottom line is ordinarily a question of the transfer of money from one party to another, family law almost always involves other very personal issues. The physical and emotional well-being of the parties and their most important relationships are at stake.

In this intense atmosphere, the attorney faces an array of professional dilemmas that have traditionally been classified under the heading of "legal ethics." The American Bar Association (ABA) has in recent decades addressed the problems of lawyers' conduct through the adoption of ethical codes proposed to the states for adoption by state bar associations. Although the ABA established a set of basic principles called the Canons of Ethics in the early part of the century, it was not until 1970, with the Model Code of Professional Responsibility, that a comprehensive code was formulated (and quickly adopted by most states). The Model Rules of Professional Conduct issued in 1983 attempted to rectify the imperfections of the Model Code. One or the other has been adopted with relatively few changes in the vast majority of states.

The two codes deal with problems of professional ethics encountered in the practice of law. Family law raises important issues primarily in the two most important areas of the codes: confidentiality and conflict of interest. Of lesser frequency, but no less problematic, are issues of attorneys' fees and romantic involvement with clients.

2.1 CONFIDENTIALITY

In seeking legal advice, individuals routinely reveal the details of conduct and transactions that are personal, private, and even secret. The delicate nature of these confidences is acute in family law. Even with no-fault divorce well established, the moral conduct of spouses becomes a frequent subject of family law. In deciding the **best interests of the child**, in dividing marital property, and in awarding alimony, courts and lawyers regularly consider the behavior of the spouses during the marriage. Personal, financial, and sexual matters that are otherwise unknown to the world may be discussed with an attorney. The details of marital stories are fascinating, often entertaining, and even disturbing. The temptation to pass these stories on is great for all but the close-mouthed gossip-hater. Nevertheless, great care must be taken to protect the confidences of family law clients.

Confidentiality is protected by the **attorney/client privilege**, which prevents an attorney from disclosing a client's confidences without the client's consent, with the exception of a few situations specified by the ethical codes. The staff of the law firm is also covered by the privilege; that is, members of the staff of a law firm may not be required to reveal confidential information or statements made by a client, at least to the extent that the staff may necessarily have access to such information. Secretaries, clerks, and paralegals are covered by the privilege. Note that this privilege is owned by the client and extends to the paralegal through employment by an attorney. If no attorney is involved, there is no privilege. For example, divorce is a prime area of services offered by independent **legal technicians**, individuals who deal directly with the public, who are not licensed attorneys and who are not supervised by attorneys. As of this writing, statements made by clients to legal technicians are not privileged. As the issue of licensing of legal technicians is addressed, the various states contemplating licensing must also address the issue of client privilege.

2.2 CONFLICT OF INTEREST

Conflicts of interest arise in two basic situations. The first occurs when the interests of the attorney conflict with the interests of a client. For example, it would be unethical for an attorney to represent the wife of a partner of the law firm in which the lawyer is employed in a divorce action; loyalty to the client would be compromised by loyalty to the law firm partner. The second situation arises when two clients are represented by the same law firm or even the same attorney. This occurs in family law when both husband and wife desire to be represented by the same attorney.

To avoid adding the significant costs of fees for two lawyers to the already troubled finances of the divorcing couple, husband and wife often seek to be represented by a single attorney, in the belief that divorce is not an adversarial process and that both are in agreement about the details of the divorce. There are serious ethical problems in representing both parties to a divorce. Although not absolutely prohibited, it is very risky for the attorney. In states that require proof of fault as a ground for divorce, or states that have fault and no-fault alternatives, the representation of both spouses presents immediate conflict and confidentiality problems. It is feasible only when there is no contest. Divorcing parties, however, are rarely in complete agreement; what may at first appear to be an amicable divorce frequently becomes hostile and bitter.

An attorney should never be in a position where there would be a duty to advise one spouse that the other is attempting to take advantage. For example, if the couple present to the attorney the terms of their agreement on the allocation of marital property, the attorney cannot reasonably advise one spouse that the agreement is disadvantageous for that spouse without compromising a duty to represent the best interests of the other client. Although an amicable divorce is desirable for the entire family, the financial interests of one spouse are inevitably in conflict with the interests of the other. Raising monthly alimony payments by $100 benefits the recipient by that amount at the same time it costs the payor that much. When there is only one pie, one person takes a piece that would otherwise be eaten by the other.

One feature of divorces that is often overlooked is the fact that the ex-spouses may well have to engage in transactions after the divorce, such as making alimony payments, dealing with custody and visitation issues, and distributing the property as agreed and decreed. Individuals who may have thought the terms of the agreement were fair when made often view them suspiciously later on. For example, inflation may make initially generous child support provisions seem insufficient later, or the noncustodial spouse may keep the children for longer periods of time than initially anticipated while still obliged to pay child support. The disgruntled client may, with some justification, point the finger at poor legal counsel. When the attorney's loyalties are divided, the accusation is difficult to defend against. At the very least, the attorney will appear to have used poor judgment in accepting multiple representation.

Representing both spouses is not only ethically suspect, it is also unwise from a practical point of view. Consider for a moment who the people are that refuse to hire attorneys for both sides. They want cut-rate legal services, they may not like or trust lawyers, and they have a naive notion of the

LEGAL TERMS

best interests of the child
The overriding consideration (the *polestar,* as it is sometimes referred to) in determining issues of child custody.

attorney/client privilege
Because of the need for full disclosure by clients, custom (and now law) dictate that such disclosures are privileged and may not be revealed by the attorney without the client's consent.

legal technicians
Those who provide legal services as paralegals but independent of attorney supervision. They walk a narrow line bordering the unauthorized practice of law.

conflict of interest
Whenever financial interests or personal relationships present any likelihood that an attorney might provide less than faithful representation to a client, a potential conflict of interest arises. Ethically, the attorney is responsible for taking appropriate action, usually declining to accept such employment.

simplicity of divorce. They do not make good clients. In most cases, couples who are simply trying to avoid a high-cost divorce can nevertheless see the wisdom of legal representation for each side, as well as the lawyer's ethical dilemma in serving two masters. In such a situation, the attorney who declines to serve both parties may ultimately represent one party, while the other seeks different counsel.

If the other side does not have an attorney, a record must be made of the attorney's advice to the other side to seek legal representation. A letter to the other spouse, as well as a statement in the settlement agreement, to the effect that the attorney represents only one party and that the other party was urged to seek legal counsel offers protection against later claims by a disgruntled party.

Rule 1.7 of the Model Rules was written broadly to cover conflict of interest in general, but it is particularly pertinent to family law. Case No. 2-1 shows the opinion of one state's bar on this subject.

MODEL RULES OF PROFESSIONAL CONDUCT

Rule 1.7 Conflict of interest; general rule.

(a)   A lawyer shall not represent a client if the representation of that client will be directly adverse to the interests of another client, unless:
   (1)   The lawyer reasonably believes the representation will not adversely affect the lawyer's responsibility with the other client; and
   (2)   Each client consents after consultation.

(b)   A lawyer shall not represent a client if the lawyer's exercise of independent professional judgment in the representation of that client may be materially limited by the lawyer's responsibilities to another client or to a third person or by the lawyer's own interest, unless:
   (1)   The lawyer reasonably believes the representation will not be adversely affected; and
   (2)   The client consents after consultation.

(c)   When representation of multiple clients in a single matter is undertaken, the consultation shall include explanation of the implications of the common representation and the advantages and risks involved.

(d)   A lawyer related to another lawyer as parent, child, sibling, or spouse shall not represent a client in a representation directly adverse to a person who the lawyer knows is represented by the other lawyer except upon consent by the client after consultation regarding the relationship.

When studying family law, one should always visualize the parties as members of an actual family. What obligations do practitioners of law have toward unrepresented children?

CASE NO. 2-1   Representing Husband and Wife

The following opinion was issued by the Professional Ethics Committee of the Florida Bar. These opinions are written in response to formal requests made by members of the Florida Bar for an opinion on a legal question the members encounter. Before publishing a final written opinion, a proposed advisory opinion is published in the Florida Bar *News,* so that interested attorneys may offer comment on the opinion. Opinion 71-45 came soon after Florida adopted no-fault divorce (dissolution of marriage). Because no-fault suggests nonadversarial proceedings, some lawyers wondered whether its advent altered the former prohibition against lawyers representing both husband and wife in a divorce. The Ethics Committee opinions are advisory and not binding on grievance committees or courts. However, an attorney who has sought an opinion and then acted in accordance with it is unlikely to be severely sanctioned at a later date.

**PROFESSIONAL ETHICS
OF THE FLORIDA BAR
OP. 71-45 (1973)
(Reconsideration)**

The new "no-fault" divorce law has in no way changed the potential adversarial nature of the proceedings between the spouses with regard to division of property, alimony, child support and child custody. Thus a lawyer cannot represent such potentially divergent interests even though the divorce statute dispenses with the necessity of alleging and proving fault or guilt as a condition precedent to dissolving the marriage contract.

The position is based on the following reasoning:

1. *A lawyer may not ignore the existence of potential conflicts of interest not apparent to his clients.*

* * *

2. *Conflicts of Interest may be so subtle as "compromising influences" or "discordant interests"; yet same may not be ignored by the lawyer.*

* * *

3. *A lawyer may not undertake the representation of clients recognizing the "possibility" that his judgment may be impaired or his loyalty divided.*

* * *

4. *A lawyer cannot both arbitrate and advocate in the same proceeding. The mere possibility of the latter role precludes the undertaking of the former role.*

* * *

[Footnote 1, p. 735:] Of course, adherence to this view does not mean that each spouse must necessarily have separate counsel of record. There can be situations in which there has been full and fair disclosure, the affairs are uncomplicated, no overreaching is present and both parties comprehend the significance of what is being done. In such cases it may be permissible for an attorney representing one spouse to prepare pleadings and, if appropriate, a settlement and custody agreement and submit the case to the court. In those instances it should be made to appear that the non-represented party chose not to employ counsel even though apprised of the advantages of doing so.

* * *

Committeeman Beverly stated the minority opinion of the committee:

* * *

I am assuming for purposes of this opinion that the spouses have been able to maintain an amicable and civilized relationship and have mutually agreed that a dissolution of the marriage is in order, for whatever reason, and have further agreed upon a distribution of the property. Under these circumstances, all that remains is for the legal relationship of husband and wife to be severed. In effect, therefore, the parties have resolved all of the issues between themselves and are simply seeking the services of an attorney to implement the dissolution for them.

Within these parameters, it is my opinion that an attorney may ethically represent both husband and wife in a proceeding for dissolution of marriage.

* * *

In my view the majority position is professionally deficient in that it fails to protect the unrepresented spouse since, unless a single attorney is allowed to represent both spouses, there is no doubt but what one spouse will be completely unrepresented in many of these cases. I cannot conceive that this is either ethical or proper when there is a reasonable solution.

CASE QUESTIONS

To clarify the ethical issues arising in multiple representation, attempt to answer the following:

1. An attorney representing both parties arranges an amicable divorce without any snags. Several months later, the ex-wife (former client) seeks the attorney's help in obtaining enforcement of

the agreement requiring the husband to execute documents transferring his interest in the former marital home to the ex-wife. May the attorney undertake this representation?

2. May the attorney who represented two parties to a divorce represent either several years later when one seeks to bring a petition to modify the monthly child support payments?

3. May the same attorney represent the husband years later when he seeks a divorce from his second wife?

4. Contrast the above with the following unusual but real situation: Attorney Robinson hires attorney Washington to obtain a divorce. Mrs. Robinson later becomes Mrs. Washington, but when this marriage fails, attorney Washington hires attorney Robinson in the subsequent divorce.

The ethical pitfalls of representing divorcing clients are well known to attorneys. Case No. 2-2 involves an adoption in which the attorney helped a young woman in distress, only to find himself embroiled in an ethical dilemma. From the decision, it would appear that the attorney acted morally and with the best of intentions, profited but little, but nevertheless got into trouble with the bar.

CASE NO. 2-2 Unethical Kindness

ARDEN v. STATE BAR OF CALIFORNIA
341 P.2d 6 (Cal. 1959)
Supreme Court of California

PER CURIAM.

In early 1954 petitioner was employed by Miss Karen Mattson, an unmarried girl 18 years old, who told him that she was pregnant and that, when the child was born, she wanted to have it adopted. Petitioner undertook to handle the problem, informing her that a public agency could handle the adoption, or that it could be handled privately. Miss Mattson preferred a private adoption. Petitioner first advised his client to tell her parents about her pregnancy, but she refused. He thereupon placed her in the home of one of his friends where she remained until the birth of the child. To assist in the deception of the parents, he arranged a false mailing address for her in Detroit.

Through the efforts of petitioner, Miss Mattson was introduced to several prospective parents. She selected a Mr. and Mrs. Abraham Cohen to be the adoptive parents of her child. At their request, and with the knowledge and consent of Miss Mattson, petitioner was employed to represent the Cohens in the adoption proceedings. Petitioner was paid $250.00 by the Cohens for this purpose. He was paid nothing by Miss Mattson.

The child was born in August of 1954, and, with Miss Mattson's consent, was immediately delivered to the Cohens. On August 26, 1954, the court appointed the Cohens guardians of the child. The petition, which had been filed by petitioner, contained the express consent of Miss Mattson to the appointment. Several days later, with Miss Mattson's knowledge and consent, petitioner filed a petition for adoption of the child on behalf of the Cohens.

In November of 1954 Miss Mattson told petitioner that she thought she now wanted to keep her child. She did not, however, request petitioner to take any legal action to revoke the guardianship or to in any way interfere with the adoption proceedings. In December, 1954, she apparently changed her mind again because, in that month, she gave her written consent to the adoption at a conference at the Los Angeles County Bureau of Adoptions.

On January 14, 1955, Miss Mattson visited the Cohens at their home and demanded $3000.00 or the return of the child. Mr. Cohen told her to call him at the petitioner's office at a designated time on the following day. She telephoned that office three times. The first two of these telephone communications were tape recorded by petitioner. In the third telephone conversation, petitioner told Miss Mattson that he had advised the Cohens not to pay her, that he had recorded their prior conversations, that the recordings showed an attempt at extortion which was a criminal offense for which she could be prosecuted, that the tapes would be available in connection with any action she might take to have her child returned, but that if the adoption went through without any action on her part to obtain the child, he would destroy the tapes. Thereafter petitioner discussed the matter of the tape recordings with the District Attorney. The nature of this discussion does not appear in the record.

* * *

The petitioner challenges some of these findings. He first challenges the finding that he "was employed by Miss Karen Mattson," on the ground that the record shows that no formal employment was ever entered into. The point is without merit. Obviously, an attorney-client relationship existed. The fact that there were no formal arrangements is immaterial. It is of some significance that petitioner, throughout the hearings before the local committee, referred to his being "hired" by Miss Mattson.

* * *

The local committee concluded that petitioner had not violated Rule 7 of the Rules of Professional Conduct, because Miss Mattson had knowledge of and consented to the petitioner's representation of the Cohens in the adoption proceedings, and also because no conflict of interests existed until some time after her consent to the adoption had been filed. This determination was correct.

Rule 7 provides that "a member of the State Bar shall not represent conflicting interests, except with the consent of all parties concerned." There is evidence in the record indicating that Miss Mattson gave her consent to petitioner's representation of the Cohens as early as June of 1954. Miss Mattson told petitioner she wanted the baby back in November of 1954, but this appears to have been merely an illustration of her variable attitude toward the adoption. She later changed her mind again and signed the consent for adoption. Under these circumstances, it cannot be said that petitioner was improperly representing conflicting interests.

Strangely enough, although the local committee found petitioner had not violated Rule 7, it found that petitioner had violated Rule 5 of the Rules of Professional Conduct, which provides that "a member of the State Bar shall not accept employment adverse to a client or former client, without the consent of the client or former client, relating to a matter in reference to which he has obtained confidential information by reason of or in the course of his employment by such client or former client."

* * *

The rationale for these decisions is that the common employment of the attorney removed the communications of the parties to one another and to the attorney from the privileged category. The communications not being deemed confidential, there is no impediment to or impropriety in the adverse representation by the attorney. . . .

The rule stated in these cases applies to the facts of the instant case. Here petitioner had been employed by both Miss Mattson and the Cohens in the adoption proceeding. As has been pointed out above, this dual representation was found to be proper. The communications from Miss Mattson to the Cohens and to the petitioner, and vice versa, were, therefore, not confidential.

It is suggested that the mere representation of both parties to an adoption, even with consent, may constitute a violation of the rules of professional conduct. On this issue the members of the Bar have expressed opposite views. In a handbook published in 1956 by the Continuing Education of the Bar entitled "Family Law for California Lawyers" it was urged that such dual representation was permissible. In the State Bar Journal of July-August 1957 (32 State Bar Journal 343) opinions to the contrary were published. The issue is a highly debatable one. No clear-cut rule on the subject has been announced. It is not proper to discipline an attorney for a violation of a claimed principle that was and is so highly debatable.

* * *

[T]he only charge found to involve [an ethical violation] is the tape recording incident. . . . It is quite obvious that [petitioner's offer to destroy the tapes if Mattson did not impede the adoption] constituted a threat. Miss Mattson's demand for $3,000 or return of the baby bordered on, if it did not constitute, attempted extortion. In the taped conversation between petitioner and Miss Mattson, petitioner told Miss Mattson that her demand was an attempt at extortion for which she could be prosecuted. Thus, it is clear that petitioner was threatening her with a prosecution unless she desisted from her threat to interfere with and overturn the pending adoption.

. . . Although petitioner is a young attorney and his conduct may have been prompted by the reprehensible actions of Miss Mattson, it is nonetheless conduct that cannot be countenanced.

The Board has recommended that petitioner be suspended for thirty days. We believe that, under the circumstances, that punishment is too severe. While the circumstances in which he acted can furnish no excuse, his motive and character and acts of his client may be considered in mitigation in determining the measure of discipline. Clearly, at all times, petitioner had the best interests of the child in mind. Miss Mattson's character has been sufficiently indicated herein. Further, we must also consider that these proceedings have been hanging over the petitioner's head for more than three years. . . .

It is our conclusion that petitioner should be disciplined by a public reprimand and that this opinion shall constitute such reprimand. It is so ordered.

2.3 ATTORNEYS' FEES

Fee arrangements between attorney and client are contracts, and, as such, are subject to the same requirements as other contracts (e.g., voidable for fraud, misrepresentation, etc.). Freedom of contract is a venerable principle underlying contract law, which expresses the notion that competent persons should be free to enter contracts for lawful purposes and bind each other legally by the promises voluntarily made. There are, of course, a number of exceptions or exceptional circumstances warranting a court's overriding or ignoring this principle. Lawyer-client contracts present such an exceptional circumstance for two reasons. First, as legal representation may be sought only from a licensed professional, those in need of legal services are not, strictly speaking, entirely free to choose their representatives. Second, the interests of the public compel the bar and the legal system to hold attorneys to special duties toward their clients, which may, under appropriate circumstances, override otherwise enforceable promises.

The attorney-client contract ordinarily calls for the exchange of services for money, a common sort of contractual arrangement. Unlike most commercial contracts, however, the attorney is bound by an ethical code which requires competent provision of services and prohibits excessive fees. The nature of legal fee arrangements contributes to a certain degree to the problems that may arise. Lawyers contract to receive payment of money in four basic forms: (1) hourly rate; (2) contingency fee; (3) fixed fee; or (4) retainer. These are often combined, as when an attorney accepts a **retainer** (i.e., a specified sum to retain, or hire, the attorney as an agent representing the client) that is simply part of a larger **fixed fee** or to cover a certain number of hours in advance. **Contingency fees**, through which a lawyer is compensated by receiving a percentage of the amount ultimately recovered, are usually unethical in family law cases. An attorney should not encourage a divorce nor obtain a stake in its outcome by making compensation dependent on the result. It would be inappropriate, for example, for an attorney to make an agreement with a wife to split the amount the attorney is able to wheedle out of the husband—clearly, the attorney would not then be agreeable to a fair property division or a reconciliation. Contingency fees are best left to personal injury cases.

Hourly fees may seem the most honest form of charge, especially in cases, like divorce, that are somewhat unpredictable in duration at the outset; but hourly fees encourage delay and the use of time-consuming tasks to generate increased fees. Naturally, unnecessary expenditure of work to generate fees is unethical, but the reasonableness of the effort is a matter of judgment and not susceptible to attack later unless clearly unreasonable. Despite the difficulties hourly fees raise, it is important for each attorney to establish an hourly rate and to maintain accurate records of time spent on every case. When courts are asked to test the reasonableness of a fee, time expended is inevitably an important factor. Also, when a divorce case becomes more complicated or prolonged than originally anticipated, the attorney may reassure the client of the reasonableness of fees by noting the time spent. Divorce tends to be a financial disaster for the parties, so they are quite sensitive to fees.

An important feature of divorce is the traditional practice of charging the wife's attorneys' fees to the husband. The tradition is derived from the old common law principle of making the husband responsible for the wife's expenditures for *necessaries,* usually food, shelter, and the like, but including legal fees as well. The tradition endured into modern times in large part because the traditional pattern of husband/provider–wife/homemaker usually meant that the family resources were acquired in the husband's name. The wife/homemaker often had little control over marital property from which to hire and pay for an attorney. Presently, courts seem more willing to question this relic of the past to examine its justification in specific cases. Even when approved, the court is obliged to determine whether the wife's fees are reasonable; it would be unfair to require the husband to pay exorbitant attorneys' fees simply because they were set out in the wife's claim. For this reason, it is important to keep records that can justify the amount of the fees. (In many cases, the actual fees may exceed those of the marital settlement agreement or the determination of the court and must be paid by the wife, assuming they are not unreasonably excessive.) In all these matters, disclosure of fees and their manner of ascertainment should be made clear to the client at the outset.

2.4 COMMUNICATION WITH THE OPPOSING SIDE

When an attorney communicates with a layperson concerning a legal matter, the layperson is often at a distinct disadvantage and the attorney may exploit the situation, pressure the layperson, or elicit information improperly. To avoid an appearance of impropriety, the attorney should avoid such contact whenever possible, especially when communicating with an opposing party.

The nature of the rules varies, depending on whether the opposing party is represented by an attorney. In many instances, one spouse will avoid the expense of an attorney when the other spouse has initiated divorce proceedings through an attorney. When the distribution of property is relatively simple, fairness is reasonably clear, and the parties are in agreement as to custody of minor children, one spouse may see no real need to consult an attorney. Whether this is a wise choice depends on the emotional maturity and legal sophistication of the unrepresented spouse. With an unrepresented opposing party, the attorney has little choice but to communicate directly, but such communication should be conducted, as much as possible, through written correspondence. The attorney can in this way create a paper trail that demonstrates the propriety of the attorney's conduct. Without pretending to represent the opposing spouse, the attorney may be ethically required to explain the legal consequences of the steps taken.

LEGAL TERMS

retainer
When used in connection with hiring an attorney, refers to an amount paid in advance to "retain" the attorney, i.e., make the attorney the agent of the client.

fixed fee
Attorneys sometimes charge flat, or fixed, fees, which are specified amounts ordinarily paid in advance or in installments.

contingency fee
In personal injury cases, attorneys often contract to provide legal services for a percentage of the final recovery. This is generally considered unethical in other areas of law, with the exception of some collections of debts.

MODEL RULES OF PROFESSIONAL CONDUCT

Rule 4.3 Dealing with unrepresented persons.

In dealing on behalf of a client with a person who is not represented by counsel, a lawyer shall not state or imply that the lawyer is disinterested. When the lawyer knows or reasonably should know that the unrepresented person misunderstands the lawyer's role in the matter, the lawyer shall make reasonable efforts to correct the misunderstanding.

An important point to note is that it is sometimes not sufficient to act properly. What may be important is how present acts could be perceived at some time in the future. In divorce cases, the spouses harbor a great deal of anger and frustration and the attorney for the opposing spouse is often viewed as a deserving target of these emotions. Because the attorney owes a high duty to clients, the court, and the general public, the onus of establishing proper conduct falls on the attorney.

When the other spouse is represented by counsel, it is improper for the attorney to communicate directly with opposing party. Although this rule has universal application, it is particularly sensitive in family law, because the parties often rely on their attorneys to shoulder much of the burden of the divorce procedure.

MODEL RULES OF PROFESSIONAL CONDUCT

Rule 4.2 Communication with person represented by counsel.

In representing a client, a lawyer shall not communicate about the subject of the representation with a person the lawyer knows to be represented by another lawyer in the matter, unless the lawyer has the consent of the other lawyer.

2.5 ROMANTIC INVOLVEMENT WITH CLIENT

It is quite natural that attorney and client, like any other two human beings, will sometimes discover a mutual romantic attraction. Their professional relationship, however, limits the attorney's freedom of choice in such a relationship. Though this subject has not been a major focus of ethical concerns in the past, the confirmation hearings of Justice Clarence Thomas in 1991 drew national attention to sexual harassment in the workplace and its impact on judicial qualifications. A number of notorious cases involving health care and mental health professionals and their patients in recent years has also made this a public issue. Lawyers have not been immune from these sorts of difficulties, and appropriate conduct is imperative.

The problem is particularly acute in divorce and family law cases. Those in the process of divorce suddenly find themselves very vulnerable and alone, frequently with a sense of personal failure and feelings of unworthiness and unattractiveness. Enter the confident and caring attorney to champion their cause and solve their problems. Is it any wonder that clients frequently imbue their attorneys with extraordinary qualities and desire a mutual attraction? On the other side, the attorney is quite naturally flattered, standing on this pedestal erected by the client (or perhaps the situation).

The ethical traps should be obvious. First, the attorney assumes a fiduciary relationship with clients in which any betrayal of trust implies unethical conduct. The burden is on the attorney to act properly and to be prepared to show that no breach of trust occurred. The attorney should even avoid situations that *might* be misconstrued by third parties. Second, romantic involvement with the client in a divorce case inevitably clouds the attorney's judgment with regard to the case itself. An attorney could be disinclined to accept the possibility of a reconciliation and the client, having found a new partner, might oppose an otherwise advantageous reconciliation. An attorney might become unduly antagonistic toward the opposing spouse or might be overly anxious to complete the divorce.

For a number of reasons, the likelihood and risk of romantic involvement with clients is less for paralegals than for attorneys. Nevertheless, the fiduciary aspect of the attorney-client relationship extends to a law firm's staff working on a case, and it is very imprudent for members of the staff to become romantically involved during the pendency of a case.

CASE NO. 2-3 Romancing a Client

The following case arose because an attorney had sexual relations with the plaintiff, resulting in an ectopic pregnancy and an operation that left the plaintiff sterile. The attorney had assured the woman that he could not make her pregnant. She sued for damages. The excerpt here, however, addresses only the ethical features of attorney-client romance.

BARBARA A. v. JOHN G.
145 Cal. App. 3d 369, 193 Cal. Rptr.
422 (1983)
California Court of Appeal

BARRY-DEAL, Associate Justice.

We decline to address another issue indirectly raised by appellant—one of first impression in California, at least as far as statutes, cases, and rules are concerned. She asserts that it is a breach of ethics for an attorney, particularly in a family law context, to induce a client to have sexual relations during the course of the representation, and she points out that other professions have imposed discipline on a member for sexual misconduct with a patient. (See, e.g., *Dresser v. Board of Medical Quality Assurance* (1982) 130 Cal.App.3d 506, 181 Cal.Rptr. 797; *Cooper v. Board of Medical Examiners* (1975) 49 Cal.App.3d 931, 123 Cal.Rptr. 563.)

We think this question is more properly directed to the State Bar of California, which so far has not publicly addressed the issue.[11]

---

11 The Board of Governors of the Oregon State Bar in June 1982 issued Legal Ethics Opinion No. 475, advisory only, stating that it is unethical for an attorney to be sexually involved with the client while representing the client in a divorce action, which of course may differ in degree from a post-dissolution modification proceeding. The discussion accompanying the opinion is as follows: "DR 5-101(A) requires that a lawyer not accept employment if the exercise of his or her professional judgment on behalf of the client may be affected by his or her own personal interest, except with the consent of the client after full disclosure. DR 5-101(A) and 2-110(B)(2) and (C)(2) also imply a duty to withdraw from employment if circumstances arise whereby the attorney's personal interests may impair his or her ability to continue to exercise independent professional judgment on behalf of the client, unless the client consents to continued representation after full disclosure. These rules recognize that to fulfill the lawyer's responsibility of fully and adequately representing the client, it is essential that the lawyer be able to exercise independent professional judgment on behalf of the client. Where there is any question about the lawyer's ability to exercise an independent professional judgment, the client must be able to give an informed consent. The lawyer representing one spouse in a dissolution proceeding cannot know with certainty whether a reconciliation is possible or is in the best interest of the client, or how the possibility of a reconciliation might be affected by an affair between the lawyer and the client. Nor can the lawyer know with certainty what reaction the client's spouse would have to learning that the lawyer is having an affair during the dissolution proceedings, or how such knowledge might affect the negotiation of property rights and, if children are involved, the right to custody. See In the Matter of Lehr and Lehr, 36 Or.App. 23, 583 P.2d 1157 (1978). The potential for prejudice to the client is immense. Moreover, the client may be unable to give a voluntary and informed consent to continued representation. The attorney-client relationship is a fiduciary relationship, one of trust. The nature of that fiduciary relationship tends to make the client intellectually and, in many cases, emotionally dependent upon the attorney. If the client becomes involved in a love affair with the attorney, that dependency would only be increased. It would appear impossible for the lawyer to carry on such an affair with the client and maintain an independent judgment about whether the affair might harm the client's interests. See DR 7-101(A)(3). Even if the attorney were able to predict the consequences of the affair and explain them to the client, it is doubtful that the client's consent to the attorney's continued representation could ever be deemed truly informed and voluntary. . . ."

2.6 THE UNAUTHORIZED PRACTICE OF LAW

The unauthorized practice of law was discussed in Chapter 1, particularly in relation to the Rosemary Furman case. This issue is particularly relevant to legal technicians who are not supervised by attorneys. Apparently, open as well as clandestine legal services are offered to the public, especially in divorce and family law cases. The *Winder* case, Case No. 2-4, draws a line between advice that constitutes legal services and activity that does not.

CASE NO. 2-4 What Is the Unauthorized Practice of Law?

STATE v. WINDER
348 N.Y.S.2d 270
(App. Div. 4th Dep't 1973)
Supreme Court, Appellate Division,
Fourth Department

The Divorce Yourself Kit offered for sale by defendant, a layman, purports to offer forms and instructions in law and procedure in certain areas of matrimonial law and the judicial process. . . . This is the essential of legal practice—the representation and the advising of a particular person in a particular situation. . . . [T]he defendant's publication does not purport "to give personal advice on a specific problem peculiar to a designated or readily identified person, and because of the absence

of the essential element of legal practice—the representation and the advising of a particular person in a particular situation" in the publication and sale of the kits, such publication and sale did not constitute the unlawful practice of law. . . . The record does fully support, however, the finding of the court that for the charge of $75 or $100 for the kit, the defendant gave legal advice in the course of personal contacts concerning particular problems which might arise in the preparation and presentation of the purchaser's asserted matrimonial cause of action or pursuit of other legal remedies and assistance in the preparation of necessary documents [which the court enjoined as the unauthorized practice of law].

CASE NO. 2-5 Malpractice

The following case is included to remind the reader that attorneys may be financially as well as professionally liable for the negligent provision of legal service, i.e., sued for **malpractice**. Although this is a civil suit brought by a client, it is indirectly grounded on an ethical violation, that is, the duty of the attorney to provide competent legal services. Note that the issue of military pension is today covered by federal law [Pub. L. No. 97-252, 96 Stat. 730 (1982)].

SMITH v. LEWIS
530 P.2d 589, 118 Cal. Rptr. 621 (1975)
Supreme Court of California

MOSK, Justice.

On February 17, 1967, plaintiff retained defendant to represent her in a divorce action against General Smith. According to plaintiff's testimony, defendant advised her that her husband's retirement benefits were not community

property. Three days later defendant filed plaintiff's complaint for divorce. General Smith's retirement benefits were not pleaded as items of community property, and therefore were not considered in the litigation or apportioned by the trial court. The divorce was uncontested and the interlocutory decree divided the minimal described community property and awarded Mrs. Smith $400 per month in alimony and child support. The final decree was entered on February 27, 1968.

On July 17, 1968, pursuant to a request by plaintiff, defendant filed on her behalf a motion to amend the decree, alleging under oath that because of his mistake, inadvertence, and excusable neglect (Code Civ. Proc., § 473) the retirement benefits of General Smith had been omitted from the list of community assets owned by the parties and that such benefits were in fact community property. The motion was denied on the ground of untimeliness.

* * *

The law is now settled in California that "retirement benefits which flow from the employment relationship, to the extent they have vested, are community property subject to equal division between the spouses in the event the marriage is dissolved." . . . In determining whether defendant exhibited the requisite degree of competence in his handling of plaintiff's divorce action, the crucial inquiry is whether his advice was so legally deficient when it was given that he may be found to have failed to use "such skill, prudence, and diligence as lawyers of ordinary skill and capacity commonly possess and exercise in the performance of the tasks which they undertake."

* * *

Of course, the fact that in 1967 a reasonable argument could have been offered to support the characterization of General Smith's federal benefits as separate property does not indicate the trial court erred in submitting the issue of defendant's malpractice to the jury. The *state* benefits, the large majority of the payments at issue, were unquestionably community property according to all available authority and should have been claimed as such. As for the *federal* benefits, the record documents defendant's failure to conduct any reasonable research into their proper characterization under community property law. Instead, he dogmatically asserted his theory, which he was unable to support with authority and later recanted, that all noncontributory military retirement benefits, whether state or federal, were immune from community treatment upon divorce. The jury could well have found defendant's refusal to educate himself to the applicable principles of law constituted negligence which prevented him from exercising informed discretion with regard to his client's rights.

As the jury was correctly instructed, an attorney does not ordinarily guarantee the soundness of his opinions and, accordingly, is not liable for every mistake he may make in his practice. He is expected, however, to possess knowledge of those plain and elementary principles of law which are commonly known by well informed attorneys, and to discover those additional rules of law which although not commonly known, may readily be found by standard research techniques. . . . In the instant case, ample evidence was introduced to support a jury finding that defendant failed to perform such adequate research into the question of the community character of retirement benefits and thus was unable to exercise the informed judgment to which his client was entitled.

* * *

In any event, as indicated above, had defendant conducted minimal research into either hornbook or case law, he would have discovered with modest effort that General Smith's state retirement benefits were likely to be treated as community property and that his federal benefits at least arguably belonged to the community as well. Therefore, we hold that the trial court . . . properly submitted the question of defendant's negligence to the jury under the instructions given. . . . The judgment is affirmed.

CLARK, Justice (dissenting).

I dissent.

The evidence is insufficient to prove plaintiff lost $100,000 from her lawyer's negligence in 1967. There is no direct evidence a well-informed lawyer would have obtained an award of the husband's pensions in the wife's divorce, nor does the record provide such inference. Rather, the state of the law and the circumstances of the parties reveal lawyer Lewis reached a reasonable result for his client in 1967.

* * *

CONCLUSION

Given the uncertain status of the law, the circumstances of the parties, and the close relationship between property division and alimony payment, an ethical, diligent and careful lawyer would have avoided litigation over pension rights and instead would have sought a compensating alimony award for any inequity, as expressly suggested by *Kinsey v. Kinsey.* . . . So far as appears, defendant secured such compensating award.

Accordingly even assuming that defendant was negligent in failing to research the pension questions, the record does not furnish a balance of probabilities that his negligence—rather than the uncertain status of the law and the availability of uncontested alimony—caused plaintiff to lose a $100,000 pension award.

* * *

I would reverse the judgment.

SUMMARY

Although family law cases are governed by the same ethical codes for attorneys as are other cases, the emotional and financial distress characteristic of family law, particularly divorce, makes certain ethical problems important. Confidentiality is especially sensitive because of the intimate details of personal relationships frequently disclosed to attorneys. Law office staff must adamantly resist the temptation to gossip. The issue of conflict of interest arises in a number of situations, but none so perplexing as the multiple representation of divorcing spouses—something to be avoided under all but exceptional circumstances.

Contingency fee arrangements are unethical in divorce cases. Other fee arrangements, whether fixed, retainer, or hourly rates, may be used alone or in combination, but clients must be informed of the nature and measure of their fees. A waning tradition of the husband paying the wife's attorneys' fees may affect the fee arrangement.

Attorneys and staff should avoid dating or romantic involvement with clients in the midst of divorce.

LEGAL TERMS

malpractice suit
A negligence suit brought against someone for negligent provision of professional services. It differs from ordinary negligence suits in that the professional is held to a higher standard of care.

QUESTIONS

1. Describe a scenario in which the following requirement of Rule 1.7 (see § 2.2) would be satisfied when the attorney was representing both spouses in a divorce:
   (a) A lawyer shall not represent a client if the representation of that client will be directly adverse to the interests of another client, unless:
      (1) The lawyer reasonably believes the representation will not adversely affect the lawyer's responsibility with the other client . . .
2. What would the attorney in question 1 say in the consultation required by Rule 1.7(a)(2) ("Each client consents after consultation")?
3. Why is representation of both spouses impracticable in states with divorce based on fault?
4. Why are legal technicians not covered by the attorney-client privilege?
5. How are contracts between attorney and client different from other contracts?
6. Why are contingency fee contracts unethical in divorce cases?
7. Why is it common practice to charge the husband for attorneys' fees his wife incurs during their divorce?
8. When may an attorney contact the other spouse in a divorce action?
9. What reasons can you give for an attorney to avoid romantic involvement with a client?
10. How could attorney Arden have protected himself from charges of unethical conduct (Case No. 2-2)?
11. If *Arden v. State Bar of California* were decided today under Rule 1.7 of the Model Rules of Professional Conduct, would the reasoning be different?

EXERCISES

Answer the questions according to the law of your state.

1. By what name is the lawyers' ethical code called?
2. What specific provisions does it contain regarding family law?
3. What authority is there for paralegals falling within the lawyer-client privilege?
4. May legal technicians provide assistance to divorcing parties? How far does assistance go?
5. May an attorney represent both husband and wife in a divorce?
6. Does your state have the equivalent of Rule 1.7 of the Model Rules?
7. What governs the amount charged by attorneys for domestic relations cases? 59 A.L.R.3d 152.

CHAPTER 3
Family Law in Historical Perspective

The First Divorced President

The conservative presidency of Ronald Reagan advocated family values, while his own family was dysfunctional. Ex-actor Reagan divorced his first wife, actress Jane Wyman, and married Nancy Davis, another actress. Children from both marriages often spoke publicly of neglect and abuse. Daughter Patti wrote a thinly veiled autobiographical novel discussing a famous dysfunctional family. From left to right are daughter-in-law Doria, son Ron, President and Nancy Reagan, and Patti Davis. An older son, Michael (not pictured) was adopted by Reagan and Wyman. Daughter Maureen Reagan (also not pictured) is, perhaps the most well-known of the President's children, since she travels in Republican political circles.

— Courtesy AP/Wide World Photos

A page of history is worth a volume of logic.

Justice Oliver Wendell Holmes, Jr.

OUTLINE

3.1 FAMILY LAW: A NEVER-ENDING STORY
3.2 THE MAKING OF FAMILY LAW
3.3 HISTORICAL ROOTS OF FAMILY LAW
3.4 THE MARRIAGE RELATIONSHIP
3.5 TERMINATING THE MARRIAGE RELATIONSHIP
3.6 CHILDREN
3.7 RIGHTS OF WOMEN
3.8 CHANGING LIFESTYLES
SUMMARY

3.1 FAMILY LAW: A NEVER-ENDING STORY

In the three centuries since the English colonization of America, no area of law has undergone more change than family law. Family and family life have changed radically and the law has changed accordingly. At the outset, it is important to note that regulation of the family by legislatures and courts has always been problematic. There is a lack of consensus over the extent to which the state should intrude into family relationships. For example, there is a strong policy dictating that the state should in some way protect children from abuse, neglect, and even economic misfortune. At the same time, traditional values hold that parental authority is essential to the integrity of the family and that the state should intrude upon or limit this authority only when absolutely necessary. Even these beliefs are not universally shared. If we find a homeless, down-on-their-luck family living temporarily in a van, should we take the children away from their parents? Does poverty justify intrusion? Should unwed mothers be given welfare? If so, may we

43

then invade the privacy of their homes to judge whether they are deserving recipients of governmental charity?

The regulation of the family involves limiting choices by law in an area of human life where choices are regarded as precious. Should individuals be free to marry, divorce, and bear children at their whim? In our society, some would place severe restrictions on each of these; others would insist that each is purely a matter of individual choice and not a concern of government; and, of course, most would argue some middle position. In recent years the issue of abortion has become a dominant theme in American law, with uncompromising, polarized views presenting a conflict that the machinery of justice cannot readily reconcile.

Sexual relations inevitably impinge on family law because they affect the nature, permanence, and stability of the family, as well as parental authority. The regulation of sexual relations is as old as human society. Nevertheless, the so-called "sexual revolution" not only defied traditional limits on sexuality, but also raised many legal issues. Should a single person be permitted to adopt a child? Should a homosexual or a homosexual couple be allowed to adopt? Should an infertile couple be permitted to contract for a surrogate mother? What form of sexual behavior may properly be prohibited? What part may adultery play in determining rights in divorce? In custody of children? Modern family law must deal with all these questions and many others.

3.2   THE MAKING OF FAMILY LAW

A brief historical sketch of the law of the family illustrates a number of points. First, family law as it exists today bears no resemblance to the law governing the family at the point of American independence. Other areas of law, such as the law of property, may be seen as a logical evolution from ancient English roots, but family law may be considered an American creation, consciously departing from English legal traditions. For example, Connecticut allowed absolute divorce long before England did. Divorce is really an American legal institution.

A second point that can be demonstrated by historical review is that family law reflects a continuous pattern of change. Change has not been merely incremental, tacking on something here and there. In its cumulative impact, it has been truly revolutionary. As we will see, revolutionary change seems to be a customary pattern in American family law. The reader is thus forewarned: *The principles expressed herein with regard to family law may well be obsolete before you have an opportunity to apply them.* This does not mean, however, that divorce will disappear or that children will cease to be adopted. The family will continue as an institution, albeit a changing one, and problems of family life will continue to be of concern to courts and legislatures. There will continue to be an area called *family law,* but its content and scope will not be easy to predict.

Finally, the study of family law presents a perplexing account of the relation between law and behavior. Legal scholars often debate the impact of law on society and, conversely, the impact of society on law. Extreme views are (1) that law is merely a passive reflection of social values, mediated somewhat by the process of lawmaking (also governed by social values), or (2) on the contrary, that law directs and controls behavior, actively changing behavior and social institutions. The history of family law in America could be used to argue either side. For example, *Roe v. Wade* effectively legalized abortion in the United States, with the result, perhaps, that more births may be intentionally aborted than those allowed to come to term. In contrast, no-fault divorce was an inevitable legislative recognition of the flood of divorces caused by people's desire to end their marriages regardless of fault on either side. In fact, today the course of law in general, and the course of family law in particular, is in part a product of the conflict between those who see law as a last resort in resolving social problems and those who would solve every problem by enacting a law.

In *American Family Law in Transition* (1983), Weyrauch and Katz argued that family law is often made in lawyers' offices rather than in courtrooms or even legislatures. Dominated as it is by divorce, family law is driven by the deals that lawyers make based on predictions of how judges would decide cases if they had to—which they rarely do. For example, in general, today father and mother are presumed under the law to be equally good custodians of children. Nevertheless, it is not uncommon to hear persons in the throes of divorce report that their lawyers have stated unequivocally that the mother always gets custody, unless she is shown to be unfit. Lawyers may negotiate on this assumption even while pretending to argue the equality expressed in court cases and statutes; for instance, the father's lawyer may seek custody of the children primarily as a point to trade in negotiation. Lawyers may make these assumptions based on past experience with a judge, or may simply be recognizing a social value, namely, that mothers are perceived as better nurturers than fathers. Thus lawyers may be anticipating decisions in such a way as to make their expectations self-fulfilling. For example, 95 percent of divorce cases with minor children result in custody awards to the mother, and the vast majority of divorce cases come before the court with a **marital settlement agreement** negotiated by the parties through their lawyers and rarely disapproved by the judge. Hence it appears that lawyers really are controlling legal outcomes.

3.3 HISTORICAL ROOTS OF FAMILY LAW

The archetypal family consists of a father, a mother, and children, all of whom are somehow related to others outside this basic nuclear family. Although now there are pressures to define *family* in much broader terms, the legal foundations of family law are premised on legitimizing a sexual relation between husband and wife conducive to engendering and nurturing offspring. Political, social, religious, and economic pressures have affected the law

LEGAL TERMS

marital settlement agreement
  Called by different names; the usual manner by wich divorcing parties contract to divide up their property. Without such an agreement, the judge would be responsible for deciding who should get what.

governing the family, but Anglo-American law has always held the family unit to be an essential element in the social network. American courts have throughout their history regarded themselves as the protectors of the family, often invoking rules on purely moral grounds.

The moral basis of family law was formalized when the Church assumed responsibility for regulating domestic relations in the late Middle Ages. At that time, marriage became a sacrament, subjecting the marital relationship to regulation by the Church. Our family law originated in the **canon law**, the law of the ecclesiastical courts. Because America did not employ ecclesiastical courts or canon law, domestic relations matters were subsumed under the jurisdiction of the courts of equity, except in colonies, like Connecticut and Massachusetts, that refused to adopt courts of equity. At the founding of the American Republic, the division between courts of equity and common law courts was still very strong. There was no common law tradition of family law except for property rights, and the common law was most appropriately charged with formal legal matters, such as the remedies for injury to person or property, for crimes, and for breach of contract.

Although the sacred relationships of status within the family ultimately shifted from canon law to equity, the common law nevertheless built a law of the family pertaining to property rights, and these rights formed an important feature of modern family law. After all, in England divorce and adoption were until relatively recent times unavailable. Divorce law, the major concern of contemporary family law, is largely a creation of American courts and legislatures, without significant precedent from England. In contrast, the common law had much to say about property rights of family members and the respective duties and obligations within the family. The legal family was clearly patriarchal and the legacy of the patriarchal family endures to this day.

3.4   THE MARRIAGE RELATIONSHIP

Until quite recently, marriage has always been predicated on a motivation to procreate. Marriage in Western societies has been monogamous from time immemorial, at least as far as the law is concerned. Thus, law has provided that male-female pairs may establish an enduring legal bond that allows sexual intimacy and encourages and protects procreation within the marital relationship. The need for numerous rules regulating monogamy attest to a common inclination to depart from its practice. Nevertheless, in earlier societies in which rank and status were largely determined by family relations, limitations on sexuality insured legitimacy, assured paternity, and presented the family as a stable unit within larger groups of kin, within an even larger community and society.

We can infer from the existence of laws of the family that those who made the laws considered its regulation important. We can also infer that such laws were necessary because many individuals and situations did not fit entirely comfortably within the constraints of society and its rules. If we look at medieval society, for example, we see how marriage fit into a feudal society organized around land and its defense, that is, an agricultural society organized under a military hierarchy. Local fiefdoms clustered around military forces that offered protection against enemies, and regional leaders promised allegiance to higher authorities. Warfare was endemic, preserving the power of military aristocracies. Wealth consisted almost entirely of control over land, which passed from one person to another by heredity, commonly to the eldest son. The titles of the nobility were held by virtue of the land to which they were entitled.

Within this rigid system, a man could occasionally advance his interests by force of arms, but the most important political moves for individuals and families were made through marriage. For the nobility, successful marriages could mean powerful alliances that might benefit both intermarrying families. For those of humbler status, marriage might simply mean the right to till a plot of land, but it might also thereby mean survival and the capacity to support a family.

In the medieval context, choice in marriage meant something quite different from what it means today. Choice could not be left to the young and inexperienced. Marriages, especially at the highest levels of society, were arranged for political reasons by the families concerned. The marriage contract was one between cooperating families rather than one between individuals exercising free choice. The betrothal rather than the wedding was the important event, because it was the contractual alliance, not the ceremonial exchange of vows, that was critical.

These were patriarchal societies in which men exercised legal authority over their wives and daughters and held all property rights. In turn, men were responsible for the acts of their dependents and also responsible to support and protect them.

The consequences of this social organization for the law of the family were great indeed. As evidence of this, we may note the perseverance of some underlying principles for centuries after feudalism disappeared in England. For example, it was not until the 19th century that American women could own property on an equal basis with their husbands, through the passage of the so-called married women's property acts in each of the states. In 1869, the Illinois Supreme Court (affirmed by the United States Supreme Court in 1872) denied Myra Bradwell a license to practice law, largely on the grounds that, as a married woman, she would not be bound by the contracts she would make with her clients.

The remnants of the medieval scheme can also be found in the law of torts. The so-called *heartbalm lawsuits* of **seduction, criminal conversation, breach of promise to marry**, and **alienation of affections** were based on a medieval view of marriage, particularly the importance of betrothal as integral to family alliances. Breach of promise to marry today may seem anachronistic: The prospective groom who broke off an engagement could be sued, and the damages could include the jilted party's lost economic advantages (i.e., what she stood to gain economically by the marriage). The

---

CAVEAT

Even if the family is politically and legally redefined in the future, lawyers, judges, and the public will continue to perceive the family in its model form, often defying attempts to redefine it.

LEGAL TERMS

canon law
  The law of the church. Domestic relations were formerly a matter for the church (divorce was rare and adoption not allowed), which was governed by canon law, observed to this day by the Catholic Church.

seduction
  A man's enticing a chaste woman into sexual intercourse without the use of force.

criminal conservation
  A cause of action in tort for adultery, brought against the outsider to the marriage who has been engaged in adultery; brought by the injured (nonadulterous) spouse.

breach of promise to marry
  A cause of action against someone who breaks off a marriage engagement. It was commonly used by women to collect damages for the loss of expected economic gain, namely, a life of luxury with a rich fiance.

alienation of affections
  A cause of action based on willful and malicious interference with the marriage relationship by a third party.

fiancé-as-meal-ticket model only makes sense in the context of marriage as a family alliance, when an engagement is broken because of a better opportunity. This is very different from engagement today, which is usually made by mutual consent regarding the central concern of love and companionship. The heartbalm actions were also premised on a world view that included predatory males seducing females, whose most prized possessions were their chastity before marriage and their fidelity thereafter. Today the legal equality of men and women rejects the paternalism of past social values, recognizing the rights of individuals to make their own sexual choices. The choice to be sexually active and the choice to marry need not be interrelated.

CASE NO. 3-1   Marital Rape

Even in the criminal law, changing societal values have had some effect. Many states have introduced statutes allowing prosecutions for rape against a husband, something that was impossible under the common law. The vision of the male as a sexual animal and the female as the reluctant participant in the sexual relationship granted the husband conjugal rights as well as legal dominion, so that rape within marriage was unthinkable. The husband-as-meal-ticket had its counterpart in the wife-as-slave picture that early law provides. Today, marital decisions, including sexual activity, take on a consensual aspect that makes coerced sex between marriage partners a criminal act.

PEOPLE v. LIBERTA
64 N.Y.2d 152, 474 N.E.2d 567,
485 N.Y.S.2d 207 (1984)
New York Court of Appeals

The assumption, even before the marital exemption was codified, that a man could not be guilty of raping his wife, is traceable to a statement made by the 17th century English jurist Lord Hale, who wrote: "[T]he husband cannot be guilty of a rape committed by himself upon his lawful wife, for by their mutual matrimonial consent and contract the wife hath given up herself in this kind unto her husband, which she cannot retract" (1 Hale, History of Pleas of the Crown, p. 629). Although Hale cited no authority for his statement it was relied on by State Legislatures which enacted rape statutes with a marital exemption and by courts which established a common-law exemption for husbands.

* * *

In New York, a 1922 decision noted the marital exemption in the Penal Law and stated that it existed "on account of the matrimonial consent which [the wife] has given, and which she cannot retract" (*People v. Meli*, 193 N.Y.S. 365, 366 [Sup.Ct.]).

Presently, over 40 States still retain some form of marital exemption for rape. . . .

We find that there is no rational basis for distinguishing between marital rape and nonmarital rape. The various rationales which have been asserted in defense of the exemption are either based upon archaic notions about the consent and property rights incident to marriage or are simply unable to withstand even the slightest scrutiny. We therefore declare the marital exemption for rape in the New York statute to be unconstitutional.

Lord Hale's notion of an irrevocable implied consent by a married woman to sexual intercourse has been cited most frequently in support of the marital exemption. Any argument based on a supposed consent, however, is untenable. Rape is not simply a sexual act to which one party does not consent. Rather, it is a degrading, violent act which violates the bodily integrity of the victim and frequently causes severe, long-lasting physical and psychic harm. To ever imply consent to such an act is irrational and absurd. Other than in the context of rape statutes, marriage has never been viewed as giving a husband the right to coerced intercourse on demand. . . .

A central problem of family law exists in the conflict between the course of the law and social and biological reality. In theory, and largely in fact, men and women are free, if they have the mental capacity and legal competence, to choose to marry whomever they wish. Historically this change is most dramatic for women, who not long ago exercised only a limited choice; once that choice was made, as married women, they lost the legal competence they might have enjoyed if they had reached the age of 21 before marrying. Today, under the law, they exercise significant rights before reaching the age of majority and their legal competence is not affected by marriage. Under the law, women have the right to consent to or refuse sexual activity, to procreate, and to terminate pregnancy. In fact, a good case could be made for the legal superiority of women in family law.

There remains, however, a disharmony between the rights enjoyed by women under the law and the allocation of the benefits these rights would seem to confer. A historical perspective may provide an explanation. A revolution in ideology and the rules that revolution produces do not immediately replace the systems and values that have been in place since time immemorial.

3.5 TERMINATING THE MARRIAGE RELATIONSHIP

If marriage was not a matter of individual free choice in earlier times, neither was divorce. In fact, divorce as we know it is a purely modern development in our legal system. Under English law, divorce was an ecclesiastical matter governed by canon law. In 1765, Blackstone described two forms of divorce, total divorce, *a vinculo matrimonii* (from the bond of matrimony), and divorce from bed and board (*legal separation*), *a mensa et thoro*. Divorce *a vinculo matrimonii* was based on some impediment to the marriage in the beginning, making the marriage invalid and its offspring illegitimate. Divorce *a mensa et thoro* arose from a valid marriage suffering from some cause, such as adultery, that justified a legal separation. Divorce *a mensa et thoro* allowed the award of alimony to the wife. At the time he wrote, Blackstone noted a recent development—the granting of total divorce by Parliament.

During the Middle Ages and into the 16th century, rich and powerful persons were able to persuade priests to grant divorces in the form of *annulment* (declaring the marriage a "nullity"), largely because the Church prohibited marriage between persons related within seven degrees. A *degree* is one link in a chain of relation; for example, a cousin counts as three degrees (father→uncle→cousin). The prohibition included in-law as well as blood relationships, and even included godparents. Among the European aristocracies, everyone was related in some way. (**Coke** reported an annulment based on the fact that the husband was godfather to his wife's cousin). The Church profited immensely from "discovering" prohibited marriages among nobles who desired to end their marriages.

Divorce in colonial America was rare and followed English patterns, with local variations. There was considerable variation among the colonies: some did not allow divorce, others adopted a liberal attitude toward divorce, and most fell somewhere in between. Family law in general and divorce law in particular were complicated by the absence of ecclesiastical courts and the fact that some areas, like New England, did not establish equity courts, which usually took on the ecclesiastical courts' former jurisdiction over family law. (Although common law courts refused to hear cases involving contracts between husband and wife, English courts of equity entertained disputes based on separation agreements involving postnuptial trusts.) Thus, colonies (and later states) that had courts of equity tended to allow total divorce *a vinculo matrimonii* in a fashion similar to annulment today (that is, declaring the marriage void *ab initio* for bigamy, infertility, and blood relationship, making offspring illegitimate) and to recognize separation agreements. In the New England colonies founded by religious dissenters, both equity and Anglican courts were rejected, and a liberal attitude toward divorce was adopted. Massachusetts and Connecticut courts granted absolute divorce for cause, such as adultery, long before such divorces were recognized in England. Desertion appears to have been a common ground for divorce or separation. In Connecticut, divorce always conferred the right to remarry. Colonial courts and legislatures were free of the English concerns over the titles, inheritance, and property divisions that were of primary importance to a legal system dominated by holders of hereditary landed estates.

Toward the end of the 17th century, parliamentary divorce was established in England and copied in some colonies. Legislative divorce continued in the American states in the 19th century without the cumbersome procedure required in England, where parliamentary divorce was grounded exclusively in adultery (by the wife only until 1801) and was necessarily preceded by a divorce *a mensa et thoro* from an ecclesiastical court and a successful suit for criminal conversation against the wife's lover.

LEGAL TERMS

Coke
Sir Edward Coke (pronounced "cook"), 1552-1634, rose to the exalted position of Chief Justice of the King's Bench, but is best known as the first complier of annotated law reports in his *Institutes*, which may well mark the beginning of modern Anglo-American law.

CASE NO. 3-2   Origins of Divorce

Ponder shows that Florida, not long after gaining statehood, was wrestling with the assignment of divorce to the appropriate branch of government.

PONDER v. GRAHAM
4 Fla. 23 (1851)
Supreme Court of Florida

SEMMES, *Justice,* delivered the opinion of the court.

* * *

The main question raised in this case, as to the power of a Legislative body, *as such,* to grant divorces, is not altogether a new one. It has been investigated by some of the American Courts, and grave constitutional questions have been necessarily involved in the discussion; and yet the question still remains an open one—opinions clashing—nothing settled. It is to be regretted that amid this conflict of opinion upon a question of such deep interest, we are unable to avail ourselves of the investigation of any one of the great jurists of our country, to relieve the subject from embarrassment and difficulty, and that while almost every other legal question of importance has had light and authority imparted to it, this, one of the most important of all, has been allowed to slumber on in doubt and uncertainty.

The Legislatures of some of the states of the Union exercise exclusive jurisdiction over this subject; one or more of them by reason, as is contended for by their courts, of the absence of any constitutional inhibition—while others claim this authority by reason, it is said, of an inherent power, analogous to that of the Parliament of Great Britain. Some exercise the power as a constitutional right, while others claim it as an original right, and without the sanction of constitutional authority.

No one doubts the right of the people by their constitution, to invest the power in the Legislature, or anywhere else but the question is, when the constitution is silent on the subject, in what department of government does this authority rest? I believe that much, if not the whole difficulty, has arisen from overlooking some of the great principles which enter into the constitutional government of the States, and from not preserving the obvious distinction between legislative and judicial functions—by confounding the *right* which a legislative body has to pass *general laws* on the subject of divorce, with the *power* of dissolving the marriage *contract.*

* * *

The act of the [council] undertakes to determine questions of fact and law exclusively within the province of the courts. If, as is contended with much reason, there were no existing causes of divorce, as set forth in the preamble to this act, then the dissolution of the marriage contract was a mere assumption of power, exercised in the most arbitrary manner.

* * *

It is said, and the doctrine is broadly intimated in several of the authorities, that a legislature in this country can grant divorces, in analogy to the Parliament of England. I can see no parallel in the two cases. Political writers in England claim for their Parliament omnipotent power. It is said that in that country "there is no written constitution, no fundamental law, nothing visible, nothing tangible, nothing real, nothing certain, by which a statute of Parliament can be tested." See 3 *Dallas Reports,* 308; and yet, with all this acknowledged and untrammelled power, it does not assert or exercise the right of dissolving the marriage contract; to the extent and in the summary mode adopted by the Legislatures of some of the States.

Parliament never decrees a divorce, *a mensa et thoro*—that power belongs exclusively to the courts. Parliament never even decrees a divorce *a vinculo,* but for adultery, and that upon a judgment *a mensa et thoro,* first pronounced by the Ecclesiastical Courts, and unless sufficient cause is shown, a verdict for damages in a Court of Common Law is requisite, before Parliament will take jurisdiction. The whole proceedings, from the libel filed in the Ecclesiastical Court, up to the final decree by Parliament, are, in every essential requisite, *judicial.* The formal petition to the House of Lords, with an office copy of the judgment and proceeding in the court, notice to the defendant, the examination of witnesses, the hearing of counsel, and the judgment pronounced, all clothe it with a judicial character, of which it is impossible to divest it—done, it is true, by Parliament, but by virtue of its omnipotent power.

* * *

In every respect in which I have been able to see this case, I can find no reason to sustain the act of the legislature. It appears by the record, that the parties were domiciled in the State of Georgia, where, it is alleged, the desertion and ill treatment occurred. The wife, living with the testator, Graham, removed to Florida—while the husband returned to Carolina, his former residence. The bill was introduced into the legislature one day, and passed the next. It is very clear that this divorce would not be recognized by the courts of Georgia or Carolina, were any rights asserted under it in those States. . . .

I am, therefore, of opinion that the act of the Legislative Council of February 11th, 1832, was in conflict with the organic law of Florida and the Constitution of the United States, and is, therefore, void.

Despite *Ponder v. Graham,* most states continued for many years to grant legislative divorces on the precedent of Parliament. Although probably more common than in England, divorce in America was certainly rare by modern standards, and the lack of judicial precedent (outside of canon law) left the legislatures free to terminate marriages. It was inevitable that the *Ponder* dichotomy between the legislative function of regulating marriage and the judicial function of deciding individual cases would become the norm. The debate over legislative divorces was part of a larger debate over the degree of control the state should exercise over the family. That debate continues today, but its premises have changed. Most states have adopted some form of no-fault divorce, making divorce much easier to obtain by lessening legislative and judicial involvement, leaving the choices to the individuals.

With independence from England, America expressed a strong antipatriarchal attitude which was reflected in a view of the family as a harmonious team of individuals, each entitled to respect. Husband and wife were partners to a family contract of their own choosing, and the laws governing this contract were similar to but distinct from other sorts of contracts. Although quite naturally borrowing from the traditional concepts of family law to be found in the canon law, lawyers, lawmakers, and judges also argued about the enforceability of the terms to that contract. For example, the courts early rejected premarital (antenuptial) contracts, because they encouraged divorce and the courts, as protectors of the family, could not countenance this development. Cohabitation agreements were also unenforceable, having an illegal purpose (fornication). As one commentator suggested, perhaps the old patriarchy was exchanged for a new judicial patriarchy.

Divorce in the new republic was fashioned out of separation (divorce *a mensa et thoro*), which established grounds for the court to order separate living, such as adultery, cruelty, abandonment, and long absence. The major difference over the old form was that this divorce based on "fault" allowed the parties to remarry, which was formerly allowed only for divorce *a vinculo*. Roughly, divorce from bed and board became an absolute divorce, while divorce *a vinculo*, equally absolute in its effect, became annulment. The distinction, as always, was based on the grounds supporting the action. Annulment is basically a contract remedy, in that it treats the marriage as a contract which is void because of some impediment to its formation, such as the prior marriage of one of the parties. Divorce, or its modern counterpart, *dissolution*, took on features of tort—suit was brought on the basis of fault and the allocation of assets resembled compensation for injuries. The 19th-century courts even developed legal defenses such as **recrimination** and **condonation**.

The movement toward no-fault divorce—divorce granted without the necessity to prove one of the parties at fault—was induced by an acceleration in the divorce rate and the inadequacy of traditional procedures. Many states allowed divorce on the grounds of cruelty or incompatibility, which permitted couples to obtain divorces on flimsy allegations uncontested by the other party. The result was essentially judgment by default, a process in which most judges were willing to participate. In states like New York, which limited grounds to adultery or were otherwise quite restrictive, or when one of the parties was uncooperative, a vacation to Reno for a few weeks could result in a Nevada divorce.

Lawyers, judges, and others had also come to realize that the adversarial process of fault divorce was harmful to the participants and inimical to reconciliation. State intrusion into the family to keep it together or set its standards was a miserable failure, and each state set about to extricate itself from this unseemly process. Although different statutes were written for different states, the basic divorce process today is probably more uniform in practice than at any time in American history.

3.6 CHILDREN

The status and rights of children were initially totally subject to the status and rights of their parents. Because English law, whether the product

LEGAL TERMS

recrimination
    A defense used by one who is sued for divorce on the grounds of adultery, claiming that the other party also engaged in adultery. Under recrimination, if both partners to a marriage were adulterers, the divorce could be denied

condonation
    Forgiveness for marital fault, commonly adultery, based on the continuation or resumption of cohabitation by the married couple.

of Parliament or judicial decisions, was forged primarily by a hereditary landed patriarchal aristocracy, the law's concerns were the aristocracy's concerns, and the laws reflected and protected its interests. As reflected in family law, the law of this elite group protected male prerogatives as head of household, exercising legal control over the family and property. The law also reflected a concern with legitimation of offspring. Just as adultery of a wife threatened paternal certainty, a man's illegitimate offspring posed a threat to the hereditary entitlements of legitimate offspring. The rules imposed were couched in terms of the sanctity of the family, but bastardy laws were unduly harsh in England, as compared with those in continental Europe and elsewhere, suggesting that more was at stake than protecting the family. Common law hostility toward adoption echoed the elite fixation on legitimacy and the primacy of inheritance by blood relatives. Here again, the English law, which did not allow adoption, departed from Roman law and the continental European tradition.

In America, the English law in this domain inevitably failed. Lacking an entrenched landed aristocracy, a democratic attitude toward property arose. The **fee tail** never took hold and **primogeniture** was not followed in law nor approved in custom. Although the sanctity of the family and the threat to inheritable property were recognized, an interest in the welfare of children caused a liberalization of laws with regard to legitimation of offspring, the legal recognition of children born out of wedlock, and the creation of Amercan adoption laws in the 19th century. Although not the first state to allow adoption, Massachusetts in 1851 set a national standard whereby adoption severed legal ties to natural parents, replaced them with bonds to the adoptive parents, and required judicial approval of the suitability of the adopting parents.

The evolution of custody and visitation reveals a similar drastic change from earlier principles. The law inherited from England invested the father with an absolute right to custody of the children. This rule went hand-in-hand with the husband/father's legal dominance and the absence of divorce among all but the most influential of persons. In this regard, divorcing men were ordinarily well equipped to provide for the needs of their children. Although America began with this premise, the law was more democratically oriented and divorce was more common and more readily available. Custody was denied fathers who could be shown to be unfit; some early cases involved paternal drunks. In the 19th century, courts began to recognize a doctrine that children "of tender years" ought to remain with their mothers. The wife/mother, as keeper of the hearth in a companionate partnership, exemplified an ideology that inevitably reversed the paternal presumption and favored the mother.

Over the years, a gradual shift away from the property rights model of custody toward the primacy of child welfare established the principle that custody should be awarded according to the "best interests of the child." No-fault divorce encouraged this development by removing children from the prize category, to be awarded to the winner of a mud-slinging contest.

Although custody battles continue to be among the nastiest of lawsuits, no-fault takes the fire out of the bad-spouse evidence and concentrates on proving the good parent. Florida adopted its version of joint custody, calling it "shared parental responsibility," in an effort to downplay parents' rights and emphasize their responsibilities. No-fault divorce gave the spouses the freedom to choose to terminate their marriages, but could not relieve the courts of the burden of deciding the welfare of dependent children.

3.7 RIGHTS OF WOMEN

Among the most drastic changes in American family law were the emancipation of women and their subsequent striving for equality in all areas of American society. Under the common law, married women could not own property nor sue or be sued in their own rights. Their legal rights were exercised, if at all, through their husbands. The legal rationale for this situation was the concept of marital unity. This principle, in accord with the symbolic sanctity of Christian marriage, held the married couple to be *indissoluble*, a unity that was not divisible. In a patriarchal and paternalistic society, it was logical that the husbands would speak for the unity, so that the seemingly ironic dictum that "husband and wife are one, and the husband is the one" was taken seriously. The following quote from *Warren v. State* gives some indication of the extent of change in the rights of women over the last century:

> The history of mankind is a history of repeated injuries and usurpations on the part of man toward woman, having in direct object the establishment of an absolute tyranny over her. To prove this, let facts be submitted to a candid world.
>
> He has never permitted her to exercise her inalienable right to the elective franchise. . . .
>
> [O]ur legislature has recognized that there can be violence in modern family life and it has enacted special laws to protect family members who live in the same household from one another's violent acts. . . .
>
> — *Warren v. State,* 255 Ga. 151, 336 S.E.2d 221, 224 (1985).

This has not simply been a result of democratization and advancing civilization; the patriarchal class system never took root comfortably in American soil. The extreme authority exercised by men in England preserved the hereditary class system. Among egalitarian farmers, frontier folk, entrepreneurs, and religious dissenters in America, the elitist legalism of England encountered deep distrust. Although American men may not have been ready for gender equality, they suspected and resented rank and privilege. It can fairly be said that Americans, even while resisting change, have always heeded legitimate cries for equal legal rights. The 19th-century married women's property acts were the most significant development in granting to women legal status akin to that enjoyed by men.

LEGAL TERMS

fee tail
  One of the estates in land that descibe the extent of ownership in Anglo-American property law. The fee tail, created by language such as "to my eldest son and the heirs of his body," was designed to insure that property would descend through blood lines in each generation. This prevented the estate from being conveyed out of the family, but resulted in many estates becoming hopelessly "entailed" and ill-suited for changing circumstances.

primogeniture
  The custom (and sometimes the law) requiring that titled estates descend to the eldest son.

Although the common law persistently took a restrictive attitude toward the legal rights of married women, courts of equity, which had early developed the **trust**, allowed married women to be the beneficiaries of trusts, and protected and enforced their rights, beginning in the 16th century. The trust enabled men of property to invest property in and protect their daughters at marriage, rather than surrendering property to a son-in-law who might turn out to be profligate or abusive. Such arrangement were called *marriage settlements* and the trusts were called *separate estates.* Still, these arrangements were established and enforced within the propertied class, and rarely affected the plight of less-wealthy women, who were generally at the mercy of their husbands. Perhaps this is why separate estates were apparently little used in America. Of course, in some states equity had not been imported, so common law principles were relied on. At any rate, as the United States became increasingly mercantile and industrial, the low status of women appeared inappropriate as well as unjust, and every state eventually enacted laws collectively known as the *married women's property acts*. Beginning in the 1830s in the Arkansas and Florida territories, various acts (the most important of which was New York's, enacted in 1848) were passed granting to married women the right to own and transfer property, to sue and be sued, to have contractual capacity, and to do business. This list of rights indicates the enormity of both the legal limitations on women in the past and the change that these acts made. In fact, the gains were so great that it took over 100 years and another women's movement to clarify, consolidate, and enforce the rights enumerated.

A second and more recent development that figured prominently in women's rights was a series of constitutional decisions by the United States Supreme Court establishing and defining an area of privacy rights, culminating in *Roe v. Wade,* 410 U.S. 113 (1973), which invalidated antiabortion statutes throughout the United States. In the process of establishing family privacy rights, the Court has given women the right to legal choices formerly denied, to the extent that women appear to have legal control over reproduction. Although this may have been a logical outgrowth of social change, the contraceptive pill first provided the means for women to control reproduction; abortion gave them the last word. Despite major changes in these areas, it is quite likely that the rest of this century, at least, will witness continued legal developments in the area of abortion.

In recent years, the entry of women in large numbers into the workplace, especially in professions formerly served by men, has radically changed the social environment in which family law must apply. The stable family with a male breadwinner and a female homemaker is found in a minority of households. Law predicated on the traditional model seems out of touch with current realities. The advent of stepparents, latchkey children, day care, single-parent families, and other nontraditional ways of raising children continue to puzzle and challenge those who make law and policy.

LEGAL TERMS

trust
   An arrangement, recognized by the law, whereby property may be given by a donor to a trustee, who manages the property on behalf of a third party called a *beneficiary.* One early form of trust was a *separate estate,* which fathers often set up for their daughters so that the son-in-law would not control the property.

Contrary to popular perceptions, American fathers traditionally took an active role in the education of their children. New styles of marital partnership may encourage a renewal of such activity.

3.8 CHANGING LIFESTYLES

Certain traditional attributes of the family, such as sexual intimacy, partnership based on love and affection, and procreation and nurture of children are presently assumed by persons who do not fit the traditional legal definition of the family, specifically single persons and homosexuals. In addition, advances in medicine and science have opened new possibilities for procreation through artificial insemination and the implantation of fertilized eggs. Meanwhile, the number of illegitimate births appears to be reaching new peaks. While this is morally confusing to much of the populace, it is especially troublesome to the law. Whereas in the past the courts relied on the fact or the appearance of marriage to establish rights and duties between husband and wife and parent and child, today many who appear to fall clearly outside even a broad definition of *family* are claiming rights, such as pension benefits, parental leave, or even the right to marry, as well as adoption.

Because the Fourteenth Amendment to the United States Constitution prohibits the states from denying any person equal protection of the laws, those who are deemed ineligible to marry or to be classified as a family may properly raise Fourteenth Amendment arguments. For example, may a state lawfully restrict adoption to heterosexual married couples? Assuming for the sake of argument that homosexual couples as well as single men and women can be shown to provide a healthy, nurturing environment for children, how can the law discriminate against them? These questions are fraught with controversy and raise powerful emotions; their legal resolution is not yet clearly delineated.

Case No. 3-3 demonstrates the kinds of unusual problems that courts face these days.

CASE NO. 3-3   My Two Moms

Mix a transvestite and artificial insemination—the result makes a good television drama and a tough judicial decision.

KARIN T. v. MICHAEL T.
127 Misc. 2d 14, 484 N.Y.S.2d 780
(N.Y. Fam. Ct. 1985)
New York Family Court

LEONARD E. MAAS, Judge.

* * *

To this rather routine-appearing Petition, the respondent has filed an Answer which sets forth as an affirmative defense the following: "2. That the respondent is a female and she is not the father of the said children. That the children were artificially inseminated."

* * *

Respondent was born on August 16, 1948, and is denominated a female named Marlene A.T. In her twenties she became increasingly unhappy with her feminine identity and attempted to change that identity and to live like a man. In pursuance thereof, she changed her name from Marlene to Michael, dressed in men's clothing and obtained employment which she regarded as "men's work." At some time prior to May of 1977, the respondent and Karin T. commenced a relationship. In May of 1977, Karin T. and Michael T., a/k/a Marlene T., obtained a marriage license in the Village of Spencerport in the County of Monroe. At that time, no birth certificate was requested of either party and a marriage license was issued.

Subsequently, Karin T. and the respondent participated in a marriage ceremony which was performed by a Minister in the Town of Parma, County of Monroe. This was evidenced by a Certificate of Marriage executed by said Minister.

Thereafter, two children were born by means of artificial insemination. The physician, prior to engaging in the procedure, had both parties execute an agreement, a copy of which is annexed hereto and made a part hereof. David T. was born October 8, 1980, and Falin T. was born January 17, 1983, as a result of the artificial insemination performed by the physician.

Subsequent to the birth of the second child in 1983, the parties separated and the respondent moved to the Monroe County area and is employed in Monroe County.

* * *

During the period of 1977 through 1983, it would appear that Karin T. and the respondent lived together in the same household and both contributed to the support of the family and to the children who are the subjects of this proceeding.

The Court has been further informed that there is presently pending in the Supreme Court of Erie County, State of New York, an action between Karin T. and the respondent to declare the "marriage" of 1977 null and void.

* * *

Neither counsel for the parties nor the Court has found any authority similar to the fact situation in this case. . . . This is a case of first impression and its resolution will carry the Court through uncharted legal waters. As a general rule only biological or adoptive parents are liable for the support of children. Where extraordinary circumstances require, Courts have held non-parents responsible for the support of children. See, *Wener v. Wener,* 35 A.D.2d 50, 312 N.Y.S.2d 815; *Lewis v. Lewis,* 85 Misc.2d 610, 381 N.Y.S.2d 631.

It is conceded that the children involved in this proceeding were born only after the respondent affixed her name to the agreement indicating she was the husband. The agreement stated in part: "a. That such child or children so produced are his own legitimate child or children and are the heirs of his body, and b. That he hereby completely waives forever any right which he might have to disclaim such child or children as his own."

In the *Wener* case, supra, husband and wife agreed to adopt a child, then living in Florida. The child was removed from its natural mother and brought to New York and commenced living with the parties. Prior to the finalization of the adoption, the parties separated and a proceeding was brought seeking support from the husband. He defended the action on the grounds that neither statute nor case law imposed liability on him for child support albeit that the lower Court had found an implied agreement to adopt. The *Appellate Division,* 35 A.D.2d at page 53, 312 N.Y.S.2d 815, stated:

> "We cannot ignore the realities of this infant's plight and blindly apply a rule which was never meant to encompass her situation. This infant was taken from her natural mother when but a few days old, albeit with her mother's consent. Her natural parents and their whereabouts are unknown (no one has ever suggested she be returned to them) and she has never been legally adopted. Still, the parties at bar are the only 'parents' she has ever known. Having brought the child into their home, they must, of necessity, shoulder the burden of her support."

However, as between the parties themselves, the primary liability for support properly rests upon the plaintiff. Having agreed to adopt the child and support her, and having treated her as his own prior to the parties' separation, the plaintiff may not now disavow all obligations and shift the entire burden onto the defendant. *It may be reasonably inferred from the evidence that the defendant would not have acquired the child and brought her into their home in the absence of the plaintiff's consent to adoption.* Therefore, the plaintiff's primary obligation rests upon the dual foundation of an implied contract to support the child and equitable estoppel" (emphasis supplied).

* * *

[B]y her course of conduct in this case which brought into the world two innocent children she should not be allowed to benefit from those acts to the detriment of these children and of the public generally.

* * *

The respondent is chargeable with the support of these children and this case is referred to the Hearing Examiner to determine the level of such support. . . .

SUMMARY

The law of the family has been changing continually throughout American history. Rejection of the elitism of English patriarchy created a family law in America that was radically different from that of the mother country. Divorce in particular seems to be a rather special American institution. It continues to be transformed under the name of no-fault divorce.

A major force in shaping family law has been the several movements for equality of rights for women. The discrepancy between rights and practice continues to generate social and legal problems.

The sexual revolution and changing lifestyles have made traditional definitions of the family untenable and the courts and legislatures deal frequently with living arrangements that defy classification. There is no sign that *family* will lose its dynamic quality.

QUESTIONS

1. What is the difference between absolute divorce and divorce from bed and board?
2. Who was responsible for family law in England before the 19th century?
3. Where were the earliest divorces granted?
4. What was the most important legal advance for women in the 19th century?
5. What other legal advances have been made by women in the United States?
6. On what basis can it be argued that family law is made in lawyers' offices rather than in the courts?
7. Why was betrothal formerly more important than the wedding?
8. What are "heartbalm" causes of action and why were they abolished?
9. Why could a woman not charge her husband with rape under the common law? Why has this changed?
10. How can it be argued that women have come to control reproduction?

EXERCISES

Answer the questions according to the law of your state.

1. Can a single person be permitted to adopt a child?
2. Can a homosexual or a homosexual couple be allowed to adopt?

3. Can an infertile couple be permitted to contract for a surrogate mother?
4. What part does adultery play in determining rights in divorce? In custody of children?
5. Does your state have a married women's property act?
6. Is divorce an equity proceeding?
7. Does your state allow heart-balm causes of action?
8. Find your state's no-fault divorce statute. Does your state allow divorce on "grounds" as well?

CHAPTER 4
Current Issues In Family Law

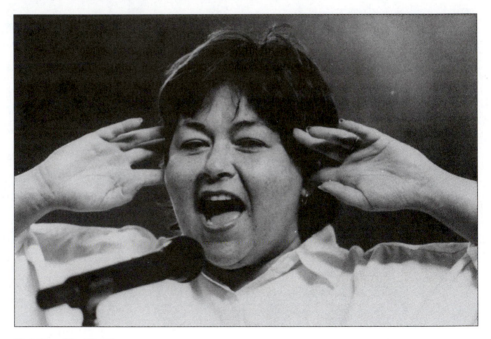

But Can She Sing?

Entertainer Roseanne Arnold, in her autobiography, Roseanne: My Life as a Woman, *discussed her difficult, often-abusive childhood. Later it was learned that Roseanne had placed her own daughter up for adoption. Frequently the theme for Arnold's television sitcom* Roseanne *explores the social issues affecting a typical working-class American family: pregnancy, homosexuality, divorce, marriage, unemployment, and financial difficulties. This chapter tracks similiar trends impacting family law today.*

— Courtesy AP/Wide World Photos.

You can sort of be married, you can sort of be divorced, you can sort of be living together, but you can't sort of have a baby.

David Shire

OUTLINE

4.1 THE FUTURE OF THE FAMILY AND THE FUTURE OF
FAMILY LAW
4.2 INCEST AND CHILD ABUSE
4.3 MEDIATION
4.4 MARRIAGE COUNSELING
4.5 DEFINITION OF FAMILY
      Who Qualifies as a Parent?
      Will the Real Parent Please Stand Up?
      Right of the Child
      Whose Child Is It Anyway?
4.6 REPRODUCTIVE RIGHTS
4.7 PRIVATE VERSUS PUBLIC CONTROL
      SUMMARY

4.1 THE FUTURE OF THE FAMILY AND THE FUTURE OF FAMILY LAW

Prophecy is an inherently dangerous pasttime, when one's forecasts are reduced to written form, but lawyers must inevitably predict the course of the law, at least where it applies to a client's case. Family law has changed steadily over the last few years and there is no reason to believe change will suddenly come to a halt, especially since family and society seem to have outpaced changes in the law. It seems inevitable, for example, from present developments that homosexuals will not continue to be denied the legal advantages of marriage. This does not mean necessarily that homosexual marriages will be allowed but rather that some of the legal benefits of marriage will be accorded to same-sex couples who declare an intention to be permanently bonded.

The need for recognition of legal benefits for unmarried couples and families, whether homosexual or heterosexual, highlights contemporary social problems. For instance, one of the reasons for the push to recognize legal bonds between unmarried partners (or allow unrestricted marriage) comes from the concern over rising healthcare costs. Until a solution to the healthcare problem is achieved, most Americans must depend upon the health insurance subsidized by public and private employers. Few can afford even brief hospitalization without some form of insurance. Family members depend upon the insurance of one or more breadwinners for their security in case of serious illness.

Educational costs have similarly risen dramatically in recent years and show no signs of abating. Most of our citizens again look to government for the solution to this problem. If the law continues to limit parental responsibility to the first 18 years of life, it is likely that the noncustodial, support-paying parent will subsidize college with reluctance. Nor is it likely that remarriage of the noncustodial parent will enhance the children's chances. Experience suggests that stepparents will avoid, restrict, or at least resent sacrifices for the sake of stepchildren.

This brings us to the social problem most associated with the family. Large numbers of children grow up with minimal contact with one parent. Self-care (*latchkey*) children and daycare warehousing of small children has become commonplace. Children of divorce share these experiences with the children of two-income parents. The economic pressures on both intact and separated families are very heavy and the interests of children must compete with other demands on their parents. In the past, social pressures and the support of the extended family operated to keep the family together—the mother at home, the father at work, and the children in line. The patterns have changed, leaving contemporary parents with little to guide them. How does a parent raise a child for a future that is unpredictable?

4.2 INCEST AND CHILD ABUSE

Child abuse and incest indicate serious problems for a self-indulgent society, ones that both tabloids and respectable media constantly report.

The Livelys' guest editorial on this "emotional subject" explains some of the facts. Paralegals who work on divorce cases may well encounter such issues— from either side—as charges of molestation and abuse are increasingly being used as legal tactics.

GUEST EDITORIAL

FAMILY CRIME

■ Excerpted from Edwin Lively and Virginia Lively,
Sexual Development of Young Children

Incest—sexual relations between persons related by blood in some degree, as defined by law—has been known throughout history, but almost always as an unacceptable activity. It is not an unknown type of behavior in any part of the world, nor is it limited to any class, race, religion, or cultural grouping. Most often those involved in an incestuous relationship are brother and sister or parent and child. Less frequently involved, at least statistically, are aunts, uncles, and grandparents. Stepfathers are sometimes found to be sexually associated with their stepchildren and this is treated as incest even though there is not a direct blood relationship. Sexual relations between blood relations who are forbidden to marry is the minimal consideration for incest, but usually is extended to a greater degree.

Vaginal intercourse is the primary focus in an incestuous relation in a family, but oral and anal sex have also been recorded in parental and kinship associations. There is a case on record of a mother having oral sex with her four-month-old son. Reports of this kind of behavior are assumed to be quite rare by most people, but recent studies suggest that frequency of incest and the forms it takes would not have been believed a few years ago. As with most forms of sexual behavior involving children, reporting of it to the public is quite sporadic, often unreliable, and limited to the extreme or bizarre incidents. The adults who participate go to great lengths to conceal their activities and children are discouraged from revealing the incestuous behavior in a variety of ways. Adults may use threats of physical punishment, or bribery with money or presents to discourage the children from exposing the relationship, but frequently the young child is unaware of the seriousness of the situation, especially if it is a parent who is involved. Often there is a love or affection among the participants and neither wishes to do anything that may cause harm or bring shame to the other (or themselves).

Young children who have become involved in incestuous situations will be less aware of the significance or

Girl with baby's head. A six-year-old girl reported to her aunt that the picture was of herself and the baby she would have when she married daddy. She said, "We love each other and we play our secret game because it feels good." This was a streetwise child who assumed much of her working mother's role at home. The mother and stepfather are now separated because of the incestuous behavior that occurred.

illegality or such behavior than older children. On the other hand, they are unlikely to be sufficiently sophisticated or secretive that they can keep it to themselves. In fact, they are quite likely to provide clues to others that unusual things have occurred. Persons who work with a small child or know the child well will quickly become aware that something different is happening in the child's life. It is not hard to persuade the young child to admit and describe the details of an incestuous relationship through careful questioning, plus careful listening to the answers.

Incest with a child six years of age or under is less common than with an older child. This is the age, however, when incestuous intentions may easily begin with games or teasing or physical expressions of affection with sexual overtones. Later any or all of these may develop into an incestuous relationship. When the specific motivation in physical expressions of love and affection is sexual arousal and gratification, and this develops over a period of time during such contacts, it is defined as incestual motivation. This kind of motivation is not present in a normal physical relationship between parent and child, even though there is frequently touching, kissing, and other such physical contacts, which are intended to express love and affection. Without the motivation of incest, this type of relationship is an integral part of the development of a healthy sexuality in a child. It is important to recognize that the adult or older person controls the nature of an association with a young child and must be held responsible for any deviations beyond acceptable limits.

The reasons a member of a family begins an incestuous relationship with a child are very difficult to ascertain in individual cases. It is very hard to obtain adequate data on which to base a theory; it is very hard to know if a sample is representative of the population who may be involved. Some women report incestuous relations with their fathers and attempt to tie it to a present situation or problem. Others report a very satisfactory involvement with the father which was not terminated until the daughter began dating or left home. Reports such as these seldom reveal any significant information about the nature and causes of incest other than to suggest that the frequency is higher than officially reported to authorities.

When incest does occur in the home, it is common, especially in the case of young children, for threats to be made to the child to prevent any public revelation. Older children may well be able to foresee the consequences of a court trial or newspaper headline and the possible imprisonment of a family member. The mother is often unaware of what is going on, especially the working mother during whose absence the incestuous behaviors take place. There are cases, however, in which the mother is fully aware of what is taking place and does nothing about it, either because of fear of harm to herself or a high degree of indifference to the child. Sexual behavior to a young child is devoid of the implications it has for older people, but it may have a degree of pleasure, a special secret, or perhaps some type of guilt feelings. The last situation will often occur if a little child has been told not to tell and then reveals the behavior. It is essential to take into account the child's welfare when an incident of incest is made public. The child will need professional counseling to help understand the recent events and to prepare for the future. Perhaps the most vital need for the child is to develop a sound sexual identity, to be able to put sex into a socially acceptable context, and to relate to other people without secrecy, shame, or a sense of wrongdoing. The thing that makes this so extraordinarily difficult is the fact that the "condemned" behavior was with a family member, a person who is integral in the establishment of a loving relationship.

One researcher cites repressive home environments as the major cause of sexual abuse of children. Many of the abusers are members of the family. When home environments are sexually restricted and repressive and emphasize traditional sex roles, sexual child abuse may occur within the family, and the children do not resist because they are taught to obey and comply. Two other factors are a possibly greater vulnerability for a little girl if there is a stepfather present, and if there is a pronounced educational inferiority on the part of the wife. Another study reported that in cases where the natural father abused a child, he was more likely to be under greater stress than an abusing stepfather (e.g., drug-user, alcoholic, mental problems, and low income).

Some experts in family law who have evaluated reports of sexual child abuse say that fathers involved in divorce cases are sometimes wrongly accused of child molestation by the wife as a legal tactic. False allegations are also made in child custody cases to avoid any kind of sharing or visitation rights. It has been estimated that the number of false charges had increased from 10 to 30 percent in recent years. It is suspected that most such charges are false, but fathers are quite vulnerable to them because of the general association of child care and protection with the mother. Extreme hostility between the parents makes the truth hard to ascertain.

Television, newspapers, magazines, and books have presented a substantial amount of material on child abuse in recent years, some quite factual and some emotion-laden, because it is an emotional subject. Certainly public awareness is higher than ever before, especially with regard to sexual child abuse. It is probably one of the most underreported crimes in our society today. The general public finds it very hard to believe that people would commit sex crimes against infants and small children and view reports of incest or sodomy with a combination of disbelief and shock. Many parents and relatives do not wish sexual incidents against their children reported because (1) it may traumatize the child and lead to ostracization and embarrassment, and (2) it may stigmatize the family as a whole.

It is believed that sexual child abuse is increasing, both in the number of cases and in the awareness of such cases. Part of the increase is attributed to a more permissive society and part of it to less direct parental supervision. The greatest publicity is usually given to incest and parental exploitation by involving the child in child pornography, but child molesting by parents, relatives, neighbors, and others who have an opportunity is considered widespread. Senator Dodd of Connecticut told a special session of congress in 1984 that one child abuse case in five involves a child under the age of seven. Estimates as to the number of children that were sexually abused in 1988 ranged from a low of 45,000 to a high of 1,000,000.

In 1986 the American Humane Association conducted a study, funded by the National Center on Child Abuse and Neglect, of 132,000 confirmed cases of child abuse. The age of the victims ranged from infancy through seventeen. Children seven or younger constituted 32.79 percent of the cases, or about one-third. The average age of the perpetrators was 32.5 with an age range from 6 to 98 years. Forty-two percent of the abusers were parents, including biological, foster, and adoptive. More than 80 percent of the perpetrators were male and more than 77 percent of the victims were female. In almost all cases, the younger children knew the abusers, who had access to them in their home, neighborhood, or school.

The fondling of a child's genitals is the most common form of sexual child abuse and is sometimes initiated when the child is an infant. Such behavior is often disguised by the adults or juveniles involved as game-playing. Some form of oral sex is also a frequent sexual activity in which children are enticed or coerced to participate. In fact, there seem to be no types of sexual abuse or sex crimes in which children have not been involved.

The reactions of children to sexual child abuse are quite varied. They may suffer from depression, anxiety, withdrawal; there may be a high degree of indifference; or there may be a positive reaction from pleasing the parents or whomever is pursuing the relationship. The reactions depend on several factors: the amount of physical trauma present, the relationship between the child and the abuser, the age of the child, the frequency of the activity, and the way the child is treated if the offense becomes public knowledge. The child may well be harmed more severely by the way people act toward him or her and the situation than the behavior itself. In addition, the personality of the child will strongly influence the nature and severity of the consequences. One of the complications in helping the child is the difficulty many people have in dealing with incest and other sexual abuses.

One commentator pointed out that children often do not allow themselves to get over the trauma of sexual child abuse because they feel guilty for some other activity or thought that occurred prior to the abuse incident. This guilt may be associated with things as elementary as taking a piece of candy without permission or not coming straight home from school. The American culture stresses punishment for misdeeds, so children can intertwine misdeeds and punishment quite easily. Unless the therapist can identify the hidden activity for which the child has assumed the guilt for the sexual abuse, progress in alleviating the feelings of wrongdoing will be slow.

If a young child is involved in sexual abuses, his or her awareness of the nature and disapproval of such activities is very restricted. One may be willing to talk about it easily, whereas older children are likely to be uncomfortable and even secretive. However, the young child may begin to exhibit some degree of regression to behaviors that had been outgrown. The child may engage in some baby talk, experience bed-wetting, or undergo a series of frightening nightmares. It is not unusual for the child to become more difficult to live with because of temper tantrums, loud-talking, the use of foul language, or becoming quite hyperactive in general.

Another possible consequence is that abused children will begin to indulge in types of sex play that they normally would not at their age. They may display seductive types of behavior toward playmates, or even adults, or they may begin masturbating frequently and sometimes quite openly. These types of behaviors are often stimulated by the television programs and movies they have seen. In other words, even the small child becomes more sexually aware after being abused. Those working with a sexually abused child have a very fine line to walk to reestablish a growth toward a healthy sexuality for the age of the child. The child must recognize that what has happened is in the past, that there is no stigmatization, and that he or she has not become abnormal; rather, life goes on and it is necessary to concentrate on learning about things to come. Abused children under six years of age need much reassurance, and promises that cannot be kept should not be made (e.g., "no one will ever hurt you again"). Most young children are able to adjust and the traumas of the abuses will disappear in a fairly short period of time.

In a broader perspective, it is clear that sexual abuse has no social, economic, or racial parameters. Until recently, it was believed that sexual abuse of children would most likely come from strangers, including the proverbial "dirty old man." The most common prevention was essentially verbal: "Don't talk to strangers," "Don't take candy from anyone you don't know," or "Don't get into any car without our permission." However, as we learn more about the sexual abuse of children, it becomes more and more apparent that the most common abusers are those who are close to the child, such as family members, relatives, and neighbors. Most of those who have been identified in court and through research have been young and consistently under the age of 50. One study found that only 10 percent of those involved were over the age of 50. It is possible to educate the young child with regard to preventing sexual abuse, but it is very difficult to identify the persons from whom the attacks may come.

4.3   MEDIATION

Mediation is one alternative to legal battle, or at least an aid to reducing conflict in the legal dissolution of marriage. It is a logical extension of the thinking that produced no-fault divorce statutes. Two goals motivated the introduction of no-fault divorce laws: (1) reduction of the destructive impact of the adversary process on divorcing partners, and (2) reduction of the burden on the courts of determining fault through a cumbersome and antiquated process. Creation of divorce without grounds based on fault, however, minimized rather than eliminated the adversarial process in divorce. Attorneys continue to represent adversarial parties in divorce and related proceedings; ethical considerations (conflict of interest and confidentiality) effectively prevent them from acting otherwise. A solution to this dilemma is offered by the procedure called *mediation* which has become particularly popular of late.

Mediation in domestic relations is simply a formalized process that has been used since time immemorial on an informal basis. Mediation uses a neutral third party to assist disputing parties in coming to an agreement regarding property disposition, child custody, and child visitation. Unlike a judge, a mediator does make decisions; unlike a lawyer, a mediator is not an advocate; unlike a therapist, a mediator does not attempt to treat marital problems. Mediation is not binding, meaning that the agreement does not constitute the final marital settlement, although it could become final. Ordinarily, the parties take the resulting mediation agreement to their attorneys for perusal. Attorneys may object to the agreement or its terms, requiring further negotiation between the parties through their attorneys to arrive at a final settlement.

Even though attorneys often serve as family mediators, they cannot properly mediate *and* represent a party to a divorce without violating basic principles of conflict of interest. Although therapists and counselors often serve as mediators, the goal of mediation is neither reconciliation nor marital therapy. A mediator may be successful in getting the parties to cooperate to the extent that reconciliation takes place, but this is simply a fortunate byproduct of the process rather than a goal of mediation. Mediation is often misconceived as either adversarial or therapeutic; it is neither.

Attorneys, negotiators, and therapists usually require additional training in mediation techniques. It is mandatory in some states for certification (or its equivalent) as a family mediator. Lawyers must learn not to take sides and view issues in terms of argumentation and therapists must learn that mediation clients have not come for treatment.

The advantages of mediation are cost-effectiveness and empowerment. Mediated divorces are typically less costly than nonmediated divorces. The hourly charge for mediators is commonly less than for lawyers and mediation usually takes less time in reaching agreement than attorney-negotiated agreements. Part of the reason for this is obvious. Mediation typically takes place in a room with the mediator, husband, and wife seated around a table discussing the terms of the marital settlement. The mediators task is to enable the parties to agree on the terms of the settlement by giving them the setting, the tools, and the skills to negotiate and by deflecting disruptive conduct and comments that interfere with cooperation ("His mother never approved of me"; "She never balanced the checkbook"). Attorneys, on the other hand, talk to their clients; call the attorneys for the other side, who then discuss the proposal with the client; call the first attorney again; and so forth. Attorneys sometimes meet together with both clients in attendance, to reach closure on issues or the agreement, but then the clients are not only paying two simultaneous legal fees, but also may have as many as four negotiators in an adversial context. The goal of mediation is closure; the goal of negotiation is winning the advantage.

Empowerment is perhaps a more significant advantage of mediation, although more difficult to measure in dollars and cents. Adversarial divorce usually entails the parties' relinquishing control of the negotiations to the attorneys. Successful mediation is a process whereby the mediator sets the stage for the parties to work out their own agreement. On a personal level, the mediation process can be very positive. Divorcing parties, typically emotionally vulnerable to begin with, become the active parties in charting their destinies rather than passive clients of fighting attorneys. This empowerment may prove a positive force in renewing some of the self-esteem lost when individuals fail at the most important feature of their lives. Additionally, because mediation teaches cooperative techniques, those who learn from their experience may be able to apply these techniques to relationships in the future. This could be especially valuable for ex-spouses who must continue to deal with each other while minor children are shared.

The major disadvantage to mediation is that it does not always work. Mediation requires interpersonal skills in the mediator, which cannot be taught to everyone. Temperament, prior training and experience, and personal prejudices may be insurmountable. A mediator might be very effective with most couples but fail miserably with others. Some couples are not mediable, having an adversarial relationship or obstinacy that defies mediation. In these situations, mediation merely adds cost by applying another layer of services for which the couple must pay. In many instances, though, this extra cost may be illusory; early studies indicate that unsuccessfully mediated divorces were significantly less costly than divorces processed without any mediation. This may be true in many cases simply because the parties have learned some skills in negotiation and compromise and have come closer to agreement, so that the time spent by lawyers in reaching the final settlement may be significantly reduced.

Nevertheless, mediation is not for everyone. Couples with extensive property holdings or businesses, which pose complex legal or financial issues, may be wasting their time in mediation, or might best be served by restricting mediation to questions regarding custody and visitation. This should give some reassurance to attorneys who fear that mediation will reduce attorney income. In fact, mediation tends to relieve the attorneys of the most unpleasant part of divorce negotiation and leave the legal issues—their primary job—for the attorneys. In fact, even when an attorney is mediating, he or she should avoid rendering legal advice during the process; mediation is not the practice of law. Mediators must be aware of some basic family law within the jurisdiction simply to avoid improper agreements, but should not go beyond simple statements of the law (for example, that alimony is generally taxed to the donee and child support is taxed to the donor). It is best to provide a handout rather than appear to interpret the law.

As federal government intrudes into family law (e.g., making it a crime to leave a jurisdiction with the intent to avoid paying child support), it becomes more important that legal advice be given. If state and federal law follow a recent trend to regulate divorce and custody, mediation may become untenable without increased licensing, certification, and policing of family mediators. Licensing and certification have already become a fixture of many jurisdictions. The respective movements to license family mediators and paralegals may coalesce soon to provide a special career track for paralegals. Perhaps baccalaureate or master's programs that include law, counseling, and mediation will spring up.

Some jurisdictions have provided by statute for judges to order mediation and delay final disposition of divorce until the couple has met with a mediator. This underscores a fundamental problem of divorce adjudication: A judge in a divorce case must make decisions based on the selected facts presented by the parties through their attorneys. Arriving at a just decision requires the wisdom of Solomon and the patience of Job. One way to lighten this task for the judge is to require mediation, with a report by the mediator as to which questions reached resolution and which did not (commonly the mediator draws up the agreement and obtains signatures from both parties). Statutory authority to require mediation is also a means for judges to compel a negotiation process from parties or attorneys who have not made a bona fide attempt to reach an agreement.

The discussions during the mediation process should be confidential and the mediator should not be compelled to testify under ordinary circumstances. The confidentiality privilege encourages the parties to negotiate without fear that offers of compromise or conciliation may later be used against them. If mediation is not confidential, it becomes an adversarial process.

4.4 MARRIAGE COUNSELING

No-fault divorce statutes may have made divorce too easy, assuming our society still values marriage and the struggle to keep marriages intact. Some courts have the authority, prior to granting divorce, to order marriage or family counseling or marital or family therapy, all of which are frequently used interchangeably. Such authority indicates that public policy favoring the preservation and stability of marriage is still viable, despite the universal acceptance of no-fault divorce. In short, although state legislatures have empowered individuals to end their marriages, public policy favors stable marriages. The increase in legislation protecting children and especially children of divorce suggests that the primary concern for marriage focuses on families with children.

Assuming the foregoing to be a correct reflection of public policy, it would seem that attorneys have an ethical as well as a moral obligation to refrain from conduct that might impede reconciliation. This may pose a dilemma, because the attorney acts primarily as an advocate for the interests a client presents. The attorney's personal judgment might well be that divorce is wrong for a couple, and yet he or she is presented with a demand to pursue a divorce. Divorce lawyers inevitably deal with counseling that transcends the legal issues of divorce. When the borders become blurred, the attorney may recommend counseling. In fact, counseling is highly advisable for divorce as well as reconciliation. Few individuals are prepared for the ordeal of divorce and its aftermath, and attorneys typically restrict their vision to the case at hand rather than the future lives of their clients. Other professionals may be better able to assist clients in such matters. Attorneys specializing in family law must at the very least acquaint themselves with competent practitioners in family therapy, so that clients may be guided to appropriate help when necessary and so that the attorneys have recourse for help with questions beyond their competence.

4.5 DEFINITION OF FAMILY

At first glance, the 1990s redefinition of the family appears to be concerned with alternative living arrangements—specifically same-sex relationships, heterosexual couples unable or unwilling to marry, and communal living arrangements including unrelated but cooperative or dependent persons. While these alternative arrangements challenge traditional legal definitions of *family*, their inclusion or exclusion from the category of family can be legally determined in three ways:

1. *Constitutional challenge.* Those presently excluded from the benefits of a legal marriage because of their status may attack governmental action or rules on the grounds that the equal protection clause of the Fourteenth Amendment to the U.S. Constitution prohibits this form of discrimination.

2. *Legislation.* The composition of the family may be redefined by the enactment of laws in state legislatures and in Congress. Amendment, reform, or redrafting of civil rights legislation could prohibit certain forms of discrimination based on marital status or might redefine qualifying members of a family. Employment, health, and housing laws could be changed to recognize different forms of the family. Marriage qualifications could be changed to allow those previously prohibited from marrying to marry. Some states have already allowed registration of unmarried individuals as a family for restricted purposes.

3. *Reinterpretation of existing law.* The courts can respond to legal challenges to existing laws by expanding the interpretation of those laws or modifying or rejecting prior interpretations to include persons previously thought to be excluded. As far as statutes are concerned, the guide to interpretation is the intent of the legislature in enacting the law. Most older statutes did not contemplate contemporary living arrangements, so intent becomes obscure and a judge may be left to speculate upon what the legislators collectively "would have" intended had they considered this problem. In the past, for example, attempted homosexual marriages have been defeated in the courts even though the statutes did not specifically require marrying parties to be of different sexes. The courts reasoned that legislators predicated the law on the only acceptable scenario of husband and wife. Today, courts could just as easily conclude that there was no intent to exclude and that the law simply enables those with contractual capacity to establish marital bonds with their attendant legal consequences.

Of course, each of these approaches may well be unsuccessful. During the early 1990s we have seen the continuation of a trend toward legal tolerance of intimate relations formerly condemned. This is counterbalanced to some extent by a backlash in some areas. The struggle will be played out in the legal and political arena, but the outcome will be tempered in large part by the direction our society takes. The future of family law has perhaps never been less certain.

Despite the considerable attention given to such questions, a number of other issues that have arisen in recent years also suggest that the family is in the process of redefinition. Like other areas of social change, change in the family is reflected in numerous changes in legal issues, as the whole field readjusts to a new ordering. The cumulative effect of many minor changes often signals major change. The inherent conservatism of the law caused by its reactive, rather than proactive, nature seems usually to favor incremental change. Nevertheless, family law has been one of the most dynamic areas of law and contemporary social issues suggest that this dynamic quality will not abate in the foreseeable future. Questions regarding parentage give some indication of the breadth of this change.

Who Qualifies as a Parent?

Although the question of who is a parent has already been addressed, it bears repetition. In the past, parents were biological parents who took the trouble to marry. Today, we have unmarried parents, nonmarital fathers, psychological parents, foster parents, adoptive parents, and a proliferation of stepparents. Each of these has an arguable claim to the status of parent; each may pursue such claims; and each may be required to meet some or all parental obligations recognized by the law. (Issues of artificial insemination, surrogacy, and paternity are treated in appendices 15B, Uniform Parentage Act, and 15C, Uniform Status of Children of Assisted Conception Act.)

Will the Real Parent Please Stand Up?

When monogamy was the norm and divorce was rare, the presumption that a woman's husband was the father of her child drew a statistically reasonable conclusion. First the sexual revolution put paternity in doubt; then reproductive medical technology advanced to the point where parenthood can be manipulated in ways lawmakers could not have contemplated in times past. A woman may be artificially inseminated; she may be implanted with a fertilized egg, whether her own or someone else's. As a consequence, a child may be born without the acquiescence, except in an indirect way, of the genetic father or the mother's husband or consort. Such technology also allows celibate or homosexual women to bear children. Future technology may make it possible for successful parthenogenesis (birth from an egg without sperm), ectogenesis (birth outside the womb), and cloning (the genetic copying of an individual). Although these possibilities would seem to present merely novel special situations, they will also test the legal definition of *parenthood.* If, for example, males are unnecessary for reproduction, should the burden of parenthood fall equally to father and mother? Does a child have a right to have a father? Does a child have a right to know or know of its father? Also along this line, challenges to the secrecy of adoption seem to be effective at present.

Right of the Child

Although child abuse and neglect have been illegal since early times, the protection afforded children came in the guise of *parens patriae,* a doctrine that gives the state authority over those suffering legal disabilities, including children. This principle is paternalistic in tradition—the state acts as the parent when the legal parents are unable or unwilling to carry out their parental duties. The state protects the child. Recently, however, many have argued that children should have rights. Unfortunately, this creates a legal anomaly: How can a person not *sui juris* (i.e., without legal capacity) have rights as against the very persons—namely their parents—who are ultimately responsible for enforcing those rights? The *Gregory K.* case may be prophetic in this regard. Children ought not to continue in the legal parent-child relationship when the parent is abusive, neglectful, or in any other way is shown to have engaged in destructive conduct toward the child.

CASE NO. 4-1   Gregory K. Makes the News

On September 27, 1992, an Orlando, Florida, court permitted a 12-year-old boy to terminate the parental rights of his natural parents and allow his foster parents to adopt him (his natural father did not oppose the adoption). The news media branded this a "divorce" brought by a child against his mother. Many observers concluded that the case was significant only because the media gave it significance. Though this may be technically true, when the media focuses its attention on a case, legal issues become social and political issues. In this instance, the case not only underlined the plight of neglected children, but also suggested the woeful inadequacies of the social services programs that deal with them.

What was unusual about this termination of parental rights was the lack of involvement of a social service agency. Typically a suit for termination of parental rights is brought by an agency, often after court authorization to act. The *Gregory K.* case was unique in giving a minor legal status to bring an action against a parent to terminate parental rights.

Gregory K. was also unique in allowing a consolidation of the termination proceeding with an adoption proceeding brought by the foster parents. Ordinarily these two proceedings would be separate; clearly the termination of parental rights is a prerequisite for the subsequent adoption. Nevertheless, there is an inherent logic in transferring parental rights from a neglectful parent to a demonstrably caring and competent parent, as was the case here.

Gregory, or Shawn, as he preferred to be called, appeared to be the master of a reasoned decision about his own future, providing further justification for the dual actions and their consolidation. The case stands as a well-publicized monument to growing recognition of the rights of children. It should not be surprising that a judge with traditional equitable discretion should engineer such a result when government agencies show a continuing inability to deal with the flood of abused, abandoned, and neglected children. It is hoped that, rather than opening the gates for a flood of lawsuits, *Gregory K.* may inspire greater attention to the role of government in an extremely serious social problem.

The Florida case did not technically "divorce" a boy from his parents. If it had, perhaps Shawn could have sought child support.

Whose Child Is It Anyway?

The several categories of parentage mentioned in this section were created by the emergence of the rights of children. The focus on fault in family law has shifted from spousal fault to parental fault. The neglect and abuse of children has received great attention recently. The increasing number of children in single-parent households or living with stepfamilies has brought the plight of children to the attention of nearly everyone. The ideal archetype of the intact family, the "happy family," can no longer serve as a general model. Along with the demise of ideal forms of the family came doubts about the roles of father and mother. It may be fair to say that parents no longer know how to be parents. The human species is the only one that offers courses and workshops in parenting.

During the 20th century in America, the authoritarian patriarchal model has been challenged not only by the movement for womens' rights but also by a powerful movement to recognize the rights of children. Symbolically, this might be represented by the change in First Ladies, from Nancy Reagan with her "Just Say No" admonitions to Hillary Rodham Clinton, who published a seminal legal article early in her career advocating increased recognition of children's rights. In 1992, national attention was focused on a seemingly unique case in Florida, the *Gregory K.* case, in which a minor effectively severed the bonds with his biological mother in favor of his foster family, opening the way for adoption by the foster family. This was tantamount to a child willingly divorcing his parents. This case might seem to be unique, but a great many children are in similar situations. In the past, Gregory's interests would have been subordinate to parental rights, with the exception of state intervention for abuse. Authority was exercised by a parent, whether it was a human parent or the state acting as parens patriae.

Parental authority is buffeted between the concern over adolescent freedom, as represented by teenage pregnancy and juvenile crime on the one hand, and serious abuse and neglect by parents on the other. The legal system will inevitably be asked to resolve this clash. It is difficult to predict the

What do you suppose is the story behind this scene of woman and child? Two-income couples and single-parent families have dramatically increased the need for all-day child care.

exact outcome, but the atmosphere changed from the 1970s, when money was steadily increased for social programs, to the 1980s and beyond, when the answer to social problems came to be criminalization of misbehavior. For instance, Florida has a law under which a parent driver may receive jail time for injury or death to a young child who is not buckled in. It is becoming a crime to be a bad parent.

4.6 REPRODUCTIVE RIGHTS

While the abortion battle continues its apparently interminable struggle over the rights of women to control reproduction by terminating pregnancy, the issue of the right to reproduce continues. As reproductive technology permits new ways of creating human beings, the question of who may reproduce raises new legal problems. In 1992, a California attorney brought an action on behalf of death-row inmates who wanted to have children. This is a logical extension of the battle for reproductive rights of persons with limited intelligence or with mental disorders. Institutionalized persons whose conduct may be controlled by governmental or private authorities are vulnerable to the impositions of a legal society. The issues generated by such situations raise the specter of Nazi genocide and other eugenics movements. These images tend to provide emotional support for recognizing constitutional rights of marriage and reproduction. From a practical standpoint, preventing death-row inmates from reproducing seems to be in society's best interest. Of all the possible candidates for reproductive limitations, this group would likely win the prize—they are neither capable of supporting their offspring nor would they likely be the genetic specimens chosen to perpetuate society. These reflections do not, however, settle the issue of whether reproductive rights may be lost by misconduct. Similarly, pragmatism suggests that free abortions ought to be provided for welfare mothers, but the politics of reproduction has gone in the opposite direction.

4.7 PRIVATE VERSUS PUBLIC CONTROL

The intersection of private and public interests creates a number of stresses for the family and for individuals. While the law seems to be making marriage, reproduction, and divorce easier to accomplish, by removing impediments and recognizing private choice, the children that result from these choices have increasingly become the concern of government and law. The federal government seems to be abandoning its traditional abstention from the domestic relations arena. In addition to the enforcement efforts discussed in chapter 12, Congress enacted a law, effective in October 1992, that makes it a crime to avoid paying child support by moving to another state. The law affects payors who are one year or $5,000 in arrears, and the penalty for a first offense could be as much as six months in jail and a $5,000 fine. Will such a law be effective in light of the complexity of interstate enforcement and the absence of state funding? Perhaps the solution will be to pay private attorneys a percentage for going after nonpaying spouses, a system currently in force in state jurisdictions. Although designed to reimburse the states for welfare payments, the system has expanded well beyond this. A lucrative business in bounty-hunting has arisen for attorneys in this area.

Does this legislation indicate a future course in the law? When government can neither fix social problems nor afford to support the victims of these problems, does privatization backed by criminal sanctions solve the problem? (Note that no jail can support a criminal for six months with a $5,000 fine, not that the fine would go to the prison anyway.) Another solution set to begin in 1994 is garnishment of paychecks of those obligated to pay child support, regardless of whether the obligor is in arrears. Although collection costs are thereby passed on to the employer, this may be the cheapest way to make collection and make it systematic. Other proposals include making the Internal Revenue Service the collection agency, beyond the present withholding of tax refunds, but increased power for the IRS is not universally welcomed. All of these measures take on a draconian or inquisitorial aspect more often associated with third-world or totalitarian legal systems.

The legal battle over educating the young is not likely to be settled in the near future. Should parents have maximum choice in their children's education, or should government not only provide education but also have absolute authority over the education of children?

SUMMARY

Family law continues to be dynamic. Family-like relationships have come to represent significant diversity, accorded recognition by the law. While the traditional family continues, the definitions of *family, parenthood,* and *childhood* are being greatly broadened. This means ultimately that new rights are recognized and old ones are changed.

Not only is the family changing in its variety, but the relationship between the family and the government is also changing. Law expresses the policies that the government extracts from and imposes on society. This will continue to be a complex process that is of necessity somewhat unpredictable.

QUESTIONS

1. Can homosexual couples enjoy employee health benefits like a heterosexual family?
2. Must a heterosexual couple marry in order to receive the benefits our society provides families?
3. How would you define the word *family*? (Do not use the dictionary.)
4. Do children have a right to parental care?
5. In the June 28, 1993, issue of *U.S. News & World Report,* John Leo, criticizing what he labeled "rights babble," noted the following:

A battered woman, abused by her husband, wrote a moving article about her experience in the *Washington Post,* but at the end she lapsed into rights talk. "Victims of this crime," she wrote, "must realize that they have the right to live in a safe, loving home." She appended a bill of rights for abused women, including the right to be angry and the right to be imperfect.

Do imperfect parents have a right to keep their children, as against a child's "right" to a "safe, loving home"? Is John Leo correct in criticizing an inclination to convert desires into legal rights?

6. Should a child be able to divorce his or her parents?
7. Can we rightfully restrict some individuals from reproducing? If so, who?
8. What are the advantages of divorce mediation?
9. What legal means can be used to bring about change in the recognition of domestic rights?
10. Should parents be able to divorce their children?

EXERCISES

Answer the questions according to the law of your state.

1. Is *family* defined in the statutes? Is it defined in different places in the statutes?
2. How do the statutes establish the qualifications for marriage? Must the couple consist of a man and a woman? If so, can you tell whether that is a recently added requirement?
3. Are there any restrictions on who may adopt?
4. Is there a statute covering surrogacy contracts?
5. Who may represent a child in a legal proceeding?

APPENDIX 4A

Uniform Putative and Unknown Fathers Act (1988)

§ 1.   Definitions.

In this [Act]:

(1)   "Man" means a male individual of any age.

(2)   "Putative father" means a man who claims to be, or is named as, the biological father or a possible biological father of a child, and whose paternity of the child has not been judicially determined, excluding:

(i)   a man whose parental rights with respect to the child have been previously judicially terminated or declared not to exist;

(ii)   a donor of semen used in artificial insemination or in vitro fertilization whose identity is not known by the mother of the resulting child or whose semen was donated under circumstances indicating that the donor did not anticipate having an interest in the resulting child;

(iii)   a man who is or was married to the mother of the child, and the child is born during the marriage [or within 300 days after the marriage was terminated by death, annulment, declaration of invalidity, divorce, or marital dissolution, or after a decree of separation was entered by a court];

(iv)   a man who, before the birth of the child, attempted to marry the mother of the child in apparent compliance with law, although the attempted marriage is, or could be declared, invalid, and:

(A)   if the attempted marriage could be declared invalid only by a court, the child is born during the attempted marriage[, or within 300 days after its termination by death, annulment, declaration of invalidity, divorce, or marital dissolution]; or

(B)   if the attempted marriage is invalid without a court order declaring its invalidity, the child is born during, or within 300 days after the termination of, cohabitation; and

(v)   a man who, after the birth of the child, married or attempted to marry the mother of the child in apparent compliance with law, although the attempted marriage is, or could be declared, invalid, and:

(A)   has acknowledged his paternity of the child in a writing filed with the [appropriate court or Vital Statistics Bureau];

(B)   with his consent, is named as the child's biological father on the child's birth certificate; or

(C)   is obligated to support the child under a written promise or by court order.

(3)   "Unknown father" means a child's biological father whose identity is unascertained. However, the term does not include a donor of semen used in artificial insemination or in vitro fertilization whose identity is not known to the mother of the resulting child or whose semen was donated under circumstances indicating that the donor did not anticipate having any interest in the resulting child.

§ 2.   Right to Determination of Paternity.

(a)   A putative father may bring an action to determine whether he is the biological father of a particular child[, in accordance with [applicable state law],] at any time, unless his paternity or possible parental rights have already been determined or are in issue in pending litigation.

(b)   An agreement between a putative father and the mother or between him and the child does not bar an action under this section[, unless the agreement has been judicially approved [under applicable state law]].

§ 3. Notice of Judicial Proceedings for Adoption or Termination of Parental Rights.

(a)   In an adoption or other judicial proceeding that may result in termination of any man's parental rights with respect to a child, the person seeking termination shall give notice to every putative father of the child known to that person.

(b)   The notice must be given

(i)   at a time and place and in a manner appropriate under the [rules of civil procedure for the service of process in a civil action in this State] or

(ii)   at a time and place and in a manner as the court directs to provide actual notice.

(c)   A putative father may participate as a party in a proceeding described in subsection (a).

(d)   If, at any time in the proceeding, it appears to the court that there is a putative father of the child who has not been given notice, the court shall require notice of the proceeding to be given to him in accordance with subsection (b).

(e)   If, at any time in the proceeding, it appears to the court that an unknown father may not have been given notice, the court shall determine whether he can be identified. The determination must be based on evidence that includes inquiry of appropriate persons in an effort to identify him for the purpose of providing notice. The inquiry must include:

(1)   whether the mother was married at the probable time of conception of the child or at a later time;

(2)   whether the mother was cohabitating with a man at the probable time of conception of the child;

(3)   whether the mother has received support payments or promises of support, other than from a governmental agency, with respect to the child or because of her pregnancy;

(4)   whether the mother has named any man as the biological father in connection with applying for or receiving public assistance; and

(5)   whether any man has formally or informally acknowledged or claimed paternity of the child in a jurisdiction in which the mother resided at the time of or since conception of the child or in which the child has resided or resides at the time of the inquiry.

(f)   If the inquiry required by subsection (e) identifies any man as the unknown father, the court shall require notice of the proceeding to be given to him pursuant to subsection (b). If the inquiry so identifies a man, but his whereabouts are unknown, the court shall proceed in accordance with subsection (b) and (g).

(g)   If, after the inquiry required by subsection (e), it appears to the court that there may be an unknown father of the child, the court shall consider whether publication or public posting of notice of the proceeding is likely to lead to actual notice to him. The court may order publication or public posting of the notice only if, on the basis of all information available, the court determines that the publication or posting is likely to lead to actual notice to him.

§ 4. Notice of Judicial Proceedings Regarding Custody or Visitation.

(a)   The petitioner in a judicial proceeding to change or establish legal or physical custody of or visitation rights with respect to a child shall give notice to every putative father of the child known to the petitioner, except a proceeding for annulment, declaration of invalidity, divorce, marital dissolution, legal separation, modification of child custody, or determination of paternity.

(b)   The notice must be given

(i)   at a time and place and in a manner appropriate under the [rules of civil procedure for the service of process in a civil action in this State] or

(ii)   as the court determines will likely provide actual notice.

(c)   If, at any time in the proceeding, it appears to the court that there is a putative father of the child who has not been given notice of the proceeding, the court shall require notice of the proceeding to be given to him pursuant to subsection (b).

(d)   If, at any time in the proceeding, it appears to the court that there may be an unknown father who has not been given notice of the proceeding, the court, in the best interest of the child, may attempt to identify him pursuant to Section 3(e) and require notice of the proceeding to be given to him pursuant to Section 3(f) and (g).

(e)   A putative father may participate as a party in a proceeding described in subsection (a).

§ 5. Factors in Determining Parental Rights of Father.

In determining whether to preserve or terminate the parental rights of a putative father in a proceeding governed by Section 3 or 4, the court shall consider all of the following factors that are pertinent:

(1)   the age of the child;

(2)   the nature and quality of any relationship between the man and the child;

(3)   the reasons for any lack of a relationship between the man and the child;

(4)   whether a parent and child relationship has been established between the child and another man;

(5)   whether the child has been abused or neglected;

(6)   whether the man has a history of substance abuse or of abuse of the mother or the child;

(7)   any proposed plan for the child;

(8) whether the man seeks custody and is able to provide the child with emotional or financial support and a home, whether or not he has had opportunity to establish a parent and child relationship with the child;

(9) whether the man visits the child, has shown any interest in visitation, or, desiring visitation, has been effectively denied an opportunity to visit the child;

(10) whether the man is providing financial support for the child according to his means;

(11) whether the man provided emotional or financial support for the mother during prenatal, natal, and postnatal care;

(12) the circumstances of the child's conception, including whether the child was conceived as a result of incest or forcible rape;

(13) whether the man has formally or informally acknowledged or declared his possible paternity of the child; and

(14) other factors the court considers relevant to the standards for making an order, as stated in Section 6(d) and (g).

§ 6. Court Determinations and Orders.

(a) If a man appears in a proceeding described in Section 3, other than as a petitioner or prospective adoptive parent, the court may:

(1) in accordance with [applicable state law],] determine whether the man is the biological father of the child and, if the court determines that he is, enter an order in accordance with subsection (d); or

(2) without determining paternity, and consistent with the standards in subsection (d), enter an order, after considering the factors in Section 5, terminating any parental rights he may have, or declaring that he has no parental rights, with respect to the child.

(b) If the court makes an order under subsection (a), the court may also make an order

(i) terminating the parental rights of any other man given notice who does not appear, or

(ii) declaring that no man has any parental rights with respect to the child.

(c) If a man who appears in a proceeding described in Section 3 is determined by the court to be the father, the court, after considering evidence of the factors in Section 5, shall determine

(i) whether a familial bond between the father and the child has been established; or

(ii) whether the failure to establish a familial bond is justified, and the father has the desire and potential to establish the bond.

(d) If the court makes an affirmative determination under subsection (c), the court may terminate the parental rights of the father[, in accordance with [applicable state law],] only if failure to do so would be detrimental to the child. If the court does not make an affirmative determination, it may terminate the parental rights of the father if doing so is in the best interest of the child.

(e) If no man appears in a proceeding described in Section 3, the court may enter an order:

(1) terminating with respect tot he child the parental rights of any man given notice; or

(2) declaring that no putative father or unknown father has any parental rights with respect to the child.

(f) If the court does not require notice under Section 3, it shall enter an order declaring that no putative father or unknown father has any parental rights with respect to the child.

(g) If a man appears in a proceeding described in Section 4 and requests custody or visitation based on a claim of paternity, the court shall either determine[, in accordance with [applicable state law],] whether he is the biological father of the child or, after considering the factors in Section 5, deny him the custody of or visitation with the child. If the court determines that he is the biological father, the court shall determine, after considering evidence of the factors listed in Section 5, whether or not to grant him custody or visitation and shall make such other orders as are appropriate. All orders issued under this subsection must be in the child's best interest.

(h) A court order under subsection (a)(2), (b), (d), or (e) terminating the parental rights of a man, or declaring that no man has parental rights, with respect to the child, is not a determination that the man is or is not the biological father of the child.

(i) [Six months] after the date of issuance of an order under this section terminating parental rights or declaring that no man has parental rights, no person may directly or collaterally challenge the order upon any ground, including fraud, misrepresentation, failure to give a required notice, or lack of jurisdiction over the parties or of the subject matter. The running of this period of limitation may not be extended for any reason.

§ 7. Short Title.

This [Act] may be cited as the Uniform Putative and Unknown Fathers Act.

ENGAGEMENTS

lody Watkins and Wayne Norville an-
the engagement of their daughter
n Watkins-Norville to Michael Curtis,
Marlene Curtis and Kevin Curtis of
o. Shannon Watkins-Norville attended
nia Polytechnic University of San Luis
graduating with a doctorate in Nu-
hysics. She lives in New York City.
ork and works at New York University.
Curtis graduated from the Institute of
California with a degree in Engineer-
lives in Amherst, New York and works
tor for the Department of Health and
Services. The two met at a physics
nce. They will be married at New York
ity. The wedding will be held in June.

and John Cage of Kansas City an-
the engagement of their daughter
Cage to Steven Fox, son of Barbara
chael Fox of Garland, Kansas. Patricia
tended Mason College of Hair and
n Kansas City. She currently lives and
n Kansas City. Steven Fox is a gradu-
oston University in Massachusetts. He
n the District Attorney's office. The
l be married May 1 in Kansas City,
They will honeymoon in Ireland.

therine Shaefer of Eagle Bluffs, an-
the engagement of her daughter
to Robert Patterson, son of Christine
arc Patterson of Tustin, California.
Shaefer, a marketing consultant, is a

Harvard Law School. He currently works for
the legal department of Stanford University.
The two will be married at the Windmill Farm.
They plan to remain in California after a long
honeymoon in Jamaica.

WEDDINGS

Shari Ellis, daughter of Sophie and Zach Ellis
of Spring Valley, Virginia, and Brian Marino,
son of Lois and Adam Marino of Colorado
Springs, were married in Colorado Springs
May 12. The Reverend Billings officiated at
the Church. The bride wore a white silk and
lace gown. The dress had a ruffled semicathe-
dral train and a bustle with pink and white
roses. The groom wore a black and white tuxedo. The reception was held at the Hilton in
Colorado Springs. Th
in Europe.

Zoe Mathison, daug
Mathison of Boulde
Kearns, son of Const
in Colorado Springs
The Reverend Jane
ceremony, held at th
bride wore ivory, as
ily, and was driven
drawn carriage. The
tuxedo, met the brid
reception, held at
tended by hundreds.
tertained the crowd. The happy couple is
honeymooning in Egypt.

Yuka Fujishima, daughter of C.W. Fujishima
and R. Fujishima, was married to Kazuteru
Murakami, son of Reiko and Haruki Murakami, in Monterey, California on May 26.
The Reverend R. Stuart officiated at the ceremony, done first in traditional Japanese style.
The bride wore a stunning kimono, the groom
a classic hakama. The second, western-style
ceremony saw the bride in a white-beaded lace
sheath with a pink obi sash. The reception was
held at the Rastafarian Reggae Bar on Light-
house Avenue. The two are honeymooning in
San Francisco.

Helen Davis, daughter of Lindsay and Daniel
Davis, was married to Keith Bronson, son of
Marie and Greg Bronson, in Hacienda, New
Mexico, on May 15. Helen Davis, who is a
graduate of New Mexico State University, is
an advertising specialist working for the U.S.
Government. Keith Bronson, a graduate of
Massachusetts Institute of Technology, is a
systems administrator for International
Computers, Inc. in Monte Vista, New Mexico.

tion was held on Mayor Carwile's grou
The couple will honeymoon in Asia.

ANNIVERSARIES

Barbara and John Slater will celebrate
10th wedding anniversary by repeating
wedding vows in the presence of a few
friends. The couple will then board an o
liner bound for the South Pacific and enj
second honeymoon.

Mary and Bruce Martin celebrated their
wedding anniversary in Breckenridge, C
rado on June 11 in the presence of family
friends. The couple were married on the is
of Maui and have lived overseas throug
their marriage. After a long second ho

ranged the festivities, flew in from New
and Montreal. Distinguished guests fron
over the world attended.

BIRTHS

Robert Christopher Halliwell, a boy,
pounds ten ounces and twenty-two inche
length, was born at 10:21 P.M. on June 2
Maria and James Halliwell. Both mother
son are doing well and will be returning
the hospital soon.

Julianna Leigh Kroft, a girl, seven pound
ounces and nineteen inches in length,
born at 8:35 P.M. on July 12, to Stephani
Lee Kroft. Mother and daughter have alr
gone home to a joyous welcome from fa
and friends.

Caroline Chase Montgomery, a girl, s
pounds 10 ounces and twenty inches in le
was born at 5:28 A.M. on July 19, to Jar
and Brian M. Montgomery. Both mother
daughter are doing well and will be retur
home next week.

CHAPTER 5
Annulment

The Royal Grimaldis of Monaco

Daughter Caroline's unhappy first marriage ended in a civil divorce from Frenchman Philip Junot. Princess Grace (former American actress Grace Kelly) spent the last years of her life pleading with the Vatican to grant Caroline a Catholic annulment. Pictured here are Princess Caroline, Princess Grace, and Prince Ranier. Chapter 5 explains another alternative to divorce: annulment.

— Courtesy AP/Wide World Photos.

I've sometimes thought of marrying—and then I've thought again.

Noel Shire

OUTLINE

5.1 ANNULMENT DEFINED
5.2 HISTORY
5.3 ANNULMENT AND DIVORCE DISTINGUISHED
5.4 VOID OR VOIDABLE?
      Marriages Generally Considered Void
      Examples of Marriages Merely Voidable
           Fraud with Regard to Essentials of Marriage
           Fraud with Regard to Inability or Unwillingness to Have Children
           Fraud on the Court or Legal Process
5.5 CONSEQUENCES OF ANNULMENT
5.6 DEFENSES

5.1 ANNULMENT DEFINED

The word *annulment* comes from the verb *annul*, which in turn comes from the word *null*, which means not valid or of no effect. *Annul*, then, means to render something void or invalid, and *annulment* is the process of making something void or invalid. When used in family law, *annulment* refers to the legal process of invalidating a marriage. This is to be distinguished from divorce or dissolution of marriage, which terminate a valid marriage. Annulment denies the validity of the marriage. This determination by the court commonly treats the marriage as if it never existed, since the marriage was void from the beginning (*ab initio*). The result of such a position may be quite harsh—it renders children born to the couple illegitimate, for instance—so most states recognize such marriages for limited purposes.

85

5.2 HISTORY

What we now refer to as annulment was originally the only form of divorce that left the parties free to remarry, i.e., divorce *a vinculo matrimonii.* Until the 19th century in England, a proceeding for divorce *a vinculo matrimonii* came within the jurisdiction of canon law and the ecclesiastical courts. In America, the absence of ecclesiastical courts resulted in a variety of approaches in the different colonies. The northeastern colonies, most notably Massachusetts and Connecticut, early recognized the need for divorce, while the southern colonies tended toward a conservatism that followed the English restriction on divorce. Having no ecclesiastical courts, the southern colonies generally had no procedure for terminating marriages.

With the founding of the United States, most states developed procedures for divorce and annulment. In some states, legislation was passed providing the rules for annulment. In other states, the courts established precedent for annulment. It was possible for the courts to create law in this area by treating marriage as a contract which, like other contracts, has certain requirements for validity. For example, for the marriage contract to be valid, both parties must have contractual capacity, but contractual capacity was defined differently for marriage than for other contracts. A person could marry below the age of majority (21 at common law) and could not contract marriage with closely related persons. More traditional challenges to contractual validity were also recognized, such as fraud in inducing a contract.

Generally, a marriage contract is not as easily voided as other contracts because the law expresses a strong presumption in favor of the validity of a marriage. In addition, the courts are reluctant to void a marriage once it has been consummated.

The significance of annulment in any given state has been related to the availability and nature of divorce or dissolution. Today the prevalence of no-fault divorce makes annulment something of an anachronism, except in unusual circumstances. Nevertheless, annulment remains an important alternative because it has different consequences than divorce.

5.3 ANNULMENT AND DIVORCE DISTINGUISHED

Conceptually, the most important aspect of the difference between annulment and divorce relates to the grounds for ending the marriage. Annulment is based on a defect in existence when the marriage was contracted. (See Case No. 5-1.) Divorce is based on grounds that arise after the marriage. For instance, it is often possible to obtain an annulment if one of the parties to the marriage was impotent or sterile at the time of the marriage (usually assuming this fact was unknown to the other party). Impotence or sterility developing after the marriage contract would not ordinarily be grounds for annulment—the complaining party would be forced to resort to divorce to get out of the marriage. (Impotence and sterility are features special to the law of domestic relations because the law traditionally viewed the purpose of the marriage contract as encouragement of the procreation of legitimate offspring.)

CASE NO. 5-1   Essentials of Marriage

A marriage contract has its own peculiarities. The *Bilowit* case provides an example of an annulment based on fraud. It provides some clues as to what the courts consider "essentials of marriage," that is, those matters that are assumed to be the subject matter of every marriage contract. Was this a marriage gone bad or one that was invalid from the start?

BILOWIT v. DOLITSKY
124 N.J. Super. 101, 304 A.2d 774 (Ch. Ct. 1973)
Superior Court of New Jersey

McKENZIE, J.C.C. (Temporarily Assigned).
On the representation of defendant that he was a practicing Orthodox Jew, plaintiff married him on January 23, 1971. Thereafter plaintiff discovered that defendant did not in fact adhere to the tenets of Orthodox Judaism and had misrepresented his religious connections to plaintiff because he was in love with her, wished to marry her, and was aware that she would not marry him otherwise. The marriage was admittedly consummated. Plaintiff seeks an annulment, and her cause of action is not contested.

Our courts have long required a more substantial quantum of fraud to entitle a party to an annulment where the marriage has been consummated than where it has not. Any kind of fraud which would render a contract voidable may be the basis for the annulment of a marriage similarly infected.

Where the marriage has been consummated, the fraud of defendant will entitle plaintiff to an annulment only when the fraud is of an extreme nature, going to one of the essentials of marriage. The language is now embodied in N.J.S. 2A:34—1(d).

As to what constitutes the "essentials" of the marriage relation, it has been observed that the guidelines are vague and not fully delineated by our decisional law. This is as it should be. What is essential to the relationship of the parties in one marriage may be of considerably less significance in another. For this reason a determination of whether a fraud goes to the essentials of the marriage must rest upon the facts in each case. . . . Here plaintiff, corroborated by her rabbi, testified that she has been a deeply religious Orthodox Jew throughout her life. Her beliefs were made known to defendant and he, representing himself to be an Orthodox Jew, agreed to follow the requirements of that religion. As testified to by the rabbi, they are many and far-reaching, touching virtually all aspects of everyday life. Although for a few weeks following the marriage defendant adhered to them, it soon became apparent that he was not in fact an Orthodox Jew, and never sincerely intended to follow that religion. Plaintiff promptly separated from him.

* * *

. . . To plaintiff the religious beliefs and convictions of her husband were essential to her marriage. She could not have properly performed the duties of a wife and mother, following the rules and teachings of her faith, without the support of a husband holding the same beliefs. Defendant, having substantially and knowingly misrepresented the same to her, and plaintiff having relied thereon in entering into the marriage, this court holds the fraud to which plaintiff was subjected to be "gross and far-reaching," . . . .

* * *

A judgment for annulment of the marriage will be entered.

Whereas divorce is effective when the decree terminating the marriage is final, annulment operates retroactively to invalidate the marriage from its beginning. This is so because the cause of action for annulment asserts some impediment to the formation of the marriage contract itself; if the contract was invalid, no marriage resulted. A divorce, on the other hand, is based on a valid marriage contract and a valid marriage. One of the important consequences of annulment is the general unavailability of alimony, which most American courts award only upon the dissolution of a valid marriage.

5.4   VOID OR VOIDABLE?

Under traditional contract theory, some contracts are deemed void and some are merely voidable. A *void* contract is not considered enforceable at any time; a *voidable* contract is valid until a court declares it invalid, even though that declaration operates retroactively to the inception of the contract. Because of the passage of time and removal of the impediment to validity, a voidable contract may become enforceable.

Marriage contracts are similarly subject to the void–voidable distinction. Although a void marriage theoretically may be ignored by all parties, because it has no existence, often a declaration of nullity or its equivalent should be sought to avoid future complications. (See figure 5-1.) Because of the special nature of the marriage contract, the grounds for invalidity are somewhat different from other contracts. (Sections 207 and 208 of the Uniform Marriage and Divorce Act (appendix 5A) provide a model version of invalid marriages.)

Marriages Generally Considered Void

Although state laws vary somewhat, some putative marriages are generally considered void. *Bigamous marriage*, in which one of the parties is already married, is one such. In Case No. 5-2, the husband brought a suit in **partition**, claiming the marriage was void because the wife had failed to divorce her first husband. The absolute rule that bigamy voids a marriage here confronts an equally powerful presumption of validity of a second

---

LEGAL TERMS

partition
Separation of shares of property. When a husband and a wife own property jointly in a form of co-ownership called *tenancy in the entireties,* a suit in partition, which would normally be available to co-owners, may not be brought. A tenancy by the entireties may only be terminated by death, divorce, or mutual conveyance by husband and wife.

marriage (the law favors presumptions validating marriage). The court is understandably reluctant to void a 25-year marriage that produced with three children.

Incestuous marriage is also generally considered void, but each state specifies what relationships may not marry (e.g., parent-child, brother-sister, aunt-nephew). See Case No. 5-3. State legislatures may define incest broadly, but the court is likely to question prohibited marriages where no blood relationship exists. See case No. 5-4.

CASE NO. 5-2 A Bigamous Marriage?

STEWART v. HAMPTON
506 So. 2d 70 (Fla. Dist. Ct. App. 1987)
District Court of Appeal of Florida

Appellant, Jewel Stewart, first married Collin Thomas in Mitchel County, Georgia in 1948. Stewart moved back to her mother's home after a few months where she resided until she moved to Florida in 1950. The only proof that the first marriage was ever legally terminated was Stewart's testimony that she had been told by her mother that Thomas had divorced her.

Stewart met Henry Hampton, appellee herein, in 1955 and married him in 1961 in Vienna, Georgia. They obtained a Georgia marriage license and were formally married. Hampton testified that he thought he was legally married to Stewart in 1961. The couple bought a home, raised three children and lived together as husband and wife for twenty-five years up to the institution of this action by Hampton to partition the home.

At the partition hearing, Stewart contended that a second marriage is presumed valid and that the burden was on Hampton to establish that the first marriage did not end in divorce. Stewart contended that Hampton had not met his burden of proof. While this is not a divorce proceeding, Hampton wanted the marriage declared void in order to get a partition. If the marriage were valid, then the property would be held as a **tenancy by the entirety** and there would be no right to partition of the home. Also, if a divorce were obtained, then the trial court could award Stewart an interest in the house as alimony.

Once a marriage is shown to have been ceremonially entered into it is presumed to be legal and valid. All presumptions necessary to make the marriage valid, including the capacity to contract, attach on proof of the ceremonial marriage and cohabitation by the parties under the belief that they were lawfully married. . . . This presumption of validity that attaches to a second marriage is one of the strongest presumptions known to the law. The party attacking the legality of the last marriage has a burden of rebutting the presumption that the marriage is valid.

* * *

Here Hampton failed to overcome the strong presumption of the validity of the second marriage and, having failed to do so, the decision below must be reversed.

COMMONWEALTH OF MASSACHUSETTS

_____   Probate and Family Court
                                     Docket No. _____

Juliet Jones

                    v.   Motion to Dismiss Complaint for Divorce

Romeo Jones

   Now comes the defendant, Romeo Jones, in the within complaint for divorce and moves this honorable court to dismiss said action in accordance with Mass. R. Dom. Rel. P. 12(b) for the reason that:
   Defendant was never validly married to plaintiff as he never obtained a divorce from his first wife, Octavia Jones, to whom he was married on 15 March, 1979 at Seneca County, State of New York and to whom he was still married when he went through a marriage ceremony with plaintiff on September 19, 1986 at Essex County, Massachusetts.

                                     Respectfully submitted,
                                     Romeo Jones, Plaintiff
                                     by His Attorneys,
                                     Divide & Conquer

                                     By _____
                                     Attila LeHun
                                     100,000 North Road
                                     New Rome, MA 02130
                                     Tel: 1-800-555-1212

[Certificate of Service follows]

FIGURE 5-1
Sample motion to dismiss complaint for divorce

Some unfortunate surprises may arise in the course of a divorce case. A defense such as that raised by this motion inevitably encourages a response that may make the case considerably complex. The plaintiff is sure to contemplate some contract and tort actions not ordinarily associated with a simple divorce.

   Mental incompetence, i.e., the lack of mental capacity to contract marriage, also usually makes a marriage by the incompetent void. Case No.5-5 suggests a wise motto: Marriage is best contracted while sober.

CASE NO. 5-3 Prohibited Marriage

In the *Catalano* case, two seemingly irreconcilable rules come into conflict. One rule states that a man may not marry his niece; the other holds that a marriage valid where made is valid everywhere. In *Catalano,* a woman attempted to collect a widow's share of her husband's estate. The majority take a traditional view of a void marriage; the dissent views the issues as having more complexity. (This is the same case that appeared in chapter 1, edited somewhat differently here.)

CATALANO v. CATALANO
148 Conn. 288, 170 A.2d 726
(1961)
Supreme Court of Connecticut

MURPHY, Justice.

* * *

The material facts are these: Fred Catalano, a widower and citizen of this state, was married on December 8, 1951, in Italy to the plaintiff, his niece, an Italian subject. Such a marriage was prohibited by § 87 of the Italian Civil Code, but since the parties obtained a legal dispensation for the marriage from the Italian authorities, it was valid in Italy. Fred returned to this country. The plaintiff remained in Italy until 1956, when she joined Fred and they came to Hartford, where they lived as husband and wife until his death in 1958. A son was born to the couple. The plaintiff claims to be the surviving spouse of the decedent and, as such, entitled to an allowance for support under the provisions of § 45-250 of the General Statutes.

. . . It has been the declared public policy of this state continuously since 1702 to prohibit marriages of uncle and niece and declare them void.

* * *

It is the generally accepted rule that a marriage valid where the ceremony is performed is valid everywhere. There are, however, certain exceptions to that rule, including one which regards as invalid incestuous marriages between persons so closely related that their marriage is contrary to the strong public policy of the domicil though valid where celebrated. . . .

The marriage of the plaintiff and Fred Catalano, though valid in Italy under its laws, was not valid in Connecticut because it contravened the public policy of this state. The plaintiff therefore cannot qualify under § 45-250 as the surviving spouse of Fred Catalano.

We answer the question propounded "No."

In this opinion BALDWIN, C.J., and KING and SHEA, JJ., concurred.

MELLITZ, Justice (dissenting).

We are dealing here with the marriage status of a woman who was validly married at the place of her domicil and who, so far as the record discloses, was entirely innocent of any intent to evade the laws of Connecticut. . . . If a marriage status resulting from a valid marriage, such as the one here, is to be destroyed, the issue bastardized, and the relations of the parties branded as illicit, it should follow only from an explicit enactment of the legislature, giving clear expression to a public policy which compels such harsh consequences to ensue from a marriage entered into under the circumstances disclosed here.

The cases cited in the majority opinion which deal with the question we have here are all cases where the parties went to a foreign state to evade the law of the domicil and the marriage celebrated in the foreign state was refused recognition in the place of their domicil when they returned to live there after the marriage. . . .

[Section 46-1] is a validating statute and declares valid the marriage of a citizen of Connecticut celebrated in a foreign country in conformity with the law of that country, provided each party would have legal capacity to contract the marriage in Connecticut. Capacity, in the sense employed in the statute, is defined in 2 Beale, Conflict of Laws § 121.6, as follows: "By capacity to enter into a marriage is meant a quality which legally prevents the person in question marrying anyone; it does not refer to some quality which prevents the particular marriage in question, though the person may marry someone else. A typical example of capacity is nonage, or having a living spouse. A typical example of a quality which prevents the particular marriage, though the person has capacity to marry, is consanguinity."

* * *

[Cases are cited from Maryland and New York recognizing foreign uncle-niece marriages even though prohibited in Maryland and New York.]

In whatever terms "capacity," under the provisions of § 46-6, may be conceived, it relates to the capacity of the parties to enter into the contract of marriage. After the marriage, the relation between the Catalanos became a status, no longer resting merely on contract. Allen v. Allen, 73 Conn. 54, 55, 46 A. 242, 49 L.R.A. 142. A contract of marriage is sui generis. "It is simply introductory to the creation of a status,

and what that status is the law determines. A contract executed in contravention of law may yet establish a status which the law will recognize, and, if one of the contracting parties were innocent of any intention to violate the law, may recognize as carrying with it in his favor the same rights and duties as if the contract had been entirely unexceptionable. In re Grimley, 137 U.S. 147, 152, 153, 11 S.Ct. 54, 34 L.Ed. 636." Gould v. Gould, 78 Conn. 242, 245, 61 A. 604, 605, 2 L.R.A., N.S., 531. Mrs. Catalano was innocent of any intent to violate our laws, and she is entitled to have recognition here of her marriage status, with all of the rights flowing from that status. The following from the opinion in Pierce v. Pierce, 58 Wash. 622, 626, 109 P. 45, aptly expresses what I conceive to be the correct view in the situation here. "We know of no public policy which will warrant a court in annulling a marriage between competent parties if there be any evidence to sustain it, and especially so where it appears that the parties have consummated the marriage, a child has been born, and the offending party has been openly acknowledged as a spouse. It will not be done unless it clearly appears that the parties willfully went beyond the jurisdiction of the courts of this state to avoid and defy our laws. It is not clear that they did so in this case."

The answer to the question in the reservation should be "Yes."

CASE QUESTIONS

1. Is the void-voidable distinction helpful here?
2. If Maine's dictum that society is evolving from relations based on status to relations based on contract is correct, is the majority or the dissent more modern? (Note that the dissent uses both terms.)

CASE NO. 5-4 *Annulment and Affinity*

BACK v. BACK
148 Iowa 223, 125 N.W. 1009 (1910)
Supreme Court of Iowa

William Back married Mrs. Dirke, a widow with a daughter by her prior husband. They had no children of their marriage. Back later divorced the former Mrs. Dirke and proceeded to marry his ex-wife's daughter. The second Mrs. Back bore William four children. The first Mrs. Back died two years after Back married her daughter. On William's death, the second Mrs. Back sued to receives her widow's share of his estate.

Iowa Code § 4936 included as incest the marriage between a man and his wife's daughter, suggesting that the second marriage here should be void. [From the court's opinion:]

We reach the conclusion, therefore, that the relationship of affinity between the decedent and plaintiff which existed during the continuance of the marriage relation between decedent and plaintiff's mother terminated when the latter procured a divorce from decedent, and after that time plaintiff was not the daughter of decedent's wife, and the marriage between them was valid.

CASE NO. 5-5 *The Soused Spouses*

MAHAN v. MAHAN
88 So. 2d 545 (Fla. 1956)
Supreme Court of Florida

The record shows that on July 2, 1955, after an afternoon and evening devoted to drinking a combination of such stimulants as beer, whiskey and gin at an establishment bearing the foreboding name of "The Caribbean," the parties, accompanied by another man, in some fashion wound up in Folkston, Georgia, late in the evening. At this point they were united in wedlock by an Ordinary of the State of Georgia. Folkston, Georgia, incidentally, appears to be the "Gretna Green" of Florida couples who are either not inclined to comply with the requirements of our laws stipulating various conditions precedent to matrimony, or for other reasons find themselves incapable of completing the marriage contract in our state. Experience has suggested that, although there are of course fortunate and happy exceptions, many of these "Folkston-Green" marriages terminate as did this one. Be this as it may, the record shows that the plaintiff was not conscious of the fact that she was married until she came to her senses at the home of her mother the afternoon of July 3, 1955.

* * *

One condition precedent to a valid and binding marriage contract is that the parties be mentally competent to enter into the contractual engagement. A party lacking the essential requirement of mental capacity may in a proper case obtain the annulment of the contract absent ratification or confirmation during a lucid interval, or upon regaining mental competency. The general rule is well stated in 35 Am.Jur., Marriage, Sec. 116, p. 254, as follows:

> Intoxication at the time of entering into a marriage, where such intoxication renders one non compos mentis and incapable of knowing the nature of the contract and its consequences, voids or invalidates the marriage or renders it voidable, depending on the effect of mental

incapacity on marriage in the particular jurisdiction. Intoxication to a less degree, however, has no such effect on the marriage."

Finding as we do, and finding further that there is no evidence of ratification or confirmation of the marriage, it is our view that the prayer of the complaint for annulment should have been granted.

[Note: Although *Am.Jur.* indicates that intoxication renders a marriage void in some states and voidable in others, the Florida court, by its reference to ratification and confirmation, seems to take the voidable path.]

Other circumstances may render a marriage void, as when at least one of the parties was below the minimum age to marry. (This situation should be distinguished from a case in which parties old enough to marry with parental consent did not obtain parental consent; theirs would be a voidable marriage.)

Examples of Marriages Merely Voidable

A marriage contract may be declared invalid by a court (with the declaration operating retroactively) for various reasons. Such an attempted marriage may be voidable for failure to meet the formal requirements for a licensed marriage, for instance. Fraud, however, is the largest category of attack on marriage through annulment proceedings. It is also the least precise and is therefore given extended treatment here.

Fraud with Regard to Essentials of Marriage

Review Case No. 5-1 and compare it with *Jordan*, Case No. 5-6. Many courts have adopted the rule that fraud as to the essentials of marriage must be of an extreme nature. This is often referred to as the *Massachusetts rule*, derived from *Reynolds v. Reynolds,* 85 Mass. (3 Allen) 605 (1862). Under this doctrine, misrepresentations of good character, health (other than

LEGAL TERMS

tenancy by the entirety
Form of co-ownership of property that can be held only by husband and wife. It has a right of survivorship (if one spouse dies, the other owns the property). States recognizing this ancient tenancy often encounter problems with creditors. It is destroyed by divorce or death but is not subject to a suit in partition, as are other forms of co-ownership.

sexually transmitted diseases and capacity to procreate), and finances do not go to the essence of the marriage. In *Reynolds,* the husband and wife married after a short courtship. Unbeknownst to the husband, the wife, who had represented herself as chaste, was already pregnant by another man. An annulment was granted to the husband. A similar result should be expected when the wife induces marriage on the basis of pregnancy allegedly caused by the husband when in fact she knows it was caused by someone else. (And if she is not sure?) Contrast this with cases in which the wife feigned pregnancy to induce marriage. Courts have been reluctant to annul such marriages. Because such misrepresentation reveals itself rather quickly, annulment is hardly necessary with today's no-fault divorce.

CASE NO. 5-6   Former Marriage Fraud

Failure to disclose a former marriage does not create an atmosphere of trust.

JORDAN v. JORDAN
115 N.H. 545, 345 A.2d 168 (1975)
Supreme Court of New Hampshire

This case arises from a petition for the annulment of a marriage on the ground that the defendant concealed his previous marriage. The petition, filed by the wife's mother and next friend, alleges the following facts: The parties were married on November 17, 1973, in St. Christopher's Roman Catholic Church, Nashua. The bride was seventeen, the husband twenty-six. On February 27, 1974, the plaintiff learned that the defendant had previously been married and returned to her parents. The plaintiff is a member of the Roman Catholic faith and is prohibited by her faith from marrying a divorced person. The petition states that the plaintiff did not know of the defendant's prior marriage at the time she married him; that she would not have married him had she known; and that she cannot live with the defendant now because of her religious beliefs and the defendant's deceit. The record contains two documents which show that the defendant

twice stated in writing prior to the marriage that this was his first marriage. The record also includes a copy of the order of the plaintiff's church annulling the marriage and a letter from a psychiatrist which concluded "that it would be detrimental toward the health and welfare of Mrs. Cathy Jordan to return to her husband." The Master (Joseph L. Clough, Esq.) found "that plaintiff was induced to marry through fraud of the defendant going to the essentials of the marriage relationship thereby making it morally and spiritually impossible for the plaintiff to fulfill her marital commitment." The master recommended that the petition be granted.

[Heath v. Heath, 85 N.H. 419, 429, 159 A. 418, 423 (1932):] "The fraudulent misrepresentations for which a marriage may be annulled must be of something essential to the marriage relation—of something making impossible the performance of the duties and obligations of that relation or rendering its assumption and continuance dangerous to health or life." . . . .

Petition granted.

Fraud with Regard to Inability or Unwillingness to Have Children

Perhaps the oldest ground for annulment known to our law has to do with sex and procreation. The law assumes procreation to be the fundamental purpose of marriage, and has even used this argument to deny marriage licenses to homosexual couples. Today the inability to procreate is ordinarily associated with annulment in terms of fraud. One of the partners may be sterile, impotent, or refuse to engage in sexual intercourse with the other partner. If the sterility or impotence was known to the other partner at the time of the marriage, no fraud was committed; if known to the sterile or impotent partner but unknown to the other, a fraud was committed. If neither partner knew, no fraud is involved, but one partner has received much less than expected under the marriage contract and may in some states be allowed to have the marriage annulled. Similarly, if one partner refuses to have sex with the other, a fraud is involved if the refusal was planned at the time of the marriage, that is, if the couple planned for children but one intended a deception. See Case No. 5-7.

CASE NO. 5-7 Impotence

The following case deals with impotence apparently unknown to the parties at the time of the marriage. This is one of the rare cases involving impotence on the part of the wife. This court recognizes the interplay between physical and psychic causes of impotence.

T. v. M.
100 N.J. Super. 530, 242 A.2d 670
(Ch. Div. 1968)
Superior Court of New Jersey

[Full title of case: T, Plaintiff, v. M, falsely called T, Defendant.]

HARTMAN, J.C.C. (temporarily assigned).

This action to annul a marriage on the ground of impotence is a case of novel impression in New Jersey and, perhaps, in this country, in that the wife, while still a virgin, with an intact hymen, suffered a miscarriage during the marriage. The husband seeks the annulment, charging his wife with being physically and incurably impotent.

The question to be determined is whether a virgin wife, capable of procreation, can legally be declared to be impotent so as to warrant annulling the marriage. I have decided this question in the affirmative and will grant the husband an annulment.

* * *

I am satisfied that the evidence supports the following findings of fact. The parties were married in this state on July 25, 1964. Numerous efforts at sexual intercourse proved to be abortive because of the inability of the female organ to permit penetration to the slightest degree. On one occasion the husband used force in his attempt to penetrate. This resulted in his ejaculating against the vulva, causing a "splash pregnancy".

The husband urged his wife to see a doctor. At first she refused to do so. She asked him to give her time, that she was nervous, that eventually it would work out. Although they continued to try, the situation did not change and the parties separated. At that time neither of them were aware that conception had taken place.

A few months thereafter the wife advised the husband that she was then prepared to see a doctor because she thought she was pregnant. In November, 1965, they both went to see Doctor George Massell, an obstetrician and gynecologist. The wife complained of abdominal cramps; she had missed a period; about two weeks before this visit to the doctor she had "spotted".

The doctor attempted to examine her pelvically by manual examination. He testified that this proved to be impossible. Two days later the doctor learned that her bleeding had progressed and he admitted her to the hospital. He again found it impossible to examine her physically but her symptoms indicated early miscarriage. In the operating room she was anaesthetized and dilated at which point it was discovered that she had an intact hymen. An incision was made into the hymen and the doctor proceeded to perform a D & C for the miscarriage.

It was the doctor's opinion that there had been no penetration by the husband beyond the hymen, and that wife was suffering from a firm, fixed, deep-seated psychological problem. When asked how a pregnancy could occur in a woman whose hymen was intact he testified that this was possible and that it was not unknown in medical science. To use his own expression, it was a "splash pregnancy".

* * *

By statute in New Jersey, impotence is a ground for nullity of marriage. N.J.S. 2A:34—1,

N.J.S.A. provides for a number of grounds for nullity. Sub-paragraph c. dealing with impotency, provides as follows:

> "The parties, or either of them, were at the time of marriage physically and incurably impotent, provided the party making the application shall have been ignorant of such impotency or incapability at the time of the marriage, and has not subsequently ratified the marriage."

Vaginismus, physical or psychical, is a recognized cause of incurable impotency in New Jersey. . . . [I]mperfect intercourse is not enough to rebut a finding of impotence. Impotency is the inability to have sexual intercourse; impotence is not sterility.

Annulment of a marriage, where the parties, or either of them, were at the time of the marriage, physically or incurably impotent, may be accomplished in one of two ways. Where the impotency was known before the marriage but was not disclosed, that marriage may be annulled at the suit of the innocent party for the fraud inherent in the non-disclosure, invoking the inherent jurisdiction of the Court of Chancery to deal with fraudulent contracts. The inherent jurisdiction of the Court of Chancery to annul fraudulent contracts has been held sufficient to include a contract of marriage. Carris v. Carris, 24 N.J.Eq. 516 (E. & A.1873): "the absence of ecclesiastical courts, the existence in the Court of Chancery of the general jurisdiction stated, and there being no provision in the Constitution for a different tribunal, and consent being a common-law essential of the marriage contract, all show that jurisdiction must embrace the right to annul such a contract for sufficient fraud." Steerman v. Snow, 94 N.J.Eq. 9, 12, 118 A. 696, 697 (Ch.1922).

The second method of approaching nullity of marriage for impotence is statutory. It lies where the disability was not known at the time of the marriage; here fraud is not involved.

Impotence was at the time of the common law a canonical disability and was treated in the ecclesiastical courts where, according to Canon 1068 of the Code of Canon Law, "inability to perform the marital act was a diriment impediment, and thus invalidated the marriage." 52 Iowa Law Review 768 (1967). There were no ecclesiastical courts in New Jersey when we adopted the common law as the law of this state; the only jurisdiction to annul a marriage for impotence was that which involved a fraudulent concealment of it. Relief from this type of marriage was, as I have stated, vested in the court of chancery pursuant to its inherent jurisdiction to annul contracts for fraud. This explains the dismissal of a suit to annul a marriage for impotence by Chancellor Runyon where no fraud was involved and the impotence was known after the marriage. See Anonymous, 24 N.J.Eq. 19 (Ch.1873). The Chancellor there held that if the jurisdiction of the Court of Chancery was to be extended to include cases of this character, it was for the legislature to decide. And the legislature did so enact in the following year, 1874, incorporating into the revision of the Divorce Act a section 4 which provided for "divorce" from the bond of matrimony in such cases of impotence. Our current statute, N.J.S. 2A:34–1, subd. c, N.J.S.A. provides the relief by way of annulment.

I have not been able to find a reported opinion in this country where a dissolution of a marriage was sought because of an impotent wife, not able to copulate yet capable of procreation.

* * *

Children are no longer bastardized in this, and in many other states, by reason of the fact that the marriage of the parents is later annulled by court action. When a judgment of nullity of marriage is declared in New Jersey, children of that marriage are not thereby rendered illegitimate except in the single instance where a marriage, not a ceremonial one, is dissolved because either party had another wife or husband living at the time of the marriage. Another statute in New Jersey legitimatizes children born out of wedlock where the natural parents thereafter intermarry, and such children enjoy all the rights and privileges that they would enjoy had they been born after the marriage. The status of such children is statutorily declared to be the same as if they were born in lawful wedlock. N.J.S.A. 9:15–1. Still another statute makes legitimate any child born of a ceremonial marriage notwithstanding the marriage be thereafter annulled or declared void. N.J.S.A. 9:15–2. Our legislature has thus declared the public policy in this state with regard to the legitimation of children. The reasons of concern expressed by Mr. Bishop as to children being bastardized would seem to have no force, in reason or logic, in present day legal thinking. Nor is it any longer valid to say that annulments of marriage result in characterizing the female as an infamous person to the world. The old scandal has lost its bite.

I have, therefore, decided that it would be unjust to hold the husband to his marriage contract. My factual reasons may be summarized as follows: (1), he was at the time of the marriage ignorant of the facts alleged; (2), his efforts to secure medical assistance for his wife were motivated by a desire to continue the marriage; (3), the blame for the failure to rectify the sexual problem may not be attributed to him; (4), his decision to disaffirm the marriage was made, and the action to annul was brought, within a reasonable time, not subject to successful attack by reason of any equitable defense of laches, whether raised by the wife (she raised no such defense) or by the court itself

(I gave thought to it and found no reason to apply it); and, (5), after his decision to disaffirm, there were no further acts nor conduct between the parties to bar the action.

The wife is impotent. Judgment of nullity will be entered in favor of the husband.

Fraud on the Court or Legal Process

Certain cases involve collusion between the parties that involves fraud on the legal system rather than fraud on the other party. This occurs with *sham marriages*, where some purpose other than marriage, cohabitation, and procreation is intended, such as marrying to qualify for a visa or legitimizing a child. When there was no intent to consummate the marriage and the marriage was not in fact consummated, annulment may be available:

> A man is entitled to annulment of the marriage where the woman goes through the ceremony merely to secure his name, with no intention of living with him, and leaves him immediately at its conclusion. But it has been held in an action for annulment on the ground of fraud that such annulment will not be granted upon evidence of denial of intercourse unless at the time of marriage there was intention not to perform marital obligations.
>
> — *35 Am. Jur.* 240

Consider *Anders v. Anders,* 224 Mass. 438, 113 N.E. 203 (1916):

> In the case at bar the respondent went through the marriage ceremony with an intention never to perform any one of the duties of a wife. She went through the ceremony solely to secure a right to bear the name of a married woman and in that way to hide the shame of having had an illegitimate child, intending to leave her husband at the church door and not see him again. That plan she carried into effect. It is settled that a contract for the sale of goods is induced by fraud and for that reason voidable where the purchaser had an intention when the contract was made not to perform his promise to pay for them. If an intention not to perform his promise renders a contract for purchase of property voidable, a fortiori the same result must follow in case of a contract to enter into "the holy estate of matrimony."

5.5   CONSEQUENCES OF ANNULMENT

Historically, annulment treated the marriage as if it had never occurred, but the harshness of this has been softened in recent times. In particular, annulment should not bastardize the offspring of an annulled marriage. The **Uniform Marriage and Divorce Act** (UMDA), in § 207(c), states:

LEGAL TERMS

Uniform Marriage and Divorce Act (UMDA)
A product of the National Conference of Commisioners on Uniform State Laws. Like other uniform laws published by this body, the UMDA is unofficial unless and until adopted by a state legislature. Nevertheless, as a state proposal for family law, it represents an up-to-date view of the law of this area and is persuasive authority in cases where existing statutes and cases do not cover an issue confronting a court.

"Children born of a prohibited marriage are legitimate." Modern values reject visiting the sins of the parents upon the children, and the law has always favored legitimacy over illegitimacy. Thus it is unlikely that any state would now create bastards retroactively.

Quite different is the situation with regard to alimony. Under the common law, it was the duty of the husband to provide for the wife, and this duty extended to legal separations, including divorce from bed and board and absolute divorce (other than an annulment). This duty, however, depended upon a valid marital contract and was therefore inconsistent with an annulment. A number of states have passed legislation allowing alimony following annulment under restricted circumstances, as when the receiving spouse is an innocent party.

Is the void–voidable distinction useful here? Although the annulment may apply retroactively as far as the bonds of matrimony between the parties, this does not necessarily mean that both parties go back to square one with regard to the whole world. Case No. 5-8 deals with the special problem of reinstatement of prior alimony following an annulled second marriage.

CASE NO. 5-8   Can Alimony be Reinstated after Annulment?

McCONKEY v. McCONKEY
216 Va. 106, 215 S.E.2d 640 (1975)
Supreme Court of Virginia

COCHRAN, Justice.

The question for our determination in this appeal is whether a wife, upon annulment of a voidable second marriage, is entitled to reinstatement of the alimony awarded her when she was divorced from her first husband.

Clara Johnson McConkey and Edward Cecil McConkey, her husband, were divorced by final decree entered September 23, 1968, by the trial court, which ordered Edward to pay Clara the sum of $200 per month as alimony. On October 16, 1971, Clara married Calvin D. Sykes. On November 5, 1971, Clara filed her bill of complaint against Sykes in the Circuit Court of the City of Norfolk seeking in the alternative an annulment of their marriage on the ground of Sykes's fraud or a divorce on the ground of his desertion. By final decree entered January 3, 1973, the marriage was annulled and declared to be "null, void and of no effect". On December 20, 1973, Clara filed her petition in the trial court against Edward for reinstatement of alimony payments that had been terminated prospectively from July 1, 1972, by order entered July 17, 1972. Clara appeals the order entered February 11, 1974, denying her petition.

Clara contends that, as her second marriage was declared void retrospectively, she should be restored to the same position and standing she enjoyed before she went through the second marriage ceremony. We do not agree.

Section 20-110 of the Code of 1950, as amended, provides: "If any person to whom alimony has been awarded shall thereafter marry, such alimony shall cease as of the date of such marriage."

We need not decide whether this statute would apply to a person to whom alimony has been awarded who thereafter is involved in a void marriage. Clara's marriage to Sykes was not void *ab initio*. There is no evidence that the marriage ceremony was invalid. The annulment was based upon fraud on the part of Sykes, so that the marriage was voidable if Clara desired to have it annulled. Pretlow v. Pretlow, 177 Va. 524, 548–49, 14 S.E.2d 381, 387 (1941).

We have drawn a distinction between void and voidable marriages. A voidable marriage is "usually treated as a valid marriage until it is decreed void." Toler v. Oakwood Smokeless Coal Corp., 173 Va. 425, 432, 4 S.E.2d 364, 367 (1939). And the parties to a voidable marriage "are husband and wife unless and until the marriage is annulled." Payne v. Commonwealth, 201 Va. 209, 211, 110 S.E.2d 252, 254 (1959).

Clara's reliance on Robbins v. Robbins, 343 Mass. 247, 178 N.E.2d 281 (1961) is misplaced. There, the court held that an annulled voidable second marriage did not relieve the first husband of his obligation to make alimony payments under a divorce decree that was silent as to the effect of remarriage. The Massachusetts statute, however, required proof of a change of circumstances before the previous award of alimony could be altered, and the court found no such change of circumstances in the case under consideration. Moreover, in Surabian v. Surabian, ___ Mass. ___, 285 N.E.2d 909 (1972), the court held, in distinguishing Robbins v. Robbins, *supra,* that where a separation agreement incorporated in a divorce decree provided that alimony should terminate upon the wife's remarriage the annulment of her voidable second marriage did not reinstate the alimony.

It has been generally held that annulment of a voidable second marriage does not entitle the wife to reinstatement of alimony payments from her first husband, where there is a statute providing that alimony shall terminate upon the recipient's remarriage. . . .

We hold that where the divorced wife enters into a subsequent voidable marriage she thereby forfeits her right to alimony from her former husband. The husband has a right to assume the validity of the second marriage and to arrange his affairs accordingly. . . .

The trial court did not err in denying Clara's petition and the judgment order is affirmed.

Affirmed.

CASE QUESTIONS

1. Many states, like Virginia, provide that remarriage terminates alimony payments. If state law terminates alimony on the basis of remarriage, can the state reinstate alimony when the remarriage is canceled? Should it?

2. The court avoids a declaration about what would happen if this were a void, rather than a voidable, marriage. In refusing to decide that issue, the court implies that alimony might be reinstated if the second marriage was void. Bigamous and incestuous marriages are the principal classes of void marriages: would it therefore make sense to assume that an alimony-paying ex-husband should continue to pay alimony when his ex-wife marries a man the ex-husband believes to still be married to another woman? If the ex-husband does stop paying alimony, and sometime later the bigamous marriage is held to be void, is the ex-husband liable for arrearages in alimony? What if the bigamous husband was an excellent provider during the period the first husband would have paid and finished paying **rehabilitative alimony**?

5.6 DEFENSES

Many states have specific statutes of limitations with regard to the grounds upon which annulment may be brought. Because most domestic relations cases are subject to equity jurisdiction, they are vulnerable to the defense of **laches**. Long-term marriages with children raise this issue.

Equity jurisdictions may also use the **clean hands doctrine.** At least one court has held the doctrine inapplicable to annulment proceedings. *Powell v. Powell,* 86 A.2d 331 (N.H. 1952).

An issue of ratification may arise when a spouse, after learning of grounds for a voidable marriage, continues to cohabit. Practically speaking, the court may view the grounds for annulment as spurious, the claimant having overlooked the defect until a suitable time. *See Stewart* Case No. 5-2.

LEGAL TERMS

rehabilitative alimony
    A modern form of alimony, ordinarily in the form of monthly payments of short duration.

laches
    The equitable equivalent of a statute of limitations. It may be used as a defense to an action in equity if the action has been unreasonably delayed to the prejudice of a party who has changed position during the delay.

clean hands doctrine
    Doctrine providing that courts of equity do not hear claims brought by claimants who have acted improperly or in bad faith.

QUESTIONS

1. In the light of wholesale reform in divorce law in recent times, why have state legislatures paid little attention to annulment?
2. Why does annulment constitute only 5 percent or less of marital dissolutions in most states?
3. How are void and voidable marriages distinguished? Are the results different?
4. Why would someone choose annulment over no-fault divorce?
5. What difference does it make whether the marriage was consummated?
6. How may a voidable marriage be ratified?
7. Why was impotence or sterility the prime traditional basis for annulment?
8. What is a "tenancy by the entireties"?
9. What is the difference between a fraud on one of the parties and a fraud on the court?
10. Who lacks legal capacity to marry?

EXERCISES

Answer according to the law of your state.

1. Which of the following is authorized?
    a. Annulment
    b. Divorce *a mensa et thoro*
    c. Divorce *a vinculo matrimonii*
    d. Legal separation

2. How do the classifications in question 1 correspond to those described in the text?

3. Is there a presumption of legitimacy for a child born after annulment? 46 A.L.R.3d 158.

4. Can a marriage be annulled for intoxication at the time of the marriage? 57 A.L.R.2d 1250.

5. Is concealment or misrepresentation of religion grounds for annulment? 44 A.L.R.3d 972.

6. Does annulment preclude spousal support? 81 A.L.R.3d 281.

7. Is sexual incapacity grounds for annulment? 52 A.L.R.3d 589.

8. Is refusal to have sexual relations or avoidance of procreation grounds for annulment? 28 A.L.R.2d 499; 4 A.L.R.2d 227.

9. Is concealment or misrepresentation of prior marriage grounds for annulment? 15 A.L.R.3d 759.

10. Is knowledge of existence of facts constituting grounds for annulment a defense to an action for annulment? 15 A.L.R.2d 706.

11. Does your state follow the "Massachusetts" rule with regard to fraud as to the essentials of marriage?

APPENDIX 5A

Uniform Marriage and Divorce Act (1973)

PART I. GENERAL PROVISIONS

§ 101. Short Title.

This Act may be cited as the "Uniform Marriage and Divorce Act."

§ 102. Purposes: Rules of Construction.

This Act shall be liberally construed and applied to promote its underlying purposes, which are to:

(1) provide adequate procedures for the solemnization and registration of marriage;

(2) strengthen and preserve the integrity of marriage and safeguard family relationships;

(3) promote the amicable settlement of disputes that have arisen between parties to a marriage;

(4) mitigate the potential harm to the spouses and their children caused by the process of legal dissolution of marriage;

(5) make reasonable provision for spouse and minor children during and after litigation; and

(6) make the law of legal dissolution of marriage effective for dealing with the realities of matrimonial experience by making irretrievable breakdown of the marriage relationship the sole basis for its dissolution.[1]

§ 103. Uniformity of Application and Construction.

This Act shall be so applied and construed as to effectuate its general purpose to make uniform the law with respect to the subject of this Act among those states which enact it.

PART II. MARRIAGE

§ 201. Formalities.

Marriage is a personal relationship between a man and a woman[2] arising out of a civil contract to which the consent of the parties is essential. A marriage licensed, solemnized, and registered as provided in this Act is valid in this State. A marriage may be contracted, maintained, invalidated, or dissolved only as provided by law.

§ 202. Marriage License and Marriage Certificate.

(a) The [Secretary of State, Commissioner of Public Health] shall prescribe the form for an application for a marriage license, which shall include the following information:

(1) name, sex, occupation, address, social security number, date and place of birth of each party to the proposed marriage;

(2) if either party was previously married, his name, and the date, place, and court in which the marriage was dissolved or declared invalid or the date and place of death of the former spouse;

(3) name and address of the parents or guardian of each party;

(4) whether the parties are related to each other and, if so, their relationship; and.

(5) the name and date of birth of any child of which both parties are parents, born before the making of the application, unless their parental rights and the parent and child relationship with respect to the child have been terminated.

(b) The [Secretary of State, Commissioner of Public Health] shall prescribe the forms for the marriage license, the marriage certificate, and the consent to marriage.

§ 203. License to Marry.

When a marriage application has been completed and signed by both parties to a prospective marriage and at least one party has appeared before the [marriage license] clerk and paid the marriage license fee of [$____], the [marriage license] clerk shall issue a license to marry and a marriage certificate form upon being furnished:

(1) satisfactory proof that each party to the marriage will have attained the age of 18 years at the time

the marriage license is effective, or will have attained the age of 16 years and has either the consent to the marriage of both parents or his guardian, or judicial approval; or, if under the age of 16 years, has both the consent of both parents or his guardian and judicial approval; and

(2) satisfactory proof that the marriage is not prohibited; [and]

[(3) a certificate of the results of any medical examination required by the laws of this State.]

§ 204. License, Effective Date.

A license to marry becomes effective throughout this state 3 days after the date of issuance, unless the [_____] court orders that the license is effective when issued, and expires 180 days after it becomes effective.

§ 205. Judicial Approval.

(a) The [_____] court, after a reasonable effort has been made to notify the parents or guardian of each underaged party, may order the [marriage license] clerk to issue a marriage license and a marriage certificate form:

[(1)] to a party aged 16 or 17 years who has no parent capable of consenting to his marriage, or whose parent or guardian has not consented to his marriage; [or

(2) to a party under the age of 16 years who has the consent of both parents to his marriage, if capable of giving consent, or his guardian.]

(b) A marriage license and a marriage certificate form may be issued under this section only if the court finds that the underaged party is capable of assuming the responsibilities of marriage and the marriage will serve his best interest. Pregnancy alone does not establish that the best interest of the party will be served.

(c) The [_____] court shall authorize performance of a marriage by proxy upon the showing required by the provisions on solemnization.

§ 206. Solemnization and Registration.

(a) A marriage may be solemnized by a judge of a court of record, by a public official whose powers include solemnization of marriages, or in accordance with any mode of solemnization recognized by any religious denomination, Indian Nation or Tribe, or Native Group. Either the person solemnizing the marriage, or, if no individual acting alone solemnized the marriage, a party to the marriage, shall complete the marriage certificate form and forward it to the [marriage license] clerk.

(b) If a party to a marriage is unable to be present at the solemnization, he may authorize in writing a third person to act as his proxy. If the person solemnizing the marriage is satisfied that the absent party is unable to be present and has consented to the marriage, he may solemnize the marriage by proxy. If he is not

satisfied, the parties may petition the [_____] court for an order permitting the marriage to be solemnized by proxy.

(c) Upon receipt of the marriage certificate, the [marriage license] clerk shall register the marriage.

(d) The solemnization of the marriage is not invalidated by the fact that the person solemnizing the marriage was not legally qualified to solemnize it, if neither party to the marriage believed him to be so qualified.

§ 207. Prohibited Marriages.[3]

(a) The following marriages are prohibited:

(1) a marriage entered into prior to the dissolution of an earlier marriage of one of the parties;

(2) a marriage between an ancestor and a descendant, or between a brother and a sister, whether the relationship is by the half or the whole blood, or by adoption;

(3) a marriage between an uncle and a niece or between an aunt and a nephew, whether the relationship is by the half or the whole blood, except as to marriages permitted by the established customs of aboriginal cultures.

(b) Parties to a marriage prohibited under this section who cohabit after removal of the impediment are lawfully married as of the date of the removal of the impediment.

(c) Children born of a prohibited marriage are legitimate.

§ 208. Declaration of Invalidity.

(a) The [_____] court shall enter its decree declaring the invalidity of a marriage ventered into under the following circumstances:[4]

(1) a party lacked capacity to consent to the marriage at the time the marriage was solemnized, either because of mental incapacity or infirmity or because of the influence of alcohol, drugs, or other incapacitating substances, or a party was induced to enter into a marriage by force or duress, or by fraud involving the essentials of marriage;

(2) a party lacks the physical capacity to consummate the marriage by sexual intercourse, and at the time the marriage was solemnized the other party did not know of the incapacity;

(3) a party [was under the age of 16 years and did not have the consent of his parents or guardian and judicial approval or] was aged 16 or 17 years and did not have the consent of his parents or guardian or judicial approval; or

(4) the marriage is prohibited.

(b) A declaration of invalidity under subsection (a)(1) through (3) may be sought by any of the following persons and must be commenced within the times specified, but in no event may a declaration of invalidity be sought after the death of either party to the marriage:

(1) for a reason set forth in subsection (a)(1), by either party or by the legal representative of the party who lacked capacity to consent, no later than 90 days after the petitioner obtained knowledge of the described condition;

(2) for the reason set forth in subsection (a)(2), by either party, no later than one year after the petitioner obtained knowledge of the described condition;

(3) for the reason set forth in subsection (a)(3), by the underaged party, his parent or guardian, prior to the time the underaged party reaches the age at which he could have married without satisfying the omitted requirement.

[Alternative A

(c) A declaration of invalidity for the reason set forth in subsection (a)(4) may be sought by either party, the legal spouse in case of a bigamous marriage, the [appropriate state official], or a child of either party, at any time prior to the death of one of the parties.]

[Alternative B

(c) A declaration of invalidity for the reason set forth in subsection (a)(4) may be sought by either party, the legal spouse in case of a bigamous marriage, the [appropriate state official], or a child of either party, at any time, not to exceed 5 years following the death of either party.]

(d) Children born of a marriage declared invalid are legitimate.

(e) Unless the court finds, after a consideration of all relevant circumstances, including the effect of a retroactive decree on third parties, that the interests of justice would be served by making the decree not retroactive, it shall declare the marriage invalid as of the date of the marriage. The provisions of this Act relating to property rights of the spouses, maintenance, support, and custody of children on dissolution of marriage are applicable to non-retroactive decrees of invalidity.

§ 209. Putative Spouse.[5]

Any person who has cohabited with another to whom he is not legally married in the good faith belief that he was married to that person is a putative spouse until knowledge of the fact that he is not legally married terminates his status and prevents acquisition of further rights. A putative spouse acquires the rights conferred upon a legal spouse, including the right to maintenance following termination of his status, whether or not the marriage is prohibited (Section 207) or declared invalid (Section 208). If there is a legal spouse or other putative spouses, rights acquired by a putative spouse do not supersede the rights of the legal spouse or those acquired by other putative spouses, but the court shall apportion property, maintenance, and support rights among the claimants as appropriate in the circumstances and in the interests of justice.

§ 210. Application.

All marriages contracted within this State prior to the effective date of this Act, or outside this State, that were valid at the time of the contract or subsequently validated by the laws of the place in which they were contracted or by the domicil of the parties, are valid in this State.

§ 211. Validity of Common Law Marriage.
ALTERNATIVE A.

Common law marriages are not invalidated by this Act.

§ 211. Invalidity of Common Law Marriage.
ALTERNATIVE B.

Common law marriages contracted in this State after the effective date of this Act are invalid.

PART III. DISSOLUTION

§ 301. Application of [Rules of Civil Practice] to Proceedings under this Act.

(a) The [Rules of Civil Practice] apply to all proceedings under this Act, except as otherwise provided in this Act.

(b) A proceeding for dissolution of marriage, legal separation, or declaration of invalidity of marriage shall be entitled "In re the Marriage of _____ and _____." A custody or support proceeding shall be entitled "In re the (Custody) (Support) of _____."

(c) The initial pleading in all proceedings under this Act shall be denominated a petition. A responsive pleading shall be denominated a response. Other pleadings, and all pleadings in other matters under this Act, shall be denominated as provided in the Rules of Civil Practice.

(d) In this Act, "decree" includes "judgment."

(e) A decree of dissolution or of legal separation, if made, shall not be awarded to one of the parties, but shall provide that it affects the status previously existing between the parties in the manner decreed.

§ 302. Dissolution of Marriage; Legal Separation.

(a) The [_____] court shall enter a decree of dissolution of marriage if:

(1) the court finds that one of the parties, at the time the action was commenced, was domiciled in this State, or was stationed in this State while a member of the armed services, and that the domicil or military presence has been maintained for 90 days next preceding the making of the findings;

(2) the court finds that the marriage is irretrievably broken, if the finding is supported by evidence that

(i) the parties have lived separate and apart for a period of more than 180 days next preceding the commencement of the proceeding, or

(ii) there is serious marital discord adversely affecting the attitude of one or both of the parties toward the marriage;[6]

(3) the court finds that the conciliation provisions of Section 305 either do not apply or have been met;

(4) to the extent it has jurisdiction to do so, the court has considered, approved, or provided for child custody, the support of any child entitled to support, the maintenance of either spouse, and the disposition of property; or has provided for a separate, later hearing to complete these matters.

(b) If a party requests a decree of legal separation rather than a decree of dissolution of marriage, the court shall grant the decree in that form unless the other party objects.

§ 303. Procedure; Commencement; Pleadings; Abolition of Existing Defenses.

(a) All proceedings under this Act are commenced in the manner provided by the Rules of Civil Practice.

(b) The verified petition in a proceeding for dissolution of marriage or legal separation shall allege that the marriage is irretrievably broken and shall set forth:

(1) the age, occupation, and residence of each party and his length of residence in this State;

(2) the date of the marriage and the place at which it was registered;

(3) that the jurisdictional requirements of Section 302 exist and the marriage is irretrievably broken in that either

(i) the parties have lived separate and apart for a period of more than 180 days next preceding the commencement of the proceeding or

(ii) there is serious marital discord adversely affecting the attitude of one or both of the parties toward the marriage, and there is no reasonable prospect of reconciliation;

(4) the names, ages, and addresses of all living children of the marriage, and whether the wife is pregnant;

(5) any arrangements as to support, custody, and visitation of the children and maintenance of a spouse; and

(6) the relief sought.

(c) Either or both parties to the marriage may initiate the proceeding.

(d) If a proceeding is commenced by one of the parties, the other party must be served in the manner provided by the [Rules of Civil Practice] and may within [30] days after the date of service file a verified response.

(e) Previously existing defenses to divorce and legal separation, including but not limited to condonation, connivance, collusion, recrimination, insanity, and lapse of time, are abolished.

(f) The court may join additional parties proper for the exercise of its authority to implement this Act.

§ 304. Temporary Order or Temporary Injunction.

(a) In a proceeding for dissolution of marriage or for legal separation, or in a proceeding for disposition of property or for maintenance or support following dissolution of the marriage by a court which lacked personal jurisdiction over the absent spouse, either party may move for temporary maintenance or temporary support of a child of the marriage entitled to support. The motion shall be accompanied by an affidavit setting forth the factual basis for the motion and the amounts requested.

(b) As a part of a motion for temporary maintenance or support or by independent motion accompanied by affidavit, either party may request the court to issue a temporary injunction for any of the following relief:

(1) restraining any person from transferring, encumbering, concealing, or otherwise disposing of any property except in the usual course of business or for the necessities of life, and, if so restrained, requiring him to notify the moving party of any proposed extraordinary expenditures made after the order is issued;

(2) enjoining a party from molesting or disturbing the peace of the other party or of any child;

(3) excluding a party from the family home or from the home of the other party upon a showing that physical or emotional harm would otherwise result;

(4) enjoining a party from removing a child from the jurisdiction of the court; and

(5) providing other injunctive relief proper in the circumstances.

(c) The court may issue a temporary restraining order without requiring notice to the other party only if it finds on the basis of the moving affidavit or other evidence that irreparable injury will result to the moving party if no order is issued until the time for responding has elapsed.

(d) A response may be filed within [20] days after service of notice of motion or at the time specified in the temporary restraining order.

(e) On the basis of the showing made and in conformity with Sections 308 and 309, the court may issue a temporary injunction and an order for temporary maintenance or support in amounts and on terms just and proper in the circumstance.

(f) A temporary order or temporary injunction:

(1) does not prejudice the rights of the parties or the child which are to be adjudicated at subsequent hearings in the proceeding;

(2) may be revoked or modified before final decree on a showing by affidavit of the facts necessary to revocation or modification of a final decree under Section 316; and

(3) terminates when the final decree is entered or when the petition for dissolution or legal separation is voluntarily dismissed.

§ 305. Irretrievable Breakdown.

(a) If both of the parties by petition or otherwise have stated under oath or affirmation that the marriage is irretrievably broken, or one of the parties has so stated and the other has not denied it, the court, after hearing, shall make a finding whether the marriage is irretrievably broken.

(b) If one of the parties has denied under oath or affirmation that the marriage is irretrievably broken, the court shall consider all relevant factors, including the circumstances that gave rise to filing the petition and the prospect of reconciliation, and shall:

(1) make a finding whether the marriage is irretrievably broken; or

(2) continue the matter for further hearing not fewer than 30 nor more than 60 days later, or as soon thereafter as the matter may be reached on the court's calendar, and may suggest to the parties that they seek counseling. The court, at the request of either party shall, or on its own motion may, order a conciliation conference. At the adjourned hearing the court shall make a finding whether the marriage is irretrievably broken.

(c) A finding of irretrievable breakdown is a determination that there is no reasonable prospect of reconciliation.

§ 306. Separation Agreement.

(a) To promote amicable settlement of disputes between parties to a marriage attendant upon their separation or the dissolution of their marriage, the parties may enter into a written separation agreement containing provisions for disposition of any property owned by either of them, maintenance of either of them, and support, custody, and visitation of their children.

(b) In a proceeding for dissolution of marriage or for legal separation, the terms of the separation agreement, except those providing for the support, custody, and visitation of children, are binding upon the court unless it finds, after considering the economic circumstances of the parties and any other relevant evidence produced by the parties, on their own motion or on request of the court, that the separation agreement is unconscionable.[7]

(c) If the court finds the separation agreement unconscionable, it may request the parties to submit a revised separation agreement or may make orders for the disposition of property, maintenance, and support.

(d) If the court finds that the separation agreement is not unconscionable as to disposition of property or maintenance, and not unsatisfactory as to support:

(1) unless the separation agreement provides to the contrary, its terms shall be set forth in the decree of dissolution or legal separation and the parties shall be ordered to perform them, or

(2) if the separation agreement provides that its terms shall not be set forth in the decree, the decree shall identify the separation agreement and state that the court has found the terms not unconscionable.

(e) Terms of the agreement set forth in the decree are enforceable by all remedies available for enforcement of a judgment, including contempt, and are enforceable as contract terms.

(f) Except for terms concerning the support, custody, or visitation of children, the decree may expressly preclude or limit modification of terms set forth in the decree if the separation agreement so provides. Otherwise, terms of a separation agreement set forth in the decree are automatically modified by modification of the decree.

§ 307. Disposition of Property
ALTERNATIVE A.

(a) In a proceeding for dissolution of a marriage, legal separation, or disposition of property following a decree of dissolution of marriage or legal separation by a court which lacked personal jurisdiction over the absent spouse or lacked jurisdiction to dispose of the property, the court, without regard to marital misconduct, shall, and in a proceeding for legal separation may, finally equitably apportion between the parties the property and assets belonging to either or both however and whenever acquired, and whether the title thereto is in the name of the husband or wife or both. In making apportionment the court shall consider the duration of the marriage, and prior marriage of either party, antenuptial agreement of the parties, the age, health, station, occupation, amount and sources of income, vocational skills, employability, estate, liabilities, and needs of each of the parties, custodial provisions, whether the apportionment is in lieu of or in addition to maintenance, and the opportunity of each for future acquisition of capital assets and income. The court shall also consider the contribution or dissipation of each party in the acquisition, preservation, depreciation, or appreciation in value of the respective estates, and the contribution of a spouse as a homemaker or to the family unit.

(b) In a proceeding, the court may protect and promote the best interests of the children by setting aside a portion of the jointly and separately held estates of the parties in a separate fund or trust for the support, maintenance, education, and general welfare of any minor, dependent, or incompetent children of the parties.

§ 307. Disposition of Property.
ALTERNATIVE B.

In a proceeding for dissolution of the marriage, legal separation, or disposition of property following a decree of dissolution of the marriage or legal separation by a court which lacked personal jurisdiction over the absent spouse or lacked jurisdiction to dispose of the property, the court shall assign each spouse's separate property to that spouse. It also shall divide community property, without regard to marital misconduct, in just proportions after considering all relevant factors including:

(1) contribution of each spouse to acquisition of the marital property, including contribution of a spouse as homemaker;

(2) value of the property set apart to each spouse;

(3) duration of the marriage; and

(4) economic circumstances of each spouse when the division of property is to become effective, including the desirability of awarding the family home or the right to live therein for a reasonable period to the spouse having custody of any children.

§ 308. Maintenance.

(a) In a proceeding for dissolution of marriage, legal separation, or maintenance following a decree of dissolution of the marriage by a court which lacked personal jurisdiction over the absent spouse, the court may grant a maintenance order for either spouse only if it finds that the spouse seeking maintenance:

(1) lacks sufficient property to provide for his reasonable needs; and

(2) is unable to support himself through appropriate employment or is the custodian of a child whose condition or circumstances make it appropriate that the custodian not be required to seek employment outside the home.

(b) The maintenance order shall be in amounts and for periods of time the court deems just, without regard to marital misconduct, and after considering all relevant factors including:

(1) the financial resources of the party seeking maintenance, including marital property apportioned to him, his ability to meet his needs independently, and the extent to which a provision for support of a child living with the party includes a sum for that party as custodian;

(2) the time necessary to acquire sufficient education or training to enable the party seeking maintenance to find appropriate employment;

(3) the standard of living established during the marriage;

(4) the duration of the marriage;

(5) the age and the physical and emotional condition of the spouse seeking maintenance; and

(6) the ability of the spouse from whom maintenance is sought to meet his needs while meeting those of the spouse seeking maintenance.

§ 309. Child Support.

In a proceeding for dissolution of marriage, legal separation, maintenance, or child support, the court may order either or both parents owing a duty of support to a child to pay an amount reasonable or necessary for his support, without regard to marital misconduct, after considering all relevant factors including:

(1) the financial resources of the child;

(2) the financial resources of the custodial parent;

(3) the standard of living the child would have enjoyed had the marriage not been dissolved;

(4) the physical and emotional condition of the child and his educational needs; and

(5) the financial resources and needs of the noncustodial parent.

§ 310. Representation of Child.

The court may appoint an attorney to represent the interests of a minor or dependent child with respect to his support, custody, and visitation. The court shall enter an order for costs, fees, and disbursements in favor of the child's attorney. The order shall be made against either or both parents, except that, if the responsible party is indigent, the costs, fees, and disbursements shall be borne by the appropriate agency.

§ 311. Payment of Maintenance or Support to Court.

(a) Upon its own motion or upon motion of either party, the court may order at any time that maintenance or support payments be made to the [clerk of court, court trustee, probation officer] as trustee for remittance to the person entitled to receive the payments.

(b) The [clerk of court, court trustee, probation officer] shall maintain records listing the amount of payments, the date payments are required to be made, and the names and addresses of the parties affected by the order.

(c) The parties affected by the order shall inform the [clerk of court, court trustee, probation officer] of any change of address or of other condition that may affect the administration of the order.

(d) If a party fails to make a required payment, the [clerk of court, court trustee, probation officer] shall send by registered or certified mail notice of the arrearage to the obligor. [If payment of the sum due is not made to the [clerk of court, court trustee, probation officer] within 10 days after sending notice, the [clerk of court, court trustee, probation officer] shall certify the amount due to the [prosecuting attorney]. The [prosecuting attorney] shall promptly initiate contempt proceedings against the obligor.]

(e) The [prosecuting attorney] shall assist the court on behalf of a person entitled to receive maintenance or support in all proceedings initiated under this section to enforce compliance with the order. The person to whom maintenance or support is awarded may also initiate action to collect arrearages.

(f) If the person obligated to pay support has left or is beyond the jurisdiction of the court, the [prosecuting attorney] may institute any other proceeding available under the laws of this State for enforcement of the duties of support and maintenance.

§ 312.   Assignments.

The court may order the person obligated to pay support or maintenance to make an assignment of a part of his periodic earnings or trust income to the person entitled to receive the payments. [The assignment is binding on the employer, trustee, or other payor of the funds 2 weeks after service upon him of notice that it has been made. The payor shall withhold from the earnings or trust income payable to the person obligated to support the amount specified in the assignment and shall transmit the payments to the person specified in the order]. The payor may deduct from each payment a sum not exceeding [$1.00] as reimbursement for costs. An employer shall not discharge or otherwise discipline an employee as a result of a wage or salary assignment authorized by this section.

§ 313.   Attorney's Fees.

The court from time to time after considering the financial resources of both parties may order a party to pay a reasonable amount for the cost to the other party of maintaining or defending any proceeding under this Act and for attorney's fees, including sums for legal services rendered and costs incurred prior to the commencement of the proceeding or after entry of judgment. The court may order that the amount be paid directly to the attorney, who may enforce the order in his name.

§ 314.   Decree.

(a) A decree of dissolution of marriage or of legal separation is final when entered, subject to the right of appeal. An appeal from the decree of dissolution that does not challenge the finding that the marriage is irretrievably broken does not delay the finality of that provision of the decree which dissolves the marriage beyond the time for appealing from that provision, and either of the parties may remarry pending appeal.

(b) No earlier than 6 months after entry of a decree of legal separation, the court on motion of either party shall convert the decree to a decree of dissolution of marriage.

(c) The Clerk of Court shall give notice of the entry of a decree of dissolution or legal separation:

(1) if the marriage is registered in this State, to the [marriage license] clerk of the [county, judicial district] where the marriage is registered who shall enter the fact of dissolution or separation in the [Registry of Marriage]; or

(2) if the marriage is registered in another jurisdiction, to the appropriate official of that jurisdiction, with the request that he enter the fact of dissolution in the appropriate record.

(d) Upon request by a wife whose marriage is dissolved or declared invalid, the court may, and if there are no children of the parties shall, order her maiden name or a former name restored.

§ 315.   Independence of Provisions of Decree or Temporary Order.

If a party fails to comply with a provision of a decree or temporary order or injunction, the obligation of the other party to make payments for support or maintenance or to permit visitation is not suspended; but he may move the court to grant an appropriate order.

§ 316.   Modification and Termination of Provisions for Maintenance, Support and Property Disposition.

(a) Except as otherwise provided in subsection (f) of Section 306, the provisions of any decree respecting maintenance or support may be modified only as to installments accruing subsequent to the motion for modification and only upon a showing of changed circumstances so substantial and continuing as to make the terms unconscionable. The provisions as to property disposition may not be revoked or modified, unless the court finds the existence of conditions that justify the reopening of a judgment under the laws of this state.

(b) Unless otherwise agreed in writing or expressly provided in the decree, the obligation to pay future maintenance is terminated upon the death of either party or the remarriage of the party receiving maintenance.

(c) Unless otherwise agreed in writing or expressly provided in the decree, provisions for the support of a child are terminated by emancipation of the child but not by the death of a parent obligated to support the child. When a parent obligated to pay support dies, the amount of support may be modified, revoked, or commuted to a lump sum payment, to the extent just and appropriate in the circumstances.

PART IV. CUSTODY

§ 401.   Jurisdiction; Commencement of Proceeding.

(a) A court of this State competent to decide child custody matters has jurisdiction to make a child custody determination by initial or modification decree if:

(1) this State

(i) is the home state of the child at the time of commencement of the proceeding, or

(ii) had been the child's home state within 6 months before commencement of the proceeding and the child is absent from this State because of his removal or retention by a person claiming his custody or for other reason, and a parent or person acting as parent continues to live in this State; or

(2) it is in the best interest of the child that a court of this State assume jurisdiction because

(i) the child and his parents, or the child and at least one contestant, have a significant connection with this State, and

(ii) there is available in this State substantial evidence concerning the child's present or future care, protection, training, and personal relationships; or

(3) the child is physically present in this State and

(i) has been abandoned or

(ii) it is necessary in an emergency to protect him because he has been subjected to or threatened with mistreatment or abuse or is neglected or dependent; or

(4) (i) no other state has jurisdiction under prerequisites substantially in accordance with paragraphs (1), (2), or (3), or another state has declined to exercise jurisdiction on the ground that this State is the more appropriate forum to determine custody of the child, and

(ii) it is in his best interest that the court assume jurisdiction.

(b) Except under paragraphs (3) and (4) of subsection (a), physical presence in this State of the child, or of the child and one of the contestants, is not alone sufficient to confer jurisdiction on a court of this State to make a child custody determination.

(c) Physical presence of the child, while desirable, is not a prerequisite for jurisdiction to determine his custody.

(d) A child custody proceeding is commenced in the [_____] court:

(1) by a parent, by filing a petition

(i) for dissolution or legal separation; or

(ii) for custody of the child in the [county, judicial district] in which he is permanently resident or found; or

(2) by a person other than a parent, by filing a petition for custody of the child in the [county, judicial district] in which he is permanently resident or found, but only if he is not in the physical custody of one of his parents.

(e) Notice of a child custody proceeding shall be given to the child's parent, guardian, and custodian, who may appear, be heard, and file a responsive pleading. The court, upon a showing of good cause, may permit intervention of other interested parties.

§ 402. Best Interest of Child.[8]

The court shall determine custody in accordance with the best interest of the child. The court shall consider all relevant factors including:

(1) the wishes of the child's parent or parents as to his custody;

(2) the wishes of the child as to his custodian;

(3) the interaction and interrelationship of the child with his parent or parents, his siblings, and any other person who may significantly affect the child's best interest;

(4) the child's adjustment to his home, school, and community; and

(5) the mental and physical health of all individuals involved.

The court shall not consider conduct of a proposed custodian that does not affect his relationship to the child.

§ 403. Temporary Orders.

(a) A party to a custody proceeding may move for a temporary custody order. The motion must be supported by an affidavit as provided in Section 410. The court may award temporary custody under the standards of Section 402 after a hearing, or, if there is no objection, solely on the basis of the affidavits.

(b) If a proceeding for dissolution of marriage or legal separation is dismissed, any temporary custody order is vacated unless a parent or the child's custodian moves that the proceeding continue as a custody proceeding and the court finds, after a hearing, that the circumstances of the parents and the best interest of the child require that a custody decree be issued.

(c) If a custody proceeding commenced in the absence of a petition for dissolution of marriage or legal separation under subsection (1)(ii) or (2) of Section 401 is dismissed, any temporary custody order is vacated.

§ 404. Interviews.

(a) The court may interview the child in chambers to ascertain the child's wishes as to his custodian and as to visitation. The court may permit counsel to be present at the interview. The court shall cause a record of the interview to be made and to be part of the record in the case.

(b) The court may seek the advice of professional personnel, whether or not employed by the court on a regular basis. The advice given shall be in writing and made available by the court to counsel upon request. Counsel may examine as a witness any professional personnel consulted by the court.

§ 405. Investigations and Reports.

(a) In contested custody proceedings, and in other custody proceedings if a parent or the child's custodian so requests, the court may order an investigation and report concerning custodial arrangements for the child. The investigation and report may be made by the court social service agency, the staff of the juvenile court, the local probation or welfare department, or a private agency employed by the court for the purpose.

(b) In preparing his report concerning a child, the investigator may consult any person who may have information about the child and his potential custodial arrangements. Upon order of the court, the investigator may refer the child to professional personnel for diagnosis. The investigator may consult with and obtain information from medical, psychiatric, or other expert persons who have served the child in the past without obtaining the consent of the parent or the child's custodian; but the child's consent must be obtained if he has reached the age of 16, unless the court finds that he lacks mental capacity to consent. If the requirements of subsection (c) are fulfilled, the investigator's report may be received in evidence at the hearing.

(c) The court shall mail the investigator's report to counsel and to any party not represented by counsel at least 10 days prior to the hearing. The investigator shall make available to counsel and to any party not represented by counsel the investigator's file of underlying data, and reports, complete texts of diagnostic reports made to the investigator pursuant to the provisions of subsection (b), and the names and addresses of all persons whom the investigator has consulted. Any party to the proceeding may call the investigator and any person whom he has consulted for cross-examination. A party may not waive his right of cross-examination prior to the hearing.

§ 406. Hearings.

(a) Custody proceedings shall receive priority in being set for hearing.

(b) The court may tax as costs the payment of necessary travel and other expenses incurred by any person whose presence at the hearing the court deems necessary to determine the best interest of the child.

(c) The court without a jury shall determine questions of law and fact. If it finds that a public hearing may be detrimental to the child's best interest, the court may exclude the public from a custody hearing, but may admit any person who has a direct and legitimate interest in the particular case or a legitimate educational or research interest in the work of the court.

(d) If the court finds it necessary to protect the child's welfare that the record of any interview, report, investigation, or testimony in a custody proceeding be kept secret, the court may make an appropriate order sealing the record.

§ 407. Visitation.

(a) A parent not granted custody of the child is entitled to reasonable visitation rights unless the court finds, after a hearing, that visitation would endanger seriously the child's physical, mental, moral, or emotional health.

(b) The court may modify an order granting or denying visitation rights whenever modification would serve the best interest of the child; but the court shall not restrict a parent's visitation rights unless it finds that the visitation would endanger seriously the child's physical, mental, moral, or emotional health.

§ 408. Judicial Supervision.

(a) Except as otherwise agreed by the parties in writing at the time of the custody decree, the custodian may determine the child's upbringing, including his education, health care, and religious training, unless the court after hearing, finds, upon motion by the noncustodial parent, that in the absence of a specific limitation of the custodian's authority, the child's physical health would be endangered or his emotional development significantly impaired.

(b) If both parents or all contestants agree to the order, or if the court finds that in the absence of the order the child's physical health would be endangered or his emotional development significantly impaired, the court may order the [local probation or welfare department, court social service agency] to exercise continuing supervision over the case to assure that the custodial or visitation terms of the decree are carried out.

§ 409. Modification.

(a) No motion to modify a custody decree may be made earlier than 2 years after its date, unless the court permits it to be made on the basis of affidavits that there is reason to believe the child's present environment may endanger seriously his physical, mental, moral, or emotional health.

(b) If a court of this State has jurisdiction pursuant to the Uniform Child Custody Jurisdiction Act, the court shall not modify a prior custody decree unless it finds, upon the basis of facts that have arisen since the prior decree or that were unknown to the court at the time of entry of the prior decree, that a change has occurred in the circumstances of the child or his custodian, and that the modification is necessary to serve the best interest of the child. In applying these standards the court shall retain the custodian appointed pursuant to the prior decree unless:

(1) the custodian agrees to the modification;

(2) the child has been integrated into the family of the petitioner with consent of the custodian; or

(3) the child's present environment endangers seriously his physical, mental, moral, or emotional health, and the harm likely to be caused by a change of environment is outweighed by its advantages to him.

(c) Attorney fees and costs shall be assessed against a party seeking modification if the court finds that the modification action is vexatious and constitutes harassment.

§ 410.   Affidavit Practice.

A party seeking a temporary custody order or modification of a custody decree shall submit together with his moving papers an affidavit setting forth facts supporting the requested order or modification and shall give notice, together with a copy of his affidavit, to other parties to the proceeding, who may file opposing affidavits. The court shall deny the motion unless it finds that adequate cause for hearing the motion is established by the affidavits, in which case it shall set a date for hearing on an order to show cause why the requested order or modification should not be granted.

PART V. EFFECTIVE DATE AND REPEALER

§ 501.   Time of Taking Effect.

This Act shall take effect [_____].

§ 502.   Application.

(a)   This Act applies to all proceedings commenced on or after its effective date.

(b)   This Act applies to all pending actions and proceedings commenced prior to its effective date with respect to issues on which a judgment has not been entered. Pending actions for divorce or separation are deemed to have been commenced on the basis of irretrievable breakdown. Evidence adduced after the effective date of this Act shall be in compliance with this Act.

(c)   This Act applies to all proceedings commenced after its effective date for the modification of a judgment or order entered prior to the effective date of this Act.

(d)   In any action or proceeding in which an appeal was pending or a new trial was ordered prior to the effective date of this Act, the law in effect at the time of the order sustaining the appeal or the new trial governs the appeal, the new trial, and any subsequent trial or appeal.

§ 503.   Severability.

If any provision of this Act or application thereof to any person or circumstance is held invalid, the invalidity does not affect other provisions or applications of the Act which can be given effect without

the invalid provision or application, and to this end the provisions of this Act are severable.

§ 504.   Specific Repealer.

The following acts and all other acts and parts of acts inconsistent herewith are hereby repealed: [Here should follow the acts to be specifically repealed, including any acts regulating:

(1)   marriage, including grounds for annulment and provisions for void marriages;

(2)   existing grounds for divorce and legal separation;

(3)   existing defenses to divorce and legal separation, including but not limited to condonation, connivance, collusion, recrimination, insanity, and lapse of time; and

(4)   alimony, child support, custody, and division of spouses' property in the event of a divorce and judicial proceedings designed to modify the financial or custody provisions of divorce decrees.]

§ 505.   General Repealer.

Except as provided in Section 506, all acts and parts of acts inconsistent with this Act are hereby repealed.

§ 506.   Laws Not Repealed.

This Act does not repeal: [Here should follow the acts not to be repealed, including any acts regulating or prescribing:

(1)   the contents of and forms for marriage licenses and methods of registering marriages and providing for license or registration fees;

(2)   the validity of premarital agreements between spouses concerning their marital property rights;

(3)   marital property rights during a marriage or when the marriage terminates by the death of one of the spouses;

(4)   the scope and extent of the duty of a parent to support a child of the marriage;

(5)   custody of and support duty owed to an illegitimate child;

(6)   the Uniform Child Custody Jurisdiction Act; and

(7)   any applicable laws relating to wage assignments, garnishments, and exemptions other than those providing for family support and maintenance.]

---

1   Note the policy expressed in § 102(6) to the effect that irretrievable breakdown be the sole ground for dissolution of marriage.

2   This language excludes same-sex marriages.

3   While preserving the invalidity of bigamous and incestuous marriages, § 207 nevertheless makes the offspring of such marriages legitimate. A bigamous marriage would be validated once the former marriage is dissolved. Sec. 207 (b).

4 Section 208 lists marriages denominated "voidable" in the text, including lack of capacity to consent to marry; impotence; underage party; prohibited marriage (e.g., bigamous, incestuous).

5 The UMDA version of *putative spouse* retains the "good faith belief" that a person was married.

6 The UMDA version of *irretrievably broken* is not pure no-fault divorce, but requires judicial inquiry into the validity of the ground. A 180-day separation prior to filing satisfies this requirement. See also § 305.

7 The separation agreement is binding on the court unless it finds the agreement to be unconscionable.

8 Section 402 expresses a modern view of the best-interest test, including, at the end the note, stating that the conduct of the custodian is irrelevant if it does not affect the child.

CHAPTER 6
Antenuptial Contracts

Jackie and Ari

The former First Lady married the Greek shipping tycoon in 1968 following the execution of a secret prenuptial agreement. Although the marriage was an unhappy one, it survived until Ari's death, at which time Jackie sought to enforce the agreement. Later Ari's estate settled for a reported $25 million. Pictured are the late multibillionaire Aristotle Onassis and Jacqueline Kennedy Onassis.

— Courtesy AP/Wide World Photos.

*And, for that dowry, I'll assure her of her Widowhood, be it that she survive me,
In all my land and leases whatsoever. Let specialties be therefore drawn
between us, That covenants may be kept on either hand.*

Shakespeare, *The Taming of the Shrew.* **Cited by Justice Burke in** *Brooks v. Brooks,*
733 P.2d 1044 (Alaska 1987) as an ancestral antenuptial agreement.

OUTLINE

6.1 BACKGROUND
6.2 WHAT SHOULD AN ANTENUPTIAL AGREEMENT CONTAIN?
6.3 WHO SHOULD HAVE AN ANTENUPTIAL AGREEMENT?
6.4 THE ANTENUPTIAL AGREEMENT AND THE PRACTITIONER
    Fairness and Conscionability
    Disclosure
    Voluntariness and Consent
    Waiver of Rights
6.5 AGREEMENTS THAT ENCOURAGE OR PROMOTE DIVORCE
6.6 SUPPORT PROVISIONS
    SUMMARY

*Some couples elect to put the terms of their marriage contracts
into a written contract, called by the alternative names antenuptial,
premarital, or prenuptial agreements or contracts. Perhaps this is a
confirmation of Maine's claim that law is moving from status to
contract. The antenuptial agreement describes the relative statuses of
husband and wife; it redefines to a greater or lesser extent the rights
and duties of the spouses that are otherwise expressed or implied by the
law. Although formerly rejected when such agreements contemplated
divorce, in recent years the courts have reversed themselves and
accepted antenuptial arrangements much like other contracts. The
special requirements imposed by the courts form much of the subject
matter of this chapter, but judicial acceptance of these agreements
implies one further step in the withdrawal of legal intervention into the
private arrangements of domestic relations. Courts and legislatures vary*

considerably, however, in the requirements they impose to make such agreements valid and enforceable.

6.1 BACKGROUND

Antenuptial agreements were not the first express marital contracts. There is a long history of marital settlements in the form of trusts set up by fathers to protect their daughters from husbands who might exploit the common law authority husbands enjoyed over their wives' property. By putting property in a trust for their daughters, fathers insulated the daughters, because the trustee held title to the property for the benefit of the daughter (and often the daughter/beneficiary had free reign over the property because the trustee had a tacit agreement with the father to respect the beneficiary's wishes). These arrangements formed part of a marriage settlement which resembled modern antenuptial agreements in the sense that the future disposition of property was planned.

At first, antenuptial contracts entered into by the parties were disfavored, because judges saw these contracts as interfering with or contravening public policy, as stated by the law that allocated rights, duties, and property within the family. Objections to the distribution of property at the death of one of the parties were grudgingly accepted when the contract was fair and had been made voluntarily by a couple who seemed to know what they were doing (the overt paternalism of the common law, which presumed that the wife was inexperienced in the niceties of law and business, reigned in most states until recently). It took much longer, however, to accept property settlements in divorce cases. As the courts (the judges) regarded themselves as the protectors of the family, a contract that contemplated divorce seemed unlawful. Even with widespread acceptance of antenuptial agreements today, courts and legislators have placed special burdens on their validity.

CASE NO. 6-1   Alaska Approves Antenuptial Agreements

In *Brooks,* the Supreme Court of Alaska was called upon for the first time to rule on the validity of antenuptial agreements. As a latecomer to the field, the court was able to draw upon cases and statutes from other states to decide the issues. The following is an excerpt from that decision, which admirably traces the history of antenuptial agreements and analyzes the policy behind the law as it once was and as it has changed.

BROOKS v. BROOKS
733 P.2d 1044 (Alaska 1987)
Supreme Court of Alaska

II. DISCUSSION

A. *The Validity of Prenuptial Agreements Made in Contemplation of Divorce*

* * *

The traditional common law view was that prenuptial agreements in contemplation of divorce[4] (hereinafter prenuptial agreements) were inconsistent with the sanctity of marriage and the state's interest in preserving marriage and maintaining the financial security of divorced persons. Courts uniformly viewed these agreements as inherently conducive to divorce[5] and as allowing a husband to circumvent his legal duty to support his wife. Thus, prior to 1970, prenuptial agreements that stipulated terms regarding alimony and property settlements upon divorce were almost universally considered void *ab initio* as contrary to public policy.[6]

Since 1970,[7] however, public policy has changed markedly.[8] Freed & Walker, *Family Law in the Fifty States: An Overview,* 19 Fam.Law Q. 331, 438 (1985–86) (hereinafter *"Overview"*). With the advent of no-fault divorce laws[9] and the changes in society such laws represent, the traditional rule has rapidly given way to the more realistic view that prenuptial agreements are not void *ab initio* but are valid and enforceable if certain standards of "fairness" are met. . . .

[T]he idea that prenuptial agreements induce divorce is anachronistic. Today, divorce is a "common-place fact of life." *Posner,* 233 So.2d at 384. As a result there is a concurrent increase in second and third marriages—often of mature people with substantial means and separate families from earlier marriages. The conflicts that naturally inhere in such relationships make the litigation that follows even more uncertain, unpleasant and costly. Consequently, people with previous "bad luck" with

domestic life may not be willing to risk marriage again without the ability to safeguard their financial interests. In other words, without the ability to order their own affairs as they wish, many people may simply forgo marriage for more "informal" relationships.

Prenuptial agreements, on the other hand, provide such people with the opportunity to ensure predictability, plan their future with more security, and, most importantly, decide their own destiny. Moreover, allowing couples to think through the financial aspects of their marriage beforehand can only foster strength and permanency in that relationship. In this day and age, judicial recognition of prenuptial agreements most likely "encourages rather than discourages marriage." *Gant,* 329 S.E.2d at 112–13.

In sum, both the realities of our society and policy reasons favor judicial recognition of prenuptial agreements. Rather than inducing divorce, such agreements simply acknowledge its ordinariness. With divorce as likely an outcome of marriage as permanence, we see no logical or compelling reason why public policy should not allow two mature adults to handle their own financial affairs. Therefore, we join those courts that have recognized that prenuptial agreements legally procured and ostensibly fair in result are valid and can be enforced. "The reasoning that once found them contrary to public policy has no place in today's matrimonial law." *Marschall,* 477 A.2d at 839.

---

4 Prenuptial agreements in contemplation of divorce must be distinguished from prenuptial agreements in contemplation of death. While the former, until recently, were held to be presumptively invalid, the latter, since the time of Shakespeare, have been considered presumptively valid because they were seen as conducive to marital tranquility and preventing unnecessary litigation. . . .

---

5 The time-honored majority rule in this country has been that contracts intended to facilitate or promote the

procurement of a divorce are illegal as contrary to public policy. Restatement (Second) of Contracts § 190 (1979). The reason prenuptial agreements were thought to promote divorce was stated in *Crouch v. Crouch,* 53 Tenn.App. 594, 385 S.W.2d 288, 293 (1964):

> [S]uch [a] contract is promotive of divorce and void on grounds of public policy. Such contract[s] could induce a mercenary husband to inflict on his wife any wrong he might desire with the knowledge that his pecuniary liability would be limited. In other words, a husband could through abuse and ill treatment of his wife force her to bring an action for divorce and thereby buy a divorce for a sum far less than he would otherwise have to pay.

See also Fricke v. Fricke, 257 Wis. 124, 42 N.W.2d 500 (1950) (such agreements invite dispute, encourage separation and incite divorce).

---

6 The policy grounds most frequently cited by the courts were that prenuptial agreements (1) are incompatible with and denigrate the marital relation; (2) tend to facilitate and induce divorce; and (3) burden the state by casting indigent spouses on public charity. *Ferry v. Ferry,* 586 S.W.2d 782, 785 (Mo.App.1979).

---

7 The case generally considered to mark the judicial watershed on prenuptial agreements is *Posner v. Posner,* 233 So.2d 381 (Fla.1970), *rev'd on other grounds,* 257

So.2d 530 (Fla.1972) (prenuptial agreement invalidated on grounds of nondisclosure).

---

8 As the West Virginia Supreme Court recently noted:
The older rule was grounded in yesteryear's sound public policy: in general, thirty years ago women did not work in the market economy; society enjoyed a consensus that favored lifetime marriage and disfavored divorce; and prenuptial agreements that limited the support obligation in favor of former wives encouraged divorce and made divorced women potential charges of the state.

Circumstances have changed dramatically in the last three decades, however. . . . [T]oday 58.7 percent of all married women are gainfully employed. . . . [W]e no longer have a society-wide consensus on the sanctity of marriage: . . . as of 1983 there were 114 divorced persons per 1,000 married persons. . . . Currently divorces are being granted . . . at the rate of approximately 1,200,000 per year. *Grant,* 329 S.E.2d at 112 (citations and footnotes omitted).

---

9 All American jurisdictions now have some form of "no-fault" divorce. Overview, supra, at 341. In Alaska, a divorce or a dissolution may be obtained on the "no-fault" grounds of "incompatibility of temperament." See AS 25.24.050(5)(C) (divorce), and AS 25.24.200(b)(1) (dissolution).

6.2 WHAT SHOULD AN ANTENUPTIAL AGREEMENT CONTAIN?

Much depends on the character of the parties and their intended relationship. Many agreements contain great detail concerning the expectations of the parties concerning the marriage. Some details may seem quite practical: "Husband will be in charge of financial recordkeeping, paying household bills promptly on a monthly basis." Some might seem unduly trivial: "Wife will prepare dinner on Monday, Wednesday, and Friday evenings while the Husband will prepare dinner on Tuesday, Thursday, and Sunday evenings, Saturday being reserved for dining out or whatever arrangement is made by mutual agreement." Some couples have even attempted to set minimum frequency of sexual contact. All of these terms are permissible, yet none of them appears to be enforceable—no court is likely to use its powers to require compliance. Nonetheless, highly detailed agreements do present a picture of the relationship envisioned by the couple and could be used later when the relationship has soured to show that one of the spouses has lived up to these conditions while the other has failed. Presumably, in no-fault divorces, such lapses merit little attention with regard to severing marital bonds, but fault remains a negotiating weapon when property settlement, custody of children, and support payments are discussed in the pretrial process.

As a concrete example, it might be apparent from the premarital agreement that it was intended that the wife would return to finish her education when the children had all entered elementary school. If the marriage terminated before she was able to accomplish this goal, the agreement would make a powerful argument in favor of rehabilitative alimony for this purpose. This would be particularly true if the agreement fairly divided rights and duties and the wife had performed her part of the bargain.

The overriding concern of the law and the legal practitioner with regard to premarital agreements is the disposition of property rights upon death or divorce. These are generally enforceable today, although controversial until quite recently, and still burdened with special requirements the courts and legislatures have seen fit to attach. It goes without saying that one of the spouses would be materially better off if the antenuptial agreement were invalid or unenforceable. More than greed is involved. At death, enforcement of the agreement usually means that persons close to the deceased but not close to the surviving spouse will get a share that would otherwise be reserved to the surviving spouse. At divorce, enforcement means that a disliked, despised, or even hated spouse will get the lion's share of property that was once enjoyed by both. Under such circumstances, it is essential that the antenuptial agreement be properly drafted.

An antenuptial agreement presents special problems not encountered with other contracts. Here we have a very special contract, one that may not take effect for decades. In some respects it is like a will, especially in making distribution of property at death. A will, however, is not a contract; it is a unilateral disposition of property and may be unilaterally revoked until the death of the testator. Nor is an antenuptial agreement a contract in the usual sense of an exchange of promises to be performed; it is really a mutual denial of rights and duties that would otherwise be imposed by law. For example, all states provide for a surviving spouse to receive a share of the decedent's estate if there is no will or to elect to take a share of the estate if dissatisfied with the will. An antenuptial agreement is the only way to circumvent this law and provide a lesser share. As a second example, California is a community property state, that is, property earned and acquired during the marriage is deemed *community property,* owned equally by husband and wife. However, in *Marriage of Dawley,* 17 Cal. 3d 342, 551 P.2d 323, 131 Cal. Rptr. 3 (1976), the Supreme Court of California held that a couple could provide in an antenuptial agreement to keep their respective properties separate, thus circumventing the law of community property.

The fact that the property distributions described by antenuptial agreements commonly do not go into effect until many years after the agreement is signed presents two problems. First, the law may change; it has been changing for several decades and is likely to continue to change as antenuptial agreements become ever more popular and used in a variety of situations.

Second, regardless of the state in which the contract was made or the state in which the couple lived, married, and were domiciled, divorce or death may take place in a state with a very different attitude toward antenuptial agreements than the one in which the contract was signed. (The sample New York antenuptial agreement in appendix 6B lists all kinds of marital property to be on the safe side.) Some protection may be afforded by including a clause requiring application of the law of the state where the contract was finalized (presumably the intended domicile of the couple). Although most states are inclined to honor such a clause, antenuptial agreements fall in an area—namely, family law—where public policy considerations are heavy, and the court may choose to ignore the clause on policy grounds.

The solution to these problems is to make a contract that would be enforceable in virtually every state. This can be done by dealing with the problems, noted later in this chapter, that have caused antenuptial agreements to be invalidated.

CASE NO. 6-2 Choice of Law

DELOREAN v. DELOREAN
221 N.J. Super. 423, 511 A2.d 1257
(Ch. Ct. 1986)

[I]t is argued that California, not New Jersey, law should be applied. The parties married and executed the agreement in California. It is hornbook law that when an agreement is silent as to which law should be applied, the validity and construction of a contract shall be determined by the law of the place of contracting. But this agreement is not silent and expressly provides that it:

> shall be construed under the laws of the State of California and enforceable in the proper courts of jurisdiction of the State of California.

[Thus,] the law of California must be applied in this case.

* * *

Where California and New Jersey law part is in their determination of what constitutes a **fiduciary** because, unlike New Jersey, California does not treat a party to an antenuptial agreement as a fiduciary on the theory that "parties who are not yet married are not presumed to share a confidential relationship." *Marriage of Dawley,* 17 Cal.3d 342, 355, 131 Cal.Rptr. 3, 551 P.2d 323 (1976). So long as the spouse seeking to set aside such an agreement has a general idea of the character and extent of the financial assets and income of the other, that apparently is sufficient in California. . . . As this court reads California law, the disclosures made by John DeLorean appear to be sufficient for purposes of enforcing this agreement.

6.3 WHO SHOULD HAVE AN ANTENUPTIAL AGREEMENT?

Certain circumstances suggest the advisability of an antenuptial agreement, but the relationship of the bride and groom will decide whether an agreement will be executed. The antenuptial agreement introduces harsh economic considerations into what is presumably a romantic relationship; it suggests that one of the parties has second thoughts about the permanence of the relationship or the sincerity of the other party. For this reason, many who might think an antenuptial agreement desirable nonetheless refuse to raise the subject.

In the past, antenuptial agreements were sought in two kinds of situations. Older persons marrying for companionship or convenience without the intention of building a family (commonly with their respective children already self-supporting) would often choose to keep their property separate, having planned for some time for the disposition of their property at death. Where both parties were affluent, neither took advantage of the other. The other situation was a May–December marriage in which the December member was rich. The antenuptial agreement gave some assurance that the May member was not a golddigger, by limiting the property to be gained in death or divorce. If this seems unfair, note that the wealthy partner could always express generosity through gift or will.

Today, it could be said that women in general ought to consider the advisability of an antenuptial agreement. Ironically, the advancement of women's rights and equality of the sexes have put women at a disadvantage in family law. Courts generally do not take the same paternalistic, protective attitude toward women that they did in decades past—women are now presumed to know what they are signing, unintimidated by their fiances or husbands; permanent alimony is uncommon; women can support themselves; widows receive no more than widowers. All this would be reasonable if men and women were truly equal in society and in the workplace, but the facts speak differently. Women receive less pay for equal work and traditional female occupations pay less than male occupations. It is far more frequent for women to work to help their husbands through school than the other way around. When families break up, the wife usually becomes the primary caregiver of the children. A relatively high divorce rate tended to create an underclass of single mothers of preschool-age children with fathers who rarely or never paid court-ordered child support. The states, under pressure from the federal government (see chapter 12), have enacted a variety of laws to facilitate enforcement of child support, but the overall effectiveness of these laws has yet to be gauged. The harsh realities of marriage and divorce argue strongly for antenuptial agreements offering some measure of protection for women, especially those intending to sacrifice career for husband or children.

Persons contemplating second marriages, especially those who have children by prior marriages, should seriously consider drawing up an antenuptial

CAVEAT

Antenuptial agreements must be in writing because of the ancient Statute of Frauds, which required that contracts to marry be in writing and signed to be enforceable.

LEGAL TERMS

fiduciary
    Person who has a high duty of loyalty, trust, and fair dealing because of a special relationship with another.

agreement. The demands on family resources will be great and nearly everyone will feel unfairly treated. When the couple plans through an antenuptial agreement for the allocation of resources, they will be forced to confront these problems and make a reasonable attempt to head off the worst scenarios. Those who grew up on the "Brady Bunch" should have a long talk with a divorce lawyer. Step relationships are difficult, often unfriendly, and sometimes downright nasty. Stepparents and stepchildren rarely foresee the depth of hostility that can arise when family members take sides.

CASE NO. 6-3   Limiting the Widow's Share

In the *Pajak* case, West Virginia gives approval to antenuptial agreements designed to protect children of a former marriage.

PAJAK v. PAJAK
182 W. Va. 28, 385 S.E.2d 384 (1989)
Supreme Court of Appeals
of West Virginia

NEELY, Justice:

[William J. Pajak, Sr., married to Patricia Schmidt in 1949 and divorced her in 1954. Their two children, Christina and Anthony, were brought up by their mother and George Poore, her second husband. William J. Pajak, Sr., married again in 1963, sired two more children, Clark and William, and divorced in 1980. In 1979, before his divorce, he wrote his last will and testament, leaving all his property to Clark and William.

Then William J. Pajak, Sr., married his third wife, Audrey, in 1982, one day after he and Audrey entered into a prenuptial agreement by which Audrey waived any and all interests in his estate. William J. Pajak, Sr., died in December 1985 and the 1979 will was offered for probate.

This case arose when Clark and William, Mr. Pajak's children by his second marriage, brought a declaratory judgment action to declare the respective rights in the estate of Clark and William on one side and Audrey on the other. Anthony Poore and Christina Poore, Mr. Pajak's two children by his first marriage, intervened in the action.

The court held that the West Virginia Code provides that wills are revoked by a subsequent marriage or divorce and that therefore the decedent died intestate. This left the remaining issue of whether the antenuptial agreement was valid, which would prevent the widow from taking her statutory share of her deceased husband's estate.]

* * *

I.

[The prenuptial agreement provides:]

IT IS, THEREFORE, NOW AGREED that for and in consideration of the marriage about to be consummated between the parties hereto, both parties hereto mutually agree:

* * *

(3) That the party of the second part similarly agrees, in the event she survives the party of the first part, she will make no claim to any part or share of the real or personal estate of which the party of the first part, dies seised, other than that as may be bequeathed her in

said first party's Will; that said party of the second part expressly waives and relinquishes all claims to dower, homestead, statutory or other right available to a widow, in and to the real and personal estate of which the party of the first part may die seised and possessed. . . .

* * *

The evidence indicates that before his marriage to Audrey, William J. Pajak, Sr., was a man of considerable wealth who had a variety of active business interests. Audrey Pajak, before her marriage, worked as an employee of Carolina Furniture Company, a retail furniture business of which Mr. Pajak was the sole owner. The pre-nuptial agreement at issue in this case was drafted by William J. Pajak, Sr.'s lawyer and was presented to Mrs. Pajak at the lawyer's office one day before the couple were married. Mrs. Pajak testified that the lawyer discussed the agreement with her briefly, and that then she signed it without reading the agreement. Mrs. Pajak testified that she did not know that she could have had the agreement reviewed by another lawyer, and that at the time she signed the agreement, she believed that she "wasn't allowed to object" to the wording of the agreement.

II.

Initially, we would point out that the case before us involves a traditional pre-nuptial agreement designed to protect the inheritance rights of children from claims made by a new wife who is not the children's mother. . . .

The reason that pre-nuptial agreements of the type Mrs. Pajak signed are favored by public policy is that they enhance, rather than detract from, opportunities to form marriage relationships in middle-age and later. Typically, a couple marries in their early twenties, has children, and through joint efforts accumulates family assets. If, then, one spouse dies, the surviving spouse may feel a duty to the deceased spouse as well as to the children to protect the assets from claims of a second spouse. Thus, without the ability to enter into enforceable, pre-nuptial agreements that protect assets from the statutory entitlement of a second spouse, an older person with money acquired with the help of his or her spouse in an earlier marriage would be reluctant to remarry. Although in the case before us Mr. Pajak was divorced, it was obvious that he wished to protect the interests of his children.

* * *

Mrs. Pajak maintains that she was unaware of the extent of Mr. Pajak's assets. However, Mr. Pajak was a successful businessman and Mrs. Pajak was aware that he owned a number of businesses, had real estate holdings, and lived reasonably well. Contrary to Mrs. Pajak's reading of the law, for a pre-nuptial agreement to be valid, it is not necessary that both parties execute a detailed, written financial statement such as is required by a bank before making a loan. Although Mr. Pajak made no great moment of regaling Mrs. Pajak with the details of his holdings, there is no evidence that he was at all secretive or in any way misled Mrs. Pajak. Therefore, we find no conduct that would amount to "fraud" such that the agreement should be set aside.

III.

Finally, Mrs. Pajak maintains that she could not understand the agreement and was not accorded an opportunity to have it examined by independent counsel. We addressed this exact problem in syllabus point 2 of *Gant v. Gant*, . . . , where we said:

> The validity of a pre-nuptial agreement is dependent upon its valid procurement, which requires its having been executed voluntarily, with knowledge of its content and legal effect, under circumstances free of fraud, duress, or misrepresentation. . . . [Independent counsel is not required by

West Virginia law. But see the sample agreement in appendix 6B (New York), paragraph 5, which recites independent legal counsel for each party.]

It appears from Mrs. Pajak's own testimony that she made no effort even to read the agreement in order to understand as much of it as she could, nor did she ask to have the agreement examined by her own lawyer. We believe that the terms of this agreement comport with the requirement of syllabus point 2 of *Gant v. Gant,* . . . in that "the terms of the agreement are understandable to a reasonably intelligent adult. . . ."

* * *

A person seeking to overcome the presumptive validity of a pre-nuptial agreement designed to protect assets for the children of a previous marriage has a heavy burden of proof.

> . . . In the field of prenuptial agreements, firm rules favoring enforceability inevitably further the public policy of encouraging middle-aged, cohabiting couples to regularize their relationships by getting married.

[*Gant v. Gant,*] 329 S.E.2d at 115.

Accordingly, the judgment of the Circuit Court of Ohio County is affirmed.

Affirmed.

MILLER, Justice, dissenting:

I trust that today's opinion does not signal a retreat from this Court's position, evolved over the last decade or so, requiring fair and just treatment for married women. [Justice Miller for several pages follows a paternalistic argument favoring protection of women. That his perspective is traditional is perhaps evidenced by the cases he cites to contradict the majority's citation of *Gant v. Gant* (1985) ("we have always strongly favored prenuptial agreements that establish property rights at death in West Virginia") by citing three cases decided prior to 1880 and one case from 1919.]

* * *

Turning to an analysis of the *Gant* factors, it is clear that this agreement is void. The testimony is that while Mrs. Pajak signed the agreement, she did so without any relevant explanation from her husband's attorney of what she was giving up. The fact that she had no advance warning of the agreement until she was taken to her husband's attorney's office the day before the wedding undercuts a claim of voluntariness. Furthermore, Mrs. Pajak received absolutely nothing under the antenuptial agreement. As stated in 41 Am.Jur.2d Husband and Wife § 298 (1968), the adequacy of the provision for the wife bears upon the fairness of the agreement: "However, adequacy of the provision for the wife is to be considered in connection with the question whether the contract is fair, and inadequacy may give rise to a presumption of fraud vitiating the agreement." (Footnotes omitted). See Annot., 27 A.L.R.2d 883 (1953).

Moreover, it seems axiomatic that to have knowledge of the agreement's contents, as *Gant* requires, there must be some reasonable disclosure of the husband's assets or at least a showing that the prospective wife had some independent knowledge of these facts. . . .

* * *

I regret to say that today's opinion does not befriend the widow who believes that justice requires a prospective husband, in the words of *Gieseler,* "to fully disclose the amount of his property and to deal fairly with his prospective bride." 117 W.Va. at 432, 185 S.E. at 848.

For these reasons, I dissent.

6.4 THE ANTENUPTIAL AGREEMENT AND THE PRACTITIONER

For the practitioner, the primary problem is to draft an antenuptial agreement that conforms to the requirements of the law while reflecting the wishes of the parties to the contract. At first glance, it might appear that the drafter of an antenuptial agreement simply needs to know appropriate state law to draft a valid antenuptial agreement. Unfortunately, antenuptial agreements pose unique problems as contracts.

1. Antenuptial agreements are not arm's-length contracts. Some states treat them as if they were; others consider the bride and groom to be in a fiduciary relationship (see *DeLorean*, Case No. 6-2, re California and New Jersey; still others exercise a paternalistic protectionist attitude toward the wife. Regardless of how the law treats these contracts, the parties themselves are ordinarily involved in a romantic relationship which makes the handling of the antenuptial agreement a very delicate matter for the practitioner.

2. Antenuptial agreements are not like standard contracts promising compensation for services or goods. Commonly, antenuptial agreements are designed to plan for the consequences of the termination of another contract—the marriage contract—by death or divorce. They are not primarily contracts calling for performance but provide instead for breach of the marriage contract. It is clear that antenuptial agreements also usually attempt to avoid the impositions of the law that would normally intervene at the termination of a marriage.

3. Antenuptial agreements may have no practical consequences in the foreseeable future. For the most important provisions of these contracts, no action will be taken until divorce or death, which may not occur for decades. The provisions of an antenuptial agreement may appear strange 20 years later when they finally come into effect. The parties are certainly in a different mood, their finances may be completely altered, and the law may have changed.

4. When the time comes to give effect to the provisions of an antenuptial agreement, the parties may live in a state with very different rules with regard to antenuptial agreements.

5. The antenuptial agreement is often not mutually satisfactory as a contract. If both parties are affluent, they may each be interested in preserving to themselves permanent control over their own property. In a great many cases, however, one party is simply relinquishing property rights that would otherwise be retained. To the lawyer preparing the agreement and retained by the more affluent party, the agreement protects the client and penalizes the client's loved one. To the attorney consulted by the party pressured to sign the agreement, the agreement almost never looks good—how may an attorney advise a client to give up valuable rights and receive nothing of material value in return? Frequently only

one attorney is consulted; as can be seen from the immediately preceding comments, that attorney must exercise self-protection while at the same time protecting the client.

The problem of framing an antenuptial agreement good for all times and all places is daunting. Nevertheless, one approach likely to be successful is to draft the agreement according to the most stringent state requirements. Because the trend in the law has been slowly but steadily toward a liberalized view allowing the parties to establish their own requirements (i.e., toward recognizing private contractual rights over protectionist and paternalistic governmental intrusion and oversight), it is unlikely that the requirements in any state will become more strict. Typically, the burdens of antenuptial agreements are concerned with fairness, disclosure, and conscionability. Voluntariness, consent, and fraud are basic features of contractual validity that apply to antenuptial agreements as well. (Section 6 of the Uniform Premarital Agreement Act, reprinted in appendix 6A, outlines these considerations and should be noted in connection with the rest of the section. See figure 6-1 for states that have adopted the Act.)

Fairness and Conscionability

Fairness is in the eye of the beholder; most courts would not rely on fairness or unfairness as a single deciding factor in the validation of an antenuptial agreement. Nevertheless, a careful reading of the many cases on antenuptial agreements leaves a strong impression that judges frequently mold their reasoning based on the equities of the case before them. For example, when a couple, each marrying for the second time, is composed of two people each comfortably affluent, an antenuptial agreement that reserves separate property to each does not seem unfair. In contrast, when one of the partners is a multimillionaire and the other without significant assets, an agreement that prevents either from making claims against the other in case of death or divorce seems distinctly unfair. Jurisdictions emphasizing fairness often use the terms "unreasonable" or "disproportionate," which would fit the second example.

> In evaluating the reasonableness of the provision for the survivor, such reasonableness must be determined as of the time of the Agreement and not by hindsight. Reasonableness will depend upon the totality of all the facts and circumstances at the time of the Agreement, including (a) the financial worth of the intended husband; (b) the financial status of the intended wife; (c) the age of the parties; (d) the number of children each has; (e) the intelligence of the parties; (f) whether the survivor aided in the accumulation of the wealth of the deceased spouse; and (g) the standard of living which the survivor had before marriage and could reasonably expect to have during marriage.
>
> — *In re Geyer,* 516 Pa. 492, 533 A.2d 423 (1987).

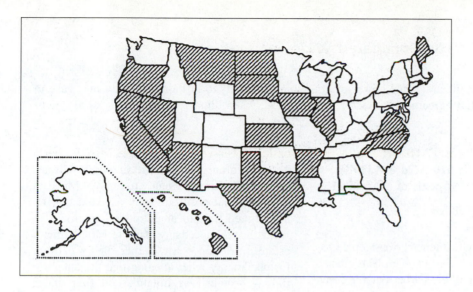

FIGURE 6-1
States adopting the
Uniform Premarital
Agreement Act

Conscionability refers to a long-standing equitable principle which holds that a court of equity will not require enforcement of an unconscionable bargain. Roughly speaking, unconscionability goes to the extremes of unfairness. In the preceding example of the multimillionaire who gives a spouse nothing, the court might find unconscionability, but giving one million out of twenty might seem unfair (that is, disproportionate) but not unconscionable. Ivana Trump's distress over receiving a mere $25 million in her postnuptial agreement with Donald Trump did not evoke pangs of anguish in most onlookers over the injustice of it all.

In most jurisdictions, unfairness, unreasonableness, and unconscionability are bargaining chips for the attorney representing the shortchanged spouse, who has little to lose except attorneys' fees in challenging the provisions of the agreement (the court either enforces the agreement or invalidates it). However, for the attorney drafting an antenuptial agreement for a prospective spouse and attempting to limit the resources going to the other spouse, the obvious solution is to make provisions that are fair. It ought not to be difficult to counsel a client to be fair to someone who is about to become the client's spouse. In some instances, a wealthy person desires some assurance that the partner-to-be is not motivated by gain. The solution at which many have arrived has been to write an antenuptial agreement that provided an increasing share based on the duration of the marriage, usually a greater dollar amount or percentage of assets for each year of the marriage. Though this may seem as if the less affluent partner is earning a share, it nonetheless demonstrates good faith on both sides.

CASE NO. 6-4   The Dominated Widower

The *Martin* case illustrates the power of equitable principles to fashion a remedy in a case in which the antenuptial agreement is clearly free of fraud, when blind adherence to it would incur a serious injustice.

MARTIN v. FARBER
68 Md. App. 137, 510 A.2d 608 (1986)
Court of Special Appeals of Maryland

GILBERT, Chief Judge.

* * *

Three days prior to their marriage on June 22, 1939, Nettie Sue Farber, then Nettie Sue Goldberg, and Morris W. Farber entered into an antenuptial agreement. The agreement provided, in essence, that Mrs. Farber would retain sole control of the property she acquired either prior to or during the marriage. Mr. Farber relinquished all rights in the property and estate of Mrs. Farber.

At the time of the execution of the agreement, Mrs. Farber was 39 years old, a widow, and the mother of two boys. Her first husband, Dr. Chester Goldberg, died in 1936. Mrs. Farber inherited property from him which included real estate located in Baltimore City. She also received from insurance proceeds more than $20,000.

Mr. Farber, although steadily employed as an electrician, had no accumulated wealth at the time of his marriage to Mrs. Farber. He did, however, continue to work until his retirement in 1967. During his forty-four year marriage to Mrs. Farber, Mr. Farber turned his paychecks over to his wife. Mrs. Farber, meanwhile, remained at home and managed the couple's household and financial affairs.

When Mrs. Farber died intestate in August, 1983, she had accumulated in her own name assets valued at approximately $275,000. The Orphan's Court for Baltimore County appointed Mr. Farber as personal representative of his deceased wife's estate. Mrs. Farber's grandchildren filed a petition in the Circuit Court for Baltimore County to remove Mr. Farber from that position. They asserted that he had signed a valid antenuptial agreement in which he renounced any claim to Mrs. Farber's estate. In response, Mr. Farber filed a petition for declaratory relief alleging that the antenuptial agreement was invalid, and that under Maryland's intestacy laws he was entitled to his share of the estate.

* * *

The Antenuptial Agreement
* * *

In determining the validity of an antenuptial agreement, a court must consider: 1) was there a fair and reasonable provision for the spouse's relinquishing his or her rights; or 2) in the absence of such provision, was there "[f]rank, full and truthful disclosure of what is being relinquished (or in lieu thereof actual knowledge otherwise available or obtained). . . ." *Hartz,* 248 Md. at 57, 234 A.2d at 871. Equally important is the question of whether the agreement was entered into freely and voluntarily. *DelVecchio v. DelVecchio,* 143 So.2d 17, 20 (Fla.1962).

* * *

The element of "reasonableness must be weighed as of the time of the execution of the agreement." Lindey, *Separation Agreements and Antenuptial Contracts,* § 90-53 (1985). Some courts, for public policy reasons, have imposed another test—one of conscionability—in order to determine the validity of antenuptial agreements, at least with regard to provisions relating to maintenance and sustenance on dissolution of marriage. Under that particular test, "such provisions may lose their legal vitality by reason of changing circumstances which render the antenuptial provisions for maintenance to be unconscionable at the time of the marriage dissolution." *Newman v. Newman,* 653 P.2d 728, 734 (Colo.Sup.Ct.1982). The Colorado Court said that,

> "even though an antenuptial agreement is entered into in good faith, with full disclosure and without any element of fraud or overreaching, the maintenance provisions thereof may become voidable for unconscionability occasioned by circumstances existing at the time time of the marriage dissolution."

Other tribunals, citing the underlying State interest in the welfare of the divorced spouse, have simply invalidated maintenance or sustenance provisions in antenuptial agreements or have held them to be altogether void. [The court then cites Oregon, Illinois and Iowa cases striking down antenuptial agreements that waived a wife's alimony]. . . .

* * *

Constructive Trust

* * *

A constructive trust has been definded as "A . . . remedy employed by a court . . . to convert the holder of the legal title to property into a trustee for one who in good conscience should reap the benefits of the possession of said property. The remedy is applied by operation of law where property has been acquired by fraud, misrepresentation, or other improper method, or where the circumstances render it inequitable for the party holding the title to retain it."

* * *

Based on the evidence presented to support Mr. Farber's assertion that his wife abused that confidential relationship by using his earnings to acquire assets which she titled or placed solely in her own name, we agree that the imposition of a constructive trust was proper. We think, however, that the trust should only be imposed to the extent that Mr. Farber's funds were used to acquire assets which were not a part of or attributable to the assets in Mrs. Farber's estate prior to the marriage of the couple. In limiting scope of the constructive trust imposed in the case *sub judice,* we are mindful of a primary purpose of that form of trust—to prevent unjust enrichment. Therefore, the constructive trust should be limited to the extent Mr. Farber is able to trace his funds into his late wife's estate. The imposition by the trial court of a constructive trust over the entire estate, without regard to the amounts actually contributed by Mr. Farber, was error. . . .

Disclosure

Disclosure may be the most problematic feature of antenuptial agreements. Different jurisdictions have treated this question in a variety of ways. The *DeLorean* case, Case No. 6-2, implies that the New Jersey court might have decided differently had it not been applying California law. The court found that California, unlike New Jersey, did not treat parties to an antenuptial agreement as fiduciaries; hence, all that was needed in California was that the spouse had "a general idea of the character and extent of the financial assets and income of the other." In New Jersey, however, "fiduciaries are required to exercise a high degree of trust, good faith and candor in their dealings with each other."

Obviously, the disclosure requirement will be met whenever full and complete disclosure is made by way of a minutely detailed listing of assets and income. In many cases, this may be tediously complex, very unromantic, and quite distasteful to both parties. In most jurisdictions approving antenuptial agreements, a ballpark figure will suffice—a good faith estimate of total wealth, perhaps with a sketch of the nature of the assets.

CASE NO. 6-5   The Cutting Edge in Antenuptial Agreements

Florida is frequently credited with creating the landslide in favor of recognizing antenuptial agreements in divorce through its decision in *Posner v. Posner,* 233 So.2d 381 (Fla. 1970), but some may wonder if it did not go too far in *Stregack.*

STREGACK v. MOLDOFSKY
474 So. 2d 206 (Fla. 1985)
Supreme Court of Florida

McDONALD, Justice.

* * *

The issue here is whether a surviving spouse may challenge an antenuptial agreement based upon fraudulent nondisclosure of assets by a decedent spouse, in light of section 732.702, Florida Statutes (1983), which requires no disclosure for a valid antenuptial agreement in probate. . . .

When Manuel Moldofsky died, his will contained no provision for his wife, Sally Moldofsky, beyond a reference to an antenuptial agreement between them. Mrs. Moldofsky filed a notice of elective share after the circuit court probate division admitted the will to probate. Susan Stregack, Mr. Moldofsky's daughter and personal representative of his estate, moved to strike the notice of elective share based upon an antenuptial agreement executed by the parties, in which Mr. and Mrs. Moldofsky waived all rights in each other's estate. Mrs. Moldofsky

then filed an action in the circuit court general jurisdiction seeking cancellation of the antenuptial agreement for fraud. The probate court struck Moldofsky's motion for elective share. Following this order, the trial court dismissed on mootness and re judicata grounds the pending action to cancel the antenuptial agreement.

The district court reversed both orders on appeal. While acknowledging that section 732.702 eliminated the disclosure requirement for an antenuptial agreement to be valid in probate, the district court held that a surviving spouse could challenge an antenuptial agreement for fraudulent nondisclosure by the deceased spouse. . . .

In *Del Vecchio v. Del Vecchio,* 143 So.2d 17 (Fla.1962), this Court held that a valid antenuptial agreement must either contain fair and reasonable provisions for the spouse waiving his or her rights or else the spouse obtaining the waiver of rights must make a full and fair disclosure of assets to the other spouse. *Id.* at 20. The legislature changed this rule be enacting subsection 732.702(2), which provides: "Each spouse shall make a fair disclosure to the other of his or her estate if the agreement, contract, or waiver is executed after marriage. *No disclosure shall be required for an agreement, contract, or waiver executed before marriage.*" (Emphasis added). We held this statute constitutional against access to courts, due process, and equal protection challenges. *Estate of Roberts,* 388 So.2d 216 (Fla.1980). . . .

In the present case, . . . the district court interpreted subsection 732.702(2) to eliminate the disclosure duty before marriage, but not the duty that any disclosure be made truthfully . . .

Nondisclosure, whether fraudulent or not, is precisely what the legislature intended to eliminate from consideration on the validity of antenuptial agreements. Many older Florida residents want to marry again but also want to keep their assets separate. Often this is the desire of both parties contemplating marriage. Section 732.702 allows complete control over assets accumulated over a lifetime without fear that a partial disclosure before marriage may trigger an unwanted disposition of those assets. We cannot accept the district court decision which rewards the totally silent spouse and punishes the spouse who attempts some disclosure.

* * *

Accordingly, we quash the decision under review. . . .

BOYD, C.J., and OVERTON, ALDERMAN, and SHAW, JJ., concur.

EHRLICH, J., dissents with an opinion, in which ADKINS, J., concurs.

EHRLICH, Justice, dissenting.

I cannot disagree with the majority when it says that "nondisclosure in any form cannot invalidate an antenuptial agreement in probate proceedings of a deceased spouse," and with its

further holding that fraudulent nondisclosure does not render the surviving spouse's signature improperly obtained. However, that is not what this case is all about. . . .

The widow attacked the validity of the agreement, claiming that decedent had affirmatively misled her as to his actual assets in obtaining her assent. . . .

The agreement provides in part that decedent "is the owner of real and personal property in his own right" and that "the agreement is entered into by the parties hereto with full knowledge on the part of each of the extent and probable value of all of the property or estate of the other."

Section 732.702, Florida Statutes[10] relieved each party from making a disclosure of his or her assets, and so long as neither made any disclosure, the agreement could not be set aside, but if either party, in my opinion, made any disclosure of his or her assets, then it was incumbent upon that party to make a truthful disclosure and one that was not misleading. The widow alleged fraud on decedent's part and the statute does not protect him from that. Whether she could have proved fraud or not is another matter.

Thus, as I see it, we are not dealing with a case of nondisclosure or fraudulent nondisclosure, but one wherein one of the parties claims that there was a disclosure in fact and that fraud was practiced. She should have had an opportunity to prove her allegations of fraud.

I dissent and would approve the opinion of the district court of appeal.

ADKINS, J., concurs.

---

[10] In pertinent part the statute provides: "No disclosure shall be required for an agreement, contract, or waiver executed before a marriage."

CASE QUESTIONS

1. Is this the wave of the future, or is it aberrant?
2. Which is better, to have an inflexible rule, as here, or to have judges imbued with great discretion?

Voluntariness and Consent

Contracts are agreements that establish rights and duties between the parties to the contract. Under traditional contract law, the contracting process involves bargaining and mutual agreement. The law enforces contracts because they are presumed to be, at least at the time of contracting, mutually agreed upon. One form of attack on contractual rights and duties is based on a lack of consent or voluntariness in the bargaining process. When the wealthy groom insists on an antenuptial agreement as a prerequisite to the marriage, the voluntary agreement of the bride is questionable. Without more than this, however, the level of evidence needed to prove coercion or duress is not reached. The bride may simply refuse to agree; the temptation of all that money may be resisted. One caution may be derived from the cases: Do not show the prospective spouse the antenuptial agreement for the first time on the morning of the wedding. In the *Lutgert* case, the court found ample reason to hold that the wife's signature was not "free and voluntary."

CASE NO. 6-6

LUTGERT v. LUTGERT
338 So. 2d 1111
(Fla. Dist. Ct. App. 1976).

[The Lutgerts] kept company for approximately a year and became engaged some four weeks prior to their marriage herein at 12:30 in the early morning hours of Friday, April 30, 1965.

An understanding of the odd hour of the marriage can be had from the events which began on Monday evening of that fateful week, April 26, when appellee husband called and suggested that they be married shortly after midnight on Thursday, April 29, provided they could book passage for an extended honeymoon cruise on the SS Constitution, scheduled to sail from New York later on that same day. The wife ecstatically agreed.

On Tuesday morning, April 27, the husband advised appellant by telephone that he had succeeded in getting passage on the Constitution and that the wedding plans could go ahead. The parties met shortly thereafter and spent the rest of that day purchasing a sable stole for her and a wedding outfit for him; getting their passports straightened out; getting blood tests; arranging for a state Court of Appeals judge to marry them; acquiring the use of V.I.P. facilities, called the 'Topflight Room' of Northwest Airlines, at the O'Hare Airport in Chicago; and inviting family and friends to the wedding.

On Wednesday, April 28, the wife purchased her trousseau, after which the parties met at their jewelers to select and fit wedding rings. Thereafter, a marriage license was procured.

The following day, Thursday, April 29, is the critical date concerning the execution of the antenuptial agreement. That afternoon the parties met again at the jewelers to finalize the sizing of the wedding rings. While they were being readied the husband took the antenuptial agreement out of his pocket and for the first time presented it to appellant and asked her to sign it. She objected, saying that it indicated

lack of trust on his part and that she didn't want the marriage to start out on such a weak footing. He made light of that suggestion, proclaiming that the agreement was of no consequence anyway since they wouldn't be getting a divorce. He joked about being married for some 80 years, getting married at their age. The wife still objected; so the husband called his Chicago lawyers, Cummings and Wyman, while still at the jewelers and apparently some conversation ensued between the lawyers and the wife after the husband put her on the telephone. . . .

In any case, following the aforementioned phone call, the wife finally agreed reluctantly to sign the agreement after the husband insisted that the wedding would otherwise be called off.

Waiver of Rights

An issue sometimes explicitly discussed, and sometimes buried in problems with unfairness, disclosure, consent, or voluntariness, concerns whether the party relinquishing rights intended to do so, or even was aware of the rights relinquished. A number of cases have involved older wealthy men with legal advisors marrying young women relatively unsophisticated in financial and legal matters. Although the law generally favors the enforcement of contracts voluntarily entered, it has also long recognized that not all contracts are freely bargained for. When there is a great discrepancy in bargaining power, the courts often view the contract with suspicion. With antenuptial agreements, we have the added tradition of protective paternalism, so that a few courts have heeded claims of women who professed ignorance or confusion over the terms of the agreement.

To avoid a later challenge of this sort, the antenuptial agreement should include mention of the rights being waived:

> Each party has been advised that under the law of Illinois and many other jurisdictions, a spouse who has not made an agreement such as this one, or one of similar effect, is, upon the death of the other spouse, entitled to receive as the surviving spouse's own property, regardless of the provisions of the deceased spouse's Will, at least one-third of all property owned by the deceased spouse at the time of death, and each understands that by this agreement each of them is relinquishing this right and all rights of every sort to participate in the estate of the deceased spouse, except to the extent provided for herein.

> *Each party hereby forever releases*, relinquishes, waives, quitclaims and grants to the other party, his or her heirs, executors, administrators and assigns, *all rights of dower or curtesy, homestead, family allowance, inheritance descent, distribution, election, spouse's award, renunciation, survivorship, community property, community interest and all other now or hereafter existing, vested, contingent, or inchoate rights, titles, claims, interest and estates which he or she now has or may hereafter have under any present or future law of any state or jurisdiction.*
>
> — *In re Byrne*, 179 Ill. App. 3d 944, 947, 535 N.E.2d 14, 16 (1989) (emphasis added).

Of course, such a waiver is most meaningful when the signatory has had the benefit of independent counsel. In such cases, the court has little justification for stepping in to rescue.

This issue has tended to involve the fundamental legal status of women. Should women be treated as legally equal, or should they enjoy protection? *In re Geyer*, Case No. 6-7, expresses this conflict in the law in the opinions of the majority and the dissenters. It also represents a step backward toward requiring an understanding of the rights being waived, aligning Pennsylvania with traditional states in imposing restrictions on antenuptial agreements.

CASE NO. 6-7 The Changing Status of Women

The *Geyer* case illustrates the conflict between status and contract, but it mostly reflects two attitudes toward women: whether they should be equal or be protected by the law. A careful reading of the opinions in this case reveals a very strong difference in the perception of women by the justices in the case.

IN RE ESTATE OF GEYER
516 Pa 492, 533 A.2d 423 (1987)
Supreme Court of Pennsylvania

McDERMOTT, Justice.

[A widow attempts to take the statutory share against the husband's will and against an antenuptial agreement.

George and Rosalie had each married and been widowed twice. They met in October 1976 and were married January 1977. He was 68, she 56. He had a son, grandchildren, and greatgrandchildren; she had three adult children. He was worth $594,000 at marriage.

Their antenuptial agreement provided:]

* * *

2. That upon the death of the first party, the second party surviving him and living with him at the said time as his wife, shall be awarded, given or bequeathed a sum of Twenty Thousand ($20,000) Dollars to provide a substantial contribution to her way of living.

3. That the first party agrees with the second party and the second party agrees with the first party that in consideration of the two previous

provisions by the first party, the second party will not make any claim to or file an election to any other portion of the first party's estate. . . .

As the surviving spouse Mrs. Geyer elected to take her statutory share of her late husband's estate. 20 Pa.C.S. § 2203. The executor asserted the antenuptial agreement referred to in the will as a bar to the appellant's statutory election.

* * *

After announcing these standards the Court [in *In re Hillegass Estate,* 431 Pa. 144 244 A.2d 672 (1968)] set forth the following principles.

> (1) An Antenuptial Agreement is presumptively valid and binding upon the parties thereto.
>
> (2) *The person seeking to nullify* or avoid or circumvent the Agreement has the burden of proving the invalidity of the Agreement by clear and convincing evidence that the deceased spouse at the time of the Agreement made *neither (a) a reasonable provision for the intended spouse, nor (b) a full and fair disclosure* of his (or her) worth.
>
> (3) In evaluating the reasonableness of the provision for the survivor, such reasonableness must be determined *as of the time of the Agreement* and not by hindsight. *Reasonableness will depend upon the totality of all the facts and circumstance at the time of the Agreement,* including (a) the financial worth of the intended husband; (b) the finanacial status of the intended wife; (c) the age of the parties; (d) the number of children each has; (e) the intelligence of the parties; (f) whether the survivor aided in the accumulation of the wealth of the deceased spouse; and (g) the standard of living which the survivor

had before marriage and could reasonably expect to have during marriage.

> (4) Full and fair disclosure does not require the disclosure of the *exact* amount of his or her property.
>
> (5) Even where there is a valid Antenuptial Agreement, this does not prohibit subsequent inter vivos gifts and testamentary bequests to a surviving spouse.

* * *

The burden in this case was on Mrs. Geyer to demonstrate by clear and convincing evidence that the agreement did not make reasonable provison for her, and that it was entered into without full and fair disclosure by the decedent.[9]

* * *

The evidence at trial, which was accepted by the trial judge, indicates that the 20,000 dollar cash gift was basically equivalent to the worth of the Navy pension of the latter was reduced to a present value lump sum. Thus these two factors basically cancel out, and we are left with the question of whether the marital residence and unspecified furnishings constituted reasonable provision for an older woman who would expect to have limited opportunities for employment after the decedent's death. We think the inescapable conclusion is that this was not reasonable.

* * *

In summary, in return for her love and affection, as well as the sacrifice of her own independence, decedent conveyed to the appellant nothing more than the equivalent of a pension she already had; a property which she would almost certainly have to get rid of; and the possibility of an unspecified amount of "furnishings". We can hardly say such a one-sided bargain represents reasonable provision under the *Hillegass* standard.

* * *

We therefore think it is fair and reasonable, as well as sound judicial policy, to require that any agreement which seeks to change the duly enacted civil policy of this Commonwealth must be based on nothing less than full and fair disclosure. Such disclosure must include both the general financial pictures of the parties involved, and evidence that the parties are aware of the stautory rights that they are relinquishing.

Accordingly, the Order of the Superior Court is reversed.

* * *

NIX, Chief Justice, dissenting.

* * *

In my view it is time that we apply the traditional rules of contract to these agreements and therefor not only discard the consideration of the adequacy of the agreement but also recognize that the traditional arm's length bargaining principle of contract law is diametrically opposed to the disclosure requirement. These agreements are nothing more than contracts and should be treated as such.

* * *

I.

The law relating to antenuptial agreements initially developed at a time when the societal norm was a marriage in which the husband had a duty to provide the economic mainstay of the family while the wife was usually relegated to the management of the home and the raising of the children. Upon the death of the husband, the surviving wife traditionally was dependent upon the assets which were left by her husband for her maintenance and support. Courts, reflecting the state interest in the protection of widows in public welfare, predicted the validity of antenuptial agreements upon the adequacy of the provision made for ". . . the wife's future security and financial protection . . . ." *Barnhart v. Barnhart,* 376 Pa. 44, 53, 101 A.2d 904, 908 (1954).

* * *

The clear underlying assumption reflected in these [early] decisions was that the intended wife was in an inferior bargaining position and therefor incapable of participating in arm's length bargaining with her future husband. Thus, when an objection was made to an antenuptial agreement the court would first look to whether there was a reasonable provision made for the intended wife. . . .

II.

* * *

[A]ntenuptial agreements are normally employed by more sophisticated parties who are well aware of the effect of such an agreement. There are individuals who, sometimes as a result of prior marriages or other relationships, acquired certain property and have definite plans for its disposition after their death—plans which they do not want interfered with as a result of the new relationship. The facts of this case provide the clearest example of parties who were, in fact, aware that their impending marriage would effect their rights in the subsequent disposition of their respective property and for that reason entered into the agreement to effectuate their plans for the disposition of the property in question.

It is quite true that there is a strong policy against one spouse attempting to disinherit the other spouse after that relationship has soured. This, of course, is the reason that the surviving spouse has been given the right to elect to take against a will providing for a testamentary disposition less favorable than that provided under the intestate laws. However, it has never been suggested that the surviving spouse cannot agree to accept a share less than the statutory provision nor is it against public policy for parties to an impending marriage to make such a condition for entering into that marriage. Indeed, the Opinion Announcing the Judgment of the Court ignores that in this very case the antenuptial agreement was initiated to satisfy the prospective wife who otherwise would have been reluctant to enter into that relationship. The purposes of such antenuptial agreements are unquestionably proper and it is the duty of courts to protect those commitments. The only legitimate issue raised in this appeal was whether or not the alleged breach of the agreement was in fact a material breach so as to nullify the agreement. In resolving this question clearly the normal rules of contract would adequately protect all the parties involved.

* * *

FLAHERTY, Justice, dissenting.

I dissent. Numerous societal changes have impacted upon family units in recent times, and the law has advances accordingly to recognize the equal status of men and women in our society. No longer are women regarded as the "weaker" party in a marriage or in society generally. Accordingly, the law has discarded presumptions and protections that arose to protect women from the inferiorities and incapacities which they were perceived as having in earlier times.

Enlightened thinking has accorded equality between the sexes, and, with that equality, it has become inconsistent to preserve special protections that arose in response to perceived inequalities. . . .

The opinion authored by Mr. Justice McDermott reaches a contrary result. Instead of applying the traditional rule of contract law that binds one to the contents of agreements entered, a contrary rule is applied, which, in effect, binds one only if it is determined that the terms, and effects, of the agreement were fully understood. This is a departure from longstanding, traditional principles of contract law. . . .

---

9 We note that the Superior Court read *Hillegass* as requiring an antenuptial agreement to make reasonable provision and to be entered into after full and fair disclosure. This was a misreading of *Hillegass* which provides that an agreement can survive if *either* (but not necessarily both) of these requirements is satisfied. *See In re Estate of Kester*, 486 Pa. 349, 353 n.4, 405 A.2d 1244, 1246 n. 4 (1979).

6.5 AGREEMENTS THAT ENCOURAGE OR PROMOTE DIVORCE

In drafting an antenuptial agreement, one must keep in mind the nearly universal public policy argument used to attack antenuptial agreements when they encourage or promote the divorce of the parties to the agreement. The rationalization that was first used to circumvent attacks on agreements contemplating divorce was that they were a form of planning that was actually conducive to marital harmony. Although this argument seems a little thin, it was palatable to many judges because it left intact the notion that an agreement could still be attacked if it facilitated the *occurrence* of divorce. As a result, antenuptial agreements commonly include language such as "in the unlikely event that the marriage should fail and the parties seek divorce . . ." and include language at the beginning such as "the parties hereto, in the interests of marital harmony do hereby agree. . . ." No court is likely to approve a contract that states, "After five years of marriage, the spouses will assess the marriage to decide whether to continue. . . ."

CASE NO. 6-8

IN RE MARRIAGE OF NOGHREY
169 Cal. App. 3d 326, 215
Cal. Rptr. 153 (1985).

[Kambiz and Farima Noghrey were married for seven and one half months. The court was asked by Farima to enforce the antenuptial agreement, designated a *ketubah* in the Jewish tradition. At trial there was some dispute over the circumstances of signing this agreement shortly before the wedding, but this was not the issue on which the court placed the greatest weight. The court held that the following provision *encouraged and promoted* divorce: "I, Kambiz Noghrey, agree to settle on Farima Human the house in Sunnyvale and $500,000 or one-half my assets, whichever is greater, in the event of divorce." In the words of the decision:]

The agreement before us . . . is not of the type that seeks to define the character of property acquired after marriage nor does it seek to ensure the separate character of property acquired prior to marriage. This agreement is surely different and speaks to a wholly unrelated subject. It constitutes a promise by the husband to give the wife a very substantial amount of money and property, *but only upon the occurrence of a divorce*. . . . Farima did testify that neither she nor her parents possessed great wealth. The prospect of receiving a house and a minimum of $500,000 by obtaining the no-fault divorce available in California would menace the marriage of the best intentioned spouse.

CASE NO. 6-9   The Spendthrift Honeymooner

The *Neilson* case used the public policy argument against promoting divorce in a rather novel way—it promoted divorce by giving the wife incentive to push the husband into divorcing her.

NEILSON v. NEILSON
780 P.2d 1264 (Utah Ct. App. 1989)
Court of Appeals of Utah

JACKSON, Judge:

* * *

FACTUAL BACKGROUND

At the time of the parties' divorce, Alfred Neilson was a sixty-seven-year-old retired business executive whose primary source of income was dividends from his shares in Texas Eastern Corporation. Carleen Neilson was a thirty-one-year-old bank employee with a college degree in finance and accounting. They met and began dating in December 1985. On January 18, 1986, she was evicted from her apartment. Upon her request and his agreement, she moved into a private bedroom in his home three days later. On February 25, 1986, they executed a document entitled "Prenuptial Agreement," which was prepared by Alfred's attorney at his request.

* * *

In the event the parties are subsequently divorced in a divorce action initiated by CARLEEN, it is understood and agreed that the only assets she shall be entitled to receive from the separate property owned by ALFRED are the shares of Texas Eastern Corporation stock which [have] theretofore been transferred to her. On the other hand, if the parties are divorced in an action initiated by ALFRED, CARLEEN shall be entitled to receive, as the only property to be transferred by the divorce to her from the separate property of ALFRED, sufficient shares of Texas Eastern Corporation stock so that she will own at the time of the divorce the same number of shares of said stock as will then be owned by ALFRED.

The wedding took place on March 1, 1986, and the marriage was consummated. In accordance with the agreement, Alfred transferred 1,272 shares of stock to Carleen at that time. . . .

After a six-day trial, the court found that Alfred had paid off $8,200 worth of Carleen's premarital debts, purchased $12,592 in wedding jewelry for her, paid $9,600 for a 1978 Corvette and another $2,000 for a watch purchased by Carleen, and paid another $5,000 for miscellaneous benefits for her. Carleen was found to have expended excessive sums of Alfred's money for her own use and benefit, without Alfred's knowledge or authorization. These unauthorized purchases overdrew Alfred's checking account by $14,000 after completely consuming his quarterly dividend check in the amount of $16,000, requiring him to sell some stock to pay those expenses and the taxes owed for the sale of the stock. While this action was pending, Carleen sold 372 shares of the stock she had received when the parties married. At the time of the decree, the proceeds from that

sale consisted of $2,000 in cash and a $10,000 time certificate of deposit in her name.

The trial court denied Alfred's petition for annulment and, with no objection from either party, treated his complaint as one for divorce, which it awarded to him on the basis of mental cruelty and irreconcilable differences. Although the trial court specifically found that the prenuptial agreement was entered into without any fraud, duress, or undue influence, it nonetheless concluded that the entire agreement was void and unenforceable as violative of public policy "for the reason that it encourages conduct designed to facilitate the breakup of a marital relationship." Alternatively, the court concluded that consideration for the prenuptial contract, a "normal marital relationship," had failed. The court then, in the exercise of its equitable powers, made a distribution of property. In addition to personal property she brought to the marriage, Carleen was awarded the following $35,600 worth of property she received during the marriage: the jewelry; the 1978 Corvette; the certificate of deposit; and the $2,000 in cash remaining from her sale of stock. Alfred was awarded his remaining personal property, including the 900 stock shares previously transferred to Carleen that she did not sell during the parties' separation. Finally, Carleen was ordered to pay her attorneys $20,000 as reasonable attorney fees.

PUBLIC POLICY

We first consider the trial court's ruling that the prenuptial agreement was void and unenforceable because it violates public policy. Under the traditional view commonly held until two decades ago, a premarital contract that even addressed the contingency of the parties divorcing in the future (e.g., by providing for a certain property division or levels of alimony or child support) was unenforceable in its entirety in all states as a contravention of the public policy favoring marriage:

Some courts believed that such agreements encouraged divorce. The conventional wisdom was that if the husband were permitted to limit the amount of property and alimony the wife could receive at divorce, he would have an economic incentive to obtain a divorce. . . .

* * *

Even in states where the traditional view of across-the-board unenforceability has been judicially or legislatively rejected, however, there are still several limits drawn from general contract law that are imposed on the enforceability of premarital contracts. These include requirements that they be voluntary, supported by consideration, made by competent parties, in compliance with any applicable statute of frauds, and consistent with public policy.

* * *

The *Restatement* standard employs a "reasonableness" factor: "A promise that tends unreasonably to encourage divorce or separation is unenforceable on grounds of public policy." *Restatement (Second) of Contracts* § 190(2) (1981). Other jurisdictions have expressly or implicitly adopted this standard as the public policy limitation on the enforceability of provisions in a premarital agreement that settle the parties' property rights upon divorce. [The court concluded that the antenuptial agreement, whereby the wife was entitled to one half of husband's stock, was unenforceable as a matter of public policy because it unreasonably tended to encourage divorce by providing the wife with an incentive to induce the husband to seek dissolution.]

CASE QUESTIONS

1. If antenuptial agreements encouraging divorce are unenforceable, would this category logically include an agreement that might encourage the wife to make the husband divorce her?
2. In considering question 1, does it seem that Carleen Neilson's post-honeymoon spending spree was designed to push Alfred to the point of divorce?
3. Alfred and Carleen knew each other less than three months before they married. She was 36 years younger than he. Immediately after marrying she went on an irresponsible spending spree, and their marriage lasted only a few months. Does this set of facts create a picture of a young golddigger and a gullible sugar daddy? Did this encourage the court to stretch the grounds for invalidating an antenuptial agreement?

6.6   SUPPORT PROVISIONS

Many states have balked at antenuptial agreements that attempt to establish support payments in case of divorce. The courts often consider this a province of the law not amenable to private agreement. (Note the provision in the Uniform Premarital Agreement Act, § 3(b), in appendix 6B.) One recurrent aspect in such cases is the fear that a divorced spouse and children will become recipients of public welfare, while the beneficiary of the antenuptial agreement's limitations maintains an affluent lifestyle.

Clearly, a reasonable provision for each spouse can allay the fears of the court, although in some states limitations on alimony may threaten the validity of the agreement. At present, it seems ill-advised to attempt to limit child support payments in case of divorce. As we shall see in subsequent chapters, children in divorce suits must be treated differently from the parents. Minor children may not represent themselves, nor are they parties to the agreement. The welfare of the children depends very much on the benevolence of the court and the law. It is unlikely that any judge would look favorably on an agreement that prospectively attempts to limit the financial responsibility of parents.

SUMMARY

Antenuptial agreements are contracts setting the terms of the marital contract. They have increased in popularity in recent years, although marriage settlements have an ancient history. In the practice of law, the important features of antenuptial agreements are concerned with the distribution of property at death or divorce. At first, antenuptial agreements were approved for property distributions at death, but an increasing number of states have approved contracts that spell out property rights at divorce. Jurisdictions that approve antenuptial agreements have tended, in recent years, to treat them in most respects like other contracts. A contract's validity may be challenged on traditional contract grounds such as voluntariness, fraud, and conscionability. Some jurisdictions, however, have been reluctant to treat antenuptial agreements like other contracts, expressing traditional public policy concerns for the stability of the family and the protection of its members. Some courts treat these agreements as if they were arm's-length transactions, like other contracts, whereas other courts impose a fiduciary relationship between prospective spouses, or at least recognize that the parties are not usually contracting as objective business persons.

A major feature of antenuptial agreements, like other aspects of family law, is the changing status of women. When women are considered independent and legally equal, the protective paternalism of traditional law seems inappropriate. Nevertheless, many courts have expressed concern over the fact that social and economic inequality continue to disadvantage women.

QUESTIONS

1. Why did the courts recognize antenuptial agreements in widowhood before they were recognized in divorce?
2. Why is it advisable to draft an antenuptial agreement with clauses satisfying the most stringent requirements of other states?
3. Who should consider drafting an antenuptial agreement?
4. How do antenuptial agreements differ from other contracts?

5. Why should an attorney avoid mention of child support in an antenuptial agreement?

6. Why should women in particular be concerned about having antenuptial agreements?

7. What is the difference between an antenuptial agreement and a premarital contract?

8. What case in which state in what year is often credited with starting the trend toward enforcing antenuptial agreements at divorce?

9. Under what circumstances would a resulting trust be appropriate in relation to a valid antenuptial agreement?

10. How has the movement for women's rights changed attitudes toward antenuptial agreements?

EXERCISES

Answer the questions according to the law of your state.

1. Can a premarital agreement be attacked when executed in close proximity to the wedding? 53 A.L.R.4th 85.

2. What is the policy with regard to "promoting" or encouraging divorce? 53 A.L.R.4th 161.

3. Must the premarital agreement be in writing, signed by the parties?

4. Is "fairness" required? (Compare *In re Geyer.*) 53 A.L.R.4th 161.

5. Can conduct during the marriage constitute abandonment or waiver of rights in an antenuptial agreement? 56 A.L.R.4th 998.

6. What degree of disclosure, if any, is required? 3 A.L.R.5th 394.

7. Is the fairness of an antenuptial agreement judged by the circumstances at the time the contract was made or at the time of divorce? 53 A.L.R.4th 161.

8. Can the lack of legal representation be grounds for avoiding a premarital agreement? 53 A.L.R.4th 85.

APPENDIX 6A

Uniform Premarital Agreement Act (1983)

§ 1. Definitions.

As used in this Act:

(1) "Premarital agreement" means an agreement between prospective spouses made in contemplation of marriage and to be effective upon marriage.

(2) "Property" means an interest, present or future, legal or equitable, vested or contingent, in real or personal property, including income and earnings.

§ 2. Formalities.

A premarital agreement must be in writing and signed by both parties. It is enforceable without consideration.[1]

§ 3. Content.

(a) Parties to a premarital agreement may contract with respect to:

(1) the rights and obligations of each of the parties in any of the property of either or both of them whenever and wherever acquired or located;

(2) the right to buy, sell, use, transfer, exchange, abandon, lease, consume, expend, assign, create a security interest in, mortgage, encumber, dispose of, or otherwise manage and control property;

(3) the disposition of property upon separation, marital dissolution, death, or the occurrence or nonoccurrence of any other event;

(4) the modification or elimination of spousal support;

(5) the making of a will, trust, or other arrangement to carry out the provisions of the agreement;

(6) the ownership rights in and disposition of the death benefit from a life insurance policy;

(7) the choice of law governing the construction of the agreement; and

(8) any other matter, including their personal rights and obligations, not in violation of public policy or a statute imposing a criminal penalty.

(b) The right of a child to support may not be adversely affected by a premarital agreement.[2]

§ 4. Effect of Marriage.

A premarital agreement becomes effective upon marriage.

§ 5. Amendment, Revocation.

After marriage, a premarital agreement may be amended or revoked only by a written agreement signed by the parties. The amended agreement or the revocation is enforceable without consideration.

§ 6. Enforcement.

(a) A premarital agreement is not enforceable if the party against whom enforcement is sought proves that:

(1) that party did not execute the agreement voluntarily; or

(2) the agreement was unconscionable when it was executed and, before execution of the agreement, that party:[3]

(i) was not provided a fair and reasonable disclosure of the property or financial obligations of the other party;

(ii) did not voluntarily and expressly waive, in writing, any right to disclosure of the property or financial obligations of the other party beyond the disclosure provided; and

(iii) did not have, or reasonably could not have had, an adequate knowledge of the property or financial obligations of the other party.

(b) If a provision of a premarital agreement modifies or eliminates spousal support and that modification or elimination causes one party to the agreement to be eligible for support under a program of public assistance at the time of separation or marital dissolution, a court, notwithstanding the terms of the agreement, may require the other party to provide support to the extent necessary to avoid that eligibility.

(c) An issue of unconscionability of a premarital agreement shall be decided by the court as a matter of law.

§ 7. Enforcement: Void Marriage.

If a marriage is determined to be void, an agreement that would otherwise have been a premarital agreement is enforceable only to the extent necessary to avoid an inequitable result.

[§§ 8 and 9 omitted.]

§ 10. Short Title.

This [Act] may be cited as the Uniform Premarital Agreement Act.

---

1 Marriage contracts traditionally fell within the Statute of Frauds, which requires a writing.

2 This provision expresses appropriate concern for the effect of an agreement on subsequent child support. Children are not parties to the agreement and the state has a legitimate concern in protecting their interests.

3 Although disclosure is provided by the Act, problems with disclosure do not impede enforcement of the contract unless its provisions are manifestly unfair, i.e., "unconscionable."

APPENDIX 6B

Antenuptial Agreement (New York)

Source: *New York Matrimonial Practice,* Willard H. DaSilva, The Practice Systems Library, The Lawyers Co-operative Publishing Co., Rochester, N.Y. (1990).

AGREEMENT made as of this _____ day of _____, 19____, between _____ ("Mathilda"), residing at _____, New York _____, and _____ ("Algernon"), residing at _____, New York _____.

WITNESSETH:

Whereas, each of the parties has known the other for a period of time, is fully satisfied with the disclosure[1] of the financial circumstances of the other, and desires to make an agreement regarding his and her property rights in consideration of the marriage to each other, and

Whereas, each party acknowledges that the other may hereafter acquire by gift and inheritance, as well as through professional endeavor and from other sources, assets and income of value, and

Whereas, each of the parties has assets and earnings, or earnings potential, sufficient to provide for his or her own maintenance and support in a proper and acceptable standard of living without the necessity of financial contributions by the other,[2] and each of the parties is aware of the hazards and risks of the continuance of earnings and the changes in assets and liabilities of the other and of the possibility of substantially changed financial circumstances of the other with the result that the earnings and/or net worth of one party is or may be substantially different from those of the other party, and

Whereas, except as otherwise herein set forth, each of the parties desires to own, hold, acquire, and dispose of property now and in the future and subsequent to their marriage to each other with the same freedom as though unmarried and to dispose of said property during their respective lifetimes or upon death or upon any other termination of the marriage without restriction or limitation in accordance with his and her own desires, and

Whereas, except as otherwise herein set forth, it is the intention of each of the parties by entering into this agreement to determine unilaterally what property, now and in the future, shall be his or her own separate property and that all of the property of each, however acquired or held, shall be free from any consideration as marital property, community property, quasi-community property or any other form of marital or community property,[3] as those terms are used and understood in any jurisdiction, including but not limited to the State of New York,

NOW, THEREFORE, in consideration of the marriage of each party to the other and the mutual promises and covenants[4] herein, the parties have mutually agreed as follows:

1. *Present property.*[5] All of the property, real, personal, and mixed, which each party has previously acquired and now holds in his or her name or possession shall be and continue to remain the sole and separate property of that person, together with all future appreciation, increases, and other changes in value of that property and irrespective of the contributions (if any) which either party might have made or may hereafter make to said property or to the marriage, directly or indirectly.

2. *Future property.* All of the property, real, personal, or mixed, which each party may hereafter acquire in his or her own name or possession shall be and remain the sole and separate property of that person, together with all future appreciation, increases, and other changes in value of that property

147

and irrespective of the contributions (if any) which either party may make to said property or to the marriage, directly or indirectly. Notwithstanding the foregoing, any property which is a gift from one party to the other shall remain the sole and separate property of the donee of the gift; and all wedding presents given to both parties shall be deemed jointly owned by the parties wherein each shall hold an undivided one-half interest.

3. *Joint property.*[6] Any property, real, personal, or mixed, which shall now or hereafter be held in the joint names of the parties shall be owned in accordance with the kind of joint ownership as title is held, and if there is no other designation, shall be held equally by the parties with such survivorship rights (if any) as may be specifically designated by the title ownership or as may be implied or be derived by operation of law other than the operation of the so-called equitable distribution law or community property or any similar law of any jurisdiction involving marital property, community property, quasi-community property, or any other form of marital or community property.

4. *Life insurance.*[7] From and after the marriage of the parties, Algernon shall maintain at his own expense a policy or policies of life insurance on his life having death benefits payable in the sum of not less than $250,000 for the benefit of Mathilda until the earlier occurrence of the death of either party or the remarriage of Mathilda (as "remarriage" is hereinafter defined), and he will not encumber said insurance whereby the death benefits which are actually payable shall be less than $250,0000. Algernon shall furnish proof of his compliance with this paragraph upon the reasonable request of Mathilda, but not more often than annually; and Mathilda, in addition, is authorized to obtain direct confirmation from any insurance carrier or employer through which said policy or policies are issued or administered.

5. *Estate rights.* Except as otherwise herein set forth, each party hereby releases, waives, and relinquishes any right or claim of any nature whatsoever in the property of the other or otherwise, now or hereafter acquired, and, without limitation, expressly forever waives any right or claim which he or she may have or hereafter acquire, whether as the spouse of the other or otherwise, under the present or future laws of any jurisdiction: (a) to share in the estate of the other party upon the death of the other party; and (b) to act as executor or administrator of the estate of the other or as trustee, personal representative, or in any fiduciary capacity with respect to the estate of the other. All rights which either party may acquire in the other's estate by virtue of the marriage, including but not limited to rights of set-off in [applicable state law], all distributive shares in [applicable state law], and all rights of election in [applicable state law], as such laws may now exist or hereafter be changed, and any similar or

other provision of law in this or any other jurisdiction are hereby waived by each party.

6. *Wills.*[8] Nothing in this agreement shall prevent or limit either party from hereafter making provisions for the other by Last Will and Testament: (a) to inherit from the estate of the other; and/or (b) to serve in any fiduciary capacity, in which event the provisions thus made in said Last Will and Testament shall control.

7. *Primary residence.*[9] In the event that Algernon should predecease Mathilda during the time when they are married to each other (as "married" is hereinafter defined), Mathilda shall have the right to continue to reside in their primary residence until the occurrence of her remarriage; provided, however, that Mathilda shall pay all expenses of every kind and nature in connection with said residence (including but not limited to all repairs, whether ordinary, extraordinary, structural, or otherwise), except only for the payment of real estate taxes and, if the primary residence is a condominium or cooperative apartment, the maintenance or common charges, as the case may be, which real estate taxes and maintenance charges or common charges, as applicable, shall be paid for by Algernon's estate as an obligation of the estate. If the primary residence is rented and occupied by the parties under a lease (not a proprietary lease of a cooperative apartment), Mathilda shall have the right to cause said lease to be transferred to her sole name, including any rent security deposited under said lease, without payment to Algernon's estate, provided that said request is made in writing to Algernon's estate representatives within ninety days after his death. This paragraph shall apply only to the primary residence of the parties and not to any other residence which they or either of them may own at the time of Algernon's death.

8. *Support.*[10] (a) In the event that the parties shall cease to be married for any reason other than Algernon's death (as "married" is hereinafter defined), Algernon, or his estate, shall pay to Mathilda as and for her support and maintenance the sum of $500 per week, commencing as of the first Friday after the parties shall cease to be married (by reason of death or otherwise) and continuing on each successive Friday thereafter. Said payments shall continue for one week for each full week that the parties are married, but in no event shall said payments continue for a period of more than 260 weeks, whereby said payments shall automatically and without further notice cease. By way of example, if the parties are married for 210 full weeks, a total of 210 weekly payments shall be made; if they are married for $20\frac{1}{2}$ weeks, 20 weekly payments shall be made. Notwithstanding the foregoing, all of said weekly payments shall sooner cease upon the earliest happening of: (i) the death of Mathilda; (ii) the remarriage of Mathilda; or (iii) the fifth anniversary date after the date when payments are required to be commenced. This paragraph shall not be construed

as an indication of any financial need on the part of Mathilda, but rather an expression by Algernon of his desire to make a contribution to the future life of Mathilda under the circumstances and provisions herein set forth.

(b) In the event that Algernon shall die while the parties are married to each other (as "married" is hereinafter defined), Algernon's estate shall pay to Mathilda as and for her support and maintenance the sum of $500 per week, commencing as of the first Friday after his death and continuing on each successive Friday thereafter until the earliest happening of: (i) the death of Mathilda; or (ii) the remarriage of Mathilda; or (iii) the fifth anniversary date after the date when payments are required to be commenced.

9. *Definitions.* The following definitions shall apply to the respective expressions whenever used in this agreement:

(a) "Remarriage" as used everywhere in this agreement shall be deemed a remarriage of Mathilda, regardless of whether said remarriage shall be void or voidable or terminated by divorce or annulment or otherwise and shall also be deemed to include circumstances whereby Mathilda shall live with an unrelated person in a husband-wife relationship (irrespective of whether or not they hold themselves out as such) for a continuous period of 60 days or for a period or periods of time aggregating 120 days or more on a noncontinuous, or interrupted, basis in any 18-month period.

(b) The time during which the parties are "married," or the period of the "marriage" of the parties, as used everywhere in this agreement, shall constitute the period of time commencing with the ceremonial marriage of the parties to each other and continuing until the earliest happening of any of the following events: (i) the commencement of a matrimonial action (as "matrimonial action" is presently defined by the [applicable state law] or any similar action or proceeding in any other jurisdiction; (ii) the divorce or legal separation (by decree or judgment or by agreement) of the parties; or (iii) the physical separation of the parties wherein either or both of the parties have commenced to live separate and apart from the other with the intent not thereafter to live together, regardless of whether that intent is expressed in writing, orally or otherwise; or (iv) the death of either party.

10. *Disclosure.* Each party has been apprised of the right to obtain further disclosure of the financial circumstances of the other party and is satisfied with the disclosure made. Each party expressly waives the right to any further financial disclosure and acknowledges that said waiver is made with the full benefit of legal counsel and knowledge of the legal consequences thereof and that neither party properly cannot, and shall not, subsequently assert that this agreement should be impaired or invalidated by reason of any lack of financial disclosure or lack of understanding or of fraud, duress, or coercion. Without limiting the generality of the foregoing, Algernon represents that his present net worth is in excess of $_____ and that his annual income is in excess of $_____, which representation admittedly is not all-inclusive and which is not intended to be relied upon by either party.[11]

11. *General provisions.* This agreement shall be construed as an agreement made and to be performed in the State of New York and cannot be changed, or any of its terms waived, except by a writing signed and acknowledged by both parties. Each party hereby consents to the personal jurisdiction of the State of New York in the event of any dispute or question regarding this agreement. Each party acknowledges receipt of a fully executed copy of this agreement, has had an opportunity to read it, and understands the same after consultation with independent counsel and is fully satisfied with the disclosure made of all of the financial circumstances of the other party. The paragraph captions in this agreement are for the purpose of convenience only and are not a part of this agreement.

12. Each party has been separately represented by an attorney[12] of his or her own choice. Mathilda has been represented by _____ [insert name and address of attorney], and Algernon has been represented by _____ [insert name and address of attorney] in connection with the negotiation, making, and execution of this agreement.

IN WITNESS WHEREOF the parties, for themselves, their heirs, next-of-kin, representatives, and assigns have executed these presents prior to their marriage to each other on the day and year first above written.

_____ L.S.
[Type name of woman]

_____ L.S.
[Type name of man]

WITNESS

_____
, Esq.

STATE OF NEW YORK   }ss.:
COUNTY OF   }

On the _____ day of _____, 19____,
before me _____ personally came _____,
to me known and known to be the individual described in and who executed the foregoing instrument, and she did duly acknowledge to me that she executed the same.

_____
Notary Public, State of New York

WITNESS

_____

, Esq.

STATE OF NEW YORK   } ss.:
COUNTY OF   }

   On the _____ day of _____, 19____,
before me _____ personally came _____,
to me known and known to be the individual described in and who executed the foregoing instrument, and she did duly acknowledge to me that he executed the same.

_____
Notary Public, State of New York

_____

1   A recitation of disclosure may be essential or merely desirable. Actual disclosure should accompany its recital.

2   This sentence suggests that the sample antenuptial agreement contemplates affluent, mature couples.

3   The all-inclusive language covering marital property contemplates emigration to another state or a change in New York law.

4   *Consideration, promises,* and *covenants* indicate language of an enforceable contract and indicate the intent to make a binding contract (especially if the parties received independent legal counsel).

5   Paragraphs 1 and 2 specify separate (rather than marital) property.

6   Any marriage inevitably acquires marital property in some form. Paragraph 3 provides for the specific category of joint property with right of survivorship. Regardless of whether such property were to be classified as marital or separate, the survivorship makes it the equivalent of marital property and it should not be the subject of dispute for failure to label it.

7   This provision is optional, but it is an excellent device to keep separate property while still providing for a surviving spouse. Either or both spouses could purchase life insurance.

8   Although an antenuptial agreement typically waives the rights of the surviving spouse, the parties are free to be more generous in their wills than in their antenuptial agreement.

9   An optional expression of care.

10   Specificity avoids ambiguity even if it sounds a little like an employment contract.

11   Paragraph 10 should settle subsequent attacks based on nondisclosure, assuming Algernon has disclosed accurately in good faith.

12   Many antenuptial agreements have been attacked for lack of legal counsel on one side.

CHAPTER 7
Postnuptial and Separation Agreements

Ivana Trump

Ivana Trump was the wife of real estate and casino developer Donald Trump of New York. She managed the Plaza Hotel for Trump during their marriage. Once asked what her salary was, Donald Trump responded that Ivana (an ex-model) could buy all the dresses she wanted.

Upon the commencement of an action for divorce, Ivana demanded significantly more than her wardrobe. A flurry of agreements during the divorce action and afterwards ensued. This chapter examines both postnuptial and separation agreements.

— Courtesy AP/Wide World Photos.

The marriage didn't work out but the separation is great.

Liz Smith

OUTLINE

7.1 POSTNUPTIAL AGREEMENTS DISTINGUISHED FROM ANTENUPTIAL AGREEMENTS

7.2 RECITAL OF CONSIDERATION

7.3 KINDS OF POSTMARITAL AGREEMENTS

7.4 SEPARATION AND SEPARATION AGREEMENTS

7.5 MERGER AND INCORPORATION: HOW DOES THE AGREEMENT FIT INTO THE DECREE?

7.6 MODIFICATION

SUMMARY

7.1 POSTNUPTIAL AGREEMENTS DISTINGUISHED FROM ANTENUPTIAL AGREEMENTS

At first glance, postnuptial agreements would seem to be governed by the same rules as antenuptial agreements, with the difference simply terminological—"post-" means *after* rather than *before*, so *postnuptial agreements* are those concluded after the wedding has taken place. The wedding, however, makes all the difference. An antenuptial agreement is really a marriage contract in which the bride and groom are setting the terms of the contract, rather than leaving them to the rights and duties that would otherwise be imposed by law. By virtue of the marriage ceremony itself, in the absence of an antenuptial agreement, the marriage contract has been sealed and legal bonds, duties, and rights have been created.

A postnuptial agreement therefore attempts to change a contract already in existence, albeit a contract the terms of which are created by the law. (Parties may also attempt to change the terms of an antenuptial agreement

153

through a postnuptial agreement.) Changing the terms of a contract after it has been made invokes different sets of rules than those employed to validate a contract in the first place, although some basic flaws, such as fraud or duress, apply in both situations.

One of the problems with postnuptial agreements lies in the concept of *consideration*. Under the classical model of contract law, consideration is required for contractual validity. Consideration remains a somewhat cloudy concept, but it is often used to denote the exchange of something of value. The easiest example is a sale of goods: At the grocery store, the patron pays money (something of value) for groceries (something of value). Value is somewhat obscure in a marriage, but love and affection, companionship, a duty to support, and other features of the marriage relationship are sufficient consideration to validate a marriage contract. It is traditional in our society for bride and groom to exchange vows (promises) at the altar.

In postnuptial agreements, consideration seems to be lacking. If, for example, the wife agrees to take less than her lawful share in case of the death of her husband, what has she received of value to compensation her for this promise? Although the courts do not always address this issue in a direct discussion of consideration, the fundamental issue of one spouse forgoing a right without anything in return has clearly concerned judges ruling on the validity of postnuptial agreements. In addition, whereas antenuptial agreements are treated in some jurisdictions as arm's-length bargains, postnuptial agreements are assumed to be negotiated by persons heavily emotionally involved and, depending on the circumstances, often in a relationship of great trust or dependence. This has encouraged the courts to view the contract as well as the concept of consideration with heightened scrutiny.

CASE NO. 7-1   Failure of Consideration

The *Dexter* case demonstrates the consideration problem with regard to postnuptial agreements. It does so, however, in distinguishing a postnuptial agreement from a separation agreement.

DEXTER v. DEXTER
7 Va. App. 36, 371 S.E.2d 816 (1988)
Court of Appeals of Virginia

KOONTZ, Chief Judge.

* * *

I. Factual Background

The parties were married on March 1, 1975, shortly after divorcing their prior spouses. No children were born to this marriage. The

disputed support agreement was executed on March 6, 1975. [Final decree of divorce entered in 1986.]

* * *

IV. The Support Agreement Issue

We turn now to the issue of the validity of the agreement. In pertinent part it provides: that the parties were married on March 1, 1975, that the wife was receiving $1,000 per month spousal support from her prior husband, that the parties are happily married and expect to continue to be married, and that "husband desires to insure wife's continued support and well-being; and therefore, agrees that if the marriage between husband and wife is terminated by separation of [sic] divorce, husband will commence to pay wife $1,000 per month from the date of separation or divorce." This agreement was executed on March 6, 1976, five days after the parties were married. They separated on October 4, 1983.

We agree with the chancellor that this postnuptial agreement was invalid for lack of consideration by Mrs. Dexter. Once married to Mr. Dexter, she no longer had a right to support from her prior husband and consequently she neither forfeited a right nor made a mutual promise in exchange for Mr. Dexter's promise of support. Accordingly, we hold the chancellor did not err in ruling the agreement invalid.

The parties cite numerous familiar cases concerning prenuptial and postnuptial agreements in which our Supreme Court has approved or disapproved such agreements based primarily on the principles of public policy to foster marriage and to invalidate agreements that have as their object to encourage or facilitate separation or divorce.

With the enactment of the Virginia Premarital Agreement Act, Code §§ 20-147 to 154, effective July 1, 1986, parties are permitted to contract with respect to, *inter alia,* spousal support and such contracts are enforceable without consideration. In 1987, Code § 20-155 was enacted to permit married persons to enter such contracts to the same extent as prospective spouses, "except that such marital agreements shall become effective immediately upon their execution." Thus, since the present case was decided by the trial court the legislature has made a significant change in the law

concerning marital agreements and specifically, consideration is not required. Code § 20-149.

In our view, these legislative changes were forecast in *Capps* [*v. Capps,* 216 Va. 378, 219 S.E.2d 901 (1975)]. There, the Supreme Court stated:

> The phrase "public policy" is vague and not susceptible to fixed rules. . . . However, we have said that it is the policy of the law " 'to foster and protect marriage, to encourage the parties to live together and to prevent separation, marriage being the foundation of the family and of society, without which there would be neither civilization nor progress. . . .' " It is because of this policy that we have held agreements, either antenuptial or post-nuptial, between husbands and wives, void when they tend to encourage or facilitate separation or divorce. However, we have also said that property settlements, when entered into by competent parties upon valid consideration for lawful purposes, are favored in the law and that we are therefore "averse to holding contracts unenforceable on the ground of public policy unless their illegality is clear and certain." Thus, the general rule is that agreements between husband and wife relating to the adjustment of property rights, even though in contemplation of divorce, are not violative of established public policy unless collusive or made to facilitate a separation or aid in procuring a divorce. 216 Va. at 380, 219 S.E.2d at 903 (citations omitted).

Subsequently in *Cooley* [*v. Cooley*], the Court continued the trend of encouraging marital settlements and upheld a postnuptial agreement for spousal support as not having been entered into for the purpose of encouraging or facilitating separation or divorce. The Court noted that when the agreement was first executed, the parties had experienced marital difficulties for three years and recognized that a separation was unavoidable, and when it was later amended, grounds for divorce already existed. 220 Va. at 752-53, 263 S.E.2d at 52.

... [F]or approximately seven years Mrs. Dexter held an agreement executed during the honeymoon days of her marriage, when no separation was contemplated, no grounds for divorce existed, and which surely, if held to be valid, would have facilitated her seeking a divorce to commence the payment of the specified support to her. Thus, we do not disagree with the trial court's determination that the agreement promoted or facilitated divorce and was invalid. . . .

7.2 RECITAL OF CONSIDERATION

To forestall later attacks on the validity of the agreement, an express statement of consideration may be good practice. These contracts are subject to public policy as viewed by the court at a particular time and place. As they are the subject of family law cases typically heard in equity, where the judge (chancellor) exercises great discretion, a clear statement of exchange of value is necessary: "In return for Husband's one-half interest in the marital residence, Wife waives any interest in Husband's retirement benefits." Such recitals not only indicate reciprocal exchanges, they also show that these marital interests were considered, negotiated, and agreed upon. Assuming both spouses retained legal counsel, the court should be disinclined to find the agreement unreasonable.

7.3 KINDS OF POSTMARITAL AGREEMENTS

Dexter, Case No. 7-1, demonstrates that the labels applied to postnuptial agreements imply different results. The legal issues of postnuptial agreements may be classified with the labels used. For example, a *property settlement agreement,* often called a *marital settlement agreement,* is executed when a couple has accepted the inevitability of divorce and has negotiated an agreement, commonly through attorneys, to specify the terms of the divorce. Some jurisdictions may refer to this simply as a *separation agreement.* Literally, a separation agreement provides for the terms of a marital separation, which need not result in divorce and was formerly more common when most jurisdictions did not grant divorces without fault and divorce itself carried stigma. Separation agreements without reference to divorce may ultimately become part of a divorce suit. Whether the parties were contemplating divorce may not be obvious from the document itself, as most courts have been reluctant to enforce contracts promoting or encouraging divorce and lawyers are understandably cautious about reference to divorce. For this reason, reference to divorce may be conspicuously absent from separation agreements.

In determining whether public policy forbids the enforcement of an agreement "promotive" of the dissolution of a particular marriage, we must look not solely to the terms of the agreement but also to the viability of the marriage in question at the time the contract was entered into. If the marriage had so deteriorated that legitimate grounds for divorce existed and if there was little hope of reconciliation, the dissolution of such a marriage is not contrary to public policy. Divorce is often, in fact, the preferred solution.

— *Glickman v. Collins,* 13 Cal. 3d 852, 533 P.2d 204,
120 Cal. Rptr. 76 (1975)

Postnuptial agreements theoretically include all of the agreements previously mentioned, but the phrase is commonly used today to distinguish agreements that do not contemplate separation or divorce. These resemble antenuptial agreements in the sense that they are executed at a time when the marriage has not failed. Sometimes they are in fact the equivalent of antenuptial agreements, intended to set the terms of the marriage but not executed in time for the wedding. Some postnuptial agreements may be tailored to changed circumstances of the marriage—one of the spouses may unexpectedly become the custodian of children by a prior marriage, or one may have achieved unexpected financial success (or disaster)—that make prior agreements or the impositions of the law unfair or impracticable. (Note that in some jurisdictions, the reasonableness of an antenuptial agreement is interpreted according to the circumstances prevailing when it is to be enforced.)

To summarize these confusing terms, *postnuptial* agreements are agreements made between spouses setting the terms of their relationship. One kind of postnuptial agreement is the *separation agreement*, which may be used when the couple has or plans immediately to permanently separate. One kind of separation agreement is the *property settlement*, which may be used when the couple plan to dissolve the marriage. The terminology is further confused by a lack of uniformity of usage among the various jurisdictions, as well as by a lack of uniformity of attitude toward the validity and enforcement of the agreements among the various jurisdictions.

A true postnuptial agreement—that is, one contracted while the marriage is still viable—is the most vulnerable, subject to the infirmities of antenuptial agreements as well as lacking consideration. When an attorney drafts such a document, it may be anticipated that many judges would be receptive to attacks on its validity. It ought to be fair and reasonable, and its validity would be aided by some expression of its justification.

7.4 SEPARATION AND SEPARATION AGREEMENTS

Jurisdictions that accept separation agreements for separation and divorce may show the same reluctance as did the Virginia court in *Dexter* to classify an agreement as postnuptial and thereby promoting divorce. To qualify as a bona fide separation agreement, the marriage must be on the verge of divorce or permanent separation. At that point, public policy arguments against promoting divorce surrender to the reality of a failed marriage and the need to resolve the problems resulting from the breakup. (Nor should we forget that disallowing planning by the parties ultimately forces the court to resolve the details of the breakup.)

A defensible separation agreement requires an actual separation of the spouses with the intent to live permanently separate or divorced. In short, husband and wife should no longer act as husband and wife. In this context, the separation agreement appears as a property settlement negotiated as the final step in the dissolution of marriage.

CASE NO. 7-2

Just how vulnerable the separation agreement is may be seen from a New Jersey case in which the spouses reconciled largely because the husband was injured in an auto accident a month after separation. They lived as husband and wife for two more years before finally seeking a divorce. In *Brazina* we see how policy and law interact. Traditional policy notions of marital duties conflict with modern policies of equality, which in turn grant couples freedom to guide their destinies. Nevertheless, the policy which asserts that the law and the courts must protect the stability of the family remains paramount. The concept of consideration is also jettisoned.

BRAZINA v. BRAZINA
233 N.J. Super. 145, 558 A.2d 69
(Ch. Ct. 1989)

We must next determine what effect, if any, does the reconciliation have upon a property settlement agreement entered into at or about the time of the separation. Earlier cases generally held that reconciliation had no effect on the validity of a property settlement agreement on the theory that:

> the promise to resume cohabitation is not, without more, even legal consideration. Unless the wife had legal justification for living separate and apart from her husband, she was under legal duty to resume cohabitation with him, notwithstanding the separation agreement, whenever he should request it.

However, that archaic philosophy is no longer followed and the modern view is that the *executory* provisions of a property settlement agreement are deemed to be abrogated by a subsequent reconciliation of the parties, unless it can be shown by the party seeking to enforce the agreement that the parties intended otherwise, but that the executed provisions of a property settlement agreement are unaffected by the reconciliation. The philosophy underpinning the theory of abrogation is that, since the policy of courts is to encourage and strengthen the bond of marriage, it is the presumed intent of the parties at the time of the reconciliation to resume the marital relationship in all respects and abrogate any prior agreements restricting or inhibiting the rights of one of the spouses, unless they indicate otherwise at the time of the reconciliation.

7.5 MERGER AND INCORPORATION: HOW DOES THE AGREEMENT FIT INTO THE DECREE?

Negotiating a contract between two unhappy spouses to end their marriage is the unpleasant task of the attorney. Unlike many other contract negotiations, the end result pleases neither side but is grudgingly accepted as a necessary evil. Nor may we expect the level of good will in performance of the terms of the agreement that come routinely in other situations. The risk of nonperformance is very high.

One other feature of property settlement agreements differs from other contracts: The agreement is ordinarily submitted to the court for court approval. The form, nature, and extent of that approval has a major impact on the future course of performance, the remedies for nonperformance, and the means to require enforcement of the terms of the agreement. One major aspect of divorce practice is planning and obtaining the divorce; the other is dealing with noncompliance with the terms of the divorce.

The parties go to the court with a contract. What they leave the court with depends upon the contract and the court. The court is asked in some way to recognize the agreement through a court decree. The court may accept the agreement wholly or in part, or it may modify or reject it. If the court accepts the agreement, the language used to accept it determines the status of the contract and its terms for the future. The court may indicate approval of the agreement as a contract, or it may adopt the agreement as its own, that is, the court may order compliance with the terms of the contract as part of its judicial order, in which case the contract is said to have *merged* in the decree.

Merger is significant because it denies the separate existence of the agreement as a contract. It becomes a court order. Despite this new status of the agreement, its terms are still interpreted by traditional contract rules and reasoning, such as rules for resolving ambiguities, discerning the intent of the parties, and the like. The difference, however, is in the treatment of problems arising under the agreement. For example, failure to perform the promises of a contract normally give rise to a suit for breach of contract seeking compensation for the breach. The failure for noncompliance with a court order, however, is contempt of court. When a parent fails to pay child support, the remedy to force compliance with court-ordered support and to collect arrearages is to petition the court to hold the obligor in contempt of court. After a hearing in which the failure to pay is established, the court may very well order the parent in arrears to jail until the arrears are paid or until some amount fixed by the court is paid to the custodian (the other parent) of the child. This is an apparent exception to the constitutional protection against imprisonment for debt, but it is rationalized in terms of defiance of an order of the court rather than failure to pay a debt.

> One serious question, as we see it, arises in this appeal: Is contempt the proper path to travel when a property settlement agreement is only ratified and confirmed by the divorce decree, without incorporating a direction that the parties comply with its terms?

The rule is plainly stated in 24 Am.Jur.2d (Divorce and Separation) § 921, p. 1049:

> "Assuming that performance of an act called for by a property settlement may be enforced by a contempt proceeding where the court distinctly orders performance, performance will not be so enforced where the decree is not to be construed as including such an order. Thus, if the decree approves a property settlement but does not order the parties to perform its obligations, the violation of the agreement is not a violation of the decree and is not a contempt of court."

The reasoning in the cited cases is that a mere approval of a property settlement agreement is not a command to pay what is due by its terms and so, therefore, there is no order of the court or decree of the court that has been violated. Furthermore, there are hovering in the background constitutional implications that a person may not be imprisoned for debt but we avoid nailing our decision to that reason. The result we then have is when a party to a divorce action, where the court has only approved and ratified the agreement, asserts nonpayment under its conditions, he or she is confined to a claim on contract, not enforceable by contempt proceedings. . . .

[The court settled the case by converting it from one for contempt to one for breach of contract.]

— *Oedekoven v. Oedekoven,* 538 P.2d 1292 (Wyo. 1975)

CASE NO. 7-3 Labeling Agreements

In his *Cases on Domestic Relations* (2d. ed. 1990), at 1275, Wadlington describes the terminological confusion:

> The terms "incorporate," "merge", "ratify", and "affirm" probably have produced the most difficulty. In some jurisdictions they have become words of art to be used with considerable care according to the result desired. In others, some of the terms may be interchangeable.

Could he have been contemplating the following language from *Sweeney's Estate?*

IN RE ESTATE OF SWEENEY
210 Kan. 216, 500 P.2d 56 (1972)
Supreme Court of Kansas

[W]e are of the opinion the intent of the subsection [of the Kansas Statutes] is to merge all matters settled by such agreement into the court's decree. The phrases "be incorporated in the decree" and "shall be confirmed in the decree" must be read together, and are intended to mean that the terms and provisions of a separation agreement are to be ratified and approved by the court by its formal consent so as to provide judicial evidence of the terms and provisions of the agreement. In *Larned v. Larned*, 98 Kan. 328, 332, 158 P. 3, it was said the definition of the word "confirm" is to make firmer, to strengthen, sanction, or ratify. By its judicial sanction through confirmation, the court makes the agreement judicial in character, entitling the parties to the full benefit of the agreement which is no longer executory but executed. When confirmed, the executed agreement is subject to enforcement pursuant to its terms and the decree of the court. In determining the effect of the decree, the agreement is properly to be considered, and this court is of the opinion the confirmation of the agreement and its merger into the decree does not abolish the contractual aspects of the agreement, but leaves the court in the position to construe the provisions of the agreement consistent with the facts and circumstances and the expressed intention of the parties.

Sweeney's Estate involved the estate of a man who died not long after a second marriage, leaving a first wife and five minor children who were entitled to support under a separation agreement incorporated into the divorce decree. Under Kansas law, support ends at the death of the paying spouse and Sweeney made no provision in his will to continue support. His first wife attempted to persuade the court that the Kansas Statutes and the separation agreement compelled the court to order continuing support. The decision follows a tortuous path, as evidenced by the preceding excerpt above, to the conclusion that neither alimony nor child support may be awarded from Sweeney's estate. Fortunately, the court's syllabus sums up the issues and the rules which were considered and decided.

Syllabus by the Court

1.   The general rule is that periodic payments of alimony to a divorced wife terminate upon the former husband's death in the absence of a provision in the settlement agreement, or in the decree, which expressly so states, or contains language which makes the intent unmistakably clear that such payments are to continue after his death.

2.   Parties to a divorce action have the right to contract in a separation agreement that alimony payments to the wife shall continue after the former husband's death, and where such agreement is approved by the court and incorporated in the decree, it may be enforceable against the husband's estate.

3.   A parent, particularly the father, has a continuing obligation to support his minor children, irrespective of any decree of divorce to that effect.

4.   At common law, a father's duty to support his children ends with his death.

5.   Parties to a divorce action who enter into a separation agreement which is confirmed by the district court and incorporated into the decree, may expressly provide in the agreement for the support, maintenance, and education of their minor children, and that upon the death of the father, child support payments may continue and be enforceable against his estate during the children's minority.

6.   In the absence of language in a separation agreement which has been confirmed by the district court and incorporated in the decree of divorce pursuant to K.S.A.1971 Supp. 60-1610(d), that an obligation on the part of the father to make periodic payments for the support, maintenance, and education of the minor children of the parties was to survive the death of the father and be paid from his estate, a decree awarding child support which merely recites that the obligation was to continue "until each of said children shall have attained his majority or until the further order of the court," does not bind the father's estate for payments accruing after his death.

7.   The record in a probate proceeding by a divorced wife to enforce claims against her former husband's estate for future monthly payments of alimony and child support accruing after his death, based upon their separation agreement, which was confirmed by the district court and incorporated in the divorce decree pursuant to K.S.A.1971 Supp. 60-1610(d), is

examined, and it is held: The separation agreement did not expressly state or contain language which clearly and unmistakably evidenced the intent that obligations for alimony and child support were to survive the death of the husband so as to bind his estate, and such claims were not valid and enforceable.

LEGAL TERMS

breach of contract
Contract remedy that ordinarily seeks compensation for injury due to failure to perform.

specific performance
Contract remedy that asks the court to order a party to the contract to perform olbigation under the contract.

modification
Agreement or orders with regard to custody and support may be changed at a later time by petitioning the court for modification.

Sweeney's Estate and cases from other jurisdictions lead us to some general principles, which have a certain logic of their own. The language of the decree should indicate whether the separation agreement is merely approved or totally merged in the decree. The term *incorporated* or the phrase *incorporated by reference* suggest a merger, but are not absolutely decisive. The determining factor is whether the terms of the agreement have been ordered by the court, and this is often far from clear.

The contract itself may indicate that it is or is not to be merged in the decree, and this direction ought to be honored subsequently unless the court has indicated otherwise. The court could in theory merge the terms of the contract into the decree, despite language in the agreement to the contrary.

When customary or permitted by the court, attorneys for the parties should submit a written order of the court for the court to adopt and sign that echoes the language of the agreement. Thus, if the agreement requests merger into the decree, the decree should express merger; when the agreement requests approval (or "incorporation") without merger, the decree should reflect this. Assuming that the parties, through their attorneys, have decided which

Child care has become a common experience of the American child. Divorce and economic forces have shifted child care institutions from care for the children of the affluent toward serving the working parent.

course to follow, it would be poor practice to allow this question to be ambiguous because of a conflict between the agreement and the decree. This invites a lawsuit over the meaning and enforcement of the terms, suggesting that the attorneys have been derelict in their draftsmanship. Of course, the judge may not go along with the plan. If so, it is essential that the court's final order be clear and unequivocal, as it supersedes the terms of the contract.

Generally, agreements that are merged no longer have independent existence—they may not be sued upon as contracts but may only be enforced as court orders. If the agreement has not been merged into the decree, it continues as a contract and may give rise to traditional remedies applying to contracts, such as **breach of contract** or a suit for **specific performance.** As discussed in the section on **modification**, court-ordered support and custody may later be subject to modification by the court, whereas a contract cannot ordinarily be modified except by mutual agreement of the parties (approved by the court where a divorce has been granted).

These rules may be viewed from the standpoint of those concerned. The party obligated to perform (e.g., a father paying support) may wish to fix the terms of payment permanently, in which case approval without merger is desirable because the terms are contractual and may not be altered without mutual agreement. A court order may later be modified. The party concerned with compliance (e.g., a custodial mother receiving child support) may want the agreement merged so that the terms may be treated as court-ordered and their breach may be remedied by a petition for contempt of court—in many jurisdictions a faster, easier, and cheaper way to seek arrearages than suit for breach of contract, although more dependent on the discretion of the judge. Whether or not the parties seek merger, it is in their interest to submit their agreement to the court for approval to assure its legally binding status and avoid later litigation over the validity of the contract itself.

CAVEAT

The most vulnerable portion of a separation agreement concerns provisions for the support and custody of children. Some jurisdictions find such provisions against public policy, especially if they are not part of a final settlement in a divorce proceeding.

CASE NO. 7-4 Merger vel non

The *Johnston* case provides a detailed discussion of the issues of incorporation and merger of a separation agreement into a court decree. *Johnston* gives another example of the ramifications of merger—because the agreement became merged in the decree, Mr. Johnston was no longer able to challenge the validity of the agreement as a contract (on the grounds of mental incompetence). The agreement was no longer a contract, but had become an order of the court.

JOHNSTON v. JOHNSTON
297 Md. 48, 465 A.2d 436 (1983)
Court of Appeals of Maryland

COUCH, Judge.

Although the parties have raised four issues in this case, the issue, as we see it, is whether a separation agreement approved and incorporated but not merged in a divorce decree may be **collaterally attacked.** For reasons to be discussed herein, we hold that it may not be where, as here, its validity is conclusively established by the decree which operates as *res judicata.*

The parties hereto were married in June of 1948 and lived together 23 years prior to separating in June of 1971. During the marriage, four children were born all of whom have now reached their majority. Subsequent to their separation, each party retained counsel and negotiated an agreement the purpose of which was "to effect a final and permanent settlement of their respective property rights." The agreement was executed by the parties in February of 1973 and provided, *inter alia,* for the support and maintenance of Mrs. Johnston and the four children, the transfer of certain property interests, the execution of testamentary designations, and the creation of various trusts. The agreement was made in contemplation of divorce proceedings and provided:

> "*This agreement shall be offered in evidence in any such suit, and if acceptable to the court, shall be incorporated by reference in the decree that may be granted therein. Notwithstanding such incorporation, this agreement shall not be merged in the decree, but shall survive the same and shall be binding and conclusive on the parties for all time.*"

(Emphasis supplied). The agreement also provided:

> "No modification or waiver of any of the terms of this agreement shall be valid unless in writing and executed with the same formality as this agreement."

Mr. Johnston filed a "Bill of Complaint for Divorce *A Vinculo Matrimonii*" in the Circuit Court for Baltimore City, specifically requesting "[t]hat the Agreement of the parties dated February 16, 1973 be incorporated by reference in any decree that may be granted herein." A "Decree of Divorce" was entered June 27, 1973, stating in relevant part:

> "It is further ADJUDGED, ORDERED AND DECREED that the Plaintiff provide for maintenance, and support of Defendant and of the infant children of the parties, all as provided in the Agreement between the parties dated February 16, 1973 and filed in this cause of action, *said Agreement being hereby approved and made a part hereof as if fully set forth herein. . . .*" (Emphasis added.)

In May, 1981, Mr. Johnston filed a "Petition to Set Aside and Void Agreement" on the basis that "consultations [with professionals] ha[d] disclosed that [he] suffered from a mental disease and/or mental defect during the negotiations and subsequent execution of the aforesaid Agreement which severely impaired [his] mental competency at that time." The petition further asserted that Mr. Johnston's mental incompetency justified the voiding of the separation agreement. . . .

(1)

We believe that the threshold issue, which neither the chancellor nor the intermediate appellate court discussed, is whether the separation agreement merged in the decree so as to be superseded by the decree.[3] The decree expressly approved and incorporated the agreement. However, the agreement explicitly provided that it was not to merge in the decree but was to survive the decree. As observed by the Supreme Court of Arizona in *McNelis v. Bruce,* 90 Ariz. 261, 367 P.2d 625, 631 (1961) (en banc):

> "It is the rule that the mere approval of a property settlement in the divorce

decree does not operate to make it a part of and enforceable as a decree. If the language of the agreement shows an intent to make it part of the divorce decree and the agreement is actually incorporated in the decree, the provisions of the agreement may be enforced as an order of the court. As soon as a property settlement agreement is incorporated into the decree the agreement is superceded [sic] by the decree and the obligations imposed are not those imposed by contract but are those imposed by the decree since the contract is merged in the decree." (Citations omitted.)

The language of the agreement in *McNelis* was similar to that in the instant case, providing: "'This agreement shall be offered in evidence in such action and if acceptable to the court shall be incorporated by reference in any decree that may be granted herein. Notwithstanding such incorporation, this agreement shall not be merged in the decree but shall survive the same and shall be binding and conclusive upon the parties for all time.'" *Id.* 367 P.2d at 631-32.

In determining whether the agreement merged in the decree so as to be modifiable by the court, the court looked to the intent of the parties, stating in pertinent part: "The foregoing clause manifests the intention of the parties to the agreement. It was not disapproved by the court but rather adopted as part of the agreement; it therefore must be taken as speaking the intention of not only the parties but of the court that the agreement was not to be merged in the judgment." *Id.* 367 P.2d at 632.

The Supreme Court of California has also had occasion to discuss the issue of merger:

> "Merger is the substitution of rights and duties under the judgment or the decree for those under the agreement or cause of action sued upon. . . . [I]t is first necessary to determine whether the parties and the court intended a merger. If the agreement is expressly set out in the decree, and the court orders that it be performed, it is clear that a merger is intended. On the other hand, the parties may intend only to have the validity of the agreement established, and not to have it become a part of the decree enforceable as such. Whether or not a merger is intended, the agreement may be incorporated into the decree either expressly or by reference. If a merger is not intended, the purpose of incorporation will be only to identify the agreement so as to render its validity res judicata in any subsequent action based upon it. If a merger is intended, the purpose of incorporation is, of course, to make the agreement an operative part of the decree." *Flynn v. Flynn,* 42 Cal.2d 55, 265 P.2d 865, 866 (1954). . . .

In our view, where, as in the instant case, the agreement provides that it shall be *incorporated but not merged* in the decree, it is patent that the parties did not intend merger and the agreement survives as a separate and independent contractual arrangement between the parties. On the other hand, where, as in *Flynn, supra,* the agreement does not include a non-merger clause and it is incorporated in the decree, the agreement is superseded by the decree. The agreement, once incorporated and merged in the decree, is enforceable through contempt proceedings and may be modified by the court. It has also been stated that where the court incorporates the agreement as a whole, including the non-merger clause, the court approves the clause against merger so that the contract survives. . . .

(2)

It has been stated that:

"Where there is a valid bilateral divorce . . . and the court approves the separation agreement, which is then incorporated in the decree, the court will be deemed to have passed on its legality, and . . . [t]he validity of the agreement is then *res judicata*. . . . To put it concretely, the husband cannot in such a case evade his obligations under the agreement by claiming that it is illegal because it was in consideration of divorce, or

that it is voidable because it was procured through fraud. Nor can the wife upset the agreement on the ground of misrepresentation or coercion. . . ."

---

3 "Merger" is defined as the "[s]ubstitution of rights and duties under judgment or decree for those under property settlement agreement." Black's Law Dictionary 892 (5th ed. 1979).

7.6   MODIFICATION

Provisions in a divorce decree for spousal and child support and the terms of custody and visitation of the children may be modified by petition at a later time, when the party requesting modification can show changed circumstances justifying the modification. The court has discretion to rewrite the conditions or terms of its decree in accordance with changed circumstances. If the court made the terms, it can change them. If, alternatively, the terms of support and custody are governed by an independent contract lacking the authority of a judicial decree, the court may not freely rewrite what the parties agreed.

We agree with the trial court that, by the terms of the separation agreement, Mrs. Swift waived any claim to alimony or a share of her husband's pension rights. Under District of Columbia law, where a separation agreement is fair and reasonable and is intended as a final disposition regarding property rights or adult support, the parties will be bound by the agreement. . . .

Since these provisions are unambiguous, Mrs. Swift is seeking what amounts to a modification of the agreement. To be sure, in certain circumstances a trial court may modify agreements which are incorporated but not merged into a divorce decree, but the authority to do so is limited. . . . Such modifications require a showing that a substantial and material change in circumstances unforeseen at the time the agreement was signed has occurred. . . .

There is also an indication in the record that the trial court may have interpreted paragraph 10 of the agreement as allowing it to make modifications as it saw fit. This paragraph states that the agreement shall be incorporated but not merged into any divorce decree and shall be "forever binding unless and until modified by a court of competent jurisdiction. . . ." . . . A separation agreement incorporated but not merged into a final divorce decree is governed by the law of contracts. . . . The standard for

LEGAL TERMS

collateral attack
An attack on a judgment or decree that uses a proceeding other than a direct challenge to the judgement or decree.

res judicata
Literally means "the thing has been decided." An affirmative defense which argues that the issues of a case have been adjudicated may not be litigated again.

modification is therefore more restrictive than it would be if the trial court were modifying a prior divorce decree or an agreement merged into that decree. . . . Paragraph 10 of the agreement clearly contemplates the more restrictive standard for modification. An interpretation allowing modifications as the trial court sees fit would render the language providing for non-merger of the separation agreement meaningless.

— *Swift v. Swift*, 566 A.2d 1045 (D.C. 1989)

SUMMARY

Postmarital contracts may be labeled *postnuptial agreements, separation agreements*, or *property settlement agreements*. Postnuptial agreements executed while the marriage is still harmonious are subject to the same hazards as antenuptial agreements, plus the challenge of lack of consideration. Separation agreements and property settlements should be executed when divorce or permanent separation is imminent, lest they be voided for promoting divorce. All these postmarital agreements are becoming more acceptable to the courts and legislatures, but considerable variation continues among the several states.

A major issue regarding agreements submitted to the courts in divorce proceedings concerns whether the agreement is merged into the final decree, so that it loses its separate existence as a contract. On the answer to this question rest the availability of modification to change the terms and the means of enforcement. If merged, contempt of court is available to enforce compliance; if not, traditional contract remedies may be necessary. If the agreement is merged so that its terms are ordered by the court, those orders may be modified as are other orders (custody and support) emanating from the court. If the agreement is not merged, the contract may be modified only by mutual agreement of the parties. The common exception to this concerns the children, whose interests most courts will not allow to be bargained away.

Because of changing law and different traditions, different jurisdictions run the gamut of rules in these matters. Careful drafting is essential.

CAVEAT

Jurisdictional differences are great. The rules expressed here and in the cases and case excerpts tend toward the more modern or progressive views. Rules and practices may differ among different districts or circuits of the same state and even among judges. This occurs in part because definitive statements of the law are often slow in coming, because relatively few cases are appealed to higher courts. It is also due to the changing nature of this area of the law. The advent of no-fault divorce has marked a retreat of the courts from controlling the terms of the dissolution of marriage toward empowering the parties to set their own terms. In light of this uncertainty, careful draftsmanship and a bit of clairvoyance are called for. Legal practitioners in divorce must keep abreast of new decisions and scrutinize materials available for practitioners as models of agreements or clauses in agreements. The specific items to be included in separation agreements are discussed in chapters 12 and 13.

QUESTIONS

To test your understanding of the chapter, sections of the Uniform Marriage and Divorce Act (UMDA) (see appendix 5A) are quoted here for comparison with the rules expressed in this chapter. Recognize that the UMDA provisions set the tone for the future and may be ahead of any actual jurisdiction. They nevertheless express a logical culmination to trends already in place and may very well become law in the near future.

Uniform Marriage and Divorce Act

Section 306. (a)   To promote amicable settlement of disputes between parties to a marriage attendant upon their separation or the dissolution of their marriage, the parties may enter into a written separation agreement containing provisions for disposition of any property owned by either of them, maintenance of either of them, and support, custody, and visitation of their children.

(b)   In a proceeding for dissolution of marriage or for legal separation, the terms of the separation agreement, except those providing for the support, custody, and visitation of children, are binding upon the court unless it finds, after considering the economic circumstances of the parties and any other relevant evidence produced by the parties on their own motion or on request of the court, that the separation agreement is unconscionable.

(c)   If the court finds the separation agreement unconscionable, it may request the parties to submit a revised separation agreement or may make orders for the disposition of property, maintenance, and support.

(d)   If the court finds that the separation agreement is not unconscionable as to disposition of property or maintenance and not unsatisfactory as to support:

   (1)   unless the separation agreement provides to the contrary, its terms shall be set forth in the decree of dissolution or legal separation and the parties shall be ordered to perform them, or

   (2)   if the separation agreement provides that its terms shall not be set forth in the decree, the decree shall identify the separation agreement and state that the court has found the terms not unconscionable.

(e)   Terms of the agreement set forth in the decree are enforceable by all remedies available for enforcement of a judgment, including contempt, and are enforceable as contract terms.

(f)   Except for terms concerning the support, custody, or visitation of children, the decree may expressly preclude or limit modification of terms set forth in the decree if the separation agreement so provides. Otherwise, terms of a separation agreement set forth in the decree are automatically modified by modification of the decree.

1.   What seems to be the only grounds for the court to disapprove a separation agreement under the UMDA? What additional grounds are mentioned in the text and cases in this chapter?

2.   Who determines whether the agreement is merged in the decree under the UMDA? Does this differ from the impression given in the text as to present practice?

3.   Does the UMDA favor merger? Is this an improvement over current practice?

4.   Why are parental duties treated separately with regard to modification?

5.   How is an agreement that is not merged (court-ordered performance) enforced under the UMDA? Does this differ from current practice?

6. Would *Johnston v. Johnston* have been decided differently if the UMDA had been adopted verbatim by Maryland?

7. If your state legislature were about to adopt these provisions of the UMDA, would you recommend prospective application, that is, that the provisions apply to agreements executed after the date of the act adopting the UMDA?

8. Would your answer to question 7 be different if you were to consider Article I, § 10(1) ("No State shall . . . pass any . . . Law impairing the Obligation of Contracts . . .")? Constitution of the United States.

EXERCISES

Answer the questions according to the law of your state.

1. Can a widow's allowance (e.g., dower, elective share) be waived through a postnuptial agreement? 9 A.L.R.3d 955.

2. Does your state law merge agreements in divorce decrees? Does it allow separation agreements to exist independently of the decree?

APPENDIX 7A

Financial Statement for Dissolution of Marriage

Source: Florida Rules of Civil Procedure, Form 1.975 (1973)

IN THE CIRCUIT COURT OF
THE _____ JUDICIAL CIRCUIT
IN AND FOR _____ COUNTY, FLORIDA

IN RE: The Marriage of:
    Husband,

                                Case No. _____

and

                                Division: _____

    Wife.

_____

FINANCIAL AFFIDAVIT

STATE OF FLORIDA
COUNTY OF _____

    BEFORE ME, this day personally appeared _____, who being duly sworn, deposes and says that the following information is true and correct according to his/her best knowledge and belief:

ITEM 1:   EMPLOYMENT AND INCOME

OCCUPATION: _____
EMPLOYED BY: _____
ADDRESS: _____
_____
_____
SOC. SEC. #: _____
PAY PERIOD: _____
RATE OF PAY: _____

AVERAGE GROSS MONTHLY INCOME FROM EMPLOYMENT	$_____
Bonuses, commissions, allowances, overtime, tips, and similar payments	$_____
Business income from sources such as self-employment, partnership, close corporations, and/or independent contracts (gross receipts minus ordinary and necessary expenses required to produce income)	_____
Disability benefits	
Workers' compensation	_____
Unemployment compensation	_____
Pension, retirement, or annuity payments	_____
Social Security benefits	_____
Spousal support received from previous marriage	_____
Interest and dividends	_____
Rental income (gross receipts minus ordinary and necessary expenses required to produce income)	_____
Income from royalties, trusts, or estates	_____
Reimbursed expenses and in kind payments to the extent that they reduce personal living expenses	_____
Gains derived from dealing in property (not including non-recurring gains)	_____
Itemize any other income of a recurring nature	_____
TOTAL MONTHLY INCOME	$_____

LESS DEDUCTIONS:

Federal, state, and local income taxes (corrected for filing status and actual number of withholding allowances)	$_____
FICA or self-employment tax (annualized)	_____
Mandatory union dues	_____
Mandatory retirement	_____
Health insurance payments	_____
Court-ordered support payments for children actually paid	_____
TOTAL DEDUCTIONS	$_____

ITEM 2:   AVERAGE MONTHLY EXPENSES

HOUSEHOLD:

Mortgage or rent payments	_____
Property taxes and insurance	_____
Electricity	_____
Water, garbage, and sewer	_____
Telephone	_____
Fuel oil or natural gas	_____
Repairs and maintenance	_____
Lawn and pool care	_____
Pest control	_____
Misc. household	_____
Food and grocery items	_____
Meals outside home	_____
Other:	
_____	_____

AUTOMOBILE:

Gasoline and oil   _____
Repairs   _____
Auto tags and license   _____
Insurance   _____
Other:
_____   _____
_____   _____

CHILDREN'S EXPENSES:

Nursery or babysitting   _____
School tuition   _____
School supplies   _____
Lunch money   _____
Allowance   _____
Clothing   _____
Medical, dental, prescription   _____
Vitamins   _____
Barber/beauty parlor   _____
Cosmetics/toiletries   _____
Gifts for special holidays   _____
Other:
_____   _____
_____   _____

INSURANCES:
Health   _____
Life   _____
Other:
_____   _____
_____   _____

OTHER EXPENSES NOT LISTED ABOVE:

Dry cleaning and laundry   _____
Affiant's clothing   _____
Affiant's medical, dental, prescription _____
Affiant's beauty parlor   _____
Affiant's gifts (special holidays)   _____
Pets:
Grooming   _____
Veterinarian   _____
Membership dues:
Professional dues   _____
Social dues   _____
Entertainment   _____
Vacations   _____
Publications   _____
Religious organizations   _____
Charities   _____
Miscellaneous   _____

Other:

_____ _____
_____ _____
_____ _____
_____ _____

TOTAL ABOVE EXPENSES: _____

PAYMENTS TO CREDITORS:

TO WHOM:	BALANCE DUE:	MONTHLY PAYMENT:
_____	_____	_____
_____	_____	_____
_____	_____	_____
_____	_____	_____

Total monthly payments to creditors: $_____
TOTAL MONTHLY EXPENSES: $_____

ITEM 3:   ASSETS (Ownership: if joint, allocate equally)

Description	Value	Husband	Wife
Cash (on hand or in banks)	_____	_____	_____
Stocks/bonds/notes	_____	_____	_____
Real estate:			
Home:	_____	_____	_____
_____	_____	_____	_____
_____	_____	_____	_____
_____	_____	_____	_____
Automobiles:			
_____	_____	_____	_____
_____	_____	_____	_____
_____	_____	_____	_____
Other personal property:			
Contents of home	_____	_____	_____
Jewelry	_____	_____	_____
Life ins./cash surrender value	_____	_____	_____
Other assets:			
_____	_____	_____	_____
_____	_____	_____	_____
_____	_____	_____	_____
TOTAL ASSETS:	$_____	$_____	$_____

ITEM 4:   LIABILITIES

Creditor	Security	Balance	Husband	Wife
_____	_____	_____	_____	_____
_____	_____	_____	_____	_____
_____	_____	_____	_____	_____
_____	_____	_____	_____	_____
_____	_____	_____	_____	_____
TOTAL LIABILITIES		$_____	$_____	$_____

_____ Affiant

SWORN TO AND SUBSCRIBED before me on

_____, 19___

_____ NOTARY PUBLIC

My Commission Expires:

CERTIFICATE OF SERVICE

I HEREBY CERTIFY that a true and correct copy of the above financial affidavit has been furnished by U.S. mail this _____ day of _____, 19___, to:

_____

APPENDIX 7B

Settlement Agreement (Georgia)

Source: *Georgia Divorce.* Copyright © 1985 by Lawyers Co-operative Publishing.

SETTLEMENT AGREEMENT
Introductory Note

The form agreement that follows includes sample provisions that should meet most common situations. It is not intended to be exhaustive. The settlement agreement offers the richest opportunity for the Attorney to be creative in resolving problems peculiar to his or her client and should be approached as a challenge rather than a routine exercise.

Items that are in parentheses are either optional or to be shaped to accommodate individual needs. In some instances, alternative provisions have been suggested. Numbers in parentheses refer to Data Packet numbers.

Special attention should be given to visitation provisions. Many agreements specify only "reasonable visitation" rights for the non-custodian. Yet, visitation is an area often fraught with conflict and vague language leads to unpredictable results. The drafter should attempt to anticipate as many common concerns as possible. Remember that the agreement typically must be operative for many years.

STATE OF GEORGIA
COUNTY OF (where executed)

AGREEMENT

THIS AGREEMENT is made and entered into this _____ day of _____, 19____ by and between _____ (hereinafter "Husband") and _____ (hereinafter "Wife").

(RECITATION OF FACTS FORMING BASIS OF AGREEMENT)

Husband and wife were lawfully married on ____, 19____, in _____ County, _____ (state), _____ and cohabited as husband and wife until _____, 19____, at which time in consequence of certain irreconcilable differences between them they separated.

(USE IF A DIVORCE HAS BEEN GRANTED)

(Husband and Wife were granted a total divorce on _____, 19____, with all questions regarding alimony, child support, child custody, visitation, division of property, and attorney's fees reserved for later determination.)

(USE IF MINOR CHILDREN ARE INVOLVED)

(Husband and wife have as issue of their marriage _____ minor child(ren), _____, age ____, and _____, age ____).

(ACKNOWLEDGMENT OF JOINT SUPPORT OBLIGATION)

(Husband and Wife acknowledge that [each of them] [husband] is gainfully employed and that they have a joint and several obligation for the care, custody, and support of their child(ren).)

(OBJECT OF AGREEMENT)

Husband and wife desire to resolve by this agreement all questions regarding alimony, child support, child custody, visitation, division of property, and attorneys' fees.

175

(GENERAL RECITATION OF CONSIDERATION)

THEREFORE, in consideration of the mutual promises and covenants herein contained, Husband and Wife do hereby agree as follows:

(THIS PARAGRAPH IS A BASIS FOR
CONTEMPT IN THE EVENT OF
FUTURE INTERFERENCE)

1.   *Future Relationship of Husband and Wife.*

Husband and wife shall (continue to) live separate and apart, and each shall be free from interference, authority and control, either direct or indirect, of the other, except as may expressly be provided in this Agreement. Without regard to the other provisions hereof, each may reside at such place or places as he or she may select and each may, for his or her own separate use and benefit, engage in any employment, business, or profession which he or she may deem advisable.

2.   *Child Custody and Visitation.*

(a)   (Husband) (Wife) shall have the [temporary and] permanent custody and control of _____, subject only to the rights of visitation hereinafter vested in (Wife) (Husband).

(OPTIONAL LANGUAGE TO AID
ENFORCEMENT OF VISITATION RIGHTS)

((b)   (The custodian) acknowledges that (he) (she), by accepting custody of said child(ren) stands in a relation of trust to said child(ren) as high as any recognized in law or equity and agrees to discharge this trust with the welfare and benefit of said child(ren) as (his) (her) pre-eminent goal.)

((c)   (The custodian) acknowledges that it is in the best interest of said child(ren) that (he) (she) (they) maintain as close a relationship with [the non-custodian] as is possible while Husband and Wife live separate and apart, and to that end agrees to foster and encourage a free, liberal, and reasonable exercise of the visitation rights hereinafter vested in (the non-custodian].)

((d)   Husband and Wife agree that it is in the best interest of said child(ren) that they continue to confer on matters respecting health, education and religious upbringing of said child(ren) and (the custodian) acknowledges that (he) (she) has an affirmative duty to keep (the non-custodian) informed of events of significance respecting said matters.)

(SAMPLE VISITATION
PARAGRAPHS)

(e)   (The non-custodian) shall have the right to visit with said child(ren) at any time mutually agreeable to Husband and Wife. In addition, (the non-custodian) shall have the following specific rights to visit with said child(ren), which rights are mutually agreed to be minimal and not exclusive:

(1)   On alternate weekends between the hours of (6:00) p.m. (E.S.T. or E.D.T.) on Friday and (6:00) p.m. (E.S.T. or E.D.T.) on Sunday, commencing on the (first) Friday following the execution of this Agreement.

(2)   For (four) weeks (28 days) during the month of June, July, and August of every year. Said weeks may be consecutive or separate at the option of (the non-custodian), provided that the first day of such visitation shall not be before the lapse of seven (7) days following completion of each child's regular school year and the last day of such visitation shall occur at least seven (7) days prior to the commencement of each child's next regular school year.

(3)   In each (even) (odd) numbered year (the non-custodian) shall have the right to visit with said child(ren) for a period of (seven) (7) consecutive days ending at [12:00, noon) (E.S.T.) on December 25.

(4)   In each (even) (odd) numbered year (the non-custodian) shall have the right to visit with said child(ren) for a period of (seven) (7) consecutive days commencing at (12:00, noon) (E.S.T.) on December 25, and ending at (6:00 p.m.) (E.S.T.) on January 1 of the next succeeding year.

Practice Guide: Similar provisions may be considered for Valentine's Day, Easter, spring vacation, July 4, Thanksgiving, or religious holidays of significance to the client.

(5)   On the birthday of each child in each (even) (odd) numbered year (the non-custodian) shall have the right to visit with said child from _____ to _____.

((6)   On any day when [the non-custodian] is not visiting with said child(ren) (he) (she) may, at (his) (her) expense, telephone the child(ren) between the hours of _____ and _____ (E.S.T. or E.D.T.).)

(7)   (The custodian) agrees to inform (the non-custodian) of the following special occasions at least twenty-four (24) hours in advance of each: birthday parties outside the (custodian's) home, religious events of significance, graduations, school open-houses, demonstrations of acquired skills (e.g., recitals, athletic events), weddings, award ceremonies, _____, and (the non-custodian) shall have the rights afforded [the custodian] to attend and participate in any such special occasion.

(RIGHT TO VISIT OUTSIDE CUSTODIAN'S HOME)

(8)   (The non-custodian) may exercise any visitation rights vested herein at any suitable location apart from (the custodian's) residence.

(PICKUP AND RETURN)

(9)   (The non-custodian) shall collect and return the child(ren) for each visitation at or to (the custodian's) home.

(EXPENSE OF VISITATION)

(10) All transportation expenses incident to exercise of visitation rights shall be borne by the (non-custodian).

(WHERE PARTIES RESIDE IN SEPARATE
AND DISTANT LOCALES)

(11) In the event that Husband and Wife should reside more than _____ miles apart, (herein provide for use of common carriers, division of expenses, collection and return sites, additional summer visitation, etc.).

Practice Guide: The trial court may prohibit removal of children from the United States, but cannot prohibit relocation to another state because the applicability of the Uniform Child Custody Jurisdiction Act provides adequate protection.

(NOTICE)

(12) (The non-custodian) shall give (the custodian) at least (twenty-four (24)) hours advance notice of each intended visitation, provided that notice for summer visitation shall be at least (thirty (30)) days in advance.

3. *Alimony and Child Support*

Practice Guide: The income tax rules applying to alimony payments have been completely changed by the Deficit Reduction Act of 1984. The following clause should satisfy the basic requirement of the new law and render the payments income to the recipient and deductible by the payor.

Alimony Only—$10,000 or less
per calendar year;
indefinite term.

(Husband) (Wife) shall pay to (Wife) (Husband) as alimony or separate maintenance payments the sum of ($_____) Dollars per month on the (first) day of each month, commencing on the (first) day of _____, 19____. Payments shall terminate on the death of (the payee) or upon remarriage of (the payee). (The payor) shall have no obligation to make any payments after the death of (the payee) to (the payee's) estate, heirs or successors, nor to make any payments in cash or property as a substitute for such payments after the death of (the payee). All payments shall be made in cash.

Husband and Wife intend that all payments made pursuant to this paragraph shall be included as income on (the payee's) income tax returns beginning in calendar year 19____ pursuant to Internal Revenue Code Section 71. Husband and Wife intend that all payments made pursuant to this paragraph shall be a deduction on (the payor's) income tax returns pursuant to Internal Revenue Code Section 215, beginning in the same calendar year.

Husband's taxpayer identification number is (insert social security number) Wife's taxpayer identification number is (insert social security number).

OR

Alimony Only—More than $10,000
per calendar year; indefinite term.

(Husband) (Wife) shall pay to (Wife) (Husband) as alimony or separate maintenance payments the sum of ($_____) Dollars per month on the (first) day of each month, commencing on the first (first) day of _____, 19____. Payments shall terminate on the death of (the payee) or upon the remarriage of (the payee). (The payor) shall have no obligation to make any payments after the death of (the payee) to (the payee's) estate, heirs or successors, nor to make any payments in cash or property as a substitute for such payments after the death of (the payee). All payments shall be made in cash.

(The payor) shall have the obligation to continue making alimony or separate maintenance payments—

[for (sixty-six) consecutive months,] or [in at least each of the six "post-separation years," as that term is defined in Internal Revenue Code Section 71(f)(4)(A),] or [until _____,19____,]

not taking into account any sooner termination of said payments contingent upon the (death, remarriage of the payee), as set forth in Internal Revenue Code Section 71(f)(1).

Husband and Wife intend that all payments made pursuant to this paragraph shall be included as income on (the payee's) income tax returns beginning in calendar year 19____ pursuant to Internal Revenue Code Section 71. Husband and Wife intend that all payments made pursuant to this paragraph shall be a deduction on (the payor's) income tax returns pursuant to Internal Revenue Code Section 215, beginning in the same calendar year.

Husband's taxpayer identification number is (insert social security number).Wife's taxpayer identification number is (insert social security number).

Practice Guide: The term of the payments may be any length, but the obligation to make payments must endure for *at least* six *calendar* years if amounts greater than $10,000 per year are to be income to the payee and deductible by the payor. There is no "minimum term rule" if the annual payments are less than $10,000.

So long as payments are made in each of the six "post-separation years" the "minimum term rule" is satisfied. Accordingly, a payment in December of the first "post-separation year," monthly payments in each of the next four "post-separation years," and a payment in January of the sixth "post-separation year" will be sufficient (as little as 50 months).

However, because of the recomputation provisions, care must be taken to ensure that payments in the sixth "post-separation year" are not more than $10,000 less than total payments in each of the five preceding "post-separation years."

OR

Alimony Only—$10,000 or less
per calendar year; fixed term.

(Husband) (Wife) shall pay to (Wife) (Husband) as alimony or separate maintenance payments the sum of ($_____) Dollars per month on the (first) day of each month, commencing on the (first) day of _____,19____ and ending with the payment to be made on the (first) day of _____, 19____. Payments shall terminate upon the death of (the payee) and (the payor) shall have no obligation to make any payments due after the death of (the payee) to (the payee's) estate, heirs or successors, nor to make any payments in cash or property as a substitute for such payments after the death of (the payee). All payments shall be made in cash.

Husband and Wife intend that all payments made pursuant to this paragraph shall be included as income as (the payee's) income tax returns beginning in calendar year 19____ pursuant to Internal Revenue Code Section 71. Husband and wife intend that all payments made pursuant to this paragraph shall be a deduction on (the payor's) income tax returns pursuant to Internal Revenue Code Section 215, beginning in the same calendar year.

Husband's taxpayer identification number is (insert social security number). Wife's taxpayer identification number is (insert social security number).

OR

Alimony Only—More than $10,000
per calendar year; fixed term.

(Husband) (Wife) shall pay to (Wife) (Husband) the total sum of $200,000 as alimony or separate maintenance payments in ten annual installments of $20,000 each payable on the (first day of June) in each year with the first such payment due on (June 1, 1985) and the last such payment due on (June 1, 1994).

Payments shall terminate upon the death of (the payee), and (the payor) shall have no obligation to make any payments due after the death of (the payee) to (the payee's) estate, heirs or successors, nor to make any payments in cash or property as a substitute for such payments after the death of (the payee). All payments shall be made in cash.

Husband and Wife intend that all payments made pursuant to this paragraph shall be included as income on (the payee's) income tax returns beginning in calendar year 19____ pursuant to Internal Revenue Code Section 71. Husband and Wife intend that all

payments made pursuant to this paragraph shall be a deduction on (the payor's) income tax returns pursuant to Internal Revenue Code Section 215, beginning in the same calendar year.

Husband's taxpayer identification number is (insert social security number). Wife's taxpayer identification number is (insert social security number).

OR

(NO ALIMONY)

(a) Neither Husband nor Wife shall recover any alimony from the other.

Practice Guide: In the event no alimony is to be paid, it is better to state that specifically to clarify the intentions of the parties.

OR

(CHILD SUPPORT ONLY)

(b) (The non-custodian) shall pay to (the custodian) for the support and maintenance of _____ the sum of _____ ($____) Dollars per month on the (first (1st) day) of each month, commencing with the (first (1st) day) of _____ and continuing until said child marries, dies, attains the age of majority (or becomes eighteen (18) years of age), or emancipated, or until custody of said child is awarded to [the non-custodian], whichever first occurs.

(Add a similar paragraph for each child.)

Practice Guide: Variants on these paragraphs are limited only by the facts of each case and the imagination of the drafter. Alimony and child support payments can be designed to decrease, increase or terminate at different times.

OR

Combined Alimony and Child Support.

Practice Guide: Unallocated alimony and child support or "Lester" payments have been rendered a high risk arrangement by the Deficit Reduction Act of 1984. If there is only one child and only one reduction this provision is still relatively safe. If there are two or more children and multiple reductions the statutory restrictions are very complex. The following sample provision is probably safe under the new rules for a one child situation.

(Husband) (Wife) shall pay to (Wife) (Husband) as alimony or separate maintenance payments and for the support of _____, the minor child of Husband and Wife, the sum of ($_____) Dollars per month on the (first) day of each month, commencing on the (first) day of _____, 19____.

On _____, 19____, said sum shall automatically be reduced to ($_____) Dollars per month. (See Practice Guide below.)

Payments shall terminate on the death of (the payee spouse), and (the payor) shall have no obligation to make any payments due after the death of (the payee) to (the payee's) estate, heirs or successors, nor to make any payments in cash or property as a substitute for such payments after the death of (the payee). All payments shall be made in cash.

Husband and Wife intend that all payments made pursuant to this paragraph shall be included as income on (the payee's) income tax returns beginning in calendar year 19____ pursuant to Internal Revenue Code Section 71. Husband and Wife intend that all payments made pursuant to this paragraph shall be a reduction on (the payor's) income tax returns pursuant to Internal Revenue Code Section 215, beginning in the same calendar year.

Husband's taxpayer identification number is (insert social security number). Wife's taxpayer identification number is (insert social security number).

Practice Guide: The date of the reduction must be greater than six months before or after the 18th birthday of the child and should not coincide with graduation or other predictable child-related events.

Payments Not to Be Alimony.

Any payment (or a fixed portion of any payment by (Husband) (Wife) to (Wife) (Husband) pursuant to paragraph _____ of this Agreement is designated as excludible from the gross income of (the payee) pursuant to Internal Revenue Code Section 71(b)(1)(B) and non-deductible by the (payor) pursuant to Internal Revenue Code Section 215. Husband and Wife agree that they will treat these payments for federal income tax purposes in accordance with this designation.

Recomputation Provisions.

Practice Guide: If economic considerations dictate that payments must be higher in the first years than in later years, or as a precautionary measure against certain hardships, a clause similar to the following can eliminate or minimize the drastic effect of the recomputation (recapture) rules. Note that the recomputation provisions do not apply to payments pursuant to temporary orders.

"In any taxable year in which an excess amount, as defined in Internal Revenue Code Section 71(f), is included by (the payor) in gross income and (the payee) is allowed a deduction for said excess amount, (the payee) shall pay to (the payor) an amount equal to (the payor's additional income tax liability) or (the payee's reduced income tax liability). Any payment pursuant to this paragraph is designated by Husband and Wife as excludible from the gross income of (the recipient) pursuant to Internal Revenue Code Section 71(b)(1)(B) and non-deductible by (the paying spouse) pursuant to Internal Revenue Code Section 215. Husband and Wife agree that they will treat payments made pursuant to

this paragraph for federal income tax purposes in accordance with this designation."

(ATTORNEY FEES)

(c) Attorney Fees: (Husband) (Wife) agrees that (Wife's) (Husband's) attorneys have performed a valuable service in representing (her) (him) in proceedings related to the case of _____ v. _____, Civil Action No. _____, in the Superior Court of _____ County, Georgia. In full discharge of [Husband's] [Wife's] obligation to pay any fees earned by said attorneys, [Husband] [Wife] agrees to pay (*Attorneys*) _____ the total sum of _____ ($_____) Dollars, payable as follows: (Set forth payment terms). (In the event (Husband) (Wife) defaults in payment of any installment, (*Attorney's*) _____ may declare the entire outstanding balance due instanter, and may pursue any available remedies to collect same.)

Practice Guide: Although attorney fees are technically a part of temporary alimony, the attorney may prefer to include them in a paragraph apart from alimony provisions. Provision for litigation expenses may also be included here. Attorney fees may be treated as alimony for income tax purposes under the Deficit Reduction Act of 1984. Care must be taken to comply with the basic alimony tax rules.

(PRIVATE SCHOOLS)

(d) As additional child support (Husband) (Wife) agrees to pay all expenses incident to or arising out of _____ attendance at [private schools] [up to a maximum of _____ ($_____) Dollars per school year.

(1) (Husband) (Wife), as a condition precedent to (his) (her) obligation under subparagraph (3(d)) shall have the right to approve the school to be attended by _____, which approval shall not be unreasonably withheld.

(2) All expenses owed pursuant to subparagraphs (3(d)) shall be billed directly to (Husband) (Wife) and (he) (she) shall pay the same within thirty (30) days of receipt of any such bill.

(MEDICAL EXPENSES)

(e) As additional child support (Husband) (Wife) shall (provide) (maintain) sufficient medical and hospitalization insurance to cover and pay all medical, drug, clinic, hospital and outpatient charges incurred for the benefit of the child(ren).

(1) (Husband's) (Wife's) obligation under this subparagraph (3(e)) includes psychological, psychiatric, dental, and orthodontic expenses.

(2) To the extent any charges incurred under this subparagraph are not covered or paid by insurance (Husband) (Wife) shall pay to (Wife) (Husband) (all) (one-half (½)) of such uninsured charges.

(3) (Husband's) (Wife's) obligation under this subparagraph (3(e)) shall terminate at the time all (his) (her) child support obligations under paragraph (3) have terminated or have been discharged in full.

(4) All bills for charges incurred under this subparagraph (3(e)) shall be forwarded directly to (Husband) (Wife) and (he) (she) shall either pay said charge or file a claim for insurance within (30) days after receipt of any such bill.

(COLLEGE EDUCATION
OR
VOCATIONAL TRAINING)

(f) As additional child support, (Husband) (Wife) shall pay all expenses incidental to or arising out of the attendance by 1.31 at a college, university or vocational school, provided:

(1) Said child is enrolled in a curriculum directed at securing an undergraduate degree or a certificate of completion of vocational training in four (4) years or less.

(2) (Husband's) (Wife's) obligation under this subparagraph (3(f)) shall terminate on the date said child attains the age of twenty-two and one half (22½) years, provided further, (he) (she) shall remain responsible for unpaid expenses incurred prior to such date.

(3) "Expenses" includes tuition and enrollment fees, official costs, books and educational supplies, room and board, transportation to and from the campus at the beginning or end of the school term or during holidays, and all incidental costs.

(4) (Husband's) (Wife's) liability under this paragraph (3(f)) shall not exceed those expenses normally incurred by a resident student at the major land-grant college in the state of _____ residence during the actual years of _____ college attendance.

4. *Division of Property.*

Practice Guide: The Deficit Reduction Act of 1984 completely altered the income tax effects of transfers of appreciated property between spouses or former spouses. No tax is now recognized on the transfer and the transferee takes the basis of the transferor in the property.

Husband and Wife intend hereby to divide equitably between them [specific property]. Husband and Wife agree that they are co-owners of [the property] and intend this division to recognize their community type ownership of this marital property wherein their respective rights vested during their marriage or on the date of commencement of [the divorce action].

(a) Residence:

Husband and Wife are co-owners of real property known as (*address*) _____ and more particularly described in Exhibit "_____", attached hereto and incorporated herein as if fully set forth (hereinafter the "Property").

(TRANSFER TO SPOUSE)

(1) (Husband) (Wife) agrees to transfer by (quit-claim) (warranty) deed all (his) (her) right, title and interest to the Property to (Wife) (Husband).

OR
(IMMEDIATE SALE WITH
DIVISION OF PROCEEDS)

(1) Husband and Wife agree to sell the Property as soon as practicable and, upon consummation of said sale, to divide the net proceeds received therefrom in equal shares between them.

OR
(DEFERRED SALE WITH
DIVISION OF PROCEEDS)

(1) (Husband) (Wife) shall have the exclusive use and possession of the Property until (*specific date*) _____ (the youngest child of the parties then residing with (the custodian) becomes eighteen (18) years of age). Upon the occurrence of (the condition) the parties shall sell the Property as soon as practicable and, upon consummation of said sale, divide the net proceeds received therefrom in equal shares between them.

("NET PROCEEDS" DEFINED)

(2) "Net Proceeds" means that sum of money remaining after subtracting from the total sale price of the Property the following items: all valid encumbrances against the Property created on or before the date of execution of this Agreement (including the deed to secure debt held by _____,) all ad valorem taxes due on the date of closing of the sale, all hazard insurance premiums due on the date of closing of the sale, all costs of sale, (including reasonable broker's commission), and (*list others*) _____ .

(DIVISION OF LIABILITY
FOR CAPITAL GAINS TAX)

Practice Guide: The capital gain tax consequences of transfers of appreciated property incident to divorce may be eliminated by legislation pending before the Congress.

(3) Any capital gains tax owed by Husband or Wife as a result of the sale of the Property shall be paid as follows: (Specify division of tax liability). (In the event (Husband) (Wife) is entitled to a deferment of any capital gains tax (he) (she) may owe by reason of the purchase of a new principal place of residence after sale of the Property (the record title

holder) shall be entitled to the benefit of said deferment in calculating the tax owed.)

Practice Guide: The language in parentheses is intended for situations such as that where one spouse is the title holder but is transferring property to the other and the transferee is responsible for the tax.

(4) During the period between execution of this Agreement and sale of the Property pursuant to paragraph (4(a)(1)):

Practice Guide: Provision should be made for the following contingencies:

(1) Use and occupancy of the property;

(2) Liability for "mortgage" payments, taxes, insurance, repairs, improvements, and other anticipated costs. Also consider whether the party paying such costs should receive a total or partial credit for those expenses and whether "net proceeds" (paragraph 4(a)(2)) should be redefined accordingly.

(3) Death, incapacity, or bankruptcy of the Husband or Wife.

(4) Allocation of tax deductions created by payment of expenses pending sale.

(b) Personal Property:

See Practice Guide preceding paragraph 4(a) supra.

(ALLOCATION OF PERSONAL PROPERTY)

(1) (Husband) (Wife) shall, from and after the date of execution of this Agreement be the owner of (the following personal property) (the personal property listed in Schedule "_____", hereto attached and incorporated as if fully set forth herein).

Practice Guide: A similar paragraph should be included for each party. Property should be identified as specifically as possible and separate provisions may be advisable for bank accounts, negotiable securities and instruments and other items of particular value. Personal property should be listed in detail on the schedules as a protection against post-divorce litigation between the former spouses.

OR

(1) Husband and Wife have amicably divided their personal property and from and after the date of the execution of this Agreement, each shall be the owner of any such property in their respective custody and control.

(RESPONSIBILITY FOR ENCUMBERED PROPERTY)

(2) Any liens or encumbrances against the property listed in Schedule(s) "_____" shall, from and after the date of this Agreement be paid by [the owner], except as otherwise specifically provided in this Agreement.

Practice Guide: Special problems concerning delivery and storage of the property should be dealt with in a separate subparagraph.

5. *Indebtedness.*

(RESPONSIBILITY FOR INDEBTEDNESS)

(a) (Husband) (Wife) henceforth shall be responsible for timely payment in full of the following debts according to their respective terms: (*list debts*)

_____.

Practice Guide: Debts should be specifically described, including creditor, balance owed, monthly or other payment amount, and account or loan number. All debts should be included. A separate paragraph should set forth the responsibility of each party.

(INDEMNIFICATION)

(b) (Husband) (Wife) agrees to indemnify (Wife) (Husband) and hold (her) (him) harmless against any claims for the debts, or any of them, set forth in paragraph (5(a)). Should (Wife) (Husband) be required to pay or defend any claim for any such debt or debts (Husband) (Wife) will pay or reimburse the full amount of such claim, together with any costs of defense, including attorney fees.

Practice Guide: If a debt is secured by certain property awarded the party not responsible for payment, provision should be made for foreclosure of the security interest.

(DEATH OF RESPONSIBLE PARTY)

(c) In the event of the death of (Husband) (Wife) prior to payment in full of all debts for which (he) (she) is responsible, pursuant to paragraph (5(a)), the remainder of any such claims shall be a charge against (his) (her) estate.

Practice Guide: In the event the debts are substantial and the party not responsible for them is a co-maker or guarantor, an insurance provision equal to the liability may be advisable.

(BANKRUPTCY OF RESPONSIBLE PARTY)

(d) In the event of the bankruptcy of (Husband) (Wife) prior to the payment in full of all the debts for which (he) (she) is responsible, pursuant to paragraph (5(a)), and which (Wife) (Husband) is a co-maker or guarantor, payment of said debts is agreed to be an alimony obligation of (Husband) (Wife) and not dischargeable.

(6) *Insurance.*

(LIFE INSURANCE OWNED)

(a) (Husband) (Wife) represents that (he) (she) is the owner of the following policies of insurance on (his) (her) life:

Insurance Policy No. Face Amount Beneficiary Encumbrance

(MAINTENANCE OF EXISTING POLICIES)

(b) (Husband) (Wife) agrees to maintain the aforesaid policies and to pay all premiums thereon when due until ((his) (her) (child support) (alimony) obligations under this Agreement are fully performed). (Husband) (Wife) further agrees to instruct (his) (her) insurers to change the beneficiaries of each such policy to (the minor child(ren) of the parties) and to further instruct said insurers to send copies of any notices pertaining to said policies to (Wife) (Husband).

(PURCHASE OF ADDITIONAL INSURANCE)

(c) (Husband) (Wife) further agrees to purchase additional insurance on (his) (her) life in the face amount of _____ ($_____) Dollars and to maintain such additional insurance and to instruct his insurer regarding beneficiaries and notices as provided in paragraph (6(b)).

(CHARGE AGAINST ESTATE)

(d) Should (Husband) (Wife) fail to maintain the requisite amount of insurance or allow encumbrances thereon to reduce the total face amount of said insurance below (_____ ($_____) Dollars) (the sum total of his remaining child support obligations under this Agreement calculated as of the instant preceding (his) (her) death) then there shall be a first charge against (Husband's) (Wife's) estate in an amount equal to (the difference between the actual and required insurance amounts) (the difference between remaining child support obligations calculated as aforesaid and the insurance actually owned less the amount of any encumbrances thereon).

Practice Guide: The attorney may wish to include provisions regarding the form of insurance (e.g., term, whole life) or permitting a decline in insurance owned to accommodate a decline in child support or alimony obligations. In addition, the beneficiary can be made the owner of all or some of the insurance or it can be held in trust.

7. *Income Tax.*

(DEPENDENCY EXEMPTION)

(a) So long as (Husband) (Wife) shall be current in all (his) (her) child support obligations pursuant to paragraph (3) of this Agreement, (he) (she) shall be entitled to claim the minor child(ren) as exemptions on (his) (her) federal and state income tax returns. (The custodial parent) hereby relinquishes the dependency exemption for (_____) for the following years: (specify). This relinquishment shall be invalid for any year in which (the non-custodian) is delinquent in payment of (his/her) child support obligation in whole or in part. Husband and Wife agree that they shall claim the dependent child exemption

consistent with this paragraph. (Custodian) agrees not to claim (child) as a dependent in (any year) in which (non-custodian) agrees not to claim (child) as a dependent in (any year) in which (he/she) is delinquent in payment of (his/her) child support obligation in whole or in part. (Note: This approach has neither been approved nor disapproved by the IRS.)

Practice Guide: The Deficit Reduction Act of 1984 provides that the party with whom a child resides for more than half of the year is generally entitled to claim the dependency exemption. To relinquish the exemption for a dependent the custodial spouse must sign a written declaration. The relinquishment may be for one year or any specified years or for all future years.

Language substantially equivalent to the form to be released by IRS should be incorporated into the Agreement.

(INDEMNIFICATION)

(b) (Husband) (Wife) indemnifies (Wife) (Husband) and shall hold (her) (him) harmless from any assessment, penalty, fine, or underpayment of federal or state income taxes owed for any taxable year during which the parties filed a joint return.

Practice Guide: If the parties are to file a joint return for a taxable year ending prior to divorce, provision should be made for preparation and filing of the return, supplying necessary information, division of refunds, and liability for underpayment.

8. *Decedent's Estate.*

(LAST WILL AND TESTAMENT)

(a) (Husband) (Wife) agrees that henceforth and while (he) (she) is in life, (he) (she) will maintain a Last Will and Testament which provides that (his) (her) estate be divided and distributed, upon (his) (her) death, in such manner that at least (one-half ($\frac{1}{2}$)) of the value of (her) (her) adjusted gross estate be bequeathed, devised or given to (the child(ren)), share and share alike.

(ADJUSTED GROSS ESTATE DEFINED)

(b) Adjusted gross estate shall be defined in accordance with provisions of the United States Internal Revenue Code and Regulations (in effect as of the date of this Agreement.)

(CHARGE AGAINST ESTATE)

(c) Subparagraph (8(a)) shall be binding on (Husband) (Wife), (his) (her) heirs, administrators, executors, trustees and assigns, whether or not such Last Will and Testament is, in fact, executed by (Husband) (Wife) and (the child(ren)) shall be entitled to property from (Husband's) (Wife's) estate having a value as defined in subparagraphs (8(a and 8(b)), regardless of the terms of (Husband's)

(Wife's) Will or whether or not such a Will is in force at (his) (her) death.

(PROVISION OF COPIES OF WILL)

(d) (Husband) (Wife) shall furnish a true copy of the provisions of (his) (her) Will effecting the intent of subparagraph (8(a)) to (Wife) (Husband) within _____ days following the execution of this Agreement, together with a certification from the preparer of said Will that those provisions are not impaired, contravened or diminished by any other provisions of (Husband's) (Wife's) Will and that those provisions are contained in (Husband's) (Wife's) Last Will and Testament. (Husband) (Wife) shall further provide (Wife) (Husband) with true copies of any codicils or other alterations in (his) (her) Will which affect those provisions, together with a similar certification.

9. *Modification and Waiver.*

(MODIFICATION BY PARTIES)

(a) A modification or waiver of this Agreement or any provision thereof shall not be effective for any purpose unless the same is made in writing and executed with the same formality as this Agreement.

(WAIVER OF STRICT PERFORMANCE)

(b) The failure of either Husband or Wife to insist upon strict performance of any provision of this Agreement shall not be construed to be a waiver of any subsequent default or performance of the same or similar nature.

(NON-MODIFICATION OF PERIODIC ALIMONY)

((c) Husband and Wife hereby waive their statutory right to future modifications, up or down, of the alimony payments provided for herein, based upon a change in the income or financial status of either party.)

OR
(MODIFICATION OF PERIODIC ALIMONY)

((c) The provisions of this Agreement pertaining to periodic alimony may be modified up or down solely in accordance with the laws of the State of Georgia in effect at the date of filing an action seeking such a modification and upon such terms or conditions as may by such laws be required or permitted.)

Practice Guide: Automatic modifications provisions may be included in the agreement and are enforceable if sufficiently definite. Percentage increases or decreases in periodic alimony payments can, for example, be tied to percentage increases or decreases in income. Waivers of modification of periodic child support by the custodian are void.

A settlement agreement which provides for automatic modification based upon changes in the consumer price index has been held enforceable.

10. *Notices.*

(FORMAL REQUIREMENTS)

(a) Any notice required to be given by this Agreement shall be deemed effective if made in writing and sent by registered or certified mail to the address of the party to be notified last given in accordance with subparagraph (10(b)).

(CHANGE OF ADDRESS)

(a) Husband's address is _____. Wife's address is: _____. Any change in Husband's or Wife's address shall be communicated to the other party in writing, together with the effective date of such change, and sent to the other party, by certified or registered mail, at the address given in this subparagraph (10(b)) or at the last address changed in accordance with subparagraph.

11. *Applicable Law.*

This Agreement shall be construed and governed in accordance with the laws of the State of Georgia.

12. *Partial Invalidity.*

If any provision or provisions of this Agreement is or are held to be invalid or unenforceable, all other provisions are, nevertheless, continued in full force and effect.

13. *Implementation of Agreement.*

Husband and Wife agree to execute any documents required to effect the terms of this Agreement and to perform any other legal act required to implement or effect the terms and intention of this Agreement.

14. *Religious Divorce.*

At the request of either Husband or Wife, the other party agrees to perform any acts and to execute any documents as may be required to obtain a divorce in accordance with the doctrines of the _____ faith.

Practice Guide: This provision is common where the parties are of the Jewish faith.

15. *Subsequent Divorce.*

No provision of this agreement shall be deemed to prevent Husband or Wife from instituting or defending a suit for divorce against either of them based on conduct occurring prior to the date of execution of this Agreement. In the event such an action is instituted, the parties shall be bound by all the provisions of this Agreement. If permissible under the rules of practice and the laws governing the court with jurisdiction of such an action, this Agreement shall be offered in evidence and it shall be incorporated in form and substance into any judgment or decree of divorce rendered by such court.

Notwithstanding any such incorporation, this Agreement shall not be merged into such judgment or decree, but shall in all respects survive the same and be forever binding and conclusive upon Husband and Wife and enforceable independently of such judgment or decree.

16. *Full Settlement.*

The provisions of this Agreement are intended and accepted by Husband and Wife as a full and final settlement of any and all rights or obligations either may have from or to the other arising out of or in any way incidental to their marriage to each other. Husband and Wife acknowledge that each has read the provisions of this Agreement and had the advice of counsel of his or her choosing and further acknowledge that each is satisfied with the provisions of this Agreement and enters into same voluntarily and without duress.

17. *Effective Date.*

This Agreement shall become fully effective and binding on the date first written above, which shall henceforth be known as the "date of execution of this Agreement."

_____(L.S.)
(Name of Husband), "Husband"

_____(L.S.)
(Name of Wife), "Wife"

Practice Guide: If the Agreement is to be recorded, two witnesses should sign opposite the signature of each spouse. The attorney may wish to indicate by signature his or her "approval" of the Agreement, especially if counsel for the opposite party is to submit the Agreement to the court.

SETTLEMENT WORKSHEET
(Sample)

Date:_____

Case Name: _____ v. _____

Firm File No. _____

1. Standard Clauses: _____

2. Periodic Alimony: $_____ /month, payable _____
   to _____.

3. Lump Sum Alimony: $_____, payable _____
   to _____.

4. Child Support: $_____ month, payable _____
   to _____.

5. Property Division: To Wife: _____

   _____

   To Husband: _____

   _____

6. Medical Insurance: _____

   _____

7. Life Insurance: $_____ face amount with _____
   _____ as beneficiary(ies).

8. Child Custody: _____ Wife _____ Husband

9. Special Provisions: _____
_____
_____
_____
_____

SETTLEMENT CLOSING STATEMENT
(Sample)

Date: _____

Case Name:_____ v. _____
Our File No. _____

1. Documents to be Executed and Delivered:

Signature Required / Complete

	Attorney	Wife	Husband	Notary
(a) Agreement	( ) Yes	( ) Yes	( ) Yes	( ) No
(b) Deed	( ) No	( ) If Grantor	( ) If Grantor	( ) Yes
(c) Automobile Title	( ) No	( ) If Owner	( ) If Owner	( ) Yes
(d) Stock Certificates	( ) No	( ) If Owner	( ) If Owner	( ) Yes
(e) Change of Beneficiary	( ) No	( ) If Owner	( ) If Owner	( ) No
(f) _____	( )	( )	( )	( )

2. Monies to be Paid:

Received

To Wife: $_____ ( )
To Husband: $_____ ( )
To Attorney: $_____ ( )

3. [Other Required Transactions]:

CHAPTER 8
Husband and Wife as Partners

Unhappily Ever After

Prince Charles and Princess Diana married in 1981 in perhaps the most heralded wedding of the century. Like many marriages between commoners, they did not live happily ever after. Royal tradition and legal restrictions prevent the couple from divorcing. She would lose custody of her sons, both heirs to the British throne, and he could lose his privileged place as heir to Queen Elizabeth II. This chapter surveys the options for commoners.

— Courtesy AP/Wide World Photos.

"It was all Mrs. Bumble. She would do it," urged Mr. Bumble;
first looking round to ascertain that his partner had left the room.
"That is no excuse," replied [attorney] Brownlow. "You were present on the occasion of
the destruction of these trinkets, and indeed the more guilty of the two, in the eye
of the law; for the law supposes that your wife acts under your direction."
"If the law suppose that," said Mr. Bumble, squeezing his
hat emphatically in both hands, "the law is a ass—a idiot."

Charles Dickens, *Oliver Twist*

OUTLINE

8.1 TOWARD A PARTNERSHIP MODEL OF MARRIAGE
8.2 PUBLIC POLICY
8.3 THE DUTY TO SUPPORT
8.4 HEARTBALM REMEDIES
    Breach of Promise to Marry
    Seduction
    Criminal Conversation
    Alienation of Affections
8.5 ALTERNATIVES TO HEARTBALM REMEDIES
8.6 THE NEW DEFENDANT: THE SPOUSE
8.7 THE NEW PLAINTIFF: THE SPOUSE
8.8 MARRIAGE PARTNERS OR BUSINESS PARTNERS?
SUMMARY

8.1 TOWARD A PARTNERSHIP MODEL OF MARRIAGE

For attorneys, marriage is commonly defined by divorce, because that is the most common setting in which marriage confronts the law. Later chapters highlight the marital remains after the funeral of divorce. This chapter, however, attempts to reveal the model of marital relations through other situations in which marital rights and duties are the subject of the law (lawsuits).

An important message that may be gleaned from legal decisions in domestic relations is that the "Father Knows Best" happy family model is no longer tenable; the borderline dysfunctional "Roseanne" show family is more likely to enter the courtroom, and may in fact be more typical of the American family.

The partnership model of the family appears to be the powerful trend of the 20th century. It provides a useful legal perspective in two ways. First, the view of husband and wife as partners conforms to modern values regarding intimate relations. Understood in the term *partners* is "equal partners," and this concept is found explicitly and implicitly in the cases and modern statutes. Second, the partnership is a metaphor for a business enterprise for profit. Partnerships are business arrangements of close, mutual, and trusting individuals who have decided to pool their talents and resources to succeed in a chosen enterprise. Husband and wife fit this model, with the additional features of a sexual relationship and procreation as a traditional goal. In fact, procreation appears to be the enterprise which the law has assigned to the spouses.

> In the instant case, it is apparent that the state's refusal to grant a license allowing the appellants to marry one another is not based upon appellants' status as males, but rather it is based upon the state's recognition that our society as a whole views marriage as the appropriate and desirable forum for procreation and the rearing of children. This is true even though married couples are not required to become parents and even though some couples are incapable of becoming parents and even though not all couples who produce children are married. These, however, are exceptional situations. The fact remains that marriage exists as a protected legal institution primarily because of societal values associated with the propagation of the human race. Further, it is apparent that no same-sex couple offers the possibility of the birth of children by their union. Thus the refusal of the state to authorize same-sex marriage results from such impossibility of reproduction rather than from an invidious discrimination "on account of sex."
>
> — *Singer v. Hara,* 11 Wash. App. 247, 522 P.2d 1187 (1974)

As implied by this excerpt from *Singer v. Hara,* changing family and sexual lifestyles in America have put pressure upon the enterprise of procreation, but the partnership model remains. Like a business partnership, a marriage may now be dissolved without the need of showing either side at fault, the issue being a fair and proper division of the resources. When children are involved, their interests may be paramount for the court, but the dissolution of partnership, viewed in material terms, remains the model for the breakup.

A partnership is really just a contract to join together in a business enterprise. The major change in family law brought about by the application of this model is the introduction of business concepts to the relationship. In the past, marriage was seen as a contract based on consent; it was an ongoing— ideally a lifelong—enterprise, designed to be mutually beneficial and satisfying. In times past, only limited choices were available to the partners. Men were assigned the task of breadwinner, usually in whatever work their fathers did, and wives were keepers of the hearth. The rules of the partnership were not open for negotiation. Society and law assigned rights and duties to husband and wife appropriate to what then seemed their natural and eternal roles in life.

Today, in America individuals and couples have a multitude of choices in terms of their personal and mutual goals and satisfactions. No longer is it possible for lawmakers, whether legislators or judges, to define the marriage contract precisely and completely. We have seen in previous chapters how couples have been given increasing power to set the terms of their relationships. In most cases husband and wife do not execute an express contract detailing the terms of their relationship. They operate as a partnership, and the terms of the partnership may be inferred from their conduct. Thus, the court may conclude from the nature of one relationship that this was a traditional family, wherein the husband assumed the duties of provider while the wife was a full-time homemaker. It might be apparent, however, that another family completely reversed the traditional roles, or lived under very different arrangements. There is mounting pressure to expand the definition of *family* in America. This is due in part to the unavailability of employee, pension, and government benefits to those who do not fit definitions of *spouse, parent,* or *child.* Homosexuals have also pushed for marital rights. As yet, however, homosexual couples have received little legal recognition.

8.2 PUBLIC POLICY

Although a couple may formally set the terms of their marriage by way of an antenuptial agreement, the law imposes certain responsibilities on the marital and family relationships. An antenuptial or postmarital contract that attempts to waive fundamental rights or duties considered to be firmly rooted in public policy is likely to be unenforceable. Nevertheless, this bedrock called *public policy* has changed dramatically in this century and continues to change (e.g., expansion of the concept of the family) as noted in § 8.1. The increasing recognition of women's rights has been a driving force for change. Women have not only entered the workforce in larger and larger numbers, but they have also entered professions, like law, from which they were once legally excluded and later effectively discouraged by social values. Many law schools now have more female than male students.

Public policy is a phrase often used in judicial decisions in family law to indicate that the state has expressed social values through its laws and policies. For example, we have seen that the courts claim a continuing concern for the stability of the family. Marital agreements that promote or encourage divorce may be denied judicial enforcement on the grounds of public policy. To a certain extent, public policy in family law merely reflects the biases of society (or maybe the judges and legislators) at any particular point in time. These biases may be called "social values," or even "natural law," but their changing character suggests that public policy is transitory. As change

DICTA

Public policy is clouded in the mysteries of the values underlying the law. Sometimes it simply means what is good for society: "Whatever is injurious to the interests of the public is void, on the grounds of public policy." Sir Nicholas Conyngham Tindal, English jurist, in *Horner v. Graves*, 7 Bing. 743 (1831).

accelerates, litigation is encouraged; the more we see judges stating that old social values have been replaced by new ones, the more litigants will press for even more changes. For example, countless cases refer to the antiquated view of the subordinate role of woman and wife. In fact, this chapter is largely devoted to the partnership model that portrays the modern wife as an equal partner with the husband. The changes in law wrought by changes in social values quite naturally encourage those ordinarily excluded from the family model, such as homosexuals, to seek legal recognition. If we are redefining the family, those who were unhappy with prior definitions will seek to have their positions considered. This discussion in the courts often invokes the mystical concept of public policy, but ultimately *public policy* is defined as the court's interpretation of the values underlying legislation (e.g., states adopting gender-neutral legislation have expressed a strong policy with regard to sexual equality), and expresses the biases of the judges framed in terms of important social values recognized by the law.

CASE NO. 8-1   Loss of Consortium

Gates v. Foley is an example of litigation designed to change the law. Under the common law a husband, but not a wife, could sue for loss of **consortium**, and this was the law of Florida until *Gates*. The inability of the wife to sue for loss of consortium was based on antiquated social and legal concepts. An enterprising attorney concluded that the law was due for a change and persuaded Mrs. Gates that it was worth pursuing well beyond the trial court, probably to the Florida Supreme Court, because lower courts, bound by prior precedents, were unlikely to go against the law as stated and the opposing party would most certainly appeal an award to Mrs. Gates.

GATES v. FOLEY
247 So. 2d 40 (Fla. 1971)
Supreme Court of Florida

ADKINS, Justice.

* * *

Plaintiff, Hilda I. Gates, sued the Defendant, alleging that the Defendant negligently operated his automobile causing a collision with an automobile operated by the husband of Plaintiff. It is further alleged that as a result of the accident Plaintiff's husband was rendered totally disabled and the Plaintiff claimed damages for "the loss of consortium and other services from her said husband."

* * *

At common law the wife could not maintain such an action. In 1950 the United States District Court of Appeal for the District of Columbia decided Hitaffer v. Argonne Company, 87 U.S.App.D.C. 57, 183 F.2d 811, 23 A.L.R.2d 1366, cert. den. 340 U.S. 852, 71 S.Ct. 80, 95 L.Ed. 624 in which the Court updated the common law of the District of Columbia by acknowledging a cause of action in the wife for loss of consortium.

This Court, in Ripley v. Ewell, 61 So.2d 420 (Fla.1952), rejected the reasoning in the Hitaffer case and followed the common law doctrine.

* * *

Since Hitaffer v. Argonne Company, *supra,* a flood of authorities in other jurisdictions have overturned the common law rule and, on various grounds, allowed the wife to recover for loss of consortium. [Footnote cites 23 states.]

* * *

We are asked to overrule Ripley v. Ewell, *supra,* as well as Wilson v. Redding, . . . , and follow the trend which has been definitely in the direction of approving the wife's cause of action for harm to the marriage relation resulting from negligent injury to her husband. See Prosser on Torts, (3rd Ed.) § 119, p. 918.

It should be specifically noted that the suit is for "loss of consortium" and not loss of support or earnings which the husband might recover in his own right. We are only concerned with loss of consortium, by which is meant, the companionship and fellowship of husband and wife and the right of each to the company, cooperation and aid of the other in every conjugal relation. Consortium means much more than mere sexual relation and consists, also, of that affection, solace, comfort, companionship, conjugal life, fellowship, society and assistance so necessary to a successful marriage. Lithgow v. Hamilton, 69 So.2d 776 (Fla.1954).

As discussed in Ripley v. Ewell, *supra,* Fla.Stat. § 2.01, F.S.A., adopts the common law of England. The Court recognized the principle that if the inability of the wife to recover in a case of this kind is due to some reason of the common law which has disappeared, the rule denying her the right to maintain the action may have disappeared with it. This principle is a part of the common law which was adopted by the Florida Statute.

The law is not static. It must keep pace with changes in our society, for the doctrine of **stare decisis** is not an iron mold which can never be changed. . . .

It may be argued that any change in this rule should come from the Legislature. No recitation of authority is needed to indicate that this Court has not been backward in overturning unsound precedent in the area of tort law. Legislative action could, of course, be taken, but we abdicate our own function, in a field peculiarly nonstatutory, when we refuse to reconsider an old and unsatisfactory court-made rule.

* * *

The recent changes in the legal and societal status of women in our society forces us to recognize a change in the doctrine with which this opinion is concerned. The Florida Constitution (1968) contained the following significant clauses:

> "All natural persons are equal before the law." Article 1, Section 2. "No person shall be deprived of life, liberty or property without due process of law." Article 1, Section 9.
>
> "The courts shall be open to every person for redress of any injury, and justice shall be administered without sale, denial or delay." Article 1, Section 21.
>
> "There shall be no distinction between married women and married men in the holding, control, disposition, or encumbering of their property, both real and personal." Article 10, Section 5.

Prior to the 1968 revision, the Florida Constitution always contained a provision that *all men* are equal before the law (Fla.Const., Declaration of Rights, § 1 (1885)); and that every person could have a remedy for injury done *him* by due course of law (Fla.Const., Declaration of Rights § 4 (1885)).

The Florida Legislature has enacted the Married Woman's Property Act (Fla.Stat., Ch. 708, F.S.A.), and the United States Congress has passed the Civil Rights Act

(U.S.C.A. Title 42, Ch. 21). Discrimination on the basis of sex has been proscribed by the United States Congress. U.S. Code Title 42, § 2000e et seq.

So it is that the unity concept of marriage has in a large part given way to the partner concept whereby a married woman stands as an equal to her husband in the eyes of the law. By giving the wife a separate equal existence, the law created a new interest in the wife which should not be left unprotected by the courts. Medieval concepts which have no justification in our present society should be rejected. We therefore hold that deprivation to the wife of the husband's companionship, affection and sexual relation (or consortium, as above defined) constitutes a real injury to the marital relationship and one which should be compensable at law if due to the negligence of another.

A husband, of course, has a cause of action for loss of consortium of his wife when she suffers personal injury through the negligence of another, Busby v. Winn & Lovett, Miami, Inc., 80 So.2d 675 (Fla.1955). No reasonable suggestion can be offered any longer to explain the disparity in the spouses' relative rights to secure damages for loss of consortium. No reasonable distinctions may be made between the wife's claim for negligent impairment of consortium and a similar claim by her husband. As consortium is defined above, the interests of the husband and wife are the same and it necessarily follows that negligent impairment of those interests by an outsider ought to have the same legal consequences.

* * *

The intangible segments of the elements comprising a cause of action for loss of consortium are equally precious to both husband and wife. The classification by sex formerly made by this Court discriminates unreasonably and arbitrarily against women and must be abolished. We recede from Ripley v. Ewell, *supra.*

* * *

The rule that we now recognize is that the wife of a husband injured as a proximate result of the negligence of another shall have a right of action against that same person for her loss of consortium. We further hold that her right of action is a derivative right and she may recover only if her husband has a cause of action against the same defendant. This means that the tortfeasor was negligent and the husband was free from contributory negligence.

* * *

The decision of the District Court of Appeal is quashed and the cause is remanded to that court with instructions to further remand same to the trial court for further proceedings not inconsistent with this opinion.

It is so ordered.

ROBERTS, C.J., and ERVIN, CARLTON, BOYD, and DEKLE, JJ., and SPECTOR, District Court Judge, concur.

The precedent that *Gates* overruled, *Ripley v. Ewell,* 61 So. 2d 420 (Fla. 1952), was a 20-year-old case from the Florida Supreme Court. The language of *Ripley* could not be sustained. It justified discrimination on grounds that would be especially offensive today, 40 years later:

> The underlying process of thinking that evolved the common-law rule seems to be that the law would allow a recovery by one person having a special property interest in the services of another when such other was injured by the wrongful act of a stranger.

It seems remarkable that, as late as 1953, the Florida Supreme Court would justify discrimination on the grounds that the husband had a special property interest in his wife's services. The court's analogies to father and child, master and servant are not very reassuring.

Ripley represented a view of the world that is no longer tenable, a world in which a wife could recover large amounts for the wrongful death of her husband but nothing for the loss of his companionship while a husband could recover for the loss of his wife's companionship but relatively little for her wrongful death. The common law held that a husband had a duty to support his wife and the wife had a duty to provide domestic services, to follow her husband in his workplace, etc. These rules were still part of Florida law in 1953.

8.3   THE DUTY TO SUPPORT

Spousal support during the marriage has changed from the unilateral duty of the husband to support the wife to duties of mutual support. The intricacies of these obligations are revealed by the liability for necessaries, which has shifted along with the duty to support.

Cases No. 8-2 and 8-3 involve a common law rule that imposes liability on a husband for debts incurred by his wife if the debts were for "necessaries," i.e., food, clothing, and shelter. In each case a hospital is suing the surviving spouse for expenses of the last illness. Although each court acknowledges that hospital expenses qualify as necessaries and each accepts an equal protection argument to abolish the common law rule, the results are diametrically opposed. Each court takes a modern view of family and society. Which provides the most "modern" rule?

LEGAL TERMS

consortium
Historically, a claim for damages due to personal injury or wrongful death of the wife. The husband brought the action against the third party who caused the injury. A major component of damages was often the loss of sexual services; although consortium is sometimes defined as conjugal affection, companionship, etc., it usually encompasses much more.

stare decisis
A Latin expression meaning "Let the decision stand." It represents the principle of precedent, the hallmark of the common law, whereby judges should decide cases based on rules set forth in prior cases involving similar facts.

CASE NO. 8 -2

SCHILLING v. BEDFORD COUNTY MEMORIAL HOSPITAL, INC.
225 Va. 539, 303 S.E.2d 905 (1983)
Supreme Court of Virginia

STEPHENSON, Justice.

In this appeal, we consider the applicability and constitutionality of the common law "necessaries" doctrine. . . .

Appellant's wife was hospitalized four times. Upon each admission, she signed a promissory note, which the hospital filled in at her discharge for the amount of its charges. The hospital requested appellant to obligate himself for his wife's expenses, but he refused. Nevertheless, the hospital listed appellant as "guarantor" on its records. A hospital billing clerk testified it was the hospital's general policy to list husbands as guarantors of their wives' accounts. Schilling testified his wife had always personally paid her medical bills with money he provided.

The necessaries doctrine holds that a husband is responsible for necessary goods and services furnished his spouse by a third party. It stems from the common law rule that a wife could not have a separate estate. A husband was entitled to his wife's domestic services and consortium and was in return liable for her support.

* * *

[T]he necessaries doctrine, which makes a husband responsible for necessities provided to his spouse, but which does not impose a similar obligation on the wife, contains a gender-based classification. Appellant argues this classification is violative of Article I, § 11 of the Virginia Constitution and the Equal Protection Clause of the Fourteenth Amendment to the Federal Constitution.

The United States Supreme Court has held that, for a sex-based classification to pass constitutional muster, it must serve an important governmental objective and be substantially related to the achievement of that objective.

[The court rejects the hospital's arguments that the necessaries doctrine serves a governmental function in promoting prompt and efficient hospital treatment.]

It is apparent the necessaries doctrine has its roots in the same, now outdated, assumptions as to the proper role of males and females in our society. It therefore creates a gender-based classification not substantially related to serving important governmental interests and is unconstitutional. The hospital urges us to extend the doctrine so it applies to wives as well as husbands, rather than abolish it. Courts in other jurisdictions have adopted this view. However, this task, if advisable, is better left to the General Assembly.

For the reasons stated, the judgment of the trial court will be reversed and final judgment entered for the appellant.

Reversed and final judgment.

CASE NO. 8 -3

JERSEY SHORE MEDICAL CENTER-FITKIN HOSPITAL v. ESTATE OF BAUM 84 N.J. 137, 417 A.2d 1003 (1980) Supreme Court of New Jersey

POLLOCK, J.
This case presents the novel question whether, in the absence of an express agreement, a widow is liable for the hospital and medical expenses of the last illness of her deceased husband. . . .

The hospital sued Mrs. Baum and the estate of Mr. Baum for the balance due on Mr. Baum's bill, contending that the common law rule that imposed liability on a husband for the necessaries furnished to his wife should be extended so that a wife would be liable for the necessaries, such as expenses of a last illness, of her husband. That contention is based on the increasing independence of women, the emerging concept of marriage as a partnership, and the belief that husbands and wives should be treated equally.

We conclude that the common law rule must yield to the evolving interdependence of married men and women and to the reality that a marriage is a partnership. Consequently, we declare that both spouses are liable for necessary expenses incurred by either spouse in the course of the marriage. As long as the marriage subsists, the financial resources of both spouses should be available to pay a creditor who provides necessary goods and services to either spouse. That conclusion comports with our belief that in most marriages a husband and wife consider themselves as a financial unit in paying necessary expenses incurred by either marital partner. However, a judgment creditor must first seek satisfaction from the income and other property of the spouse who incurred the debt. If those financial resources are insufficient, the creditor may then seek satisfaction from the income and property of the other spouse.

I

The common law rule imposing liability on a husband for his wife's necessaries derived from the husband's obligation to support his wife. That duty arises not from principles of contract law, but from the marriage relation and the public policy of the State. The husband's duty developed in an era when a wife depended on her husband for support and, in exchange, provided him with her services and society. A wife had no duty at common law to support her husband.

The husband's duty to support his wife led to the imposition of liability on him for necessaries furnished to her. The basis of liability for expenses incurred by the wife was the husband's presumed failure to provide adequate support. There is no doubt that the cost of hospital and medical care qualifies as a necessary expense. Accordingly, in the converse of the present case, a widower was found liable for the payment of the expenses of the last illness of his wife. However, a wife was not bound to pay the expense of the last illness of her husband unless she assumed that obligation.

* * *

III

In support of its argument that wives should be liable for the debts of their husbands, the hospital relies on *Orr v. Orr,* 440 U.S. 268, 99 S.Ct. 1102, 59 L.Ed.2d 306 (1979). In *Orr,* the United States Supreme Court held that a statute under which husbands, but not wives, might be ordered to pay alimony, violated the equal protection clause of the Fourteenth Amendment to the United States Constitution. *Orr* followed a line of cases in which the Supreme Court rejected gender-based classifications.

* * *

IV

A modern marriage is a partnership, with neither spouse necessarily dependent financially on the other. Many women have shed their traditional dependence on their husbands for active roles as income earners.

* * *

Normally a person is not liable for the debt of another in the absence of an agreement. The imposition of liability based on marital status alone is an exception to that rule. Nonetheless, it is a justifiable exception. The reasonable expectations of marital partners are that their income and assets are held for the benefit of the marital partnership and, incidentally, for creditors who provide necessaries for either spouse. However, it would be unfair to accord the same rights to a creditor who provides necessaries on the basis of an agreement with one spouse as to a creditor who has an agreement with both spouses. In the absence of such an agreement, a creditor should have recourse to the property of both spouses only where the financial resources of the spouse who incurred the necessary expense are insufficient. Marshalling the marital resources in that manner grants some protection to a spouse who has not expressly consented to that debt.

V

... Mrs. Baum properly assumed that she incurred no liability when the hospital provided services to her husband, and the hospital did not expect payment from her in providing those services. Since both parties relied on the prior law when the expense was incurred, it would be unfair to apply the rule retrospectively. . . .

On the record before us, there is no basis to hold Mrs. Baum liable for her husband's obligation to the hospital. We conclude that our holding should be applied prospectively. . . .

We affirm the summary judgment in favor of defendant.

Many states have enacted legislation, referred to as *family-expense statutes,* aimed at protecting creditors of husband or wife. Washington provides an unexceptionable example:

> The expenses of the family and the education of the children including stepchildren, are chargeable upon the property of both husband and wife, or either of them, and in relation thereto they may be sued jointly or separately. *Provided,* That with regard to stepchildren, the obligation shall cease upon the termination of the relationship of husband and wife.
>
> — Wash. Rev. Code § 26.16.205.

The Supreme Court of Washington, in *State v. Clark,* 88 Wash. 2d 533, 563 P.2d 1253 (1977), held that this covered expenses of a wife's appeal of felony and misdemeanor convictions (controlled substances and marijuana). In so deciding, the court cited with approval an older Colorado case that held the husband liable for "necessaries" for the expense of an appeal of his wife's second-degree murder conviction. In that case, the court made an analogy of an unusual nature:

> We have said that plaintiff is entitled to have the judgment of conviction reviewed by this court and the necessity for expenses incurred therewith is as apparent and as vital as would be medical expenses incurred in case of her illness. Suffering and anguish resulting from her conviction may be as serious and disastrous as bodily ailments. The trial court found that plaintiff is destitute and that her husband is financially able to bear the expenses incurred in reviewing her conviction.
>
> — *Read v. Read,* 119 Colo. 278, 202 P.2d 953 (1949).

8.4 HEARTBALM REMEDIES

A drastic change in attitude with regard to the legal image of the family is reflected in a relaxed treatment of extramarital sexuality. No-fault divorce reflects this, as adultery was formerly a major ground for divorce. Traditionally alimony was denied an adulterous wife. Sex was a primary feature in the so-called *heartbalm* remedies, a class of tort suits based on wrongful interference in family relations.

There are four principal actions classed as heartbalm actions: breach of promise to marry, alienation of affections, seduction, and criminal conversation (each defined in chapter 3). They have slowly fallen by the wayside under a variety of attacks as discriminatory (equal protection, Fourteenth Amendment), violative of rights of privacy now considered part of the Constitution, and often simply because they seem inappropriate to modern values and mores. The demise of heartbalm remedies exemplifies both a major change in marriage, family, and sexual mores, and a different relationship between legal institutions and the family. Each is treated in this section. The reader should attend to the arguments in terms of the picture they paint of marriage and the family. If marriage is a contract and a partnership, it is a very different one than it once was.

DICTA

The expression *criminal conversation* does not bring to mind adultery, but in fact it is the civil cause of action that corresponds to the criminal action called *adultery* (a crime very rarely prosecuted). It is the legal revenge of the cuckold.

Breach of Promise to Marry

The tort of breach of promise to marry was the first to go. It really does not fit in well with the others, which are based on wrongful interference with marital relations; breach of promise to marry attempts to remedy a failed engagement rather than a failed marriage. It is of historical interest because it emphasizes the primacy of the engagement rather than the marriage. At a much earlier time in history, marriages were arranged, couples often engaged in sexual relations after the engagement, and a woman who was spurned was often rendered ineligible to marry. In more recent times, the action fell into disrepute because the measure of damages included the loss of expected economic advantage—the woman was entitled to received the support she would have received if she had married. Some courts argued that this meant that a rich man was better off marrying and divorcing quickly than breaking off an engagement. The public policy ground asserted for abolition of this cause of action is that it is better for the law to encourage breaking an engagement by one who recognizes that a mistake is about to take place. In view of the increase in the rate of divorce, this seems a practical approach.

Seduction

Seduction originated as an action brought by a father against one who seduced his daughter. Traditionally, seduction required a previously chaste female. Marriage between the seducer and the seduced barred further prosecution. Most states did not allow the action if the woman had reached the age of consent. Today the appropriate action falls within the criminal statutes— punishment for statutory rape rather than compensation for loss of services seems more appropriate when a young girl has fallen victim to a predatory older male.

Criminal Conversation

Like seduction, the crux of criminal conversation is illicit sexual intercourse, except that criminal conversation involves adultery with a married woman rather than fornication with a minor female. In common with seduction, this cause of action seems to make women the property of men and is offensive to modern social and legal notions of equality. On its way to obsolescence, this action sometimes went through a stage in which equal protection required that women could be plaintiffs as well as men.

CASE NO. 8-4   Criminal Conversation

Fadgen describes briefly the rise and fall of this cause of action in Pennsylvania. Note Justice Manderino's concurring opinion arguing a constitutional right of privacy. The Pennsylvania Supreme Court here sounds uncharacteristically modern.

FADGEN v. LENKNER
469 Pa. 272, 365 A.2d 147 (1976)
Supreme Court of Pennsylvania

JONES, Chief Justice.

* * *

This Court last reviewed an action [for criminal conversation] similar to the one presently at bar in 1959. In *Karchner v. Mumie,* 398 Pa. 13, 156 A.2d 537 (1959), the Court upheld a jury verdict in favor of the plaintiff-wife based upon the tort of criminal conversation where appellant-defendant had sought reversal on the ground that the cause of action as developed at common law was only available to married men as against an erring spouse's paramour. The Court reasoned that the Married Women's Property Act of June 8, 1893, P.L. 344, *as amended* by the Act of May 17, 1945, P.L. 625, mandated the extension to married women of the right to bring such an action on their own behalf. *Id.* at pp. 15–17, 156 A.2d at pp. 538–39.

It is clear, however, that first step directed towards fusing the ancient with the "modern" of 1959 was not sufficient revitalization such as

to weather the rapid legal and societal changes witnessed over the past fifteen years. We might look back and well appreciate that, absent the benefit of attitudes reflected in the passage of the Equal Rights Amendment, the Court in 1959 nevertheless laudably rejected the fictitious notion that a wife, like a servant, was the personal property (chattel as it were) of the husband and that an action in criminal conversation was a right sacrosanct to none but the master. Still, the Court's extension to married women of the right to bring such a cause of action only delayed what today demands; that is, the total abolition of a pious yet unrighteous cause of action.

* * *

One of several civil actions directed at protecting against intentional interferences with the marital relationship, criminal conversation comes closest in form to a strict liability tort. The cause of action is made out upon plaintiff's proof that while married to plaintiff, plaintiff's spouse and the defendant engaged in at least a single act of sexual intercourse without the consent of plaintiff. There are but two possible complete defenses to the action: one, obviously, is an outright denial by the defendant of having had any such relation with plaintiff's spouse; the other occurs upon proof that the *plaintiff* consented to the adulterous relation.

It is no defense to the action, however, that the plaintiff's spouse consented nor in fact that the spouse was the aggressor or seducer. *Sieber v. Pettit,* 200 Pa. 58, 49 A. 763 (1901); *During v. Hastings,* 183 Pa. 210, 38 A. 627 (1897). As to the former, it was thought at common law that a wife was not competent to give her consent so as to defeat her husband's interest. *Tinker v. Colwell,* 193 U.S. 473, 483, 24 S.Ct. 505, 48 L.Ed. 754 (1903). As to the justification for eliminating the defense that the wife initiated and pursued the adulterous relationship, in addition to the belief at common law that she was incapable of prejudicing her husband's rights, the law burdensomely presuming the superiority of men over women chastized:

> "The man who breaks up the home of his neighbor by debauching his wife, rendering his children worse than motherless, is not excused because he is weak, and, being tempted by the woman, falls."

Seiber v. Pettit, 200 Pa. 58 at 67, 49 A. 763 (1901).

> "... it is but the old cowardly excuse set up by the first man, 'The woman gave me of the tree, and I did eat.' It did not save from the penalty the first defendant, and cannot, under the law, save this one."

Id. at p. 69, 49 A. at 765. . . .

We, of course, in no way condone sexual promiscuity and continue to hold the institution of marriage in the highest regard. However, the reasoning developed at common law behind stripping a defendant of all defenses to an action in criminal conversation, save the plaintiff's consent, no longer merits endorsement.

. . . "Those actions for interference with domestic relations which carry an accusation of sexual misbehavior—that is to say, criminal conversation, seduction, and to some extent alienation of affections—have been peculiarly susceptible to abuse. Together with the action for breach of promise to marry, it is notorious that they have afforded a fertile field for blackmail and extortion by means of manufactured suits in which the threat of publicity is used to force a settlement. There is good reason to believe that even genuine actions of this type are brought more frequently than not with purely mercenary or vindictive motives; that it is impossible to compensate for such damage with what has derisively been called 'heartbalm'; that people of any decent instincts do not bring an action which merely adds to the family disgrace; and that no preventive purpose is served, since such torts seldom are committed with deliberate plan." Prosser, *supra,* at 887 and authorities cited therein.

* * *

The Order of the court below is vacated and the case remanded for the entry of judgment in favor of the appellant. The civil cause of action based upon the tort of criminal conversation is hereby abolished.

Each party to bear own costs.

MANDERINO, Justice (concurring).

I concur in the result reached by the majority opinion because I believe that result mandated by the decisions of the United States Supreme Court in *Roe v. Wade,* 410 U.S. 113, 93 S.Ct. 705, 35 L.Ed.2d 147 (1973), in which the court held that the right of privacy was broad enough to preclude interference by the state in a woman's decision whether or not to terminate her pregnancy, and in *Cleveland*

Board of Education v. La Fleur, 414 U.S. 632, 94 S.Ct. 791, 39 L.Ed.2d 52 (1974). In the latter case the court stated its recognition "... that freedom of personal choice in matters of marriage and family life is one of the liberties protected by the Due Process Clause of the Fourteenth Amendment."

Alienation of Affections

Although the tort of alienation of affections was not part of the English common law, it was established in every state except Louisiana. This cause of action (unlike criminal conversation) is descriptively named; it is a wrongful interference in the marital relationship by a third party (the defendant)—it is an injury to consortium. Like criminal conversation, however, it has been used frequently in the past by disappointed or vengeful spouses against their partner's paramours. Equally common as defendants have been family members, namely, in-laws, who have intruded in the marital relationship to the point that a spouse claims a compensable injury to the relationship.

Although this action is also very much in disfavor among the state legislatures, it bears an interesting resemblance to the tort action for wrongful interference with business (or contractual) relations. It remains to be seen whether alienation of affections may be replaced by interference with business relations as marriage comes more to be viewed as a contractual partnership. Chief Justice Reynoldson or the Iowa Supreme Court suggested as much in his dissent to the Court's abolition of the cause of action: "Even if marriage is viewed merely as a 'civil contract' ... , the majority opinion is a departure from our modern recognition of the tort of wrongful interference with contractual relations." *Fundermann v. Mickelson,* 304 N.W.2d 790 (Iowa 1981). But Justice Harris, writing for the majority, succinctly stated the classic legal argument against heartbalm remedies: "In the last analysis we think the action should be abolished because spousal love is not property which is subject to theft .... [P]laintiffs in such suits do not deserve to recover for the loss of or injury to 'property' which they do not, and cannot, own." *Id.*

8.5 ALTERNATIVES TO HEARTBALM REMEDIES

Our courts are not yet ready to treat the marital relationship purely as a business partnership. Not only the importance of the family as the building block of society but also the special nature of intimate relations urge a continued recognition of this relationship as special and worthy of protection. It is not surprising that the courts and legislatures disfavored suits brought for sexual misconduct, especially when the spouse in a failing marriage engaged willingly in adultery. For such actions to endure, the wife must be envisioned as the special slave or property of her husband and the mindless victim of a predatory seducer. Although many may entertain this view, it is politically, socially and legally untenable.

Nevertheless, some intrusions into marital and family relations are sufficiently outrageous to evoke remedial steps by the courts and legislatures. When husband and wife work together at a family business, wrongful interference with business relations may be appropriate, depending on the facts of the case. When Robert Bear was "shunned" by the Reformed Mennonite Church, members of the church could no longer do business with him and his wife and his children could not speak to him. The Supreme Court of Pennsylvania acknowledged that he had stated a cause of action for alienation of affections as well as tortious interference with business relationships. *Bear v. Reformed Mennonite Church,* 462 Pa. 330, 341 A.2d 105 (1976). Among the local elders of the church were Bear's closest in-laws.

Nor is *Bear* an isolated instance of suits against religious institutions and their representatives for interference in the marital relationship. Intentional infliction of emotional distress is a likely candidate to replace the heartbalm actions of the past. This was tried and rejected by the Supreme Court of Ohio in a case brought by a husband whose wife had an affair with the Lutheran minister to whom they had gone for marital counseling. *Strock v. Presnell,* 38 Ohio St. 3d 207, 527 N.E.2d 1235 (1988). The court also rejected clergy malpractice in *Strock,* but this is likely to be an attempted basis for suit in other states in situations where professionals, such as physicians, psychotherapists, or lawyers, occupy fiduciary relationships in which vulnerable clients are sexually exploited.

At least one court has apparently approved invasion of privacy as an alternative to alienation of affections (see Case No. 8-5).

CASE NO. 8-5 *Invasion of Privacy*

Husband and wife were estranged by members of the Tridentine Latin Rite Church, an offshoot of the Roman Catholic Church. Leading local members happened to be the wife's sister and mother.

O'NEIL v. SCHUCKARDT
112 Idaho 472, 733 P.2d 693 (1986)
Supreme Court of Idaho

HUNTLEY, Justice.

* * *

Since the many ill effects of the suit for alienation of affections outweigh any benefit it may have, we both affirm the ruling of the trial court and abolish the cause of action in Idaho.

II. INVASION OF PRIVACY

Invasion of privacy occurs when one intentionally intrudes, physically or otherwise, upon the solitude or seclusion of another or his private concerns or affairs. There is liability for such an intrusion if it would be highly offensive to a reasonable person. An intrusion may occur without physical invasion, for example, as by eavesdropping by means of wiretapping, or by persistent and unwanted phone calling. Clearly, however, there must be something in the nature of a prying or intrusion. Also, that which is intruded into must be, and be entitled to be, private. See *Prosser and Keeton on Torts,* § 117 (5th Ed., 1984).

* * *

The trial court herein instructed the jury: A person's "right of privacy" encompasses various rights recognized to be inherent in our concept of ordered liberty and such rights prevent governmental (and private) interference in intimate personal relationships or activities, freedoms of [the] individual to make fundamental choices involving himself, his family, and his relationships with others.

Jerry O'Neil contends that defendants' actions constituted an invasion of his and his wife's domestic privacy and that defendants' actions invaded the domestic privacy of his children.

The jury heard testimony that when Jerry O'Neil came to Coeur d'Alene to see his family, Pauline and the children did not see him for more than a few minutes at a time, and did not spend time with him without a chaperone. Jerry testified that church officials purposefully kept his family from seeing him, and, in fact, for a period of time later during their visit to Coeur d'Alene, hid his family from him at the residence of another church member. O'Neil testified that church officials lied to him or to Pauline or to both of them, telling him that he would have to join the church in order to marry Pauline again, but telling Pauline that all Jerry needed to do was take instruction and agree to raise the children as Catholics. Sister Mary Bernadette wrote a letter to Jerry in which she stated that Jerry must accept the religion "heart and soul" before he could marry Pauline again.

Before Pauline returned to Kalispell to live with Jerry and the children, she, Jerry and Father Chicoine had a meeting outside Bishop Schuckardt's residence. Father Chicoine told Pauline then that if she found herself giving in to Jerry and acting as a wife, that it was her duty to leave him. After they returned to Kalispell, Pauline spent long hours praying with the children, and refused to talk to Jerry alone.

Aside from his own testimony about actions of church members towards his wife, Jerry O'Neil presented testimony from Barbara Strakel, director of the Cult Awareness Center in Coeur d'Alene. Strakel described for the jury the characteristics of and techniques employed by cults. She testified that the practices of the Fatima Crusade have many similarities to those of a cult. The emphasis of her testimony was that the extreme and often abusive behavior of religious cults in general, and this cult in particular, can rise to the level of wrongful and malicious conduct which the courts consider actionable in an alienation of affections suit.

. . . David O'Neil, Jerry and Pauline's son, testified that after his parent's divorce, he and his siblings attended masses and other church meetings with and at the instigation of their mother, grandmother, aunt and other church members. . . . He also stated they had been told by members of the religious community that Jerry O'Neil's religion was wrong and that they should pray for their father's conversion. Further they were told that their father was not a true father or someone they could depend on, and that these statements changed the children's attitude toward their father. . . .

* * *

The jury had before it substantial competent evidence from which to conclude that the plaintiffs had established a claim and right to damages for invasion of privacy. Therefore, the trial court erred in entering judgment n.o.v. on that cause of action.

Accordingly, the verdict awarding the five children $50,000 each is reinstated, and the trial court, on remand, is directed to enter judgment thereon.

However, as to the $250,000 verdict awarded Jerry Bryant O'Neil, the special verdict form and record make it impossible to determine what portion thereof was awarded for alienation of affection and what portion was awarded for invasion of privacy. Therefore, the award cannot stand, and the case is remanded

for new trial on the husband's cause of action for invasion of privacy.

Similarly, the $500,000 punitive damage award cannot stand because it is impossible to determine from the special verdict form what portion thereof, if any, was awarded on the basis of the cause of action for alienation of affections.

* * *

Affirmed in part, reversed in part, and remanded for further proceedings consistent herewith.

SHEPARD and BISTLINE, JJ., concur.

8.6 THE NEW DEFENDANT: THE SPOUSE

At common law, a married woman could neither sue nor be sued, so suits between husband and wife were theoretically impossible. From this and the policy rationalization that interspousal suits would destroy the family came the American doctrine of **interspousal immunity** from tort suit. The demise of the common law notion of marital unity, the married women's property acts, and several movements for equal rights for women led not only to contractual and partnership models of marriage but also to marital partners as individuals in their own rights who could injure and be injured. Most states have found immunity from suit based on a person's status quite difficult to defend in the last part of the 20th century.

As a practical matter, tort suits against spouses are brought in a scenario that includes or sets the stage for divorce. The divorce lawyer must then consider the advisability of such a suit and determine when to bring each suit for maximum effect for the client. Although no-fault divorce seems universal, fault plays a large part in divorce negotiations, for a number of reasons. A tort suit may be one way of threatening the opposing spouse and obtaining a more favorable settlement. Would this be ethical?

The difficulty for the courts may consist in achieving an equitable result when marital property is subject to distribution in divorce as well as to judgment claims in a tort suit.

LEGAL TERMS

interspousal immunity
This is really a subspecies of "intrafamilial immunity," which held that members of an immediate family could not sue each other for tort. Under the earlier common law this was not possible anyway because the father as head of household was the only member of the family who was sui juris, that is, he was the sole legal agent within the family, he could sue and be sued in behalf of the family or its members.

CASE NO. 8-6   Spousal Immunity

The following case presents most of the arguments in favor of retaining spousal immunity. The policy arguments favoring abolition deal primarily with hostility to an immunity based on status; our legal system strongly advocates the principles that all persons are equal before the law and that for every injury there is a remedy.

S.A.V. v. K.G.V.
708 S.W.2d 651 (1986)
Supreme Court of Missouri

RENDLEN, Judge.

This appeal concerns Missouri's longstanding rule of interspousal immunity for tort actions, discussed at length in *Townsend v. Townsend*, 708 S.W.2d 646 (1986). This case differs from *Townsend* in that appellant charges her husband with negligence as well as an intentional tort. We now decide if spousal immunity should continue as a bar to negligence actions or whether it too should be removed as we have done for the intentional tort in *Townsend*. For reasons hereinafter discussed we hold that the archaic doctrine of spousal immunity is no longer available as a bar to negligence actions and the cause is remanded for reinstatement of plaintiff's (appellant's) petition.

The trial court dismissed appellant's petition against respondent in which it was alleged that during the marriage, respondent contracted *herpes praeputialis* and transmitted the disease to appellant. Appellant's three-count petition alleges that respondent willfully, recklessly and negligently transmitted the disease to appellant without informing her of his infection. Count III concludes with the allegation "[t]hat [d]efendant's negligence . . . is the proximate and direct cause of [p]laintiff's contracting this disease, herpes, and thereby suffering injury and damage. . . ."

* * *

In *Townsend v. Townsend,* we considered § 451.290, RSM 1978, as well as earlier case law and found that the rationale for the previously controlling decision of *Rogers v. Rogers,* 265 Mo. 200, 177 S.W. 382 (1915), was no longer persuasive, nor valid. We held that *Rogers* and subsequent cases following the *Rogers* rule were no longer to be followed.

It is generally argued that total abolishment of interspousal immunity will clog courts with trivial suits, disrupt family harmony and result in collusive claims. Respondent in the present case is particularly concerned that tort claims will be duplicative of property settlements and judgment obtained in dissolution of marriage proceedings.

The "flooding" of the courts argument collides with the requirement that courts must provide a forum to redress legitimate and compensable injuries. Further, that argument has been tested and apparently found wanting in thirty jurisdictions which have totally abolished the doctrine of interspousal immunity. Particularly instructive is a case decided by the Supreme Court of New Jersey which first curtailed the doctrine with respect to negligent operation of motor vehicles, *Immer v. Risko,* 56 N.J. 482, 267 A.2d 481 (1970) and thereafter abolished the doctrine entirely. *Merenoff v. Merenoff,* 76 N.J. 535, 388 A.2d 951 (1978). Not only was the New Jersey Supreme Court undeterred in expanding its earlier decision, but, after eight years of experience in an area where potential for fraudulent claims is said to be highest, that court found the "adversary system . . . equal to the task of screening out fraudulent claims." *Id.* 388 A.2d at 961.

A similar argument is made that removal of the bar will lead to a rash of claims of the "unwanted kiss" and "rolling pin" variety.[3] It cannot be said it is beyond the capacity of our courts to examine and on a case-by-case basis define or adjust the duty of care required between married persons to accommodate the "give-and-take" of married life. It seems remarkably inconsistent to argue that connubial bliss will be disrupted to the breaking point by a spouse filing a tort action and in the same breath argue against removing the spousal immunity doctrine because such couples might unite for purposes of collusive claims.

It is particularly important to note that the bar to interspousal tort suits has been curtailed in a variety of cases in Missouri during the last fifty years with no apparent ill effect. . . .

Finally, respondent contends that dissolution of marriage proceedings between the parties affords appellant an adequate avenue of redress. While there are distinct differences between the division of marital property between spouses and awards of damages for an injury, to the extent that conduct of the spouses is taken into account in division of marital property pursuant to § 452.330.1(4), RSMo Supp.1984, the dissolution decree might be admissible in the subsequent tort action subject to usual constraints of relevance, competence and with a careful eye to questions of causation and speculativeness of damages. The same may hold true for the dissolution proceeding if that action follows trial of the tort claim.

In conclusion, we join the majority of our sister states who have taken this step before us. . . .

The judgment is reversed and the cause remanded to the trial court with direction to reinstate plaintiff's petition.

* * *

WELLIVER, Judge, concurring in part and dissenting in part.

* * *

. . . I agree that where there is an intentional tort committed by one spouse against the other there is no sufficient justification for retaining the doctrine. Marital harmony already has been disturbed, and the civil justice system is capable of distilling collusive and insubstantial suits such as the "unwanted kiss" (battery) type of case. . . .

[Welliver reiterates the major arguments of those opposed to abolishing spousal immunity, namely, that] (1) lawsuits destroy family harmony and encourage escalating trivial injuries, and (2) allows collusive suits, e.g., "this really results in a joint venture," with "the husband calling his insurance agent, the wife calling her lawyer and both entertaining visions of better days ahead." *Shook v. Crabb,* 281 N.W.2d 616, 621-22 (Iowa 1979) (LeGrand, J., dissenting).

Has the law progressed so far that now twelve jurors can decide whether a husband should have been more careful when he brought home a vicious dog that he hoped to train but which in the meantime bit the husband's spouse?[1]

---

3 These expressions are shorthand descriptions of those instances when a spouse allegedly subjects the other to minor physical abuse, possibly constituting trivial torts, and often were alleged as general indignities which, when accumulated, might be considered as grounds for divorce under the old "divorce" statutes. . . .

---

1 See also "Great Moments in Domestic Relations," Fortune 114 (April 14, 1986).

CASE QUESTIONS

1. In a companion case, *Townsend v. Townsend,* reported immediately before *S.A.V. v. K.G.V.,* the same court abolished spousal immunity for intentional torts such as battery. Is there a stronger argument for immunity in one class of torts over the other?
2. Is this suit simply a way to punish the husband for adultery, which is no longer punished under no-fault divorce?

8.7   THE NEW PLAINTIFF: THE SPOUSE

With the abandonment of the concept of marital unity and interspousal immunity, it is evident that a wife may sue those who have injured her, including her husband. We have transformed husband and wife from an indissoluble sacred unity into a joint venture for profit. The result is that those contemplating divorce must be circumspect in their behavior and their planning. This, in turn, suggests that attorneys should advise their clients to take defensive measures to build their cases for possible dissolution. Not only is one's spouse a potential knot-breaker, but he or she may also be an adversary in a tort suit.

CASE NO. 8-7

"He who lies down with dogs wakes up with fleas."

ZYSK v. ZYSK
239 Va. 32, 404 S.E.2d 721 (1991)
Supreme Court of Virginia

COMPTON, Justice.

The question for decision in this civil appeal is whether participation in the crime of fornication, in violation of Code § 18.2-344, bars recovery in tort for injuries resulting from that criminal act.

Appellant Lynn L. Zysk instituted this action against appellee Heinz Rudolph Zysk, her husband, seeking recovery in damages for alleged personal injuries and other losses caused by the defendant's conduct prior to the marriage. The defendant filed a demurrer, which the trial court sustained. We awarded the plaintiff this appeal from the court's August 1988 order dismissing the action.

We will summarize the allegations of the motion for judgment in accord with the familiar principle that a demurrer admits the truth of all properly pled material facts. The plaintiff alleged that the parties were married in May 1986 and that they permanently separated about eight months later. She asserted that, shortly before the marriage, "the parties engaged in consensual sexual intercourse." Further, she alleged, "unbeknownst to the Plaintiff, the Defendant was at that time infected with the Herpes Simplex Type 2 virus, and he was a carrier thereof."

In addition, the plaintiff asserted that defendant "was fully aware that he was so infected." She claimed that the infection "was at its active stage and thus was highly contagious at the time the parties engaged in sexual intercourse." She also alleged that at no time prior to the intercourse did the defendant inform the plaintiff of his condition "nor did he attempt to take any precautions whatsoever to prevent the transmission of the virus to the Plaintiff."

As a result, the plaintiff alleged, she became infected with the virus which "is a permanent and incurable condition." She sought judgment in damages for alleged personal injuries, economic losses, and emotional distress on the grounds that defendant engaged in intentional and negligent conduct.

Code § 18.2-344 provides: "Any person, not being married, who voluntarily shall have sexual intercourse with any other person, shall be guilty of fornication, punishable as a Class 4

misdemeanor." In sustaining the demurrer, the trial court implicitly adopted defendant's contention that the plaintiff, a participant in the unlawful act of fornication, is barred from recovering damages resulting from the act. We hold that the trial court was correct.

Virginia follows the general rule that "a party who consents to and participates in an immoral or illegal act cannot recover damages from other participants for the consequence of that act." *Miller v. Bennett*, 190 Va. 162, 164-65, 56 S.E.2d 217, 218 (1949) (wrongful death action against abortionist held barred when plaintiff's decedent consented to abortion, or attempted abortion, performed in violation of Virginia's then general anti-abortion criminal statute). The foregoing principle applies to all civil actions, whether in tort or in contract.

* * *

The facts set forth in the motion for judgment demonstrate that the plaintiff's claim against the defendant clearly is barred by settled Virginia law. The very illegal act to which the plaintiff consented and in which she participated produced the injuries and damages of which she complains.

CASE QUESTIONS

1. There is no indication of a divorce action, but the parties separated after eight months of marriage and had been separated for three years by the time this case was decided. In a divorce action, she would not be likely to receive much in the way of a settlement because of the brevity of the marriage. Now that wives may sue husbands (in most states), is a tort suit sometimes more lucrative than a divorce action?

2. Is this the modern equivalent of seduction or breach of promise to marry? That is, did he seduce her with the promise of a permanent relationship that was fraudulent? Was her infection the modern equivalent of the loss of chastity, something much less valuable than in former times?

3. Is the court backward in its condemnation of premarital sex? Do you think the court is really expressing a sexist attitude that an unmarried woman who engages in unsafe sex is to blame for getting infected? Perhaps the court is afraid of setting a precedent for future AIDS suits?

CASE NO. 8-8

States differ on the issue of whether spouses may sue each other in tort, although interspousal immunity was universal early in this century.

HILL v. HILL
415 So. 2d 20 (Fla. 1982)
Supreme Court of Florida

OVERTON, Justice.

The district court certified to us, as a question of great public importance, whether this Court should modify the doctrine of interspousal immunity, which bars recovery by one spouse against the other, to allow recovery for intentional torts.

* * *

We hold that the protection of the family unit and its resources requires us to answer the question in the negative and reject a change in the interspousal immunity doctrine at this time. In doing so, however, we emphasize that the trial judge in a dissolution proceeding has authority to require an abusive spouse to pay necessary medical expenses and the authority to consider any permanent injury or disfigurement or loss of earning capacity from such abuse when setting alimony. We also point out that in this circumstance we are unable to modify our immunity doctrine as we did with parental immunity in *Ard v. Ard,* 414 So.2d 1066 (Fla. 1982), because insurance coverage is not available for intentional torts.

The present factual situation illustrates the need to retain the present immunity doctrine. This proceeding is the result of a tragic domestic relations custody dispute, complicated by the possibility that one spouse has a mental condition which may require treatment. The parties were married in August of 1972 and had a child in 1973. The wife had two children by a prior marriage. The parties separated in September, 1978, and have since had a contentious relationship concerning the custody of their minor child.

A dissolution proceeding was pending in another division of the circuit court when the wife instituted this action for malicious prosecution, false imprisonment, and abuse of process. . . . The final and principal allegation is that the husband sought to have her involuntarily committed for mental illness and that he succeeded in doing so for a one-day period. . . .

The husband responded with the affirmative defenses that his actions were done on the advice of counsel and that he had probable cause to have his wife committed. As grounds, he asserted that his wife had previously experienced a mental breakdown requiring her confinement in a straitjacket; that she had been previously committed for mental incompetency for three and one-half months; that she followed a charismatic movement, devoting much of her time to religious writing inspired by divine trances. . . . The husband supported his assertions in part with an affidavit from the family minister:

> I am a minister, and I have talked with Mrs. Hill at the request of her husband. She appears mentally sick, which expresses itself in fanatic religious behavior. Believes God is speaking to her verbally. She annointed [sic] the cat with oil before the children. She feels her husband is demon possessed. . . .

The record further reflects that the wife had a history of mental problems, having been declared incompetent and confined to a mental hospital prior to her marriage, and that, after the marriage, she was under the care of a psychiatrist and diagnosed as a paranoid schizophrenic.

* * *

Interspousal tort immunity is a judicial doctrine established to protect the family unit. Historically, under Biblical, Roman, and English common law, the "family" has had certain responsibilities, obligations, and special protections. Many of these are presently contained in our constitution, statutes, and judicially established doctrines.

* * *

The family continues to be an unofficial sociological governmental structure necessary and vital to our free, independent society. We look with great concern upon societies that break up the family unit and entrust children to the state for education and training. Protection of the family unit is a significant public policy and we are greatly concerned by any intrusion that adversely affects the family relationship or the family resources. That is the reason we rejected abolition of the interspousal immunity doctrine in *Raisen v. Raisen*. We emphasize, however, that the purpose of the doctrine is to protect family harmony and resources, not to shield the wrongful acts of a spouse, whether negligent or intentionally tortious, and not to protect insurance companies.

* * *

Our concern is in what manner the abolition of this common law doctrine will affect the family unit, including children and the family resources. We conclude that the abolition would be detrimental to the family as a whole.

* * *

We conclude that in Florida the protection of the family unit and family resources, including the needs of minor children, merits a continuation of the interspousal immunity doctrine for intentional torts. In reaffirming the doctrine, we have taken into consideration and emphasize the authority of the trial judge in a dissolution proceeding to direct the offending spouse to pay the necessary medical expenses not covered by insurance and the judge's authority to consider any permanent injury, disfigurement, or loss of earning capacity caused by an intentional tort in establishing appropriate alimony under section 61.08, particularly that provision which provides "the court may consider any other factor necessary to do equity and justice between the parties."

For the reasons expressed, we approve the decision of the district court of appeal in this case.

It is so ordered.

BOYD, ALDERMAN and McDONALD, JJ., concur.

SUNDBERG, C.J., and ADKINS, J., dissent.

[The Florida legislature abrogated interspousal immunity for battery in 1985, Fla. Stat. § 745.235.]

8.8 MARRIAGE PARTNERS OR BUSINESS PARTNERS?

The sum of what has been discussed thus far in this chapter strongly suggests that husband and wife might well view themselves as adversaries rather than lovemates. From the legal viewpoint, marital partners and attorneys may view marriage as a prelude to divorce or worse. The mutually supportive, sacred and blessed, intimate partnership is singularly absent from modern law.

A middle ground, perhaps, is the business partnership model. This view has always been implied in the community property states, where property acquired during coverture is owned equally. Equitable distribution states have reached a similar position with the presumption of the equal value and contribution of both spouses, regardless of their economic contribution (see chapter 10). Both these schemes, however, are economic, concerned with the distribution of assets without consideration of fault. No-fault divorce minimizes the noneconomic relationship so that dissolution of marriage very much resembles the dissolution of a business partnership. Under the common law, the contribution of the husband was classified as "support," a duty and noncompensable; the contribution of the wife in services was gratuitous, a gift and nonrefundable.

A business partnership is an organization in which a duty of loyalty is owed among the partners. Partners may not act against the interests of the partnership nor the interests of other partners. When the partnership breaks up, it is assumed that the assets were equally shared, unless the partnership agreement indicated otherwise. If we accept these underlying principles as the general rules or customs of business partnerships, we can see that they could readily apply to a marriage partnership. The most important feature of this model concerns the meaning of being a partner, namely, equality of authority, responsibility, and ownership. The marital partnership has develped from a master-servant model toward one of equality.

CASE NO. 8-9 Louisiana Wives Become Partners

We have referred occasionally to the common law doctrine that the husband exercised legal authority for the marital unity. Louisiana, unique in its civil code tradition, did not inherit the common law but nevertheless employed a similar concept in its community property regime. In fact, it held on to the "head and master" concept until quite recently.

KIRCHBERG v. FEENSTRA
450 U.S. 455, 101 S. Ct. 1195 (1981)
United States Supreme Court

Justice MARSHALL delivered the opinion of the Court.

In this appeal we consider the constitutionality of a now superseded Louisiana statute that gave a husband, as "head and master" of property jointly owned with his wife, the unilateral right to dispose of such property without his spouse's consent. Concluding that the provision violates the Equal Protection Clause of the Fourteenth Amendment, we affirm the judgment of the Court of Appeals for the Fifth Circuit invalidating the statute.

I

In 1974, appellee Joan Feenstra filed a criminal complaint against her husband, Harold Feenstra, charging him with molesting their minor daughter. While incarcerated on that charge, Mr. Feenstra retained appellant Karl Kirchberg, an attorney, to represent him. Mr. Feenstra signed a $3,000 promissory note in prepayment for legal services to be performed by appellant Kirchberg. As security on this note, Mr. Feenstra executed a mortgage in favor of appellant on the home he jointly owned with his wife. Mrs. Feenstra was not informed of the mortgage, and her consent was not required because a state statute, former Art. 2404 of the Louisiana Civil Code Ann. (West 1971), gave her husband exclusive control over the disposition of community property.[1]

* * *

While Mrs. Feenstra's appeal from the District Court's order was pending before the Court of Appeals for the Fifth Circuit, the Louisiana Legislature completely revised its code provisions relating to community property. In so doing, the State abandoned the "head and master" concept embodied in Art. 2404, and instead granted spouses equal control over the disposition of community property. La.Civ. Code Ann., Art. 2346 (West Supp.1981). . . .

Because [the former] provision explicitly discriminated on the basis of gender, the Court of Appeals properly inquired whether the statutory grant to the husband of exclusive control over disposition of community property was substantially related to the achievement of an important governmental objective. The court noted that the State had advanced only one justification for the provision—that "[o]ne of the two spouses has to be designated as the manager of the community." The court agreed that the State had an interest in defining the manner in which community property was to be managed, but found that the State had failed to

show why the mandatory designation of the husband as manager of the property was necessary to further that interest. The court therefore concluded that Art. 2404 violated the Equal Protection Clause. . . .

II

. . . Instead the burden remains on the party seeking to uphold a statute that expressly discriminates on the basis of sex to advance an "exceedingly persuasive justification" for the challenged classification. *Personnel Administrator of Mass. v. Feeney,* 442 U.S. 256, 273, 99 S.Ct. 2282, 2293, 60 L.Ed.2d 870 (1979). See also *Wengler v. Druggist Mutual Ins. Co., supra,* 446 U.S., at 151, 100 S.Ct., at 1546. Because appellant has failed to offer such a justification, and because the State, by declining to appeal from the decision below, has apparently abandoned any claim that an important government objective was served by the statute, we affirm the judgment of the Court of Appeals invalidating Art. 2404.

* * *

Accordingly, the judgment of the Court of Appeals is affirmed.

So ordered.

[Justice Marshall noted that Louisiana has modified the managerial rules in its matrimonial property regimes.]

---

[1]   Article 2404, in effect at the time Mr. Feenstra executed the mortgage in favor of appellant, provided in pertinent part: "The husband is the head and master of the partnership or community of gains; he administers its effects, disposes of the revenues which they produce, and may alienate them by an onerous title, without the consent and permission of his wife." This provision has been repealed. . . .

In the past, the breadwinner/homemaker division of family labor put the wife in a particularly disadvantageous position when the marriage was dissolved. Because the assets were owned and earned by the husband, the wife merely received what the court considered owing to her by way of the husband's duty of support. A wife and mother may have labored day and night for her family without earning a penny and was therefore not considered to have contributed economically to the family. This view has generally reversed itself to the extent that the contributions of both spouses are generally considered equal—or, in another way of putting it, both spouses probably contributed 100 percent of their energies and resources to the marriage and the family. This being so, fairness would suggest a 50–50 split.

> Either spouse may contribute either by working in the market place or by working as a homemaker. The fact that in one marital venture a spouse is gainfully employed in the market place and pays a housekeeper to rear the children and keep house is not distinguishable from the spouse who devotes his or her full time to the profession of homemaker.
>
> — *Brown v. Brown,* 300 So. 2d 719 (Dist. Ct. App. 1974).

This image of the marital partnership not only brings it very much in line with basic principles of business partnership, but also advances equality of the sexes and expresses the ideal of companionate marriage that reflects the choices and decisions that those now entering marriage frequently contemplate.

CASE NO. 8-10

A wife's assumption of her husband's surname at marriage is a custom, *not* a law.

IN RE MILLER
218 Va. 939, 243 S.E.2d 464 (1978)
Supreme Court of Virginia

I'ANSON, Chief Justice.

Petitioner, Polly Christine (Brewer) Miller, petitioned the court below . . . to resume the use of her maiden name. The petition was denied, and petitioner contends that the trial court abused its discretion in denying her application.

The record shows that the petitioner's maiden name was Polly Christine Brewer. Upon her marriage to John Miller, she took his surname. There were no children born of the marriage, but petitioner and her husband stated in the sworn supplementary petition they had agreed that any children thereafter born of the marriage would be given their father's surname. Petitioner alleged that the change of name was not sought for any dishonest, illegal, or fraudulent purpose. She stated that she desired to resume her maiden name of Brewer because that is the surname by which she is commonly known. She had also embarked on a career in accounting and is known among her colleagues and clients by her maiden name. A number of creditors extended credit to petitioner and her husband in the surname of Miller, but she stated her intention to notify all her creditors of the change of name.

The trial court, in a memorandum opinion, assigned the following reasons for denying petitioner's application:

(1) ... Even though petitioner announced her intention to notify her creditors of the change of name, the creditors would not have adequate protection if she inadvertently failed to notify them, and thereafter changed her residence.

(2) There is no compelling need for a change of name.

(3) The proposed name change contravenes society's substantial interest in the easy identification of married persons.

(4) Petitioner's as-yet-unborn children would be substantially burdened in explaining to their peers why they did not have their mother's name and why their mother and father had different names.

(5) Petitioner could satisfy her desire for a separate professional career under the provisions of Code § 59.1-69, et seq., relating to transaction of business under an assumed name.

Code § 8-577.1 provides that a change of name may be granted in the "discretion" of the trial court, but it does not set forth any guidelines or criteria for the exercise of that discretion. *Strikwerda* presented us our first opportunity to consider the limits of this discretion.

... [T]he English common law is in force in Virginia, except as altered by statutes, and that Code § 8-577.1 did not change the common-law principles to be considered in petitions filed by married women seeking to resume their maiden names.

Under the common law, a person may adopt any name he or she wishes, provided it is not done for a fraudulent purpose or does not infringe upon the rights of others. Although a married woman customarily assumes her husband's surname, there is no statute requiring her to do so.

* * *

There is nothing in Code § 8-577.1, or in the common law, requiring a showing of a compelling need to justify a change of name. Such a requirement would be inconsistent with the common-law principle that names may be changed in the absence of a fraudulent purpose. . . .

* * *

To reason that a name change of the mother would have an embarrassing effect on her children is pure speculation.

* * *

We hold that the trial court abused its discretion in denying the applicant's petition to resume her maiden name. Such discretion is not unbridled. Exercise of the discretion must be based on evidence, not speculation, that a change of name would infringe upon the rights of others.

For the reasons stated the judgment of the trial court is reversed, and the case is remanded for entry of an order granting the application for the change of name.

Reversed and remanded.

SUMMARY

Although marital rights and duties are commonly legally defined in the process of divorce, the model of the American family may be gleaned from a number of areas of law in which rights and duties have been the subject of litigation. We see, for instance, that the legal image of the family has changed from one in which the breadwinner/homemaker–master/servant model from the common law has been changed to one much more resembling a business partnership in which legal rights and duties are equally shared. Whereas the husband formerly owed a duty of support and the wife the duty of domestic service, the duty to support is now equally shared. A steady abolition of the common heartbalm remedies has taken place, reflecting a change in women's status from that of legal incompetent and something akin to their husband's property into fully capable legal partners in marriage. The demise of interspousal immunity also reflects the changed status of women, who may now redress their own injuries, even against their husbands.

QUESTIONS

1. Does the abolition of spousal immunity reintroduce fault to divorce?
2. When divorces were granted on the basis of fault, the distribution of property and alimony could be adjusted totake into account the conduct of the wrongdoer. Is the institution of a tort suit a better way to "punish" a bad spouse?
3. How does the nature of wrongdoing change from fault grounds of the past to tort suits in the present?
4. Is there a marriage in which intentional infliction of mental distress has not occurred?
5. How does the concept of consortium fit into the modern model of the family? Does it fit the business partnership model?
6. Would you advise divorce for the wife of a terminally ill husband facing large medical costs?
7. Is the expense of an appeal for a felony conviction included in necessaries chargeable to a spouse's assets?
8. How is a marital partnership different from or similar to a business partnership?

EXERCISES

Answer the questions according to the law of your state.

1. What is the status of interspousal tort immunity? 92 A.L.R.3d 901.
2. Is there a right of action for loss of consortium? 46 A.L.R.3d 880; 36 A.L.R.3d 900 (loss to wife).
3. Is the husband solely liable for necessaries? 20 A.L.R.4th 196.
4. What defenses does a husband have to civil suit by his wife for support? 10 A.L.R.2d 466.
5. May a wife obtain compensation for services rendered to her husband?
6. Are so-called heartbalm actions available?
7. If a cause of action for breach of promise to marry is available, what damages are allowed for recovery? 73 A.L.R.2d 553.
8. Does the law recognize husband-wife partnership agreements?

CHAPTER 9
Cohabitation and Marriage Alternatives

Beware the Toothbrush!

The famous "palimony" case involving actor Lee Marvin and Michelle Triola Marvin was settled by the California Supreme Court. The court expressed willingness to honor verbal agreements between unmarried partners who share property acquired while living together are valid and binding. Michelle Triola, who legally changed her surname to Marvin, once remarked, "If a man wants to leave a toothbrush at my house, he can damn well marry me." This chapter explores life before and after the famous case of Marvin v. Marvin.

— Courtesy AP/Wide World Photos.

Saw a wedding in the church and strange to see what delight we married people have to see these poor fools decoyed into our condition.

Entry in Samuel Pepys's *Diary* for December 25, 1665

OUTLINE

9.1 INTRODUCTION
9.2 COMMON LAW MARRIAGE
9.3 CONFLICT OF LAWS AND COMMON LAW MARRIAGE
9.4 MODERN EQUIVALENTS TO COMMON LAW MARRIAGE
9.5 PUTATIVE MARRIAGE
9.6 PRESUMPTION OF MARRIAGE AND MARRIAGE BY ESTOPPEL
9.7 COHABITATION AGREEMENTS
9.8 *MARVIN* AND ITS PROGENY
9.9 *MARVIN*'S FIRST COUSINS
9.10 LESSONS FROM *MARVIN* AND ITS PROGENY
SUMMARY

9.1 INTRODUCTION

The stereotype of a legal marriage is framed in technical terms—a couple is married who have the capacity to marry and who register their marriage at the courthouse. They have a marriage license and are therefore legally married. Of course, there may be a flaw in the marriage, such as a prior undissolved marriage, but, excepting such situations, there is a tendency to perceive the license as the *sine qua non* of marriage. The wedding ceremony may symbolically and ritually join husband and wife, but the license is the essential legal document making the marriage official.

At the same time, it is recognized that today many couples engage in relationships that have all the attributes of marriage *except* the license. Among these are some who make no pretense of their lack of a license, while others hold themselves out as husband and wife and are perceived as such.

Still others fall somewhere in between; for instance, they admit the lack of a license, but she uses his surname.

At an earlier period in American history, **consensual unions** were quite common, especially on the frontier where clergy and courts were few and far between. This gave rise to the common law marriage, which, once established, was just as legally binding as a licensed marriage. As we have seen in prior chapters, the law favors marriage—that is, it will presume that a marriage exists whenever feasible. The law also favors legitimacy, which bolsters the presumption of marriage to avoid making offspring illegitimate. It is no wonder, then, that in an era of consensual unions and erratic or nonexistent recordkeeping, a legal vehicle for establishing marriage and legitimating children would arise.

Perhaps it is not surprising, either, that in the modern era of careful recordkeeping, most states have seen fit to abolish common law marriage and rely more on licenses and records. Thus we find many cases that would in former times have been common law marriages but no longer qualify. Judges are frequently faced with situations begging for some recognition of marital status. For example, a couple maintains a long-term relationship, has children, and is believed by their community to be married. When he dies, technically his "widow" is not entitled to any widow's or survivor's property or benefits. Judges have discovered a number of means to provide an equitable result.

On the other hand, in recent years, many couples have deliberately chosen not to marry even though their relationships have a character resembling most marriages. (Kurt Russell and Goldie Hawn, as well as other celebrities, come to mind.) Still others seem to be engaged in what was formerly called "trial marriage," that is, living together as an experiment in contemplation of marriage. A number of other living arrangements also seem to have developed.

Perhaps nothing is more important to the emotional development of a child than love and encouragement. Does family law play any part in this need?

All these relationships present the same problems that occur in marriage when they end by separation or death. What property belongs to whom? What happens to any children born of the relationship? (The latter question is addressed in the chapters devoted to children, chapters 12 through 15.) The law and the decisions that have arisen in this area tell us about our vision of marriage and family, at least in legal terms.

9.2   COMMON LAW MARRIAGE

As the name suggests, common law marriage was largely a creation of custom and the courts, although some legislatures have established the requirements for common law marriages. The basic requirements are fourfold:

1. *Capacity* to marry.
2. A present, mutual *agreement* to permanently enter the marriage relationship to the exclusion of all other relationships.
3. Public recognition of the relationship as a marriage, "holding oneself out as husband and wife" (*repute*).
4. Public assumption of marital duties and cohabitation (*cohabitation*).

Of these, repute and cohabitation distinguished common law marriage from other forms of marriage. Agreement could be inferred from repute and cohabitation; in the common law of England, the agreement to take each other as husband and wife was the basis for establishing a marriage. In Pennsylvania at least, the magic words of agreement were sufficient to make a marriage, and the words need not have been formal. From the words, "Now you have the ring and you are my wife." "That is fine. I love it.", the Supreme Court of Pennsylvania held that the parties were married. *Rosenberger Estate,* 362 Pa. 153, 155, 65 A.2d 377, 379 (1949).

A common law marriage may take time to establish by repute and cohabitation. Some states that codified the requirements gave a specific time period, such as cohabitation for four or seven years. Once a common law marriage has been established, however, it *relates back,* that is, the couple is deemed married from the outset of the period in which the marriage was established. This establishes the legitimacy of children born to the relationship, but presents problems with ownership of property acquired during the period in which the marriage was germinating. Because common law marriages are informal arrangements lacking official documentation, the existence of a common law marriage may not be discovered through record searches and may present real estate title problems later.

The *Suggs* and *Boswell* cases (Case Nos. 9-1 and 9-2) demonstrate how important time frames are in establishing a common law marriage.

CAVEAT

Although a state may have abolished common law marriage, the practitioner may not necessarily rest easy on the subject. A couple may have established a common law marriage prior to the date of abolition; a property title may be affected by a common law marriage at some time in the past. Knowing the date and effect of abolition in your state can avoid malpractice.

LEGAL TERMS

consensual union
   One of many terms used to refer to a marriage-like union that lacks official or recorded legal recognition. It is relatively stable and potentially permanent and often results in offspring.

CASE NO. 9-1   Timing Is Everything

IN RE SUGGS' ESTATE
405 So. 2d 1360 (Fla. Dist. Ct.
App. 1981)
Court of Appeals of Florida

ORFINGER, Judge.

. . . The personal representative denied the allegations of the marriage, and asserted affirmatively that appellant was not the common law wife of decedent because she was married to another man until April 26, 1968; therefore, she was not competent to become the common law wife of decedent until a time after January 1, 1968, when common law marriages were abolished in Florida. . . .

The two essentials of a common law marriage are capacity and mutual consent. There is competent evidence in the record to support the court's finding that appellant was not the common law wife of decedent, and was thus not his surviving spouse. Because she was married to another on the date when common law marriages were no longer valid in Florida, she lacked the capacity to enter into a common law marriage with decedent while such marriages were still recognized.

Appellant further contended that when she and decedent purchased some real estate in 1971 and took title in the names of "Eugene N. Suggs and Frances Mary Suggs, his wife," she and decedent became tenants by the entirety even if there was no marriage, and thus she was entitled to the entire ownership as the surviving tenant. The trial court held otherwise.

Except for estates by the entirety, a conveyance to two or more persons creates a tenancy in common unless the instrument creating the estate expressly provides for the right of survivorship. § 689.15, Fla.Stat. (1971). A conveyance to spouses as husband and wife creates an estate by the entirety in the absence of express language showing a contrary intent. *Losey v. Losey,* 221 So. 2d 417 (Fla.1969). If appellant had established a valid common-law marriage, the deed in question would have been sufficient to create the estate by the entirety.

* * *

The judgment appealed from is AFFIRMED.

CASE NO. 9-2

BOSWELL v. BOSWELL
497 So. 2d 479 (Ala. 1986)
Supreme Court of Alabama

JONES, Justice.

* * *

The trial court, after hearing testimony without a jury, entered a final decree, which reads, in part:

"Marjorie brings this action to obtain the allotments due a widow. The Executor of the Estate of S.C. Boswell objects upon the ground that Marjorie is not the widow of S.C.

"The conflict in the evidence relates to the issue of whether a common law marriage existed between Marjorie and S.C. after removal of any impediment to a lawful union.

"The court has considered the evidence as it relates to the conduct of Marjorie and S.C. over the approximate 37 or 38 years of living together to determine the attitude of each with respect to marriage. The court concludes from the conflicting evidence that by habit, repute, and cohabitation Marjorie Boswell and S.C. Boswell lived in matrimonial cohabitation and she is entitled to the allotments due a widow of S.C. Boswell."

This Court has recently reaffirmed the requirements for a common-law marriage in Alabama in *Etheridge v. Yeager*, 465 So. 2d 378 (Ala. 1985). In that opinion, citing various cases as precedent, we held that while no ceremony or particular words are necessary, there are common elements which must be present, either explicitly expressed or implicitly inferred from the circumstances, in order for a common-law marriage to exist. Those elements are: 1) capacity; 2) present, mutual agreement to permanently enter the marriage relationship to the exclusion of all other relationships; and 3) public recognition of the relationship as a marriage and public assumption of marital duties and cohabitation.

Appellant argues, however, that the evidence before the trial court negated any finding of a common-law marriage between Marjorie and S.C. Boswell. Appellant contends that because Marjorie and Arthur Fair were ceremonially married in 1944 and were never divorced, and because Marjorie did not begin living with S.C. until 1946, they did not make a present agreement, in good faith, to live together as husband and wife, nor were they capable of doing so. Appellant bases his contention on several Alabama cases.

* * *

We do not argue with these decisions, nor with Appellant's argument that both a present agreement to live together as husband and wife and the capacity to so agree are requisites of a legal common-law marriage. Yet, it is equally true that the record reflects undisputed evidence that Arthur Fair died in June 1983, and that Marjorie and S.C. continued to live together for more than one year until S.C.'s death in 1984. Therefore, upon the death of Arthur Fair, any impediment to the common-law marriage of S.C. Boswell and Appellee ceased to exist. See *Walker v. Walker*, 218 Ala. 16, 117 So. 472 (1928). S.C. Boswell and Appellee continued to live together, holding themselves out as husband and wife, following Arthur Fair's death, thereby mutually agreeing to a common-law marriage.

* * *

The judgment appealed from is affirmed.

9.3   CONFLICT OF LAWS AND COMMON LAW MARRIAGE

Because each state has its own law of domestic relations, problems occasionally arise with regard to the validity of marriages and divorces from other states. As we saw in *Catalano v. Catalano* in chapter 5, the general rule is that one state will recognize as valid a marriage that was valid where performed. This rule would be required by the **full faith and credit clause** of the U.S. Constitution even if it were not a general rule. This still leaves another problem of interpretation of **foreign** law. This is called a *conflict-of-laws problem;* that is, one state, to determine what law applies in a given situation, first looks at its own rules for choosing what state law to apply. Once it has determined what state law applies, it interprets the law of that state. Specifically, if California must determine whether Jane is a widow of James, when Jane claims that they were married in Alabama, the California court would examine California conflict-of-laws principles—which indicate that it must determine the validity of the marriage by the laws governing at the time of the marriage in the state of Alabama. If the marriage was valid in Alabama, it is valid in California.

Ordinarily this is not a problem, because most people have capacity to marry when they marry and they have a ceremonial, licensed marriage. Only under rare circumstances will this be questioned in another state. Unfortunately, a significant minority of couples either lacked the capacity to marry (e.g., one of the partners was already married) or failed to meet the statutory requirements for a license, usually by not obtaining one. The problem does not end there, because lack of a license or capacity is not necessarily fatal to marital status. The state asked to validate the marriage (California in the preceding example) may or may not conclude that the other state (Alabama) would have deemed the couple married. One might expect that this process would be rather mechanical except in unique situations. Nevertheless, we must recognize that a judge from one state interpreting the laws of another state may enjoy a higher degree of freedom than when determining local law.

Common law marriage illustrates the forces at work in such situations. About three-quarters of the states have abolished common law marriages (see figure 9-1). These states, however, have not found common law marriage so abhorrent to their public policy as to refuse to recognize common law marriages from other states. If a couple qualified for common law marriage elsewhere, they should be deemed married everywhere. In most instances, however, no court action is taken until the parties separate or one dies. In our example, California would not have the benefit of any adjudication of the validity of the marriage from Alabama and would of necessity have to rule on its validity based on Alabama law. (Full faith and credit is not really involved in this example, as the court is not asked to enforce a decree of another court.) One might suppose that judges in a state hostile to common law marriage would show little tolerance for an out-of-state common law marriage. Whether a common law marriage existed depends as much on the court's determination of the facts—i.e., the conduct of the partners—as it does on foreign law.

A look at the cases suggests that the merits of each case, or perhaps the merits of each relationship, govern the result. It should also be noted here, as will be shown in subsequent sections of this chapter, that states having abolished common law marriages have used a number of other devices to assign marital rights and duties to legally flawed marriages.

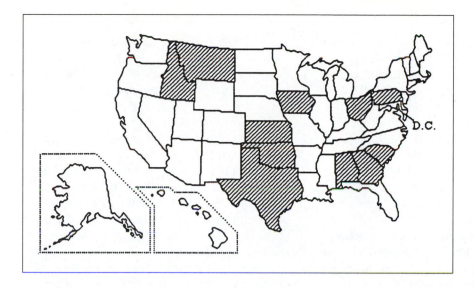

FIGURE 9-1
States recognizing
common law marriage
Source: Areen, *Cases
and Materials on
Family Law*
(3d ed. 1992).

CASE NO. 9-3   Married by Motel in Pennsylvania

The *Renshaw* case strains law and logic to the fullest in order to find a marriage. Note that the issue was Social Security benefits for a widow.

RENSHAW v. HECKLER
787 F.2d 50 (2d Cir. 1986)
United States Court of Appeals

GEORGE C. PRATT, Circuit Judge:

This appeal presents a single question: did the Secretary of Health and Human Services and the district court err in determining that, under Pennsylvania law, plaintiff Edith L. Renshaw was not the common-law wife of the decedent Albert Renshaw, and therefore not entitled to widow's insurance benefits under Title II of the Social Security Act? . . .

BACKGROUND

After a brief courtship following their respective divorces from other individuals, Albert and Edith Renshaw began living together on July 5, 1958 in Baltimore, Maryland. Although the couple did not have a formal ceremonial marriage, Mrs. Renshaw testified that when she and Mr. Renshaw began living together they agreed to live "just as though [they] were married" and that they considered themselves "husband and wife". The evidence supports her assertion.

Edith immediately adopted the last name Renshaw and a short time later, changed the name on her social security card—the only identification she had at that time—to reflect her new status. The couple told friends and relatives that they had been married, and introduced each other to relatives, friends, and acquaintances as husband and wife.

Mr. Renshaw gave Mrs. Renshaw a wedding band shortly after they began to live together, and throughout the 21 years they lived together they celebrated July 5 as their marriage anniversary. The couple never separated or broke up, and Mrs. Renshaw testified that neither ever had relationships with others during this time. Moreover, the couple filed joint tax returns as husband and wife, and Mr. Renshaw listed Mrs. Renshaw as his wife and beneficiary on his life insurance policy.

Immediately after their marriage the Renshaws lived in Maryland for several months. After that, they moved to Buffalo, New York, where they lived for the next twenty years. During this time, the couple had one child, Lorna Gail Renshaw.

On approximately eight occasions between 1968 and 1975, the Renshaws drove to Virginia and North Carolina to visit relatives. Since the visits required a lengthy drive each way, the Renshaws always spent the night at the Port Motel in Port Treverton, Pennsylvania, a state that recognizes common-law marriage. Their daughter always accompanied them on these trips; on occasions when Mr. Renshaw's mother was in Buffalo, she also traveled with them.

* * *

DISCUSSION

. . . Section 216(h)(1)(A) of the Social Security Act, 42 U.S.C. § 416(h)(1)(A), provides that an applicant is the widow of an insured individual if the courts of the state in which the insured individual was domiciled at the time of his death would find that the applicant and insured individual were validly married at the time of his death. Since Mr. and Mrs. Renshaw were domiciled in New York at the time of his death, New York law governs her status as a widow.

Although New York does not itself recognize common-law marriages, a common-law marriage contracted in another state will be recognized as valid in New York if it is valid where contracted. The law to be applied in determining the validity of such a marriage is the law of the state in which the marriage occurred.

Since plaintiff claims that she contracted a common-law marriage with her husband in Pennsylvania during their travels through the state, the appropriate law to apply is the law of Pennsylvania.

The Commonwealth of Pennsylvania recognizes the institution of common-law marriage. *In re Estate of Stauffer*, 504 Pa. 626, 476 A.2d 354, 356 (1984). Believing that common-law marriage is a fruitful source of perjury and fraud, however, the Pennsylvania courts have imposed a heavy burden on one who grounds his or her claim on an allegation of common-law marriage. *Id.*

Generally, a common-law marriage may be created by uttering words in the present tense with the intent to establish a marital relationship, *Commonwealth v. Sullivan*, 484 Pa. 130, 398 A.2d 978, 980 (1979); but where no such utterance is proved, Pennsylvania law also permits a finding of marriage based on reputation and cohabitation when established by satisfactory proof. *In re Estate of Wagner*, 398 Pa. 531, 159 A.2d 495, 498 (1960).

. . . [T]he magistrate . . . noted that "if the facts had shown that the Renshaws lived their lives primarily in Pennsylvania, and conducted themselves there as the evidence indicates they conducted their lives in New York, their marriage would be declared a valid common-law marriage by a Pennsylvania court." . . . [H]owever, "at best only 16 days out of Mr. Renshaw's lifetime were spent in Pennsylvania [and] the overwhelming bulk of the supporting evidence rests on actions taken outside of Pennsylvania in non-common law states." . . . [T]he magistrate concluded that absent proof of some present intent to marry while in Pennsylvania, the parties had not contracted a valid common-law marriage under Pennsylvania law.

The facts admittedly present a unique situation. Although we have found no

Pennsylvania cases directly on point, New York courts have recognized valid common-law marriages under similar factual situations. We think that a New York court would find that the Renshaws had contracted a valid common-law marriage in Pennsylvania. . . .

The Renshaws lived as husband and wife for 21 years, had a child, and were accepted as married by family and friends. This would have satisfied the basic requirements of cohabitation and repute required for common law marriage. However, the court was forced to look for a connection with a state that recognized common law marriages. Mrs. Renshaw appears a sympathetic litigant. All she was claiming was the Social Security benefits every widow would be entitled to; she was not taking anything away from anyone else. (Would the court have found a marriage if she were claiming dower and thereby cutting Mr. Renshaw's children out of his will?)

Compare *Renshaw* with *Byers v. Mount Vernon Mills, Inc.,* 268 S.C. 68, 231 S.E.2d 699 (1977), in which the husband had married while a prior wife was still alive. Six years later he divorced his first wife, and five years after that he left the second wife for a third. The court held that the second marriage was not valid because he had still been married to his first wife. The court held that the second relationship could have been a common law marriage if the couple had made a new agreement after he divorced his first wife. Pennsylvania apparently also follows this rule:

> Where . . . the relationship between the parties began while at least one party was married to a third person, the courts will presume that the parties continued to live together unmarried even after the impediment to their marriage had been removed. Clear and convincing evidence of a change of status is required to rebut this presumption [which the court found sufficient by evidence that the husband showed his common law wife a copy of the decree of divorce from his first wife, saying, "Now we're legally married," to which she said "It's about time. That's just what we were waiting for."].
>
> — *In re Garges,* 474 Pa. 237, 378 A.2d 307 (1977).

In Arizona, in *Grant v. Superior Court,* 27 Ariz. App. 427, 555 P.2d 895 (1976), a motel stay in Texas did not make a marriage, despite the couple's attempt to do so at the time (an agreement followed by telling everyone they were husband and wife when they returned to Arizona). The court concluded that they had not cohabited in Texas, and "merely stepping across the state line" did not allow them to avoid the Arizona law. But the court also indicated that it would recognize a common law marriage validated in another state.

The Kentucky court similarly refused to validate a marriage made by exchange of vows and rings in an Ohio motel. *Vaughn v. Hufnagel,* 473

CAVEAT

In practice, such situations arise more often than one would suspect. Pensions, worker's compensation, social security, and other benefits of death or injury, not to mention personal injury suits and insurance, may make it worthwhile to determine whether a surviving spouse ever lived as a spouse in a jurisdiction that recognized common law marriages.

S.W.2d 124 (Ky. 1971). *Renshaw* thus appears slightly aberrant; the federal court in New York seemed anxious to make a marriage, whereas South Carolina, Arizona, and Kentucky took a more restrictive attitude. *Grant* and *Vaughn* reflect a common judicial hostility toward those who cavalierly attempt to evade the law of their domicile ("it takes more than riding across the Ohio River to make [a marriage] legal").

9.4   MODERN EQUIVALENTS TO COMMON LAW MARRIAGE

With most states abolishing common law marriage, unions that would formerly have been granted marital status were put in limbo. Although in many instances the parties disdained family values or merely neglected to obtain a license, many others had a good faith belief that they were married.

> The Parkinsons were Roman Catholics. She divorced him and he separated but several years later moved back in with his former wife and their children. Although they planned to remarry, their priest refused to remarry them on the grounds that they could not get a divorce in the Catholic Church and were still married in the eyes of God. Although this was apparently correct under Canon Law of the Church, it was not legally correct under New Jersey law, which required them to obtain a new license in order to be legally married. When she was denied dependency benefits under workmen's compensation, the court held her to be a *de facto* wife by virtue of being a "good faith wife." "The test of the relationship of husband and wife should not be quite the same in the context of [worker's compensation], designed to supply a social need and to remedy a social evil, as in the area of familial law where questions of property, inheritance, legitimacy of offspring and the like rightly demand a more rigid adherence to conventional doctrine."
>
> — *Parkinson v. J.&S. Tool Co.,* 64 N.J. 159, 313 A.2d 609 (1974).

The Parkinsons met all the traditional requirements of a common law marriage plus the belief that they were actually married. Note also that the court explicitly softens the requirements for worker's compensation in contrast to situations where property rights between individuals might be adjudicated. It is easier to recognize the status of surviving spouse when the rights involved pertain to proceeds from an insurance plan or a government treasury than it is when funds are removed from one person for the benefit of another.

9.5   PUTATIVE MARRIAGE

A *putative marriage* is a marriage that is invalid for some reason but which is given some effects of a valid marriage. Although the requirements of a putative marriage vary from state to state, the principal requirements are (1) a good faith belief in the validity of the marriage by at least one of the partners, and (2) an attempted ceremonial marriage. Under the early canon law, the concept seems to have been an attempt to protect those who went through what they believed to be a valid church wedding, which later turned out to be invalid. In the United States, putative marriage was first associated with states having some civil law background from Spain or France—earliest in Louisiana, but also notable in California and Texas. Although it is also frequently associated with community property states, it has spread in recent years to a number of common law, separate property states, such as Illinois, Colorado, Minnesota, and Montana. This popularity is due in large part to the Uniform Marriage and Divorce Act (UMDA), § 209, which encourages the statutory adoption of putative marriage.

UNIFORM MARRIAGE AND DIVORCE ACT

Section 209. Any person who has cohabited with another to whom he is not legally married in the good faith belief that he was married to that person is a putative spouse until knowledge of the fact that he is not legally married terminates his status and prevents acquisition of further rights. A putative spouse acquires the rights conferred upon a legal spouse . . . . If there is a legal spouse or other putative spouses, rights acquired by a putative spouse do not supersede the rights of the legal spouse or those acquired by other putative spouses, but the court shall apportion property, maintenance and support rights among the claimants as appropriate in the circumstances and in the interests of justice.

Note that the UMDA does not require a ceremony, although traditionally this was important. Note also that the putative status terminates when the spouse learns of the invalidity of the marriage, conforming to the rule that has generally developed in the law of putative marriage.

Because putative marriage has developed in a number of different states with different legal traditions, results in specific relationships vary by jurisdiction. The contrast with common law marriage is nevertheless clear. The principal motivation for the development of putative marriage was originally the protection of women who married men who had some impediment to contracting a valid marriage (most usually a prior, undissolved marriage). These women married in good faith only to find themselves without any rights.

If both husband and wife attempted marriage in good faith, both qualified as putative spouses. If only one was in good faith (e.g., the husband knew his claim of a prior divorce was false), only the good faith spouse could qualify as a putative spouse. When the invalidity of the marriage became apparent, the putative status terminated, as indicated in UMDA § 209. In community property states, where the putative marriage doctrine evolved, this meant that a putative spouse could share marital earnings for a period and then, when the putative status ended, return to separate property ownership for subsequent income.

CASE NO. 9-4   Marrying Out of State

The *Levie* case illustrates the serious ramifications of an imperfectly contracted marriage. When Grant V. Levie died without a will (*intestate*), his estate passed by intestate succession to his widow and his heirs. Did he have a "widow?"

IN RE ESTATE OF LEVIE
50 Cal. App. 3d 572,
123 Cal. Rptr. 445 (1975)
California Court of Appeal

CHRISTIAN, Associate Justice.

. . . The [lower] court determined that respondent was a putative spouse and that she was entitled to receive all the property acquired by decedent during the supposed marriage and one third of the other property of decedent.

The petition to determine heirship was submitted on stipulated facts, as follows:

1.   Grant V. Levie died intestate on November 30, 1973, in San Mateo County, State of California, being then a resident of said County and State;

2.   Grant V. Levie had more than one child surviving him at the time of his death, all of such children having been the issue of the marriage between Grant V. Levie and Elnora Levie, which marriage was terminated by a valid divorce prior to 1964 in the State of California;

3.   Sherrey E. Hankins is one of the said children of Grant V. Levie, surviving him at the time of his death;

4.   Grant V. Levie and Belva Levie entered into a marriage ceremony in Reno, Nevada on December 8, 1972, and at such time both parties in good faith thought they were entering into a valid marriage;

5.   Said marriage ceremony was performed in conformance with all the procedural requirements of Nevada law, and is a valid marriage unless invalid because Belva Levie and Grant V. Levie were related as first cousins at the time of their marriage;

6.   Grant V. Levie and Belva Levie were at the time of their marriage in fact related as first cousins, their natural fathers being brothers;

7.   Grant V. Levie and Belva Levie were both residents of the State of California at the time of said ceremony;

8.   Subsequent to said marriage until the death of Grant V. Levie, Belva Levie and Grant V. Levie lived together continuously as husband and wife and held themselves out as such to all the world;

9.   Prior to said marriage ceremony, Grant V. Levie had accumulated substantial separate property which he possessed at the time of said ceremony; and

10.   Subsequent to said ceremony, Grant V. Levie and Belva Levie may have accumulated some property which would have been community if their marriage [were] recognized as valid in California.

Decedent and respondent, as first cousins, could lawfully have been married in California (Civ.Code, § 4400). But it is conceded by respondent that the marriage ceremony performed in Nevada was invalid in that state because of the parties' consanguinity (Nevada

Rev. Stats., § 122.020). Appellant in turn concedes that respondent, as a putative spouse, was entitled to succeed under Probate Code section 201 to all property which would have been community property if the marriage had been valid.

Appellant contends, citing Civil Code section 4104, that because the attempted marriage was void in Nevada, the state where contracted, it is void in California. It is true that the statute (and a predecessor enactment, former Civil Code section 63) do not speak expressly of the invalidity in California of a marriage which was void where performed. But the statute by implication adopts the common law rule that "the law of the place of marriage controls the question of its validity." (*Colbert v. Colbert* (1946) 28 Cal. 2d 276, 280, 169 P.2d 633, 635; see 52 Am.Jur.2d, Marriage, § 80; 6 Witkin, Summary of California Law, Husband and Wife, § 28, p. 4898.)

* * *

Respondent contends that even if the invalidity of the marriage be conceded she should be permitted, as a putative spouse, to receive under Probate Code section 221 a surviving spouse's share of the separate property of the decedent. No authority is cited for this proposition; respondent points to the intention expressed in the Family Law Act to exclude concepts of fault and punishment from any influence in the determination of family property rights (citing *In re Marriage of Cary* (1973) 34 Cal. App. 3d 345, 109 Cal. Rptr.

862). But the right of a putative spouse, to succeed to an interest in property which would have been community property but for the invalidity of the marriage is not based on concepts of fault. It is derived instead from "(e)quitable considerations arising from the reasonable expectation of the continuation of benefits attending the status of marriage entered into in good faith . . ." (*Vallera v. Vallera* (1943) 21 Cal. 2d 681, 685, 134 P.2d 761; also see *Estate of Krone* (1948) 83 Cal. App. 2d 766, 189 P.2d 741). No California decision has been found, suggesting that a putative spouse is entitled to succeed, under Probate Code section 221, to an interest in any property which the decedent owned before the putative marriage. The equities connected with property acquired during the putative marriage do not apply, as the joint efforts of the putative spouses did not contribute to the acquisition of previously held property; to recognize in the putative spouse an interest in previously held property of the decedent would unjustifiably disregard the statutory scheme governing intestate succession of separate property. (Prob. Code, § 220 et seq.)

The order is reversed with directions to enter a new order limiting the award to respondent of property, acquired during the putative marriage, which would have been community property if the marriage had been valid.

CASE QUESTIONS

1. What would Belva's share of the estate have been if they had married in California?
2. What would Belva's share have been if California recognized common law marriage, assuming their cohabitation and repute sufficed to make such a marriage?

3. Belva made a public policy argument based on the establishment of no-fault divorce in California. Was there substance to this argument, which the court readily dismissed? Perhaps she was ahead of her time?

4. How long were Grant and Belva married? Could this have influenced the court? (You might want to consider *Sousa v. Freitas,* discussed below.)

Manuel Sousa Freitas married Maria Jacinto de Sousa in the Azores Islands, Republic of Portugal, in 1908. Three years later he moved to California, leaving his wife and son in the Azores. In 1915 he changed his name legally to Manuel S. Freitas. In Portuguese custom, the father's surname precedes the mother's surname, so that he would have been known principally by the name Sousa. This is important because when he divorced Maria a year later, the publication of the proceedings under the name Freitas was not recognized by anyone in the Azores nor did Maria recognize herself as defendant Maria Sousa Freitas, as she was never known by this name. When Manuel died in 1962, these facts became known, and in the probate of his estate it was concluded that this divorce was obtained fraudulently and was therefore invalid. As a result, Manuel's subsequent marriage to Catherine in 1919 was invalid. Their 43-year cohabitation was deemed a putative marriage. Manuel left a will leaving his entire estate to Catherine.

The court gave three-fourths of the estate to Catherine and one-fourth to Maria, with the following reasoning: Catherine and Manuel accumulated this property through their mutual efforts so that half of the estate was hers, the other half was Manuel's, or rather Manuel-and-Maria's community property, so that Maria got her share or one fourth of the estate. The remaining one-fourth passed by will to Catherine.

— The preceding is a summary taken from *Sousa v. Freitas,*
10 Cal. App. 3d 660, 89 Cal. Rptr. 485 (1970).

Query: Would the court have followed the same reasoning if the facts were the same but Manuel had been married to Maria for 43 years and to Catherine for 3?

9.6 PRESUMPTION OF MARRIAGE AND MARRIAGE BY ESTOPPEL

We have seen already that the law presumes the validity of marriage—a presumption described by some as one of the strongest known to the law. This presumption also applies to a second (or third) marriage. That is, when someone marries more than once, the later marriage is presumed valid. In effect, this may presume that the former marriage was dissolved or the former spouse died; the court may infer facts necessary to validate the second marriage. Although the presumption is rebuttable, when it comes to proving that a prior spouse was *not* divorced, absolute proof may be quite difficult.

In states that have abolished common law marriage but have not adopted putative marriage, in appropriate cases, the presumption of marriage may be applied to create a functional equivalent of the common law marriage. For example, although a marriage license or court records may be produced to prove the validity of a marriage, the failure to produce such evidence does not disprove the existence of a marriage. In a sympathetic case, where, for instance, a widow claims a long-term marriage but cannot produce documentary evidence, the court may use the presumption of a valid marriage. This is better than a putative marriage (for the widow) because the marriage is valid for all purposes, whereas a putative marriage merely benefits from certain attributes ("civil effects") of marriage for the period to which it applies.

Marriages have on occasion been validated by estoppel. In cases of apparent bigamous marriages, where two people claim property rights as surviving spouses, the court may estop one of the parties from making claims inconsistent with prior behavior. For example, a claimant who entered into a second marriage was estopped from making a claim as a surviving spouse of her first husband (the court may also "presume" that there was a valid divorce from the first marriage). In one case, a first wife was estopped from asserting widow's claims because she knew of the second wife (who married in the good faith belief that her husband was divorced), as well as the failure of a divorce action to go to a final decree, but said nothing and made no claims during the lifetime of her husband. The husband lived with his second wife for 20 years prior to his death in 1962. *Mason v. Mason,* 174 So. 2d 620 (Fla. Dist. Ct. App. 1965).

Though the presumption of marriage and marriage by estoppel may operate to revive the abolished common law marriage in specific circumstances, they leave considerable discretion to the court. Common law marriage was considerably more secure where the elements of cohabitation and repute were clearly present.

CASE NO. 9-5   Marriage (Divorce?) by Estoppel

Estoppel is the law's way of saying, "You can't have your cake and eat it, too."

IN RE ESTATE OF BUTLER
444 So. 2d 477 (Fla. Dist. Ct. App. 1984)
District Court of Appeal of Florida

LEHAN, Judge.

* * *

The issue is whether the trial court correctly applied the doctrine of estoppel to prevent Georgia Mae Butler from asserting her rights as a widow of the deceased. We affirm.

The decedent and Georgia Mae were married in 1946. They lived together for a short time and then separated in 1947. Although the marriage was never legally dissolved, Nathaniel told Georgia Mae that he had "bought" a divorce. Georgia Mae believed him.

In 1950, Georgia Mae married James Whitfield in a ceremonial marriage performed by a judge in Sarasota County. Georgia Mae had two children by Whitfield and later had three children by three different men. Georgia Mae continued to be known as Georgia Mae Whitfield until some time after Nathaniel Butler's death. Georgia Mae never attempted to obtain a divorce from Nathaniel Butler.

Nathaniel Butler married Rosa Belle Butler in 1963 after telling Rosa Belle that he was divorced from Georgia Mae. Rosa Belle believed him. Rosa Belle and Nathaniel lived together continuously as husband and wife until Nathaniel's death in 1975. During this time Rosa Belle and Nathaniel had one child and adopted one child, both children taking the name of Butler and living with Rosa Belle and Nathaniel. The two children were minors at the time of Nathaniel's death. The marital domicile was titled in the joint names of Rosa Belle and Nathaniel, and the couple lived in that house continuously from 1965 until Nathaniel's death.

At some point Georgia Mae found out that she and Nathaniel had never actually been divorced. The record does not show when Georgia Mae learned this and does not show whether she learned it before or after Nathaniel's death. Georgia Mae did know that Nathaniel had married Rosa Belle. Georgia Mae saw and talked with Nathaniel about once a year up until his death.

Nathaniel died in 1975. On December 29, 1981, Georgia Mae filed a petition for administration of his estate, seeking as surviving spouse appointment as personal representative.

Rosa Belle filed objections to the petition. After a hearing, the trial court found that Georgia Mae was estopped from asserting her rights as widow. The court found Rosa Belle to be more deserving and entitled to Nathaniel's estate.

On appeal, Georgia Mae argues that the cases relied upon by the trial court for the doctrine of estoppel are different in nature from the facts of this case because in those cases the person estopped acted in blatant and wanton disregard of the institution of marriage or was of such reprehensible character as to shock the conscience of the court. . . . In *Nedd v. Starry*, 143 So. 2d 522 (Fla. 1st DCA 1962), the husband separated from the wife after about one and a half years of marriage and approximately one year later entered into a bigamous ceremonial marriage. Two months after that marriage he left without getting a divorce and bigamously married a third time. The chancellor in the case noted also that the husband commonly had sexual relations with other women during his travels. The chancellor stated that misconduct of such a flagrant and inexcusable character showing a repudiation of marital obligations will estop the person from enjoying the rights of marriage. . . .

Rosa Belle cites *Minor v. Higdon*, 215 Miss. 513, 61 So. 2d 350 (1952), cited with approval by the Florida Supreme Court. . . . In *Minor* the court prevented a surviving wife from claiming under her deceased husband's estate where the wife had remarried without obtaining a divorce from the husband. The wife, Zelma, testified that she did not know at the time of her second marriage that her first husband had not obtained a divorce from her. "But this is no excuse for her contracting a bigamous marriage relationship with a second husband. Zelma did know that [her first husband] was still alive, and that he was living in the same or an adjoining county, and that she had not obtained a divorce from him, and that she had not been served with a summons in any divorce proceeding that he may have instituted against her. Zelma's marriage to Clarence Robinson under these circumstances constituted a complete repudiation of her marital status as the wife of Will Minor." 61 So. 2d at 353.

In affirming the judgment of the trial court, we recognize that the Florida cases cited involve bigamy committed knowingly by the claiming spouse while the record in this case indicates that Georgia Mae believed herself to be divorced from Nathaniel when she married James Whitfield. However, as in *Minor v. Higdon,* at the time Georgia Mae entered into her second marriage, she knew that her first husband was still alive and that *she* had not obtained a divorce from him and that she had not been served with any papers in any divorce

proceeding that he may have instituted. Georgia Mae's marriage to James Whitfield and her subsequent actions constituted a repudiation of her marital status as the wife of Nathaniel Butler. The evidence does not show when Georgia Mae learned there had been no divorce, but Georgia Mae lived as if she had been divorced from Nathaniel and made no attempt to represent herself as his wife until six years after Nathaniel died. Georgia Mae, after having taken advantage of the "divorce" that Nathaniel told her he had bought, cannot now claim the benefits of a marriage which she herself has repudiated by her subsequent conduct. Analogous to *Nedd v. Starry, supra,* Georgia Mae's abandonment of the marriage relationship with Nathaniel operates to estop her from asserting rights under that marriage.

AFFIRMED.

The *Garduno* case, Case No. 9-6, tests one's understanding of common law and putative marriages and even hints strongly at presumption of marriage and divorce. Texas recognizes both common law and putative marriages, and *Garduno* reveals that the two forms of marriage may even alternate during one long relationship.

CASE NO. 9-6 Every Which Way But Married

GARDUNO v. GARDUNO
760 S.W.2d 735 (Tex. Ct. App. 1988)
Court of Appeals of Texas,
Corpus Christi

KENNEDY, Justice.
Roberto Garduno appeals from the judgment of the trial court finding that he and Margarita Garduno, appellee, had entered both putative

and common law marriages to each other between 1980 and 1986. The court granted appellee's petition for divorce, awarded her certain property held by the couple during those years, and ordered appellant to pay arrearages on a temporary support order entered earlier. Appellant brings six points of error challenging the sufficiency of the evidence to show that a putative or common law marriage ever arose, the court's award of property to appellee based on a putative or community property interest, and the court's order for temporary support of appellee.

According to her testimony, appellee met appellant in the latter part of 1979, shortly after she divorced her former husband with whom she had lived in Mexico. Appellant told appellee that he was divorced also at that time. In early 1980, appellee moved into a condominium unit that appellant owned in Brownsville. Appellant moved into the same unit around the middle of the year, and the two lived there together and represented themselves to others as husband and wife from that time until appellee moved out in 1986.

In January of 1981, appellee learned from appellant's daughter that he was still married to a woman who lived in Mexico. Appellant, however, assured her that he would divorce his wife and that he intended to marry appellee. Appellant then attempted to divorce his wife through the Mexican courts. In April 1984 he obtained a Mexican divorce decree which he showed to appellee. However, appellant's Mexican divorce lawyer informed him shortly thereafter that the divorce had been set aside by an appellate court, which appellant also told appellee.

Finally, appellant petitioned for divorce in Texas and a decree was signed on December 3, 1985. The couple continued to live together until appellant physically assaulted appellee in the spring of 1986. Appellee then moved out of the condominium unit and petitioned for divorce. Appellee also petitioned for a temporary support order, which was not made a part of the record on appeal.

During the course of their relationship, the couple acquired a large amount of property, including a 1986 Volkswagon with title in both names and used primarily by appellee, a 1985 Cadillac used primarily by appellant, a $100,000 certificate of deposit which was put in appellant's name in trust for appellee, a vacation time share plan in both names, and 1,500 shares of stock in United Amore's, Inc. . . .

In points one, two, and seven appellant complains that the trial court erred in finding that either a putative or a common law marriage arose during the period of the couple's relationship. Point one complains that a putative marriage could not have arisen, because appellee was aware of appellant's prior undissolved marriage. Points two and seven challenge the sufficiency of the evidence to establish the existence of a common law marriage after appellant divorced his first wife. . . .

The elements of a common law marriage are: (1) a present agreement to be husband and wife; (2) living together as husband and wife; and (3) holding each other out to the public as such.

A putative marriage is one that was entered into in good faith by at least one of the parties, but which is invalid by reason of an existing impediment on the part of one or both parties. A putative marriage may arise out of either a ceremonial or common law marriage. The effect of a putative marriage is to give the putative spouse who acted in good faith the same right in property acquired during the marital relationship as if he or she were a lawful spouse. However, there being no legally recognized marriage, property acquired during a putative marriage is not community property, but jointly owned separate property.

It is clear from the evidence that appellant's prior marriage was an impediment to a valid common law marriage to appellee, until the divorce became final on January 3, 1986. The parties could still have entered a putative marriage, however, during the times that appellee was unaware of the prior marriage or believed it had been terminated.

In January 1981 appellee first became aware of appellant's prior marriage. Appellee had knowledge of this impediment for the remainder of the prior marriage, with the exception of a short period in the spring of 1984 when she believed that the marriage had been dissolved by a Mexican divorce. These two periods of the relationship, before January 1981 and during the spring of 1984, provide the potential for a putative marriage. We next look to see if a common law agreement can be found or inferred during either period.

Taking only the evidence favorable to the court's decree, there was cohabitation and holding out to the public from the middle of 1980 to April or May of 1986. This is without real dispute in the evidence, although appellant claims that the holding out was done selectively only to strangers, out of some sort of respect for appellee. Under Texas Family Code § 1.91(b) the agreement to be married may be inferred if cohabitation and holding out to the public are found. However, an agreement cannot be implied contrary to direct evidence which definitely shows that there was no such agreement. Direct evidence of an agreement by the parties to present cohabitation and future marriage is insufficient; there must be a present agreement to be married.

In the present case, appellee admits that the parties talked about the status of their relationship from before the time the court found that they began cohabitation. The nature of their conversations and actions relevant to an agreement about their status are as follows:

> January '80—appellant told appellee "that I should always be telling everyone that we were married. Especially the ladies of the tennis club, so that I could be having some respect while, *until we married*."
>
> Sometime in '80—appellant gave appellee a diamond *engagement ring*.
>
> March '81—A few days after appellee found out that appellant was

still married, in January 1981, she went to live with her family in Saltillo, Mexico, for two months. Appellant came down for her, told her that he was in the process of divorcing his wife, and "he said for me to go back *to get married* with him. . . ."

> In the following question, appellee's counsel sought to establish an agreement during the period after appellee returned with appellant to Brownsville and while appellant was trying to divorce his wife: "Q. During that period, did he ever tell you that you were to continue, you were to continue together with him because *you were his wife?* A. Yes. . . ."
>
> April '82—on a trip through Mexico appellant and appellee purchased two inscribed rings (Roberto 5-12-82 and Margarita 5-12-82, as was the custom for wedding rings in Mexico) for the following purpose: "Well, [appellant] was always concerned about the social aspect. He asked me to tell everybody, whoever asked me a question on the both that *we had just gotten married.*"

The initial understanding that the parties had in January of 1981 was, in her own words, that appellee was to represent herself as appellant's wife for the purpose of avoiding embarrassment *until* the two got married. This indicates that appellant had the intention to marry appellee in the future, but did not consider himself, or agree to be, married to her at that time or at any time before appellee discovered the prior marriage. There could have been no putative marriage during this period.

The question now becomes whether either of the parties' actions after that time suggest that they later changed their understanding of the relationship and agreed to be married. The engagement ring and proposal to *get married* in March of 1981 still assume a future marriage. However, the exchanging of wedding rings in 1982 and the new affirmation that appellee should tell "everyone . . . that we had just gotten married," was some evidence that appellant at that time agreed to be married to appellee. In addition, appellee's testimony that appellant had told her that "[she was] his wife," sometime after the couple returned to Brownsville in 1981, also suggests a present agreement to be married. We find that there is sufficient evidence to show a common law agreement after 1982. If appellee in good faith believed that appellant's divorce had become final in 1984, there would also be sufficient evidence to show a putative marriage after that date.

The good faith of the putative spouse is generally a fact question. When the spouse is unaware of a prior undissolved marriage, good faith is presumed. However, when the putative spouse is aware that a former marriage existed at one time, the question becomes one of the reasonableness of that party's belief that the former marriage has been dissolved. A putative spouse may believe in good faith that a prior marriage has been dissolved by divorce, even though in the eyes of the law it has not. See *Dean v. Goldwire,* 480 S.W.2d 494 (Tex. Civ. App.—Waco 1972, writ ref'd n.r.e.). In *Dean,* the putative spouse was shown papers represented to her as a Mexican divorce decree, though they did not effect a divorce. In the present case, appellee saw a Mexican divorce decree that she believed to be valid in April of 1984. Sometime shortly thereafter, she learned from a phone call appellant received from a Mexican lawyer that the divorce had been set aside by the Mexican courts. However, appellee testified that neither she nor appellant believed this to be true.

The courts of Louisiana have discussed the concept of putative marriage perhaps more extensively than those of any other state. As in Texas, in Louisiana a putative marriage arises when one of the parties enters a void marriage in the good faith belief that no impediment exists. *Succession of Chavis,* 211 La. 313, 29 So. 2d 860 (1947). The party's good faith is a question of fact and will not be vitiated by "unconfirmed rumors or mere suspicions . . . so long as no certain or authoritative knowledge of some legal impediment comes to him or her." *Id.,* 29 So. 2d at 862. When reliable knowledge of an impediment does come to the party, however, he cannot simply declare his disbelief of this information and continue as if it were untrue, but is then under a duty to investigate further: "a party alleging good faith cannot close her eyes to information or her ears to suspicious circumstances. She must not act blindly or without reasonable precaution." *Id.,* 29 So.2d at 863.

In the present case appellee was no longer acting in good faith after she learned through appellant's lawyer that the Mexican divorce had been set aside. At this point, any putative marriage that may have arisen came to an end. Moreover, we have no evidence to suggest that during the period of time between the initial Mexican decree and appellee's knowledge of its being set aside the parties acquired any of the property now in dispute. For this reason, it is irrelevant whether such a putative marriage temporarily arose.

Finally, we must determine whether there was sufficient evidence to show that after appellant's divorce in 1986 the parties entered a valid common law marriage. Under Texas Family Code § 2.22, a marriage which was void by reason of a prior marriage becomes valid after the prior marriage is dissolved "if since that time the parties have lived together as husband and wife and represented themselves to others as being married." This provision applies to common law as well as ceremonial marriages. For the reasons discussed above, we find that there was sufficient evidence to show a common law agreement after 1982, and thus to show a common law marriage when the parties continued to cohabitate and hold themselves out as married after appellant's 1986 divorce. . . .

9.7 COHABITATION AGREEMENTS

The final set of situations involving unofficial unions concerns cohabiting partners who have no intention of either the pretense or the actuality of marriage. These are couples who do not qualify for marital status and do not seek marital rights. They nevertheless become involved with the law over a dispute as to property. Both partners may have contributed to the property, although it appears only one is holder of title; sometimes one claims property rights based on a contractual remedy. These situations differ in their legal arguments from those who attempt to obtain marital rights such as pensions, worker's compensation, or social security by arguing a broad definition of *spouse, widow,* or *family*. These latter are often decided on dependency status or simple equity, as they do not involve interfering with the distribution of assets among competing claimants. Nevertheless, some couples may fall in the first category (cohabitants) who believed they were, or pretended to be, married when they are domiciled in states hostile to recognizing informal marriages (common law, putative, presumption of marriage).

Cohabitants may not have a marital agreement, but they may have—or at least argue they had—a contractual arrangement. This could consist of an actual cohabitation agreement in writing, which the parties executed when they began to live together. They might have had an oral agreement or an implied agreement. They might have cooperated in a business venture in such a way as to suggest some sort of business partnership remedy. In relationships that last for many years, funds inevitably become commingled, so that it is difficult to attribute individual ownership of specific assets. When the relationship fails or terminates because of death, the partner who appears to have been shortchanged may well seek a legal remedy.

Litigants face two principal hurdles in bringing suit:

1. Cohabitation is illegal in most states, assuming the term includes illicit sexual activity. Courts are disinclined to put their blessings on these relationships.
2. The court, the traditional protector of marriage and family, hesitates to create a marital-like relationship when the couple has defied social convention and legal procedure.

Thus, courts are not inclined to resolve issues where the parties voluntarily declined the appropriate legal means to establish their respective rights and duties. Only when the equities indicate a clear injustice will be done are the courts likely to interfere.

The increasing numbers of single, working parents often means children are escorted to and from schools and child care by grandparents or other members of the child's extended family.

On the other hand, American society seems to have chosen to accept wide freedom in intimate relationships and a new tolerance toward alternative lifestyles. The law inevitably follows social mores. In addition, cohabiting partners should be free to make contracts. In most states the laws against fornication and adultery are rarely, if ever, enforced. Cohabitation is only technically a crime. As long as compensation is not sought for sexual services and the substance of the claim is independent of the sexual aspects of the relationship, a contract between the parties should be honored by the courts. If someone hired a maid or a cook, their contract would be honored without regard to incidental sexual activity.

One other feature of these relationships bears mentioning. Although (nonsexual) services of a spouse are often gratuitous, and were at one time presumed to be so under law, the same argument fails in a cohabitation arrangement. A person may not expect compensation for washing the dishes or taking out the trash, but neither does one expect to go unrewarded for contributions to the overall prosperity of the enterprise. Obviously, the strongest cases are those in which one of the parties has made clear contributions that have demonstrably increased the assets of the other; in other words, the more the relationship resembles a business partnership, the more likely the court is to ignore the cohabitation relationship.

CASE NO. 9-7   Cohabiting Partners

The existence of a sexual relationship between two unmarried individuals does not prevent them from having a business relationship recognized by the law.

SUGGS v. NORRIS
88 N.C. App. 539, 364 S.E.2d 159 (1988)
Court of Appeals of North Carolina

WELLS, Judge.

The overriding question presented by this appeal is whether public policy forbids the recovery by a plaintiff partner to an unmarried but cohabiting or meretricious relationship, from the other partner's estate, for services rendered to or benefits conferred upon the other partner through the plaintiff's work in the operation of a joint business when the business proceeds were utilized to enrich the estate of the deceased partner.

* * *

We now make clear and adopt the rule that agreements regarding the finances and property of an unmarried but cohabiting couple, whether express or implied, are enforceable as long as sexual services or promises thereof do not provide the consideration for such agreements. Moreover, where appropriate, the equitable remedies of constructive and resulting trusts should be available as should recovery under a quasi-contractual theory on *quantum meruit.*

* * *

Moreover, plaintiff's efforts must not have been gratuitous as is generally presumed where services are rendered between family or spousal members.

In the present case, the evidence clearly showed that the plaintiff had from 1973 until the death of the decedent in 1983 operated a produce route for and with the decedent. According to several witnesses' testimony, plaintiff had worked decedent's farm, disced and cultivated the soil, and harvested and marketed the produce. Plaintiff, working primarily without the decedent's aid, drove the produce to various markets over a 60 mile route. She handled all finances and deposited them in the couple's joint banking account. Finally, the evidence showed that the decedent, an alcoholic, depended almost entirely on plaintiff's work in the produce business and as well her care of him while he was ill. Because of plaintiff's efforts the couple had amassed seven vehicles valued at $20,000; some farm equipment valued at $4,000; $8,000 in cash in the account, and all debts which had attached to the farm when plaintiff began working with decedent in 1973 were paid—all due to plaintiff's efforts. Additionally, plaintiff testified that when she began work with the decedent in 1973 she believed they were partners and that she was entitled to share in one-half the profits.

The foregoing evidence clearly establishes a set of facts sufficient to have submitted a quasi-contractual issue to the jury and from which the jury could have inferred a mutual understanding between plaintiff and the decedent that she would be remunerated for her services. Plaintiff's efforts conferred many years of benefits on the decedent and the decedent, by all accounts, willingly accepted those benefits.

[The court affirmed the jury's award to Darlene Suggs.]

9.8 MARVIN AND ITS PROGENY

Suggs v. Norris cites with approval a line of cases that traces its roots to *Marvin v. Marvin,* 18 Cal. 3d 660, 557 P.2d 106, 134 Cal. Rptr. 815 (1976), the first "palimony" case and one that ran through many appeals. *Marvin* involved the termination of a seven-year relationship between the movie star Lee Marvin and Michelle Triola Marvin. Michelle sued on an alleged oral contract under which Lee and Michelle had agreed to share their earnings during their relationship. The California Court of Appeals and the California Supreme Court accepted the proposition that cohabitants could contract in such a fashion if the contract was not grounded on meretricious (that is, illicit sexual) services. Without condoning such relationships, the courts held that contracts independent of such considerations were enforceable. The California court also went through a list of equitable remedies or devices designed to remedy unjust enrichment or compensate a cohabitant for services rendered, including the quantum meruit measure of damages applied in *Suggs*.

Unlike Darlene Suggs, Michelle Triola had not contributed to Lee's success, and the court found that she had been amply compensated for the limited services she had provided. Michelle's case was especially weak; her allegations that she had given up a lucrative singing career to accompany Lee were unsubstantiated; the evidence she provided of an oral agreement was ambiguous at best. Ironically, although Michelle did not prevail, the decisions established the willingness of the California courts to provide a remedy to cohabiting partners, provided they had a valid express (written or oral) contract, an implied contract, or some claim of contribution that deserved restitution or compensation, whether it was labeled quantum meruit, quasi-contract, or constructive trust.

What the California court failed to do was to equate cohabitants with married partners. Although in a way *Marvin* seems to resurrect common law marriage in California (even though the case states it is not resurrecting it), it is clear that Michelle's attempt to obtain the equivalent of community property was rejected by the court. She could recover if only she could show merit to her case.

The California courts were faithful to their pronouncements. In *Jones v. Daly,* 122 Cal. App. 3d 500, 176 Cal. Rptr. 130 (1981), a suit based on a cohabitation agreement between two men, to share equally in property acquired by their joint efforts, was dismissed by the court. In this instance the surviving partner alleged as his consideration for the contract that he would "render his services as a lover, companion, homemaker, traveling companion, housekeeper and cook." The inclusion of "lover" in the allegations of the complaint proved fatal to the suit—it showed that compensation was sought for sexual services.

On the other hand, the fact that Jonne Alderson (see Case No. 9-8) admitted that part of her "role" was sexual partner did not prove equally fatal.

CASE NO. 9-8   Marvin v. Marvin, the Next Generation

ALDERSON v. ALDERSON
180 Cal. App. 3d 450, 225 Cal. Rptr. 610 (1986)
California Court of Appeal, First District

MERRILL, Associate Justice.

[Jonne and Steve Alderson, although not formally married, lived together as husband and wife for 12 years, during which time they had 3 children. Jonne asks for an equal division of real property acquired during the relationship.]

* * *

Comparing the nonmarital situation to that of the putative spouse, the court said: "[A]lthough parties to a nonmarital relationship obviously cannot have based any expectations upon the belief that they were married, other expectations and equitable considerations remain. The parties may well expect that property will be divided in accord with the parties' own tacit understanding *and that in the absence of such understanding the courts will fairly apportion property accumulated through mutual effort*. We need not treat nonmarital partners as putatively married persons in order to apply principles of implied contract, or extend equitable remedies; *we need to treat them only as we do any other unmarried persons*." ([Marvin v. Marvin, 18 Cal. 3d], at p. 682, 134 Cal.Rptr. 815, 557 P.2d 106, emphasis added.) "There is no more reason to presume that services are contributed as a gift than to presume that funds are contributed as a gift; in any event the better approach is to presume . . . 'that the parties intend[ed] to deal fairly with each other.' " (*Id.*, at p. 683, 134 Cal.Rptr. 815, 557 P.2d 106.)

"In summary, we believe that the prevalence of nonmarital relationships in modern society and the social acceptance of them, marks this as a time when our courts should by no means apply the doctrine of the unlawfulness of the so-called meretricious relationship to the instant case. As we have explained, the nonenforceability of agreements expressly providing for meretricious conduct rested upon the fact that such conduct, as the word suggests, pertained to and encompassed prostitution. *To equate the nonmarital relationship of today to such a subject matter is to do violence to an accepted and wholly different practice*." (*Ibid.*, emphasis added.)

In the instant case, the trial court ruled in favor of Jonne and held that she was entitled to an undivided half interest in the parties' properties. In so ruling, the court impliedly found that the parties' conduct over the twelve-year period they were together, evidenced an implied contract between them to share equally any and all property acquired during the course of their relationship, as alleged in the complaint. The court also impliedly found this contract to be legal and enforceable under *Marvin* and not resting on "a consideration of meretricious sexual services." Our review of these findings necessarily begins and ends with the question of whether or not they are supported by substantial evidence. After fully examining the record before us, we have determined that they are.

Evidence that the parties impliedly agreed to share equally in their acquisitions includes the following: Jonne's testimony to this effect; the fact that the parties held themselves out socially, as well as otherwise, as husband and wife; the fact that Jonne and the couple's three children, in fact, took Steve's surname; the fact that the pair pooled their financial resources and then drew upon the same to purchase the subject properties; the fact that the decision to purchase said properties was, in most cases, made jointly; the fact of Jonne's participation in the properties other than financial (she kept the books on the properties, helped repair and fix up the properties, paid the bills and collected the rents); and finally, the fact that title to ten of the properties was taken by Jonne and Steve jointly and in the case of seven of these purchases, was taken as husband and wife.

Evidence that consideration for the implied agreement between the parties did not rest on meretricious sexual services includes the absence of any evidence to the contrary and Jonne's own testimony.[1] Said testimony establishes that the implied agreement between Jonne and Steve was very general and nonspecific. The parties never bothered to actually spell out the terms of their agreement or the consideration therefor. Jonne testified that her part of the consideration was to be Steve's wife and to do "whatever a wife does." However, she also said, "if you took one specific thing away, there [were] so many other things that we both did, one wouldn't make any difference, or two or three."

Such an agreement can hardly be deemed the type disapproved in *Marvin.* A contract based on "many . . . things," no one of which is in itself crucial, is not the same as one based upon a consideration of meretricious sexual services. Before a nonmarital contract is to be deemed unenforceable under *Marvin,* it must be found to explicitly rest upon a consideration of meretricious sexual services and even then the contract will fail "only to the extent" that it does so. Here, there is no evidence that the agreement between Jonne and Steve, or any part thereof, explicitly rests upon such a consideration.

Nor does the fact that the couple engaged in sexual relations and that Jonne perceived this as part of her "role" alter this conclusion. As the *Marvin* court pointed out, the fact that a man and woman live together without marriage, and engage in a sexual relationship, does not in itself invalidate agreements between them relating to their earnings, property or expenses. (*Marvin v. Marvin, supra,* 18 Cal.3d at pp. 670-671, 134 Cal.Rptr. 815, 557 P.2d 106.) In today's society when so many couples are living together without the benefit of marriage vows, it would be illogical to deny them the ability to enter into enforceable agreements in respect to their property rights.

[The court concluded that Jonne was entitled to a half interest in the property.]

------

[1] "[Defense Counsel]:   Q. Mrs. Alderson, in your complaint, you decribed that you had a contract with Mr. Alderson by which you would share the ownership of all of the property you acquired during the time you lived together, is that a fair statement of what you are saying in the case?

"A.   Yes.

"Q.   According to the terms of your contract you were going to do something for the property you were to acquire, is that correct?

"A.   I was going to do something?

"Q.   Yes. You each were going to do things for each other, is that correct?

"A.   You mean both to work and—

"Q.   Yes.

"A.   Uh huh.

"Q.   For instance, you were going to cook for you and Mr. Alderson, is that right?

"A.   I was. I was his wife. I mean, whatever a wife does.

"Q.   Okay. Well, let me list the things that a wife does and ask you if that's what you understood you were going to do as part of this contract, all right. Did you understand that as part of your contract you were going to cook?

"A.   I—as far as a contract, written, saying I did this and he did this, we just were living together as we were married. We did anything that any other married couple did and we pooled together resources, we saved money, we didn't buy things so we had money to buy houses.

"Q.   Let me ask this: Was it your understanding that you were going to stay home and cook for the time you lived together as long as you didn't work, and Mr. Alderson was going to go out and earn the money?

"A.   There was no such understanding. If I had a job, I worked and we—it was our money. If I didn't have a job, I had children to take care of.

"Q.   Let me explain what I am driving at. In every contract the parties have some understanding as to what each are going to do. If I hire someone to paint my house, my understanding is that he is going to paint the house and his understanding is that I pay him, say, a thousand dollars. And I am asking you whether you had an understanding that you were supposed to do certain things, or were expected to do certain things and if you don't do those things, then this would be an extreme disappointment by Mr. Alderson. That's what I am try-ing—driving at. If you had not cooked and refused to cook at all times, would your living arrangement have continued?

"A. Yes, I mean it would—if I had a broken arm and couldn't cook, I wouldn't expect him to leave me.

"Q. Would you expect him to give you half of every-thing—

"A. Yes, there were many things, if you took one spe-cific thing away, there was so many other things that we both did, one wouldn't make any difference, or two or three.

"Q. All right. You told me that you had a contract with Mr. Alderson, is that correct, or did you have a contract?

"A. I don't know what you mean by contract, an agreement written on paper?

"Q. No.

"A. Verbal contract?

"Q. Yes.

"A. We were living together. We were living—I mean, we were married and anything any other married couples do, we were just the same. We had higher ex-pectations than some because we wanted property; we wanted investments; we wanted things for the future for the kids.

"Q. Let me ask you this: As far as your understanding went you were going to be getting half of everthing Mr. Alderson earned, is that correct?

"A. It was ours. There was no—I mean, if left the house there was no talk of my leaving as far as me get-ting half and him getting half, was both or ours. If something happened to him it was all mine, if some-thing happened to me it was all his. . . .

"Q. Let me ask about the—about the role of a wife. As you performed your duty in the house, did that in-clude being the cook for the family, the housekeeper, the companion of Mr. Alderson, the lover of Mr. Alder-son and the mother of the children?

"A. Yes.

"Q. Were all of those essential parts of being a wife, as you understood them?

"A. Yes."

CASE QUESTIONS

1. How is this different from a common law marriage?
2. The properties in question were purchased through the joint efforts of the two partners. Jonne signed quitclaim deeds to them when Steve was about to throw her out and threatened her with bodily harm. If you were the judge, would you let Steve get away with this?
3. Why did Steve's attorney's cross-examination fail to win the suit for Steve?

9.9 MARVIN'S FIRST COUSINS

When *Marvin* opened the door, it opened all the way. As long as a suit was not grounded on sexual services, litigants could use almost any theory of recovery based on contract remedies. Many other states were reluctant to go along. North Carolina followed *Marvin* when faced with a compelling case (*Suggs v. Norris,* Case No. 9-7)—Darlene Suggs kept the business going while she cared for her dying alcoholic boyfriend. A similarly compelling case in Illinois *Hewitt v. Hewitt,* 77 Ill. 2d 49, 394 N.E.2d 1204 (1979), found the Illinois Supreme Court rejecting *Marvin.* In *Hewitt,* the "wife" ac-cepted her physician "husband's" promises of lifelong commitment, bore and raised his (their) children, and assisted him in his career, but neglected to be-come formally married. In rejecting her suit, the court expressed its concern for preserving marriage and the possibility of resurrecting common law marriage, which had been abolished by the legislature. Public policy (and morality) was uppermost in the minds of the justices:

> The issue of unmarried cohabitants' mutual property rights . . . cannot appropriately be characterized solely in terms of contract law, nor is it limited to considerations of equity or fairness as between the parties to such relationships. There are more public policy questions involved in determining whether, under what circumstances, and to what extent it is desirable to accord some type of legal status to claims arising from such relationships. Of substantially greater importance than the rights of the immediate parties is the impact of such recognition upon our society and the institution of marriage. Will the fact that legal rights closely resembling those arising from conventional marriages can be acquired by those who deliberately choose to enter into what have heretofore been commonly referred to as "illicit" or "meretricious" relationships encourage formation of such relationships and weaken marriage as the foundation of our family-based society?
>
> — *Hewitt v. Hewitt,* 77 Ill. 2d 49, 394 N.E.2d 1204 (1979).

In 1987, Wisconsin was faced with a cohabitation in many respects like that in *Hewitt*—the "wife" took the "husband's" name, bore his children, and gave up her job to be a homemaker on promises of support. Comparing *Marvin* and *Hewitt,* the Wisconsin Supreme Court in *Watts v. Watts,* 137 Wis. 2d 506, 405 N.W.2d 303 (1987) rejected *Hewitt*'s public policy argument and adopted an approach analogous to *Marvin. Watts* not only permitted the plaintiff to sue on an express or implied contract, but also permitted her to sue on the basis of unjust enrichment:

> In Wisconsin, an action for unjust enrichment, or quasi contract, is based upon proof of three elements: (1) a benefit conferred on the defendant by the plaintiff, (2) appreciation or knowledge by the defendant of the benefit, and (3) acceptance or retention of the benefit by the defendant to retain the benefit.

Watts noted that Illinois and Wisconsin were different in other respects. Illinois still allowed divorce based on fault, whereas Wisconsin had gone to pure no-fault; Illinois still had criminal sanctions for nonmarital cohabitation, whereas Wisconsin had abolished these in 1983. Thus, Illinois had a stronger policy argument for discouraging nonmarital cohabitation.

9.10 LESSONS FROM MARVIN AND ITS PROGENY

As in any area of evolving law, the law with regard to the legal consequences of cohabitation is difficult to predict in any specific case. In contrast, the cases provide a fairly clear picture of the advice an attorney should give in advance to a couple who plan to live together without a formal marriage ceremony or registration, who are nevertheless concerned about future property rights. A written agreement that spells out what is expected of each party and their respective shares in property acquired in the future should be executed. The existence of an express, provable contract should preclude the necessity to search for means to establish property rights later on through quasi-contract, quantum meruit, unjust enrichment, or constructive trusts. An express contract would be the most likely to be acceptable in jurisdictions as yet unfavorable to cohabitation.

Any agreement should avoid any hint that intimate relations are part of the arrangement. The more businesslike the arrangement appears, the more likely it is that a court will enforce an agreement setting its terms. In practice, clients are more likely to seek advice from an attorney when a relationship is ending than when it is beginning, unless the attorney is a member of a Beverly Hills celebrity law firm, in which case the opposite might be true. At present, cohabiting partners who seek a provider-homemaker arrangement may see different judicial attitudes in different jurisdictions. There are distinct dangers for the homemaker side of the arrangement. If a female, she is likely to be denied full community property rights in some states and not entitled to equitable distribution in others. Presently wives often receive rehabilitative alimony and sometimes permanent alimony. It is unlikely that court will award rehabilitative payments to paramours; even California in *Marvin* rejected this idea, and California is the most liberal in awarding property to cohabitants. A male homemaker is probably at an even greater disadvantage, because our society still views with great disfavor a man living off the earnings of a woman.

Although unromantic, the legal advice for those entering intimate relations of any kind is much the same:

> Trust your husband, adore your husband, and get as much as you can in your own name.
>
> — Joan Rivers

SUMMARY

Many cases have arisen in which cohabiting couples are not officially married. They may present themselves to the world as husband and wife or they may flout convention and brashly admit they are simply living together. As such relationships endure, the couple inevitably pools resources and sometimes bears children. When death or divorce intervene to end the relationship, issues of the property rights of the widowed or spurned spouse arise. Because there is no marriage, marital property and marital rights were not established. Often the courts are asked to intervene and provide a just settlement.

The oldest resolution to this problem was common law marriage, which arose at a time when clergy and courthouses were often hard to find. Common law marriage could be created voluntarily by the agreement of the parties, who thereafter held themselves out as husband and wife. Nearly all states adopted this form of marriage in the 19th century and treated such arrangements on a par with licensed marriages. In the 20th century, most states abolished common law marriages. Informal marriages still present a problem, though, even in the states that have abolished common law marriages, because those states must recognize common law marriages established in other states still recognizing them.

The states with some civil law background, most notably Louisiana, Texas, and California, which also are community property states, have recognized a relationship called putative marriage. In general, the basic requirements for this relationship consist of a good faith belief, at least on the part of one partner, that a valid marriage has been created and some sort of marriage ceremony has been performed. Several common law-separate property states have recognized putative marriage, partly under the influence of the Uniform Marriage and Divorce Act's § 209, which encourages its recognition and does not require a ceremonial marriage. Putative marriage does not establish a legal marriage, but treats the relation like a marriage as far as property rights for the period during which there was a good faith belief in a valid marriage.

A number of courts have used the fictional device of presumption of marriage or estopped a cohabitant from claiming an invalid marriage in order to create a marriage where the equities strongly favor a party who would be unfairly treated if no marriage were recognized.

For those who make no pretense of a valid marriage, property rights are still murky. California recognized the legality of contracts between cohabitants, as long as the contracts were not grounded in compensation for sexual services, in the landmark case of *Marvin v. Marvin*. Most states either have not caught up with California or have rejected its basic premises on the public policy that supports the institution of marriage. This promises to be a fertile area for litigation and lawmaking in the years to come. As a practical matter, attorneys drafting cohabitation agreements should attempt to create a picture of a businesslike arrangement and should avoid any implication of sexual services as part of the agreement. Attorneys with clients attempting to obtain rights from a cohabitation must attempt to characterize the relationship as a business partnership in which sex was independent of the purpose of the relationship. If a surviving spouse attempts to obtain pension or welfare benefits, most courts have taken a more liberal view of cohabitation when they find deserving cases, e.g., a long-term, good faith relationship with an elderly dependent who would face poverty without the benefits.

QUESTIONS

1. Why would a state that has abolished common law marriage recognize a marriage meeting the requirements for a common law marriage in another state?
2. John and Mary went through a ceremony conducted by a person claiming to have authority to marry as a minister of the Universal Life

Church. After five years of living together, John and Mary discover the man had no such authority and their marriage is not officially registered with the state.

    a. Would they have a putative marriage in a state recognizing such marriages?

    b. Would they have a common law marriage in a state recognizing common law marriages?

    c. If John left Mary, how would the effect of the cohabitation be treated differently, in terms of property between the partners, if it qualified as a putative marriage, as opposed to a common law marriage?

    d. How would the treatment be different if John and Mary were legally married?

3. Describe a situation in which the presumption of marriage might be an effective approach to winning property rights for a client.

4. Describe a situation in which marriage by estoppel might be accepted by a judge.

EXERCISES

Answer the questions according to the law of your state.

1. Does your state recognize common law marriages? If not, when (if ever) did it abolish them?

2. Does your state recognize putative marriages?

3. Has your state adopted UMDA § 209 (putative marriages)?

4. Is there a presumption of validity of a second marriage? 14 A.L.R.2d 7.

5. What are the rights and remedies of a man and woman living together with regard to property accumulated during their relationship? 31 A.L.R.2d 1255.

6. When cohabiting partners separate and one claims property against the other, can temporary support be ordered during the pendency of the suit? 35 A.L.R.4th 409.

7. What are the respective rights of lawful and putative spouses in a deceased spouse's estate? 81 A.L.R.3d 6.

elody Watkins and Wayne Norville an-
e the engagement of their daughter
on Watkins-Norville to Michael Curtis,
f Marlene Curtis and Kevin Curtis of
go. Shannon Watkins-Norville attended
rnia Polytechnic University of San Luis
o, graduating with a doctorate in Nu-
Physics. She lives in New York City,
ork and works at New York University.
el Curtis graduated from the Institute of
r, California with a degree in Engineer-
lives in Amherst, New York and works
ctor for the Department of Health and
Services. The two met at a physics
nce. They will be married at New York
sity. The wedding will be held in June.

e and John Cage of Kansas City an-
the engagement of their daughter
Cage to Steven Fox, son of Barbara
chael Fox of Garland, Kansas. Patricia
ttended Mason College of Hair and
in Kansas City. She currently lives and
n Kansas City. Steven Fox is a gradu-
Boston University in Massachusetts. He
n the District Attorney's office. The
ll be married May 1 in Kansas City,
They will honeymoon in Ireland.

therine Shaefer of Eagle Bluffs, an-
s the engagement of her daughter
to Robert Patterson, son of Christine
arc Patterson of Tustin, California.
Shaefer, a marketing consultant, is a

Harvard Law School. He currently works for
the legal department of Stanford University.
The two will be married at the Windmill Farm.
They plan to remain in California after a long
honeymoon in Jamaica.

WEDDINGS

Shari Ellis, daughter of Sophie and Zach Ellis
of Spring Valley, Virginia, and Brian Marino,
son of Lois and Adam Marino of Colorado
Springs, were married in Colorado Springs
May 12. The Reverend Billings officiated at
the Church. The bride wore a white silk and
lace gown. The dress had a ruffled semicathe-
dral train and a bustle with pink and white
roses. The groom wore a black and white tuxedo. The reception was held at the Hilton in
Colorado Springs. Th
in Europe.

Zoe Mathison, daug
Mathison of Boulde
Kearns, son of Const
in Colorado Springs
The Reverend Jane
ceremony, held at th
bride wore ivory, as
ily, and was driven
drawn carriage. The
tuxedo, met the brid
reception, held at
tended by hundreds.
tertained the crowd
honeymooning in Egypt.

Yuka Fujishima, daughter of C.W. Fujishima
and R. Fujishima, was married to Kazuteru
Murakami, son of Reiko and Haruki Murakami, in Monterey, California on May 26.
The Reverend R. Stuart officiated at the ceremony, done first in traditional Japanese style.
The bride wore a stunning kimono, the groom
a classic hakama. The second, western-style
ceremony saw the bride in a white-beaded lace
sheath with a pink obi sash. The reception was
held at the Rastafarian Reggae Bar on Light-
house Avenue. The two are honeymooning in
San Francisco.

Helen Davis, daughter of Lindsay and Daniel
Davis, was married to Keith Bronson, son of
Marie and Greg Bronson, in Hacienda, New
Mexico, on May 15. Helen Davis, who is a
graduate of New Mexico State University, is
an advertising specialist working for the U.S.
Government. Keith Bronson, a graduate of
Massachusetts Institute of Technology, is a
systems administrator for International
Computers Inc. in Monte Vista, New Mexico.

tion was held on Mayor Carwile's gr
The couple will honeymoon in Asia.

ANNIVERSARIES

Barbara and John Slater will celebrate
10th wedding anniversary by repeating
wedding vows in the presence of a few
friends. The couple will then board an
liner bound for the South Pacific and e
second honeymoon.

Mary and Bruce Martin celebrated their
wedding anniversary in Breckenridge,
rado on June 11 in the presence of fami
friends. The couple were married on the
of Maui and have lived overseas throu
their marriage. After a long second h

and Montreal. Distinguished guests fro
over the world attended.

BIRTHS

Robert Christopher Halliwell, a boy,
pounds ten ounces and twenty-two inch
length, was born at 10:21 P.M. on June
Maria and James Halliwell. Both mothe
son are doing well and will be returning
the hospital soon.

Julianna Leigh Kroft, a girl, seven poun
ounces and nineteen inches in length
born at 8:35 P.M. on July 12, to Stephani
Lee Kroft. Mother and daughter have a
gone home to a joyous welcome from f
and friends.

Caroline Chase Montgomery, a girl,
pounds 10 ounces and twenty inches in l
was born at 5:28 A.M. on July 19, to Ja
and Brian M. Montgomery. Both mothe
daughter are doing well and will be ret
home next week.

PART THREE

Breaking the Contract

CHAPTER 10
Property Settlements

Donald Trump and Marla Maples

Following his property settlement with former wife, Ivana, "The Donald" was free to publicly romance actress Marla Maples of Broadway's Will Rogers Follies. This on-again, off-again relationship resulted in a pregnant Maples. In contrast to the Trumps, more typical property settlements are examined in this chapter.

— Courtesy AP/Wide World Photos.

Whoever said "Marriage is a 50-50 proposition" laid the foundation for more divorce fees than any other short sentence in our language.

Austin Elliot

OUTLINE

10.1 INTRODUCTION

10.2 JUDICIAL DISCRETION

10.3 THE EROSION OF JUDICIAL DISCRETION

10.4 NO-FAULT DIVORCE

10.5 COMMUNITY PROPERTY STATES AND COMMON LAW (OR EQUITABLE DISTRIBUTION) STATES

10.6 WHAT IS PROPERTY AND WHAT IS NOT PROPERTY?
Husband's versus Wife's Perceptions of Divorce
Title versus Partnership
If It's Property, Is It Marital Property?
Professional Licenses and Professional Degrees

10.7 WHAT IS IT WORTH?

10.8 DISSIPATION DOCTRINE

10.9 PRACTICE
SUMMARY

10.1 INTRODUCTION

The picture presented in this chapter is inherently confusing. The rules and policies regarding the distribution of marital assets at divorce show inconsistencies among different states and within each state, as well as over time. Perhaps courts and legislatures are attempting to do the impossible—introduce fairness to relationships where the partners themselves despaired of fairness, however much they tried to achieve it. In addition, courts and legislatures are attempting to establish general rules to allocate family wealth in a society in which values with regard to both family and wealth are highly fragmented.

251

The disarray in which we find statutes and decisions echoes the confusion characterizing the contemporary marriage relationship. Family law seems to be driven by issues rather than consensus. The area of property settlements shows this issue orientation in the evolving law of pension rights for the nonemployee spouse, for reimbursement to one spouse for contribution to the education and professional career of the other spouse, and in the equal value of homemaking and breadwinning.

Although some issues are legislatively supported, such as child support enforcement, much of the law is initiated through litigation. This has significant ramifications. First, rules and policies are tied to the peculiarities of individual cases. Second, the absence of consensus and rule requires that judges continue to exercise great discretion, creating uncertainty in each case, which in turn threatens to lead to litigation because lawyers cannot make reliable predictions of outcomes. Lawyers play a dynamic role in divorce.

This chapter discusses the distribution of assets upon divorce. The subject covers existing assets in the form of property and continuing obligations in the form of alimony (spousal support). Chapter 11 discusses alimony, which enters the discussion here only when necessary to explain asset distribution. This separation into two chapters is artificial; attorneys and their clients must examine both property distribution and alimony as part of the whole settlement scheme. Because of their importance and complexity, however, both subjects deserve at least a chapter of their own.

The goal of property distribution at divorce is fairness to the parties. The modern phrase *equitable distribution* embodies the principle of fairness. As values change, the perception of fairness changes. In earlier times, when women had very limited opportunities to produce income, it seemed fair that the husband assume the duty of economic support for the family. This continued after divorce because the former wife was likely to be impoverished without alimony. This entitlement to permanent alimony was necessary because she acquired no property rights while married. Even after divorce, she was likely to receive only support during her lifetime, with little else in the way of property rights. Today this scheme is hopelessly antiquated, but not long ago it fit the model of family and society.

Social change is not always synchronized with changes in values. For example, equality of the sexes under the law, which contemporary courts uniformly recognize as inherent in public policy, has yet to see a corresponding equality in employment and the marketplace. (Some would also argue that we are far from achieving equality under the law.) Because divorce courts deal with the reality of divorce cases as well as the abstract principles called laws, judges often must balance fairness in principle with fairness in fact.

10.2 JUDICIAL DISCRETION

Traditionally, because domestic relations cases arose in equity, judges enjoyed great discretion in molding their decisions to be fair to the parties. In recent years, state legislatures have been active in divorce legislation, frequently establishing specific guidelines for the distribution of property and thus intruding on judicial discretion. Nevertheless, courts have often sought to encourage consistency by treating certain matters as governed by established rules.

The effect of rules is influenced by the appellate process. When a party to a divorce case is dissatisfied with the trial court's decree, an appeal may be grounded on two possible errors of the lower court:

1. If the decision was within the **discretion** of the judge, the appellant may claim that there was an **abuse of discretion**.
2. If the judge followed a principle of law, the appellant may argue that the law was incorrectly stated or applied.

The standards by which the trial judge's actions are measured are very different in these two situations. Discretion signifies a wide latitude in the exercise of judgment. To establish that there was an abuse of discretion by the trial judge, an appellant would ordinarily have to show that discretion was exercised in an unreasonable fashion, was irrationally exercised, or was based on improper considerations. Of course, ultimately an appellate court must decide whether an abuse of discretion occurred, and this calls for a judgment involving discretion on the part of the appellate court. Nevertheless, appellate courts are reluctant to interfere with the exercise of discretion unless it is clearly unreasonable. Extreme measures are inherently suspect. For example, if a court must determine the frequency of visitation between a noncustodial father and his children, many factors may be weighed to come up with a plan of visitation. To prohibit visitation without justification or to allow visitation at any time at the pleasure of the father would seem to be beyond the reasonable exercise of discretion. Just how close the scheme must be to these two extremes to constitute an abuse of discretion cannot be precisely stated. Query: If the award of 100 percent of a father's income for child support is unreasonable, is an award of 50 percent unreasonable? Of 70 percent? Of 90 percent? Appeals based on abuse of discretion commonly face an uncertain outcome and ought not to be pursued without a very persuasive case.

When a disappointed party appeals judicial action as an incorrect application of the law, the standard is less flexible. The appellate court is bound to uphold the law. If it concludes that the trial court was incorrect in its application or statement of the law, the appellate court will require action in accordance with its reading of the law. The doctrine expressing this standard is often called **substitution of judgment**, by which is meant that the appellate court replaces the lower court's judgment with its own, in contrast to the deference shown to a lower court's exercise of discretion. For example, when the trial court in the *Marvin v. Marvin* palimony case (see chapter 9) could not find a basis for a contract remedy for Michelle Marvin, it awarded her $104,000 for rehabilitation. The court of appeal saw no legal basis in this obvious analogy to rehabilitative alimony in divorce:

LEGAL TERMS

discretion
A trial court's freedom to exercise its judgment (discretion). Many of the most important areas of family law, such as distribution of assets, the amount of alimony, and custody of children, allow great discretion to the trial court judge or chancellor.

abuse of discretion
"A manifest abuse of discretion is a decision manifestly unreasonable or exercised on untenable grounds or for untenable reasons. It is one that no reasonable person would have made." *Marriage of Tower*, 55 Wash. App. 697, 780 P.2d 863 (1989).

substitution of judgment
On questions of law (in contrast to questions of fact), an appellate court need not defer in any manner to the lower court, and may *substitute its judgment* for that of the lower court when they disagree on the law. Distinguish this from areas of discretion, in which the appellate court defers to the lower court unless there is an abuse of discretion.

> The award . . . must be supported by some recognized underlying obligation in law or in equity. A court of equity admittedly has broad powers, but it may not create totally new substantive rights under the guise of doing equity.
>
> — *Marvin v. Marvin*, 122 Cal. App. 3d 871, 176 Cal. Rptr. 555 (1981).

When feasible, appeal is grounded on an incorrect application of the law, because the exercise of discretion is so difficult to attack.

CASE NO. 10-1   Equal or Equitable?

When a trial court is asked to divide up property equitably, its discretion is difficult to challenge effectively.

IN RE MARRIAGE OF TOWER
55 Wash. App. 697, 780 P.2d 863 (1989)
Court of Appeals of Washington

WINSOR, Judge.

* * *

Theresa and Hugh Tower were married in 1969. They had two children, A., born in 1973, and B., born in 1979. In approximately 1977, Theresa was diagnosed as having multiple sclerosis. The trial court found that by 1988, this progressively debilitating disease "substantially limited" Theresa's activities.

Theresa filed a petition for dissolution that went to trial in January 1988. The trial court awarded the parties joint legal and physical custody of the children. Under the decree, the children spend approximately equal time with Hugh and Theresa.

The decree requires Hugh, who at time of trial had a net monthly income of $2,100, to pay Theresa $621 per month in child support, to maintain health and dental insurance for the children, and to pay for the children's clothing, incidental school expenses, membership fees, school lunches, and other miscellaneous expenses. The child support obligation is subject to annual adjustments in accord with the Washington State Uniform Child Support Guideline Schedule.

At time of trial, the parties' most significant assets were a house, valued by the trial court at $54,000, and Hugh's vested TIAA retirement account, valued at approximately $62,000. The house was subject to a $21,500 mortgage and needed between $3,000 and $4,000 in repairs. The TIAA account is inaccessible to Hugh until he retires or leaves his current employment.

The trial court awarded the house to Theresa and the retirement account to Hugh. The court also awarded Theresa $8,091 in personal property; Hugh received $5,976 in personal property. Thus, Theresa's net award was $40,591 and Hugh's was $67,976.

The trial court found Theresa's disability caused by multiple sclerosis to be a basis for awarding maintenance and ordered Hugh to pay Theresa $100 per month until A. is emancipated. At that time, the maintenance award will increase to $350 per month. Upon B.'s **emancipation**, the award will increase to $700 per month. The decree provides that the maintenance award "shall be deemed permanent maintenance, but shall terminate by [Theresa's] remarriage or cohabitation or by her death." Although Theresa allegedly incurred attorney fees in excess of $10,000, the trial court made a fee award against Hugh of $1,200.

PROPERTY AWARD

On appeal, Theresa first contends that in making its property distribution, the trial court abused its discretion by awarding Hugh a disproportionate share of community property. Although this contention presents a close question, we affirm the award as being within the broad discretion granted the court.

A trial court making a property division in a dissolution proceeding is charged with making a "just and equitable" distribution of property. To that end, the court is to consider the nature and extent of community and separate property, the duration of the marriage, and each spouse's economic circumstances. The parties' relative health, age, education, and employability may also be considered. "A paramount concern is the economic condition in which the decree will leave the parties."

A property distribution need not be equal to be "just and equitable". "The key to an equitable distribution of property is not mathematical preciseness, but fairness." Fairness is attained by considering all circumstances of the marriage and by exercising discretion, not by utilizing inflexible rules.

The trial court's considerable discretion in making a property division will not be disturbed on appeal absent a manifest abuse of that discretion. A manifest abuse of discretion is a decision manifestly unreasonable or exercised on untenable grounds or for untenable reasons. It is one that no reasonable person would have made.

* * *

The net result of the entire decree, including maintenance and child support provisions, is that the parties will probably have approximately equal monthly disposable incomes, at least until the youngest child is emancipated.[2] Hugh has 63 percent of the property; Theresa has only 37 percent. Such a disproportionate community property award in favor of the only spouse with any significant earning capacity would be an abuse of discretion were it not balanced by long term maintenance. The property division is affirmed.

---

[2]   At time of trial, Hugh's monthly approximate net income was $2,100. From this amount, he is to pay maintenance and child support in the amount of $721, and all clothing, insurance, and other incidental costs associated with the children. Hugh, who has joint physical custody of the children, will also pay for approximately 50 percent of their food. Theresa's $721 monthly income under the decree is supplemented by $316 per month in social security disability benefits.

10.3   THE EROSION OF JUDICIAL DISCRETION

In recent years state legislatures have been active in divorce legislation. A major focus of legislation has been establishing guidelines for *equitable distribution,* the means for the division of assets upon divorce. As these laws become more specific, they naturally diminish the degree of discretion enjoyed by the judiciary. Such legislation attempts to set the rules for fairness. In large part, the legislatures have been motivated by the need to protect the welfare of dependent spouses, usually wives, after divorce, since the advent of no-fault divorce left them generally without the means to hold a conniving spouse accountable unless the jurisdiction continued to permit the pleading of

LEGAL TERMS

emancipation
  The status of a minor when he or she is free of parental control, most commonly upon reaching the age of majority, but also in most states by marriage or when self-supporting and living separately from parents.

fault grounds. When divorces were framed in adversary terms, judges imbued with great discretion could adjust the property settlement, including alimony, according to the merits of the case, considering the history of the marriage. No-fault divorce tends to focus on identifying the property belonging to the partners and dividing it according to the rules developed by the courts or enacted by the legislatures. Whereas the older model treated divorce much like a tort suit, in which assets shifted from the wrongdoer to the injured party, the new scheme treats married couples as if they were terminating an amicable business partnership. The role of the judge appears more mechanical.

No-fault divorce may work fairly for married professionals without children; each is likely to fare according to the dictates of the marketplace. They can divide up the property they acquired during the marriage on a more or less equal basis. The result is far different for the homemaker with children, in what is commonly now called a traditional family. Where the husband (but rarely the wife) pursues a career while the wife bears and raises the children, divorce perpetuates this allotment of tasks, but usually leaves the husband with fewer responsibilities toward the family. Once he meets his support obligations—which often are not fulfilled—he is free to advance his status. The ex-wife, however, is usually in a poor position to pursue a career with the same degree of freedom and is responsible for the welfare of the children. Treating husband and wife as business partners assumes an equality of opportunity and status that is often lacking.

Courts and legislatures have responded by treating the noneconomic contributions of the homemaker as equal to the economic contributions of the income-producer. Ironically, the effort to hone the rules for dividing marital assets has spawned litigation. When distribution was formerly within the discretion of the trial court, the results were difficult to challenge if they presented even a modicum of fairness. In contrast, when the law specifies the rules of distribution, many arguments arise as to application of the rules and their interpretation. For example, equitable distribution usually divides assets into marital property and nonmarital, or separate, property. *Marital property* includes income and earnings during the marriage and the property acquired with that income. *Separate property* includes property owned by one of the marital partners prior to the marriage and usually property inherited by or given to one of the partners. This dual classification encourages litigation, as one party will attempt to classify property as separate property while the other wants it classified as marital property. The dispute is aggravated by questions of appreciation in value of separate property and the income that property has produced. For example, suppose that the husband came into the marriage with a fledgling business. After reinvesting years of profits from the business, the husband claims in his divorce action that he should get the entire business as his separate property. Whereas the judge formerly had discretion to adjust the distribution of assets in fairness to the parties, today the issues come down to an interpretation of the rules fashioned by court and legislature. Such a win-or-lose proposition invites litigation.

Despite growing limitations on judicial discretion, its role in family law is still very great. The uncertainty that this discretion creates puts pressure on lawyers and their clients to reach an agreement rather than to put their fates in the hands of a judge.

10.4 NO-FAULT DIVORCE

In times past, one would have expected a chapter or two in a family law text titled "Divorce." Today, obtaining a divorce is theoretically easy, because all states have some form of no-fault divorce (meaning that one party may get a divorce even if the other party objects). It is no longer necessary to include a lengthy discussion of the "grounds" for divorce or dissolution. In a recent edition of their annual survey of family law in the *Family Law Quarterly,* Freed and Walker commented that "activity concerning grounds for divorce is almost nonexistent due to the current availability of no-fault grounds in all states." There is still some variation on this theme; many states continue to allow divorce based on fault, along with a no-fault option. Some states premise no-fault on a certain period of separation. No-fault may be designated by "marriage irretrievably broken," "irreconcilable differences," or "incompatibility," but each rests on the assertion by at least one spouse that no chance remains for reconciliation.

Although different jurisdictions vary in terms of the proof required to show the total collapse of the marital relationship, no-fault encourages judges to undertake only a limited inquiry into the relationship. Five- and ten-minute hearings are common. Fault is rarely the basis for the divorce action, but it enters into negotiations over property, support, and child custody, all subjects deserving extended discussion.

10.5 COMMUNITY PROPERTY STATES AND COMMON LAW (OR EQUITABLE DISTRIBUTION) STATES

Throughout the history of family law, lawyers have been accustomed to dividing the states into jurisdictions with community property principles and the so-called common law jurisdictions (figure 10-1). Actually, only Louisiana can legitimately claim to be a non-common law jurisdiction, tracing its roots directly to the civil law systems of Spain and France. In California, Texas, and the other community property states, this aspect of family law represents the borrowing of a concept rather than a system of law. Common law states in this context are also referred to as *separate property states,* and today the widespread adoption of equitable distribution statutes has encouraged the use of a distinction between community property states and equitable distribution states.

DICTA

The abbreviated divorce hearing is premised on both parties' being represented by attorneys and having negotiated a property settlement agreement. When either of these elements is lacking, a judge must take care to make sure that neither party is unfairly treated.

CAVEAT

The differences between community property and separate property states in the past may have been exaggerated. The partnership model in the 19th century was not an equal partnership. Texas and California, for example, preserved premarital separate property as a measure to protect wives who, although sharing in ownership, did not share equal rights to the management of community property.

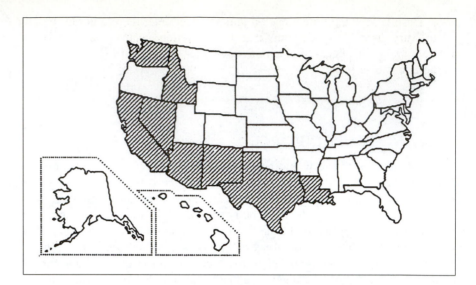

FIGURE 10-1

Community property states

One of the major motivations for enacting equitable distribution legislation was to give official recognition to the noneconomic contributions of homemakers. The differential in economic contribution, then, gives way to an assumption of equality of effort by the partners to a marriage, in much the way that business partners are treated as equal partners. In community property states, the income and earnings of both husband and wife during the marriage are owned equally and acquisitions made with this income are also owned equally. Upon divorce, the couple's assets (with some exceptions) ought to be divided roughly equally, under both schemes. In fact, equitable distribution borrowed the partnership model from the community property states. In 1984, Wisconsin adopted a community property law modeled on the Uniform Marital Property Act (UMPA). The UMPA was designed to apply to property during marriage rather than divorce and elected a community property scheme. The UMPA was a product of the National Conference of Commissioners on Uniform State Laws, the entity that constructed the Uniform Marriage and Divorce Act, which in § 307 proposes equitable distribution and community property alternatives. It is worthy of note that this group chose a community property scheme as the model proposed for all states. This is a reflection of the nearly universal acceptance of the partnership model.

Equitable distribution today is a legislative product that evolved in many instances from judicial decisions, which moved steadily toward an equal division of property acquired during the marriage, excepting property acquired as gift or by will or inheritance. The statutes stress equity over equality, providing guidelines for judicial division of property. The Massachusetts and Florida statutes are exemplary.

MASS. GEN. L. CH. 208 § 34 (1988)

§ 34 Alimony and Assignment of Property; Considerations.

Upon divorce or upon a complaint in an action brought at any time after a divorce, whether such a divorce has been adjudged in this commonwealth or another jurisdiction, the court of the commonwealth, provided there is personal jurisdiction over both parties, may make a judgment for either of the parties to pay alimony to the other. *In addition to or in lieu of a judgment to pay alimony, the court may assign to either husband or wife all or any part of the estate of the other.* In determining the amount of alimony, if any, to be paid, or in fixing the nature and value of the property, if any, to be so assigned, the court, after hearing the witnesses, if any, of each party, shall consider the length of the marriage, the conduct of the parties during the marriage, the age, health, station, occupation, amount and sources of income, vocational skills, employability, estate, liabilities and needs of each of the parties and the opportunity of each for future acquisition of capital assets and income . . . [emphasis added].

FLA. STAT. 61.075 (1989)

Equitable distribution of marital assets and liabilities.

(1)   . . . [T]he court shall set apart to each spouse that spouse's nonmarital assets and liabilities and shall distribute between the parties the marital assets and liabilities in such proportions as are equitable after considering all relevant factors, including

(a)   The contribution to the marriage by each spouse, including contributions to the care and education of the children and services as homemaker.

(b)   The economic circumstances of the parties.

(c)   The duration of the marriage.

(d)   Any interruption of personal careers or educational opportunities of either party.

(e)   The contribution of one spouse to the personal career or education opportunity of the other spouse.

(f)   The desirability of retaining any asset, including an interest in a business, corporation, or professional practice, intact and free from any claim or interference by the other party.

(g)   The contribution of each spouse to the acquisition, enhancement, and production of income or the improvement of, or the incurring of liabilities to, both the marital assets and the nonmarital assets of the parties.

(h)   *Any other factors necessary to do equity and justice between the parties* [emphasis added].

Under both statutes, great discretion continues to rest in the hands of trial judges, albeit buried in catch-all clauses. These are guidelines rather than rules. The final phrase in the Florida statute is a grant of broad discretion to the court. Seemingly, the legislature significantly diminished discretion by requiring consideration of the specific listed factors to be considered in distributing property, but by including the final phrase, the legislature gave back what it appeared to have taken away. With the same sweep of the pen, it also reintroduced fault, which it abolished elsewhere as grounds for dissolution. After all, equity and justice certainly would suggest that a philandering husband receive less and that a neglectful, alcoholic wife is less deserving of the presumed 50–50 split. Nor was this a casual afterthought; following another list of "relevant economic factors," the legislature included the following phrase with regard to alimony: "The court may consider any other factor necessary to do equity and justice between the parties." Fla. Stat. § 61.08(2) (1989).

CASE NO. 10-2   You Always Hurt the One You Love

New York also has a catch-all clause in its equitable distribution statute. The *Brancoveanu* case simply begs for reconsidering fault in dispensing marital assets.

BRANCOVEANU v. BRANCOVEANU
145 A.D.2d 395, 535 N.Y.S.2d 86 (1988)
Supreme Court, Appellate Division,
Second Department

MEMORANDUM BY THE COURT.

* * *

The parties, both immigrants from Romania, were married on August 5, 1976. There are two infant children of the marriage. The husband is a practicing attorney who had been an attorney in Romania and who was admitted to the New York Bar in 1978. The wife had been a practicing dentist in Romania for 10 years before emigrating in 1976. She married the husband within days of her arrival in this country. The wife became certified to practice dentistry here in November 1978 and immediately opened her own practice in December of that year. After the marriage, the parties bought a two-family home in Rego Park, Queens. The wife initiated an action for divorce in 1982 but the action was discontinued by stipulation dated July 27, 1983. The instant action was commenced in 1984 by the husband. The wife asserted a counterclaim for a divorce on the ground of cruel and inhuman treatment.

With respect to the husband's initial argument that the wife should not have been granted a divorce on the ground of cruel and inhuman treatment, we note that the evidence adduced at the trial amply supported the trial court's determination. Competent evidence established that the husband attempted to engage a person to murder the wife and dispose of the body; that he had continually threatened her and had struck her causing her to seek emergency medical treatment; that he called her a "whore" and a "lesbian" in the presence of her children and others; that he made continual threats over the years that he would kill her; and that he caused her to be falsely incarcerated for a period of almost five hours. These facts amply support the grant of the divorce to the wife.

The husband, on the other hand, was not entitled to a divorce on the ground of cruel and inhuman treatment as he failed to allege, much less prove, that the wife was guilty of conduct which would make it unsafe or improper for him to continue to cohabit with her.

* * *

Although the general rule is that marital fault is not a relevant consideration under the equitable distribution provisions of the Domestic Relations Law, there are situations where the marital misconduct is so egregious and shocking to the court that it is compelled to invoke its equitable power so that justice may be done between the parties. This is one of those rare cases.

There was testimony received at both the pendente lite hearing and at trial from Arsene Silviu, an admitted former instructor at a Romanian terrorist camp, that the husband had attempted to engage him to murder the wife. Silviu gave detailed testimony as to how the husband initially approached him with a proposal that he give perjured testimony against the wife. Later, the husband took Silviu to Bath, Maine, and showed him an out-of-the-way bridge from which the wife's corpse, weighted with stones, could be dropped after Silviu killed her in New York. The husband told Silviu that he could procure a gun and paid $500 to Silviu to think about it. The husband's offer was $20,000. After learning that Silviu told the wife of his machinations, the husband offered Silviu $5,000 to change his testimony.

Pursuant to Domestic Relations Law § 236(B)(5)(d)(13), in determining an equitable distribution of marital property, the courts are empowered to consider, in addition to the 12 factors which are listed, "any other factor which the court shall expressly find to be just and proper" in its distribution of the marital assets. The trial court herein considered the other 12 factors enumerated in the statute along with the husband's fault and determined that, under the unique factual circumstances herein, equity does not permit the husband to share in the dental practice which the wife built through her own diligent labor. We agree that a great injustice would result if the husband, who unsuccessfully contrived to have his wife murdered, was granted an award of a portion of the value of her dental practice. . . .

In community property states, the general rule is that property acquired during the existence of the *community* (that is, the marriage) is owned equally unless received by gift, will, or inheritance. Property owned before the marriage is separate property along with gifts, inheritances, and property passing by will from one side of the family. Important problems arise in terms of separate property, such as its increase in value, whether it has been **commingled** with community property in such a way as to lose its separate property status, whether a spouse contributed to enhance the value of separate property, and whether income from separate property is itself separate property. Unfortunately, the various states have chosen to answer these issues in different ways.

In equitable distribution states, the issues of equity and equality arise upon divorce; during **coverture** title is not held jointly unless acquired jointly. Title, however, may be irrelevant when equitable distribution takes place; the fact that title technically lies in the hands of one spouse does not prevent the property from being included as marital assets subject to division between the spouses. In community property states, ownership is shared as property is acquired. This has important ramifications for widowhood, as a surviving spouse has presumably acquired half ownership in community property. In divorce, the issues may not so much involve the fairness of the distribution as they do the identification of community and separate property.

LA CIV. CODE ANN. (WEST 1988)

Art. 2335. Classification of property.

Property of married persons is either community or separate.

Art. 2336. Ownership of community property.

Each spouse owns a present undivided one-half interest in the community property. Nevertheless, neither the community nor things of the community may be judicially partitioned prior to the termination of the regime.

During the existence of the community property regime, the spouses may, without court approval, voluntarily partition the community property in whole or in part. In such a case, the things that each spouse acquires are separate property.

Art. 2338. Community Property.

The community property comprises: property acquired during the existence of the legal regime through the effort, skill, or industry of either spouse; property acquired with community things or with community and separate things, unless classified as separate property under Article 2341; property donated to the spouses jointly; natural and civil fruits of community property; damages awarded for loss or injury to a thing belonging to the community; and all other property not classified by law as separate property.

LEGAL TERMS

commingle
　To mix funds from one source with funds from another source, making them untraceable to their original source. If a husband puts his funds or the proceeds from his property in a joint bank account with his wife, or they pool funds to make a purchase, a commingling has taken place.

coverture
　The status of being a married woman; the period from the beginning to the end of marriage.

Statutory schemes such as that of Louisiana seem to provide an easy formula for property division, but life is far too complex for the legislative imagination, and judges in community property states are also concerned about the fairness of the division of assets. *Lynch v. Lynch,* Case No. 10-3, demonstrates what may happen under unusual circumstances. In *Lynch* a serious question arose concerning the actual termination of the community, and the court noted that a different result might be achieved in other community property states. The court was faced with the interesting question of how to distribute good fortune.

CASE NO. 10-3 Lady Luck Smiles on Mrs. Lynch

It is best to win the lottery *after* the divorce is final.

LYNCH v. LYNCH
164 Ariz. 127, 791 P.2d 653 (1990)
Court of Appeals of Arizona

FIDEL, Judge.

A man who won the lottery before the pending dissolution of his marriage seeks to reverse the trial court's grant of half his winnings to his wife. We hold that the winnings were community property and affirm . . . .

FACTS

Michael Lynch (husband) and Bonnie Lynch (wife) were married in 1968. Their only child was born in 1971. The couple separated in 1985, and within a year husband began living with a woman named Donna Williams. Wife filed for dissolution shortly after.

Wife's petition was uncontested, and at a default hearing on February 10, 1987, wife testified that the marriage was irretrievably broken. A decree of dissolution is ordinarily entered at the conclusion of a default hearing. However, on February 10, the trial court took the matter under advisement and, on February 19, vacated the hearing because husband had received untimely notice.[1]

On February 21, husband and Donna Williams won a $2.2 million jackpot in the Arizona State Lottery. Each owned half a share of the winning ticket. Wife then filed an amended petition in the unconcluded dissolution seeking half of husband's share. This time husband answered, the case went on to trial, and in the ultimate decree of dissolution the trial court awarded wife half of husband's lottery share.

Husband has appealed the trial court's ruling on three grounds.[2] By each argument, he attempts to establish that the parties acquired no community property after February 10, 1987, when the invalid default hearing was held. First, he argues that a marital community lasts only as long as the parties' "will to union" and that these parties' will to union had ended by the time of wife's testimony on February 10 that the marriage was irretrievably broken. Second, he argues that, by this testimony, wife waived her community interest in his future acquisitions. Last, he contends that, because wife's lawyers gave untimely notice of the February 10 hearing, wife is estopped from denying that the marital community ended on that date.

We consider each argument in turn.

COMMUNITY DURATION

When an Arizona spouse acquires an asset before marital dissolution, Arizona law treats the asset as community property unless it falls within one of several statutory exceptions. This "bright line" rule is established by A.R.S. § 25-211, which provides: "All property acquired by either husband or wife *during the marriage,* except that which is acquired by gift, devise or descent, is the community property of the husband and wife." (Emphasis added.) A marriage endures in Arizona—and thus the acquisition of community property continues—"until the final dissolution is ordered by the court."

In some jurisdictions, acquisition of community property ceases when spouses begin to live "separate and apart." In Arizona, however, demarcation by decree "avoids the factual issue of when the couple began living apart, and provides appropriate treatment for the on-again-off-again manner in which some couples try to resolve their differences and patch up their marriages."

An Arizona couple that wishes to end the acquisition of community property before (or without) dissolution has a statutory means to do so. A.R.S. § 25-313(B) provides for entry of a decree of legal separation that terminates "community property rights and liabilities . . . as to all property, income and liabilities received or incurred after [its] entry." In the absence of a decree of legal separation, however, acquisition of community property continues in Arizona until the decree of dissolution is filed. . . .

[The court then rejects husband's argument based on the "will to union" doctrine, a Spanish rule which holds that property acquired after the "union of the wills" has ceased would not be community property.][5]

WAIVER

Husband makes the related argument that wife waived any interest in his further acquisitions on February 10 when she testified that the marriage was irretrievably broken, expecting a decree of dissolution to issue on that date. We disagree. Waiver is the "intentional relinquishment of a known right." Wife surely waived her interest in husband's acquisitions beyond the dissolution of their marriage, but her waiver went no further. She did not relinquish what might accrue to the marital community if the marriage lasted beyond its anticipated end.

* * *

CONCLUSION

This case displays the hand of chance. Fortune favored husband with a jackpot, but, because his marriage had not ended, fortune dealt his wife a share. Though the lottery was a windfall, spouses marry for better or for worse and share no less in windfalls than in labor's wages. Husband claims that his marriage ended equitably, though not formally, before the winning ticket was acquired. We have given our reasons for rejecting his arguments. The judgment of the trial court is affirmed.

---

[1] Wife's counsel had mistakenly notified husband that the default hearing was scheduled for February 9. After recognizing the mistake, counsel sent a corrected notice that February 10 was the hearing date. This second notice, however, was delivered on February 4, and did not give husband the full notice that our rules require. Written notice of a default hearing nust be provided "at least three days prior to the hearing." Weekends, holidays, and the date of delivery are excluded. . . . February 4 was the excluded date of delivery, the 7th and 8th were excluded weekend days and the 9th was an excluded holiday. This left only February 5 and 6, which did not constitute the three days prior notice specified by the rules.

---

[2] Husband died on October 30, 1989, during the pendency of this appeal. Donna L. Lynch, his personal representative, was substituted as appellant . . . . We will refer in this opinion to husband's arguments, though they are now maintained by his personal representative.

---

[5] We note, however, that even if the will to union doctrine were routinely considered in equitable division, there would be a reasonable basis for the trial court to

determine that the parties' will to union lingered through the dissolution in this case. The parties separated in early 1985, but continued to discuss reconciliation through and beyond July of 1986, when wife petitioned for dissolution of their marriage. In November of 1986, husband called on wife to arrange his release from jail. Wife posted bail, brought him clothes, and took him to her home. When asked why she would go through this, wife said: "[B]ecause whenever he is in trouble he calls me always. And because I've taken care of him for 22 years." As late as March of 1987, after the aborted default hearing and husband's lottery win, wife assisted husband in a medical emergency, checked him into an alcoholic rehabilitation program, and agreed to join him in family counseling.

10.6 WHAT IS PROPERTY AND WHAT IS NOT PROPERTY?

The house, the silverware, the stereo—these are property and in most instances can be valued fairly easily. What about a professional degree? The value of goodwill in a business? What about items that have potential value or potential profit? Husband finishes a book under contract, but it has not been published. The book took four years to write; he took summers off from teaching to finish it, spent $5,000 on computers and supplies to help him, paid a student to conduct library research for him, and incurred various other expenses. If the husband is merely to receive royalties from the sale of the book, is this property even before the book is published? If it is, should the wife have property rights in the book? If so, how does the court award them? What if the husband has written a book not under contract, which he intends to market to a publisher? Assuming he presently has a copyright on the book, is this property? Is it property that should be divided at divorce? What if the husband got the idea for the book and wrote several chapters of it before he married? Is his wife entitled to anything?

The partnership model reveals its weaknesses here. In most marriages, except for those that have lasted many years, the primary resources consist of the family residence and the human potential of the family members. Except for the fortunate few who need not wait and the unfortunate for whom waiting is of no avail, the marital career calls for a long period of sacrifice, savings, and investment leading to prosperity and security. Commercial partnerships may resemble this pattern, but the nature of the commitments and the rewards are often noneconomic in nature. The family is characterized by a special altruism in which parents sacrifice so that others, their children, will benefit. This is best accomplished when an extraordinary level of trust and cooperation is achieved between spouses.

When the marriage is terminated prematurely, a division of the current assets rarely resolves the marital partnership issues. Children are left with parents whose capacity for parenting has been distinctly diminished. The economic goals of the union are unfulfilled. Long-term goals, such as prosperous retirement, college education for the children, and a successful business or profession, have not been achieved and are likely injured.

DICTA

Equitable distribution jurisdictions have a similarly inconsistent treatment of property acquired after separation but before a final decree of divorce.

Husband's versus Wife's Perceptions of Divorce

A common source of frustration for divorce attorneys derives from the differing perceptions of rights to marital assets of husband and wife. This is particularly true in states without community property law, as residents tend to assume traditional values and laws under which property-owning husbands were favored and homemaking was not valued economically. It is wise to assess the expectations of the partners and to educate those who misconceive the law.

Husband and wife tend to view the outcome of divorce differently. Political and social ideology notwithstanding, traditionally the husband in America carried primary responsibility for the economic welfare of the family and the wife carried primary responsibility for the children and domestic needs. It should not be surprising, then, that wives were far more likely to sacrifice career, profession, and economic achievement for the general welfare of the family. This put them at a distinct disadvantage in divorce when their contributions were domestic duties and child-rearing—noneconomic and therefore difficult to value. The husband's contributions may be gleaned from the tax returns. It may be that the wife's greatest contribution has been contributing to her husband's success, which he can claim but she cannot. The husband may view the family assets as his own if he earned most of the money to acquire them. The wife, on the other hand, is likely to feel that she has suddenly been cheated out of the full reward for her services. Meanwhile, she usually becomes the primary or sole caregiver of the children, further impoverishing her.

The course of divorce rarely runs smooth. Parties may be obliged to ask the court to require the other party to behave properly or simply to keep away. The motion in figure 10-2 is designed to require a spouse to leave the marital home during the pendency of the divorce and is accompanied by an affidavit of plaintiff in support of the motion to vacate, which details the reasons for the motion (usually that the spouse has become disruptive or even dangerous).

Other situations demand other settlements. Ivana Trump, furious over the paltry $25 million she was to receive under a postmarital agreement she signed with Donald Trump, vowed to sue. Their lawyers negotiated a settlement. Admitting that Ivana was a significant business asset and assistant in the Trump business, it was still difficult to feel outrage at the prospect of a $25 million settlement. After all, Donald furnished the capital and the business acumen that made all those millions—a statement that often represents the husband's point of view. From another point of view, Donald, who may have been worth a billion, was leaving his dutiful wife for Marla Maples, a young paramour. His greatest financial successes were accomplished while Ivana was by his side as a business and marital partner.

Perceptions may well be changing. Morning television personality, Joan Lunden, expressed indignation over payments to be made to her impecunious ex-husband. Perhaps it is natural that the income-producer expects to walk away from the marriage with the lion's share of the assets. Modern legal trends dictate otherwise.

Title versus Partnership

In former times, common law states tended to distribute property in divorce to the titleholder. Because men held title, they received the major portion of the assets of the family. The wife was protected by the husband's duty to support his wife permanently, whether married or divorced, so that permanent alimony was the general rule, at least when the wife was not at fault. She was also protected by dower, which gave her a widow's share in the real property of the family, and late in the 19th century homestead laws protected her against her husband's creditors. The system gave men the property but

---

COMMONWEALTH OF MASSACHUSETTS

_____ Probate and Family Court
Docket No. _____

Juliet Jones

             v. Motion to Vacate the Marital Home
Romeo Jones

Now comes the plaintiff, _____, in the above-entitled action and moves that this honorable court enter an order requiring the defendant to vacate the marital home, in accordance with M.G.L. Chapter 208, Section 34B, for the reason the health, safety and welfare of the plaintiff and minor children would be endangered by failure to enter such an order, as can be seen more fully in the affidavit of plaintiff filed herewith and incorporated herein by reference.

                           Respectfully submitted,
                           Juliet Jones, Plaintiff
                           by Her Attorneys,
                           Veni, Vidi, & Vici

                           By _____
                           Julio Cesar
                           10 Via Appia
                           New Rome, MA 02130
                           Tel: 1-800-Et-2-Brute

[Certificate of Service follows]

FIGURE 10-2
Sample motion to vacate the marital home

imposed upon them obligations to protect the women. The modern partnership model attempts to recognize the equality of men and women and leave title preferences behind.

Nevertheless, the partnership model does not remedy the inequality, even though it is based on a notion of equal partners. Because the model converts an intimate relationship into a business relationship, the economic contributor has the greater advantage. Let us examine some scenarios to see how this can be true.

1. Husband is poor to destitute. Wife pays for divorce.
2. Husband is salaried worker. Wife gets pittance that is left after husband's living expenses are subtracted.
3. Husband is chief executive officer of a large corporation. Wife will have uphill battle proving that those stock options will someday be worth something. Meanwhile, he postpones the big bonuses until after the divorce.
4. Husband is a successful entrepreneur; the business is worthless unless he is at the helm. Wife gets the house, the kids, and two years' rehabilitative alimony.
5. Husband is a thoracic surgeon. Wife is reimbursed for putting him through medical school.

The system is not sexist, in the sense that if the roles are reversed, the husband fares no better and probably fares worse. It *is* discriminatory, in the sense that the dependent spouse is usually the wife, so that the burden of failure of the partnership tends to fall heavily on women.

If It's Property, Is It Marital Property?

Although judges are concerned about fairness, they are most comfortable when dealing in terms of property or property rights. For example, one of the most notable issues in family law in recent years has been the recognition of pension rights on behalf of the nonemployee spouse. The fairness issue was most poignantly illustrated by military divorcees. It sometimes happened that a woman would follow her husband from base to base for 19 years, dutifully fulfilling the assigned role of officer's helpmate, playing bridge and serving sherry to the colonel's wife, only to be divorced and completely cut out of her husbands retirement benefits. Meanwhile, his new wife acquired all the benefits without any of the pain. If we use the title ideology, the husband/employee acquires all the entitlement and any dependents have merely derivative rights. If we follow the partnership ideology, the husband was not merely an employee but was supported, encouraged, and advanced in his career-enterprise by a sacrificing wife. Although the partnership model may well be closer to the truth in military families, it is still merely another means to translate behavior into property rights. Although the U.S. Supreme Court, in *McCarty v. McCarty,* 453 U.S. 210 (1981), held military pensions to be separate property, Congress made this ruling ineffective when it passed the Uniformed Services Former Spouse's Protection Act (USFSPA) 10 U.S.C. § 1408, effective February 1, 1983. The USFSPA provided that state courts would decide military pension benefits according to state law. Nearly all community property states and most equitable distribution states allow some spousal claim on pension benefits. As in so many areas of family law, however, jurisdictional peculiarities make accurate generalization impossible.

Property owned separately prior to marriage would ordinarily continue to be owned separately under either community property or common law schemes. Property may change, however: it can be sold and the proceeds reinvested, or conveyed to the nonowning spouse as a gift or as jointly owned property. Any income it produces could be considered separate property or marital property, depending on the circumstances and the jurisdiction. Persons desiring to maintain separate property as such should be scrupulously careful to avoid any suggestion of marital characteristics. Although clearly separate at one time, property may be reclassified by the court if an intent to treat it as marital property can be found. This is not a mechanical process; the judge attempts to treat the parties fairly in terms of the entirety of circumstances. The status of property in some cases may be so clear that a judge has no choice but to characterize property as separate or marital, but in marriages of more than short duration, family finances commonly become a joint effort, making the issue of separate property arguable.

It has been argued that community property jurisdictions treat the matter differently from equitable distribution jurisdictions. Because community property protected the wife in her separate property, the courts may take a restrictive view of marital property. That conclusion probably bucks contemporary trends. In equitable distribution jurisdictions, a broad inclusion of property as marital property is favored, as the overriding goal of fairness is difficult to achieve if major assets are removed from the overall calculation.

Transmutation is a label some courts have adopted to characterize the transformation, translation, and transfiguration of separate property into marital property.

CAVEAT

A successful person is often in a position to maximize his or her share of the divorce split. In preparation for the divorce, husband and wife prepare financial summaries of their income, assets, debts, and liabilities. A person who owns a business can often seriously distort the economic picture of the business by making large expenditures in the business.

CASE NO. 10-4 A Horse Is a Horse, of Course

South Carolina has shown the greatest hostility toward divorce of any American jurisdiction. Although the state legalized divorce for a few years in the 19th century, from 1878 to 1949 South Carolina did not allow divorce. In *McDowell* the South Carolina equivalent of no-fault (an extended separation) is used by the wife while the husband sues on the grounds of physical cruelty. The circumstances of the case explain why the court was sympathetic to the husband and so did not include the marital residence as marital property. The Court of Appeals, however, had some difficulty transmuting a horse.

McDOWELL v. McDOWELL
300 S.C. 96, 386 S.E.2d 468
(Ct. App. 1989)
Court of Appeals of South Carolina

CURETON, Judge:

* * *

Jacqueline McDowell filed for a divorce on the ground of one year continuous separation. Ronald McDowell counterclaimed for a divorce based upon physical cruelty. He also sought alimony, equitable division, and attorney fees. . . .

PHYSICAL CRUELTY

Jacqueline McDowell argues the court erred in granting a divorce on the ground of physical cruelty. . . .

Mr. McDowell and three other people came to Mrs. McDowell's residence at about ten o'clock at night. She was alone and did not have a telephone. She had not seen Mr. McDowell in almost six months. She testified a car without lights appeared several times in the road by her home and she was frightened because someone had tried to break in previously. She carried her pistol with her to answer the door. Mr. McDowell was present with his son. They had a discussion about the car. She testified Mr. McDowell was acting out of character but she did not see any weapons. He turned to leave after she refused to give him the car. He turned back to say something to her when he was about six feet away and she testified the gun went off accidentally. She did admit during testimony that she would have shot him if he had come within a certain distance of her.

A single assault by one spouse upon the other spouse can constitute physical cruelty. The assault must, however, be life threatening or must be either indicative of an intention to do serious bodily harm or of such a degree as to raise a reasonable apprehension of great bodily harm in the future. A divorce on the ground of physical cruelty will not be granted when the physical cruelty is provoked by the complaining spouse and the physical cruelty is not out of proportion to the provocation. The family court heard the testimony and observed the witnesses. We find sufficient evidence in the record to support the findings and conclusions of the family court awarding the divorce on the ground of physical cruelty. The single assault was certainly life threatening and indicative of an intention to do serious bodily harm. Although the discussion between Mr. and Mrs. McDowell may have been heated the evidence does not support the assertion Mr. McDowell provoked the shooting.

ALIMONY

The family court awarded Mr. McDowell $200 per month in periodic alimony. The court found he had suffered serious and disabling injuries from the shooting. . . .

After a review of the record we affirm the award of alimony. Although the marriage was relatively short a consideration of the other factors relevant to an alimony award supports the decision of the court. . . .

EQUITABLE APPORTIONMENT

The marital property of the parties consisted of certain horses and equestrian equipment acquired during the marriage. Mrs. McDowell assigns error to the valuation of certain horses, the inclusion of one horse in the marital estate, and the apportionment of the marital estate on a fifty-fifty basis.

Mrs. McDowell did not challenge the inclusion of five horses in the marital estate but disputed the court's valuation of the horses. Basically, she claims the horses were either sold for relatively low values or given away in exchange for their board fees. Mr. McDowell gave his opinion of the value of the horses. Mrs. McDowell asserts his values are not reliable because of his lack of expertise. No independent witness testimony was admitted into evidence. The values assigned by the trial court are either between the values assigned by the parties or coincide with the testimony of Mr. McDowell. The trial judge weighed the testimony and judged the credibility of the parties. The values assigned by the judge are within the values cited by the parties. We find no abuse of discretion after examining the record.

Mrs. McDowell asserts the court erred in including one horse, Slash Valentine, in the marital estate. She claims she owned this horse before the marriage and it was not transmuted into marital property as the court found. Both parties testified the horse was owned by Mrs. McDowell before the marriage. This horse was bred with another horse purchased by the parties. There is testimony from Mr. McDowell that both parties cared for the horse and marital funds were utilized to support this horse as well as the other horses acquired during the marriage.

Transmutation continues as a viable doctrine under the Equitable Apportionment of Marital Property Act. Property which is nonmarital at the time of its acquisition may be transmuted into marital property (1) if it becomes so commingled with marital property as to be untraceable; (2) if it is titled jointly; or (3) if it is utilized by the parties in support of the marriage or in some other manner so as to evidence an intent by the parties to make it marital property.

Mr. McDowell bears the burden of demonstrating the transmutation of this horse from nonmarital to marital property. The record contains little specific evidence regarding this matter. Certainly, the horse did not become commingled and untraceable. There is no evidence it was jointly titled. There is no evidence it was used in support of the marriage. The only evidence concerning the horse is that it was used for breeding purposes and its upkeep came from marital funds. On this record we find Mr. McDowell has failed to carry his burden of proving this horse was transmuted into marital property.

Mrs. McDowell . . . claims error in the fifty-fifty division. . . . The court did not consider the home where they resided as part of the marital estate. While the record is not entirely clear it appears Mr. McDowell owned the home before the marriage. . . . Upon review of the entire record we do not find any abuse of discretion by the family court in the apportionment of the marital estate on a fifty-fifty basis.

* * *

The decision of the family court is AFFIRMED AS MODIFIED.

Professional Licenses and Professional Degrees

One example of the failure of the partnership model to achieve equitable results is the disappointed professional spouse. Because of the cost of a professional education and the advanced age at which professionals commence their careers, many choose to marry while in college, agreeing that one spouse will support the other through professional school. The reality of the sacrifice is harsh, and devotion to one spouse's career at the expense of the other can rarely be adequately compensated. This sacrifice is premised on the bright financial future that a professional license often brings. The scenario is often part of a lifelong plan under which one spouse sacrifices for the other in the expectation that future financial security will allow one spouse to leave the workforce to raise the couple's children. The injustice is particularly acute when a divorce is sought soon after the acquisition of professional credentials but before wealth has been acquired. The financial affidavit of the professional provides little to distribute to the other spouse.

If this scenario seems farfetched, we must ask why every major jurisdiction has enacted or considered legislation to deal with such situations. In the last 20 years, the courts have fashioned a number of remedies to compensate the self-sacrificing spouse. The basic problem faced by the courts is that the professional spouse looks forward to prosperity due in large part to the nonprofessional spouse, who is left behind older, perhaps wiser, but no richer for the experience. To compensate the nonprofessional spouse with minimal generosity, the court must look into a crystal ball and project future earnings. In short, the court is asked to grant one spouse a property interest in the other's license or degree. Although a license has value to its possessor, in the sense that income is thereby obtainable and potential earnings are greatly enhanced, the license is not property in the usual sense—it is personal, nontransferable, and cannot be sold or converted into valuable property. Nearly all courts have been uncomfortable with this problem because of their unwillingness to treat professional licenses as property. The solution has usually been found in the distribution of assets, if any, or in the guise of alimony. One notable exception has been New York, as shown in Case Nos. 10-5, 10-6, and 10-7.

CASE NO. 10-5   Dr. O'Brien Shares His License

New York has charted its own course in compensating the spouse who sends a mate through professional school to get a license.

O'BRIEN v. O'BRIEN
66 N.Y.2d 576, 489 N.E.2d 712,
498 N.Y.S.2d 743 (1985)
Court of Appeals of New York

SIMONS, Judge.

In this divorce action, the parties' only asset of any consequence is the husband's newly acquired license to practice medicine. The principal issue presented is whether that license, acquired during their marriage, is marital property subject to equitable distribution under Domestic Relations Law § 236(B)(5). . . .

I

Plaintiff and defendant married on April 3, 1971. At the time both were employed as teachers at the same private school. Defendant had a bachelor's degree and a temporary teaching certificate but required 18 months of postgraduate classes at an approximate cost of $3,000, excluding living expenses, to obtain permanent certification in New York. She claimed, and the trial court found, that she had relinquished the opportunity to obtain permanent certification while plaintiff pursued his education. At the time of the marriage, plaintiff had completed only three and one-half years of college but shortly afterward he returned to school at night to earn his bachelor's degree and to complete sufficient premedical courses to enter medical school. In September 1973 the parties moved to Guadalajara, Mexico, where plaintiff became a full-time medical student. While he pursued his studies defendant held several teaching and tutorial positions and contributed her earnings to their joint expenses. The parties returned to New York in December 1976 so that plaintiff could complete the last two semesters of medical school and internship training here. After they returned, defendant resumed her former teaching position and she remained in it at the time this action was commenced. Plaintiff was licensed to practice medicine in October 1980. He commenced this action for divorce two months later. At the time of trial, he was a resident in general surgery.

* * *

Defendant presented expert testimony that the present value of plaintiff's medical license was $472,000. . . . [The expert] also gave his opinion that the present value of defendant's contribution to plaintiff's medical education was $103,390. . . .

The court, after considering the life-style that plaintiff would enjoy from the enhanced earning potential his medical license would bring and defendant's contributions and efforts toward attainment of it, made a distributive award to her of $188,800, representing 40% of the value of the license, and ordered it paid in 11 annual installments of various amounts beginning November 1, 1982 and ending November 1, 1992. . . .

II

The Equitable Distribution Law contemplates only two classes of property: marital property and separate property. The former, which is subject to equitable distribution, is defined broadly as "all property acquired by either or both spouses during the marriage and before the execution of a separation agreement or the commencement of a matrimonial action, *regardless of the form in which title is held"* (Domestic Relations Law § 236[B][1][c] [emphasis added]; see § 236[B][5][b], [c]). Plaintiff does not contend that his license is excluded from distribution because it is separate property; rather, he claims that it is not property at all but represents a personal attainment in acquiring knowledge. He rests his argument on decisions in similar cases from other jurisdictions and on his view that a license does not satisfy common-law concepts of property.

* * *

Section 236 provides that in making an equitable distribution of marital property, "the court shall consider: * * * (6) any equitable claim to, interest in, or direct or indirect contribution made to the acquisition of such marital property by the party not having title, including joint efforts or expenditures and contributions and services as a spouse, parent, wage earner and homemaker, and *to the career or career potential* of the other party [and] * * * (9) the impossibility or difficulty of evaluating any component asset or any interest in a business, corporation or profession" (Domestic Relations Law § 236[B][5][d][6], [9] [emphasis added]). Where equitable distribution of marital property is appropriate but "the distribution of an interest in a business, corporation or *profession* would be contrary to law" the court shall make a distributive award in lieu of an actual distribution of the property (Domestic Relations Law § 236[B][5][e] [emphasis added]). The words mean exactly what they say: that an interest in a profession or professional career potential is marital property which may be represented by direct or indirect contributions of the non-title-holding spouse, including financial contributions and nonfinancial contributions made by caring for the home and family.

CASE NO. 10-6

McGOWAN v. McGOWAN
142 A.D.2d 355, 535 N.Y.S.2d 990 (1988)
Supreme Court of New York,
Appellate Division

BRACKEN, Justice Presiding.

It is now settled that where, during a marriage, one spouse begins and completes a medical education, the professional license which is conferred in recognition of the completion of that education qualifies as marital property which is subject to equitable distribution pursuant to Domestic Relations Law § 236(B)(5) (*O'Brien v. O'Brien,* 66 N.Y.2d 576, 498 N.Y.S.2d 743, 489 N.E.2d 712). In the present case, two questions have arisen, both of which require determination of the scope of the rule of the *O'Brien* case. First, it is necessary to decide whether a teaching certificate, conferred during the parties' marriage but as the result of an educational program which had been completed prior to the marriage, may constitute marital property. Second, we must decide whether an academic degree may, for the purposes of equitable distribution, be considered analogous to a professional license.

Any difficulty that may be thought to exist in deciding these issues is markedly diminished by considering that the rationale espoused by the *O'Brien* court is essentially founded upon the concept that a professional license is a thing of value mainly, if not solely, because of the "enhanced earning capacity it affords the holder" (*O'Brien v. O'Brien, supra,* at 588, 498 N.Y.S.2d 743, 489 N.E.2d 712). Since an academic degree may, under various circumstances, similarly enhance the earning potential of its holder, we see no valid basis upon which to distinguish such degrees from the professional licenses which pursuant to *O'Brien* are subject to equitable distribution. Also, considering that the enhancement of one spouse's earning capacity is the thing of value subject to equitable distribution pursuant to the *O'Brien* case, we conclude that such enhancement of earning capacity is acquired when it is actually achieved, that is, when the work that gave rise to it is finally completed, not at some later point when the completion of that work is formally recognized by the conferral of a degree or license.

We therefore hold that the teaching certificate conferred upon the plaintiff wife in the present case, which reflects certain achievements which she had attained before her marriage to the defendant, is not marital property. We also hold that the Masters Degree which was subsequently conferred upon her is marital property, since it reflects the successful completion of a course of study undertaken during the marriage.

CASE NO. 10-7

GOLUB v. GOLUB
139 Misc. 2d 440, 527 N.Y.S.2d 946
(Sup. Ct. 1988)

SILBERMANN, J.

* * *

Plaintiff . . . contends that her celebrity status [as a model] is neither "professional" nor a "license" and hence not an "investment in human capital subject to equitable distribution." . . .

In *O'Brien,* the fact that the professional license itself had no market value was irrelevant. It is the enhanced earning capacity that the license affords the holder that is of value.

* * *

O'Brien is the law. If it is to remain as good law, the rule should be uniformly applied. There seems to be no rational basis upon which to distinguish between a degree, a license, or any other special skill that generates substantial income.

* * *

This court . . . holds that the skills of an artisan, actor, professional athlete or any person whose expertise in his or her career has enabled him or her to become an exceptional wage earner should be valued as marital property subject to equitable distribution. . . .

Although other states have declined to follow *O'Brien,* regarding it as tied to the specific language of the New York statute, the problem remains. Some states courts have simply declared that licenses are not property, not even the special form of marital property *O'Brien* created. Such declarations leave the nonprofessional spouse to seek a remedy in alimony, if available. Some state legislatures have chosen to specify contributions to career as a factor to be considered in equitable distribution:

> (d) Any interruption of personal careers or educational opportunities of either party.
> (e) The contribution of one spouse to the personal career or education opportunity of the other spouse.

* * *

> (g) The contribution of each spouse to the acquisition, enhancement, and production of income or the improvement of, or the incurring of liabilities to, both the marital assets and the nonmarital assets of the parties.

— Fla. Stat. § 61.075

This contrasts with California, which casts spousal contributions in terms of community property; that is, one spouse is expending community property for the enhancement of a personal career:

> (b) Subject to the limitations provided in this section, upon dissolution of marriage or legal separation:

(1) The community shall be reimbursed for community contributions to education or training of a party that substantially enhances the earning capacity of the party. The amount reimbursed shall be with interest at the legal rate, accruing from the end of the calendar year in which the contributions were made.

(2) A loan incurred during marriage for the education or training of a party shall not be included among the liabilities of the community for the purpose of division pursuant to Section 4800 but shall be assigned for payment by the party.

— California Civil Code § 4800.3 (community contributions to education or training)

Many states continue to view this as an alimony problem, because it involves future earnings rather than property that can be valued in the present. The advantage of alimony is that it can be manipulated to achieve reimbursement if the professional's assets are presently inadequate. The disadvantages are that present payment is more secure than future payment and alimony may later be decreased.

The professional license problem raises a number of other issues. If the spouse contributes to an enhanced career, should some form of compensation, restitution, or reimbursement be forthcoming? Should a spouse have a share in the other spouse's career? This extends the business model to careers in general; a personal career becomes a business in which a spouse has a permanent stake. Reality and values collide here. Traditionally our legal system has helped individuals to reap the fruits of their labor. The law has also protected the dependent spouse, and recent trends have highly valued the support contribution of the homemaker. Translating an intimate, trusting, mutual relationship into a commercial enterprise is nowhere more awkward than when attempting to adjust the earning potentials of the spouses to achieve an equitable division of assets. When substantial money is involved and novel circumstances are present, litigation is virtually inevitable.

10.7 WHAT IS IT WORTH?

The valuation problem is a practical as well as a legal one. Even in the simple divorces, husband and wife will dispute over the value of the property to be divided and the extent of their obligations. Honest disclosure is not to be expected, and attorneys protecting their client's interests will encourage them to furnish the lowest possible values for their assets and the highest possible for their debts. Meanwhile, the figures furnished by the other side must be investigated thoroughly for accuracy. In fact, the attorney must be on guard lest the client fraudulently hide, disguise, or transfer personal, marital, or business assets.

This adversarial environment is exacerbated by the existence of extensive assets consisting of business, pensions, and professional earning potential. Placing a dollar value on these can be extremely difficult. Accountants must be consulted and may be called to testify if the case goes to trial. The cost of divorce in disputed valuations can be very great, yet the attorney who does not fully explore all avenues for the client risks a malpractice suit.

Consider the fundamental problems in valuing pension rights. What portion of the pension may be attributed to the marital regime? What will the pension be worth when finally received? What would have been the nonemployee spouse's share? What is this share worth in present dollars? Or what should be paid at some later date (actual or potential retirement date)? How should the employee spouse pay this amount? These questions may not be answered mechanically. The farther in the future the retirement lies, the more questionable the answers.

CASE NO. 10-8   No Laughing Matter

The *Piscopo* case presents the extreme problems of equitable distribution. Can "celebrity goodwill" be treated like business goodwill as marketable property that can be distributed upon divorce? What is its worth?

PISCOPO v. PISCOPO
232 N.J. Super. 559, 557 A.2d
1040 (1989)
Superior Court of New Jersey,
Appellate Division

ASHBEY, J.A.D.

This is an appeal from the provisions of a judgment of divorce between plaintiff entertainer and comedian Joseph and defendant Nancy Piscopo. The novel issue raised by the trial judge's holding is that the marital property included plaintiff's "celebrity goodwill." *See Piscopo v. Piscopo*, 231 N.J.Super. 576, 580-581, 555 A.2d 1190 (Ch.Div.1988).

At trial plaintiff claimed that the goodwill attributed to his celebrity status was not an asset subject to equitable distribution. On appeal he concedes that celebrity goodwill could be a distributable marital asset. His argument is personal, that his reputation as a celebrity could not be related to probable future earnings, but only to possible future earnings. Defendant asserts that the goodwill associated with plaintiff's status as a celebrity is an intangible but quantifiable asset recognizable by analogy to well-accepted New Jersey case law, and therefore an equitably distributable marital asset.

Irwin Marks, C.P.A., was appointed by the trial judge to value plaintiff's business and pension interests and to calculate the value, if any, of celebrity goodwill and the actual disposable income of plaintiff. Marks had experience as an accountant for famous entertainment personalities. He rendered two reports and testified at trial.

Marks found that substantially all of plaintiff's earned income flowed through Piscopo Productions, Inc., with plaintiff's compensation from the corporation determined at the end of each year. Marks said the valuation of plaintiff's business was analogous to valuing any other professional corporation. He used three out of five years of income from which to derive an average adjusted net income of $288,150 and average adjusted gross receipts of $635,452.

Marks had never valued the business of a show business personality. He had familiarized himself with publications and with custom of the trade, which was to take a percentage of the celebrity's average gross earnings and to apply an appropriate discount. He calculated plaintiff's celebrity goodwill by taking 25% of his average gross earnings over the three year period. He applied no further discount. He said that by using the figure of 25%, he had already discounted the applicable percentage based upon his experience and training. Marks attributed to plaintiff's celebrity goodwill a value of $158,863.

Under *N.J.S.A.* 2A:34-23, the court may "effectuate an equitable distribution of the property, both real and personal, which was legally and beneficially acquired by them or either of them during the marriage." While no New Jersey case has held that celebrity goodwill is a form of "property" to be distributed within the meaning of the statute, goodwill is a legally protected interest.

In the context of equitable distribution, the leading case holding that goodwill is a distributable asset is *Dugan v. Dugan,* 92 N.J. 423, 457 A.2d 1 (1983). In *Dugan* the Supreme Court held that the goodwill attributed to the solely owned professional corporation of a lawyer was subject to equitable distribution, despite the fact that ethical considerations prevented plaintiff from selling his practice. The Court said that business goodwill existed although the business depended entirely upon the skill of one person and had no book value. *Id.* at 429, 457 A.2d 1. The Court defined goodwill as "essentially reputation that will probably generate future business." *Ibid.* The Court said further:

> . . . [goodwill] does not exist at the time professional qualifications and a license to practice are obtained. A good reputation is earned after accomplishment and performance. Field testing is an essential ingredient before goodwill comes into

being. Future earning capacity *per se* is not goodwill. However, when that future earning capacity has been enhanced because reputation leads to probable future patronage from existing and potential clients, goodwill may exist and have value. When that occurs the resulting goodwill is property subject to equitable distribution.

The trial judge in this case analogized the celebrity goodwill of plaintiff to the professional goodwill of *Dugan. Piscopo v. Piscopo,* 231 N.J.Super. at 580, 555 A.2d 1190 (slip opinion at 5). Plaintiff distinguishes *Dugan* on the ground that a successful professional has a reliable future income, whereas show business is volatile. The *Dugan* Court said, however, that the valuation of goodwill is not measured by future earnings, but by past earning capacity and the probability that such past earnings will continue. *Dugan v. Dugan,* 92 N.J. at 433, 457 A.2d 1.

Contrary to plaintiff's contention, "the possible" earnings which the *Dugan* Court distinguished from "probable" earnings referred to earnings from a new license or degree untested in the marketplace. Plaintiff's record of past earning was undisputed. It was also undisputed that whatever plaintiff had achieved as a celebrity had taken place during the marriage. While the trial judge recognized that it would be difficult to value plaintiff's celebrity goodwill, that difficulty would not affect its includability in the marital estate.

The trial judge said:

> . . . The Court cannot countenance the anomaly that would result if one branch of Chancery vigorously protected plaintiff's person and business from another's "unjust enrichment by the theft of [his] goodwill," *Ali v. Playgirl, Inc.,* 447 F.Supp. 723, 729 (S.D.N.Y.1978), while another branch

deprived a spouse from sharing in that very same protectible interest. [*Piscopo v. Piscopo,* 231 N.J.Super. at 579, 555 A.2d 1190 (slip opinion at 4)].

The trial judge also cited authority in which a person's name and likeness had been recognized as a property right and given legal protection.

In her opinion, the trial judge also cited a New York case, *Golub v. Golub,* 139 Misc.2d 440, 527 N.Y.S.2d 946 (Sup.Ct.1988), where the court ruled on a similar question. The financial issues there stemmed from the divorce of actress and model Marisa Berenson. The New York court recognized her earning potential as an asset and held that her spouse was entitled to a share of its value. Unlike plaintiff, Berenson had established a successful modeling and acting career before the marriage, but during the course of the marriage her earnings appreciated, due, in part, as the court found, to the husband's efforts. (The husband was an attorney.) The court held that this increase in value was marital property subject to equitable distribution (the court did not use the term "goodwill"). The New York court said:

> . . . There seems to be no rational basis upon which to distinguish between a degree, a license, or any other special skill that generates substantial income. In determining the value of marital property, all such income generating assets should be considered if they accumulated while the marriage endured. If one spouse has sacrificed and assisted the other in an effort to increase that other spouse's earning capacity, it

should make no difference what shape or form that asset takes so long as it in fact results in an increase earning capacity. . . .

> The noncelebrity spouse should be entitled to a share of the celebrity spouse's fame, limited, of course, by the degree to which that fame is attributable to the noncelebrity spouse. The source of the fame must still be traced to the marital efforts [139 Misc.2d at 446-447, 527 N.Y.S.2d at 950 (citation omitted)].

The court-appointed accountant in the case before us calculated the value of plaintiff's corporation by including plaintiff's goodwill and the trial judge also so allocated the goodwill in her oral opinion. In her published opinion, however, and in the final judgment of divorce, the trial judge separately listed the asset.

Plaintiff contends, and we agree, that New York law differs materially from ours and from that of other states because in New York the value of a license alone is considered marital property. Plaintiff's reliance on *Lynn v. Lynn,* 91 N.J. 510, 453 A.2d 539 (1982), and on *Mahoney v. Mahoney,* 91 N.J. 488, 453 A.2d 527 (1982), however, is misplaced. We accept the accountant's analysis which conforms to ours and to that of the majority of states concerning the value in a marital estate of a business which is based upon personal competence. Plaintiff had such a business, the earnings of which were undisputed, and which he conceded had value.

We agree with the Family Part that the goodwill value of plaintiff's business was a distributable marital asset and affirm that part of the judgment.

10.8 DISSIPATION DOCTRINE

One of the most recent developments in asset distribution in divorce is the recognition of responsibility for depletion of marital assets. In equitable distribution states, this translates into an argument that *but for* the wrongful depletion of assets by one spouse, those assets would be available for distribution at divorce. Suppose, for example, that one spouse was overly fond of gambling and quite unsuccessful at this endeavor. Suppose as well that the other spouse was purposefully deceived about the extent of gambling and the extent of losses incurred, discovering upon divorce that $100,000 of marital assets had been foolishly squandered in gambling. Would this justify an award to the innocent spouse of $50,000 more than would otherwise have been awarded, as a return of that spouse's share of the dissipated assets? This raises the issue of fault in a new, but logically consistent, form: Fairness requires that marital assets be apportioned fairly in accord with the subtraction from, as well as the addition to, the partnership. New York specifically provides for dissipation as a factor in equitable distribution: "the wasteful dissipation of assets by either spouse." Domestic Relations Law § 236 Part B (5)(d)(11).

CASE NO. 10-9   Waste Not, Want Not

Spouses not only contribute to marital assets, but they may also destroy them. Under appropriate circumstances, this may affect the distribution of assets in divorce.

BOOTH v. BOOTH
7 Va. App. 22, 371 S.E.2d 569 (1988)
Court of Appeals of Virginia

COLEMAN, Judge.

. . . Equitable distribution in divorce cases in Virginia is a recent creature of statute. Judicial construction of the statute is in its infancy. The many questions concerning the scope, intention and application of the act are now only beginning to be answered. Wayne Booth's appeal of a $565,000 monetary award to his former wife raises some questions under the act which we have not previously addressed.

In 1964, Wayne Booth and Helen Cash married. Two children were born of their marriage. Mrs. Booth left the marital home on August 1, 1982. She filed for divorce on August 4, 1982. On January 13, 1983, Mrs. Booth filed a motion in the divorce proceeding for an equitable distribution award. She filed an amended complaint on May 16, 1984, seeking a divorce on the ground of a one year separation.

* * *

II. *Considerations in Determining Amount of Award*

We next decide whether the trial judge erred in considering evidence of the waste of marital assets and evidence of attorneys' fees in determining the amount of the monetary award.

Mr. Booth argues Mrs. Booth's award should be reduced because the trial court failed to consider her "waste" of $146,000 of marital assets. Although not an exclusive definition, "waste" may be generally characterized as the dissipation of marital funds in anticipation of divorce or separation for a purpose unrelated to the marriage and in derogation of the marital relationship at a time when the marriage is in jeopardy. Just as a court may consider positive contributions to the marriage in making an equitable distribution award, it can also consider "negative" contributions in the form of squandering and destroying marital resources. The goal of equitable distribution is to adjust the property interests of the spouses fairly and equitably. The mechanism to accomplish that goal is the monetary award. To allow one spouse to squander marital property is to make an equitable award impossible. On the other hand, at least until the parties contemplate divorce, each is free to spend marital funds. To decide a question of dissipation of marital assets, we must accommodate these conflicting interests in the marital estate.

Normally, only property owned by the parties at the time of the last separation is classified as marital property. In the case of assets wasted or dissipated in anticipation of separation or divorce, however, equity can only be accomplished if the party who last had the funds is held accountable for them. The funds necessarily must be considered marital assets held by the party guilty of waste. The trial judge then may consider that one party has wasted assets as a factor when the judge determines the amount of the award. Code § 20-107.3(E)(2) (contributions to the care and maintenance of marital properties).

Mr. Booth presented evidence that Mrs. Booth removed $146,000 from the marital resources. Mrs. Booth then explained her use of those funds. The trial judge specifically considered the question of waste as a factor under Code § 20-107.3(E)(11), which allows the court to consider factors other than those enumerated when such consideration is necessary or appropriate to reach an equitable decision. He found that $60,000 of the $146,000 was wasted when lost in a speculative stock market venture. Mrs. Booth did not challenge that ruling. The remainder, which Mrs. Booth used to pay legal fees and to support herself and her son, was not wasted. . . .

10.9 PRACTICE

Two factors in the area of property settlements have a major impact on the practice of law, both creating uncertainty of outcome. First, the changing nature of the law makes outcomes difficult to predict. As new statutes are passed and new decisions change precedent, the lawyer must analyze these changes in relation to clients' circumstances. For instance, it might have been unthinkable a few years ago to seek rights in the "goodwill" of the professional spouse's practice—but it might be negligent not to attempt to negotiate over this today, in many jurisdictions. The dynamism of family law means not only that an attorney must keep current with developments in the local jurisdiction, but also that developments in other states are important as well in suggesting new theories of law and future trends. After *O'Brien,* lawyers in other states naturally raised the same issues to see whether courts in their states would follow New York's lead.

Second, the degree of discretion still enjoyed by judges in family law cases also makes outcomes difficult to foresee. A judge will allocate property based on a combination of policy as stated in the statutes and the cases, social values as perceived or felt by the judge, and personal bias (often unconscious). If the judge is a feminist, a sexist, had a fight with the spouse that morning, went through a nasty divorce last month—all these factors may affect the outcome. The uncertainty this produces pressures attorneys to resolve marital disputes short of trial. A property settlement agreement is the most satisfactory method of achieving this because it is based on agreement of the parties, grudging though it may be, rather than the judge's best guess as to what is fair. As a result, the property issues are most often raised in the lawyer's office and are settled through the negotiating and mediating skills of the lawyers. In this way, attorneys are making law and defining social values. Even when they cannot agree and must go to trial, lawyer-practitioners are largely responsible for the direction of the law, as much of family law begins with litigation.

Valuation problems have made settlement more complex than in the past. The inclusiveness of marital property under equitable distribution compels attorneys to search for valuable property, no matter how abstract in form. The speculative nature of pensions, goodwill, and licenses requires accountants and lawyers to argue the figures. Values will begin highly inflated—negotiation downward is easy, negotiation upward nearly impossible.

Despite the universality of no-fault divorce, marital misconduct remains a potent threat in the arsenal of the divorce attorney. This is unfortunate because it makes the process nasty for all concerned and borders on blackmail. Legal professionals must guard against exceeding ethical and legal limitations when using misconduct as a bargaining device.

SUMMARY

The distribution of assets at divorce is treated differently in different states, but the underlying goal is fairness to the parties. A major theme of distribution has been the effort to protect dependent spouses and more recently to value homemaking in the distribution of marital assets. The questions that arise in this context concern classification and valuation. Are future pension benefits or professional licenses classified as property? If they are property, are they marital property that can be distributed at divorce? What are they worth? Although no-fault divorce commonly makes misconduct of a spouse largely irrelevant with regard to obtaining a divorce, fault is relevant in most states to the allocation of marital assets, either because the statutes explicitly make it so or because judges continue to exercise significant discretion, often by virtue of catch-all clauses in the divorce statutes ("the court may consider any factor necessary to do equity and justice to the parties").

In community property states, property acquired during the marriage is owned equally, so disputes in divorce concern whether property is community or separate property (the latter consisting of property owned prior to the marriage or acquired during the marriage by gift, will, or inheritance). Separate property can be transmuted into community property by transfer, by gift, or by commingling funds so as to render them untraceable as separate property.

Community property embodies a partnership model that has been borrowed in so-called common law states with the label *equitable distribution.* This scheme is designed to treat the partners fairly, especially considering domestic contributions equal to financial contributions. Although equitable distribution generally takes a broad, inclusive view of marital property, the distinction between marital and separate property is similar to community property.

QUESTIONS

1. What is the overriding goal of the distribution of marital assets?
2. Under what circumstances may an appellate court substitute its judgment for that of the trial court?
3. On what basis may the exercise of discretion by the trial court judge be appealed?
4. What part of the country contains nearly all of the community property states? Why?
5. Why do equitable distribution states tend to be broad in their inclusion of marital property?
6. Why was the partnership model adopted over the title model in dissolution?
7. Which states first expressed a partnership ideology?
8. What are the weaknesses of the partnership model in asset distribution?
9. What is transmutation?
10. How does the dissipation doctrine work?

EXERCISES

Answer the questions according to the law of your state.

1. Can the court consider the needs of the children in the division of property at divorce? 19 A.L.R.4th 239.
2. What is the treatment of a spouse's professional degree or license in the division of marital property? 4 A.L.R.4th 1294.
3. How does change of domicile affect property previously acquired as separate or community property? 14 A.L.R.3d 404.

4. How are future interests in real estate or trust property valued at divorce? 60 A.L.R.4th 217.

5. Is it proper to award divorcing spouses co-ownership of a business? 56 A.L.R.4th 862.

6. Can dissipation of marital assets prior to divorce be considered in property division? 41 A.L.R.4th 416.

7. How are pension and retirement benefits treated with regard to property division at divorce? 94 A.L.R.3d 176.

8. How is life insurance valued at divorce? 55 A.L.R.4th 14.

The following questions apply specifically to states having either community property or equitable distribution principles.

9. What form of equitable distribution does your state have? 41 A.L.R. 4th 481.

10. How is the appreciation of separate property treated at divorce? 24 A.L.R.4th 211.

11. What is the status of profits from a business run as separate property in a community property state? 29 A.L.R.2d 530.

12. Is community property liable for antenuptial debts? 68 A.L.R.4th 877.

CHAPTER 11
Spousal Support

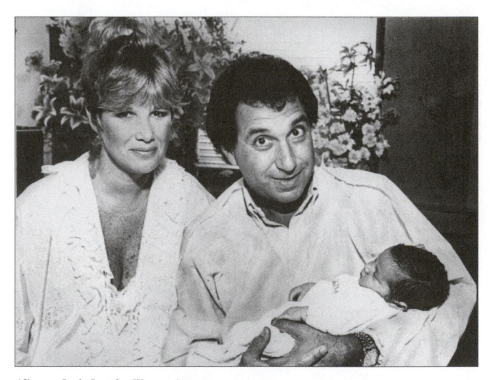

Alimony Isn't Just for Women Anymore

Popular co-host of ABC's Good Morning America, *Joan Lunden, settled her divorce suit against television producer Michael Krauss by agreeing to pay him $3 million. Lunden had previously been paying Krauss $28,000 a month in temporary alimony and expenses. With the divorce finalized, both Lunden and Krauss agreed to joint custody of the two daughters. This chapter surveys spousal support as it existed yesterday and impacts today.*

— Courtesy AP/Wide World Photos.

The claim for alimony ... implies the assumption that a woman is economically helpless.

Suzanne LaFollette (*Concerning Women*, 1926)

OUTLINE

11.1 ALIMONY AND PUBLIC POLICY
11.2 TERMINOLOGY
11.3 ALIMONY IS DISCRETIONARY
11.4 ALIMONY IS MODIFIABLE
11.5 THE THRESHOLD QUESTION: NEED OF THE RECIPIENT
11.6 THE SECOND QUESTION: ABILITY TO PAY
11.7 STATUTORY GUIDELINES
11.8 PERMANENT ALIMONY IN DECLINE
11.9 FAULT
11.10 TERMINATION UPON REMARRIAGE
11.11 REIMBURSEMENT ALIMONY
11.12 TAX CONSIDERATIONS
11.13 ENFORCEMENT
11.14 MODIFICATION
11.15 CHANGED CIRCUMSTANCES
SUMMARY

At divorce, financial obligations are allocated in three forms: distribution of assets, child support, and spousal support (alimony). Chapter 10 discussed asset distribution; this and the next chapter cover the two forms of support, beginning with alimony. These arrangements are part of a negotiated package, the intricacies of which depend on the law and the circumstances of the parties. In the last chapter, the conclusion was drawn that present payment is better than the promise of future payment—the bird-in-the-hand argument. Yet, as we have seen with professional licenses, many persons who have limited resources today will be affluent tomorrow. A bird in the bush is better than no bird at all. Other factors may influence how resources pass from one spouse to the other, some practical, like taxes, and others personal.

11.1 ALIMONY AND PUBLIC POLICY

Alimony has weaker policy grounds than child support, which is justified by the inability of minor children to support themselves. The age at which this should end is arbitrary, having been reduced two decades ago from 21 to 18 years of age. Asset distribution (chapter 10) is justified on the basis of contribution, despite the difficulty in setting guidelines. Alimony is a remnant of the time when husbands supported wives for life, whether married or divorced. Divorce meant a divorce from bed and board (*a mensa et thoro*). Annulment was the only practical means to sever the bonds of matrimony, and annulment meant the marriage was void, so that support was not available. With the introduction of divorce *a vinculo matrimonii* in the United States, alimony carried over from separate maintenance. Based on the husband's duty of support, alimony was originally available only to women. In 1979, the United States Supreme Court, in *Orr v. Orr,* 440 U.S. 268, held that Alabama's limitation of alimony to women violated the equal protection clause of the Fourteenth Amendment in discriminating against men (most states had already neutered alimony provisions).

Opponents of alimony include men who accuse women of looking for a steady meal ticket and some feminists who view alimony as a demeaning remnant of female economic servitude. The policy supporting alimony conflicts with the ideology of sex equality, female independence, and self-sufficiency. Although alimony today is ordered in only a small minority of divorce cases, its existence creates the illusion that women in a dependent or disadvantaged status are supported by their ex-husbands. Statistical data portray a very different picture, one of impoverished single mothers and neglectful fathers. Practically speaking, alimony is an issue in divorce with the affluent, where attorneys balance financial interests through a variety of devices, principally alimony, child support, and asset distribution.

From a rational-legal perspective, alimony is logically inconsistent with the body of law and offends the policy of sex equality. From a practical perspective, it is the only handy device for a judge to even the disadvantages suffered by women in our society, both as homemakers and as income-producers.

11.2 TERMINOLOGY

Despite some inconsistency in the use of terms, the following definitions are generally understood by the American legal profession. *Support* is a generic term referring to the duty of support, the duty of a husband to support his wife and of parents to support their children. *Postdivorce support* more commonly refers to child support, but *alimony* is also a form of support, derived from the original duty of lifetime support on the part of the husband. Alimony may be expressed as spousal support. Many states today use the term *maintenance* in preference to alimony, and statutory provisions are indexed accordingly. *Separate maintenance* traditionally referred to spousal support in cases of divorce from bed and board rather than total divorce. *Alimony* comes from a Latin term meaning sustenance or support.

Three terms are used with reference to the duration of alimony. *Permanent alimony* implies periodic payments during the lifetimes of the ex-spouses, terminating at the death of one spouse or (usually) by the remarriage of the recipient of the alimony. *Temporary alimony* has a limited duration, referring to alimony *pendente lite* ("pending suit") and designed to carry a dependent spouse through the divorce proceeding. It terminates with the order of divorce. *Rehabilitative alimony* is distinguished by its purpose, namely, to provide the recipient a limited period, typically one to two years of assistance, to achieve a position of self-sufficiency. Rehabilitative alimony arose as a means to help homemakers to begin or to re-enter their careers, training, or education. It is seen by many as a means to compensate the homemaker for the career sacrifice. In some cases a spouse has acquired no significant employment record or skills, except as "charwoman and babysitter," as put by a California appellate judge, and rehabilitative alimony provides a limited time to learn the employment game.

Alimony is also classed by manner of payment as either *periodic* or *lump sum.* Periodic payments are more common, usually consisting of monthly payments. This form of payment is consistent with the underlying purpose of alimony, which is support. *Lump-sum* alimony refers to a specific total amount, usually paid at one time, but lump-sum alimony may also be paid in installments. Lump sum is also referred to as *alimony in gross* and in some jurisdictions is considered to be a property distribution rather than alimony. On the other hand, a later payment of lump sum may be appropriate when existing property is insufficient and some feature of the relationship (e.g., wife put husband through law school) calls for restitution in some form. Because alimony is taxed to the recipient, a lump-sum arrangement may have tax advantages.

11.3 ALIMONY IS DISCRETIONARY

Because there is no right to alimony, the award of alimony falls within the discretion of the court. Alimony thus becomes very difficult to appeal because the trial court judge can readily find a basis for justifying alimony. Unless the amount is unreasonable or the award itself is unsupported by the circumstances of the case as presented to the trial court, appellate courts are unlikely to reverse the lower court. This has the effect of encouraging settlement agreements prior to trial when uncertainty is great. Alimony is not favored by the courts, even though most judges are aware that women fare worse in the job market than men. On any given day, it is difficult to predict whether a judge will view a wife as a deserving but disadvantaged

CAVEAT

Alimony is not available in all states. Texas does not have it. Indiana allows it only in cases of mental or physical disability.

homemaker or a lazy parasite. The judge has a very limited picture of the marriage, one that has been carefully framed by the lawyers to put their clients in the best light. The decision is likely to drastically affect the economic well-being of both parties, so they and their attorneys generally prefer to reach an agreement rather than gamble on the judge.

11.4 ALIMONY IS MODIFIABLE

Alimony may be modified by petition to the court when changed circumstances justify a modification. This is a serious practical matter when negotiating the settlement. Although little risk is incurred in the distribution of property, great risk is incurred with an award of alimony. What began as two years, alimony may be extended to four; what appeared to be reasonable support when ordered may be decimated by inflation or may be reduced when the payor becomes unemployed and seeks reduction or termination of alimony. In addition the record of payment by those obligated to pay alimony is poor, and it is clear that alimony actually remains uncertain even when agreed upon by the parties or ordered by the court. After child support, alimony is the most common subject of postdivorce litigation. In short, alimony is the least reliable form of divorce payment. Modification is treated in more detail in § 11.14.

CASE NO. 11-1   Terminology Test

Robinson shows that labels make a difference. If the maintenance (alimony) is classified as in gross (lump-sum), modification is not available, which provides an additional reason for its use. *Robinson* strains the use of terms to its limits.

MARRIAGE OF ROBINSON
184 Ill. App. 3d 235, 539 N.E.2d
1365 (1989)
Appellate Court of Illinois, Fifth District

Justice GOLDENHERSH delivered the opinion of the court:

Respondent, Billy J. Robinson, appeals from the judgment of the circuit court of Shelby County denying his motion to terminate temporary maintenance. The circuit court found that the maintenance order was maintenance in gross and as such was non-modifiable. On appeal respondent raises the issue whether the

trial court erred in determining that the maintenance order was an order providing for maintenance in gross.

On May 26, 1983, petitioner, Donna Robinson, filed a petition for dissolution of marriage. On June 18, 1985, the court entered a memorandum judgment regarding the property division, which stated:

"9—That Temporary Maintenance should be awarded to WIFE, to allow her to rehabilitate herself, to allow for the transitional period, to allow her to undergo educational and/or job-training experience, and to allow her to obtain employment. The Court orders HUSBAND to pay to WIFE said maintenance as follows:

$1500.00 per month, beginning July 1, 1985, for 24 months; and $750.00 per month, beginning July 1, 1987, for the next 36 months.

Same is to be payable from the income, or the property, or both, of HUSBAND."

In the court's July 12, 1985, judgment, it amended the memorandum judgment regarding the $750 monthly maintenance. Instead of 37 months, the court amended to state, "$750 per month on July 1, 1987 and on the 1st day of the next 35 months thereafter. Thereafter, Plaintiff shall be barred of further maintenance from Defendant."

In dividing the marital property, the court also awarded:

"In addition thereto, the Court directs that WIFE receive cash in the amount of $175,000.00; and orders that same be paid by HUSBAND to WIFE as follows: $10,000.00 by August 1, 1985, $15,000.00 by October 1, 1985, and $150,000.00 to be paid in ten (10) annual principal installments of $15,000.00 each, plus annual interest payments to likewise be payable at the annual rate of 10%, payable from July 1, 1985 on the said remaining unpaid principal; said payments of principal and interest to be due and payable on the 1st day of July of each year, commencing on July 1, 1986. The Court orders that a lien attach to the 400 acre farm to secure the payments herein provided for."

In addition to the above payments, the court denied petitioner's request for permanent maintenance and granted temporary maintenance to her as set forth hereinabove. Later, on September 27, 1985, the court entered an order which in part amended the maintenance. The order stated that the maintenance payments would terminate upon death or remarriage of petitioner.

On October 1, 1987, respondent filed a petition for termination of temporary maintenance alleging that he "has experienced a substantial reduction in income since the Judgment of Dissolution of marriage was entered." The hearing on the motion was held on November 6. Thereafter, the court entered an order in the docket sheet finding that the temporary maintenance cannot be modified because it was maintenance in gross. From this order, respondent appeals.

The question before this court is whether the trial court erred when it determined that the maintenance order was for maintenance in gross and as such non-modifiable. Respondent argues that section 510 of the Illinois Marriage and Dissolution of Marriage Act (the Act) does not distinguish between maintenance and maintenance in gross, and as such, all maintenance orders are modifiable under appropriate circumstances. Petitioner responds that the order was rehabilitative maintenance in gross [translation: "lump sum rehabilitative alimony"] because, for one reason, the trial court held that respondent lacked credibility and dissipated marital assets.

* * *

This court agrees that:

"An order for rehabilitative maintenance should satisfy three objectives. First, it should encourage and enable a formerly dependent spouse to become self-supporting. Second, it should allow for the continuation of maintenance on review if the spouse is genuinely unable to be self-supporting. Third, it should allow for a reduction or termination if an able recipient fails to make a diligent attempt to become self-sufficient. An order which meets all of those objectives will be fair to both parties and consistent with the letter and spirit of section 504 of the Illinois Marriage and Dissolution of Marriage Act."

While rehabilitative maintenance enables a once-dependent spouse to be independent, maintenance in gross is used where an award of periodic maintenance is not feasible. In *In re Marriage of Freeman* (1985), 106 Ill.2d 290, 88 Ill.Dec. 11, 478 N.E.2d 326, the supreme court found that maintenance in gross has the same meaning as alimony in gross under the former Act and further found that periodic maintenance is different from maintenance in gross.

In this case, the order and the circumstances reveal that the court ordered not maintenance in gross but rather rehabilitative maintenance. . . . [T]he trial court's order specifically stated that the purpose of these payments was to enable petitioner to rehabilitate herself, support herself during a transitional period and permit her to undergo educational and/or job training experience or obtain employment. This court finds that the trial court erred when it determined that the temporary maintenance award was actually non-modifiable maintenance in gross. Accordingly, this court finds that the order is modifiable upon a showing of change of circumstances and remands this cause for further proceedings.

CASE NO. 11-2   When Lump Sum Is Not Lump Sum

The *Low* case shows the interrelationship of the elements of property settlements. Presumably, lump-sum alimony (maintenance) is not subject to modification. That apparently is the rule in Kentucky, but *Low* provides a lesson in the discretion inherent in courts of equity.

LOW v. LOW
777 S.W.2d 936 (Ky. 1989)
Supreme Court of Kentucky

LAMBERT, Justice.

This Court granted discretionary review to reconsider our decision in *Dame v. Dame*, Ky., 628 S.W.2d 625 (1982), in order to determine whether the occurrence of any circumstance authorizes the trial court to modify a lump sum maintenance award.

The essential facts of this case are uncomplicated. In 1984 the marriage of appellant Judy Kay Low and appellee Burnell Ray Low

was dissolved. By the terms of the decree and as a part of the division of marital property, appellee was required to execute an interest-bearing promissory note in favor of appellant for the sum of $11,600 and being payable in monthly installments of five hundred dollars. The trial court also determined that maintenance should be awarded and required appellee to pay appellant the sum of fifty dollars per week for a period of three years. No appeal was taken from this decree.

* * *

While maintenance and interest payments were ongoing, but before resumption of principal payments upon the note, appellee filed a voluntary petition in bankruptcy. He listed the note to appellant as an indebtedness and the bankruptcy court granted him discharge of this obligation. In the same proceeding appellee sought and obtained exemption of his employee pension account of about $35,000, the parties' principal marital asset and the primary basis for allocation of the promissory note to appellant.

Upon the occurrence of this event, the parties went back to court. Appellant sought an increase in child support, an increase and extension of maintenance, and attorneys' fees. Upon consideration of the evidence and in a thorough opinion, the trial court decided the issues presented. An increase in child support was denied. As to maintenance, the trial court held that the bankruptcy proceeding amounted to "a change of conditions that is (so) substantial and continuing as to require the court to provide some relief." On this basis the duration of maintenance was extended for two years beyond its original termination date and appellant was awarded attorney's fees.

On appeal, the judgment of the trial court was reversed. Accurately characterizing the original maintenance order as a "lump sum award" [Court of Appeals: "fixed sum payable over a specified period of time."] and relying on our decision in *Dame,* the Court of Appeals held that modification was not permissible.

By virtue of the provisions of KRS 403.200, maintenance may not be awarded until account has first been taken of the assignment and division of property. . . . Thus, any award of maintenance being wholly dependent upon the value of property received by the spouse seeking maintenance, it necessarily follows that a proper award is impossible unless the trial court can be reasonably assured that its determination of property ownership will be realized.

* * *

As previously discussed, a strong nexus exists between property awarded and maintenance. In a proper application of the statutes, the trial court should formulate a comprehensive plan for allocation of resources in an equitable manner. Upon occasion, however, extraordinary events may intervene which render full compliance with the decree impossible and defeat the scheme formulated by the court. As a result, one party may reap a windfall while the other is left to suffer. In equity and good conscience, this Court cannot approve prospective application of one provision of a decree when another and essential provision of the same decree has failed entirely.

In the case at bar, an examination of the original decision of the trial court reveals a carefully formulated plan to equitably divide marital property and allocate scarce resources for the benefit of the parties and their children. Under this plan, and in addition to her modest earnings, appellant was awarded child support, maintenance, and the $11,600 note payable in monthly installments of $500. Under the law, the value of the note and the income it provided were considered by the court in determining the amount and duration of maintenance. Upon discharge of the note in the bankruptcy proceeding, an essential element of the trial court's formulation was eliminated. As such, the maintenance award was left without a sufficient legal predicate. Upon confrontation with such a circumstance and with due regard for the requirements of KRS 403.250, the trial court properly entertained the motion for modification of maintenance to compensate for loss of the note.

* * *

Accordingly, the opinion of the Court of Appeals is reversed, and the order of the trial court is reinstated in every respect.

11.5 THE THRESHOLD QUESTION: NEED OF THE RECIPIENT

Need of the recipient and ability of the payor to pay alimony are the two questions that must be resolved prior to an award. There must be some justification for alimony based upon the need of the recipient before questioning the ability to pay. Alimony is part of the package, including child support and the distribution of property. Alimony is awarded in a minority of cases but is probably the subject of negotiation in most divorces where the wife is represented by an attorney. As a practical matter, the division of the marital property may be fairly obvious, and the only bargaining chip for the less affluent spouse may be alimony, which may be relinquished or reduced as part of the bargaining process. When the marriage has produced children, the wife commonly becomes the primary caregiver, invoking the concern and sympathy of the court. When the children are very young, alimony is an appropriate addition to child support to help the mother until the children are in school. Because alimony is based on need, the single mother is in the best position to argue in favor of alimony. This may be palatable to the husband/father as well, as alimony is most commonly rehabilitative and of short duration. In the negotiation process, alimony may be viewed as preferable to a higher level of child support. Because alimony is taxed to the recipient, it is excludable from gross income of the payor for tax purposes, which makes it an efficient way to transfer wealth from the more prosperous spouse to the less prosperous spouse.

If mutual interest does not result in an agreement for alimony, and the issue is submitted to the court, the first focus of inquiry will be the need of the party seeking alimony. The scenario involving the single mother, the caregiver of preschool children who has foregone a career to raise a family, is the classic picture and is likely to result in a court decision to award alimony. Traditionally, alimony was justified on the husband's duty of support, which continued after divorce because of the inability of the wife to find suitable employment and the risk that the ex-wife would become a public charge. Alimony, then, was a form of private welfare. Young mothers and older homemakers continue to be economically disadvantaged, which accounts in large part for the retention of alimony. This may also explain why husbands are so rarely awarded alimony. Our society still disdains men living off the earnings of women, a fact that may account for the rarity of alimony to males and also for the lesser amount men usually receive when it is ordered. Physical and mental disability often constitute the need required by alimony.

CASE NO. 11-3   Husbands Can Have Alimony, Too

What do we do when a poor man marries (and is divorced by) an heiress?

PFOHL v. PFOHL
345 So. 2d 371 (Fla. Dist. Ct. App. 1977)
District Court of Appeals of Florida

HUBBART, Judge.

* * *

On May 28, 1966, the parties were married. At the time of the marriage, the wife owned a one-third interest in a trucking company given to her by her father, which interest she sold in 1972 for seven million dollars. The husband had no assets going into the marriage except for a one-half interest in one hundred shares of Sears Roebuck stock. He had been employed for four and one half years as a toy salesman for Strombecker Toy Co. earning a salary of approximately $9,000—$10,000 a year plus expenses and bonus. . . .

The parties lived a life of extreme luxury and comfort during a marriage which lasted nine years prior to the parties' final separation. The wife supported the family at first through contributions from her father, and from 1972-75 from her own separate estate.

* * *

The so-called "no fault" divorce law enacted by the Florida Legislature in 1971, represents a significant, but not totally radical departure from the historic conception of alimony. . . .

Under this statute, it is provided for the first time that a wife may be required to support her husband through alimony payments. This is in keeping with the current social trend toward establishing a more equitable relationship between the sexes.

* * *

Although this historic change in alimony law is far-reaching and we have not yet [charted] its full effects, we can at least begin by stating that a husband's entitlement to alimony must stand on the same criteria as that of a wife. To be entitled to alimony, the husband must show a financial ability by the wife to pay for such an award coupled with a demonstrated need of the husband for support, taking into consideration the standard of living shared by the parties to the marriage.

* * *

The wife throughout these proceedings has attacked the husband's life style as parasitic and has warned that he should not be able to parlay such an existence into a $120,000 alimony award. The same criticism could be made of a good many wives who upon dissolution of a tragically flawed marriage have received alimony awards. We pass no judgment on the morality or social value of the marriage herein. Many Americans might very well regard the conduct of either party to this marriage with some cynicism. The work ethic is, after all, deeply ingrained in our mores. But we must take the marriage as we find it without passing judgment on the life style of either party. In a free society, there is room enough for many kinds of marriages, including this one. If and when such a marriage dissolves, it must be accorded equal treatment according to the standards for determining alimony set for all marriage dissolutions.

Moreover, the limited nature of the alimony awards herein should allay any fears that it will encourage any type of parasitic conduct. The husband has hardly been given a meal ticket for life; he has been given a temporary and limited assist to rehabilitate himself to a position of eventual self-support based on a demonstrated need. In this, we can find no abuse of discretion.

Absence of need may be established by proof that the spouse has reached her career potential or is self-supporting, sometimes by virtue of a property distribution that has left her financially independent. As alimony is ultimately a matter of judicial discretion, the judge may sidestep the need issue, emphasizing other issues. Nor must the recipient spouse fall below the poverty level to justify alimony. In fact, neither party should be required to substantially reduce its standard of living; need is measured relative to the standard of living during the marriage.

11.6 THE SECOND QUESTION: ABILITY TO PAY

In many jurisdictions, courts have historically declared that the test of proper provision for a divorced spouse was whether the standard of living enjoyed during the marriage could be maintained. It does not take much thought to realize that when a couple splits up, into two homes with two utility bills, two grocery bills, and so on, costs rise without a corresponding rise in income. In response to unreasonable demands for alimony, a spouse will argue that resources are limited, despite a showing of need on the part of the spouse requesting alimony. In fact, alimony contests evoke cries of poverty from both sides, both of which should be treated with considerable skepticism by the other.

11.7 STATUTORY GUIDELINES

Although need and ability to pay are the central questions underlying alimony, many states have translated these into guidelines or factors to consider by the court when awarding alimony. Many states have adopted statutes similar to Uniform Marriage and Divorce Act § 308.

(a) In a proceeding for dissolution of marriage, legal separation, or maintenance following a decree of dissolution of the marriage by a court which lacked personal jurisdiction over the absent spouse, the court may grant a maintenance order for either spouse only if it finds that the spouse seeking maintenance:

(1) lacks sufficient property to provide for his reasonable needs; and

(2) is unable to support himself through appropriate employment or is the custodian of a child whose condition or circumstances make it appropriate that the custodian not be required to seek employment outside the home.

(b) The maintenance order shall be in amounts and for periods of time the court deems just, without regard to marital misconduct, and after considering all relevant factors including:

(1) the financial resources of the party seeking maintenance, including marital property apportioned to him, his ability to meet his needs independently, and the extent to which a provision for support of a child living with the party includes a sum for that party as custodian;

(2) the time necessary to acquire sufficient education or training to enable the party seeking maintenance to find appropriate employment;

(3) the standard of living established during the marriage;

(4) the duration of the marriage;

(5) the age and the physical and emotional condition of the spouse seeking maintenance; and

(6) the ability of the spouse from whom maintenance is sought to meet his needs while meeting those of the spouse seeking maintenance.

— Uniform Marriage and Divorce Act (1973), § 308

Some states have largely adopted § 308, adding or subtracting items. The New York Domestic Relations Law § 236 Part B (6)(a)(9) added wasteful dissipation of marital property by either spouse. Kentucky omitted the marital misconduct language of 308(b) in Ky. Rev. Stat. § 403.200. Wisconsin Stat. § 767.26 (1979-80) added:

(7) the tax consequences to each party

(8) the contribution by one party to the education, training or increased earning power of the other.

When Florida established no-fault divorce by statute in 1972, the adultery of the recipient could be considered as a factor in setting alimony. Subsequent case law employed the "any other factor to do equity and justice" element to consider a spouse's sexual misconduct. Finally, the Florida Legislature added that the "court may consider the adultery of either spouse and the circumstances thereof in determining the amount of alimony." Fla. Stat. § 61.08(1) (1989). Virginia banned alimony for adulterous spouses until 1988, when it allowed alimony "if the court determines from clear and convincing evidence, that a denial of support and maintenance would constitute a manifest injustice, based upon the respective degrees of fault during the marriage and the relative economic circumstances of the parties." Va. Code Ann. § 29-107.1.

11.8 PERMANENT ALIMONY ON THE DECLINE

Permanent alimony is disfavored in most states; it flies in the face of contemporary policies of sexual equality and self-sufficiency. There remain, nevertheless, many women who married long ago under very different premises. It was not until well into the 1960s that the women's movement began to open up professions and business to large numbers of women. Those who married prior to this accepted homemaker status as a lifetime career, premised on the lifetime duty of support shouldered by husbands. It was no disgrace, then, for a woman to have minimal work experience throughout her adult life. For such women to be thrust into the workforce at 55 or 60 years of age certainly violated the contract upon which the marriage was founded. Permanent alimony is appropriate in such cases, especially when the husband

Young mothers often face the dilemma of choosing between providing their young children with personal attention and security or working full-time to provide the essentials of living: clothing, food, and shelter.

has a good job and a good retirement plan. Permanent alimony is also appropriate when a spouse is physically or mentally impaired to the extent that economic self-sufficiency is out of reach. Permanent alimony is rare in other circumstances.

In the case at hand, both parties are young, both are in good health, and both are or can be self-supporting. The marriage having been dissolved, it does not appear desirable to have their lives bound together by financial ties which may continue for their lifetimes if the defendant does not remarry. On the other hand, the marriage did endure for about 9 years and during that time the defendant made substantial contributions to the future economic well-being of the parties. The parties at the time of the separation had just reached the point where they would begin to reap some of the economic rewards of their efforts. The defendant would have liked to have had the marriage continue. These considerations lead us to believe that the alimony to be awarded the defendant should be substantial, but in the light of the ages of the parties and the capacity of the defendant to ultimately be self-supporting in a teaching or secretarial capacity, we think the award should be payable over a relatively shorter period of time than that made by the trial court. [Instead of permanent alimony, which the majority called an "annuity," the court awarded $10,000 for ten years. The dissenting justice was outraged at this amount and accused the majority of reintroducing fault to divorce.]

— *Magruder v. Magruder,* 190 Neb. 573, 209 N.W.2d 585 (1973)

11.9 FAULT

Most people hoped that no-fault divorce would put an end to the public display of husbands and wives attacking each other. By providing divorce without the requirement of proof of fault, it was thought that the process would become nonadversarial. By the time no-fault was introduced, in many states uncontested divorces were processed using sham arguments on the grounds of "extreme cruelty." Judges would listen halfheartedly to a brief account of one spouse's nastiness, the nasty spouse would decline to cross-examine or present a defense, and a divorce would be granted. No-fault obviated the need for such a charade, making the process more honest and more efficient.

Fault, however, has re-emerged in contests over equitable distribution (see chapter 10) and especially in awarding alimony. Currently rehabilitative alimony is favored in most jurisdictions over permanent alimony. Because an award of alimony is based first on the need of the recipient, requesting rehabilitative alimony encourages painting a picture of the long-suffering home-maker, abused and neglected by a prodigal, philandering husband. Because the award also depends on the exercise of judicial discretion, the judge must be convinced of the justice of making the award. Alimony resembles compensation for injury with the possibility of punitive damages. In this guise, alimony disputes echo the unpleasant exchange of charges of misconduct that characterized divorce based on fault.

A review of modern cases on alimony reveals that fault on the part of a wife is most commonly constituted by illicit sexual conduct or unconventional living arrangements (implying illicit sexual conduct). In earlier times, when the duty of support was lifelong, adulterous women were routinely denied alimony. No-fault divorce attempted to avoid the voyeuristic inquiry into the private lives of divorcing couples, but sexual misconduct has become an integral part of proceedings in which economic resources are at stake. Even when alimony is decreed, sexual behavior of the recipient is a frequent issue in petitions for modification.

11.10 TERMINATION UPON REMARRIAGE

The parties may make specific provisions for alimony in a settlement agreement, in which case the court will interpret the intent of the parties by traditional interpretation-of-contract principles. Nowadays, settlement agreements commonly provide for a termination of alimony upon remarriage and use language to include cohabitation. Recipients of alimony have sometimes sought to avoid termination of payments, especially when the paramour has minimal resources. Ex-husbands have shown a universal distaste for supporting ex-wives with live-in companions. Some states provide for the termination of alimony by statute. Louisiana provides not only for termination upon remarriage but also for "open concubinage." The law has been generally unsympathetic to demands for support from ex-wives who remarry or cohabit. A distinction is sometimes made between permanent alimony and rehabilitative alimony, especially if the latter is clearly intended for education and training. The argument in such a case may be made that the alimony does not stem out of an obligation to support but instead is designed to assist the recipient to prepare herself to be productive and self-sufficient. Even remarriage does not undermine the intent of the agreement. Many states that provide for termination on remarriage also allow the parties to agree that it will continue regardless of remarriage.

CASE NO. 11-4   Ohio Avoids the Trap of Quasi-Polygamy

Alimony usually terminates upon remarriage, but as we have seen in previous chapters, *marriage* is not always easy to define. Here the Ohio court, in a state that still recognizes common law, knows a marriage when it sees one.

FAHRER v. FAHRER
36 Ohio App. 2d 208, 304 N.E.2d
411 (1973)
Court of Appeals of Ohio,
Hamilton County

SHANNON, Judge.

* * *

This matter came before the court on a motion for a rule instructing defendant, the appellee herein, to show cause why he should not be held in contempt for failure to pay installments of alimony as provided in the decree of divorce dissolving the marriage of plaintiff, the appellant, and defendant. . . .

The parties filed a stipulation below and from it we have extracted certain essential facts. The marriage occurred in Cincinnati, Ohio, in 1943 and was dissolved in 1966. Prior to the decree, the parties entered into a separation agreement which was incorporated by reference into the decree. The defendant paid the sum of four hundred dollars per month to the plaintiff as alimony in accordance with the agreement and decree for approximately five years. In June 1971, defendant filed an affidavit in the cause in the court of common pleas

stating that he had reasonable grounds to believe that the plaintiff had remarried, and he terminated the alimony payments.

After the divorce, plaintiff moved to Florida and began an association with one Roger C. Thayer. On December 17, 1970, she and Thayer applied for a marriage license in Florida and it was issued to them, but there is no record that a marriage ceremony was performed. However, both plaintiff and Thayer admit they booked passage on a steamship and occupied the same stateroom, and when they returned from the cruise took up residence in plaintiff's apartment. The name on the mailbox then was changed from J. L. Fahrer to Mr. and Mrs. Roger C. Thayer and, ultimately, to Roger C. and Jean L. Thayer. It is also admitted that they maintain joint savings and checking accounts, that each is the beneficiary of an insurance policy on the life of the other, and that they hold themselves out in the community where they live as man and wife. Further, it is stipulated that common-law marriage is not recognized in Florida.

The inquiry here must center upon the interpretation to be given Section 3 of the separation agreement, which provides:

"Husband shall pay to the Wife as alimony for *her support and maintenance* the sum of Four Hundred Dollars ($400.00) per month, commencing July 1, 1966, and continuing until Husband or Wife dies, or should Husband or Wife be divorced, *until Wife remarries.*" (Emphasis ours.)

* * *

Beginning on page 282 of the opinion, 159 N.E.2d on page 435, the court quoted with approval Alsop v. Commissioner of Internal Revenue (C.C.A.3, 1937), 92 F.2d 148, to this extent:

"Though it is generally stated that the remarriage of the wife does not automatically release the former husband from the duty of supporting her (19 C.J. 625), her remarriage is almost universally held to be sufficient grounds for an order suspending or abrogating further payments of alimony upon application therefor by the former husband. * * * (Citing many authorities.)

"* * * It has been held that 'good public policy would not compel a divorced husband to support his former wife after she has become another man's wife, except under extraordinary conditions, which she should be required to prove,' and that 'the cases wherein the alimony should be continued after the remarriage are extremely rare and exceptional.' "

In Ohio, the elements essential to the establishment of a common-law marriage are: "(1) a mutual agreement to marry in praesenti, made by parties competent to marry; (2) accompanied and followed by cohabitation as husband and wife; (3) a holding of themselves out as husband and wife in the community in which they move; and (4) being regarded as husband and wife in the community in which they move."

The evidence set forth in the stipulation and the several depositions is such as to leave no doubt in our minds that the relationship between the plaintiff and Roger C. Thayer constitutes a common-law marriage under the law of Ohio. Further, we are convinced that when the parties entered into the separation agreement and when it became part of the decree of divorce, the intent of the parties was that "remarry" should mean remarry in a manner which would result in a marriage considered valid in Ohio.

It is significant that in her deposition the plaintiff, when asked why she and Thayer applied for a marriage license but claimed not to have had a marriage ceremony performed, said:

"Q. Well, the only reason then you didn't go ahead and have the ceremony performed was that you could continue to collect the $400 alimony?

"A. Because I couldn't continue. I'd [nothing] else.

"Q. That was the reason, wasn't it?

"A. Oh, well, sure, yeah, yeah."

* * *

We hold that the plaintiff has entered into a relationship with a man which if maintained in Ohio would constitute a valid marriage and, therefore, she must be said to have remarried within the meaning of the agreement made part of the decree.

Further, we hold that the public policy as established by the Supreme Court has not changed and the conclusion is inescapable that the marriage to a man whom we must, from the record, presume to be capable of supporting her constitutes an election on the part of the plaintiff to be supported by that new husband and an abandonment of the provision for alimony from the defendant. . . .

"A contrary decision would result in what might well be described as: quasi-polygamy by court order."

* * *

Judgment affirmed.

Apparently the Supreme Judicial Court of Massachusetts is disinclined to require alimony continued for a quasi-polygamist:

> The cohabitation clause in question allowed the termination of alimony payments in the event that the plaintiff lived with a man "so as to give the outward appearance of marriage." It focused on the possibility of the plaintiff's sharing a home with a man, and it contemplated that that might occur in either of two ways: in a way that would create the appearance that the plaintiff and the man were married, or in a way that would not create such an appearance. Clearly, the parties thought that a man and a woman could live together in a way that would normally be associated with being married without their actually being married and without claiming or acknowledging a marriage relationship. It is difficult to conceive of what conduct the parties contemplated if that conduct did not at least include the plaintiff's sharing a bedroom with a man on a regular basis for approximately three years.

> — *Bell v. Bell,* 393 Mass. 20, 468 N.E.2d 859 (1984)

CASE NO. 11-5　Termination by Cohabitation

Termination of alimony upon remarriage was justified in earlier times on the grounds that remarriage meant that the new husband was now bound to support his wife, terminating the ex-husband's duty of support. Today this may be implicit in case of remarriage, but a new argument is also forthcoming. If the ex-wife moves in with a new husband or paramour, she either moves into his residence, reducing the need of the ex-husband to furnish her support, or the new man moves into her quarters, which means that the ex-husband is supporting his replacement.

**O'CONNOR BROS. ABALONE CO.
v. BRANDO
40 Cal. App. 3d 90, 114 Cal. Rptr.
773 (1974)
Court of Appeal, Second District**

COMPTON, Associate Justice.

In July of 1968, in connection with the annulment of their marriage, Marlon and Movita Brando executed a written agreement purporting to settle certain financial matters and child custody rights.

As a part of that agreement Marlon undertook to make monthly payments of $600 for the support of the minor children and monthly payments of $1400 for the support of Movita. Only the latter payments to Movita are in issue here.

[O'Connor Bros. Abalone Co. was attempting to collect a judgment (against Movita) of $55,000 by joining Marlon on the grounds that he owed Movita arrears under their agreement.]

* * *

The resolution of this dispute turns on whether, under the terms of the agreement between Marlon and Movita, her conduct was such as to terminate Marlon's obligation to make further payments. The crucial provision in the agreement is as follows:

"(a) Defendant agrees to pay or cause to be paid to Plaintiff, the amount of $1,400.00 per month commencing on the first day of the calendar month next succeeding the month in which this Agreement is executed and continuing for a period of one-hundred fifty-six (156) months, or *until she remarries or dies, whichever occurs sooner. For the purposes of this Agreement, 'remarriage' shall include, without limitation, Plaintiff's appearing to maintain a marital relationship with any person, or any ceremonial marriage entered into by Plaintiff even though the same may later be annulled or otherwise terminated or rendered invalid."* (Emphasis added.)

In reliance on this "remarriage" clause, Marlon ceased to make the payments in April 1971. He contends that in 1968, Movita entered into a relationship with one James Ford which relationship was within the provisions of the term "remarriage" as defined in the Agreement.

* * *

The evidence in the trial left little doubt that Movita and Ford enjoyed a relationship of substantial duration, which relationship bore the objective indicia of marriage. By their own admission they engaged in frequent sexual intercourse. Ford kept his clothes at the residence in Coldwater Canyon, he ate meals there, many of which he prepared. Ford frequently purchased groceries for their meals by charging them to Movita's account at the market, he drove her cars and was authorized to use her charge account at one of the major department stores.

* * *

The trial court's finding that they "lived" together is well supported. The further finding that such relationship could not be reasonably interpreted as indicating that Ford and Movita were in fact married apparently flowed from the absence of any evidence that they told anyone they were married.

* * *

We here summarize the position of the respective parties. O'Connor contends, and the trial court concluded, that the phrase "appearing to maintain a marital relationship" means a holding out by Movita that she was in fact married or conduct on her part that would imply a marriage in fact. According to this version, a meretricious relationship, no matter how intimate and enduring, would not terminate the obligation for support payments so long as it was made clear to the world that Movita and her paramour were *not* married. . . .

According to Marlon the Agreement means a "marital type" relationship and such interpretation is necessary to avoid what he sought to avoid, i.e., the possibility that Movita's male companion, in sharing Movita's shelter, bed and board, would also benefit from the support payments which Marlon was providing.

* * *

Clearly the purpose of the Agreement was not to circumscribe Movita's sexual activity per se as she was free to engage in sexual intercourse with other men. The Agreement sought to embrace actual ceremonial marriages on the one hand and on the other, relationships which were not marriages but which had the attributes of marriage such as companionship of substantial duration, the sharing of habitation, eating together and sexual intimacy. The characterization of such a relationship as "marital" does not depend on whether third persons are led to believe the existence of a ceremonial marriage. In fact, public belief that Movita and Ford were actually married would be less demeaning to Marlon than their conduct of "living" together while disavowing an actual marriage.

What is important here from the standpoint of the objectives of the Agreement is that such a relationship creates the strong probability that the male partner will derive benefit from the support payments. And that, in fact, is what occurred here. . . .

We interpret the phrase "appearing to maintain a marital relationship" as including the appearance of "living together" under circumstances such as existed here, whether or not there is the appearance of marriage in fact. This appears to us to be the only possible reasonable interpretation of the Agreement.

CASE QUESTIONS

1. Does it make a difference that this agreement was made in connection with an annulment rather than a divorce?
2. Is this a moral question or an economic one? Does it matter? If it is moral, then Movita loses because she is engaged in an illicit relationship. If it is economic, she loses because either she is benefiting from support from Ford or she is using Marlon's money to support an unintended beneficiary (Ford). Is this analysis correct?
3. How would you phrase a clause in a property settlement agreement to effectively terminate alimony obligations when the ex-spouse cohabits?

11.11   REIMBURSEMENT ALIMONY

In chapter 10, *O'Brien* was presented as New York's answer to the professional license problem. Other states have been reluctant to label professional licenses property or even marital property. Another solution has recently been proposed which creates a new species of alimony labeled "reimbursement alimony." *In re Marriage of Francis,* Case No. 11-6, not only addresses the issue but also clearly distinguishes the contemporary goals of property distribution and alimony, including a cogent analysis of the difference between rehabilitative and reimbursement alimony. In light of the general rejection of *O'Brien,* we may cautiously predict that *Francis* will be representative of a line of cases that will resolve a problem that has plagued the courts for some time.

CASE NO. 11-6   Reimbursement Alimony

Although some states have provided by statute for consideration of contribution to education and career in the award of property or alimony, *Francis* distinguishes reimbursement alimony as nonmodifiable, nonterminable-by-remarriage, lump-sum alimony, a distinction that may be adopted by courts elsewhere.

IN RE MARRIAGE OF FRANCIS
442 N.W.2d 59 (Iowa 1989)
Supreme Court of Iowa

NEUMAN, Justice.

This appeal involves the thorny economic issues surrounding what has come to be called the "advanced degree/divorce decree"[1] dissolution of marriage action.

On the day he was admitted to medical school, appellant Thomas Francis proposed marriage to appellee Diana Mora Francis. Like countless couples before them, they pledged to one another their support and commitment to a shared future. Six years and two children later, however, their marriage is at an end. And while Tom stands at the threshold of his career as a physician specializing in family practice, Diana ponders her future from the vantage point of one who has helped support the family through medical school and two years of residency on the modest income generated by her in-home day care business.

The fighting issue, as framed by the trial court and reiterated by the parties on appeal, is this: What compensation, if any, should Diana receive for her contribution to Thomas' increased earning capacity due to his education received during the marriage? For over a decade this court has recognized that a spouse's contribution to that increased earning potential is a factor properly considered in the award of alimony and an equitable division of the parties' assets. Yet precisely because each dissolution action must be decided on its unique facts and circumstances, no predictable method of valuing that contribution or distributing the fruits of that increased potential has been settled upon.

Here the trial court awarded Diana a $100,000 lump sum property award payable with interest in ten annual installments, along with a three-year rehabilitative alimony award totaling $54,000. . . .

I.   Several well settled rules guide our decision. Principal among them is the rule that an advanced degree or professional license *in and of itself* is not an asset for property division purposes.

Nevertheless, the future earning capacity flowing from an advanced degree or professional license is a factor to be considered in the division of property and the award of alimony.

Prior Iowa cases have interchangeably used property awards and alimony as means of compensating a nonprofessional spouse for the contribution made to the other spouse's advanced degree or professional license.

It must be remembered, however, that the purposes of property division and alimony are not the same. Property division is based on each partner's right to "a just and equitable share of the property accumulated as the result of their joint efforts." Alimony, on the other hand, is a stipend to a spouse in lieu of the other spouse's legal obligation for support.

Recently, such court-ordered stipends have taken on new forms to accommodate the broad range of functions that alimony may serve. . . .

In [long-term marriages], life patterns have largely been set, the earning potential of both parties can be predicted with some reliability, and the contributions and sacrifices of the one spouse in enabling the other to attain a degree have been compensated by many years of the comfortable lifestyle which the degree permitted. Traditional alimony analysis works nicely to assure equity in such cases.

In another kind of recurring case, . . . where divorce occurs shortly after the degree is obtained, traditional alimony analysis would often work hardship because, while both spouses have modest incomes at the time of divorce, the one is on the threshold of a significant increase in earnings. Moreover, the spouse who sacrificed so the other could attain a degree is precluded from enjoying the anticipated dividends the degree will ordinarily provide. Nonetheless, such a spouse is typically not remote in time from his or her previous education and is otherwise better able to adjust and to acquire comparable skills, given the opportunity and the funding. In such cases, alimony analysis must become more creative to achieve fairness, and an award of "rehabilitative" or "reimbursement" alimony, not terminable upon remarriage, may be appropriate.

With these principles in mind, we consider the contentions of the parties.

* * *

As previously stated in this opinion, alimony has traditionally taken the place of support that would have been provided had the marriage continued. A calculation of future earning capacity, in a case like the present one, essentially represents a value placed on the income to be derived from the advanced degree achieved during the marriage. The amount that

would have been the student spouse's contribution to the future support of the parties is logically tied, if not wholly determined by, future earning capacity. Thus the court's duty to look at the future earning capacity of the spouses tracks more closely with a concern for loss of anticipated support, reimbursable through alimony, than through division of as-yet-unrealized tangible assets.

The alimony of which we speak is designed to give the "supporting" spouse a stake in the "student" spouse's future earning capacity, in exchange for recognizable contributions to the source of that income—the student's advanced education. As such, it is to be clearly distinguished from "rehabilitative" or "permanent" alimony.

Rehabilitative alimony was conceived as a way of supporting an economically dependent spouse through a limited period of re-education or retraining following divorce, thereby creating incentive and opportunity for that spouse to become self-supporting.

Because self-sufficiency is the goal of rehabilitative alimony, the duration of such an award may be limited or extended depending on the realistic needs of the economically dependent spouse, tempered by the goal of facilitating the economic independence of the ex-spouses. As in the case of "traditional" alimony, payable for life or so long as a spouse is incapable of self-support, a change in status (e.g., remarriage) may alter the support picture and warrant a modification.

"Reimbursement" alimony, on the other hand, which is predicated upon economic sacrifices made by one spouse during the marriage that directly enhance the future earning capacity of the other, should not be subject to modification or termination until full compensation is achieved. Similar to a property award, but based on future earning capacity rather than a division of tangible assets, it should be fixed at the time of the decree. In recognition of the personal nature of the award and the current tax laws, however, a spouse's obligation to pay reimbursement alimony must terminate upon the recipient's death.

We think the case before us exemplifies the situation calling for an award of reimbursement alimony rather than a property settlement. Not only does such an award bear a closer resemblance to support than a division of assets, alimony carries tax benefits to the payor and assurance to the payee that the award will not be discharged in bankruptcy. The trial court's decree must be modified accordingly.

* * *

[There follows a lengthy discussion of the figures offered by an expert witness establishing the proper amount to be awarded as reimbursement.]

The district court's order for rehabilitative alimony commencing August 1, 1988, is affirmed as modified by the reduction to one year and increase in amount to $1000 per month. . . .

AFFIRMED AS MODIFIED.

CARTER, Justice (dissenting in part).

I believe the trial court was correct in concluding that the type of spousal reimbursement which is the primary issue on this appeal has all of the attributes of a property settlement. I would treat is as such rather than characterizing it as alimony.

ANDREASEN, J., joins this partial dissent.

---

1 An apt, but somewhat cynical, label derived from one coined by the Wisconsin Supreme Court in *Haugan v. Haugan,* 117 Wis.2d 200, 206, 343 N.W.2d 796, 799-800 (1984).

11.12 TAX CONSIDERATIONS

A major concern of the transfer of marital resources is the tax consequences of the scheme. Ordinarily alimony goes from an affluent payor to a recipient with more limited resources, for example, a former homemaker returning to complete an education. Alimony is deductible from the payor's taxable income but taxed to the recipient. When the payor has substantial income and the recipient has none, a significant tax savings may be gained. For this reason, many spouses will arrange for limited child support and generous alimony, as child support is taxed to the payor. If the alimony is rehabilitative, child support may be appropriately adjusted, if necessary, following the period of alimony payments. Because of the tax savings, many well-to-do couples avoided child support altogether or made an arrangement in which the child support was insignificant compared to the alimony. Judges understood the arrangements and generally approved them. The Internal Revenue Service and Congress, however, were unhappy about certain abuses and the revenue lost by the national treasury.

In 1985, Congress defined *alimony* to prevent child support passing for alimony to save taxes. The label used by the property settlement or the judicial order will not protect the taxpayer if the payment does not meet the requirements. Payment must be made in money, as opposed to services or other forms of property. Payor and recipient must live in separate residences.

CAVEAT

As with equitable distribution, a valuation problem arises when a spouse is reimbursed for contribution to education, career, or professional license. *Francis* and *O'Brien* contain discussions of legal aspects of valuation in this situation. These and other cases should be consulted by the practitioner urging or challenging such reimbursement. These cases may be won or lost on the quality of the presentation of economic data.

Payments must terminate on the death of the recipient. Payments contingent on events relating to a child or children (e.g., marriage or economic independence) will cause the payments to be treated as child support. Payments exceeding $10,000 per year must continue for at least six years, excepting cases of death of either party or remarriage of the recipient.

Pre-1985 divorces are treated somewhat differently. Agreements are enforceable if they provide for periodic payments of a period of more than ten years. As time goes on, only a few cases of permanent periodic alimony will raise any questions. Also, alimony payments from income from business and property may be treated differently.

11.13 ENFORCEMENT

The traditional means for enforcing payment of alimony is through contempt of court proceedings. This raises the threat of imprisonment for nonpayment, but most judges are reluctant to further burden the jails except for egregious disregard of court orders. Because contempt sanctions are discretionary, there is no certainty that a delinquent payor will be seriously threatened; judges vary considerably from those who routinely lock up delinquents to those who never do so. The delinquent's argument is that he or she cannot earn any money while in jail. Many judges nevertheless lock up delinquents, making the condition of their release a stipulated payment of arrears. One judge in Tallahassee, Florida, followed a policy of ordering some reasonable payment for release and commented, "To my knowledge, none of them has ever spent the night in jail."

Recordkeeping is essential in establishing arrearages. If payment may be made through the court, this is advisable for both sides, to avoid or refute accusations of payment or nonpayment, (assuming the court records are accurate). The court's record of payments as of the day of the hearing should be obtainable from the clerk and is very difficult to challenge.

Other civil remedies may also be available, but are often more costly and cumbersome to obtain. For example, one of the most effective means of collecting support is through **garnishment** of wages, so that the support goes from the employer directly to the alimony recipient.

11.14 MODIFICATION

Periodic alimony is subject to change by way of a *petition for modification*. Alimony may be increased or decreased by modification, unless otherwise agreed or ordered. Property settlement agreements may include a clause waiving the right to sue for modification at a later date. Such a clause may or may not be enforceable in a given jurisdiction—a waiver of rights is viewed with some suspicion by the courts. On the one hand, the clause was probably bargained for by the attorneys for the respective parties. On the other hand, public policy intervenes to protect parties from the harshness of bargains made during the trying circumstances of divorce.

An increase in alimony by petition for modification is premised on proof by the alimony recipient of two elements: changed circumstances and the ability of the payor to pay. A decrease in payments is also premised on changed circumstances, either a decrease in the need of the recipient or a decrease in the ability to pay by the payor (usually through forces beyond his or her control).

> [After marrying a well-to-do second wife, Curt Fried quit working and then challenged the lump-sum alimony awarded his first wife.] Although the court cannot look to the present wife's assets as a source for the appellant's alimony requirements, it can consider the fact that appellant has declined to seek employment because his living expenses have been furnished by his present wife when determining what efforts appellant should make in order to provide periodic alimony. To put it another way, while there is nothing wrong in appellant not seeking employment because his present wife's circumstances make it unnecessary, this does not obviate his obligation to pay alimony commensurate with what he might reasonably be expected to earn had he chosen to seek employment. The choice is his. He can seek to continue to borrow from his wife, or he can go to work.
>
> — *Fried v. Fried,* 375 So. 2d 46 (Fla. Dist. Ct. App. 1997)

11.15 CHANGED CIRCUMSTANCES

As a practical matter, the single mother of minor children can usually make an effective argument for changed circumstances, unless her own resources have increased substantially. As children grow older, they become more expensive, and inflation aggravates budget problems. Fixed payments are worth less, while the ex-husband is likely to have increased his income over time. Requests for continuation or increase in alimony are best coupled with child support claims. (We are probably close to the day when childless women will simply not receive alimony unless elderly or disabled.)

In accordance with this general principle, courts have recognized "changed circumstances" that warrant modification in a variety of settings. Some of them include

(1) an increase in the cost of living
(2) increase or decrease in the supporting spouse's income
(3) illness, disability or infirmity arising after the original judgment
(4) the dependent spouse's loss of a house or apartment
(5) the dependent spouse's cohabitation with another
(6) subsequent employment by the dependent spouse
(7) changes in federal income tax law.

Courts have consistently rejected requests for modification based on circumstances which are only temporary or which are expected but have not yet occurred.

CAVEAT

In any divorce involving substantial assets or payments, or complex business or property transactions, a sophistication in tax matters is absolutely necessary. Tax law is subject to change at any time. Difficult problems are referred to specialists in tax law.

CAVEAT

Postdivorce bankruptcy poses special problems. Alimony and child support are not dischargeable in bankruptcy, thus protecting the recipient. Support may come in many forms, though. While the bankruptcy court makes the final determination on what is and what is not support (as opposed to property settlement), a party foreseeing a bankruptcy on the part of the alimony debtor may wish to draft the agreement with this in mind.

LEGAL TERMS

garnishment
A statutory procedure diverting payment of debts from a third party, typically an employer. For example, an ex-wife might be able to garnish her ex-husband's wages, so that part of the payment would go directly to her. Because the procedure is statutory, state statutes should be consulted.

> When children are involved, an increase in their needs, whether occasioned by maturation, the rising cost of living or more unusual events has been held to justify an increase in support by a financially able parent.
>
> — *Lepis v. Lepis,* 83 N.J. 139, 416 A.2d 45 (1980)

CASE NO. 11-7   No More Mister Nice Guy

Changed circumstances do not always warrant modification of alimony. Despite the various philosophical arguments about the meaning of fault versus no-fault divorce, courts of equity traditionally are governed by justice rather than strict adherence to technical rules. The clean hands doctrine ("He who comes into equity must do so with clean hands") allows the chancellor in equity to deny a remedy to one who has acted improperly. This doctrine may occasionally reintroduce fault into divorce cases, but the fact situation in *Waskin* argues persuasively for the retention of the clean hands doctrine—the good guys and the bad guys are here easily distinguishable.

WASKIN v. WASKIN
484 So. 2d 1277 (Fla. Dist. Ct. App. 1986)
District Court of Appeal of Florida

DANIEL S. PEARSON, Judge.

If, as the cases tell us, the clean hands doctrine prevents a court of equity from relieving a former husband of his obligation to pay alimony to his former wife where the decrease in the former husband's financial ability to pay (the requisite substantial change in circumstances) has been brought about by the former husband's voluntary acts of, for example, permitting a thriving medical practice to be closed down and making no effort to seek other employment, see *Kalmutz v. Kalmutz,* 299 So.2d 30 (Fla. 4th DCA 1974); increasing his spending, *Coe v. Coe*, 352 So.2d 559 (Fla. 2d DCA 1977); or otherwise willfully divesting himself of the ability to pay, *Bowen v. Bowen,* 471 So.2d 1274 (Fla. 1985), then, most assuredly, the clean hands doctrine should have prevented the entry of the order under review which, inter alia, reduced the former husband's alimony and child support obligations established by the

1976 final judgment of dissolution as modified on appeal and as upwardly modified by the trial court in 1980.

We have no quarrel with the trial judge's finding that Robert Waskin showed "a substantial decrease in his financial ability dating back to October of 1983." Certainly there is ample evidence to support his findings that, beginning in October 1983, Waskin spent $70,000 ($35,000 of which was borrowed from his sister) in newly-incurred attorneys' fees and lost a substantial number of patients and staff privileges at nursing homes and hospitals, which losses caused a severe drop in Waskin's income and thus his ability to meet certain existing obligations. The trial judge's conclusion, however, that this extraordinary expenditure on attorneys' fees and the reduction in income from the medical practice were matters beyond Waskin's control is, in our view, totally unwarranted.

The events of October 1983 which led to Waskin's subsequent financial ills are fully recounted in our recent opinion in *State v. Waskin*, 481 So.2d 492 (Fla. 3d DCA 1985). There we reversed the dismissal of a criminal information charging Waskin with soliciting someone to murder his former wife, Gloria Waskin, the appellant here. In resurrecting the charge and returning the case for trial, we set out in detail the conversation between Waskin and the prospective hitman (in actuality, Tom Tretola, an undercover police officer), a conversation which, we noted, Waskin conceded took place. We concluded that

> "[t]he conversation between the defendant and Tretola in the present case is, at the very least, susceptible of being understood by reasonable fact-finders as meaning that the defendant *requested* or *encouraged,* if not actually *hired,* Tretola to murder the ex-Mrs. Waskin. The fact that the time of performance was not agreed upon or even that it was postponed for several months, or that payment of money was not immediately made, does not mean that no *request* or *encouragement* occurred, or even that no agreement—hiring—had taken place. . . . Indeed it appears that the defendant's request to postpone the hit was not occasioned by any disagreement about the figure of $10,000, but rather was motivated by the defendant's professed need to have sufficient time to amass the cash for payment without calling attention to his plan by borrowing. Where, as here, the defendant clearly requested that Tretola do away with his ex-wife, neither the lack of agreement about the price, or lack of payment, makes any difference."

State v. Waskin, 481 So.2d at 498 (emphasis in original). As a result of Waskin's request that Tretola do away with the former Mrs. Waskin, Waskin was arrested and charged; as a result of the charge, he hired an attorney and paid him $70,000; and, as a result

of the attendant publicity, he lost patients and institutional affiliations, and thus income.

We have little difficulty concluding that Waskin's voluntary act in seeking to do away with his ex-wife—the epitome of unclean hands—was the cause of his financial woes. What Waskin did to bring about his financial downfall is, quite obviously, far more condemnable than closing down a lucrative practice, failing to seek gainful employment, or going on spending sprees. It does not matter in this proceeding whether Waskin is ultimately convicted of the crime with which he is charged, even as it did not matter, the trial court's finding to the contrary notwithstanding, that when Waskin's motion to modify was filed and ruled upon, the criminal charges against him then stood dismissed.[2] Whether a criminal jury concludes beyond a reasonable doubt that Waskin is guilty of solicitation, or, as happened, a trial judge in the criminal division concludes that Waskin's conversations with Tretola did not go far enough to become a crime, is simply not important in this matter of Waskin versus Waskin. What is important here is that the conversation between Waskin and Tretola indisputably occurred, that Waskin admittedly believed that Tretola was a "hitman," and that in the conversation Waskin indisputably requested Tretola to do away with the ex-Mrs. Waskin. Under these circumstances, it can be readily said that Waskin's acts brought about his own arrest and prosecution, as well as the financial consequences of those events, whatever the outcome of the criminal proceeding.[3]

Accordingly, we reverse the order below insofar as it reduced the alimony and child support payments and relieved Waskin of the responsibility to pay the monthly mortgage on the marital home. As counsel for the former wife correctly observes, the bitter irony of the trial court's ruling is that, in effect, it requires the children and former wife to defray the cost of Waskin's attorney, a result no less ironic than, as in the well-known anecdote, taking pity on the orphan who killed his parents.

* * *

Reversed and remanded.

———————————

2 We disagree entirely with the trial court's conclusion that:

"(E) Husband is entitled to this modification as his change in circumstances [was] due to acts which as a matter of law did not constitute a crime and as he did not purposefully divest himself of funds or purposefully put himself in a disadvantaged financial position through frivolous spending or indulgence, and [was] as a result of Husband's begin taken off the staff of nursing homes, notwithstanding his presumption of innocence, and then finding of innocence as a matter of law, he therefore is not directly responsible."

———————————

3 A different question would be presented if, for example, Waskin's defense to the charges was that no such conversation soliciting the murder of his ex-wife occurred. It might then be argued upon his exoneration that the adverse publicity resulting in loss of business and the expenses of defending himself were matters not caused by him and over which he had no control.

SUMMARY

Alimony (maintenance) originated from the husband's lifelong duty to support his wife, whether married or divorced. Today either husband or wife may receive alimony. In recent times courts and legislatures have come to disfavor permanent alimony and alimony in general. Most awards of alimony today come in the form of periodic payments lasting a few months or years, classified as rehabilitative alimony and designed to return a homemaker to the job market; that is, to help a dependent spouse get through the post-divorce period of adjustment to self-sufficiency. Lump-sum alimony is occasionally awarded, often to provide compensation for contributions by one spouse, such as one spouse working to put the other through professional education. Alimony is part of a more comprehensive plan dividing the resources and obligations of the spouses; the distribution of assets and child support are the other two important economic ingredients of this plan.

Alimony is characterized by a high degree of discretion on the part of the judiciary, although most states have recently provided more or less detailed guidelines for judges to weigh in awarding alimony. Alimony is principally based on the need of the recipient and the ability to pay of the spouse making support payments. Need is a relative concept, depending to a large degree on the standard of living enjoyed during the marriage. Alimony is usually terminated by the death of either party or by the remarriage of the recipient. Depending on the jurisdiction, this may be waived in the property settlement agreement.

A postdivorce procedure, in the form of a petition for modification, is available to increase or decrease alimony or to extend or shorten the period during which payments are made. The key element in a successful suit for modification is proof of *changed circumstances* justifying the modification.

For the recipient of alimony to obtain an upward modification, it must be shown also that the payor has the ability to pay the increased amount.

QUESTIONS

1. What form of alimony is most commonly awarded today?
2. What is the difference in concept between rehabilitative and reimbursement alimony?
3. What is the policy argument against permanent periodic alimony?
4. Under what circumstances is permanent periodic alimony justified?
5. What part does fault play, if any, in the award of alimony?
6. What part does discretion play in alimony awards?
7. What would best qualify for the changed circumstances required for modification of alimony?
8. How is modification of alimony best avoided in advance?
9. What factors are most commonly used to determine the amount of alimony awarded?
10. How is alimony terminated?

EXERCISES

Answer the questions according to the law of your state.

1. May an adulterous wife receive permanent alimony? 86 A.L.R.3d 97.
2. Can the former wife's sexual misconduct subsequent to divorce warrant modification of alimony? 98 A.L.R.3d 453.
3. Does a change in financial condition of husband or wife warrant modification of alimony? 18 A.L.R.2d 10.
4. How is the adequacy of a combined award of alimony and a division of property in divorce measured? 55 A.L.R.4th 14.
5. What role does fault play in an award of alimony? 86 A.L.R.3d 1116.
6. Does a husband have a right to alimony? 66 A.L.R.2d 880.
7. What are the tax considerations of alimony? 51 A.L.R.3d 461.
8. Is interest due on unpaid alimony? 33 A.L.R.2d 1455.
9. May visitation rights be withheld for failure to make alimony payments? 51 A.L.R.3d 520.
10. Who may institute civil contempt proceedings for failure to comply with an order for payment of alimony? 61 A.L.R.2d 10951.

CHAPTER 12
Child Support

The Children's Hour

President Bill Clinton speaking to members of the President's Task Force on National Health Reform. His wife, Hillary Rodham Clinton, was named to chair the task force. Before her husband's election, Hillary was chairperson of the political advocacy group Children's Defense Fund. This chapter discusses the various issues involving child support, including the expensive components—health insurance and benefits.

— Courtesy AP/Wide World Photos.

Soon, society may have to decide that parenting is a socially worthy career and not just private folly.

Professor Harry Krause

OUTLINE

12.1 PARENTAL DUTY TO SUPPORT
12.2 NEED AND ABILITY TO PAY
12.3 SINGLE PARENTS
12.4 COLLEGE EDUCATION
12.5 HEALTH CARE
12.6 CHILD SUPPORT AND REMARRIAGE
12.7 PARENTS IN ARREARS: THE ENFORCEMENT PROBLEM
12.8 CHILD SUPPORT GUIDELINES
12.9 THE CHILD "TAX"
12.10 INTERSTATE ENFORCEMENT
12.11 URESA
SUMMARY

After divorce, one parent usually becomes the primary caregiver of the children. When one parent is responsible for the physical custody of the children more than the other, the primary caregiver is entitled to contribution for providing more than her or his share of support. Today both parents are obligated to support their children, and that obligation is measured in terms of their respective ability to pay and the needs of the children. Legal issues with regard to child support range from the basic questions of how much support should be paid and how to collect arrearages to questions of who should pay and what should be covered. Legislation in this area has focused on establishing precise guidelines for payments and the means to enforce them.

315

12.1 PARENTAL DUTY TO SUPPORT

The English common law was surprisingly silent about the duty of a father to support his children. Perhaps this was considered a fundamental element of natural law that did not require restatement. Some have argued that the duty of support as found in the law evolved from the English poor laws, which were designed to prevent the poor from becoming a burden on the state. During the marriage, failure to support may be remedied by child neglect and abuse statutes, but postdivorce support echoes this early origin in enforcing a private welfare system.

In 1992, it was commonly reiterated as fact that 20 percent of American children live in conditions of poverty. It is clear that many in our country are poor, many are homeless, and a great many children live with one parent with little or no financial support from the other parent. We also have many children who will never know their fathers. In short, although children are by nature vulnerable, we have a large number of children who are particularly vulnerable because of some parental deficit. How to deal with this problem is a public policy matter and ultimately a legal matter. The problem is complicated by the changing nature of the American family, particularly the high rate of divorce as compared with the past.

Policy choices about supporting children are based on social values, which in turn are often supported by stereotypes. The stereotypes of the deadbeat dad and teenage pregnancy underscore a common attitude toward childbearing and the duties incurred. The two stereotypes convey a perception of fault that relieves society of responsibility for its children. Our social services agencies are empowered to go after the father who is in arrears on his support payments and to scrutinize the lifestyle of the promiscuous teen. Our political and legal systems seem to be saying that children are not the responsibility of society or the state.

The private welfare concept is also revealed in the extent of the duty of support. Like spousal support during marriage, parental support extends only to necessaries. In fact, contemporary controversy over parental support for a college education appears in some courts as an argument over whether a college education is a "necessary" or not.

As the duty of support was first legally recognized, it applied only to the father. In the 20th century, the duty of support was extended to mothers, who were *secondarily* liable for support. This concept was destined to fall, as focus on the equal protection clause of the Fourteenth Amendment was applied with greater force to legal distinctions based on sex. For example, *Conway v. Dana,* 456 Pa. 536, 318 A.2d 324 (1974), hailed changing values, declaring the presumption of paternal support "a vestige of the past and incompatible with the present recognition of equality of the sexes." Despite judicial recognition of equality of the sexes, statistics indicate that it is almost always accurate to refer to the single-parent caregiver as "she" and the child support payor as "he." The continuing discrepancy between legal and political ideals causes a tension in family law that promises further litigation.

Unmarried fathers are also obligated to support their offspring. Adoptive parents are legally bound to support their adoptive children, because adoption severs the legal bond between a child and its natural parents and treats the child as having the same legal relationship to its adoptive parents as a natural child would have. There is even a trend toward recognizing stepparents' legal obligations to support their stepchildren (*see M.H.B. v. H.T.B,* Case No. 12-1).

> *After 26 years of marriage* the parties were each granted a divorce on the grounds of *incompatability* [sic]. The trial court divided the marital assets, awarded custody of two minor children to the appellant wife, and disallowed child support [emphasis added]. . . .
>
> At the time of the divorce the appellant was earning about $500 to $550 per month. The appellee's gross monthly income was $3,672. There were two minor children placed in appellant's custody. The youngest, a 12 year old, was adopted by the parties and was receiving $411 per month social security from the benefits of her deceased natural mother. The trial court considered this in determining that the appellee need not contribute to the support of his adopted daughter. The effect of the trial court's order was to require the 12 year old to support herself. This was error.
>
> — *Graham v. Graham,* 761 P.2d 1298 (Okla. Ct. App. 1988)

CASE NO. 12-1 Extending the Private Welfare System

Under special circumstances, stepparents may be obligated to support their stepchildren. The *M.H.B.* case seems to open the door wide to stepparent liability. Is the case a product of psychologizing parenthood or preserving the private welfare system?

M.H.B. v. H.T.B.
100 N.J. 567, 498 A.2d 775 (1985)
Supreme Court of New Jersey

PER CURIAM.
The members of the Court being equally divided, the judgment of the Appellate Division is affirmed.
HANDLER, J., concurring.
We have recently recognized that upon a divorce, one spouse may be obligated under principles of equitable estoppel to provide financial support for his or her stepchildren who are the children of the other spouse. *Miller v. Miller,* 97 N.J. 154, 167, 478 A.2d 351 (1984). In this

appeal, we consider the circumstances that can give rise to an equitable estoppel forbidding a divorced stepparent from denying the validity of a previous voluntary commitment to provide financial support for a stepchild. The child in this case was born while the defendant was married to the child's mother. However, the defendant knew shortly after the child's birth that he probably was not her natural father. Nevertheless, throughout the marriage and for five years following the divorce, the defendant consistently conducted himself as the child's father, successfully gained the child's love and affection, and established himself as the little girl's parental provider of emotional and material support. Under such circumstances, I believe that the stepfather is obligated to provide continuing financial support for his stepchild.

* * *

[Marilyn (M.H.B.) and Henry (H.T.B.) married and had two children, after which Marilyn had an extramarital affair by which she conceived K.B. Henry separated. A six-month reconciliation did not work.]

I am satisfied, as was the trial court, that the evidence in this case establishes that Henry, from the time of K.B.'s birth, engaged in a voluntary and knowing course of conduct with respect to K.B., which constituted in its purpose and effect an affirmative representation that he was her natural father. It is also abundantly clear that the child K.B., as well as her mother Marilyn, relied upon Henry's purposeful conduct and depended upon him for support. Further, it cannot be disputed that the reliance by K.B. was detrimental in the sense of the financial, as well as personal, harm she would suffer if Henry were permitted to disavow his representations, repudiate the expectations he created, and evade the responsibilities he had assumed. Under these circumstances he is equitably estopped from denying a continuing obligation to provide child support on behalf of K.B.

* * *

For the reasons expressed, I would affirm the judgment below. Chief Justice Wilentz and Justice O'Hern join in this opinion.

POLLOCK, J., concurring in part and dissenting in part.

As Justice Handler's concurrence acknowledges, this case is controlled by our opinion last term in *Miller v. Miller*, 97 N.J. 154, 478 A.2d 351 (1984), which was published after the judgment of the Appellate Division. *Miller* recognized that the primary duty to support a child rests on the natural parent, but that in certain circumstances a stepparent could be estopped to deny such a duty. Specifically, we stated in *Miller* that it is only when a stepparent "actively interferes with the children's support from their natural parent that he or she may be equitably estopped from denying his or her duty to support the children." *Id.* at 169, 478 A.2d 351. Today's concurring opinion, however, would impose on a stepparent a duty of support not on the basis of estoppel but of a perceived emotional bonding between stepparent and child. From that premise, the opinion then proceeds to force the facts of the present case within its expanded interpretation of *Miller*.

* * *

Accordingly, [*Miller*] held that a stepparent could be equitably estopped from denying an obligation to support a stepchild on proof of three conditions. First, the stepparent must have made a representation to either the children or the natural parent that he or she would provide support. Second, that representation must have been relied on by either the children or the natural parent. We declined to rely on these two conditions alone to establish estoppel because such a rule would penalize a "stepparent who tried to create a warm family atmosphere with his or her stepchildren." Consistent with that concern, we imposed a third condition, one that required a showing that "the children will suffer future financial detriment as a result of the stepparent's representation or conduct that caused the children to be cut off from their natural parent's financial support." Such financial detriment could be shown if the custodial parent cannot locate or does not know the whereabouts of the natural parent, or cannot obtain legal jurisdiction over the natural parent, and the natural parent's unavailability is attributable to the actions of the stepparent. Thus, a stepparent is responsible for the unavailability of a natural parent only when he or she takes "positive action interfering with the natural parent's support obligation."

* * *

I continue to be counselled by *Miller's* warning not to impose a child-support obligation on a stepfather merely because he developed a close relationship with the stepchildren. Without further proof, I would not alter *Miller's* requirement that when the natural parent can be located and is financially able, he or she remains principally responsible to pay permanent child support.

The concurring opinion in the present case reflects the understandable desire to spare K.B. the painful knowledge that Henry is not her biological father. As painful as that discovery may be, however, it is inevitable that one day K.B. will learn the facts. . . .

12.2 NEED AND ABILITY TO PAY

Like alimony, child support is based on (the children's) *need for support* and (the parent's) *ability to pay.* Because the mother is liable for support, her resources may be considered in the amount ordered to be paid by the father. Similarly, when the father has custody of the children, the mother may be ordered to pay child support to the father.

Unlike alimony, the resources of the beneficiary have only a limited impact on the award. A child's resources (e.g., a trust set up by grandparents) do not ordinarily reduce the parental obligation for furnishing necessaries, but might persuade the court that even a well-heeled parent need not be obligated for the expenses of higher education, arguably a necessary in some jurisdictions.

The relation between child support and the marital settlement agreement also differs from alimony. Although some jurisdictions honor a waiver of future right to modify the amount of alimony, the child has neither negotiated nor agreed to the terms of the agreement. If the parents act in concert against the interests of the child, the court is responsible for looking out for the child. If need increases, the court will not be bound by the waiver in the agreement.

Some courts have also declared that children are entitled to share in the good fortune of their parents. "Need" is a relative concept. The courts do not limit parental contributions to necessaries after divorce. In this instance, the child of divorce may be entitled to more (but usually receives less) than the child of an intact family, who has only a right to necessaries. The rationale is that a child should not be required to drastically reduce an accustomed lifestyle simply because one of the parents has moved to other quarters.

DICTA

American society presents innumerable instances of a general attitude holding individuals responsible for sexual behavior and reproduction. The raging abortion controversy and Planned Parenthood pickets spring to mind. Our law strongly suggests that children are a burden to society, one that society should pass on to those who are "to blame." Children are apparently the product of depravity, insufficient sexual restraint, lack of birth control, and lack of social responsibility. Does this bode well for the future of America?

12.3   SINGLE PARENTS

Professor Harry Krause has cogently argued that child-bearing in America is foolish. Raising children is costly at best—a financial catastrophe for divorced mothers and a damnable drain on divorced fathers. Whereas marriage has been described as a financial venture of considerable risk (partnership model), bearing children is an activity that no honest financial planner would recommend. The cost to women who choose to be homemakers for even a few years is enormous. The cost incurred is not simply for the nurture of children, substantial though that is; the deficit in career is so great that child-bearing can be justified only by some primitive addiction to passing on ones genes. As women find more opportunities for jobs and pay equal to men, the price of children becomes too high for a woman of any promise. When the risk of divorce is added to the calculus, it is a wonder that any rational woman chooses to bear children.

Krause highlights the dilemma by showing how social security discourages child-bearing:

> . . . out in the "real world," the mother's childless sister has been building up social security credits [through employment] which ultimately will have to be earned and paid—by none other than the mother's children who are thereby rendered that much less able to contribute to her! The mother, on the other hand, will not have earned any social security entitlement in her own right and, indeed, her derivative right as a widow or divorced wife is under challenge from those who would save the social security system by removing from eligibility those who have not contributed cash. . . .
>
> Soon, society may have to decide that parenting is a socially worthy career and not just private folly.
>
> — Harry Krause, *Family Law in a Nutshell* (2d ed. 1986).

Professor Krause points out that the two areas under greatest pressure in child support cases (excluding enforcement of nonpayment) are higher education and health costs. These are the two back-breakers for parents, for both intact families and families of divorce. He points out that these two areas are assumed as state responsibilities in other advanced countries. In the 1992 presidential election, education and national health care became important issues for the first time. Resolution of these issues will dramatically affect the family and family law.

12.4   COLLEGE EDUCATION

As an increasing proportion of our population attends college, higher education becomes more and more necessary as a prerequisite to employment. Reduction of the age of majority to 18 has relieved parents of support obligations during those years in which most youths attend college. Funding a college education has not been a legal duty of parents in an intact family, who are legally only responsible for providing necessaries. The high cost of a college education today makes it difficult for any family to absorb the cost without the income of two parents. In his syndicated financial column, Malcolm Berko periodically reiterates his argument that parents would be foolish to fund their children's college educations. He argues that those who are in a position to save should be saving to protect their old age, considering the likelihood that the social security system may be bankrupt.

Ironically, the noncustodial divorced parent may in some jurisdictions be required to finance the children's college education. There is a strong trend toward considering higher education a necessary and therefore something for which the court can order payment. This seems not to have carried over to parents in intact families, who enjoy considerable freedom in their expenditures on their children. Nor has this apparently carried over to requiring a custodial parent to fund higher education (though the custodial parent's resources should at least be considered when apportioning the burden of support).

CASE NO. 12-2 Paying for College for an Ungrateful Daughter

Should the one who pays child support have any say in the plans the child has to spend that support on a college education?

RIEGLER v. RIEGLER
259 Ark. 203, 532 S.W.2d 734 (1976)
Supreme Court of Arkansas

JONES, Justice.

This is an appeal by Nicholas W. Riegler, Jr. from a chancery court order in which he contends that the chancellor erred in awarding child support payments and college payments to an adult child where there was no contract. The parties to this proceeding were divorced in 1966 and this is the fourth appeal to this court growing out of the divorce litigation. . . .

The parties had five daughters when the divorce was granted in 1966. Four of the daughters at that time were minors under 18 years of age. Their custody was awarded to the appellee Mrs. Riegler and the appellant was ordered to pay to the appellee alimony and support money for the four minor children. During the intervening years since the divorce three of the four

minor children went to live with the appellant and have attained their majority. The youngest daughter remained with the appellee and also reached her majority on October 31, 1974.

* * *

A part of what we said when this matter was first before us in 1967 (*Riegler v. Riegler*, 243 Ark. 113, 419 S.W.2d 311) is pertinent to the decision we reach in the matter now. In the 1967 opinion we said:

"The matter of the children's college education was deferred for a later decision. What we have to say in Part V of this opinion may be pertinent if that question comes up in the future.

V. The decree for separate maintenance awarded Mrs. Riegler $600 a month 'for maintenance of herself and the four children now in her custody.' In the interval between that decree and the one now being reviewed Mrs. Riegler spent a total of $3,187.68 for college educational expenses of her oldest daughter, who was of age when the separate maintenance decree was entered, and for similar expenses of her next daughter, who reached 18 before the rendition of the later decree. The chancellor directed Dr. Riegler to repay $2,749.00 of those outlays.

That direction was an error. Ordinarily a mother who spends more for child support than the court has allowed her cannot recover the excess, because an award of child support ought not be increased retroactively. She should apply in advance for a larger allowance. *Gant v. Gant,* 209 Ark. 576, 191 S.W.2d 596 (1946). On the other hand, a father may by contract bind himself to go beyond the decree in supporting a daughter who has reached her majority. *Worthington v. Worthington,* 207 Ark. 185, 179 S.W.2d 648 (1944). Mrs. Riegler insists that the proof establishes such a contract on Dr. Riegler's part.

We do not so find. Dr. Riegler testified, as most fathers would, that he wanted all his children to have a college education. We do not read his testimony, however, as embodying an agreement to pay the expenses now at issue. To the contrary, he said that if he paid for his daughters' higher education he expected them to treat him with the respect due a father and to counsel with him about their college training. He complained, among other things, that his oldest daughter had told him to go to hell and had declared that the only thing he had to do with her education was to give her the money to spend as she chose. On the proof as a whole Mrs. Riegler did not sustain the burden of proving an agreement for support over and above the allowance made by the separate maintenance decree."

[On cross-examination, the daughter] said she had decided to attend the University of Tennessee because a number of her friends were attending that university, and that she had not discussed those plans with her father. She said she simply had not had time to discuss her plans with her father; that he had his medical practice to attend to and she was not in town enough to discuss her plans with him.

'Q. You went ahead and made your plans without even finding out if he wanted to send you to the University of Tennessee?

A. It seems to me it would be up to my choice where I would like to go to college.' "

* * *

The appellant in the case at bar gave his three older daughters a college education after they attained their majority, but they discussed with him the college of their choice and they complied with reasonable restrictions he prescribed for them while attending college. The question in the case at bar as to the youngest daughter is not whether appellant is morally obligated to assist her financially while attending college, but the question is whether he is *legally* obligated to do so under the evidence in this case. . . .

In *Missouri Pacific Railroad Company et al. v. Foreman,* 196 Ark. 636, 119 S.W.2d 747 (at page 651 of the Arkansas Reports) we said: "Ordinarily, there is no legal obligation on the part of a parent to contribute to the maintenance and support of his children after they become of age." A significant word in the above quotation is the word "ordinarily," showing that the Court realized there might be circumstances which could impose on a parent the duty to support a child after such child became of age. . . .

In *Petty v. Petty,* 252 Ark. 1032, 482 S.W.2d 119 (1972), this court reversed a chancellor's decree terminating child support for an 18 year old child. But in that case we pointed out that the girl was "disabled and unable to earn a livelihood." In [another case], we affirmed a chancellor's order continuing child support for an 18 year old girl until she finished high school. The "circumstances of necessity" to justify the order were pointed out as follows:

> "Had the chancellor terminated the appellant's support payments for Dinah Gale as soon as she became of age, it may be assumed, as far as this record shows, that she would have been forced to drop out of high school to support herself, there being no obligation on the part of either of her parents for her continued maintenance. We know, by common knowledge, that a high school diploma is of almost inestimable value to a young person who seeks to make his or her own living. The appellant, as a result of having taken no appeal from the supplementary October decree and as a result of having offered no new testimony at the hearing with respect to the modification of that decree, is not in a position to contend that he has suffered an undue hardship by having to support his daughter during the six months between her coming of age and her graduation from high school. Upon the facts of this case—and our decision of course is limited to those facts—we sustain the chancellor's slight extension of the appellant's minimum duty to support the older child."

* * *

The decree is reversed as to the $350 per month child support until graduation from college and in all other respects the decree is affirmed.

Reversed in part on appeal and affirmed on cross-appeal.

One of the problems with providing for college education is ascertaining in advance what the cost will be or what a parent is willing and able to provide. General promises of support may fail as ambiguous contractual terms. Fixed amounts may commit the promisor but turn out to be inadequate several years later. In *Rumbaugh v. Rumbaugh,* 229 Neb. 652, 428 N.W.2d 500 (1988), the Nebraska Supreme Court held the following paragraph in an agreement to be sufficiently clear to be enforceable:

> The respondent further agrees that when said child graduates from high school, he will pay the yearly cost of the college education for said child for a maximum of 4 years beyond high school, said yearly total costs not to exceed the normal cost then in effect for attendance at the University of Nebraska at Lincoln, or one of the state public schools in Nebraska; that this cost will include, but not be limited to, tuition, mandatory or other special fees, book costs, [sorority costs,] and the like, but will not cover clothing or food costs. . . .

12.5 HEALTH CARE

Payment for health care for children is potentially the most critically important feature of support. As the divided family almost inevitably becomes poorer after divorce, while health care costs follow a never-ending upward spiral, painful choices must be made. The noncustodial parent who was required under the agreement or court order to provide health insurance may neglect this duty or lose the job that provided affordable health insurance. Serious illness can drive a family to destitution or physical neglect.

Health care became a serious issue in the 1992 presidential elections. Whether health care can be provided to all Americans by one means or another is a policy question that will take some time to answer. In the meantime, divorce settlements must address this issue with regard to minor children.

> As additional child support (Husband)(Wife) shall (provide)(maintain) suffecient medical and hospitalization insurance to cover and pay all medical, drug, clinic, hospital and outpatient charges incurred for the benefit of the children.
>
> (1) (Husband's)(Wife's) obligation under this subparagraph includes psychological, psychiatric, dental, and orthodontic expenses.
> (2) To the extent any charges incurred under this subparagraph are not covered or paid by insurance (Husband)(Wife) shall pay to (Wife)(Husband) (all)(one-half) of such uninsured charges.
> (3) (Husband's)(Wife's) obligation under this subparagraph shall terminate at the time all (his)(her) child support obligations under paragraph (#) have terminated or have been discharged in full.
> (4) All bills for charges incurred under this subparagraph shall be forwarded directly to (Husband)(Wife) and (he)(she) shall either pay said charge or file a claim for insurance within thirty (30) days after receipt of any such bill.
>
> — Excerpt from a model version of a property settlement agreement, *from* McGough, *Georgia Divorce,* (The Practice Systems Library, Lawyers' Co-operative Publishing Co. 1986).

Provision for the contingency of a policy lapse is also desirable. Health insurance is commonly considered a part of child support and could be part of the payment made to the custodial parent, who would then be responsible for maintaining the policy. Unreliable, hostile, or distant parents may warrant more stringent measures. Obviously, continuing coverage is critical when one or more children have existing medical problems that will incur significant costs sometime in the future.

12.6 CHILD SUPPORT AND REMARRIAGE

Divorced parents remarry, sometimes to other divorced parents, often bearing more children and thereby creating step relationships and half-siblings ("Yours, Mine, and Ours"). The person paying child support faces the dilemma of too many demands on personal income and resources. Past and present spouses tend to show little sympathy for each other and their respective children. Society and the law hold fathers responsible for all their children: If he could not support the children of his first marriage, he should not have remarried, much less continued procreating. Phrased neutrally, the "first family first" doctrine argues that the level of support established for children of a prior marriage should not be diminished by the parent's choice to have additional children. Although support is normally modifiable based on changed circumstances of the parties, this is an apparent exception. It is difficult to defend a principle that penalizes innocent children of the "fault" of their parents, and a trend may be developing toward apportioning resources in a humane and rational way to serve the interests of all the children. Stepchildren traditionally had little claim on the stepfather's resources, presumably because they were being supported by their natural parents. For a particularly poignant example of an application of the first family first doctrine, see *Donohue v. Getman,* Case No. 12-3.

12.7 PARENTS IN ARREARS: THE ENFORCEMENT PROBLEM

Both law and society have been unforgiving in the pursuit of fathers who are in arrears in their child support payments. Little attention has been given to errant mothers, perhaps because the overwhelming majority of custodial parents are mothers supporting their children without a court order to do so. In 1992, the popular media suddenly became aroused by the "deadbeat dad" problem, after many years of federal and state action designed to step up enforcement of child support orders. The motivation for government action was not a simple and direct response to the woeful record of support payments, although statistics in that regard demanded attention and action. State, and especially the federal, governments aimed at reducing the government's share in welfare payments to single-parent families. In many instances public assistance provided support when fathers failed to meet their legal support obligations. New laws provided means for collecting arrears that could then be credited to amounts that had been paid, mostly through Aid to Families of Dependent Children (AFDC), in the form of welfare.

These efforts were begun primarily through the Office of Child Support Enforcement (OCSE) of the U.S. Department of Health and Human Services, beginning in 1974, and are presently collecting several billion dollars yearly. The federal government furnishes funds for state enforcement programs at the same time that it imposes requirements on them if they are to receive the funds. Amendments to the law (the Federal Enforcement Initiative of 1974) in 1984 and 1988 added more requirements and made more drastic the means of enforcement. AFDC applicants assign their uncollected support rights to the state and must assist efforts to collect. The states must maintain records and the federal government also maintains records to assist in locating parents in arrears.

CAVEAT

When representing the custodial parent, an attorney should insist that child support obligations be insured, usually through life insurance on the life of the payor. This should be in the settlement agreement along with a clause that allows a claim against the estate for unpaid support.

DICTA

Passing the fault of the parents on to their children has a long history in Western society; recall Adam and Eve and the doctrine of original sin. In more recent times, illegitimate children were not only socially stigmatized but were also deemed *filius nullius* (the child of no one) and so did not enjoy the legal rights ordinarily accorded family members.

Health care for children (as for
everyone) will be a major theme
of law and politics for the
remainder of this century.

Under the new requirements imposed on the states, new state laws must
require employee withholding of child support from paychecks of those in arrears. Arrears in excess of $1,000 must be deducted from state and federal in-
come tax refunds by the Internal Revenue Service (IRS). Under the 1988
amendments, new orders for support or orders modifying support will cause
support payments to be automatically deducted from paychecks, whether the
payor is in arrears or not. The 1988 amendments also provide new standards
for paternity and provide federal funds for paternity testing, in an obvious effort to make unwed fathers financially responsible for their offspring.

Professor Krause points out that these new efforts may come at a time
when collection efforts have reached maximum efficiency. Collection efforts
have shifted from their original focus, so that now 50 percent of those receiving collection assistance from the government are not on the welfare rolls. To
pursue indigent, absent, or unemployed fathers with a vengeance may be
throwing good money after bad. Congressional data indicate that some states
spend more to collect than they collect, and many others come close. Additional efforts appear counterproductive:

> We could debate at length the relative effectiveness of specific enforce-
> ment techniques, from wage withholding to extraction and imprison-
> ment. . . . We could discuss the U.S. Supreme Court's recent struggle

with contempt sanctions, civil or criminal, in *Hick ex rel. Feiock v. Feiock,* 108 S.Ct. 1423 (1988). But I think that the better enforcement debate is all but over. With mandated, formula-based setting of support obligations, with payroll deduction of support owed, and with computer-provided nationwide access to support-owing parents, the law now provides an effective arsenal for imposing the obligation as well as collecting child support. Continuing complaints that child-support collections remain inadequate can no longer expect much response by passage of better enforcement laws.

— Krause, "Child Support Reassessed: Limits of Private Responsibility and the Public Interest," 24 *Fam. L.Q.* 1 (1991).

So much attention has been given to the single mother and her plight and so little given to the absent father that it has encouraged generalization from those fathers who have simply avoided supporting their children through indifference, malice, or egotism. Placing blame on all divorced fathers encourages the implementation of mechanical formulas and severe remedies. Focusing on providing for the children by giving assistance to their hitherto neglected custodians, the mothers, has ignored a number of issues with regard to fathers that will occupy the courts over the next few years. A sampling:

Should arrears continue to accumulate when the delinquent father is laid off or loses his job without his fault? Should they continue to accumulate when the father takes de facto custody of one or more children?

Should a father obligated to pay child support be allowed downward modification when a stepfather has assumed some of the support?

May the father-obligor switch to more fulfilling but lower-paying work? *See McQuiddy v. McQuiddy,* 238 Pa. Super. 390, 358 A.2d 102 (1976), in which a construction worker obtained modification downward when he began the less lucrative practice of law.

12.8   CHILD SUPPORT GUIDELINES

One of the most far-reaching requirements of the 1984 amendments provided: "Each state, as a condition for having its State plan approved under this part, must establish guidelines for child support award amounts within the state. The guidelines may be established by law or by judicial or administrative action." Although need and ability to pay are the foundation for determining the amount of child support the noncustodial parent must pay, a powerful movement toward establishing statutory (sometimes judicial) guidelines has resulted in numerous schemes, from criteria to formulas to lengthy tables, by which to calculate child support.

CASE NO. 12-3 Hard Cases Make Bad Law

Donohue v. Getman may be an example of the old legal adage that hard cases make bad law, meaning that cases with strong equities on both sides are difficult to resolve fairly and the resulting rule may not be a good one to apply to other cases. This case raises issues that will require scrutiny in the next few years. One issue concerns the meddling of the federal government in what have traditionally been state matters, specifically family law. Here South Dakota enacted statutory guidelines for child support in order to receive federal money.

A second issue involves rule versus discretion. In his concurring but argumentative opinion, Justice Henderson rails against guidelines that invade traditional areas of judicial discretion, namely, the appropriate amount of child support. This issue would be largely academic were it not for the fact that the approach we use to solve the issue will ultimately affect a great multitude of our children.

DONOHUE v. GETMAN
432 N.W.2d 281 (S.D. 1988)
Supreme Court of South Dakota

MILLER, Justice.

Virginia Getman Donohue appeals from an order which set Richard Getman's child support payments at $120 per month. We reverse.

FACTS

Richard and Virginia were divorced in 1982. At that time, Richard received physical custody of their three children. Both parties subsequently remarried, and their new spouses either have custody of or pay child support for children from prior marriages.

In 1986 the trial court reexamined the custody situation and awarded sole legal and physical custody of the parties' three children to Virginia. The court denied Virginia's request for child support, finding that Richard did not have the means or ability to make support payments.

Shortly thereafter, Virginia petitioned the trial court for child support based on the guidelines set forth in SDCL 25-7-7, since Richard was receiving worker's compensation and social security disability benefits totaling $1,405.33 per month. The trial court found that Richard is totally disabled within the meaning of worker's compensation and social security

law. Richard has a severe degenerative condition of the spine and a herniated disc; as a result, he suffers pain, has occasional blackouts, and is experiencing atrophy of his arms. Richard has undergone surgery at least four times due to these problems, and his present wife cannot work because she must stay at home to take care of him. The trial court also found that the children of Richard's new spouse are experiencing medical problems which will require surgery, and Richard will be obligated to pay those medical bills. The trial court concluded that even though the statutory guidelines would require Richard to pay between $539 and $578 per month in child support (based on a monthly income of $1,405.33), he should pay only $120 per month. The trial court gave the following reasons for its deviation from the guidelines: Richard's medical condition and total disability; his monthly expenses and large indebtedness; his future medical expenses; his inability to hold any kind of gainful employment; and the medical condition of his stepchildren, which will require further expenditures of money.

ISSUE

Did the trial court abuse its discretion by deviating from the child support guidelines found at SDCL 25-7-7?

DECISION

This court will not disturb an award of child support unless it clearly appears that the trial court abused its discretion. Virginia argues that the trial court abused its discretion when it failed to enter findings with regard to all five factors listed in SDCL 25-7-7 before deviating from the guidelines. Virginia also contends that it was an abuse of discretion to allow expenses from Richard's second family to be used as a reason for deviation from the guidelines. We agree.

SDCL 25-7-7 states in part:

> These guidelines shall be used in setting child support. *Deviation from the guidelines may be made only upon the entry of specific findings based upon the following factors:* (1) Financial condition of the parents, including, but not limited to, income of a new spouse or contribution of a third party to the income or expenses of that parent; (2) The standard of living of the child; (3) The age and special needs of the child; (4) The effect of provisions relating to custody and visitation; or (5) Child care. (emphasis added)

Very recently, in *Bruning v. Jeffries,* 422 N.W.2d 579 (S.D. 1988), we addressed the guidelines set forth in SDCL 25-7-7 and stated:

> As the above quoted portion of SDCL 25-7-7 indicates, *there may be no deviation from the guidelines unless there is an entry of specific findings regarding the five listed factors....*

Here, the trial court entered findings regarding the financial condition of Richard and his second family, but none on the financial condition of Virginia or the other four factors listed in SDCL 25-7-7. We hold that the failure of the trial court to address these factors constitutes an abuse of discretion. . . .

Furthermore, it is well settled that a parent's responsibility to support his children is paramount; other debts are secondary. This includes obligations resulting from remarriage. . . .

We therefore reverse the order of the trial court and remand for reconsideration of Richard's child support obligations pursuant to SDCL 25-7-7.

HENDERSON, Justice (specially concurring).

* * *

With a total monthly income of $1,405.33, this father should pay more than $120 per month. A reversal should be premised upon honored precedent in this Court, not an artificial schedule. . . .

* * *

Now, having agreed with the majority court's ruling, I wish to express the primary reason for my special concurrence which, essentially, is to attack the nightmare, created in South Dakota, which establishes dollar amounts for minimum and maximum support depending upon income. . . .

Rather than to submit the trial judges of this state, or any state, to being schedule-automatons, I would pursue a judicial philosophy of recognizing fundamental law. Organic law. Judges should be imbued with judicial discretionary power springing from experience, clothed with constitutional power, and centered on vibrant blood cells stimulating the brain. Then, when one of these damnable schedules makes no sense, as they do in so many factual situations, the judge can trigger his brain rather than . . . push a button. His Honor belongs to the judiciary and has the right, belonging to the judiciary, to be a full participant in the Doctrine of Separation of Powers. He or she need not, because the Legislature says so, make decisions affecting the lives of children, and mothers, and fathers, by employing the rigidity of mathematical analysis by percentages; nor need His Honor decide the fate of human beings by sterile, mathematical extrapolation of tables foisted upon him by a new mood swing in Congress sugarcoated with dollars.

12.9 THE CHILD "TAX"

Some states have chosen to legislate a schedule of support payments rather like the federal income tax schedules. The parallels are quite striking, as exemplified by Florida Statutes § 61.30. Paragraph (2)(a) includes a list of items to be included in "gross income," much like what would be included in a income tax return. Subsection (3) lists "allowable deductions" designed to arrive at a net income. The net incomes of both parents are added together; their monthly combined income is then found on the schedule and the appropriate figure for child support is determined by the number of children supported. For example, if Wife has a net monthly income of $1,000 and Husband $1,500, their combined net income would be $2,500. If they had three children, the "minimum child support need" would be $1,036. This is the amount, plus or minus 5 percent, that the parents need to support the children (they may spend as much more as they wish, of course). Each parent's share is based on his or her percentage of the net monthly income, in this case 40 percent (1,000/2,500) for Wife and 60 percent (1,500/2,500) for Husband. If Wife had custody of the children, Husband's child support would be $621 (.60 × $1,036).

The tax metaphor is further bolstered by the financial affidavit that must accompany the pleadings (Fla. Stat. § 61.30(12)). Section 61.30(7)–(10) provides various bases for adjusting the child support according to the specific circumstances of a given case.

The statute departs from the tax model when it comes to judicial discretion. Although it makes the calculation as mechanical as possible, the statute nevertheless reserves discretion for the judge ("the trier of fact"). Section 61.30(10)(i) provides:

> Any other adjustment which is needed to achieve an equitable result which may include, but not be limited to, a reasonable and necessary existing expense or debt. Such expense or debt may include, but is not limited to, a reasonable and necessary expense or debt which the parties jointly incurred during the marriage.

This curious language gives the judge discretion at the same time as it suggests the areas in which the discretion might be exercised. That this is an attempt to limit the exercise of discretion by judges is made clear in the first section of the statute:

The trier of fact may order payment of child support in an amount different from such guideline amount upon a written finding, or a specific finding on the record, explaining why ordering payment of such guideline amount would be unjust or inappropriate.

The requirement of written findings justifying a variance from the amount in the schedule suggests the grounds for appealing such a variance on the basis of abuse of discretion. When a judge gives a justification on a basis not within the enumerated categories, reversible error may be found. From a cynical point of view, this might seem to require the judge to mold the justification to the exceptions given by the legislature. The judge may also adjust the property distribution and alimony to achieve a calculated result.

The loopholes, however, cannot dispel the reality of the guidelines. Judges depart from the guidelines at the risk of reversal. Although the figures are in one sense arbitrary, they are no more arbitrary than the figures judges calculated in the past and the guidelines have the advantage of uniformity and public scrutiny. The result is much less argument over child support; any lawyer proposing support at variance from the guidelines faces an uphill fight. Arguments over the accuracy of income statements or the special circumstances of the case continue, but the starting point is the schedule of support payments. As a practical matter, this may also be useful in dealing with a client who has unreasonable expectations with regard to child support.

One of the disadvantages of the schedule is that it must frequently be reviewed; the urgency of this task depends in large degree on economic inflation (or deflation). The task of review should be well within the competence of the legislature. Although the guidelines may have originated with federal arm-twisting, detailed schedules are an experiment that aims directly at reforming the past chaos surrounding support awards. The guidelines facilitate attorney negotiation, trial decision, and appellate review.

Ironically, the guidelines cannot resolve the issue for which they were originally encouraged by the federal government—privatizing child support for our poorest citizens is futile. The schedule loses its validity at the lowest end where one finds welfare families. The statute reserved case-by-case decision for the poorest families and for those with combined incomes in excess of $100,000 (raised in 1991 from $50,000).

DICTA

Comprehensive guidelines with a "tax" schedule like Fla. Stat. § 61.30 involve periodic tinkering by the legislature. Like taxation, this involves moving resources from one pocket to another. The transfer is based on values and premises about the family, about parenthood, and about government involvement in the family. The values underlying the transfer of wealth will change in time, requiring more tinkering.

FLORIDA STATUTES § 61.30. CHILD SUPPORT GUIDELINES

(1) (a) The child support guideline amount as determined by this section presumptively establishes the amount the trier of fact shall order as child support in an initial proceeding for such support or in a

332 Part Three Breaking the Contract

proceeding for modification of an existing order for such support, whether the proceeding arises under this or another chapter. The trier of fact may order payment of child support in an amount different from such guideline amount upon a written finding, or a specific finding on the record, explaining why ordering payment of such guideline amount would be unjust or inappropriate.

(b) . . .

(2) Income shall be determined for the obligor and for the obligee as follows:

(a) Gross income shall include, but is not limited to, the following items:

[There follow 14 numbered categories of income.]

(b) Income shall be imputed to an unemployed or underemployed parent when such employment or underemployment is found to be voluntary on that parent's part, absent physical or mental incapacity or other circumstances over which the parent has no control. In the event of such voluntary unemployment or underemployment, the employment potential and probable earnings level of the parent shall be determined based upon his or her recent work history, occupational qualifications, and prevailing earnings level in the community; however, the court may refuse to impute income to a primary residential parent if the court finds it necessary for the parent to stay home with the child.

(c) Aid to families with dependent children benefits shall be excluded from gross income.

(3) Allowable deductions from gross income shall include:

(a) Federal, state, and local income tax deductions, adjusted for actual filing status and allowable dependents and income tax liabilities.

(b) Federal insurance contributions or self-employment tax.

(c) Mandatory union dues.

(d) Mandatory retirement payments.

(e) Health insurance payments.

(f) Court-ordered support for other children which is actually paid.

(4) Net income for the obligor and net income for the obligee shall be computed by subtracting allowable deductions from gross income.

(5) Net income for the obligor and net income for the obligee shall be added together for a combined net income.

(6) The following schedules, plus or minus 5 percent, shall be applied to the combined net income to determine the minimum child support need:

Combined Monthly Available Income	Child or Children					
	One	**Two**	**Three**	**Four**	**Five**	**Six**
$500	48	48	49	49	50	50
550	93	94	95	96	97	98
600	138	139	141	142	144	145
650	154	185	187	189	191	193
700	166	230	233	235	238	240
750	177	274	279	282	285	288
800	188	292	325	328	332	335
850	199	309	371	375	379	383
900	210	327	409	421	426	430
950	221	344	430	468	473	478
1000	231	359	450	507	520	525
2000	437	677	847	956	1042	1113
2050	447	693	868	979	1067	1140
2100	457	709	887	1000	1091	1166
2150	467	724	906	1021	1114	1191
2200	476	739	924	1042	1136	1215
2250	485	754	943	1063	1159	1240
2300	495	768	961	1084	1182	1264
2350	504	783	980	1105	1205	1288
2400	514	798	999	1126	1228	1313
2450	523	813	1017	1146	1251	1337
2500	532	828	1036	1167	1274	1362
7650	1110	1721	2159	2432	2651	2831
7700	1113	1725	2164	2437	2657	2838
7750	1115	1729	2169	2443	2663	2844
7800	1118	1733	2174	2448	2669	2850
7850	1120	1736	2178	2454	2675	2856
7900	1123	1740	2183	2459	2681	2863
7950	1125	1744	2188	2465	2687	2869
8000	1128	1748	2193	2470	2693	2875
8050	1130	1751	2197	2476	2699	2881
8100	1133	1755	2202	2481	2705	2888
8150	1135	1759	2207	2487	2711	2894
8200	1138	1763	2212	2492	2717	2900
8250	1140	1766	2216	2498	2723	2906
8300	1143	1770	2221	2503	2729	2913
8350	1145	1774	2226	2509	2735	2919
8400	1148	1778	2231	2514	2741	2925

[Schedules are condensed here for reproduction.]

For combined monthly available income less than the amount set out on the above schedules, the parent should be ordered to pay a child support amount, determined on a case by case basis, to establish the principle of payment and lay the basis for increased orders should the parent's income increase in the future.

(7) Child care costs incurred on behalf of the children due to employment or job search of either parent shall be added to the basic obligation. Child care costs shall not exceed the level required to provide quality care from a licensed source for the children.

(8) Each parent's percentage share of the child support need shall be determined by dividing each parent's net income by the combined net income.

(9) Each parent's actual dollar share of the child support need shall be determined by multiplying the minimum child support need by each parent's percentage share.

(10) The court may adjust the minimum child support award, or either or both parent's share of the minimum child support award, based upon the following considerations:

* * *

(i) Any other adjustment which is needed to achieve an equitable result which may include, but not be limited to, a reasonable and necessary existing expense or debt. Such expense or debt may include, but is not limited to, a reasonable and necessary expense or debt which the parties jointly incurred during the marriage.

* * *

(12) Every petition for child support or for modification of child support shall be accompanied by an affidavit which shows the party's income, allowable deductions, and net income computed in accordance with this section. The affidavit shall be served at the same time that the petition is served. The respondent shall make an affidavit which shows the party's income, allowable deductions, and net income computed in accordance with this section. The respondent shall include his affidavit with the answer to the petition.

(13) For purposes of establishing an obligation for support in accordance with this section, if a person who is receiving public assistance is found to be noncooperative as defined in § 409.2572, the IV-D agency is authorized to submit to the court an affidavit attesting to the income of the custodial parent based upon information available to the IV-D agency.

(14) The Legislature shall review the guidelines established in this section at least every 4 years, beginning in 1993.

12.10 INTERSTATE ENFORCEMENT

The multipicity of jurisdictions in the United States poses special problems when father and mother reside in different states, and both may reside in states other than the one that ordered the child support and set the terms of divorce and custody. The full faith and credit clause of the U.S. Constitution requires the courts of one state to honor and enforce the orders of courts of other states. In cases in which arrearages have been reduced to judgment, and a court has held that the one obligated to pay child support owes the amount specified in the judgment, a foreign court should have no hesitancy in enforcing the judgment in its full amount. Payments that have not been reduced to judgment, however, are open to challenge. Although arrearages ought to be routinely enforceable, because they were ordered by a court, some states allow unpaid support to be modified. If the state ordering the payments allows retroactive modification, the state asked to enforce the order need not treat this as a final judgment—the foreign court has the same authority as the original court. Nevertheless, we should not expect a court to invite litigation by questioning a foreign court's judgment unless the circumstances are compelling.

12.11 URESA

Uniform Reciprocal Enforcement of Support Act (URESA) and its latest version, the "Revised" version (RURESA), was another product of the National Conference of Commissioners on Uniform State Laws, the body that formulated the UMDA. URESA was formulated because of the national problem with interstate enforcement of child support orders. URESA has been adopted, with some variations, in every state (see figure 12-1). URESA provides a means of enforcement when defaulted payments have not been reduced to judgment, as well as when the defaulting obligor has been found in contempt of court. (Appendix 12A includes all the major provisions of URESA and should be consulted for statutory details.) It is a means by which the recipient of child support payments may bring an action in her own state to be tried in the state of the debtor. This solves the problem of lack of personal jurisdiction over the debtor by the state of the creditor and saves the creditor the expense of traveling to the debtor's state. A complaint is filed in the appropriate court in the creditor's state. The complaint is forwarded to the court having jurisdiction over the debtor-defendant and the case is tried there, with a local official representing the creditor.

Once the case is decided, the state ordering compliance receives the payments and forwards them to the court of the creditor. Failure to pay by the creditor subjects him to the usual sanctions (contempt, garnishment, etc.) available in the state with personal jurisdiction over the defendant.

Unwed fathers may also be subject to URESA. If paternity has already been adjudicated, they may be treated the same as divorced fathers. URESA also provides for the responding state to adjudicate paternity.

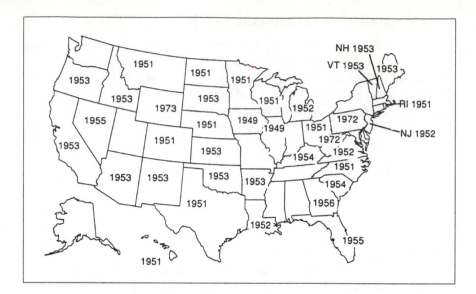

FIGURE 12-1
Date of effect of
URESA in adopting
states

CASE NO. 12-4   URESA

URESA often invokes thorny problems of differences between the laws of different jurisdictions.

STATE *EX REL.* McDONNELL
v. McCUTCHEON
337 N.W.2d 645 (Minn. 1983)
Supreme Court of Minnesota

PETERSON, Justice.

Jean E. McDonnell, petitioner below (hereafter plaintiff), a resident of Colorado, commenced a Uniform Reciprocal Enforcement of Support Act (URESA) proceeding in the courts of that state, seeking to recover accrued and ongoing child support. The file was transmitted to the District Court of Washington County, where respondent James T. McCutcheon (hereafter defendant) resides.

The facts relevant to this appeal are essentially undisputed and may be briefly stated. The parties were divorced in New York by order

dated April 16, 1970. Pursuant to a separation agreement, custody of their then 6 ½-year-old child was awarded to plaintiff, subject to defendant's right of visitation at specified times. The decree obligated defendant to pay child support of $25 per week ($40 per week during such time as plaintiff attended school to obtain her teaching degree) until the child reached age 21, and an additional amount equal to 10% of any increases in defendant's gross earnings. The current amount of child support according to the terms of the New York decree would be $426 per month. Defendant has made fairly regular child support payments of $100 per month, except for August 1980 to May 1981, when the child lived with defendant and attended school in Minnesota. The parties agree that the total arrearages through December

1981 would be $24,717, if the New York decree were fully enforced.

In the district court, plaintiff sought an order awarding her the full amount of arrearages accrued, as well as $426 per month ongoing support as specified in the New York order. Defendant argued that his duty of support was negated by plaintiff's wrongful removal of the child in 1974 from New York to Colorado.

1. Our study of the purposes and provisions of URESA persuades us that in a standard URESA action, in which ongoing support is sought, the duty of support is to be determined by the law of the responding state without regard to orders or judgments of foreign courts. Minn.Stat. § 518C.28 (1982) provides that "[d]uties of support applicable under sections 518C.01 to 518C.36 are those imposed under the laws of the state where the obligor was present for the period during which support is sought." The foreign order may, however, be used as evidence that the obligor does in fact owe a duty of support. Minn.Stat. § 518C.16 (1982) provides that "[i]f the action is based on a support order issued by another court, a certified copy of the order shall be received as evidence of the duty of support * * *." We read this language to mean that a foreign order is evidence that the obligor's relationship to the obligee gives rise to a duty to support; the language does not compel a responding state to award the same *level* of support. Any support payments made by an obligor pursuant to a foreign URESA order must be "credited against amounts accruing or accrued for the same period under a support order" made by a court of this state. Because all fifty states have similar reciprocal legislation, when a Minnesota court orders payments to be made under URESA, those payments constitute a credit against amounts accruing under foreign orders.

URESA is designed to help obligees obtain support expeditiously and economically. When foreign decrees are sought to be enforced, modified, or nullified, courts are confronted with difficult questions of foreign law. By refusing to consider foreign orders in standard URESA actions, these disadvantages are avoided. For these reasons, we adopt the view of those courts which have held that a responding state may independently determine an appropriate level of support to impose on the obligor. We therefore hold that in a standard URESA action, a trial court is not bound to enforce the ongoing support provisions of a foreign decree. Instead, the court is required by Minn.Stat. § 518C.28 (1982) to apply our domestic law, which in the instant case is found in relevant part at Minn.Stat. § 518.17, subd. 4 (1982).

Applying the foregoing principles to this case, we conclude that the part of the order setting ongoing support at $160 per month was not an abuse of discretion. Although we disapprove the trial court's emphasis on denial of visitation and the lack of a memorandum explaining its decision, our own examination of the records and proceedings, including the parties' relative financial positions, the projected costs of college education, and the child's scholarships and prospects for summer employment, does not indicate the sum of $160 per month is unreasonable, and it is therefore affirmed.

2. Our holding in this case, we reiterate again, does not imply that persons who have foreign support orders are unable to enforce them in this state. An obligee who relies on a foreign order and who seeks enforcement of the amount therein prescribed, without having first reduced it to judgment in the foreign state. . . , should register the order. . . . Brockelbank has noted the distinction between standard and registered proceedings and the options open to an obligee with a foreign support order who seeks support in another state:

The remedies of this part [Registration of Foreign Support Orders] are in addition to other remedies provided in the Act * * *. This means, of course, that plaintiff has a choice. She may proceed under Part III [Civil Enforcement] and bring the ordinary reciprocal action, petition filed in the initiating state based on the duty of support growing out of the support order, mail delivery to a court in the responding state, hearing and issue of a support order *as justice may require in the latter state*. . . . [I]n a standard URESA action, a responding state is not bound to conform its order to a foreign order. The foreign order may, however, be enforced if it is registered. . . .

Appellant in this standard URESA action seeks to recover arrearages of support which accrued month by month over a period of some 10 years, apparently on the theory that New York would require such a payment. We are not convinced New York law would do so. . . .

In 1979 New York enacted a statute which provides:

> When it appears to the satisfaction of the court that a custodial parent receiving alimony or maintenance pursuant to an order, judgment or decree of a court of competent jurisdiction has wrongfully interfered with or withheld visitation rights provided by such order, judgment or decree, the court *in its discretion* may suspend such payments or cancel any arrears that may have accrued during the time that visitation rights have been or are being interfered with or withheld.

We see no justification for requiring a Minnesota court to do what New York itself might not do. But more importantly, we believe that such difficult questions should be litigated in the more formal context of a registration proceeding rather than in the standard URESA action. . . .

Affirmed.

SUMMARY

Divorce of mother and father raises the problem of maintenance of the children. Although the father alone was once charged with responsibility for support of the children, contemporary law holds both mother and father responsible for the support of their children. Fathers of children born out of wedlock are also liable for support. The primary issue of this chapter concerns the measure of financial support required of the noncustodial parent. After divorce, the mother most frequently becomes the primary caregiver of the children—they live at her residence, eat the food she buys for them. The noncustodial parent, usually the father, must then compensate the custodial parent for support. This question of transferring money from one parent to the other is the most common focus of cases on child custody.

In the past, child support was awarded, and its amount determined, largely through the exercise of judicial discretion, after each side argued the equities of the case. Most divorces with children have been concluded with settlement agreements that fixed child support obligations as part of the package of financial distribution, including alimony and the distribution of assets, and child support in any given case should be reviewed in the light of the total allocation of resources. Agreements, however, are negotiated with an eye on the factors that the courts in the past and the legislatures today give as the determining issues in fixing the amount of support.

Under the influence of federal initiatives, largely in response to a national scandal in support delinquency, the states have been pressured to establish guidelines for child support as well as recordkeeping and enforcement. This is part of a movement privatizing child support, motivated by the desire of those in government to repay welfare payments with support money from parents in arrears. Federal funds for enforcement and other aspects of the welfare program administration are premised on establishing guidelines. So successful has this collection been that half of those now receiving help in collecting support are not welfare recipients.

As child support enforcement reaches its effective limits, signs of new problems are beginning to show. The plight of the impoverished mother is by now well known. The plight of the absent father, the out-of-work father, and the negligent father looms on the horizon. This in turn raises the question of societal responsibility for children. The most obvious issues of social and political responsibilities toward children are revealed in the cost of higher education and health care. These promise to be political issues of the next decade for both parents of intact families and divorced parents.

QUESTIONS

1. When a custodial parent spends more on children than the child support she is receiving, may she recover excess expenses from the paying parent? (*See Riegler v. Riegler*, Case No. 12-2).
2. How is need measured in child support determinations?
3. Under what circumstances might a stepfather be responsible after divorce for supporting his stepchild?
4. Is a parent obligated to support a child who has enough property to support herself?
5. Can child support be retroactively modified upward? Downward?
6. How should health care expenses be handled in a divorce?
7. When a noncustodial father obligated for child support remarries and has additional children by his second wife, can he successfully petition for a decrease in the support owed to the children of his first marriage?
8. How does URESA help to obtain child support?
9. What is the motivation for funding social agencies to collect child support arrearages?
10. What are the advantages of statutory child support schedules?

EXERCISES

Answer the questions according to the law of your state.

1. Can a change in the financial circumstances of parent or child serve as a ground for modification of child support? 89 A.L.R.2d 7.
2. Does remarriage provide a basis for modification of child support? 43 A.L.R.2d 363; 89 A.L.R.2d 106.
3. What is a stepparent's postdivorce duty to support a stepchild? 44 A.L.R.4th ____ .
4. Can contempt proceedings be brought for arrearages in child support after the child reaches the age of majority? 32 A.L.R.3d 888.
5. How does the death of a parent affect an order for child support? 18 A.L.R.3d 1126.
6. How is the adequacy of a child support award measured? 27 A.L.R4th 864; 27 A.L.R.4th 1038.
7. Can the payor of child support be credited for voluntary expenditures on the child? 47 A.L.R.3d 1031.
8. Does the child have the right to enforce a property settlement agreement? 34 A.L.R.3d 1357.
9. Where does the expense of education fit into the divorce decree? 56 A.L.R.2d 1207.
10. Does the marriage of a minor child terminate the parent's support obligations? 35 A.L.R.4th 355.

APPENDIX 12A

Revised Uniform Reciprocal Enforcement of Support Act 1968 (RURESA)

PART I. GENERAL PROVISIONS

§ 1. Purposes.

The purposes of this Act are to improve and extend by reciprocal legislation the enforcement of duties of support.

§ 2. Definitions.

(a) "Court" means the [here insert name] court of this State and when the context requires means the court of any other state as defined in a substantially similar reciprocal law.

(b) "Duty of support" means a duty of support whether imposed or imposable by law or by order, decree, or judgment of any court, whether interlocutory or final or whether incidental to an action for divorce, separation, separate maintenance, or otherwise and includes the duty to pay arrearages of support past due and unpaid.

(c) "Governor" includes any person performing the functions of Governor or the executive authority of any state covered by this Act.

(d) "Initiating state" means a state in which a proceeding pursuant to this or a substantially similar reciprocal law is commenced. "Initiating court" means the court in which a proceeding is commenced.

(e) "Law" includes both common and statutory law.

(f) "Obligee" means a person including a state or political subdivision to whom a duty of support is owed or a person including a state or political subdivision that has commenced a proceeding for enforcement of an alleged duty of support or for registration of a support order. It is immaterial if the person to whom a duty of support is owed is a recipient of public assistance.

(g) "Obligor" means any person owing a duty of support or against whom a proceeding for the enforcement of a duty of support or registration of a support order is commenced.

(h) "Prosecuting attorney" means the public official in the appropriate place who has the duty to enforce criminal laws relating to the failure to provide for the support of any person.

(i) "Register" means to [record] [file] in the Registry of Foreign Support Orders.

(j) "Registering court" means any court of this State in which a support order of a rendering state is registered.

(k) "Rendering state" means a state in which the court has issued a support order for which registration is sought or granted in the court of another state.

(l) "Responding state" means a state in which any responsive proceeding pursuant to the proceeding in the initiating state is commenced. "Responding court" means the court in which the responsive proceeding is commenced.

(m) "State" includes a state, territory, or possession of the United States, the District of Columbia, the Commonwealth of Puerto Rico, and any foreign jurisdiction in which this or a substantially similar reciprocal law is in effect.

(n) "Support order" means any judgment, decree, or order of support in favor of an obligee whether temporary or final, or subject to modification, revocation, or remission, regardless of the kind of action or proceeding in which it is entered.

§ 3. Remedies Additional to Those Now Existing.

The remedies herein provided are in addition to and not in substitution for any other remedies.

§ 4.   Extent of Duties of Support.

Duties of support arising under the law of this State, when applicable under section 7, bind the obligor present in this State regardless of the presence or residence of the obligee.

PART II.   CRIMINAL ENFORCEMENT

§ 5.   Interstate Rendition.

The Governor of this State may

(1)   demand of the Governor of another state the surrender of a person found in that state who is charged criminally in this State with failing to provide for the support of any person; or

(2)   surrender on demand by the Governor of another state a person found in this State who is charged criminally in that state with failing to provide for the support of any person. Provisions for extradition of criminals not inconsistent with this Act apply to the demand even if the person whose surrender is demanded was not in the demanding state at the time of the commission of the crime and has not fled therefrom. The demand, the oath, and any proceedings for extradition pursuant to this section need not state or show that the person whose surrender is demanded has fled from justice or at the time of the commission of the crime was in the demanding state.

§ 6.   Conditions of Interstate Rendition.

(a)   Before making the demand upon the Governor of another state for the surrender of a person charged criminally in this State with failing to provide for the support of a person, the Governor of this State may require any prosecuting attorney of this State to satisfy him that at least [60] days prior thereto the obligee initiated proceedings for support under this Act or that any proceeding would be of no avail.

(b)   If, under a substantially similar Act, the Governor of another state makes a demand upon the Governor of this State for the surrender of a person charged criminally in that state with failure to provide for the support of a person, the Governor may require any prosecuting attorney to investigate the demand and to report to him whether proceedings for support have been initiated or would be effective. If it appears to the Governor that a proceeding would be effective but has not been initiated he may delay honoring the demand for a reasonable time to permit the initiation of a proceeding.

(c)   If proceedings have been initiated and the person demanded has prevailed therein the Governor may decline to honor the demand. If the obligee prevailed and the person demanded is subject to a support order, the Governor may decline to honor the demand if the person demanded is complying with the support order.

PART III.   CIVIL ENFORCEMENT

§ 7.   Choice of Law.

Duties of support applicable under this Act are those imposed under the laws of any state where the obligor was present for the period during which support is sought. The obligor is presumed to have been present in the responding state during the period for which support is sought until otherwise shown.

§ 8.   Remedies of State or Political Subdivision Furnishing Support.

If a state or a political subdivision furnishes support to an individual obligee it has the same right to initiate a proceeding under this Act as the individual obligee for the purpose of securing reimbursement for support furnished and of obtaining continuing support.

§ 9.   How Duties of Support Enforced.

All duties of support, including the duty to pay arrearages, are enforceable by a proceeding under this Act including a proceeding for civil contempt. The defense that the parties are immune to suit because of their relationship as husband and wife or parent and child is not available to the obligor.

§ 10.   Jurisdiction.

Jurisdiction of any proceeding under this Act is vested in the [here insert title of court desired].

§ 11.   Contents and Filing of [Petition] for Support; Venue.

(a)   The [petition] shall be verified and shall state the name and, so far as known to the obligee, the address and circumstances of the obligor and the persons for whom support is sought, and all other pertinent information. The obligee may include in or attach to the [petition] any information which may help in locating or identifying the obligor including a photograph of the obligor, a description of any distinguishing marks on his person, other names and aliases by which he has been or is known, the name of his employer, his fingerprints, and his Social Security number.

(b)   The [petition] may be filed in the appropriate court of any state in which the obligee resides. The court shall not decline or refuse to accept and forward the [petition] on the ground that it should be filed with some other court of this or any other state where there is pending another action for divorce, separation, annulment, dissolution, habeas corpus, adoption, or custody between the same parties or where another court has already issued a support order in some other proceeding and has retained jurisdiction for its enforcement.

§ 12.   Officials to Represent Obligee.

If this State is acting as an initiating state the prosecuting attorney upon the request of the court [a state department of welfare, a county commissioner, an overseer of the poor, or other local welfare officer] shall represent the obligee in any proceeding under this Act. [If the prosecuting attorney neglects or refuses to represent the obligee the [Attorney General] may order him to comply with the request of the court or may undertake the representation.] [If the prosecuting attorney neglects or refuses to represent the obligee, the [Attorney General] [State Director of Public Welfare] may undertake the representation.]

§ 13.   Petition for a Minor.

A [petition] on behalf of a minor obligee may be executed and filed by a person having legal custody of the minor without appointment as guardian ad litem.

§ 14.   Duty of Initiating Court.

If the initiating court finds that the [petition] sets forth facts from which it may be determined that the obligor owes a duty of support and that a court of the responding state may obtain jurisdiction of the obligor or his property it shall so certify and cause 3 copies of the [petition] and its certificate and one copy of this Act to be sent to the responding court. Certification shall be in accordance with the requirements of the initiating state. If the name and address of the responding court is unknown and the responding state has an information agency comparable to that established in the initiating state it shall cause the copies to be sent to the state information agency or other proper official of the responding state, with a request that the agency or official forward them to the proper court and that the court of the responding state acknowledge their receipt to the initiating court.

§ 15.   Costs and Fees.

An initiating court shall not require payment of either a filing fee or other costs from the obligee but may request the responding court to collect fees and costs from the obligor. A responding court shall not require payment of a filing fee or other costs from the obligee but it may direct that all fees and costs requested by the initiating court and incurred in this State when acting as a responding state, including fees for filing of pleadings, service of process, seizure of property, stenographic or duplication service, or other service supplied to the obligor, be paid in whole or in part by the obligor or by the [state or political subdivision thereof]. These costs or fees do not have priority over amounts due to the obligee.

§ 16.   Jurisdiction by Arrest.

If the court of this State believes that the obligor may flee it may

(1)   as an initiating court, request in its certificate that the responding court obtain the body of the obligor by appropriate process; or

(2)   as a responding court, obtain the body of the obligor by appropriate process. Thereupon it may release him upon his own recognizance or upon his giving a bond in an amount set by the court to assure his appearance at the hearing.

§ 17.   State Information Agency.

(a)   The [Attorney General's Office, State Attorney's Office, Welfare Department or other Information Agency] is designated as the state information agency under this Act. It shall

(1)   compile a list of the courts and their addresses in this State having jurisdiction under this Act and transmit it to the state information agency of every other state which has adopted this or a substantially similar Act. Upon the adjournment of each session of the [legislature] the agency shall distribute copies of any amendments to the Act and a statement of their effective date to all other state information agencies;

(2)   maintain a register of lists of courts received from other states and transmit copies thereof promptly to every court in this state having jurisdiction under this Act; and

(3)   forward to the court in this State which has jurisdiction over the obligor or his property petitions, certificates, and copies of the Act it receives from courts or information agencies of other states.

(b)   If the state information agency does not know the location of the obligor or his property in the state and no state location service is available it shall use all means at its disposal to obtain this information, including the examination of official records in the state and other sources such as telephone directories, real property records, vital statistics records, police records, requests for the name and address from employers who are able or willing to cooperate, records of motor vehicle license offices, requests made to the tax offices both state and federal where such offices are able to cooperate, and requests made to the Social Security Administration as permitted by the Social Security Act as amended.

(c)   After the deposit of 3 copies of the [petition] and certificate and one copy of the Act of the initiating state with the clerk of the appropriate court, if the state information agency knows or believes that the prosecuting attorney is not prosecuting the case diligently it shall inform the [Attorney General] [State Director of Public Welfare] who may undertake the representation.

§ 18.   Duty of the Court and Officials of This State as Responding State.

(a)   After the responding court receives copies of the [petition], certificate, and Act from the initiating court the clerk of the court shall docket the case and notify the prosecuting attorney of his action.

(b) The prosecuting attorney shall prosecute the case diligently. He shall take all action necessary in accordance with the laws of this State to enable the court to obtain jurisdiction over the obligor or his property and shall request the court [clerk of the court] to set a time and place for a hearing and give notice thereof to the obligor in accordance with law.

(c) [If the prosecuting attorney neglects or refuses to represent the obligee the [Attorney General] may order him to comply with the request of the court or may undertake the representation.] [If the prosecuting attorney neglects or refuses to represent the obligee, the [Attorney General] [State Director of Public Welfare] may undertake the representation.]

§ 19.   Further Duties of Court and Officials in the Responding State.

(a) The prosecuting attorney on his own initiative shall use all means at his disposal to locate the obligor or his property, and if because of inaccuracies in the [petition] or otherwise the court cannot obtain jurisdiction the prosecuting attorney shall inform the court of what he has done and request the court to continue the case pending receipt of more accurate information or an amended [petition] from the initiating court.

(b) If the obligor or his property is not found in the [county], and the prosecuting attorney discovers that the obligor or his property may be found in another [county] of this State or in another state he shall so inform the court. Thereupon the clerk of the court shall forward the documents received from the court in the initiating state to a court in the other [county] or to a court in the other state or to the information agency or other proper official of the other state with a request that the documents be forwarded to the proper court. All powers and duties provided by this Act apply to the recipient of the documents so forwarded. If the clerk of a court of this State forwards documents to another court he shall forthwith notify the initiating court.

(c) If the prosecuting attorney has no information as to the location of the obligor or his property he shall so inform the initiating court.

§ 20.   Hearing and Continuance.

If the obligee is not present at the hearing and the obligor denies owing the duty of support alleged in the petition or offers evidence constituting a defense the court, upon request of either party, shall continue the hearing to permit evidence relative to the duty to be adduced by either party by deposition or by appearing in person before the court. The court may designate the judge of the initiating court as a person before whom a deposition may be taken.

§ 21.   Immunity from Criminal Prosecution.

If at the hearing the obligor is called for examination as an adverse party and he declines to answer upon the ground that his testimony may tend to incriminate him, the court may require him to answer, in which event he is immune from criminal prosecution with respect to matters revealed by his testimony, except for perjury committed in this testimony.

§ 22.   Evidence of Husband and Wife.

Laws attaching a privilege against the disclosure of communications between husband and wife are inapplicable to proceedings under this Act. Husband and wife are competent witnesses [and may be compelled] to testify to any relevant matter, including marriage and parentage.

§ 23.   Rules of Evidence.

In any hearing for the civil enforcement of this Act the court is governed by the rules of evidence applicable in a civil court action in the _____ Court. If the action is based on a support order issued by another court a certified copy of the order shall be received as evidence of the duty of support, subject only to any defenses available to an obligor with respect to paternity (Section 27) or to a defendant in an action or a proceeding to enforce a foreign money judgment. The determination or enforcement of a duty of support owed to one obligee is unaffected by any interference by another obligee with rights of custody or visitation granted by a court.

§ 24.   Order of Support.

If the responding court finds a duty of support it may order the obligor to furnish support or reimbursement therefor and subject the property of the obligor to the order. Support orders made pursuant to this Act shall require that payments be made to the [clerk] [bureau] [probation department] of the court of the responding state. [The court and prosecuting attorney of any [county] in which the obligor is present or has property have the same powers and duties to enforce the order as have those of the [county] in which it was first issued. If enforcement is impossible or cannot be completed in the [county] in which the order was issued, the prosecuting attorney shall send a certified copy of the order to the prosecuting attorney of any [county] in which it appears that proceedings to enforce the order would be effective. The prosecuting attorney to whom the certified copy of the order is forwarded shall proceed with enforcement and report the results of the proceedings to the court first issuing the order.]

§ 25.   Responding Court to Transmit Copies to Initiating Court.

The responding court shall cause a copy of all support orders to be sent to the initiating court.

§ 26.   Additional Powers of Responding Court.

In addition to the foregoing powers a responding court may subject the obligor to any terms and conditions proper to assure compliance with its orders and in particular to:

(1) require the obligor to furnish a cash deposit or a bond of a character and amount to assure payment of any amount due;

(2) require the obligor to report personally and to make payments at specified intervals to the [clerk] [bureau] [probation department] of the court; and

(3) punish under the power of contempt the obligor who violates any order of the court.

§ 27. Paternity.

If the obligor asserts as a defense that he is not the father of the child for whom support is sought and it appears to the court that the defense is not frivolous, and if both of the parties are present at the hearing or the proof required in the case indicates that the presence of either or both of the parties is not necessary, the court may adjudicate the paternity issue. Otherwise the court may adjourn the hearing until the paternity issue has been adjudicated.

§ 28. Additional Duties of Responding Court.

A responding court has the following duties which may be carried out through the [clerk] [bureau] [probation department] of the court:

(1) to transmit to the initiating court any payment made by the obligor pursuant to any order of the court or otherwise; and

(2) to furnish to the initiating court upon request a certified statement of all payments made by the obligor.

§ 29. Additional Duty of Initiating Court.

An initiating court shall receive and disburse forthwith all payments made by the obligor or sent by the responding court. This duty may be carried out through the [clerk] [bureau] [probation department] of the court.

§ 30. Proceedings Not to Be Stayed.

A responding court shall not stay the proceeding or refuse a hearing under this Act because of any pending or prior action or proceeding for divorce, separation, annulment, dissolution, habeas corpus, adoption, or custody in this or any other state. The court shall hold a hearing and may issue a support order pendente lite. In aid thereof it may require the obligor to give a bond for the prompt prosecution of the pending proceeding. If the other action or proceeding is concluded before the hearing in the instant proceeding and the judgment therein provides for the support demanded in the [petition] being heard the court must conform its support order to the amount allowed in the other action or proceeding. Thereafter the court shall not stay enforcement of its support order because of the retention of jurisdiction for enforcement purposes by the court in the other action or proceeding.

§ 31. Application of Payments.

A support order made by a court of this State pursuant to this Act does not nullify and is not nullified by a support order made by a court of this State pursuant to any other law or by a support order made by a court of any other state pursuant to a substantially similar act or any other law, regardless of priority of issuance, unless otherwise specifically provided by the court. Amounts paid for a particular period pursuant to any support order made by the court of another state shall be credited against the amounts accruing or accrued for the same period under any support order made by the court of this State.

§ 32. Effect of Participation in Proceeding.

[Participation in any proceeding under this Act does not confer jurisdiction upon any court over any of the parties thereto in any other proceeding.]

§ 33. Intrastate Application.

This Act applies if both the obligee and the obligor are in this State but in different [counties]. If the court of the [county] in which the [petition] is filed finds that the [petition] sets forth facts from which it may be determined that the obligor owes a duty of support and finds that a court of another [county] in this State may obtain jurisdiction over the obligor or his property, the clerk of the court shall send the [petition] and a certification of the findings to the court of the [county] in which the obligor or his property is found. The clerk of the court of the [county] receiving these documents shall notify the prosecuting attorney of their receipt. The prosecuting attorney and the court in the [county] to which the copies are forwarded then shall have duties corresponding to those imposed upon them when acting for this State as a responding state.

§ 34. Appeals.

If the [Attorney General] [State Director of Public Welfare] is of the opinion that a support order is erroneous and presents a question of law warranting an appeal in the public interest, he may

(a) perfect an appeal to the proper appellate court if the support order was issued by a court of this State, or

(b) if the support order was issued in another state, cause the appeal to be taken in the other state. In either case expenses of appeal may be paid on his order from funds appropriated for his office.

PART IV.   REGISTRATION OF FOREIGN
SUPPORT ORDERS

§ 35.   Additional Remedies.

If the duty of support is based on a foreign support order, the obligee has the additional remedies provided in the following sections.

§ 36.   Registration.

The obligee may register the foreign support order in a court of this State in the manner, with the effect, and for the purposes herein provided.

§ 37.   Registry of Foreign Support Orders.

The clerk of the court shall maintain a Registry of Foreign Support Orders in which he shall [file] foreign support orders.

§ 38.   Official to Represent Obligee.

If this State is acting either as a rendering or a registering state the prosecuting attorney upon the request of the court [a state department of welfare, a county commissioner, an overseer of the poor, or other local welfare official] shall represent the obligee in proceedings under this Part.

[If the prosecuting attorney neglects or refuses to represent the obligee, the [Attorney General] may order him to comply with the request of the court or may undertake the representation.] [If the prosecuting attorney neglects or refuses to represent the obligee, the [Attorney General] [State Director of Public Welfare] may undertake the representation.]

§ 39.   Registration Procedure; Notice.

(a)   An obligee seeking to register a foreign support order in a court of this State shall transmit to the clerk of the court

(1)   three certified copies of the order with all modifications thereof,

(2)   one copy of the reciprocal enforcement of support act of the state in which the order was made, and

(3)   a statement verified and signed by the obligee, showing the post office address of the obligee, the last known place of residence and post office address of the obligor, the amount of support remaining unpaid, a description and the location of any property of the obligor available upon execution, and a list of the states in which the order is registered. Upon receipt of these documents the clerk of the court, without payment of a filing fee or other cost to the obligee, shall file them in the Registry of Foreign Support

Orders. The filing constitutes registration under this Act.

(b)   Promptly upon registration the clerk of the court shall send by certified or registered mail to the obligor at the address given a notice of the registration with a copy of the registered support order and the post office address of the obligee. He shall also docket the case and notify the prosecuting attorney of his action. The prosecuting attorney shall proceed diligently to enforce the order.

§ 40.   Effect of Registration; Enforcement Procedure.

(a)   Upon registration the registered foreign support order shall be treated in the same manner as a support order issued by a court of this State. It has the same effect and is subject to the same procedures, defenses, and proceedings for reopening, vacating, or staying as a support order of this State and may be enforced and satisfied in like manner.

(b)   The obligor has [20] days after the mailing of notice of the registration in which to petition the court to vacate the registration or for other relief. If he does not so petition the registered support order is confirmed.

(c)   At the hearing to enforce the registered support order the obligor may present only matters that would be available to him as defenses in an action to enforce a foreign money judgment. If he shows to the court that an appeal from the order is pending or will be taken or that a stay of execution has been granted the court shall stay enforcement of the order until the appeal is concluded, the time for appeal has expired, or the order is vacated, upon satisfactory proof that the obligor has furnished security for payment of the support ordered as required by the rendering state. If he shows to the court any ground upon which enforcement of a support order of this State may be stayed the court shall stay enforcement of the order for an appropriate period if the obligor furnishes the same security for payment of the support ordered that is required for a support order of this State.

§ 41.   Uniformity of Interpretation.

* * *

§ 42.   Short Title.

This Act may be cited as the Revised Uniform Reciprocal Enforcement of Support Act (1968).

§ 43.   Severability.

* * *

CHAPTER 13
Child Custody

The Ultimate Prize

Roxanne Pulitzer went through a much-publicized divorce and custody battle with Palm Beach millionaire Peter Pulitzer. Both parents sought custody of twin five-year-old sons in a trial that involved allegations of drug abuse, infidelity, and other sordid pleasures of the very rich and famous. Child custody should be determined "in the best interest of the child," which is the theme of this chapter.

— Courtesy AP/Wide World Photos.

Many people (especially men) begin with a political conviction that women ought to be equal to men economically, from which they leap to the insupportable conclusion that women are equal to men economically. It then follows that women can support children as well as men can and that whoever wants the children can pay for them.

Justice Neely, *David M. v. Margaret M.*, 182 W. Va. 57, 385 S.E.2d 912 (1989)

OUTLINE

13.1 FACTORS CONFOUNDING CUSTODY DECISIONS
13.2 HISTORICAL OVERVIEW
13.3 TYPES OF CUSTODY
13.4 BEST INTERESTS OF THE CHILD
13.5 PRESUMPTIONS
13.6 MISCONDUCT
13.7 MODIFICATION
13.8 VISITATION
13.9 THE NATURAL FATHER
13.10 RIGHTS OF NONPARENTS (THIRD PARTIES) TO CUSTODY
13.11 UNIFORM CHILD CUSTODY JURISDICTION ACT
13.12 PARENTAL KIDNAPPING PREVENTION ACT
     SUMMARY

Although no-fault divorce attempted to do away with contested divorces, it left unchanged the most brutal aspect of the adversarial system in divorce cases: the fight over custody of minor children. Although equitable distribution and alimony retained a potential for accusations of fault, custody contests always raise issues of character and fault. If a jurisdiction follows the old maternal preference (tender years doctrine) *or its modern counterpart, the* primary caregiver rule, *the contest ultimately devolves upon the mother's fitness to have the children, countered, of course, by the mother's attack on the father's fitness. If a jurisdiction adheres to the presumably gender-neutral* best interests of the child doctrine, *the contest reduces to the question of which is the better parent. Custody contests tend to be very nasty*

349

because the stakes are so high. The personal integrity of each parent is challenged and the victor gains control over the children.

The best approach to deciding custody is far from clear. Competing legal doctrines, psychological theories, and social policies have left a difficult problem in a state of confusion. Because of the importance of this subject and the dynamics of the competing policy issues, this subject is divided into two parts. The first part consists of an overview of the law of child custody. The second part, chapter 14, consists of cases and commentary on this subject.

13.1 FACTORS CONFOUNDING CUSTODY DECISIONS

Custody questions are very special in the law, for a variety of reasons.

1. *Those most deeply affected, namely minor children, are not parties to the lawsuit.* An apparent exception occurs when the court appoints a **guardian ad litem** to represent the child's interests in the case. Usually, however, the guardian ad litem merely makes recommendations to the judge and has limited authority (with the degree of authority depending upon the jurisdiction). Otherwise, the children must depend upon their battling parents and a puzzled judge to protect their interests.

2. *The parties to the dispute tend to be driven by the most primitive and least rational of motives.* It is a maxim that "family law deals with good people at their worst." The rules of fair play, decency, honesty, and truthfulness are less likely to be honored in custody disputes than in any other area of law.

3. *Each case presents unique issues.* No two families are alike. The variable needs of children and the diversity of personalities of parents combine to provide a wide array of situations.

4. *Today there is an inherent conflict in the attempt to enforce gender equality in the one area where gender is most critical and most relevant.* The equal protection clause of the Fourteenth Amendment and the political movement for sex equality demand that mothers and fathers be treated equally with regard to custody, but equality of the sexes is not echoed in the personal beliefs or practices of most people. If there are differences between the sexes, they are most important in the area of the family. Women can run companies and heavy equipment, men can be secretaries and nurses, but we have yet to fashion a man who can give birth and suckle his child.

5. *Children are the pawns in a political struggle between men and women.* The struggle exists at both personal and societal levels. Parents fight not only for care of the children but for control over them (and perhaps each other). In the larger arena, children play a symbolic role in the clash between the old patriarchy and the movement for women's rights.

6. *Decision-making by the court is based on fact-finding involving facts not yet in existence (along with some historical facts greatly distorted by the parties and their attorneys).* Whereas lawsuits ordinarily involve the resolution of a conflict over past events—a physical injury at work, a broken

contract, a dispute over title—custody suits are decided on a prediction of the future welfare of the children. This problem is compounded by the fact that the court sees good people at their worst, often making it difficult to assess the character and stability of those involved.

7. *Custody decisions are based on psychological and sociological principles as well as the law.* These principles may be based on the folk wisdom of the judge, in which case the judge's conscious and unconscious biases play a major role. These principles may rely on academic theories of psychology, psychiatry, and sociology, perhaps the least reliable of the sciences, in terms of predictability, and the sciences with the least internal consensus and consistency. Lawyers and judges are trained and are accustomed to deal with problems through the objective analysis of fact and the application of legal principle by argument, reasoning, and value consensus. Custody issues are presented in a far different format.

13.2 HISTORICAL OVERVIEW

The English common law carried on the Western European tradition of Roman law, which gave a father absolute control over his children. Because the father-husband enjoyed and exercised legal rights on behalf of the family, his duty of support was balanced by custodial rights. As a practical matter, in the absence of divorce (except for the rich and powerful), this division was reasonable in light of the relative vulnerability of women and their inability to seek gainful employment. In America, where divorce was early recognized, issues of custody and support became problems for ordinary people. As the idea of family became cast in the companionate mold, with the wife responsible for home and children, the father's right to custody was disputed and lost, particularly for children of "tender years." The ideal family isolated mother and small children from the coarse and corrupting world of work and business. Mothers were delicate and innocent nurturers, the appropriate custodians of young children.

Not until the 20th century was this custodial double standard challenged. The movement for equality of women caused two ideological changes in the legal view of custody. First, if the sexes are equal and should have equal rights, as embodied in the equal protection clause of the Fourteenth Amendment, the tender years doctrine could no longer stand. Second, as the country grew more prosperous and new opportunities for employment for women arose, the judicial opinions began to argue that women were no longer unable to join men in the workplace. The appropriate custodian of the children then became a matter of choice, giving rise to the ultimate standard, the *best interests of the child.*

The final stage in this evolution, and one still far from complete, grew out of the best interests doctrine and a growing interest in children stemming from the emphasis in psychology and psychotherapy on the influence childhood has over the development of personality. The view of the child as a more or less resilient (if sinful) student of its parents has changed to that of

LEGAL TERMS

guardian ad litem
  Person appointed by the court to represent a minor or incompetent in a lawsuit.

victim of its parents, in varying degrees mentally and perhaps physically crippled by incompetent "parenting." According to this view, the worst thing parents can do to children, short of pathological abuse, is to divorce each other.

If we accept this picture of the infliction of harm upon the innocent, the only reasonable response is protection. Instead of focusing upon parental rights—awarding custody and determining rights of access for the noncustodial parent—the focus shifts to parental duties. The parents, or at least one of them, may choose to end their relationship, and they may negotiate the consequences of that dissolution, but minor children have no choice and must rely on their parents to protect their interests during the divorce process, just as they must rely on their parents during the marriage. The law, however, can adjust the rules of the process to minimize the harm to the children and to maximize their chances for the future. One approach employed by many states has been the development of joint custody, premised on the notion that children will be better off if they have meaningful relationships with both parents. Under this scheme, both parents must share in the decision making over the vital concerns of the children, and both must have frequent contact with the children.

There is a fundamental weakness in the premise of joint custody: We are asking two individuals who were unable to cooperate effectively while married to cooperate after the destructive ordeal of divorce. Fortunately, most parents continue to love their children long after they have lost their love for each other, and hence may be able to cooperate for the sake of the children. That, at least, is the hope that joint custody offers.

13.3 TYPES OF CUSTODY

Discussion of the basic forms of custody may obscure the details of marital settlement agreements. The parents may create a specialized allocation of rights and duties regarding the children, subject only to the law and the court's approval. Provisions of this contract that the court deems to be in the best interests of the children should be approved and enforced. Nevertheless, the court should be more solicitous of the children's welfare than it might be with regard to either spouse's welfare. Thus the court might not be concerned that a wife has agreed to less than she seems to deserve, but it ought to be concerned when inadequate provision is made for the children. This is a contract to which the children are not parties and did not agree.

Occasionally, a distinction between physical and legal custody is relevant. *Legal custody* fixes responsibility in one or both parents and establishes or implies rights. When only one parent has legal custody, that parent has the legal authority for decision making, exclusive of the other parent. *Physical custody* refers to the child's residence. It is possible, for example, for the mother to have physical custody while both father and mother have legal custody.

1. *Sole custody.* When only one parent has custody of a child, the arrangement is called sole custody. The other parent is ordinarily accorded rights of visitation, but the child is under the control of one parent.

2. *Divided or alternating custody.* The children live with one parent part of the year and the other parent for the remainder of the year. As children move back and forth, custody shifts back and forth between the parents, so that the parent at their residence has sole custody while the children are living there. In rare instances, the arrangement specifies that the children will stay in the same residence while the parents take turns living with them. This is seen as a means of preventing dislocation of the children while allowing maximum contact with both parents.

3. *Split custody.* When the children are split between the parents—some living with the father, others with the mother, and each parent having sole custody of the children in his or her care—the arrangement may be called split custody. The term may also be applied to the situation previously described as divided custody. A general policy disfavors splitting siblings.

4. *Joint custody.* A modern trend in family law is joint custody, an arrangement in which both parents share rights and responsibilities for the children. The children may still have a primary residence, so that access to the children resembles a sole-custody-with-visitation situation, or the arrangement may resemble divided or split custody. The importance of joint custody is its legal consequences—both parents are responsible for the children. The recent popularity of joint custody is derived in part from the new focus on parental responsibility rather than rights and an effort to involve the former noncustodial parent in decisions involving the children's welfare. If the children have a primary residence, it is still appropriate to refer to a custodial and a noncustodial parent. Some states have gone so far as to presume that joint custody is in the best interests of the children, imposing sole custody only when one parent is found to be an unfit parent. Other states have merely indicated a preference for joint custody. During the 1980s, a majority saw fit to provide for joint custody.

CAVEAT

Terminology varies from state to state. *Split custody* may be used to refer to what is called *divided custody* in this text; one case even referred to it as "time-share." "Shared" custody may refer to joint or divided custody. Florida calls joint custody *shared parental responsibility* to emphasize the focus on rights of the children rather than parents.

13.4 BEST INTERESTS OF THE CHILD

Case after case insists that the "polestar" of custody decisions is the *best interests of the child.* This is a significant departure from the older common law paternal rights approach, but the common law rule really acted as a presumption in favor of the father and existed in an era when divorce was rare. Today, despite the best interests standard, custody decisions are made in the context of presumptions, preferences, and legislative and judicial guidelines. For example, the tender years doctrine, popular during the latter part of the 19th century and most of the 20th, expressed a presumption or preference, depending on the state, that young children should be in the custody of their mothers. The rule arose in the context of increasing divorces and sole custody. Not until the last two decades have the states seriously considered joint custody as a legitimate or preferred approach. Formerly, one of the divorcing spouses was given physical and legal control over the minor children of the marriage and the other was granted visitation rights.

Originally, the best interests doctrine gave judges carte blanche to make awards of custody. Proving abuse of discretion was nearly impossible without guidelines or standards to measure the exercise of discretion. Any reasonably intelligent judge could select facts from the record to justify an award of custody. In fact, this underscores the principal dilemma of custody awards: Mother and father are usually equally good or bad parents, so that in awarding custody the judge must often "pick and probe and scrutinize often petty testimony in an effort to find some articulable difference which will support a painful and difficult choice" (Chief Justice Bakes, in *Moye,* Case No. 13-1).

The determination of the best interests of the child came to be governed by certain policies established by judicial custom, which so were frequently repeated in judicial justifications for awards that they could serve as bases for reversal on abuse of discretion. For example, although the tender years doctrine was not a presumption, it was a preference or a policy from which a judge would depart only with a clearcut reason to favor the father. Practically speaking, a father wanting custody had to prove the mother "unfit," which meant addicted to drugs or alcohol, insane or nearly so, a child abuser, or an adulteress (this last a hangover from patriarchal double standards)—in short, "an emotional cripple or a moral leper, preferably both."

The courts recognized parental rights to be superior to those of third parties. Initially this applied only to fathers of legitimate or legitimized children, but later, on constitutional equal protection grounds, this recognition was extended to nonmarital fathers. Unwed fathers were still at a disadvantage, however, because another policy against removing children from their accustomed locale could be used to argue best interests. The more recent concept of psychological parent could also be used against a natural father who had been absent during most of the child's life.

Another policy often invoked was designed to prevent splitting siblings. The courts favored placement of adolescent children with their same-sex parents. Some attention was given to the wishes of the children, especially if they were 14 or older, but most courts recognized that children could be cajoled, bribed, or fooled into bad choices or preferences and refused to give them the final say. Given these customs or policies, along with the vague best interests test, most judges could fashion a decision that comported with policy and did not appear to be an abuse of discretion.

UNIFORM MARRIAGE AND DIVORCE ACT § 402

The court shall determine custody in accordance with the best interest of the child. The court shall consider all relevant factors, including:

1. The wishes of the child's parent or parents as to his [or her] custody;
2. The wishes of the child as to his [or her] custodian;
3. The interaction and interrelationship of the child with his [or her] parent or parents, and his [or her] siblings;
4. The child's adjustment to his [or her] home, school, and community;
5. The mental and physical health and integrity of all individuals involved.

The court shall not consider conduct of a proposed custodian that does not affect his [or her] relationship to the child.

[The gender-neutral additions in brackets appear in recent statutory versions.]

Many states have adopted the language of UMDA § 402 nearly verbatim. Idaho adds a sixth factor ("The need to promote continuity and stability in the life of the child"), as does Colorado ("The ability of the custodian to encourage the sharing of love, affection, and contact between the child and the noncustodial party"). Kentucky does not insert the gender-neutral "his or her" language, but lengthens the first sentence ("The court shall determine custody in accordance with the best interest of the child *and equal consideration shall be given to each parent*").

Some states have left nearly absolute discretion with the judge, as did Massachusetts:

> In making an order or judgment relative to the custody of children pending a controversy between their parents, or relative to their final possession, the rights of the parents shall, in the absence of misconduct, be held to be equal, and the happiness and welfare of the children shall determine their custody or possession.

> — Mass. Gen. L. ch. 208, § 31 (1988).

CASE NO. 13-1 May an Epileptic Parent Have Custody?

Surely the best interests of the children includes putting them in the care of someone physically capable of caring for them. That certainly is covered in paragraph 5 of § 402 of the UMDA. It is part of the Idaho statute and was an issue in the case of *Moye v. Moye.* What if one parent was only partially disabled but the other was fully able and both appeared to be good parents? Objectively speaking, would it not be an abuse of discretion to award custody to the partially disabled parent?

MOYE v. MOYE
102 Idaho 170, 627 P.2d 799 (1981)
Supreme Court of Idaho

DONALDSON, Justice.

Appellant Lynnae Denise Moye and respondent Terry Andrew Moye were married December 28, 1974. Two children were born of this marriage, a girl, now 4½ years old, and a boy, now 2½ years old. The parties separated on October 16, 1978 and on the following October 20, the appellant-mother filed for divorce. Pending the outcome of the divorce proceeding, the mother retained custody of the children under a temporary award made by a lawyer-magistrate.

* * *

On April 4, 1979, Judge Norris, citing a personal bias developed because of the publicity of the case, withdrew and submitted the matter for reassignment.

* * *

(1) In the instant action, the appellant-mother's basic contention is that Judge Norris abused his discretion in granting custody to the father because the judge based his order primarily upon the fact that appellant suffers from epilepsy. She also argues that pursuant to the Tender Years Doctrine, she should have received custody.

Upon review, we do not find that the Norris order is in error simply because the mother's physical ailment was a consideration in the judge's formulation of the custody grant. The rule in Idaho is that in determining the custody of a minor child, the child's welfare and best interest is of paramount importance. This rule is substantiated by case law. It follows that the

physical condition of a parent is a valid consideration in a "best interests" approach. Accordingly, such a consideration made by a court does not in itself present an incident of error.

Whether there has been abuse of discretion in the custody grant, however, is a matter of inquiry which goes beyond merely looking at a court's consideration of a parent's physical health. An abuse of discretion by the trial court occurs when the evidence is insufficient to support its conclusion that the welfare and interests of a child will be best served by a particular custody award. *It follows that an abuse of discretion may also occur where the court overemphasizes one factor,* such as a parent's physical condition, thereby similarly failing to support its conclusion that the welfare and interests of a child will be best served by a particular custody award. [Emphasis added.] In the instant case, we find this latter abuse of discretion.

Specifically, the evidence presented and so found by the trial court, that the appellant-mother suffers from epilepsy which is controlled to a degree through medication, that she requires nine to ten hours of sleep per night, that she has migraine headaches and that she has post-seizure lack of energy, does not, under the circumstances as they appear on the record, sufficiently support the court's conclusion that it is in the best interest of the children to vest custody in the respondent-father. The court did make some findings as regards the status of the respondent-father but the court's apparent overemphasis of but one consideration, that being the mother's physical condition, convinces this Court that all other relevant factors impacting upon the best interests of the children were not duly considered or, if they were, it was not so reflected upon the record.[2] We therefore reverse the Norris order and remand to the district court for further proceedings. Pending resolution of the custody issue by the district court, the Lodge decree granting joint custody pursuant to stipulation shall remain in effect except for that portion of the decree requiring that an adult female be with appellant during visitation times, a burden we find to have been imposed without any substantial evidence to support it. We observe further that the Tender Years Doctrine, that custody of a child of tender years should be vested in the mother, has limited impact in Idaho law. To the extent previous case law exists which suggests a preference for the mother as custodian of a child of tender years, the preference exists only when all other considerations are equal. As we have previously held, the considerations made by the trial court are incomplete and the preference is therefore inapplicable.

Reversed and remanded. Costs to appellant. No attorney fees awarded.

* * *

BAKES, Chief Justice, dissenting:

I respectfully dissent, well aware of the need to remove the burdensome social stigma which has so undeservedly attached itself to epilepsy and epileptics, a stigma founded solely on fear and ignorance. It is my sincere belief, however, that this case is not the appropriate vehicle to rectify those historical inequities.

One point cannot be overstressed: no one has taken Lynnae Moye's children from her because she is an epileptic. Nothing could be farther from the truth. When a district judge awards custody to one of the parents in a divorce case, it is not necessarily because the other parent is not fit. In the ordinary custody case, both parents are loving, capable and determined to raise their children in a proper manner. That does not help the judge who, with the best interests of the child at heart, must pick and probe and scrutinize often petty testimony in an effort to find some articulable difference which will support a painful and difficult choice. When the judge makes that choice, he or she is not taking the children away from the non-custodial parent, nor is that parent found to be unfit. The judge is merely awarding custody to one parent according to the best interests of the child as he views it. This difficult choice is necessitated by the parents' divorce, not by their shortcomings as parents.

[Discussion of details of the findings with regard to the father.]

There is, on the other hand, not a single finding which in any way indicates it would be in the children's better interest to have custody vested in the appellant. The lack of findings in that regard is supported by a corresponding lack of evidence in the record.

I fear, against hope, that today's opinion will make it very difficult for a parent whose spouse is an epileptic to obtain custody of his or her children, their best interests notwithstanding. While I can understand the majority's desire to rectify an unfounded historical stigmatization, I see no need to reverse a district court's custody order well supported by the record, quite apart from the epilepsy issue. I cannot help but wonder whether today's result would be different had this case not been inaccurately cast as a single-issue cause célèbre. I would affirm.

---

1 It is interesting to note that the legislature has now statutorily recognized the best interest in rule in I.C. § 32-717 (Supp.1980): "Custody of children: Best interest. In an action for divorce the court may, before and after judgment, give such direction for the custody, care and education of the children of the marriage as may seem necessary or proper in the best interests of the children. The court shall consider all relevant factors which may include:

1. The wishes of the child's parent or parents as to his or her custody;

2. The wishes of the child as to his or her custodian;

3. The interaction and interrelationship of the child with his or her parent or parents, and his or her siblings;
4. The child's adjustment to his or her home, school, and community;
5. The mental and physical health and integrity of all individuals involved; and
6. The need to promote continuity and stability in the life of the child."

2 The Norris order contained ten findings of fact. Six of those findings deal with the mother's physical health. One other finding is that each of the parties loves the children. Only the remaining three concern the status of the father and one, finding number eight, contains what we consider to be irrelevant comments by the court concerning the father's attitude towards dry diapers.

CASE QUESTIONS

1. Does the phrase "overemphasizes one factor" seem to be a weak test for abuse of discretion? Compare this with: "[A]n abuse of discretion is not merely an error of judgment but if in reaching a conclusion the law is overridden or misapplied, or the judgment is manifestly unreasonable, or the result of partiality, prejudice, bias, or ill-will as shown by the evidence or the record, discretion is abused."

2. The Idaho Coalition of Advocates for the Disabled and the Idaho Epilepsy League filed **amicus curiae briefs** in the case. The original decision brought negative publicity concerning the trial judge's award of custody to the father. A *Washington Post* article dated January 29, 1979, reported as follows:

   A 24-year-old mother who is seeking a divorce cannot keep custody of her two children because she is an epileptic, a district court judge in the farming community of Weiser, Idaho, has ruled. The unusual decision, which came early this month, has resulted in a storm of protest from epilepsy groups. . . .

   Following the Idaho Supreme Court decision, an Associated Press release reported that Lynnae Moye's attorney, Larry Hunter "cited a California Supreme Court case that states it is improper for a court to make a decision on whether a parent can properly care for his or her children on the basis of a physical problem." The court cited no California case. If the statement attributed to Hunter was an accurate rendition of a California decision, does it make any sense? Wouldn't one of the most important factors in custody be whether a parent were physically capable of caring for the children?

   a. Would it be proper to deny custody to a parent with AIDS?
   b. Would it be proper to deny custody to a parent with a physical addiction to cocaine? Alcohol? Tobacco?
   c. Would it be proper to deny custody to a parent who is a paraplegic? Who is blind? Deaf?

3. Should the trial court judge refuse the offer to present evidence of the physical attributes of a parent seeking custody? How can a judge avoid "overemphasizing" one of the factors?

13.5 PRESUMPTIONS

One way to limit judicial discretion, or at least to subject it to greater scrutiny, is to adopt *presumptions*. For example, California made a statutory presumption that joint custody is in the best interests of the child and provided that, when a party requested reasons for granting or denying joint custody, the court was required to give them; merely stating that it was in the best interests of the child would not suffice.

13.6 MISCONDUCT

The behavior of a parent is a pertinent factor in custody awards. Formerly, the adultery of the mother could cause her to lose custody; a strict moral code was in force, including a double standard censuring extramarital conduct on the part of a wife and mother. Not only was a woman "at fault" with regard to the divorce itself, but the moral code presumed that her conduct would have a bad impact on the children. This sometimes overcame the preference in favor of awarding custody to the mother. More recently, however, sexual misconduct has generally been abandoned as grounds to deny custody unless the father can demonstrate that the mother's sexual behavior has a detrimental impact on the children. The issue continues to be cloudy, however, because judges have very different perceptions of improper sexual conduct and different beliefs about the impact of parental sexuality on children. The conditions of custody and visitation may be quite detailed and specific in the marital settlement agreement and the decree of the court. More often, the issue is raised with regard to sexual behavior following divorce and before the mother's remarriage, as *Parrillo* and *Livesay*, Case Nos. 13-2 and 13-3, demonstrate. In both cases it is apparent that the parents continued to fight after the divorce. What is not clear is whether any of the parents were primarily concerned with custody of the children, or were merely serving their own egos and agendas.

LEGAL TERMS

amicus curiae brief
In some instances, most commonly on appeal to a high court, interested persons or groups may petition the court to submit briefs as a "friend of the court" (*amicus curiae*), and this request is usually granted. Such briefs indicate that the dispute has ramifications extending beyond the parties themselves, as when certain groups are concerned that an unfavorable precedent might be set.

CASE NO. 13-2 No Hanky-Panky

In *Parrillo*, the court takes a narrow view of a mother's sexual freedom. The father is not seeking custody but a limitation on overnight visits by the boyfriend.

PARILLO v. PARILLO
554 A.2d 1043 (R.I. 1989)
Supreme Court of Rhode Island

KELLEHER, Justice.
This Family Court appeal introduces us to Justin and Carla Parrillo, their three minor

children, and Carla's live-in lover, Joseph DiPippo. Justin and Carla Parrillo were divorced by a final judgment of divorce entered in the Family Court in mid-May 1986. At that time their oldest child was thirteen and their youngest was eight. Physical possession of the children was awarded to Carla, with Justin having reasonable visitation rights. In early June 1986 Carla returned to the Family Court, seeking to modify the final judgment by establishing specific times when Justin could exercise his visitation rights at a location away from what had been the marital domicile. Justin responded by filing a motion to modify the final judgment by having Carla restrained from permitting any "unrelated males" to stay overnight at her residence.

The respective motions came on for a hearing before a Family Court justice in late October 1986. Carla told the trial justice that Justin began to harass her once he learned she was dating Joseph. Carla acknowledged that Joseph would remain overnight "[o]nce or twice a week behind closed doors." Carla saw no risk to the children, who were present when Joseph was staying overnight, because, she explained, the daughters slept in separate bedrooms about twenty feet away from her bedroom and the son's bedroom was downstairs. When asked if Joseph wore his pajamas in front of the children, Carla explained that when Joseph stayed overnight, he wore a jogging suit. She explained to the trial justice that the children liked Joseph but that she had no intention of marrying him in the near future.

Justin began to reduce his support payments once he learned that Joseph was making his nocturnal visitations.

With the consent and in the presence of counsel, the trial justice met with the three children in his chambers. All the children said they got along well with Joseph, although the son did say that there were times when he did not like him.

In a bench decision given immediately after the presentation of the evidence, the trial justice stated that the children "appear to be well cared for" and that he could not fault the mother's care of her children. However, he did observe that Joseph's overnight visits, in the presence of the children, were not conducive to their general well-being, at least in terms of their psychological welfare. The trial justice did observe that if Carla married Joseph, he would become the children's stepfather and the cohabitation[1] issue would become moot.

The trial justice directed Carla to refrain from allowing any "unrelated males" to stay overnight at her residence when the children were present.

Carla argues that the trial justice erred when he entered the order because there was no evidence showing that her sexual relationship "with her lover" was not conducive to the psychological well-being of her children. Again, Carla's counsel also emphasizes that when a female custodial parent is otherwise deemed fit and there is an absence of any evidence indicating that her sexual relationship with her companion has had an identifiable adverse effect upon her minor children, the trial justice may not infer that such relationship is not conducive to her children's best interests.

* * *

A small number of courts have held that the sexual misconduct of the custodial parent, while the children are present in the home, is adequate reason to modify the custody decree, even in the absence of any evidence of detrimental effect on the children. However, the vast majority of courts considering the issue decline to adopt this approach and instead consider the parent's misconduct as a factor in determining the best interests of the children.

These courts hold that an award of custody will not be modified absent a showing that the parent's living arrangement has a detrimental effect upon the children.

This court, in *Vieira v. Vieira,* 98 R.I. 454, 204 A.2d 431 (1964), approved a change of custody from the mother to the father because six days after granting the father's petition for a divorce on the grounds of gross misbehavior, the mother and the children spent the night at a New Hampshire motor lodge. Present at the lodge was the male whose association with the mother caused the divorce. This court, in commenting on the trial justice's action, observed "it cannot seriously be questioned that the best interests of these children could no longer be served by continuing their custody in their mother. The harmful effect of her conduct on children of tender years and at impressionable ages cannot be doubted." *Id.* at 458, 204 A.2d at 433.

However, in this dispute no change in custody has been ordered by the Family Court. In entering the order that was without question directed at Joseph, the trial justice, in simple and direct language, ordered the mother to forgo any overnight visitations with Joseph on those occasions when the children are present. We cannot fault the trial justice's actions. Joseph may still visit the marital domicile overnight, with the exception of those times when the children are with their mother. Notwithstanding the views of Carla's appellate counsel to the contrary, we see no great constitutional issue in this controversy.

The mother's appeal is denied and dismissed. The order entered by the Family Court is affirmed.

---

1   In using the term "cohabitation," we are referring to sexual relations.

CASE QUESTION

1. What other reasons could the ex-husband have for seeking limitations on sexual encounters between his ex-wife and her lover?

13.7   MODIFICATION

Custody awards may be modifiable, like alimony and child support, but modification is more difficult to obtain than with alimony and child support, because of the reluctance of judges to switch custody and remove a child from a stable environment. Many states have adopted a provision similar to the UMDA's § 409, which prohibits a modification of custody for two years following a custody order, absent a showing of danger to the child posed by its environment. The most common form of modification attack is one addressed to the sexual misconduct of a custodial mother, the "moral leper" approach used to gain custody at divorce. When the single mother begins to court, the ex-husband may use this to seek custody (and sometimes as a device to negotiate support payments downward). In former times, courts concluded without proof that extramarital sexual encounters by the mother

CAVEAT

Although state appellate courts may take a modern view of the ex-wife's sexual liaisons, trial courts tend to reflect community standards, which still apply a double standard. Mothers are well-advised to exercise considerable discretion to avoid legal battles. Many ex-husbands do not react well to replacement as lover and father.

automatically created an immoral environment for the children. Sensitivity in the courts to the impropriety of a sexual double standard, along with focusing on the welfare of the child rather than the rights of the parents, has reversed this custom. Today a mother's sexuality does not justify modification of custody without a clear showing that the mother's conduct has an effect on the children.

CASE NO. 13-3   Modification

In *Livesay,* the father seeks modification of custody. Dates are significant—divorced in October, suit for modification in November, mother remarries in December, hearing in January. The dates imply that (1) the father is still fighting the divorce battle, and (2) the mother either rushed into marriage or had developed a strong attachment to Mr. Livesay before she was divorced. The mother had a fairly common response to a fairly common custody attack based on cohabitation—she married the boyfriend.

LIVESAY v. HILLEY
190 Ga. App. 655, 379 S.E.2d 557 (1989)
Court of Appeals of Georgia

POPE, Judge.

We granted Tina Hilley Livesay's application to appeal an order of the Superior Court of Madison County changing custody of the parties' three-year-old daughter to the natural father.

The record shows that the parties were divorced on October 7, 1987 and custody of the minor child was awarded to the mother. On November 20, 1987, the father filed a petition seeking a change in custody contending there had been a material change in circumstances affecting the welfare of the child based on the assertion that the mother was living with a man to whom she was not married. Although appellant did not dispute the fact of cohabitation, and admitted that Tommy Livesay began living with her and the minor child in late October, she contended that such relationship was not meretricious because she and Livesay had entered into a common law marriage. The appellant and Livesay were subsequently married in a ceremony held on December 19, 1987.

On January 5, 1988, a hearing was held on appellee-father's change of custody petition. At that hearing appellant presented witnesses who testified that around late October or early November the parties introduced themselves as common-law husband and wife. Appellant testified that she and Livesay did not have a ceremonial marriage when they began living together in October "because we wanted to make sure [the minor child] would adjust before we got into something that she was not ready for or that we were not ready for. . . ."

Following the hearing the superior court entered an order finding that the parties had not entered into a common law marriage when they began cohabiting in late October. The court also found that the minor child had been adversely affected by these living arrangements and transferred custody to the father. The court denied the appellant's motion for new trial and we granted her application for discretionary appeal.

1.   Appellant first enumerates as error the trial court's finding that the ceremonial marriage subsequent to the common-law marriage

precluded the validity of the latter. Although a letter attached to the court's order suggests that it questioned the necessity of such a ceremony in light of the appellant's contention that she was married pursuant to the common law, in its order the court relied not on this factor but on appellant's testimony that she and Livesay wanted to ensure that the child would adjust to having Livesay in the home. Based on this testimony the court found "that at the time [appellant and Tommy Livesay] began living together [they] did not have a present intention to be married, but rather the possibility of marriage in the future based upon whether or not the minor child . . . was comfortable with Mr. Livesay." We agree with the trial court that the evidence, specifically the testimony of the mother, supports the trial court's conclusion that at the time they began living together appellant and Livesay lacked the requisite present intent to marry and hence a valid common-law marriage was not shown. Consequently, this enumeration is without merit.

2. It does not necessarily follow, however, that the trial court correctly concluded that a change of custody was warranted under the facts of this case. "'The award of custody of a child of the parties in a divorce decree is conclusive unless there have been subsequently to the decree new and material changes in the conditions and circumstances *substantially affecting the interest and welfare of the child.* Though the trial judge is given a discretion, he is restricted to the evidence and unauthorized to change the custody where there is no evidence to show new and material conditions that affect the welfare of the child. . . . (Emphasis supplied.)" *Evans v. Stowe,* 181 Ga.App. 489, 491, 352 S.E.2d 811 (1987).

[The court points out the lack of substance of any evidence of harm to the child.]

. . . There being no evidence showing a material change of circumstances or conditions affecting the welfare of the child, the court [abused its discretion] in awarding custody to the [father].

Judgment reversed.

CASE QUESTIONS

1. Does this case help to explain why the UMDA requires a two-year wait before filing a suit for modification?
2. Was the mother penalized for consistently considering the best interests of her child?

13.8 VISITATION

The package of custody rights ordinarily contains provisions for *visitation,* which is the term used to describe the rights of access to the children by the noncustodial parent. Even in cases of joint custody, one parent is usually the physical custodian of the children. Sometimes physical custody can shift, as when the mother has custody for the school year and the father has custody for the summer. Visitation is a delicate subject, because the degree of cooperation between the parents dictates the degree of detail required by the agreement. Ideally, the noncustodial parent will want frequent access to the children and the custodial parent will encourage the maintenance of a parental relationship for the sake of the children; psychological studies suggest this is very important for the emotional well-being of the children. In such cases, the parents can cooperate and the agreement may be primarily useful to settle special disputes, such as access on holidays.

In many instances, continued hostility between the parents may make visitation a painful process. Not only do ex-spouses fight each other through the children, but one, typically the custodial parent, may aim at severing the parental relationship with the other parent. Remarriage commonly makes such situations worse; the new stepparent may give support either for the fight to eliminate the other parent or may want to minimize contact between his or her spouse and the children. For a stepparent, stepchildren represent a continuing need for contact between the ex-spouses and a potential drain on resources.

Denial of visitation rights may be remedied by contempt-of-court proceedings. Bringing such a suit commonly results in an agreement to abide by duties outlined in the separation agreement or the court decree. Interference with visitation has also been used in many states to terminate alimony payments. Many fathers consider that denial of visitation justifies termination of child support payments. Although such a denial might be regarded as a change of circumstance justifying modification of child support, this must be done through the court; a father who fails to pay child support may discover that he is in contempt of court.

13.9 THE NATURAL FATHER

When children are born to unmarried parents, a special set of problems arises. On the one hand, there is no body of law from which to fashion rights

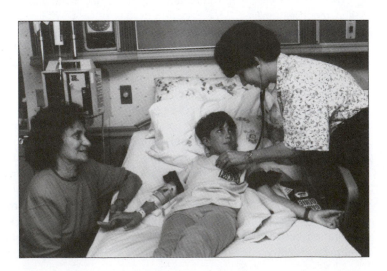

Among the hardest hit by rising health care costs are the children of uninsured parents, many of them single parents. Is this an issue in family law?

of the unofficial family. On the other, the recognition of Fourteenth Amendment equal protection rights has generated a continuing inquiry into discrimination against the relationships within a nonmarital family. As a general rule, we may say that nonmarital relationships should not invoke different treatment. The unwed father should have the same rights as a man married to his child's mother. Although it may pose a moral issue for some, the nonmarital family does not pose a legal quandary when it is an intact family or even when an intact family splits up. In many cases, however, the illegitimate child is the product of a relatively brief relationship, sometimes terminating prior to the child's birth. This may constitute abandonment of a relationship that was never established except biologically.

With the establishment of support obligations on the part of unwed fathers, reciprocal visitation rights would seem essential to those who demand some logic from the law. If both parents have duties, rights should not be reserved solely to the mother. Such a discrimination violates the equal protection clause by discriminating against the unwed father on both sex and marital status grounds. With this in mind, the states have sometimes reluctantly recognized visitation rights on the part of unwed fathers. This has been easiest when a de facto family existed, that is, father, mother, and child lived together for some time as a unit resembling a marital family. The other extreme arises when a father who was absent during pregnancy, birth, and dirty diapers suddenly wants to claim his paternal rights, much to the consternation of the mother. Courts sympathetic to mothers in such situations have reached for concepts like abandonment to prevent intrusion by the father. As with other custody questions, the standard is the best interests of the child, which leaves the nagging question of whether it is better for the child to know its father late than never at all.

CAVEAT

Although it is fairly easy to offer reasons why visitation was impeded ("He showed up drunk to pick up the kids"), it is hard to justify neglecting to pay child support over any lengthy period of time.

DICTA

A careful reading of custody cases often suggests that many cases are decided on social class and lifestyle bias. This is quite apparent in older cases expressing values of the past, particularly the sexual double standard applied against women. Today, bias often creeps in when the court refers to the favorable environment furnished by one parent over the other.

CASE NO. 13-4   Your Lifestyle Is Showing

The *Worden* case provides many clues to the way in which custody questions are decided, combining social values (bias and prejudice included) and law (including "policy"). This is a test of going behind the scenes by reading between the lines. An analysis is offered following the case. See if you can find the hidden clues.

WORDEN v. WORDEN
434 N.W.2d 341 (N.D. 1989)
Supreme Court of North Dakota

VANDE WALLE, Justice.
    Linda Worden appealed from a divorce judgment awarding custody of Elizabeth Ann Thurston (Beth) and Christopher James Worden to James D. Worden. We affirm the award of Christopher's custody to James, reverse the award of Beth's custody to James, and remand for entry of judgment placing Beth in Linda's custody.

James and Linda were married on December 16, 1985. They are the natural parents of Christopher who was born on May 21, 1985. At the time of the marriage Linda's daughter, Beth, born October 1, 1981, was four years old. Robert Jeffrey Murren is Beth's father and, although he does not exercise visitation rights, his present support obligation is $75 per month. James has not adopted Beth.

During the course of James and Linda's marriage, Linda has had primary responsibility for Beth and Christopher's daily care, while James has held various types of employment, including construction work, truck driving, and general farm labor.

The parties separated during July 1987 when James began living with another woman with whom he currently resides. Linda is currently unemployed and relies primarily on public assistance for her source of income. She has had four separate residences since the separation; an apartment that was condemned, a mobile home from which she was evicted for failure to pay rent, and a residence which she shared with eleven other persons, including her children and a boyfriend. Linda now resides alone with her two children in a one-bedroom apartment.

The trial court found that it would be in both children's best interests to be placed in James's custody with reasonable visitation for Linda. The court also found that there existed exceptional circumstances, "namely, the unstable lifestyle of [Linda] and the failure of the [natural] father to visit with his daughter," to warrant placing Beth in James's custody. On appeal Linda asserts that the trial court's award of custody is clearly erroneous.

In a divorce proceeding the trial court must award custody of a minor child based upon a determination of the best interest and welfare of the child. The trial court's custody determination is a finding of fact which will not be set aside on appeal unless it is clearly erroneous.

The trial court specifically found that James has a more stable lifestyle than Linda and that he has the facilities and resources, such as a home, a motor vehicle, and employment, suitable for providing care for minor children. The trial court determined that it would be in Christopher's best interest to be placed in James's custody. We are not left with a definite and firm conviction that the trial court made a mistake in this regard. We conclude, therefore, that the trial court's finding is not clearly erroneous and accordingly we will not disturb the trial court's placement of Christopher in James's custody.

A more complicated legal problem exists regarding Beth's custody. Beth is Linda's natural daughter but is neither James's natural nor adopted child. In addition, James's presence in Beth's life has been short-lived and sporadic. Beth was four years old when Linda and James were married and she was not yet six years old when James and Linda separated.

Parents have the right to the custody and companionship of their children superior to that of any other person. When there is a custody dispute between a natural parent and a third party the test is whether or not there are exceptional circumstances which require that in the best interest of the child, the child be placed in the custody of the third party rather than with the biological parent. The court cannot award custody to a third party, rather than the natural parent, under a "best interest of the child" test unless it first determines that "exceptional circumstances" exist to trigger the best-interest analysis. Absent exceptional circumstances the natural parent is entitled to custody of the child even though the third party may be able to offer more amenities.

In this case the trial court found that the mother's unstable lifestyle and the natural father's failure to visit Beth constituted exceptional circumstances.

This court has not attempted to narrowly define or circumscribe the exceptional circumstances which must exist to permit a court to consider placing custody of a minor child with a third party rather than the natural parent. However, each case in which such a placement has been upheld by this court has involved a child who has been in the actual physical custody of the third party for a sufficient period of time to develop a psychological parent relationship with that third party. No such circumstances exist in this case.

Prior to these proceedings, Beth has spent her entire life, with minor exceptions, in Linda's custody and care. There is no evidence that Beth has formed a psychological parent relationship with James or any other third party. We conclude, therefore, that the trial court's finding of exceptional circumstances to place Beth in James's custody rather than with Linda is clearly erroneous.

We are aware that the decision we make today results in a split-custody arrangement with Beth in Linda's custody and her half-brother, Christopher, in James's custody. Although there was testimony that Beth and Christopher get along well, there was no evidence in the record that serious detriment would occur to either by placing them in separate homes. Whether the need to place siblings in the same household could ever, in itself, constitute exceptional circumstances which would justify custody placement in a third party rather than with a natural parent is a question we need not resolve. In this case there is simply no evidence to show that a split-custody arrangement is not in the children's best interests.

Where a natural parent's fitness to provide a minimal standard of adequate care for a child is at issue, proceedings under the Uniform Juvenile Court Act, Chapter 27-20, N.D.C.C., are available to protect and safeguard the interests of both parent and child. If Linda's "unstable lifestyle" to which the trial court refers is serious enough to raise an issue of child deprivation, appropriate proceedings can be commenced under Chapter 27-20, N.D.C.C. It is improper to deprive Linda of Beth's custody on the ground of unfitness in these proceedings, because parental fitness is not the appropriate test.

We affirm Christopher's custody placement with James, reverse Beth's custody placement with James, and remand for entry of judgment placing Beth in Linda's custody.

CASE ANALYSIS

Blackletter law:

1. Custody is awarded based on the best interests of the child.
2. Parents have a right to custody as against third parties.
3. In order for a third party to gain custody from a natural parent, exceptional circumstances must be shown.
4. A stepfather who is neither the biological father nor the adoptive father of a child must be treated as any other third party with regard to the preceding rules.
5. A third party proven to be a psychological parent might obtain custody under the best interests standard.
6. Although there is a strong policy against splitting the custody of siblings, this policy does not override the disability of a third party.

The rules enumerated here explain why the court could not give James custody, although it very much disapproved of Linda. We know it disapproved of Linda because of the gratuitous statements about her living arrangements, not to mention her propensity for getting pregnant while unmarried. All this apparently persuaded the trial judge that James should have custody of his stepdaughter. The supreme court, however, saw no right in James to such an arrangement and suggested the alternative of administrative action under the Uniform Juvenile Court Act if Beth were subject to deprivation.

CASE QUESTIONS

1. Do James and Linda seem like the kind of people who would hire a parade of psychiatrists and psychologists to prove or disprove that James was a "psychological parent"?
2. What did the court mean by "It is improper to deprive Linda of Beth's custody on the ground of unfitness in these proceedings, because parental fitness is not the appropriate test"?

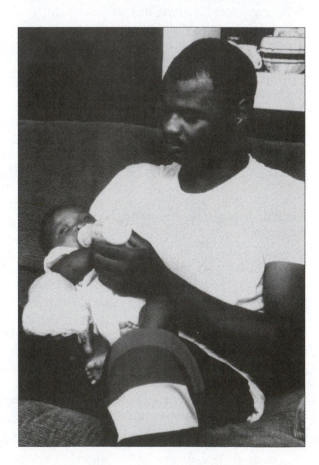

Traditional stereotypes declared the mother to be the nurturing parent, but social change has allowed and encouraged fathers to perform many of the tasks formerly the exclusive domain of the women of the family. Should the law favor the mother as the custodian of children after divorce?

13.10 RIGHTS OF NONPARENTS (THIRD PARTIES) TO CUSTODY

The best interests of the child analysis breaks down somewhat when we are confronted with a custody battle between a parent and a third party. Typically these arise when someone other than a natural parent (e.g., grandparents, foster parents, stepparents), have served as caregivers for the children. Usually the contest is between the father and the third party, as the father is more often the noncustodial parent after divorce or in a nonmarital situation. If the mother dies or is incapacitated, a change in custody may be necessary.

Traditionally, the law recognized parents' rights to custody over others. A child in the custody of its divorced mother would automatically go to its father upon the death of the mother. Today, although the rights of natural parents have first priority, the court may choose to award custody to a third party if such a situation is clearly (according to the court) in the best interests of the child.

CASE NO. 13-5 Dad versus the Grandparents

Harold Painter's wife and daughter died in a car crash in 1962. Harold had difficulty raising his son Mark and asked his deceased wife's parents, the Bannisters, to take Mark in 1963. When Harold remarried in November 1964, he asked for Mark to return, but the Bannisters refused, and a custody battle ensued. In assessing Mark's best interests, the court ruled in favor of the Bannisters. The following excerpts reveal the court's social class and lifestyle preferences.

PAINTER v. BANNISTER
258 Iowa 1390, 140 N.W.2d 152 (1966)
Supreme Court of Iowa

Stuart, Justice.

* * *

The Bannister home provides Mark with a stable, dependable, conventional, middleclass, middlewest background and an opportunity for a college education and profession, if he desires it. It provides a solid foundation and secure atmosphere. In the Painter home, Mark would have more freedom of conduct and thought with an opportunity to develop his individual talents. It would be more exciting and challenging in many respects, but romantic, impractical and unstable. . . .

Our conclusion as to the type of home Mr. Painter would offer is based upon his Bohemian approach to finances and life in general. . . . His main ambition is to be a free lance writer and photographer. . . . In the 10 years since he left college, he has changed jobs seven times.

* * *

The psychiatrist classifies him as "a romantic and somewhat of a dreamer" . . . .

* * *

Mr. Painter is either an agnostic or atheist and has no concern for formal religious training. . . .

He is a political liberal and got into difficulty in a job at the University of Washington for his support of the activities of the American Civil Liberties Union in the university news bulletin.

* * *

These matters are not related as a criticism of Mr. Painter's conduct, way of life or sense of values. An individual is free to choose his own values, within bounds, which are not exceeded here. They do serve however to support our conclusion as to the kind of life Mark would be exposed to in the Painter household. We believe it would be unstable, unconventional, arty, Bohemian, and probably intellectually stimulating.

[The court then goes on to explain why it credits the psychiatrist's testimony favoring the Bannisters despite the trial court's criticisms. The trial court's award of custody to the father was reversed. *Sequel:* Mark was allowed to visit his father in California. His wish to live with his father was then honored by his grandparents and Harold was awarded custody in 1968 by a California court. The court's disparaging comments about Harold's freelance writing prospects were disproved by Harold's book, *Mark, I Love You,* published in 1969.]

13.11   UNIFORM CHILD CUSTODY JURISDICTION ACT

It should be clear by now that the outcome of custody disputes could be radically different in different states. In the past, a parent could grab the children, run to another state, and thwart the other parent's custodial rights not only by hiding but also by making the recovery of the children dependent on a cumbersome process in which state jurisdiction became a legal issue of considerable complexity. The Uniform Child Custody Jurisdiction Act (UCCJA) (see appendix 13A) was proposed to ameliorate this situation, discourage child snatching, and provide a uniform basis for jurisdiction that could be applied reciprocally by the states. In 1983, Massachusetts became the 50th state to adopt the UCCJA. (See figure 13-1.)

Although the full faith and credit clause of the U.S. Constitution requires each state to recognize the judicial acts of other states, a major exception has been based on challenges to the jurisdiction of the state making the original order. The UCCJA attempts to minimize such challenges, or at least encourage their prompt and uniform disposition, by spelling out the bases for jurisdiction.

The UCCJA resolves three problems that arose in the past. First, jurisdiction was commonly premised on the physical whereabouts of the child, which encouraged child snatching and interstate flight, as well as forum-shopping. Second, parents often attempted to undo custody orders by seeking modification in another state. Although full faith and credit applied to the original order, this did not prevent another state from assuming jurisdiction for the sake of modification. Third, the Act promotes swift enforcement of the custody orders of other states.

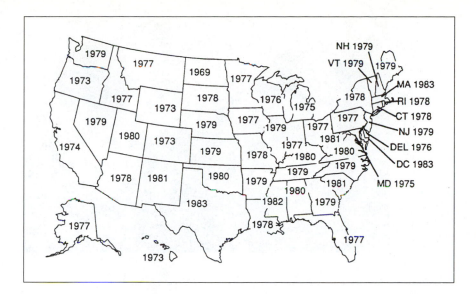

FIGURE 13-1
Date of effect of
UCCJA in adopting
states

The heart of the UCCJA is the determination of jurisdiction over child custody. Three grounds for jurisdiction form the basic jurisdictional requirements of the UCCJA. First, the Act defines the *home state* of the child as the state in which the child has lived with its parent for at least six consecutive months ending no later than six months before the commencement of the action. Even if the child is removed from the state, it remains the home state if it meets these criteria and one parent continues to reside there. This effectively prevents a child-snatching parent from changing jurisdiction in most instances. Of course, it is incumbent upon the other parent to bring an action within six months after removal of the child.

Second, jurisdiction may lie in the state with the most significant contacts with the child. There are many instances in which a child has important ties to a place, friends, school, relatives, and the like, so that it is clear that this place was the natural home in the past and is likely to be for the future, despite the child's present location.

Third, a state may assume jurisdiction even when the home state and significant contacts provisions do not apply, if the child is physically present and is abandoned, abused, or dependent. See UCCJA § 3, reproduced in appendix 13A.

13.12 PARENTAL KIDNAPPING PREVENTION ACT

The Parental Kidnapping Prevention Act (PKPA) was the congressional response to the child-snatching problem. The Act provides specifics for the full faith and credit that must be accorded to custody decrees of other states, that is, it tells when a decree must be enforced. It provides criteria for

In the modern family, sibling bonds are often a primary factor in a child's security. The law has always shown a strong preference for keeping children together in the aftermath of divorce.

jurisdiction very similar to those in the UCCJA. If the criteria are met, a sister state cannot modify the resulting decree. This means that the state originally exercising jurisdiction in accordance with the PKPA criteria will retain jurisdiction. Jurisdiction may shift only when neither the child nor any party claiming custody rights resides in that state. The PKPA confers jurisdiction on the federal courts over disputes that would not have been considered within their jurisdiction in the past.

The federal government also entered this domain by expanding the Federal Parent Locator Service from its original mission (to aid in child-support cases) to cover child-snatching situations.

In 1988, the Hague Convention on the Civil Aspects of International Child Abduction became effective in the United States, along with Canada, Australia, and several European countries. The object of the Convention was to deter international child snatching by returning the child to his or her country of residence. It does not otherwise propose to adjudicate the disputes.

SUMMARY

Child custody disputes tend to be the most emotionally charged problems that lawyers face. The drama of the situation and the emotions of the parties create this atmosphere, but child custody questions also have unique features and legal problems. Ultimately the lawyers must negotiate, or the judge decide, how the parent-child relationship will be structured in the future. The children have relatively little say in the matter and the principles that apply provide considerable discretion for the judge. Preference as to the parental custodian has changed from father to mother to both. The states vary significantly on the principles that guide their decisions and the preferred form of custody. Gender-neutral language is found in the cases and the statutes, but the mother is the overwhelming choice as custodian, both when custody is negotiated in lawyers' offices and when it is fought in court.

Fault returns when custody of children is at stake. Fathers desiring custody will attempt to totally discredit mothers. Mothers frequently retaliate in kind, making this kind of battle very nasty.

The problem of child snatching and moving to another jurisdiction has been remedied in large part by all states' adoption of the Uniform Child Custody Jurisdiction Act, which provides the grounds for jurisdiction and discourages would-be forum-shoppers. The federal government has entered the fray with the Parental Kidnapping Prevention Act, which parallels the UCCJA and removes much of the incentive for interstate child snatching.

QUESTIONS

1. Referring to UMDA § 402, can we apply the guidelines for awarding custody to an unwed father? (Consider children born from a *de facto* family relationship and those born as a result of "one-night stands.")

2. How do the Kentucky and Massachusetts additions to UMDA § 402 apply to nonmarital partners?

3. What is the tender years doctrine and what is its current status?

4. What is the difference between shared, joint, split, and alternating custody?

5. To what extent is the physical health of a parent a factor in awarding custody?

6. What are the priorities with regard to custody rights based on relationship to a child?

7. What is the purpose of the Uniform Child Custody Jurisdiction Act?

8. What federal act is aimed at deterring child snatching?

9. What are the principal differences in nature between domestic relations actions and other kinds of lawsuits?

10. The law traditionally questioned a mother's fitness when she had been an adulteress. Today the appropriate issue is whether the mother's conduct is detrimental to the child. But what about other forms of sexual misconduct? Consider the following:

    On September 6, 1992, the *Gainesville (Fla.) Sun,* published a release from the Associated Press about a circuit court in Sanford, Florida facing a custody case in which the father was seeking custody of his son, who was in the custody of his ex-wife. The father "feels more comfortable as a woman" and wants his son to call him "mom." Apparently the son approves the metamorphosis and wants to live with Dad: "She [the father] is more comfortable, and she still cares about me. I want to live with her. I love her like a mom." According to the account, the court ruled against the father on the grounds that sufficient change of circumstance had not been shown and the best interests of the child favored retention of custody by the mother, although the father's sexual identity seems not to have played a significant part.

The report was based on an interview conducted by the Orlando *Sentinel,* which did not release the names of the parties in order to protect the son. It reported that the father had not undergone a sex-change operation.

Query: If a father chooses to undergo a sex-change operation—a so-called sexual reassignment—and a court reclassifies him as female, as some courts have been willing to do, would he (she?) stand on the same footing as the birth mother for application of the tender years doctrine? If a homosexual can get custody, why not a transsexual?

EXERCISES

Find the statutory provision in your state for child custody and compare it to UMDA § 402.

Answer the questions according to the law of your state.

1. Does the statute provide specific guidelines?
2. Does it add to or subtract from UMDA § 402?
3. May race be used as a factor in the award of custody? 10 A.L.R. 4th 796.
4. Does your state permit split, divided, or alternate custody? 92 A.L.R. 2d 695.
5. Does a custodial parent's sexual conduct justify modification of custody? 100 A.L.R.3d 625.
6. Can the physical capacity of a parent be considered in your state in awarding custody? 3 A.L.R.4th 1044.
7. Does your state follow the lead of the UMDA in requiring a waiting period following the divorce before a petition for modification can be brought?
8. Can a change in financial conditions serve as grounds for modification? 89 A.L.R.2d 7.
9. What are the respective custodial rights of a stepparent versus a non-resident natural parent? 10 A.L.R.4th 767.
10. How does a parent's mental health affect the award of custody? 74 A.L.R.2d 1073.

APPENDIX 13A

Uniform Child Custody Jurisdiction Act (1968)

§ 1. Purposes of Act; Construction of Provisions.

(a) The general purposes[1] of this Act are to:

(1) avoid jurisdictional competition and conflict with courts of other states in matters of child custody which have in the past resulted in the shifting of children from state to state with harmful effects on their well-being;

(2) promote cooperation with the courts of other states to the end that a custody decree is rendered in that state which can best decide the case in the interest of the child;

(3) assure that litigation concerning the custody of a child take place ordinarily in the state with which the child and his family have the closest connection and where significant evidence concerning his care, protection, training, and personal relationships is most readily available, and that courts of this state decline the exercise of jurisdiction when the child and his family have a closer connection with another state;

(4) discourage continuing controversies over child custody in the interest of greater stability of home environment and of secure family relationships for the child;

(5) deter abductions and other unilateral removals of children undertaken to obtain custody awards;

(6) avoid re-litigation of custody decisions of other states in this state insofar as feasible;

(7) facilitate the enforcement of custody decrees of other states;

(8) promote and expand the exchange of information and other forms of mutual assistance between the courts of this state and those of other states concerned with the same child; and

(9) make uniform the law of those states which enact it.

(b) This Act shall be construed to promote the general purposes stated in this section.

§ 2. Definitions.

As used in this Act:

(1) "contestant" means a person, including a parent, who claims a right to custody or visitation rights with respect to a child;

(2) "custody determination" means a court decision and court orders and instructions providing for the custody of a child, including visitation rights; it does not include a decision relating to child support or any other monetary obligation of any person;

(3) "custody proceeding" includes proceedings in which a custody determination is one of several issues, such as an action for divorce or separation, and includes child neglect and dependency proceedings;

(4) "decree" or "custody decree" means a custody determination contained in a judicial decree or order made in a custody proceeding, and includes an initial decree and a modification decree;

(5) "home state" means the state in which the child immediately preceding the time involved lived with his parents, a parent, or a person acting as parent, for at least 6 consecutive months, and in the case of a child less than 6 months old the state in which the child lived from birth with any of the persons mentioned. Periods of temporary absence of any of the named persons are counted as part of the 6-month or other period;

(6) "initial decree" means the first custody decree concerning a particular child;

(7) "modification decree" means a custody decree which modifies or replaces a prior decree, whether made by the court which rendered the prior decree or by another court;

(8) "physical custody" means actual possession and control of a child;

(9) "person acting as parent" means a person, other than a parent, who has physical custody of a child and who has either been awarded custody by a court or claims a right to custody; and

(10) "state" means any state, territory, or possession of the United States, the Commonwealth of Puerto Rico, and the District of Columbia.

§ 3. Jurisdiction.

(a) A court of this State which is competent to decide child custody matters has jurisdiction to make a child custody determination by initial or modification decree if:[2]

(1) this State

(i) is the home state of the child at the time of commencement of the proceeding, or

(ii) had been the child's home state within 6 months before commencement of the proceeding and the child is absent from this State because of his removal or retention by a person claiming his custody or for other reasons, and a parent or person acting as parent continues to live in this State; or

(2) it is in the best interest of the child that a court of this State assume jurisdiction because

(i) the child and his parents, or the child and at least one contestant, have a significant connection with this State, and

(ii) there is available in this State substantial evidence concerning the child's present or future care, protection, training, and personal relationships; or

(3) the child is physically present in this State and

(i) the child has been abandoned or

(ii) it is necessary in an emergency to protect the child because he has been subjected to or threatened with mistreatment or abuse or is otherwise neglected or dependent; or

(4)(i) it appears that no other state would have jurisdiction under prerequisites substantially in accordance with paragraphs (1), (2), or (3), or another state has declined to exercise jurisdiction on the ground that this State is the more appropriate forum to determine the custody of the child, and

(ii) it is in the best interest of the child that this court assume jurisdiction.

(b) Except under paragraphs (3) and (4) of subsection (a), physical presence[3] in this State of the child, or of the child and one of the contestants, is not alone sufficient to confer jurisdiction on a court of this State to make a child custody determination.

(c) Physical presence of the child, while desirable, is not a prerequisite for jurisdiction to determine his custody.

§ 4. Notice and Opportunity to be Heard.

Before making a decree under this Act, reasonable notice and opportunity to be heard shall be given to the contestants, any parent whose parental rights have not been previously terminated, and any person who has physical custody of the child. If any of these persons is outside this State, notice and opportunity to be heard shall be given pursuant to section 5.

§ 5. Notice to Persons Outside this State;
Submission to Jurisdiction.

(a) Notice required for the exercise of jurisdiction over a person outside this State shall be given in a manner reasonably calculated to give actual notice, and may be:

(1) by personal delivery outside this State in the manner prescribed for service of process within this State;

(2) in the manner prescribed by the law of the place in which the service is made for service of process in that place in an action in any of its courts of general jurisdiction;

(3) by any form of mail addressed to the person to be served and requesting a receipt; or

(4) as directed by the court including publication, if other means of notification are ineffective.

(b) Notice under this section shall be served, mailed, or delivered, or last published [at least 10, 20] days before any hearing in this State.

(c) Proof of service outside this State may be made by affidavit of the individual who made the service, or in the manner prescribed by the law of this State, the order pursuant to which the service is made, or the law of the place in which the service is made. If service is made by mail, proof may be a receipt signed by the addressee or other evidence of delivery to the addressee.

(d) Notice is not required if a person submits to the jurisdiction of the court.

§ 6. Simultaneous Proceedings in Other States.[4]

(a) A court of this State shall not exercise its jurisdiction under this Act if at the time of filing the petition a proceeding concerning the custody of the child was pending in a court of another state exercising jurisdiction substantially in conformity with this Act, unless the proceeding is stayed by the court of the other state because this State is a more appropriate forum or for other reasons.

(b) Before hearing the petition in a custody proceeding the court shall examine the pleadings and other information supplied by the parties under section 9 and shall consult the child custody registry established under section 16 concerning the pendency of proceedings with respect to the child in other states. If the court has reason to believe that proceedings may be pending in another state it shall direct an inquiry to the state court administrator or other appropriate official of the other state.

(c) If the court is informed during the course of the proceeding that a proceeding concerning the custody of the child was pending in another state before the court assumed jurisdiction it shall stay the proceeding and communicate with the court in which the other proceeding is pending to the end that the issue may be litigated in the more appropriate forum and that information be exchanged in accordance with sections 19 through 22. If a court of this State has made a custody decree before being informed of a pending proceeding in a court of another state it shall immediately inform that court of the fact. If the court is informed that a proceeding was commenced in another state after it assumed jurisdiction it shall likewise inform the other court to the end that the issues may be litigated in the more appropriate forum.

§ 7. Inconvenient Forum.[5]

(a) A court which has jurisdiction under this Act to make an initial or modification decree may decline to exercise its jurisdiction any time before making a decree if it finds that it is an inconvenient forum to make a custody determination under the circumstances of the case and that a court of another state is a more appropriate forum.

(b) A finding of inconvenient forum may be made upon the court's own motion or upon motion of a party or a guardian ad litem or other representative of the child.

(c) In determining if it is an inconvenient forum, the court shall consider if it is in the interest of the child that another state assume jurisdiction. For this purpose it may take into account the following factors, among others:

(1) if another state is or recently was the child's home state;

(2) if another state has a closer connection with the child and his family or with the child and one or more of the contestants;

(3) if substantial evidence concerning the child's present or future care, protection, training, and personal relationships is more readily available in another state;

(4) if the parties have agreed on another forum which is no less appropriate; and

(5) if the exercise of jurisdiction by a court of this state would contravene any of the purposes stated in section 1.

(d) Before determining whether to decline or retain jurisdiction the court may communicate with a court of another state and exchange information pertinent to the assumption of jurisdiction by either court with a view to assuring that jurisdiction will be exercised by the more appropriate court and that a forum will be available to the parties.

(e) If the court finds that it is an inconvenient forum and that a court of another state is a more appropriate forum, it may dismiss the proceedings, or it may stay the proceedings upon condition that a custody proceeding be promptly commenced in another named state or upon any other conditions which may be just and proper, including the condition that a moving party stipulate his consent and submission to the jurisdiction of the other forum.

(f) The court may decline to exercise its jurisdiction under this Act if a custody determination is incidental to an action for divorce or another proceeding while retaining jurisdiction over the divorce or other proceeding.

(g) If it appears to the court that it is clearly an inappropriate forum it may require the party who commenced the proceedings to pay, in addition to the costs of the proceedings in this State, necessary travel and other expenses, including attorneys' fees, incurred by other parties or their witnesses. Payment is to be made to the clerk of the court for remittance to the proper party.

(h) Upon dismissal or stay of proceedings under this section the court shall inform the court found to be the more appropriate forum of this fact or, if the court which would have jurisdiction in the other state is not certainly known, shall transmit the information to the court administrator or other appropriate official for forwarding to the appropriate court.

(i) Any communication received from another state informing this State of a finding of inconvenient forum because a court of this State is the more appropriate forum shall be filed in the custody registry of the appropriate court. Upon assuming jurisdiction the court of this State shall inform the original court of this fact.

§ 8. Jurisdiction Declined by Reason of Conduct.

(a) If the petitioner for an initial decree has wrongfully taken the child from another state or has engaged in similar reprehensible conduct the court may decline to exercise jurisdiction if this is just and proper under the circumstances.

(b) Unless required in the interest of the child, the court shall not exercise its jurisdiction to modify a custody decree of another state if the petitioner, without consent of the person entitled to custody, has improperly removed the child from the physical custody of the person entitled to custody or has improperly retained the child after a visit or other temporary relinquishment of physical custody. If the petitioner has violated any other provision of a custody decree of another state the court may decline to exercise its jurisdiction if this is just and proper under the circumstances.

(c) In appropriate cases a court dismissing a petition under this section may charge the petitioner with necessary travel and other expenses, including attorneys' fees, incurred by other parties or their witnesses.

§ 9. Information under Oath to be Submitted to the Court.

(a) Every party in a custody proceeding in his first pleading or in an affidavit attached to that pleading shall give information under oath as to the child's present address, the places where the child has lived within the last 5 years, and the names and present addresses of the persons with whom the child has lived during that period. In this pleading or affidavit every party shall further declare under oath whether:

(1) he has participated (as a party, witness, or in any other capacity) in any other litigation concerning the custody of the same child in this or any other state;

(2) he has information of any custody proceeding concerning the child pending in a court of this or any other state; and

(3) he knows of any person not a party to the proceedings who has physical custody of the child or claims to have custody or visitation rights with respect to the child.

(b) If the declaration as to any of the above items is in the affirmative the declarant shall give additional information under oath as required by the court. The court may examine the parties under oath as to details of the information furnished and as to other matters pertinent to the court's jurisdiction and the disposition of the case.

(c) Each party has a continuing duty to inform the court of any custody proceeding concerning the child in this or any other state of which he obtained information during this proceeding.

§ 10. Additional Parties.

If the court learns from information furnished by the parties pursuant to section 9 or from other sources that a person not a party to the custody proceeding has physical custody of the child or claims to have custody or visitation rights with respect to the child, it shall order that person to be joined as a party and to be duly notified of the pendency of the proceeding and of his joinder as a party. If the person joined as a party is outside this State he shall be served with process or otherwise notified in accordance with section 5.

§ 11. Appearance of Parties and the Child.

(a) The court may order any party to the proceeding who is in this State to appear personally before the court. If that party has physical custody of the child the court may order that he appear personally with the child.

(b) If a party to the proceeding whose presence is desired by the court is outside this State with or without the child the court may order that the notice given under section 5 include a statement directing that party to appear personally with or without the child and declaring that failure to appear may result in a decision adverse to that party.

(c) If a party to the proceeding who is outside this State is directed to appear under subsection (b) or desires to appear personally before the court with or without the child, the court may require another party to pay to the clerk of the court travel and other necessary expenses of the party so appearing and of the child if this is just and proper under the circumstances.

§ 12. Binding Force and Res Judicata Effect of Custody Decree.

A custody decree rendered by a court of this State which had jurisdiction under section 3 binds all parties who have been served in this State or notified in accordance with section 5 or who have submitted to the jurisdiction of the court, and who have been given an opportunity to be heard. As to these parties the custody decree is conclusive as to all issues of law and fact decided and as to the custody determination made unless and until that determination is modified pursuant to law, including the provisions of this Act.

§ 13. Recognition of Out-of-State Custody Decrees.

The courts of this State shall recognize and enforce an initial or modification decree of a court of another state which had assumed jurisdiction under statutory provisions substantially in accordance with this Act or which was made under factual circumstances meeting the jurisdictional standards of the Act, so long as this decree has not been modified in accordance with jurisdictional standards substantially similar to those of this Act.

§ 14. Modification of Custody Decree of Another State.

(a) If a court of another state has made a custody decree, a court of this State shall not modify that decree unless (1) it appears to the court of this State that the court which rendered the decree does not now have jurisdiction under jurisdictional prerequisites substantially in accordance with this Act or has declined to assume jurisdiction to modify the decree and (2) the court of this State has jurisdiction.

(b) If a court of this State is authorized under subsection (a) and section 8 to modify a custody decree of another state it shall give due consideration to the transcript of the record and other documents of all previous proceedings submitted to it in accordance with section 22.

§ 15. Filing and Enforcement of Custody Decree of Another State.

(a) A certified copy of a custody decree of another state may be filed in the office of the clerk of any [district court, family court] of this State. The clerk shall treat the decree in the same manner as a custody decree of the [district court, family court] of this State. A custody decree so filed has the same effect and shall be enforced in like manner as a custody decree rendered by a court of this State.

(b) A person violating a custody decree of another state which makes it necessary to enforce the decree in this State may be required to pay necessary travel and other expenses, including attorneys' fees, incurred by the party entitled to the custody or his witnesses.

§ 16. Registry of Out-of-State Custody Decrees and Proceedings.

The clerk of each [district court, family court] shall maintain a registry in which he shall enter the following:

(1) certified copies of custody decrees of other states received for filing;

(2) communications as to the pendency of custody proceedings in other states;

(3) communications concerning a finding of inconvenient forum by a court of another state; and

(4) other communications or documents concerning custody proceedings in another state which may affect the jurisdiction of a court of this State or the disposition to be made by it in a custody proceeding.

§ 17. Certified Copies of Custody Decree.

The Clerk of the [district court, family court] of this State, at the request of the court of another state or at the request of any person who is affected by or has a legitimate interest in a custody decree, shall certify and forward a copy of the decree to that court or person.

§ 18. Taking Testimony in Another State.

In addition to other procedural devices available to a party, any party to the proceeding or a guardian ad litem or other representative of the child may adduce testimony of witnesses, including parties and the child, by deposition or otherwise, in another state. The court on its own motion may direct that the testimony of a person be taken in another state and may prescribe the manner in which and the terms upon which the testimony shall be taken.

§ 19. Hearings and Studies in Another State; Orders to Appear.

(a) A court of this State may request the appropriate court of another state to hold a hearing to adduce evidence, to order a party to produce or give evidence under other procedures of that state, or to have social studies made with respect to the custody of a child involved in proceedings pending in the court of this State; and to forward to the court of this State certified copies of the transcript of the record of the hearing, the evidence otherwise adduced, or any social studies prepared in compliance with the request. The cost of the services may be assessed against the parties or, if necessary, ordered paid by the [County] State.

(b) A court of this State may request the appropriate court of another state to order a party to custody proceedings pending in the court of this State to appear in the proceedings, and if that party has physical custody of the child, to appear with the child. The request may state that travel and other necessary expenses of the party and of the child whose appearance is desired will be assessed against another party or will otherwise be paid.

* * *

§ 26. Short Title.

This Act may be cited as the Uniform Child Custody Jurisdiction Act.

---

1 The "purposes" listed form a general indictment of the morass of jurisdictional problems encountered prior to acceptance of the UCCJA. They also describe the abuses of that confusion by determined parents. Shining through the list is a determined effort to resolve jurisdictional problems in ways least detrimental to the children involved.

2 Paragraph (a) describes the criteria for determining whether a state should assume jurisdiction over a custody dispute when asked to do so. A careful reading of the provisions reveals that a broad range of discretion may be exercised, but the criteria are sufficiently clear in their intent to present firm guidelines in the exercise of that discretion. As long as the courts of each state respect each other, the UCCJA should be evenhanded and fair in its execution.

3 Paragraphs (b) and (c) present a departure from the usual basis for jurisdiction—physical presence within the state—in response to past attempts by parents to escape from the control of one jurisdiction by invoking another. Abduction and hiding continue to be a threat to the orderly resolution of custody disputes, but the UCCJA has furnished the means to minimize manipulation of different jurisdictions.

4 This section covers the problems arising from parties initiating suits in different states. Note the advantage accorded to the state of the earliest filing.

5 In this section, the Act formalizes the criteria to be used for inconvenient forum, a traditional challenge to the appropriateness of venue (the place where jurisdiction should be exercised).

CHAPTER 14
Issues in Child Custody

Three Views Through the Years

We are informed by the first elementary books we read, that all authority of the father is superior to that of the mother. It is the doctrine of all civilized nations. It is according to the revealed law and the law of nature, and it prevails even with the wandering savage, who has received none of the lights of civilization.

> — Chief Justice Sharkey, *Foster v. Alston,* 7 Miss. (6 How.) 405, 463 (1842)

[A] court of common law will not go so far as to hold nature in contempt, and snatch helpless, puling infancy from the bosom of an affectionate mother, and place it in the coarse hands of the father. The mother is the softest and safest nurse of infancy, and with her it will be left in opposition to this general right of the father.

> — *Helms v. Franciscus,* 2 Bland Ch. (Md.) 544 (1830)

Nor is the child's best interest controlled alone by comparing the depth of love and affection between the child and those who vie for its custody. Instead, in ascertaining the child's best interest, the court is guided by principles which reflect "considered social judgments in this society respecting the family and parenthood."

> — Chief Judge Breitel, *Bennett v. Jeffreys,* 387 N.Y.S.2d 821 (1976)

Issues in this chapter should generate substantial discussion.

If you've never been hated by your child, you've never been a parent.

Bette Davis

OUTLINE

14.1 INTRODUCTION
14.2 JOINT CUSTODY
    Mayer v. Mayer
    Beck v. Beck
14.3 PRIMARY CAREGIVER RULE
    David M. v. Margaret M.

14.1 INTRODUCTION

Family law is in flux because the American family is in flux and our values concerning the family are in flux. Child custody may present the extreme of uncertainty in family law, for the many reasons enumerated in the beginning of the last chapter. Chapter 13 presented many of the dominant rules applying to child custody, disguising the indeterminacy of the very rules presented. In many jurisdictions, the judge has nearly absolute discretion over awarding custody as long as the justification presents plausible reasons grounded in policy stated as law. We live in a time when the law in most jurisdictions pretends to be gender-neutral with regard to custody, yet most scholars and practitioners agree that about 90 percent of the contested custody cases result in the mother gaining custody and about the same percentage results from custody by mutual, albeit often strained or reluctant, agreement.

This chapter raises many questions and offers some answers that seem inherently flawed. There is considerable consensus concerning custody decisions—they should be made in the "best interests of the children." This polestar of family law has proven a very difficult point from which to navigate, however. The decision requires a degree of clairvoyance that judges do not

381

profess to possess. Should judges then turn to psychiatrists and psychologists to look into their crystal balls?

The cases presented in this chapter should challenge the reader's thoughts and emotions. In contrast to other chapters, annotations are interposed in the text, rather than following at the ends of the cases. "Queries" are questions meant to provoke the reader or challenge statements or conclusions in the text. "N.B." stands for *nota bene,* or "note well," a comment pertinent to the accompanying text.

14.2 JOINT CUSTODY

The first two cases in this chapter mark New Jersey's foray into joint custody. The first case acknowledges the equity court's authority to order joint custody under appropriate circumstances. Four years later, *Beck* adopts a judicial preference for joint custody, rejecting the adoption of a presumption in favor of joint custody. The distinction between a preference and a presumption is significant because a presumption places a much higher burden of persuasion on a party seeking sole custody. The judiciary usually reserves presumptions for questions about which public policy is clear and uncontroverted, such as the presumptions of legitimacy or the validity of marriage. In 1981, joint custody was not so well accepted that a presumption was appropriate.

Mayer and *Beck* are informative because of their lengthy discussions of the advisability of joint custody. All three of the cases reported in this chapter are remarkable for their citation of secondary sources. Because they are carving out new ground, they cannot rely on precedent from their own jurisdictions or a consensus from other states that would allow a narrower analysis of statutes and judicial decisions.

MAYER v. MAYER
150 N.J. Super. 556, 376 A.2d 214 (1977)
Superior Court of New Jersey,
Chancery Division

DUFFY, J. S. C.

[Plaintiff wife and defendant husband married in 1962 and separated on December 1, 1973. Plaintiff wife filed for divorce June 5, 1975, based on 18 months' separation. The parties were divorced November 23, 1976. Two children, Dana, 13 years old, and William, 11, were in the custody of wife. Husband was a New Jersey attorney but was also active in developing real estate.

Wife had recently had an operation for cancer and was under continuing medical and psychiatric care. She was a licensed real estate sales agent and was affiliated with a local agency, but she had not had a significant income from those efforts.

The court awarded the plaintiff the marital residence and certain personal property by way of equitable distribution, with the plaintiff to be solely responsible for the mortgage, taxes, and upkeep of the home. The court also fixed the amounts of alimony and child support the defendant was to pay the plaintiff; he was to provide a policy insuring his life in an amount of at least $50,000, naming the children as irrevocable beneficiaries, to be maintained until the younger shall have become emancipated, as well as health and medical insurance for them, including major medical coverage, to be maintained until each was emancipated. In addition, he was responsible for any extraordinary medical expenses incurred by the plaintiff for the treatment of her cancer.

The court suggested joint custody because of the wife's health problems. The wife was also planning to relocate to Pittsburgh. The wife, in her summation, requested that the court's order of joint custody, if entered, name one parent as the "primary custodian as a matter of law." The husband "welcome(d) dual custody" in his summation.]

Two questions are thus presented. Can this court order joint custody, that is, does the court have the authority to do so? If so, then in what fashion can an order of joint custody, if appropriate, best be implemented?

. . . [T]he concept of joint custody has never been fully explored in any reported decision of our courts. The time is ripe for a full review of the legal and statutory bases for an award of custody, in general and joint custody, in particular.

. . . [T]he Legislature has vested in this court the authority to make such order, after judgment of divorce or maintenance, "as to the care, custody, education and maintenance of the children, or any of them, as the circumstances of the parties and the nature of the case shall render fit, reasonable and just * * *."

N.J.S.A. 2A:34-23. Clearly, this legislative grant of authority would include the authority to order "joint," "divided" or "split" custody. Assuming, therefore, that the circumstances of the parties and the nature of the case render an award of joint custody, "fit, reasonable and just," there is no reason why such an order should not be entered.

New Jersey is in the majority of states which follow the traditional "best interests of the child" rule in custody determinations. The "best interests" doctrine was first announced by Judge (later Justice) Brewer in *Chapsky v. Wood,* 26 Kan. 650 (1881), in which the Kansas Supreme Court repudiated the rule which held that the rights of parents were primary over those of third parties to custody of their children. The doctrine gained popularity after the decision in *Finlay v. Finlay,* 240 N.Y. 429, 148 N.E. 624 (1925), in which the New York Court of Appeals held that the Chancellor acted as *parens patriae* to do what is best for the interests of the child.

* * *

Other standards for placement of custody have been proposed, but they have not yet had as wide acceptance as the "best interests" test has had. Goldstein *et als.* propose the "least detrimental available alternative." Goldstein, Freud and Solnit, *Beyond the Best Interests of the Child* (1973). This choice would maximize,

> * * * (i)n accord with the child's sense of time, the child's opportunity for being wanted and for maintaining on a continuous, unconditional, and permanent basis a relationship with at least one adult who is or will become the child's psychological parent. (at 99)

"Sense of time," "opportunity for being wanted" and "psychological parent" are terms of art coined by the authors.

QUERY

Does the adoption of the concept *psychological parent* as a term of art to be used in custody decisions automatically require the employment of (highly paid) psychological experts whenever it is brought into question?

Another approach is that of John Batt, who approaches child custody questions "from a psychologically oriented child development standpoint." Batt, "Child Custody Disputes: A Developmental—Psychological Approach to Proof and Decisionmaking", 12 *Willamette L.J.* 491 (1976). He proposes that the court take into account five phases of development of the human child before making a custody placement. The phases generally follow the growth of the child from infancy to young adulthood.

QUERY

Should judges base legal principles on theories from the psychological sciences? If so, which theories should be applied?

The "best interests" standard was authoritatively announced in New Jersey in 1944 by the *Armour* decision and has since been followed by our courts. Other formulations of the "best interests" test require the court to consider the safety, happiness and physical, mental and moral welfare of the child.

The court has broad discretion in dealing with the custody of a child, being always aware that the welfare and happiness (best interests) of the child [sic] is the controlling consideration.

The court will consider the wishes of an infant child as to custody, if the child is of an age and capacity to form an intelligent preference as to custody. The preference of the young child has a place, although not a conclusive place, in determining custody.[2]

Commentators have suggested that a prerequisite to an award of custody should be the appointment of independent counsel for the child so as to safeguard his or her rights. Comment, "A Child's Right to Independent Counsel in Custody Proceedings: Providing Effective 'Best Interest' Determination through the Use of a Legal Advocate," 6 *Seton Hall L.Rev.* 303 (1975); Inker and Peretta, "A Child's Right to Counsel in Custody Cases, 5 *Fam.L.Q.* 108 (1971). While this court has assigned independent counsel for children in the past, such a procedure, which entails considerable expense, should be utilized only where the interests of the child are truly adverse to those of the parent(s). One example of such adverse interest would be the situation where neither parent is a fit custodian. That is not the case here.

QUERY

Is a nonlawyer guardian ad litem a reasonable alternative?

To which parent, then, should custody be awarded? Our courts have long recognized that custody of a child of tender years ordinarily is awarded to the mother if she is a fit and proper person. The theory is that the mother will take better and more expert care of the small child than the father can. These considerations must always be considered subordinate, however, to what is truly in the child's best interest.

In the present case the question is not so much "to which parent should custody be awarded" as it is "should custody be awarded to both parents?" Nelson states that

Where both parents are suitable persons to have the custody of their children and are devoted to them, they should be given as nearly equal rights to the custody of the children as is practical and compatible with the convenience, education and welfare of the children, since it is against public policy to destroy or limit the relation of parent and child and the child is entitled to the love and training of both parents.
[2 Nelson, *Divorce and Annulment* (2 ed. 1961), § § 15, 17, at 256-57].
N.J.S.A. 9:2-4 makes it clear that, with regard to an order or judgment of custody,
* * * the rights of both parents, in the absence of misconduct, shall be held to be equal, and they shall be equally charged with their care, nurture, education and welfare, and the happiness and welfare of the children shall determine the custody or possession.

This statutory grant of equal rights in both parents to custody effectively reversed the holding of the common law wherein the father had the preferred right to custody of his minor child, unless disqualified for some reason.

Our case law is replete with decisions reaffirming the existence of equal rights to custody in both parents. One of our later cases holds that the parental right to the care of his or her child is a fundamental right subject to constitutional protection.

Notwithstanding the enlightened views of the Legislature and the courts of this State, no authoritative decision has ever been rendered by our courts on the subject of joint custody. It cannot be said, however, that joint ("dual," "alternating," "divided," "split") custody enjoys great popularity across the country. Decisions on joint custody in other jurisdictions demonstrate either a guarded acceptance or a clear dislike for the concept. See *Annotation,* 92 A.L.R.2d 691 (1963).

N.B.

Since the rendition of this opinion and A.L.R. article, a majority of states have expressed approval of joint custody in a variety of ways and degrees.
   Note the age of the cases, especially those contra.

Courts approving joint custody generally agree that a child is entitled to the love, nurture, advice and training of both mother and father. The experience is said to give the child the experience of two separate homes. *Brock v. Brock,* 123 Wash. 450, 212 P. 550 (Sup.Ct.1923); *Mullen v. Mullen,* 188 Va. 259, 49 S.E.2d 349 (Sup.Ct.App.1948). Courts disapproving the concept point to the possibility of resentment against the parents who shuffle the child back and forth, *State ex rel. Larson v. Larson,* 190 Minn. 489, 252 N.W. 329 (Sup.Ct.1934), the development of a sense of insecurity, *Heltsley v. Heltsley,* 242 S.W.2d 973 (Ky.Ct.App.1951), and the destructive effect of instability in the human factors affecting a child's emotional life. *Kaehler v. Kaehler,* 219 Minn. 536, 18 N.W.2d 312 (Sup.Ct.1945).

Two principles can be distilled from the reported cases. The first is that the primary consideration in an award of joint custody is the welfare and best interest of the child. *Bergerac v. Maloney,* 478 S.W.2d 111 (Tex.Civ.App.1972); *Brocato v. Walker,* 220 So.2d 340 (Miss.Sup.Ct.1969); *Davis v. Davis,* 354 S.W.2d 526 (Mo.App.1962). The second principle is that decision must depend upon the facts of the particular case. *Merrill v. Merrill,* 83 Idaho 306, 362 2P.2d 887 (Sup.Ct.1961); *Andrews v. Geyer,* 200 Va. 107, 104 S.E.2d

747 (Sup.Ct.App.1958); *Stillmunkes v. Stillmunkes,* 245 Iowa 1082, 65 N.W.2d 366 (Sup.Ct.1954).

Several factors are said to affect the decision to award joint custody. Among these are the wishes of the parents, as in *Ward v. Ward,* 88 Ariz. 130, 353 P.2d 895 (Sup.Ct.1960), where the court stated that a sincere desire on the part of the parent to share his child's companionship should not be lightly dismissed. Another important factor is the age of the child, the general rule being that the courts should not divide the custody of a child of tender years. Even this rule is not absolute, as in *Lutker v. Lutker,* 230 S.W.2d 177 (Mo.App.1950), where joint custody of a 2 1/2-year-old was approved, largely because of the devotion of the parents to the child and the short distance between their respective homes.

The distance between the homes of the parents becomes an important factor if the distance is such as to prevent visitation by the noncustodial parent. In that case an award of joint custody may be appropriate. *Maxwell v. Maxwell,* 351 S.W.2d 192 (Ky.Ct.App.1961).

Assuming that an order of joint custody is appropriate, most courts hold that a frequent shifting from home to home is unnecessarily harmful to the child and should not be permitted. Thus, in *Mason v. Mason,* 163 Wash. 539, 1 P.2d 885 (Sup.Ct.1931), the court condemned an order of joint custody which gave custody of a two-year-old to the mother from noon on Sunday to noon on Thursday, and to the father from Thursday noon to Sunday noon. The Court said, "Thus the child becomes a perpetual traveler. This constant change in environment, discipline and control undoubtedly would prove to be harmful to the child." *Id.* at 886.

An award giving primary custody to one parent and giving the other parent custody on alternate weekends has been upheld. *Murnane*

v. Murnane, 14 A.D.2d 943, 221 N.Y.S.2d 28 (App.Div.1961); *Robertson v. Robertson,* 140 Cal.App.2d 784, 295 P.2d 922 (Ct.App.1956).

Courts sometimes disapprove custody arrangements which alternate custody between the parents for equal periods of time, especially where such shifts interfere with schooling. In *McLemore v. McLemore,* 346 S.W.2d 722, 92 A.L.R.2d 691 (Ky.Ct.App.1961), an award of joint custody which shifted three young children every week was terminated because of the intolerable burden such frequent, though equal, shifts placed on the children. Periods of time of 6 months and 12 months have been approved for pre-school children. *Travis v. Travis,* 163 Kan. 54, 180 P.2d 310 (Sup.Ct. 1947); *Ramsden v. Ramsden,* 32 Wash.2d 603, 202 P.2d 920 (Sup.Ct.1949).

The most widely accepted form of joint custody award is the one wherein one parent has custody during school months and the other custody during the summer. *Annotation,* 92 A.L.R.2d 691, § 11(a), at 726 (1963). This form of award solves the problem of distance between the homes of the parents and generally avoids frequent shifts in custody. The attitude of courts granting this form of custody is well illustrated by *Fago v. Fago,* 250 S.W.2d 837 (Mo.App.1952), where it was said:

> The pleasure and benefit of friendly association with both parents should be accorded to a child. . . . She needs to have the benefit of her father's guidance, love and affection as well as that of her mother and grandmother. . . . It will be a broadening and valuable experience for (the child) to spend a part of each summer in the State of New York with her father, leaving ten months of the year for the exertion on (the child) of the beneficent influence of mother, grandmother and aunt in her

customary home surroundings in St. Louis. (at 842-43)

There is no doubt that the distance between the homes of the parents was an important factor in that case. Accord, *Stockton v. Stockton,* 459 S.W.2d 532 (Mo.App.1970); *Stanfield v. Stanfield,* 350 P.2d (Okl.Sup.Ct.1960); *Barrier v. Brewster,* 349 S.W.2d 823 (Ky.Ct.App. 1961); *Dworkis v. Dworkis,* 111 So.2d 70 (Fla.App.1959).

In the present case, the minor children are 13 and 11 years of age and attend school in this State. Plaintiff has requested permission to move to Pittsburgh, Pennsylvania, to be near her parents. Under these circumstances, if plaintiff were given sole custody, visitation by defendant would be both difficult and expensive.

The children are not of such tender years that an award of joint custody would be detrimental to them. They are entitled to know, love and respect their father just as much as they know, love and respect their mother. No order of sole custody in the mother, even with unlimited visitation by the father, could possibly give these children the contact with their father that they need and have a right to. For that reason the court orders that the parties shall have joint custody of the children. Plaintiff will have physical custody from September to June, and defendant will have physical custody during July and August.

Plaintiff's request to move to Pittsburgh is granted. Defendant shall be permitted visitation one weekend a month in the Pittsburgh area during the school year. In addition, defendant shall have free access to the children via telephone at a reasonable hour and for reasonable lengths of time.

Defendant's visitation shall also include a four-day period of visitation during the Christmas and Easter vacations at either location. The parties are, of course, free to supplement this minimum visitation schedule as they may wish and are able to agree upon. Costs of transportation of the children between New Jersey and Pennsylvania will be borne equally by the parties.

[The court approved over $12,000 of the wife's attorneys' fees to be paid by the husband.]

---

2   In the present case the court did not interview the infant children of the marriage. No evidence was adduced that either child preferred one parent over the other. The court is convinced that the parties have been careful to refrain from making the minds of the children their battleground. They have thus avoided creating the discord, mistrust and misery which forces a child to make a choice between his or her parents.

BECK v. BECK
86 N.J. 480, 432 A.2d 63 (1981)
Supreme Court of New Jersey

The Superior Court, Chancery Division, Passaic County, ordered, sua sponte, the "joint custody" on a "time-sharing" schedule of two minor children. The Superior Court, Appellate Division, reversed and remanded and certification was granted by the state supreme court.

CLIFFORD, J.

The parties to this matrimonial action have been granted joint legal and physical custody of their two adopted female children. Although neither party requested joint custody, the trial court nevertheless found such an arrangement to be in the best interests of the children.[1] On appeal by defendant-wife, the Appellate Division found in her favor, reversing and remanding the joint custody decree with directions to award sole custody to her as the children's mother and liberal visitation rights to their father, and to make an appropriate upward adjustment of child support. *Beck v. Beck,* 173 N.J.Super. 33, 413 A.2d 350 (1980). We granted certification 84 N.J. 451, 420 A.2d 348 (1980), to review that determination because of the novel and important questions presented.

N.B.

Although there is considerable acceptance among the states of joint custody agreed upon by both parents, imposition of joint custody on unwilling parents has been seriously questioned.

I

The initial issue is whether courts are authorized to decree the joint custody of children. The pertinent statute provides courts with broad authorization for custody determinations in divorce proceedings:

> * * * (T)he court may make such order * * * as to the care, custody, education and maintenance of the children, or any of them, as the circumstances of the case shall render fit, reasonable and just * * *. [N.J.S.A. 2A:34-23.]

This provision evinces a legislative intent to grant courts wide latitude to fashion creative remedies in matrimonial custody cases. *Cf. Clemens v. Clemens,* 20 N.J.Super. 383, 389-90, 90 A.2d 72 (App.Div.1952) (Superior Court also has inherent jurisdiction over custody matters as successor to former Court of Chancery). The language of the statute is sufficiently broad to include the authority to decree joint custody. See *Mayer v. Mayer,* 150 N.J.Super. 556, 561, 376 A.2d 214 (Ch.Div.1977).

Moreover, parents involved in custody controversies have by statute been granted both equal rights and equal responsibilities regarding the care, nurture, education and welfare of their children. See N.J.S.A. 9:2-4. Although not an explicit authorization of joint custody, this clearly related statute indicates a legislative preference for custody decrees that allow both parents full and genuine involvement in the lives of their children following a divorce. This approach is consonant with the common law policy that "in promoting the child's welfare, the court should strain every effort to attain for the child the affection of both parents rather than one." *Turney v. Nooney,* 5 N.J.Super. 392, 397, 69 A.2d 342 (App.Div.1959). See also *Clemens, supra,* 20 N.J.Super. at 391, 90 A.2d 72 (N.J.S.A. 9:2-4 is merely declaratory of pre-existing common law rule). Hence, joint custody comports as well with the established policy of this state.

II

The use by the courts of custodial arrangements other than sole custody is not new. In the early cases of many jurisdictions custody was routinely divided when both parents sought it. See *Annot.,* 92 A.L.R.2d 695, 698 (1963). Shortly after the turn of the century, however, this practice began to be questioned. *Id.* Nevertheless, some courts have continued to fashion such remedies when deemed appropriate. See

Bratt, *Joint Custody,* 67 Ky.L.J. 271, 282 n.45 (1979).

In recent years the concept of joint custody has become topical, due largely to the perceived inadequacies of sole custody awards and in recognition of the modern trend toward shared parenting in marriage. Sole custody tends both to isolate children from the noncustodial parent and to place heavy financial and emotional burdens on the sole caretaker, usually the mother, see Bratt, *supra,* 67 Ky.L.J. at 275; Miller, "Joint Custody," 13 *Fam.L.W.* 345, 354-57 (1979), although awards of custody to the father, especially in households where both parents are employed outside the home, are more common now than in years past. Moreover, because of the absolute nature of sole custody determinations, in which one parent "wins" and the other "loses," the children are likely to become the subject of bitter custody contests and post-decree tension. *Id.* at 355. The upshot is that the best interests of the child are disserved by many aspects of sole custody.

Joint custody attempts to solve some of the problems of sole custody by providing the child with access to both parents and granting parents equal rights and responsibilities regarding their children. Properly analyzed, joint custody is comprised of two elements: legal custody and physical custody.[2] Under a joint custody arrangement, legal custody, the legal authority and responsibility for making "major" decisions regarding the child's welfare is shared at all times by both parents. Physical custody, the logistical arrangement whereby the parents share the companionship of the child and are responsible for "minor" day-to-day decisions, may be alternated in accordance with the needs of the parties and the children.

At the root of the joint custody arrangement is the assumption that children in a unified family setting develop attachments to both parents and the severance of either of these attachments is contrary to the child's best interest. See Bratt, *supra,* 67 *Ky.L.J.* at 296-97; Folberg & Graham, "Joint Custody of Children Following Divorce," 12 *U.Calif.D.L.Rev.* 523, 535 (1970). Through its legal custody component joint custody seeks to maintain these attachments by permitting both parents to remain decision-makers in the lives of their children. Alternating physical custody enables the children to share with both parents the intimate day-to-day contact necessary to strengthen a true parent-child relationship. See Bratt, *supra,* 67 *Ky.L.J.* at 299-300; Greif, 49 *Am.J.Orthopsych.* 311, 315 (1979).

Joint custody, however, is not without its critics. The objections most frequently voiced include contentions that such an arrangement creates instability for children, causes loyalty conflicts, makes maintaining parental authority difficult, and aggravates the already stressful divorce situation by requiring interaction between hostile ex-spouses. See Miller, *supra,* 13 *Fam.L.W.* at 366-68; 2 Foster & Freed, *Law and the Family,* § 29.6A (Supp.1981). Although these same problems are already present in sole custody situations, see Bratt, *supra,* 67 *Ky.L.Rev.* at 305-06, some courts have used these objections either to reject or strictly limit the use of joint custody.

Because we are persuaded that joint custody is likely to foster the best interests of the child in the proper case, we endorse its use as an alternative to sole custody in matrimonial actions. We recognize, however, that such an arrangement will prove acceptable in only a limited class of cases, as set forth more particularly in part VII of this opinion. But despite our belief that joint custody will be the preferred disposition in some matrimonial actions, we decline to establish a presumption in its favor or in favor of any particular custody determination.[3] Our concern is that a presumption of this sort might serve as a disincentive for the meticulous fact-finding required in custody cases. See Folberg & Graham, *supra*, 12 *U.Calif.D.L.Rev.* at 577. Such fact-finding is particularly important in these cases because the very interplay of parents and children that gives joint custody its potential value also creates complications different from those found in sole custody arrangements. Some of those complications are dramatized by the instant case.

N.B.

Whether "meticulous fact-finding" is worthwhile is a major issue addressed by David M., in § 14.3.

III

The parties were married in July 1963. Their two daughters, Lauren, now age twelve, and Kirsten, now age ten, were adopted in infancy. Plaintiff-husband is a successful commercial photographer. Defendant-wife works as a part-time student teacher supervisor at a local college. Since February 14, 1976, when Mr. Beck left the marital residence, the girls have resided with their mother subject to periodic visitation by their father.

In September 1977 plaintiff-husband filed a complaint for divorce based on eighteen months separation. N.J.S.A. 2A:34-2(d). He sought liberal visitation rights but not custody of the children. Defendant answered and counterclaimed for divorce on grounds of desertion. N.J.S.A. 2A:34-2(b). The initial proceeding was concerned solely with financial matters pertaining to alimony, child support and equitable distribution. The issue of custody appeared to be settled by the pleadings until April 12, 1979 when in the course of its decision the trial court decreed sua sponte that both legal and physical custody would be shared by the parties.[4]

The court supported the decree with reference to the "uniqueness" of this case. It found the parties to be "sophisticated," with a generally "positive attitude between themselves with regard to the girls"; that plaintiff's income is sufficient to support two households; that the children's ages presented no obstacle; that the proximity of the residences would enable continuity of schooling despite changes in physical custody; that the prior visitation arrangement had been maintained "with no difficulty whatever" between the parties; and, finally, that because the girls were adopted, they needed "the benefit, contact, and security of both parents."

Shortly thereafter, defendant moved for an order amending the findings and judgment of the trial court on the issue of joint custody. Plaintiff opposed the motion and both parties filed lengthy certifications. After reviewing the certifications and hearing argument, the trial court ordered a plenary hearing on the issue of custody. At the hearing defendant testified and also produced a child psychiatrist to testify on her behalf. Plaintiff chose not to testify himself, although he had done so extensively during the first proceeding, but offered three experts in support of his lately-adopted position favoring joint custody: a school psychologist, a clinical psychologist, and a psychiatric social worker. Also, in the course of the hearing the court for the first time met privately with the girls. As might be expected, the expert testimony on each side varied. Because of the acutely fact-sensitive nature of custody determinations, we offer more extended discussion of the expert testimony adduced at the hearing than might otherwise suffice.

Dr. Jerome Goodman, the expert called on behalf of Mrs. Beck, testified that he had interviewed the children and their mother and concluded that custody should remain with

Mrs. Beck. Dr. Goodman reasoned that adopted children have a special need for security and that joint custody, particularly alternating physical custody, reduced constancy and hence would cause the children to experience insecurity. He noted that the parents' differing approaches to child rearing would aggravate this problem, the mother being highly structured and the father much less so. He also emphasized the desirability of having a "woman in the home" to provide identification and guidance for the girls and that there is "no substitute for mother" in such a role. Dr. Goodman thought alternating custody was artificial and contrived in nature and would be a source of embarrassment to the children. Given the fact that the girls were well-adjusted at the time of the hearing, he advised retaining the status quo. He expressed a general opposition to alternating physical custody, characterizing it as a "hokey arrangement" and "very risky." Although his qualifications as an expert regarding adopted children and child custody in general were unimpeachable, Dr. Goodman conceded that his exposure to joint custody was rather superficial.

The testimony of plaintiff-husband's expert clinical psychologist, Dr. Leonard Abramson, was offered to establish that the father was a fit parent. Based upon an interview with Mr. Beck and on certain psychological tests, the doctor testified that he found plaintiff to be "mature and well adjusted." He described Mr. Beck as "sensitive, flexible, non (sic) compulsive or rigid, not overly gregarious" and having a genuine interest in the welfare of the children.

On the issue of the advisability of joint custody for the Becks plaintiff offered the expert testimony of Dr. Warren Clark, a school psychologist and a proponent of such arrangements. He favored joint custody in this case based on his opinion, formed after interviewing Mr. Beck and the children, that it would foster the children's relationship with both parents and would have a long-term beneficial impact on the girls' development as young women. In his view, because the children would become aware that their mother is their only "real" parent in the sense of making decisions about their lives, mere visitation rights granted to a noncustodial "zoo daddy" would not be conducive to the development of a father-daughter relationship. He was confident that the children, being adjusted, intelligent, and having affection for both parents, would be able to adapt to joint custody without difficulty.[5] Although he acknowledged the risks involved in joint custody, Dr. Clark stressed that the risk inherent in sole custody, namely, the girls' loss of their relationship with their father, was equally serious.

Noting that the children expressed opposition to the joint custody decree, Dr. Clark attributed their reaction to the fact that they misunderstood joint custody as something that would deprive them of their mother and their home. He predicted that once it went into effect, the girls would recognize the arrangement not only as retaining what they had before but as adding something more—an additional home. Dr. Clark felt that differences in child rearing practices do not necessarily militate against joint custody determinations and that children can understand that different people will set different standards for them. According to Dr. Clark it is inconsistent treatment from one parent that tends to cause problems for children.

Finally, Dr. Clark noted that the ideal joint custody arrangement would be one arrived at by agreement between the parties. Nevertheless, in the absence of such an agreement, joint custody could successfully be carried out by court decree provided the parents put the best interest of the children first and were provided with certain "ground rules" governing the custody arrangement. Dr. Clark, however, had had no experience with the particular physical custody arrangement proposed in this case.

Regarding joint custody generally, Mr. Beck presented the testimony of Dr. Judith Greif, a psychiatric social worker who has conducted independent research on the topic. Dr. Greif had not interviewed any of the Beck family members, but her testimony supported much of Dr. Clark's previous testimony. She testified that as long as both parents are fit, "the most important thing is to maintain the child's open and meaningful access to both parents." Furthermore, in her opinion it was contrary to the best interests of the children to deprive them of an adequate parent simply because the other is deemed better. Visitation, for Dr. Greif, was not "meaningful contact." She stressed that the continuity of relationship allowed by alternating physical custody is more important than the discontinuity of physical environment caused by it.

N.B.

Dr. Greif's testimony echoes the prime arguments of proponents of joint custody.

Dr. Greif's research indicated that joint custody can work even where the parents are openly hostile toward one another as long as both parents care about their children. In her words, "there needs to be good input to the children, there need not be such good input between the parties." None of the joint custody cases studied by Dr. Greif involved adopted children.

At the conclusion of the plenary hearing the trial court reiterated its prior findings and modified its original decision. Viewing the issue in terms of the importance of fatherhood in the lives of the two girls, it concluded that the lack of real contact with the father would have negative developmental effects, particularly because the girls are adopted. Although recognizing the "impeccable" qualifications of Dr. Goodman, the court found him unpersuasive. It found more rational the viewpoints of Drs. Greif and Clark and hence adopted their conclusions.

The trial court stressed that although defendant's care of the girls was more than adequate, she is limited by an inability to be both a mother and a father. It found Mrs. Beck to be a "sensible" person, but also somewhat bitter and "stiff lipped" and more partisan than plaintiff, whom he described as "a rather * * * relaxed type of man." Noting that Mrs. Beck "honestly objects to the plan because she contends she cannot cooperate with her former husband," the court concluded, based on the testimony of Dr. Greif, that an amicable relationship between the parties is "comparatively unimportant and not essential" as long as the parties "are looking out for the best interests of the children."[6]

QUERY

A major objection raised against joint custody is the inability of the parents to cooperate. Does the court suggest in footnote 6 that the mother is trying to sabotage joint custody by suddenly creating an uncooperative atmosphere?

Referring to this state's policy of seeking maximum visitation by the non-custodial parent in sole custody cases and to N.J.S.A. 9:2-4, which gives both parents equal rights to custody, the trial court concluded that "there is a real purpose of fatherhood as well as motherhood." Furthermore, it distinguished between custodial time and visitation, describing the former as "meaningful contact" and the latter as "entertainment time." It saw the contact and involvement of the girls with two fit, concerned parents as "going to be what's good for the girls." Finally, it reiterated that this case is uniquely suitable to joint custody and ordered that the parents share "joint control and supervision" of the children with alternating physical custody for four months.[7] It also provided for counselling services for the family.

IV

* * *

Plaintiff-husband contends that the determination of the trial court was well within its discretion, consistent with a developing body of case law, and uniquely appropriate to the facts of this case. He challenges the action taken by the Appellate Division, urging particularly that the burden of proof should not have been imposed on him and that the court exceeded the proper scope of review. On the other hand defendant-wife argues that the joint custody decree is without basis in law and unwarranted by these facts, that the trial court gave insufficient weight to the preference of the children, and that it erred in raising the custody issue *sua sponte.*

V

We find the determination of the Appellate Division to be fundamentally flawed in two respects. As a matter of law, reliance on *Sorentino I,* an adoption case, is inappropriate when the issue before the court is that of an initial child custody determination in the divorce context. In addition, we hold that the record in this case reveals sufficient credible evidence to support the decision of the trial court.

In respect of the *Sorentino I* argument, it must be kept in mind that in adoption matters the adoptive parent seeks the permanent termination of the child's relationship with the natural parent. Because such a permanent and drastic action is viewed as potentially harmful to the child, the party seeking to change the status quo has the burden of proving that the child will not suffer serious psychological harm. In contrast, post-divorce custody determinations seek to some extent to provide the children with access to both parents and to avoid alienation from either one. Hence, sole custody decrees almost invariably grant visitation rights to the noncustodial parent. Moreover, our courts have imposed a duty on the custodial parent to be active in aiding and encouraging the sincere efforts of the noncustodial parent "to enhance the mutual love, affection and respect between himself and his child." Since post divorce custody decrees seek to preserve, not destroy, parent-child attachments, the procedural safeguards provided by *Sorentino I* are not applicable.

QUERY

Should the criteria for custody be different for adoption than for divorce?

In addition, the Appellate Division's application of *Sorentino I* to this case misconstrues the notion of status quo. Our concern in that case was not for the physical attributes of custody, but rather for the psychological, emotional and relational "status quo" of a child about to be separated from the only parents it had ever known. See *Sorentino I, supra,* 72 N.J. at 133, 367 A.2d 1168. In this case the record indicates that the children have maintained a close relationship with both parents. The Appellate Division's approach would ignore the relationships between the children and their father and focus on the physical custody aspect of the post-separation living arrangement as the status quo—an ill-advised elevation of form over substance.[8]

* * *

We view the testimony of Drs. Greif and Clark, summarized above, . . . as constituting sufficient credible evidence upon which the trial court could reasonably have reached its decision. We certainly find no basis for the Appellate Division's apparent conclusion that only Mrs. Beck and Dr. Goodman were credible witnesses. If anything, the record reflects that whereas Drs. Greif and Clark were quite knowledgeable about the concept of joint custody, Dr. Goodman was only superficially familiar with it. . . . [T]he Appellate Division appears to have engaged in an unwarranted independent analysis of the trial court record.

VI

The question of whether a trial court may make a sua sponte custody determination need not long detain us. The paramount consideration in child custody cases is to foster the best interests of the child. . . . It would be incongruous and counterproductive to restrict application of this standard to the relief requested by the parties to a custody dispute. Accordingly, a sua sponte custody determination is properly within the discretion of the trial court provided it is supported by the record. However, we emphasize again the desirability of the trial court giving the parties an opportunity to address any new issues raised by the court. . . .

VII

The factors to be considered by a trial court contemplating an award of joint custody require some elaboration. . . . [W]e perceive that the necessary elements will coalesce only infrequently.

A

First, before embarking on a full-blown inquiry into the practicability of a joint custody arrangement, the court must determine whether the children have established such relationships with both parents that they would benefit from joint custody. For such bonds to exist the parents need not have been equally involved in the child rearing process. See Bratt, *supra,* 67 *Ky.L.J.* at 296. Rather, from the child's point of view it is necessary only that the child recognize both parents as sources of security and love and wish to continue both relationships.

B

Having established the joint custody arrangement's potential benefit to the children, the court must focus on the parents in order to determine whether they qualify for such an arrangement. At a minimum both parents must be "fit" that is, physically and psychologically capable of fulfilling the role of parent. Miller, *supra,* 13 *Fam.L.W.* at 369. In addition, they must each be willing to accept custody, see Bratt, *supra,* 67 *Ky.L.J.* at 303, although their opposition to joint custody does not preclude the court from ordering that arrangement. Rather, even if neither party seeks joint custody, as long as both are willing to care for the children, joint custody is a possibility.[9]

The most troublesome aspect of a joint custody decree is the additional requirement that the parent exhibit a potential for cooperation in matters of child rearing. This feature does not translate into a requirement that the parents have an amicable relationship. Although such a positive relationship is preferable, a successful joint custody arrangement requires only that the parents be able to isolate their personal conflicts from their roles as parents and that the children be spared whatever resentments and rancor the parents may harbor. See Folberg & Graham, *supra,* 2 *U.Calif.D.L.Rev.* at 550. Moreover, the potential for cooperation should not be assessed in the "emotional heat" of the divorce.

If the parents outside of the divorce setting have each demonstrated that they are reasonable and are willing to give priority to the best interest of their child, then the judge need only determine if the parents can separate and put aside any conflicts between them to cooperate for the benefit of their child. The judge must look for the parents' ability to cooperate and if the potential exists, encourage its activation by instructing the parents on what is expected of them. [*Id.* at 580.]

The necessity for at least minimal parental cooperation in a joint custody arrangement presents a thorny problem of judicial enforcement in a case such as the present one, wherein despite the trial court's determination that joint custody is in the best interests of the child, one parent (here, the mother) nevertheless contends that cooperation is impossible and refuses to abide by the decree. Traditional enforcement techniques are singularly inappropriate in a child custody proceeding for which the best interests of the child is our polestar. Despite the obvious unfairness of allowing an uncooperative parent to flout a court decree, we are unwilling to sanction punishment of a recalcitrant parent if the welfare of the child will also suffer. However, when the actions of such a parent deprive the child of the kind of relationship with the other parent that is deemed to be in the child's best interests, removing the child from the custody of the uncooperative parent may well be appropriate as a remedy of last resort. See *Dodd v. Dodd,* 93 Misc.2d 641, 403 N.Y.S.2d 401, 406 (Sup.Ct.1978); *cf. Sheehan v. Sheehan, supra,* 51 N.J.Super. at 291, 143 A.2d 874 (even in sole custody case, if custodial parent desires to retain custody, he or she must aid and encourage efforts of noncustodial parent to enhance mutual love, affection and respect between that parent and the child).

In *Dodd,* the Supreme Court of New York found that a fourteen month interim joint custody arrangement had failed because of the hostility between the parents. In awarding sole custody to the mother, the court characterized her as "more flexible and conciliatory" than the father and noted that "placing custody with Mrs. Dodd will maximize the role which both parents should play in their children's lives." 93 Misc.2d 641, 403 N.Y.S.2d at 406. Although an award of sole custody to Mr. Beck in this case may be a closer question (in *Dodd,* the mother had also been the primary caretaker of the children, as was the mother here), it cannot be ruled out as a potential enforcement tool, albeit one to be considered only after all other measures have failed.

C

In addition to the factors set forth above, the physical custody element of a joint custody award requires examination of practical considerations such as the financial status of the parents, the proximity of their respective homes, the demands of parental employment, and the age and number of the children. Joint physical custody necessarily places an additional financial burden on the family. Although exact duplication of facilities and furnishings is not necessary, the trial court should insure that the children can be adequately cared for in two homes. The geographical proximity of the two homes is an important factor to the extent that it impinges on school arrangements, the children's access to relatives and friends (including visitation by the noncustodial parent), and the ease of travel between the two homes. Parental employment is significant for its effect on a parent's ability properly to care for the children and maintain a relationship with them. The significance of the ages and number of the children is somewhat unclear at present, *see, e.g., Miller, supra,* 13 *Fam.L.W.* at 374, and will probably vary from case to case, requiring expert testimony as to their impact on the custody arrangement.

If joint custody is feasible except for one or more of these practical considerations, the court should consider awarding legal custody to both parents with physical custody to only one and liberal visitation rights to the other. Such an award will preserve the decision-making role of both parents and should approximate, to the extent practicable, the shared companionship of the child and non-custodial parent that is provided in joint physical custody.

D

Finally, as in all custody determinations, the preference of the children of "sufficient age and capacity" must be accorded "due weight." N.J.S.A. 9:2- 4; *Lavene v. Lavene,* 148 N.J.Super. 267, 271, 372 A.2d 629 (App.Div.1978). This standard gives the trial court wide discretion regarding the probative value of a child's custody preference.

Our review of the record indicates that the trial court gave proper consideration to the preference expressed by the children, eight and ten years old at the time of trial. After interviewing them privately, the court stated for the record that the children were sincere and honest in their desire to remain with their mother. However, observing that they expressed love for both parents and wanted to continue visitation with their father, the court concluded that they had been "persuaded" to make their statements of preference and that the defendant's negative attitude toward joint custody had "consciously or unconsciously spilled over" to the children.[10] Given this conclusion and the tender years of the children, a determination that did not fully accommodate their express wishes was not unreasonable.

VIII

Having found the decision of the trial court to be based on sufficient credible evidence, we would ordinarily reinstate it. However, in child custody cases we are always mindful that our task is to act in the best interests of the child as presently situated. Over two years have elapsed since the original decree of joint custody. Although we uphold that decree as originally made, we recognize that the facts and relationships upon which it was based may have changed dramatically. Therefore, we remand this case to the trial court for further fact-finding and a determination consonant with this opinion. We admonish the court to make a speedy but thorough investigation into the present circumstances of the parties and their children using whatever procedural mechanism and hearing what further testimony, if any, is deemed necessary so that this matter may be expeditiously and properly laid to rest.

The judgment of the Appellate Division is reversed and the case remanded to the trial court. We do not retain jurisdiction.

---

1   In his pleadings plaintiff-husband sought only "liberal" visitation rights. He has since indicated a willingness to accept joint custody.

---

2   Joint custody must be distinguished from "alternating" custody (an arrangement in which parents alternate both physical and legal custody) and "split" custody (in the case of two or more children, each parent is awarded sole custody of one or more of the children). See Folberg & Graham, "Joint Custody of Children Following Divorce," 12 *U.Calif.D.L.Rev.* 523, 525-30 (1979); Miller *supra*, 13 *Fam.L.Rev.* at 360-61.

---

3   We reject the notion that divorce dissolves the family as well as the marriage. *Contra, Braiman v. Braiman,* 44 N.Y.2d 584, 378 N.E.2d 1019, 1022, 407 N.Y.S.2d 449 (N.Y.1978). Both the legislation and case law of this state are designed to encourage parent-child interaction following divorce. *Supra* at 65. This policy is based on the best interests of the child and not on any notion of parental rights.

---

4   We pause here to note that when a trial court determines to provide a remedy that exceeds or substantially differs from the relief requested in the pleadings, a more advisable course of action would be to notify the parties regarding any new issues raised thereby and to provide an opportunity for the parties to address those

issues before a decision is rendered. *See, e.g., Mayer v. Mayer,* 150 N.J.Super, 556, 560, 376 A.2d 214 (Ch.Div.1977), in which the suggestion of joint custody was made by the court during settlement negotiations.

---

5 He noted that they spoke negatively about their father only in response to questions regarding the custody decree.

---

6 We observe that the problem of noncooperation arose only in the wake of the initial joint custody decree. The parties cooperated satisfactorily in the pre-divorce visitation routine, and Mrs. Beck does not object to future visitation rights being given the girls' father provided she is granted sole custody.

---

7 The rationale offered for the four month period was that "it gives the girls an opportunity to settle in" and "it happens to take care of alternating holidays."

---

8 The key element here is the character or quality of the parent-child relationship. In the absence of the type of relationship adverted to *infra,* joint custody would be inappropriate. Moreover, when seeking joint custody after an initial custody determination has been made, even a parent enjoying such a relationship must satisfy the same burden of proof as applies to anyone seeking to change a custody decree, namely, a change of circumstances warranting modification. *See Mimkon v. Ford,* 66 N.J. 426, 438, 332 A.2d 199 (1975); *M.P. v. S.P.,* 169 N.J.Super. 425, 431, 404 A.2d 1256 (App.Div.1979).

---

9 Although joint custody may be less likely to succeed if ordered by the court than if achieved by the parents' agreement, court-ordered joint custody is likely to be no more prone to failure than court-ordered sole custody following a divorce custody proceeding. See Folberg & Graham, *supra,* 12 *U.Calif.D.L.Rev.* at 579.

---

10 The court noted, for example, that Mrs. Beck permitted the children to read the court papers and apparently pointed out inconsistencies in Mr. Beck's certifications; thus the girls characterized him as a "liar."

14.3 PRIMARY CAREGIVER RULE

David M. v. Margaret M. is a remarkable opinion in several respects. The issue in the case seems to be a question of fact-finding, namely, whether the evidence of sexual misconduct on the part of the wife was sufficient to support the lower court's finding that she was unfit to have custody of her six-year-old son. The Supreme Court of Appeals, West Virginia's highest court, reverses on this point with very little discussion. The remainder of the opinion is a lengthy discussion of the primary caregiver rule, the modern version of the maternal preference or tender years doctrine—purged of sexual preference in language but not in effect—assuming that the primary caregiver is ordinarily found to be the mother. Justice Neely assumes a role of advocacy for the rule, arguing for its efficiency as well as its fairness. The crux of the argument, however, concerns psychology. Justice Neely writes with remarkable candor concerning the abuses of the family law process by husbands using expert psychological witnesses paid to draw conclusions favorable to the husbands.

In some respects this opinion is reminiscent of pre-no-fault days when judges decried the difficulty of finding one or the other side at fault in proceedings that encouraged gross distortions of the truth. The turmoil and

There must be a better way to grow up than "warehoused" in a crib at substandard child care. How should society and the law treat this issue?

expense of such proceedings may have added little to the judge's ability to find the truth or distinguish the better spouse from the worse. Neely's advocacy is prompted in part by the competing trend toward joint custody, which Neely would reserve for the few cases in which the parents wanted such an arrangement and showed an ability to cooperate in making it work.

Justice Neely's candor invites attack. The presentation is strongly biased toward wives. The conclusions are based on studies and theories of the psychological sciences viewed by many legal scholars with skepticism. The conclusions are also based on unsupported views of the mother-child relationship and "experience," presumably gained in family law practice. The annotations reveal important weaknesses in the reasoning, to the extent that the argument may appear inconclusive. Nevertheless, Justice Neely's statements about men, women, and children are probably largely true and the conclusions may well be sound. This discussion deserves serious consideration.

DAVID M. v. MARGARET M.
182 W. Va. 57, 385 S.E.2d 912 (1989)
Supreme Court of Appeals
of West Virginia

NEELY, Justice:
Margaret M. appeals from a divorce order entered by the Circuit Court of Wood County that awarded David M. custody of their son, Timothy, age six.[1] Mrs. M. contends that the Circuit Court erred in adopting the findings of the family law master which held that although Mrs. M. was the primary caretaker of the child, she was not a fit and suitable person to have permanent care and custody of the child. We agree with Mrs. M. and reverse the trial court's ruling.

The parties were married on 4 August 1979 and lived together in Wood County until 7 September 1988. Mr. M. filed a complaint alleging cruel and inhuman treatment or, in the alternative, adultery and seeking custody of their son, then age five. In her answer, Mrs. M. denied the allegations, filed a counterclaim alleging irreconcilable differences and sought custody of their son. Mr. M., in his reply to the counterclaim, admitted that irreconcilable differences existed between the parties.

The case was referred to a family law master and by agreement of the parties the case was bifurcated with only the divorce and the custody issues to be heard, reserving all other issues for further proceedings. After a hearing on the matter, the family law master found: (1) irreconcilable differences existed between the parties; (2) Mrs. M. was the primary caretaker; (3) Mrs. M. had committed adultery on two occasions over two years; and (4) Mrs. M. was not a fit and suitable person to have custody of the child. The Circuit Court adopted the findings and conclusions of the family law master, granted the parties a divorce, and awarded Mr. M. custody of their child, subject to reasonable visitation rights.

In the present case, although the primary caretaker parent rule as described in *Garska v. McCoy,* 167 W.Va. 59, 278 S.E.2d 357 (1981), appears to have been followed, the primary caretaker was denied custody through a broad interpretation of the fitness requirement. We have noted that our very narrow exception to the primary caretaker rule has of late developed a voracious appetite which, if left unchecked, will allow it to eat the rule. We write today to reaffirm and clarify the benefits of the primary caretaker parent rule to assist the family law masters and the circuit courts in reaching the best interests of the child by applying the primary caretaker parent presumption and its limited requirement of fitness. When properly applied, the primary caretaker parent presumption reduces sharp practices in custody negotiation, prevents fathers and mothers from being penalized on account of their gender, and avoids custody battles that are so unwieldy and intrusive that they make the lives of a divorcing couple and their children even more miserable than they otherwise would be.

N.B.

The rule effectively limits judicial discretion. Apparently lower court judges and masters had latched onto the fitness exception to regain their lost authority.

I

In the nineteenth century, and in the early part of this century, the law gave fathers custody of their children after divorce, particularly when mothers were held at fault in breaking up the marriage. That rule was a logical extension of the inferior legal status of women, the husband's property right in his family's labor, and the husband's absolute obligation to support his children. Even a hundred years ago, however, this rule made little sense in light of human emotions and society's expectation that children would be raised by women. Consequently, it was abolished in this century. By 1950, it was almost always the rule that a mother was the preferred custodian of young children if she was a fit parent.

But the behavior that different courts characterized as evidencing "fitness" differed dramatically. In application, the rule of maternal preference allowed judges substantial leeway to take a mother's fault into consideration in the award of custody. It was frequently the case, therefore, that sexual "promiscuity" (a term that tends to mean different things when applied to women than to men, with women getting the short end of the double standard) on the part of the woman would cause a court to declare her "unfit."

Currently, all parental rights in child custody matters are subordinate to the interests of the innocent child. The polestar in child custody cases is the welfare of the child. We have repeatedly acknowledged that the child's welfare is the paramount and controlling factor in all custody matters.

In *J.B. v. A.B.,* we examined our custody presumption in favor of mothers in light of our concern for the welfare of the child and found:

> The welfare of the child seems to require that if at all possible we avoid subjecting children to the trauma of being wrenched away from their mothers, upon whom they have naturally both emotional and *physical* dependency.

Id. 161 W.Va. at 338-39, 242 S.E.2d at 253 (emphasis in original).

Today, the presumption in favor of mothers is rapidly eroding because the maternal preference presumption discriminates against fathers on the basis of sex. In the 1980 amendment to W.Va.Code, 48-2-15, the legislature provided in relevant part:

> ... There shall be no legal presumption that, as between the natural parents, either the father or the mother should be awarded custody of said children but the court shall make an award of custody solely for the best interest of the children based upon the merits of each case.

Although in *Garska, supra,* 167 W.Va. at 70, 278 S.E.2d at 363, we abolished the gender-based presumption, we reaffirmed our holding in *J.B. v. A.B.,* "except that wherever the words 'mother,' 'maternal,' or 'maternal preference' [were] used" some variation of the term "primary caretaker parent" should be substituted.

In jurisdictions that retain some type of maternal preference in awarding custody of very young children, the maternal preference has become largely a tie breaker. The emerging rule is that all custody disputes be decided on their individual merits, with the parent whom the judge considers the most competent receiving custody. At first glance, this emerging rule seems to make sense, since some fathers are excellent parents and some mothers are child abusers.[9] Unfortunately, however, this individualized, sex-neutral approach poses serious problems because the welfare of the child is often lost by the distorted incentives created by the divorce settlement process. Substantial research has confirmed that young children, as a result of intimate interaction, form a unique bond with their primary caretaker. This unique attachment to a primary caretaker is an essential cornerstone of a child's sense of security and healthy emotional development.[10]

> At the earliest stage, [the attachment to a primary caretaker] is critical to the child's learning to place trust in others and to have confidence in her own capacities. Later, it plays a central role in the child's capacity to establish emotional bonds with other persons. The sense of trust in others and in self that the attachment provides may also affect the child's development of intellectual and social skills. The growing child passes through many developmental stages, each requiring her to acquire critical skills and capacities. ... The original bond of the child with the primary caretaker is believed to have an important continuing effect on the child's ability to pass through each stage with success.[11]

QUERY

Does this imply that the father-child relation is unnecessary or an interference with the child's well-being?

Thus, the young child's welfare can be best served by preserving the child's relationship with the primary caretaker parent. Without a presumption in favor of the primary caretaker parent, the process—or even the prospect—of sorting out custody problems in court affects those problems, usually for the worse.

The unpredictability of courts in divorce matters offers many opportunities for a parent (generally the father) to minimize support payments and gain leverage in settlement negotiations. The most effective, and hence the most generally used, tactic is to threaten a custody fight. The effectiveness of the threat increases in direct proportion to the other parent's unwillingness to give up custody. Because women, much more than men, are preeminently interested in custody, seemingly gender-neutral custody rules actually serve to expose women to extortionate bargaining at the hands of their husbands.

A sizable body of research has confirmed that mothers are much more likely than fathers to feel close to their children. In 1977, Sharon Araji of Washington State University published a study entitled "Husbands' and Wives' Attitude-Behavior Congruence on Family Roles."[12] In that study, she asked her subjects their opinion on the proper division of family labor and then asked how such work was in fact divided in their households. More than two-thirds stated that child-care labor should be equally divided. When asked about actual performance, however, those same people overwhelmingly responded that it was the woman in their household who bore the brunt of child-care duties. Shared responsibility for child care would seem more a cosmopolitan pretension than a reality in most settings.

QUERY

Does "feeling close to children" equate with accepting the "brunt of child-care" duties?

Another study done at the University of Nevada that same year found that the division of labor within households is resistant to change. Furthermore, the responsibility for child care was among the duties least often shared. To the extent that husbands participated in child care at all, they were more likely to be involved in playing, baby-sitting and disciplining rather than in such day-to-day tasks as feeding, changing and bathing. The Nevada study is also significant in that it examined cohabiting couples as well as married ones. One might expect that those cohabiting would show more progressive attitudes in the division of domestic responsibilities, but the study found that such couples nonetheless hewed closely to the sexual stereotypes of the world in which they grew up.

QUERY

If "primary caregiver' is gender-neutral, why are mothers caregivers and fathers baby-sitters?

Such was also the case with couples in which the women were highly career-oriented. Even among such couples, it was found, both spouses generally assumed that the woman would be the one primarily responsible for child care. A crucial finding was that the decision to take primary responsibility for the children was frequently a voluntary one for women, who saw parenting as a fundamental element of a successful female life.

Still, just because most women strongly desire custody and most men do not doesn't mean that such is the case in every instance. Fathers who want to retain the companionship of their children and who believe that they would be better single parents than their wives expect the judicial system to operate on the basis of more refined principles than simple statistically-based discrimination.

Fathers are now demanding that courts award custody based on an individualized inquiry into their specific situations. This appears reasonable on its face. But when we understand the costs of such an inquiry, and appreciate as well just how much sinister bargaining is carried out in the shadow of such an unpredictable, case-specific system, we must think again. And, as part IV, infra, will demonstrate, our conclusions in this regard are now shared by a growing number of states.

N.B.

Justice Neely implies that those few fathers who feign interest in their children are really cynically manipulating the mothers to accept less child support in exchange for custody.

II

The individualized approach might be ideal if it were costless and if courts actually considered the relative merits of the parents in each case. In fact, however, the individualized approach is intrusive, time-consuming and inherently distortive in its effect. And, because the vast majority of divorces are settled without ever reaching court,[16] very few custody arrangements receive even the dubious benefit of a judicial determination that they are in the "best interests of the child."

Under the individualized approach to the "best interests of the child" standard, custody, when contested, goes to the parent who the court believes will do a better job of child rearing. This standard is a substitute for the maternal preference rule or its gender-neutral successor, the primary caretaker parent rule. It operates as well in those states retaining a weak maternal preference, with that preference being only a tie breaker. In order to assign custody, the court must explore the dark recesses of psychological theory to determine which parent will, in the long run, do a better job.

However, this undertaking inevitably leads to the hiring of expert witnesses—psychologists, psychiatrists, social workers and sociologists.[17] These experts are paid by the parties to demonstrate that one or the other (coincidentally, always the client) is the superior parent in light of his or her personality, experience and aptitude for parenting. The experts will advance the theory that whatever positive aspects of personality their client possesses are preeminently important to successful single-parent child-raising.[18]

Expert witnesses are, after all, very much like lawyers: They are paid to take a set of facts from which different inferences may be drawn and to characterize those facts so that a particular conclusion follows. There are indeed cases in which a mother or father may appear competent on the surface, only to be exposed after perfunctory inquiry as a child abuser. Under truly careful inquiry, such discoveries might be made more often. Such careful inquiry, however, is almost impossible in the real world because it requires experts who combine competence and integrity in a way that is seldom found, at least in courtrooms. The side with the stronger case can afford to hire only competent experts with profound integrity; the side with the weaker case, on the other hand, wants impressively glib experts who are utterly devoid of principles. When both parents are good parents, the battle of the experts can result only in gibberish.

N.B.

Are expert witnesses as bad as lawyers or are lawyers as bad as expert witnesses?

No issue is more subject to personal bias than a decision about which parent is "better." Should children be placed with an "open, empathetic" father or with a "stern but value-supporting" mother? The decision may hinge on the judge's memory of his or her own parents or on his or her distrust of an expert whose eyes are averted once too often. It is unlikely that the decision will be the kind of individualized justice that the system purports to deliver.

Even when the judge, like most judges, has an intuitive grasp of the difference between good testimony and bunkum, the process is itself destructive. Judges in states that have a "best interests of the child" standard or a weak maternal presumption must allow days of testimony from a parade of highly paid experts before finally rendering a decision. In most cases, the judge ends up deciding that the mother is closer to the children and awards custody accordingly. Yet the hearings, as generally irrelevant as they are to the outcome, are bad in and of themselves because the very process of preparing experts to testify increases the hardship for all concerned. See *Garska, supra,* 167 W.Va. at 65, 278 S.E.2d at 361.

In order for a psychiatrist or psychologist to testify in court about so-called personality integration or similar psychological phenomena, the expert must interview parents and children, conduct tests and perhaps observe the litigants in a family setting. This very exercise can undermine the mental health of the children as well as the emotional stability of the parents. *Id.* When an elaborate custody battle is anticipated, the experts will create painful situations in their efforts to substantiate the testimony they have been paid to give. In much the same way that an artillery battery can "liberate the hell out of" a peaceful hamlet, experts can create emotional imbalances in the very children they are trying to "protect."[19]

In the child custody context, children fall into one of three groups, depending on their age. Children under six years of age are called "children of tender years": They are the most dependent on their parents, but they usually cannot articulate an intelligent opinion about their custody. Children between six and fourteen are also dependent on their parents, but they can usually articulate a preference regarding custody arrangements and explain their reasons.[20] By the age of fourteen a child takes on many of the qualities of an adult; in most cases, unless geography interferes, a child over fourteen will decide for himself or herself the parent with whom he or she wants to live, regardless of what a court says.[21]

N.B.

The three stages of childhood are borrowed from legal tradition rather than psychology. Although a child did not reach majority under the common law until 21 years of age, 14 was considered the age of reason, after which a person could be held accountable for intentional acts. Children under seven years were considered incapable of criminal intent. Between 7 and 14, accountability was a matter of individual maturity, intelligence, and experience.

Children over the age of six might seem to be the best available experts on the subject of how the parents and children get along. Usually, however, children do not want what is best for them; they want what is pleasant.[22] If children are permitted to influence decisions about custody simply by stating a preference, the parents are placed in the position of being competitive bidders in a counterfeit currency. For the children, the results are seldom positive.[23] That is because the litigation process is not neutral, but has its own peculiar and dangerous side effects. Unlike other litigation that sorts out rights and obligations based on facts frozen in time, custody decisions are predictions of what is best for the child—predictions based on facts constantly changing in part as a result of the litigation process.[24] If the divorce drags through the trial and appellate courts for two years, the lawsuit itself may wound or destroy the very children whose welfare is supposed to be at its center. In addition, money that would have been available to ease the transition from joint household to separate households is diverted instead to lawyers, court fees and expert witnesses.

Once a custody battle is contemplated, the relationship between parents and children usually changes for the worse. The overriding need to prepare for court will dominate the lives of both parents and if the children are to be polled—either directly through court testimony or indirectly through the probing of experts— each parent is probably going to attempt to poison the other's well.

The degree to which children suffer during divorce is a widely discussed subject. The slowly grinding machinery of the courts inevitably exacerbates the emotional stresses that result from the simple fact of divorce. Among the damaging effects of custody litigation are uncertainty, painful psychological probing (e.g., "Who do you love more, Mommy or Daddy?"), and competitive parental bribery. The magnitude of these effects is a direct function of the time it takes to conclude the proceedings.

Damage in these matters is magnified by the different meaning time has for children as opposed to adults. Events that transpired in childhood can be remembered in meticulous detail, while similar events, for an adult, are largely a blur. When a person is forty, a year represents one-fortieth of his or her life; for someone who is five, a year represents one-fifth. Divorce is by its very nature traumatic not only in terms of the mother's and father's separation but also in terms of new male and female companions for each entering the scene. If the children have no idea with whom they will live or under what terms or even where, the consequent uncertainty is likely to undermine their ability to function. Their relations with other children may suffer, their ties to the community may be threatened, and the stress they are under can cause academic failure.[26]

The harms of courtroom custody battles happen only in a relatively small minority of divorces because the vast majority of divorce cases are settled out of court. However, the possibility of a courtroom custody battle also causes problems in out-of-court settlement negotiations.

Divorce decrees are typically drafted for the parties after compromises reached through private negotiation. These compromises are then approved by a judge, who generally gives them only the most perfunctory review. The result is that parties (usually husbands) are free to use whatever leverage is available to obtain a favorable settlement. In practice this tends to mean that husbands will threaten custody fights, with all of the accompanying traumas and uncertainties discussed above, as a means of intimidating wives into accepting less child support, alimony or distribution of marital property than is sufficient to allow the mother to live and raise the children appropriately as a single parent.[28] To some extent the uncertainty in the amount of child support payments is limited by the application of the guidelines required by W.Va.Code, 48A-2-8 [1986].[29] The guidelines for child support awards are set forth in 6 *W.Va.Code of State Rules* 78-16-1 to 78-16-20 (effective May 2, 1988). Because women are usually unwilling to accept even a minor risk of losing custody, however, such techniques, despite the guidelines, are generally successful because the guidelines establish minima and do not apply to alimony or property distribution.

Under any purportedly gender-neutral system, women on statistical average come out of divorce settlements with the worst of all possible results: They get the children, but insufficient money with which to support them. They are forced to scrape along to support their families at inadequate standards of living, and the children are forced to grow up poor, or at least poorer than they should be. Yet the negotiation dynamic is seldom discussed, despite its importance in promoting the growth of a rapidly-expanding class of poor people, the female-headed household.

An important reason that little attention has been given to the effect of in-court rules on out-of-court bargaining is that views on divorce are informed more by wishful thinking than by the facts of life. Many people (especially men) begin with a political conviction that women ought to be equal to men economically, from which they leap to the insupportable conclusion that women are equal to men economically. It then follows that women can support children as well as men can and that whoever wants the children can pay for them.

In the real world, however, women are much poorer than men, and this pattern is highly resistant to change.[31] The cost of child care itself is a major economic burden placed on single mothers. Single mothers, who start with unequal earning power, also provide child care—care that involves great amounts of time that could be spent earning money.[32] But the unfairness only begins there, as so many women are forced to accept lower child support and alimony payments in order to be sure of getting the children (and the accompanying economic burden) at all.

The everyday occurrence of children being traded for money should be sufficient in and of itself to prompt a reevaluation of a system that turns custody awards into bargaining chips. The fact that such trading also has contributed to the impoverishment of women makes the need for change still more urgent. What is needed is a standard for custody awards that assures the welfare of the child without encouraging such pernicious bargaining, but which also does not discriminate by gender.

III

Most of the problems of child custody litigation can be avoided by not litigating the issue in the first place. It is here that the wisdom of the old maternal preference, or its gender-neutral alternative, the "primary caretaker parent presumption," becomes apparent. The primary caretaker presumption severely limits opportunities for using child custody litigation as a bargaining chip.

West Virginia law does not permit a maternal preference. But we do accord an explicit and almost absolute preference to the "primary caretaker parent" of young children, *Garska, supra,* at 68, 278 S.E.2d at 362. We have defined the "primary caretaker" as the parent who:

> . . . has taken primary responsibility for, inter alia, the performance of the following caring and nurturing duties of a parent: (1) preparing and planning of meals; (2) bathing, grooming and dressing; (3) purchasing, cleaning, and care of clothes; (4) medical care, including nursing and trips to physicians; (5) arranging for social interaction among peers after school, i.e.

transporting to friends' houses or, for example, to girl or boy scout meetings; (6) arranging alternative care, i.e. babysitting, day-care, etc.; (7) putting child to bed at night, attending to child in the middle of the night, waking child in the morning; (8) disciplining, i.e. teaching general manners and toilet training; (9) educating, i.e. religious, cultural, social, etc.; and, (10) teaching elementary skills, i.e., reading, writing and arithmetic.

Id. at 69-70, 278 S.E.2d at 363.

This list of criteria usually, but not necessarily, spells "mother." That fact reflects social reality; the rule itself is neutral on its face and in its application. When women pursue lucrative and successful careers while their husbands take care of the children, those husbands receive the benefit of the presumption as strongly as do traditional mothers. Furthermore, where both parents share child-rearing responsibilities equally, our courts hold hearings to determine which parent would be the better single parent.[33] This latter situation is rare, but is evidence of the actual gender-neutrality of the primary caretaker presumption.

QUERY

Are the first two sentences of this paragraph logically consistent?

Our rule inevitably involves some injustice to fathers who, as a group, are usually not primary caretakers. There are instances when the primary caretaker will not be the better custodian in the long run. Yet there is no guarantee that the courts will be able to know, in advance and based on the deliberately distorted evidence that characterizes courtroom custody proceedings, when such is the case. And, notwithstanding its theoretical imperfections, the primary caretaker parent presumption acknowledges that exhaustive hearings on relative degrees of parenting ability rarely disclose any but the most gross variations in skill and suitability. Permitting such hearings inevitably has distortive effect on the parties' behavior, and is likely to lead to potentially disastrous emotional trauma for all concerned if the case goes to court.

Any rule concerning custody matters will be gender-biased, in effect if not in form. An allegedly gender-neutral rule that permits exhaustive inquiry into relative degrees of paternal fitness is inevitably going to favor men in most instances. This bias follows from the observed pattern that in consensual divorces where there is no fight over money—either because there isn't any or because there is enough to go around—women overwhelmingly receive custody through the willing acquiescence of their husbands. Experience teaches that if there is any chance that the average mother will lose her children at divorce, she will either stay married under oppressive conditions or trade away valuable economic rights to ensure that she will be given custody.

In West Virginia we intend that generally the question of which parent, if either, is the primary caretaker of minor children in a divorce proceeding is to be proven with lay testimony from the parties themselves and from teachers, relatives and neighbors. In most cases, the question of which parent does the lion's share of the chores can be answered satisfactorily and quickly. Once the primary caretaker has been identified, the only question is whether that parent is a "fit parent." In this regard, the court is not concerned with assessing relative degrees of fitness between the two parents such as might require expert witnesses, but only with whether the primary caretaker achieves a passing grade on an objective test. That issue does not require experts.

To be a fit parent, a person must: (1) feed and clothe the child appropriately; (2) adequately supervise the child and protect him or her from harm; (3) provide habitable housing; (4) avoid extreme discipline, child abuse, and other similar vices; and (5) refrain from immoral behavior under circumstances that would affect the child. In this last regard, restrained normal sexual behavior does not make a parent unfit. The law does not attend to traditional concepts of immorality in the abstract, but only to whether the child is a party to, or is influenced by, such behavior. Whether a primary caretaker parent meets these criteria can be determined through nonexpert testimony, and the criteria themselves are sufficiently specific that they discourage frivolous disputation.

Furthermore, since *J.B. v. A.B., supra* note 5, we have divided children into the three age groups. With regard to children of tender years, the primary caretaker presumption operates absolutely if the primary caretaker is a fit parent. However, with those children able to formulate an intelligent opinion about their custody, our rule becomes more flexible. In exceptional cases when the trial judge is unsure about the wisdom of awarding the children to the primary caretaker, he or she may ask the children for their preference and accord that preference whatever weight he or she deems appropriate. Such an interview, because of the problems in asking children about their parental preference, should not, however, be routine and neither party may demand such an interview as a matter of right. When the children's testimony is necessary, the trial judge should seek to minimize the damage by talking to the children on record but outside their parents' presence. Thus, the "experts" who can rebut the primary caretaker presumption are principally the children, although in extraordinary circumstances a judge may seek or allow expert testimony. The judge is not, however, required to hear the testimony of the children, and will usually not do so, particularly if he or she suspects bribery or undue influence. Nonetheless, by allowing the children to be acceptable experts in our courts, an escape valve is provided in unusually hard cases.

Finally, once a child reaches the age of fourteen, the child is permitted to name his or her guardian if both parents are fit. Often, as might be expected, this means that the parent who makes the child's life more comfortable will get custody; however, there is little alternative because children over fourteen who are living where they do not want to live will become unhappy and ungovernable anyway. In all three cases, the parent who receives custody is primarily responsible for making decisions concerning the child and for providing the child's permanent home. The other parent, however, is usually accorded liberal visitation rights, including the right to have the child during holidays, part of the summer, and some weekends.

Although the primary caretaker parent presumption may appear cut-and-dried and insufficiently sensitive to the needs of individual children, it serves the welfare of the child by achieving stability of care in the child's life, reducing the uncertainty of custody decisions, limiting the invasiveness of the custody determination process and reducing the expense of domestic litigation. Because litigation *per se* can be the cause of serious emotional damage to children (and to adults), we consider the primary caretaker parent presumption to be in the best interests of children. Even more important, children cannot be used as pawns in fights that are actually about money because a lawyer can tell a primary caretaker parent that, if fit, that parent has *absolutely no chance* of losing custody of very young children. The result is that questions of alimony, property distribution, and child support are settled on their own merits.

QUERY

Is this an argument for "no-fault" custody?

IV

When we adopted the primary caretaker presumption in *Garska,* only [Oregon] relied upon a determination of primary caretaker in reaching custody decisions. Since then the Supreme Court of Minnesota, citing *Garska,* adopted a primary caretaker parent presumption for custody of young children. *Pikula v. Pikula,* 374 N.W.2d 705 (Minn.1985). . . .

[There follows a discussion of various states that have considered the West Virginia rule with varying degrees of approval although without adopting a primary caretaker presumption.]

Many jurisdictions have turned to joint custody to solve divorce-related custody problems.[40] Under joint custody, divorced parents have equal time with the children and equal say in decisions about their schooling, religious training and lifestyle.[41] Joint custody, however, does not solve the problem of extortion in the settlement process because many mothers find shared custody as unacceptable as complete loss of custody.

N.B.

Without applying the maternal preference, the tender years doctrine, or the primary caregiver presumption, many courts will nevertheless award custody or residential care to the mother because, as a society, we believe mothers are better nurturers on balance than fathers and that maternal care is somehow more important to a child than paternal care. In addition, judges are naturally inclined to favor the closest parent-child bond, which, as Justice Neely points out, usually spells "mother."

QUERY

If Mom is to get custody anyway, doesn't it make sense and save time and money to have a presumption in her favor? Is this Neely's most powerful argument?

Joint custody works well when both parents live in the same neighborhood or at least in the same city, and so long as they can cooperate on child-rearing matters. Divorcing couples on their own often agreed to joint custody in the past, long before court-ordered joint custody became a public issue. When joint custody is by agreement, the same cooperative spirit that animated the underlying agreement will usually allow the parents to rear a child with no more antagonism than is experienced in most married households.

Voluntary joint custody, however, must be distinguished from court-ordered joint custody. A court can order that custody be shared, but it cannot order that the parents stop bickering, stop disparaging one another, or accommodate one another in child-care decisions as married persons would. And if parents do not live close to one another, joint custody can place an intolerable strain on a child's social and academic life if one parent is not willing to allow the other to supply a more-or-less permanent home.

Furthermore, parents must constantly give permission for one thing or another. Who decides whether the child can have a driver's license at age sixteen? Who decides when the child can date, under what conditions, and with whom? When the parents violently disagree—and particularly when they disagree because there are continuing fights left over from the marriage—the child is likely to be left hopelessly confused as the parents are played off one against the other. We do not authorize court-ordered joint custody today over the objection of a primary caretaker parent, although parents may agree to such an arrangement. As we said in Syllabus point 4 of *Lowe v. Lowe,* _____ W.Va. _____, 370 S.E.2d 731 (1988):

> A cardinal criterion for an award of joint custody is the agreement of the parties and their mutual ability to co-operate in reaching shared decisions in matters affecting the child's welfare.

V

In the present case, the record established that Mrs. M. was the primary caretaker parent of the child. Mrs. M. (1) bathed, groomed and dressed the child, (2) purchased, cleaned and cared for his clothes, (3) organized and purchased his food, (4) secured medical attention, when needed, (5) missed work to nurse the child, and (6) put the child to bed, attended to him in the middle of the night and awakened him in the morning. We note that the father assisted in some of the cooking, and both parents were responsible for disciplining, educating and teaching general manners and elementary skills.

In Syllabus Point 4, *J.B. v. A.B.,* 161 W.Va. 332, 242 S.E.2d 248 (1978), as modified by *Garska, supra,* 167 W.Va. at 70, 278 S.E.2d at 363, we discussed the relationship between a parent's adultery and parental fitness.

> Acts of sexual misconduct by a [primary caregiver], albeit wrongs against an innocent spouse, may not be considered as evidence going to the fitness of the [caregiver] for child custody unless [his or] her conduct is so aggravated, given contemporary moral standards, that reasonable [persons] would find that [his or] her immorality, *per se,* warranted a finding of unfitness because

of the deleterious effect upon the child of being raised by a [primary caregiver] with such a defective character.

Although the record contains evidence of three acts of marital misconduct, two of which were adultery, there is no evidence that Mrs. M.'s marital misconduct was known to the child or damaged the child. We have repeatedly held that a "circuit court may not base a finding of parental unfitness solely on the ground that the parent is guilty of sexual misconduct." *Bickler, supra* note 2, _____ W.Va. at _____, 344 S.E.2d at 632. Mrs. M. testified that two of the instances occurred about midnight when the child was asleep and the third occurred after the child and his stepbrother left to visit a neighbor and was concluded before the children returned home. Although evidence of marital misconduct, this restrained normal sexual behavior does not make Mrs. M. an unfit parent.

The circuit court was clearly wrong in its position that the three instances of sexual misconduct, occurring over two years, warranted a finding of unfitness, without evidence establishing that the child was harmed or that the conduct *per se* was so outrageous, given contemporary moral standards, as to call into question her fitness as a parent. *J.B. v. A.B., supra* note 5, 161 W.Va. at 345, 242 S.E.2d at 256. The absence of such evidence requires reversal.

Accordingly, for the reasons set forth above, the judgment of the Circuit Court of Wood County with respect to the granting of a divorce is affirmed, but with respect to the award of custody is reversed and this case is remanded with directions to enter an order consistent with this opinion.

Affirmed in part; Reversed in part; and Remanded with directions.

[1] Mr. M. has two other children from a previous marriage, Matthew and Jason, who live with their mother.

[9] Despite popular perceptions to the effect that child abusers are predominantly male, women are just as likely to be abusers as are men. See D. Gil, *Violence Against Children* 117 (1970). *See also* Schwartz, Book Review, 2 *Yale L. & Pol'y Rev.* 179, 183-84 (1983).

[10] See J. Goldstein, A. Freud and A. Solnit, *Before the Best Interests of the Child* 31-35 (1979); Wexler, "Rethinking the Modification Child Custody Decrees," 94 *Yale L.J.* 757, 799 (1985); Leonard & Provence, "The Development of Parent-Child Relationships and the Psychological Parent," 53 *Conn.B.J. 320, 326 (1979).*

[11] Chambers, "Rethinking the Substantive Rules for Custody Disputes in Divorce," 83 *Mich.L.Rev.* 477, 530 (1984). Professor Chambers also notes that these observations present the strongest case for a presumption of custody of young children with the primary caretaker parent. However, Professor Chambers believes that the substantial emotional bonds a child forms with secondary caretakers are undervalued.

[12] 39 *J.Marr. & Fam.* 309 (1977).

[16] Over 90 percent of divorces are uncontested. This means that the granting of the divorce is *pro forma* and routine, with all of the important decisions made out of court—usually in law office negotiations. In the case of middle-class and rich clients, failure to contest usually means a settlement has been reached. *N.Y. Law Journal,* July 11, 1984, at 1, col. 1.

[17] See Bolocofsky, "Use and Abuse of Mental Health Experts in Child Custody Determinations, 7 *Behav.Sci. & L.* 197 (1989) (indicating an overreliance by mental health professionals on questionable sources of data and the inadequacies of clinical judgment in child custody evaluations).

[18] See Ziskin & Faust, "Psychiatric and Psychological Evidence in Child Custody Cases," 24 *Trial* 44 (August 1989) for a discussion on the use of scientific and professional research to dispute the expertise of mental health professionals and to question the validity of their evaluations.

[19] S. Goldstein & A. Solnit, *Divorce and Your Child* 64 (1984). See also Chambers, *supra* note 11, at 569. "Litigation imposes heavy emotional and finanancial costs on families. Unlike most other forms of litigation the parties to this dispute generally continue to deal with each other after it is over: The 'loser' is entitled to visitation over a long period of years."

[20] In *J.B. v. A.B., supra* note 5, 161 W.Va. at 340, 242 S.E.2d at 253, we stated: "The concept of 'tender years' is some what elastic; obviously and infant in the suckling stage is of tender years, while an adolescent fourteen years of age or older is not. . . . Between the two extremes are children who are more or less capable of expressing a preference concerning their custody."

[21] "[A]n adolescent fourteen yars of age or older . . . has an absolute right under W.Va.Code, 44-10-4 [1923] to nominate his own guardian." *J.B. v. A.B., supra* note 5, at 340, 242 S.E.2d; *Shimp v. Shimp* — W. Va.,—, 366 S.E.2d 663 (1988); Ga.Code Ann., 19-9-1(a) (Supp. 1988) (child fourteen or older may choose parent unless parent is unfit); Ohio Rev. Code Ann. 3109.04 (Baldwin 1983) (child twelve years or older may choose parent unless court finds parent unfit).

[22] Scott, Reppucci & Aber, "Children's Preference in Adjudicated Custody Decisions," 22 *Ga.L.Rev.* 1035, 1055 (1988) (a child's preference may be influenced by "transitory anger at the 'guilty' parent or the entertainment by a "week-end" parent).

[23] Mnookin & Kornhauser, "Bargaining in the Shadow of the Law, 88 *Yale L.J.* 950 (1979).

[24] The sheer complexity of custody decisions means that the measurement process itself changes the thing that is measured. Lack of neutrality in measuring things is a recurring problem in many areas of human endeavor. In physics the problem is known as the Heisenberg uncertainty principle—which refers to Werner Heisenberg's discovery that it is impossible to measure both the speed and the location of an electron simultaneously because the measuring devices themselves affect the speed and location being measured. Heisenberg, "Uber den anschaulichen inhalt der quantentheoretische Kinematik und Mechanik," 43 *Z.Phys.* 172 (1927); see also A. Zee, *Fearful Symmetry: The Search for Beauty in Modern Physics* 140 (1986). A similar principle applies to divorce cases—measuring family problems usually makes these problems worse.

[26] J. Despert, *supra* note 25, at 116-50; J. Goldstein, A. Freud & A. Solnit, *supra* note 25, at 37-39. See also sources cited at note 25, *supra.* Cf. Okpaku, "Psychology: Impediment or Aid in Child Custody Cases?" 29 *Rutgers L.J.* 1117, 1140-41 (1976) (lack of conclusive

empirical research in the area of children's reaction to custodial discontinuity); Dembitz, "Beyond Any Discipline's Competence" (Book Review)., 83 *Yale L.J.* 1304, 1309-11 (1974) (continuity of the custodial arrangement not always of supreme importance) (reviewing J. Goldstein, A. Freud & A. Solnit, *Beyond the Best Interests of the Child* (1973)).

28 *See Garska, supra* in text, 167 W.Va. at 66-68, 278 S.E.2d at 360-62, for a discussion of the Solomon Syndrome—the phenomenon that "the parent who is most attached to the child will be willing to accept an inferior bargain."

29 Each state is required by federal law to establish guidelines for child support amounts, effective 1 October 1987. 42 U.S.C. 667 (Supp. IV 1986). *See also* 45 C.F.R. 302.56 (1988).

31 "[Single] [w]omen maintaining families are far more likely to be unemployed than husbands or wives, their average (median) family income is less than half that of married couples, and they are five times as likely to be in poverty." Bureau of Labor Statistics, U.S. Dep't of Labor, *Women at Work: A Chartbook* 26 (1983). This gap seems to be widening. U.S. Commission on Civil Rights, *Disadvantaged Women and Their Children: A Growing Crisis* 6 (1983) (hereinafter cited as "Disadvantaged Women"). *See also* Bureau of Labor Statistics, U.S. Dep't of Labor, Women & Work (August 1987) (noting that ninety percent of persons on welfare are women and children); *N.Y.T.* February 26, 1988 at 1, col. 1, reporting a study by the Congressional Budget Office that found although median adjusted family income overall rose twenty percent from 1970 to 1986, family income for single mothers with children rose only two percent.

32 Of economically active women ages 25-34 with no spouse present, those without children worked an average of 1,966 hours annually, while those with children worked from 1,171 hours (for those with four or five children) to 1,775 hours (for those with one child). Smith, "Estimating Annual Hours of Labor Force Activity," 106 *Monthly Lab.Rev.* 13, 19 (Feb.1983). This hardship is compounded in several ways. First, in order to work full-time, working mothers must obtain child care, which (unless relatives or friends are available regularly) is always expensive and often prohibitively so. Disadvantaged Women, *supra* note 31, at 12-13, 63. Second, in general "[w]omen are segregated in a few occupations that pay low wages and have little promotion potential." *Id.* at 63. And third, there is evidence that the pressures of raising a family alone and beating back poverty are major sources of emotional stress. *Id.* at 52. Note also that women acting as single parents "are also in the category of persons who are least likely to receive preventive health care or adequate care during illness." *Id.* Men, on the other hand, largely avoid the economic pitfalls afflicting divorced women. *Id.* at 12. For more on the psychological strains suffered by working women, see J. Westman, *supra* note 3, at 105, and Johnson & Johnson, "Attitudes Toward Parenting in Dual Career Families," 134 *Am.J. Psychiatry* 391 (1977).

33 *Garska, supra* in text; *T.C.B. v. H.A.B.*, —W.Va. —, 317 S.E.2d 174 (1984) (upholding a finding of joint primary caretakers and an award of custody to the father).

40 Over half the states have adopted legislation dealing with joint custody awards within the last several years. See Scott & Derdyn, "Rethinking Joint Custody," 45 *Ohio St.L.J.* 455, 456 n. 5 (1984). Some laws require court approval of voluntary joint custody arrangements, absent unusual circumstances. Others authorize courts to enter joint custody orders over the objections of either or both parties. Some could be read as creating a legislative presumption for joint custody even over the objections of either or both parties. *Id.* at 457 n. 9, 471 n. 73.

41 Actually, in many cases one parent will provide the permanent residence of the child while other aspects of child-raising are shared evenly. Generally, the parent with whom the child is staying at the time will make day-to-day decisions (e.g., permission for school outings), with major decisions being shared between the two. See generally Folberg & Graham, "Joint Custody of Children Following Divorce," 12 *U.C.D.L.Rev.* 523 (1979) (thoroughly documented discussion of joint custody plans, including history and prevailing attitudes).

QUESTIONS

Before leaving this difficult policy area, let us consider some issues raised by other writers.

From Tender Years to Psychological Parent.

> [T]he Supreme Court of Connecticut [in *Seymour v. Seymour,* 180 Conn. 705 (1980)] used a panoply of modern vocabulary, such as "nurturing parents," "psychological parents," and "parenting ability," to reach its decision to uphold the custody award favoring the mother. One wonders whether all this judicial reasoning was necessary to arrive at the quite possibly foregone conclusion. . . . The hearing was largely ritualistic, with its show of seemingly plausible and progressive steps, such as the appointment of counsel for the minor child and seven trial days of extensive hearing with expert opinions by a psychiatric social worker, family relations officer, and two psychiatrists. Of these experts two favored the father, one the mother, and one felt it made no difference which parent was awarded custody. The trial court, predictably, favored the expert statement preferring the mother and, equally predictably, was upheld on appeal.
>
> — Weyrauch & Katz, *American Family Law in Transition* (1983)

Weyrauch and Katz suggest that the foray into psychology by the Connecticut court in *Seymour* may have been prompted by the fact that the mother and father, armed with highly paid expert witnesses, were urbane and sophisticated and would have found a more genuinely stated judicial preference for the mother unacceptable.

Query: Does New England urbanity preclude Justice Neely's down-to-earth approach. As Professor Krause puts it: "From West Virginia, the 'primary caretaker rule' is emerging as a thinly disguised variant of the maternal preference." Is "psychological parent" a disguised variant of the maternal preference more palatable to more urbane states?

Then there is the solution to the hard choice of parents proposed by the trio that invented the "psychological parent": "A judicially supervised drawing of lots between two equally acceptable psychological parents might be the most rational and least offensive process for resolving the hard choice." J. Goldstein, A. Freud, & A. Solnit, *Beyond the Best Interests of the Child* 153, n.12 (1973).

Query: Could an appellate court countenance a lower court flipping a coin to decide the fate of the children? Would that be an abuse of discretion?

Joint or Sole Custody? Results from studies of the effects of joint custody have only recently begun to emerge. Though definitive conclusions are still premature, some tentative conclusions are worth repeating:

No evidence emerged from this study [of maternal, paternal, and joint custody] that would support a legal presumption for maternal custody. . . . The only variable that predicted poorer adjustment in children was parental conflict . . . My conclusion, based on these fifty families, is that joint custody at its best is superior to single-parent custody at *its* best.

— Deborah Anne Luepnitz, *Child Custody* (1982)

Children who are part of a joint custody or frequent visitation arrangement in which there is chronic conflict between divorced parents are more likely to be emotionally, behaviorally, and socially disturbed than children in sole custody or those whose parents are cooperative.

— Judith S. Wallerstein & Janet R. Johnston, "Children of Divorce," 11 *Pediatrics in Review* 197 (Jan. 1990)

Joint legal custody is neither the solution to the problem of divorce nor a catalyst for increasing conflict in divorcing families.

— Catherine R. Albiston, Eleanor E. Maccoby, & Robert R. Mnookin, "Does Joint Legal Custody Matter?," *Stanford Law & Policy Review* 167 (Spring 1990)

Query: May we then draw the tentative conclusion that joint custody is good when parents can cooperate and bad when they continue to fight? If this were the focus of inquiry, could we determine this without resorting to expensive testimony from suspect expert witnesses?

What about the Father?

Even laymen are inclined to think that most men do not want custody of their children and therefore do not lose anything if custody is automatically awarded to the mother. However, it is a myth that fathers walk away from their family after a divorce unscathed. In fact, many men experience a "severe sense of loss" after divorce which often leads to physical and psychological manifestations.

— Judith B. Jennison, "The Search for Equality in a Woman's World," *Rutgers Law Review* (Summer 1991)

[I]n the usual pattern, fathers lose wife, home and children, and end up with only visitation rights and support obligations. Some men become so overwhelmed by these difficulties that sooner or later they just give up and stop seeing their children.

— Folber & Graham, "Joint Custody of Children Following Divorce," 12 *U.C. Davis Law Review* 523 (1979)

Query: Have we been fair to fathers? Does our system of divorce leave fathers emotionally deprived and mothers economically impoverished?

Is This a Legal Problem?

Query: Does the present process primarily fill lawyer's and expert's pockets, without contributing to justice, relevance, truth, or the welfare of parents and children? If so, would we be better off relegating the custody problem to other institutions?

Query: Would the process be improved suddenly if either a presumption in favor of the primary caregiver or a presumption in favor of joint custody were adopted, rather than attempting to perfect "guidelines," "factors," or discretion?

Query: Is the "best interests of the child" a bad standard?

EXERCISES

Answer the questions according to the law of your state.

1. What are the rights of a putative father to custody? 45 A.L.R.3d 216.
2. What are the considerations in a contest between parents and grandparents over custody? 25 A.L.R.3d 7; 29 A.L.R.3d 366; 31 A.L.R.3d 1187.
3. Is an award of joint custody proper? 17 A.L.R.4th 1013.
4. Is the primary caregiver role a factor in custody awards? 40 A.L.R. 4th 812.
5. Does remarriage justify modification of custody? 43 A.L.R.2d 363.

CHAPTER 15
Adoption and Related Matters

The Infamous "Baby M" Case

Surrogate mother Mary Beth Whitehead and her family flee reporters at the family court division of the Bergen County Superior Court in Hackensack, New Jersey. She told the judge that she should be allowed to keep custody of her baby because the father might be her own husband and not the man who agreed to pay her $10,000 to be artificially inseminated and carry the baby to term. The surrogacy controversy began with the Baby M case. This case, as well as adoption-related topics, is discussed in this chapter.

— Courtesy AP/Wide World Photos.

The most interesting thing in the world is another human being who wonders, suffers, and raises the questions that have bothered him to the last day of his life, knowing he will never get the answers.

Will Durant

It's time that people realized that adoption is for children, not infertile adults.

Annette Baran, psychotherapist, (referring to baby Jessica (DeBoer), quoted in *Time*, July 19, 1993, at 49)

OUTLINE

15.1 ADOPTION: AN OVERVIEW
15.2 THE PARTIES
    Blood Relatives
    Foster Parents
    Stepparents
    Childless Strangers
    Nonmarital Fathers
15.3 SURROGACY
15.4 FACTORS INFLUENCING ADOPTION AND THEIR CONSTITUTIONAL IMPLICATIONS
    Religion
    Race
    Legal Bonds
15.5 EQUITABLE ADOPTION
15.6 DEPENDENCY PROCEEDINGS
    SUMMARY

15.1 ADOPTION: AN OVERVIEW

Adoption creates bonds of parent and child between persons who did not previously have this relationship. Ordinarily this involves the severance of legal bonds between a child and its natural parent or parents, and substitution of a new parent or parents, with all the legal consequences of the parent-child relationship. (See appendix 15A, for the language proposed under

417

Uniform Adoption Act § 14, by which one set of parents is substituted for another.)

Adoption was not recognized in England until 1926. The American law of adoption traces its roots to Massachusetts statutes of 1851. Until recently, adoption was primarily concerned with finding children for childless couples; providing parents for children was an incidental benefit. As the focus of public policy has turned away from parental rights toward the interests of children, some reorientation has taken place. An early issue in the law of adoption was the degree to which judicial intervention was appropriate. Today governmental administrative agencies concern themselves with the adoption process, and legislatures have enacted increasing numbers of laws to regulate the adoption process.

Government has entered the adoption process in favor of children with special needs, creating subsidies so parents whose resources would otherwise be insufficient can adopt children. The National Conference of Commissioners on Uniform State Laws published the Uniform Adoption Act in 1953 (and revised it in 1969; see appendix 15A and figure 15-1) and the Department of Health, Education, and Welfare proposed a model act for the states called "An Act for the Adoption of Children."

15.2   THE PARTIES

Other than the status of adulthood, states place few statutory requirements on the prospective adopting parent. Administrative or judicial approval, however, is another matter. The law has been reluctant to grant anyone a right to adopt, but clear preferences may be found in the law and in

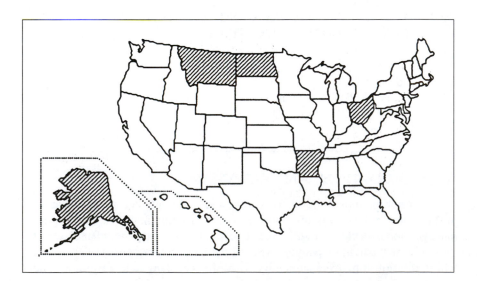

FIGURE 15-1
States adopting the
Uniform Adoption Act

the decisions approving and disapproving particular adoptions. An examination of some of the most common situations will help to clarify the adoption picture.

Blood Relatives

Intuition suggests that blood relatives make the best caregivers of children. By custom, orphans become the wards of their close relatives; someone is expected to come forward to take charge of the children. For divorced parents with minimal resources or for working single mothers, parental duties may be overwhelming; hence, children are often placed in the care of grandparents or their aunts and uncles. Although this may be a purely temporary placement, with legal custody remaining with the parent or parents, the desire to adopt may arise for many reasons. With orphans, de facto adoption may be followed by legal adoption. The court or agency looks for the same factors applicable to custody disputes—wholesome environment, continuity of care (same home, school, neighborhood, etc.), keeping siblings together, and so on. Divorce raises an added complication, as the natural parents may fight the adoption. Assuming consent to the adoption, however, blood relatives are highly favored.

Foster Parents

Children who have been placed in the care of strangers may remain with them via adoption even though foster care administered through the state is commonly conditioned on the foster parents not attempting to become adoptive parents.

Stepparents

One of the most common relationships involved in adoption is that of stepparent. The typical scenario consists of a stepfather who is actively involved in raising his wife's children by a former marriage, with the natural father mostly or completely absent and perhaps totally neglecting support obligations. Adoption seems most appropriate when the children have developed a filial attachment toward their stepparent which is reciprocated with affection and support. The parents may regard adoption with favor because other children have been born to the marriage or as a vehicle for renaming the child, although a name change may be accomplished without adoption. The greatest stumbling block to such an adoption is the denial of consent by the natural parent. Though such a denial may be overcome by a court finding that abandonment or neglect operated to sever the bonds between parent and child, the law so strongly favors continuance of the biological bond as a legal bond that lack of consent, in many instances, is fatal to the adoption process.

If the natural parent has visited the child on regular, albeit infrequent, occasions and made a reasonable effort to support, lack of consent will almost always prevent adoption. Adoption severs the natural parents' rights with regard to the child—something the courts are extremely reluctant to do. Because nonconsent can thwart even the dutiful stepparent, who has the most persuasive claim to adopt, the rule against unconsented adoption applies with even greater severity to other nonrelatives who wish to adopt.

Childless Strangers

Couples unable to bear children are most likely to go to adoption agencies or lawyers to seek children to adopt. Adoption agencies are usually extensively regulated and subject to statutory restriction. Potential adoptive parents are in theory carefully scrutinized both for the environment they can provide and for their capacity to be good parents. The process may be lengthy and cumbersome, so many prospective parents employ attorneys to facilitate the process.

Nonmarital Fathers

Until recent years, fathers of illegitimate offspring (children born out of wedlock) had no rights or legal relationship with their children. With the advent of financial responsibility through paternity suits, the fathers could expect to have parental rights as well. Visitation rights began to be granted, and custody was possible when the mother died or her custody was detrimental to the child. Still, because the father had not married the mother and usually had not otherwise acknowledged paternity, his rights inevitably threatened the maternal bond. Courts and legislatures have to balance recognizing the special place of the mother and depriving the father of rights. *Stanley v. Illinois,* 405 U.S. 645 (1972), was a landmark decision recognizing rights of the unwed father. *Stanley* struck down as unconstitutional an Illinois statutory scheme whereby an unwed father was presumed to be "unfit" and that did not allow the father an opportunity to be heard. Three children were involved, born of a long-term relationship between Joan and Peter Stanley. When Joan died, the State of Illinois appointed guardians for the children over Peter's protestations. The U.S. Supreme Court could not approve this procedure:

> [W]e are here not asked to evaluate the legitimacy of the state ends, rather, to determine whether the means used to achieve these ends are constitutionally defensible. What is the state interest in separating children from fathers without a hearing designed to determine whether the father is unfit in a particular disputed case? We observe that the State registers no gain towards its declared goals when it separates children from the custody of fit parents.

CASE NO. 15-1 *Rights of Unwed Fathers*

Despite its invalidation of the Illinois statute in *Stanley v. Illinois,* the Supreme Court later showed its willingness to place some limitations on the rights of unwed fathers.

QUILLOIN v. WALCOTT
434 U.S. 246, 98 S. Ct. 549 (1978)
United States Supreme Court

Mr. Justice MARSHALL delivered the opinion of the Court.

The issue in this case is the constitutionality of Georgia's adoption laws as applied to deny an unwed father authority to prevent adoption of his illegitimate child. The child was born in December 1964 and has been in the custody and control of his mother, appellee Ardell Williams Walcott, for his entire life. The mother and the child's natural father, appellant Leon Webster Quilloin, never married each other or established a home together, and in September 1967 the mother married appellee Randall Walcott. In March 1976, she consented to adoption of the child by her husband, who immediately filed a petition for adoption. Appellant attempted to block the adoption and to secure visitation rights, but he did not seek custody or object to the child's continuing to live with appellees. Although appellant was not found to be an unfit parent, the adoption was granted over his objection.

In *Stanley v. Illinois,* 405 U.S. 645, 92 S.Ct. 1208, 31 L.Ed.2d 551 (1972), this Court held that the State of Illinois was barred, as a matter of both due process and equal protection, from taking custody of the children of an unwed father, absent a hearing and a particularized finding that the father was an unfit parent. The Court concluded, on the one hand, that a father's interest in the "companionship, care, custody, and management" of his children is "cognizable and substantial," *id.,* at 651-652, 92 S.Ct., at 1212-13, and, on the other hand,

that the State's interest in caring for the children is "*de minimis*" if the father is in fact a fit parent, *id.,* at 657- 658, 92 S.Ct., at 1215-1216. *Stanley* left unresolved the degree of protection a State must afford to the rights of an unwed father in a situation, such as that presented here, in which the countervailing interests are more substantial.

I

Generally speaking, under Georgia law a child born in wedlock cannot be adopted without the consent of each living parent who has not voluntarily surrendered rights in the child or been adjudicated an unfair parent. Even where the child's parents are divorced or separated at the time of the adoption proceedings, either parent may veto the adoption. In contrast, only the consent of the mother is required for adoption of an illegitimate child. Ga.Code § 74-403(3) (1975). To acquire the same veto authority possessed by other parents, the father of a child born out of wedlock must legitimate his offspring, either by marrying the mother and acknowledging the child as his own, § 74-101, or by obtaining a court order declaring the child legitimate and capable of inheriting from the father, § 74-103. But unless and until the child is legitimated, the mother is the only recognized parent and is given exclusive authority to exercise all parental prerogatives, § 74-203, including the power to veto adoption of the child.

Appellant did not petition for legitimation of his child at any time during the 11 years between the child's birth and the filing of Randall Walcott's adoption petition. However, in response to Walcott's petition, appellant filed an application for a writ of habeas corpus seeking visitation rights, a petition for legitimation, and an objection to the adoption. Shortly thereafter, appellant amended his pleadings by adding the claim that §§ 74-203 and 74-403(3) were unconstitutional as applied to his case, insofar as they denied him the rights granted to married parents, and presumed unwed fathers to be unfit as a matter of law.

* * *

II

* * *

The fact that appellant was provided with a hearing on his legitimation petition is not, however, a complete answer to his attack on the constitutionality of §§ 74-203 and 74-403(3). The trial court denied appellant's petition, and thereby precluded him from gaining veto authority, on the ground that legitimation was not in the "best interests of the child"; appellant contends that he was entitled to recognition and preservation of his parental rights absent a showing of his "unfitness." Thus, the underlying issue is whether, in the circumstances of this case and in light of the authority granted by Georgia law to married fathers, appellant's interests were adequately protected by a "best interests of the child" standard. We examine this issue first under the Due Process Clause and then under the Equal Protection Clause.

A

* * *

We have little doubt that the Due Process Clause would be offended "[i]f a State were to attempt to force the breakup of a natural family, over the objections of the parents and their children, without some showing of unfitness and for the sole reason that to do so was thought to be in the children's best interest." *Smith v. Organization of Foster Families,* 431 U.S. 816, 862-863, 97 S.Ct. 2094, 2119, 53 L.Ed.2d 14 (1977) (Stewart, J., concurring in judgment). But this is not a case in which the unwed father at any time had, or sought, actual or legal custody of his child. Nor is this a case in which the proposed adoption would place the child with a new set of parents with whom the child had never before lived. Rather, the result of the adoption in this case is to give full recognition to a family unit already in existence, a result desired by all concerned, except appellant. Whatever might be required in other situations, we cannot say that the State was required in this situation to find anything more than that the adoption, and denial of legitimation, were in the "best interests of the child."

B

Appellant contends that even if he is not entitled to prevail as a matter of due process, principles of equal protection require that his authority to veto an adoption be measured by the same standard that would have been applied to a married father. In particular, appellant asserts that his interests are indistinguishable from those of a married father who is separated or divorced from the mother and is no longer living with his child, and therefore the State acted impermissibly in treating his case differently. We think appellant's interests are readily distinguishable from those of a separated or divorced father, and accordingly believe that the State could permissibly give appellant less veto authority than it provides to a married father.

* * *

For these reasons, we conclude that §§ 74-203 and 74-403(3), as applied in this case, did not deprive appellant of his asserted rights under the Due Process and Equal Protection Clauses. The judgment of the Supreme Court of Georgia is accordingly,

Affirmed.

CASE NO. 15-2   When in Doubt, Get a Blood Test

Lest you think that unwed fathers have undue advantages in family law, the *Ruth* case is provided to dispel that illusion.

RUTH v. FLETCHER
237 Va. 366, 377 S.E.2d 412 (1989)
Supreme Court of Virginia

THOMAS, Justice.

The central issue in this appeal is whether Harry Theodore Fletcher (Ted), successfully proved a case of intentional infliction of emotional distress against Patricia Ann Wilson Ruth (Patty). Ted alleged that Patty intentionally convinced him that she was pregnant with his child; that she fostered the development of a bond of love and affection between Ted and the child; that she caused Ted to pay monthly child support in return for visitation rights; that she persuaded Ted's parents that the child was their grandchild; and that when it suited Patty's purposes, she cut off Ted's visitation rights and proved that he was *not* the child's father, thus, causing Ted severe emotional distress. The case was tried to a jury which returned a $35,000 verdict in Ted's favor, upon which judgment was entered.

The proper disposition of this case is controlled by our decision in *Womack v. Eldridge*, 215 Va. 338, 210 S.E.2d 145 (1974). There, we recognized for the first time in Virginia a cause of action for intentional infliction of emotional distress unaccompanied by physical injury. We set forth the elements of the tort in the following language:

> We adopt the view that a cause of action will lie for emotional distress, unaccompanied by physical injury, provided four elements are shown: *One,* the wrongdoer's *conduct was intentional or reckless.* This element is satisfied where the wrongdoer had

the specific purpose of inflicting emotional distress or where he intended his specific conduct and knew or should have known that emotional distress would likely result. *Two,* the *conduct was outrageous and intolerable* in that it offends against the generally accepted standards of decency and morality. This requirement is aimed at limiting frivolous suits and avoiding litigation in situations where only bad manners and mere hurt feelings are involved. *Three,* there was a *causal connection between the wrongdoer's conduct and the emotional distress. Four,* the emotional *distress was severe.*

Id. at 342, 210 S.E.2d at 148 (emphasis added). Further, we pointed out in *Womack* that it was for the court to determine in the first instance whether the conduct complained of could reasonably be regarded as so extreme and outrageous as to permit recovery. *Id.*

Having stated the guiding legal principles, we set forth the facts in the light most favorable to Ted, who prevailed at trial. Ted and Patty met in late 1979 or early 1980. They dated frequently and developed a relationship which involved frequent sexual relations. They maintained their separate residences; his in the District of Columbia, hers in northern Virginia.

They engaged in sexual relations in the first part of September 1980. During that same time period, and within "three, four [or] five" days of engaging in sexual relations with Ted, Patty also engaged in sexual relations with a bartender who worked at a nightclub where Patty worked as a waitress. In October, Patty learned she was pregnant. Her first thought was that the bartender was the father. She met with him, advised him of her pregnancy, told him she wanted to get an abortion, and asked him for money. He said he would give her money when he got paid the following week.

During the next week, Patty thought the matter over, concluded that the child might be Ted's, and decided to keep the baby. When she called the bartender to advise him that she had changed her mind and did not need money from him for an abortion she found that his phone was disconnected and that he was nowhere to be found. She concluded that the bartender had taken a "hike" because he did not want to be involved with the situation.

In late October or early November 1980, Patty told Ted she was pregnant. He asked her whether there was a possibility that the child was not his. She admitted that she had engaged in a single sexual encounter with the bartender. She assured Ted, however, that based on what her doctor had told her about how far her pregnancy had advanced and based on her own calendar, she had determined to her own satisfaction that the child was Ted's. She told Ted that she had made that determination because the probable date of conception was one of the dates in September on which they had had sexual relations.

Patty told Ted's parents that she was going to make them grandparents. She also told mutual friends of Ted and hers that she was carrying Ted's child. She asked Ted to help her by giving her both emotional and financial support. She asked him to attend "Lamaze" childbirth classes with her, to be her childbirth "coach," and to be present when the child was born.

Although initially he did not provide financial support, Ted did most of the other things Patty asked of him. He attended the childbirth classes. At his urging, she decided not to have the child in Virginia, but to have it at George Washington University Hospital in Washington, D.C., which was directly across the street from Ted's apartment. Two weeks before the due date of June 13, 1981, at Ted's urging, Patty moved into his apartment so they could be close to the hospital and ready to go at a moments notice. They agreed upon a first name for the baby.

On June 13, 1981, precisely as predicted, Patty went into labor and the two walked across the street to the hospital. A boy was born that day. Ted stayed with Patty throughout labor and delivery. After the child was born, Ted went out in the hall, with tears in his eyes, to advise his mother who had waited at the hospital with him. He also allowed his name to be placed on the birth certificate as the baby's father. Later that day, Ted went into the hospital nursery to hold the baby.

The next day when Ted visited the nursery, he noticed that the baby had an "I.V." tube in its arm. When he asked why, he was told that Patty had had a fever at the time the child was born and that the baby had an elevated white blood cell count. Ted became alarmed because he associated an elevated white blood cell count with leukemia. Ted discussed the matter with the doctor, who explained that a high white blood cell count sometimes occurred when there was a significant difference in blood type between the mother and child.

The doctor explained further that Patty's blood was type "B" while the baby's blood was type "O." This revelation caught Ted off guard because he knew his own blood was type "A." The doctor recognized the concern in Ted's face and explained "dominant and recessive" blood type characteristics. He said that Patty was type "B" dominant, type "O" recessive, and that one of Ted's parents must have been type "O" in order for the baby to be type "O." Ted called his mother who told him that she was type "A," but that Ted's father was type "O." This answer satisfied Ted.

Ted then talked with Patty about the baby's "I.V." and the blood type information. Patty became angry, because she thought Ted, in an effort to determine whether the child was his, had gone behind her back to check on the child's blood type. She stated to Ted: "[He] is your child. I don't want— I'm not happy about the fact that you have asked for a blood type as if to imply that you are not sure he's your child. He is your child and that's the end of that."

Shortly after the baby was born, Ted's father decided to establish a trust fund for the child. Ted's mother urged Ted to take a definitive blood test to be sure the child was his. Ted told his mother he would ask Patty about it. When he did, Patty said "Absolutely not. This is the second time this has come up. I don't want to hear another word of it. He's your child." Patty threw a tantrum and told Ted, "I don't want you ever to bring the topic up again. I'm tired of hearing it. I'm tired of this, that and the other."

Patty left the hospital and moved in with her parents. Her parents did not welcome Ted because he was not providing financial support to their daughter. For eight to nine months after the child was born, Ted did not provide financial support. He did talk with Patty on the phone and would come to visit on occasion.

In February 1982, Patty asked Ted for $200 per month in financial support. In return, he asked for visitation rights every other weekend. Patty complained that this was too frequent. Ted replied that perhaps $200 per month was too much money. Patty responded by saying she wanted $200 per month and that if Ted did not provide it, she could take him to court to get it and might possibly get more than $200 per month. She called later to apologize and agreed to the visitation he had requested, so long as he paid the $200 per month. Ted began making such payments in March 1982. He continued the payments until June 1985.

As the child grew older, Patty noticed that he did not share any physical similarities with Ted. In 1983, Patty had a chance encounter with the bartender and noticed that her son looked remarkably like the bartender. She began to have doubts about whether Ted was her son's father but she never expressed those doubts to Ted.

In the meantime, a deep, loving relationship grew between Ted and the child. On his weekend visitations, Ted would take the child to Ted's mother's home where she would read him books. The child liked trains. Ted took him on train rides and decorated a room at Ted's apartment with trains. On occasion, Patty would ask Ted's mother to baby-sit "her grandson." The child called Ted "daddy" and would spontaneously hug Ted and tell him, "I love you, daddy." Ted, his brother, and his parents all became attached to the child.

Patty married Michael Ruth in July 1984. In September or October of that year, Patty advised Ted that she and her husband did not need his monthly support payments any longer. Ted said he did not want to stop making the payments because he did not know what effect that might have on his legal rights to the child, so he continued to pay.

Sometime in 1984, Ted started dating Irene Kennedy, whom he married in 1986. In June 1985, Irene met with Patty to plan a vacation trip involving Ted, Irene, and the child. In that conversation, Patty asked Irene how she thought Ted would react if her husband, Michael, wanted to adopt the child. Irene replied that Ted would be "vehemently opposed," and would not give his consent. Patty asked Irene not to tell Ted of the discussion since Patty and her husband had not yet made up their minds about the adoption.

On June 27, 1985, Patty told Ted that she was stopping visitation, that Ted would not be allowed to see the child again, and that she and her husband were filing for adoption. Ted refused to give his consent. He said he would fight for the legal right to see the child.

Patty and her husband, Michael, initiated adoption proceedings in July 1985. Patty filed affidavits in which she stated that Ted was not the child's father but that the bartender was. Within the confines of that proceeding, at Ted's request, a Human Leukocyte Antigen (HLA) test was performed which proved that Ted was not the child's father, but that the bartender was. Ted's visitation rights were terminated by court order.

Ted was asked whether he thought Patty had told him he was the father of the child in order deliberately to hurt him. He replied, "I don't think so, not deliberately to hurt me." He also said that when she called to advise him of the adoption, she was crying. As she talked to him, she asked him why he was not yelling and screaming. He replied, "Because I can hear in your voice, Patty, this is the hardest thing you have ever done." According to Ted, she answered "You are right. You are absolutely right."

On the basis of the foregoing facts, Patty was found liable for intentional infliction of emotional distress. In our opinion, these facts are insufficient to prove the cause of action.

[The court proceeds to review the history of the newly recognized tort of intentional infliction of emotional distress, emphasizing the reluctance of the courts to allow recovery for emotional injury in the absence of a physical injury and the strict limitations on recovery based in part on the fact that such injuries are relatively easy to fake.]

We fail to discern from this record any proof that Patty's conduct was "intentional or reckless." There is no proof that she set out to convince Ted that the child was his, and to cause him to develop a loving relationship with the child so that in the end, she could hurt Ted by taking the child away from him forever. Such proof was required to satisfy the "intentional or reckless" prong of the *Womack* test. *Id.* Therefore, we hold that the trial court erred in entering judgment in favor of the plaintiff. In light of this, we will reverse the judgment of the trial court and enter judgment here in favor of the defendant.

CASE QUESTIONS

1. If Patty did not intentionally set up Teds ultimate emotional injury, did she not act recklessly cause this harm? "Reckless" was a term used alongside "intentional" in reference to *Womack v. Eldridge,* on which *Ruth v. Fletcher* is premised.
2. Does justice cry out for a remedy for Ted?
3. Is there any other basis on which to recover for injuries to Ted?

15.3 SURROGACY

The Uniform Status of Children of Assisted Conception Act, (appendix 15C) provides a model act for surrogacy contracts, both for states recognizing such contracts and for those desiring to prohibit them.

Because of the *Baby M* case in 1988, much public attention was directed at so-called surrogacy contracts. In contrast to adoption by strangers, which may involve contracts and negotiations, surrogacy contracts have the added element that the natural father will take custody of the child, while the mother relinquishes custody in favor of adoption by the natural father's wife. Conception is ordinarily produced by artificial insemination with the contracting father's sperm or by implanting a fertilized ovum in the surrogate mother. In the former case the child-bearer is the biological mother, but not in the latter case. The problem with surrogacy arrangements is the fact that they appear to be simple contracts that could be enforced in court by traditional contract remedies—but the subject matter is unique. From one point of view, surrogacy contracts appear to be agreements to sell babies, something that is clearly illegal. Nevertheless, because the natural fathers are assuming custody, they cannot be said to be buying anything—their children are something to which they have a right. These contracts have also been considered offensive because they imply that women's bodies may be rented for a period of time and because they may promote exploitation of the poor by the rich. Additionally, surrogacy involves the psychobiology of rending an infant from its natural mother, whose feelings and state of mind have undoubtedly changed considerably since the time of contracting. For all these, and perhaps other, reasons, the *Baby M* case, in which a surrogate mother changed her mind after the birth of the child, awakened a diversity of intense emotional and intellectual responses. Many state legislatures jumped to pass special legislation to regulate surrogacy contracts.

CASE NO. 15-3   Baby M

MATTER OF BABY M
109 N.J. 396, 537 A.2d 1227 (1988)
Supreme Court of New Jersey

Wilentz, C. J.

* * *

The contract provided that through artificial insemination using Mr. Stern's sperm, Mrs. Whitehead would become pregnant, carry the child to term, bear it, deliver it to the Sterns, and thereafter do whatever was necessary to terminate her maternal rights so that Mrs. Stern could thereafter adopt the child. Mrs. Whitehead's husband, Richard, was also a party to the contract; Mrs. Stern was not. Mr. Whitehead promised to do all acts necessary to rebut the presumption of paternity under the Parentage Act. Although Mrs. Stern was not a party to the surrogacy agreement, the contract gave her sole custody of the child in the event of Mr. Stern's death. Mrs. Stern's status as a nonparty to the surrogate parenting agreement presumably was to avoid the application of the baby-selling statute to this arrangement.

Mr. Stern, on his part, agreed to attempt the artificial insemination and to pay Mrs.

Whitehead $10,000 after the child's birth on its delivery to him. In a separate contract, Mr. Stern agreed to pay $7,500 to the Infertility Center of New York ("ICNY"). The Center's advertising campaigns solicit surrogate mothers and encourage infertile couples to consider surrogacy. ICNY arranged for the surrogacy contract by bringing the parties together, explaining the process to them, furnishing the contractual form, and providing legal counsel.

* * *

One of the surrogacy contract's basic purposes, to achieve the adoption of a child through private placement, though permitted in New Jersey, "is very much disfavored." Its use of money for this purpose—and we have no doubt whatsoever that the money is being paid to obtain an adoption and not, as the Sterns argue, for the personal services of Mary Beth Whitehead—is illegal and perhaps criminal. . . . In addition to the inducement of money, there is the coercion of contract: the natural mother's irrevocable agreement, prior to birth, even prior to conception, to surrender the child to the adoptive couple. Such an agreement is totally unenforceable in private placement adoption. Even where the adoption is through an approved agency, the formal agreement to surrender occurs only *after* birth and then, by regulation, only after the birth mother has been offered counseling. . . .

The foregoing provisions not only directly conflict with New Jersey statutes, but also offend long-established State policies. These critical terms, which are at the heart of the contract, are invalid and unenforceable; the conclusion therefore follows, without more, that the entire contract is unenforceable.

* * *

The surrogacy contract is based on principles that are directly contrary to the objectives of our laws. It guarantees the separation of a child from its mother; it looks to adoption regardless of suitability; it totally ignores the child; it takes the child from the mother regardless of her wishes and her maternal fitness; and it does all of this, it accomplishes all of its goals, through the use of money.

* * *

With the surrogacy contract disposed of, the legal framework becomes a dispute between two couples over the custody of a child produced by the artificial insemination of one couple's wife by the other's husband. Under the Parentage Act the claims of the natural father and the natural mother are entitled to equal weight, *i.e.,* one is not preferred over the other solely because he or she is the father or the mother. The applicable rule given these circumstances is clear: the child's best interests determine custody.

[The court then approves the trial court's findings to the effect that custody should be awarded to Mr. Stern was based on credible evidence, and awards custody to Mr. Stern.]

We have decided that Mrs. Whitehead is entitled to visitation at some point, and that question is not open to the trial court on this remand. The trial court will determine what kind of visitation shall be granted to her, with or without conditions, and when and under what circumstances it should commence. . . .

15.4 FACTORS INFLUENCING ADOPTION AND THEIR CONSTITUTIONAL IMPLICATIONS

Although approval of adoption is premised on the best interests of the child, this test may be entirely obscured by the coalescence of prejudice, law, and politics. The greatest human problem in adoption is matching childless parents with unrelated adoptable children. The fact that there are many willing parents and many needy children does not mean that supply meets demand, or vice versa. Care should be taken to ensure the welfare of the children. This, however, is determined by the values and perceptions attached to the welfare of the child. Is it against the child's interest, for instance, for her to be brought up by parents of a different race? Is it harmful for him to be raised in a household adhering to a religion different from the child's previous experience or the religion of his natural parents? These two questions, more than any others, have intruded most on the legal issues surrounding the placement of children.

Religion and race questions arise under two different provisions of the U.S. Constitution. The First Amendment guarantees the free exercise of religion and has been interpreted in recent times to express an extreme separation of church and state. Convincing arguments have been made to the effect that a legal preference for matching the religion of a child with that of her adoptive parents—as well as a legally ordered neutrality—would represent an establishment of religion by the state. The equal protection clause of the Fourteenth Amendment prohibits discrimination, particularly on the basis of race.

Religion

The First Amendment provides that "Congress shall make no law respecting an establishment of religion, or prohibiting the free exercise thereof." Although Congress is specifically named, the U.S. Supreme Court has interpreted the language of the First Amendment to apply to the states as well. In modern times the courts have erected stringent standards to maintain the separation of church and state. Under these circumstances, it may seem odd that many states express a statutory preference for religious matching of children with their adoptive parents; that is, a preference is shown for placing children in homes having the same religious affiliation as that of the child or the child's natural parents. By maintaining such preferences, the state makes placing children more difficult, as each couple looking for a child to adopt has a smaller pool of children from which to choose. Religious matching departs from the best interests of the child doctrine by placing a limitation or hurdle on the free selection of the best home for a child.

New York has the longest history of religious matching and goes the farthest in its statute. Not only do the statutes require adoption agencies to place children with adoptive parents of the child's religion "whenever practicable," but they also require that children be placed by agencies run by members of the same religion as the child, "when practicable." If a child is placed with parents of a faith other than that of the child, the judge is required to explain what required such a decision. New York also provides that the parental wishes of an unwed mother or of both parents of a child born in wedlock be honored when practicable, considering the best interests of the child, and raises a presumption in favor of the parents' religion if no desires have been expressed.

Laura Schwartz, in the *Family Law Quarterly* (Summer 1991), notes that such religious preferences discriminate on the basis of both religion and race. Although many Jewish couples are interested in adoption, far fewer Jewish babies, proportionately, are put up for adoption. Similarly, the relatively smaller number of Protestant adoption agencies leaves black children, who are predominantly Protestant, without the benefit of Catholic and Jewish foster-care agencies, even though they are subsidized by the city.

Although such laws and practices look very much like establishment of religion through state support, the courts have turned a blind eye to such arguments in the past when the statutes purported to make such preferences contingent on the best interests of the child. Religion-matching policy, however, suggests adherence to the parental rights tradition of the past. Of course, when parents voluntarily agree to adoption by a known party, they may exercise choice over the prospective parents. When the child is under the care of the state or an agency, the parents' wishes presumably become subordinate to child's needs.

CASE NO. 15-4   Matching Religion with Adoptive Parents

In re Goldman arises under a statute similar to the New York statutes just discussed. Keep in mind that the result of this decision was to refuse adoption by the only parents the children had known, even though the adopting parents wanted to adopt and the natural mother favored the adoption.

IN RE GOLDMAN
331 Mass. 647, 121 N.E.2d 843 (1954)
Supreme Judicial Court of
Massachusetts

QUA, Chief Justice.

* * *

[Massachusetts law states] as follows: "In making orders for adoption, the judge when practicable must give custody only to persons of the same religious faith as that of the child. In the event that there is a dispute as to the religion of said child, its religion shall be deemed to be that of its mother. If the court, with due regard for the religion of the child, shall nevertheless grant the petition for adoption of a child proffered by a person or persons of a religious faith or persuasion other than that of the child, the court shall state the facts which impelled it to make such a disposition and such statement shall be made part of the minutes of the proceedings."

The petitioners obtained the children when they were about two weeks old from the hospital where they were born and have had them ever since. All of the evidence bearing on the ability of the petitioners to care for the twins . . . tended to show that the petitioners have a good home and sufficient means, are fond of the twins, and are giving them adequate care. The judge found that the petitioners are well equipped financially and physically to bring up the twins, and that they have treated them as their own children and intend to care for them and educate them to the best of their ability. The judge further found that the mother and "the natural father" of the twins are Catholics. There was ample evidence to support this finding. The mother did not cease to be a Catholic, even if she failed to live up to the ideals of her religion. If that were the test of belonging to a religious faith it is feared that few could qualify for any faith. The petitioners are of the Jewish faith and intend to bring up the twins in that faith. The mother has consented in writing on both petitions to the adoptions prayed for. She has never seen or spoken to the petitioners, but she has stated that she knew they were Jewish and was satisfied that the twins should be raised in the Jewish faith. The petitioners were informed by their attorney before they took the twins of the law relative to religion in adoptions, but they decided to take a chance that the petitions would be allowed. The petitioners have dark complexions and dark hair. The twins are blond, with large blue eyes and flaxen hair.

* * *

The judge also found that "there are in and about the city of Lynn [which is near the residence of the petitioners] many Catholic couples of fine family life and excellent reputation who have filed applications with the Catholic Charities Bureau for the purpose of adopting Catholic children of the type of the twins, and are able to provide the twins with a material status equivalent to or better than that of the petitioners, and with whom the twins could be placed immediately." This finding was in effect a finding that it was "practicable," within the meaning of that word in [the state law] § 5B to "give only to persons" of the Catholic faith. . . .

Some argument is advanced that there was here no "dispute" as to the religion of the twins and from that it is apparently sought to draw a conclusion that the religion of the mother should be disregarded. It would seem that there is a "dispute," since the guardian ad litem, as the representative of the children, contends that their religion is Catholic, while the petitioners at one stage in their argument seem to contend that it is not. But even if there is no "dispute" we think that for purposes of § 5B these twins, too young to choose a religion for themselves, must be deemed to belong to the Catholic faith for reasons hereinafter stated.

* * *

It is contended that § 5B is unconstitutional as a law "respecting an establishment of religion, or prohibiting the free exercise thereof," contrary to the First Amendment to the Constitution of the United States, and as in some manner contrary to art. 2 of our Declaration of Rights and to art. 11 and art. 46, § 1, of the Amendments to the Constitution of this Commonwealth. With this we cannot agree. All religions are treated alike. There is no "subordination" of one sect to another. No burden is placed upon anyone for maintenance of any religion. No exercise of religion is required, prevented, or hampered. It is argued that there is interference with the mother's right to determine the religion of her offspring, and that in these cases she has determined it shall be Jewish. Passing the point that so far as concerns religion she seems to have consented rather than commanded and seems to have been "interested only that the babies were in a good home," there is clearly no interference with any wish of hers as long as she retains her status as a parent. It is only on the assumption that she is to lose that status that § 5B becomes operative. The moment an adoption is completed all control by the mother comes to an end.

We do not attempt to discuss the philosophy underlying the concept that a child too young to understand any religion, even imperfectly, nevertheless may have a religion. We have no doubt that the statute was intended to apply to such children, and that in such instances the words "religious faith * * * of the child" mean the religious faith of the parents, or in case of "dispute" the faith of the mother. There is nothing new in this idea. In the leading case of *Purinton v. Jamrock,* 195 Mass. 187, at page 200, 80 N.E. 802, 18 L.R.A.,N.S., 926, it was said long before the enactment of the statute that the parents' religion was prima facie the infant's religion. It was also there decided that weight should be given to that religion in matters of adoption. The present statute merely ascribes somewhat more weight than was before ascribed to the religion of the natural parents in the matter of making a decree for adoption. If neither parent had any religion we suppose the statute would have no application. It has no effect after the adoption is completed. The principle that children should, in general, be adopted within the faith of their natural parents has received widespread approval, as is attested not only by such decisions as *Purinton v. Jamrock* but also by the fact that most of the States now have statutes more or less similar to § 5B. We are not prepared to hold either such decisions or the statute unconstitutional.

Decree affirmed.

CASE QUESTION

1. Can any inferences be drawn from the sentence: "The petitioners have dark complexions and dark hair. The twins are blond, with large blue eyes and flaxen hair."?

Race

The practice of matching adoptive parents with children on the basis of race has had a rocky road. In former times, Southern states prohibited interracial adoption. In recent times, such racial discrimination has been struck down by the U.S. Supreme Court on the basis of the equal protection clause. Because minority children are overrepresented in the pool of children waiting for adoption, many of them have been adopted or sought for adoption by persons of a different racial background. Also in recent years, some members of the black community have begun to view this development with concern. The National Association of Black Social Workers described interracial adoption as a "blatant form of racial and cultural genocide." They argue that not only does placement of black children in white homes remove the children from the black community, but such placement also deprives the children of the socialization they need to survive in a racist society. This latter claim is contested by some interracial adoption studies, but the point remains that removal of children from the traditionally disadvantaged group by the more advantaged whites is viewed by some as a new form of racism. It remains to be seen whether minority groups will be able to sustain exclusionary laws analogous to the segregationist laws of the dominant group, only recently abolished.

CASE NO. 15-5 Adoption into Racially Mixed Marriage

The *Palmore* case is a custody case, but adoption necessarily entails custody and is similarly based on the best interests standard. Whether *Palmore* applies with full force to cases of adoption is not clear, but the reasoning would seem logically to be equally relevant to the adoption process.

PALMORE v. SIDOTI
466 U.S. 429, 104 S. Ct. 1879,
80 L. Ed. 2d 421 (1984)
United States Supreme Court

Chief Justice BURGER delivered the opinion of the Court.

We granted certiorari to review a judgment of a state court divesting a natural mother of the custody of her infant child because of her remarriage to a person of a different race.

I

When petitioner Linda Sidoti Palmore and respondent Anthony J. Sidoti, both Caucasians, were divorced in May 1980 in Florida, the mother was awarded custody of their three-year-old daughter.

In September 1981 the father sought custody of the child by filing a petition to modify the prior judgment because of changed conditions. The change was that the child's mother was then cohabiting with a Negro, Clarence Palmore, Jr., whom she married two months later. . . .

[T]he court made a finding that "there is no issue as to either party's devotion to the child, adequacy of housing facilities, or respect[a]bility of the new spouse of either parent." The court then addressed the recommendations of the court counselor, who had made an earlier report "in [another] case coming out of this circuit also involving the social consequences of an interracial marriage. *Niles v. Niles,* 299 So.2d 162." *Id.,* at 25. From this vague reference to that earlier case, the court turned to the present case and noted the counselor's recommendation for a change in custody because "[t]he wife [petitioner] has chosen for herself and for her child, a life-style unacceptable to her father *and to society.* . . . The child . . . is, or at school age will be, subject to environmental pressures not of choice."

The court then concluded that the best interests of the child would be served by awarding custody to the father. The court's rationale is contained in the following:

"The father's evident resentment of the mother's choice of a black partner is not sufficient to wrest custody from the mother. It is of some significance, however, that the mother did see fit to bring a man into her home and carry on a sexual relationship with him without being married to him. Such action tended to place gratification of her own desires ahead of her concern for the child's future welfare. *This Court feels that despite the strides that have been made in bettering relations between the races in this country, it is inevitable that Melanie will, if allowed to remain in her present situation and attains school age and thus more vulnerable to peer pressures, suffer from the social stigmatization that is sure to come."* App. to Pet. for Cert. 26-27 (emphasis added).

The Second District Court of Appeal affirmed without opinion, 426 So.2d 34, thus denying the Florida Supreme Court jurisdiction to review the case.

II

The judgment of a state court determining or reviewing a child custody decision is not ordinarily a likely candidate for review by this Court. However, the court's opinion, after stating that the "father's evident resentment of the mother's choice of a black partner is not sufficient" to deprive her of custody, then turns to what it regarded as the damaging impact on the child from remaining in a racially-mixed household. This raises important federal concerns arising from the Constitution's commitment to eradicating discrimination based on race.

The Florida court did not focus directly on the parental qualifications of the natural mother or her present husband, or indeed on the father's qualifications to have custody of the child. The court found that "there is no issue as to either party's devotion to the child, adequacy of housing facilities, or respect[a]bility of the new spouse of either parent." *Id.*, at 24. This, taken with the absence of any negative finding as to the quality of the care provided by the mother, constitutes a rejection of any claim of petitioner's unfitness to continue the custody of her child.

The court correctly stated that the child's welfare was the controlling factor. But that court was entirely candid and made no effort to place its holding on any ground other than race. Taking the court's findings and rationale at face value, it is clear that the outcome would have been different had petitioner married a Caucasian male of similar respectability.

A core purpose of the Fourteenth Amendment was to do away with all governmentally-imposed discrimination based on race. Classifying persons according to their race is more likely to reflect racial prejudice than legitimate public concerns; the race, not the person, dictates the category. Such classifications are subject to the most exacting scrutiny; to pass constitutional muster, they must be justified by a compelling governmental interest and must be "necessary . . . to the accomplishment" of its legitimate purpose.

* * *

It would ignore reality to suggest that racial and ethnic prejudices do not exist or that all manifestations of those prejudices have been eliminated. There is a risk that a child living with a step-parent of a different race may be subject to a variety of pressures and stresses not present if the child were living with parents of the same racial or ethnic origin.

The question, however, is whether the reality of private biases and the possible injury they might inflict are permissible considerations for removal of an infant child from the custody of its natural mother. We have little difficulty concluding that they are not. The Constitution cannot control such prejudices but neither can it tolerate them. Private biases may be outside the reach of the law, but the law cannot, directly or indirectly, give them effect. "Public officials sworn to uphold the Constitution may not avoid a constitutional duty by bowing to the hypothetical effects of private racial prejudice that they assume to be both widely and deeply held."

This is by no means the first time that acknowledged racial prejudice has been invoked to justify racial classifications. In *Buchanan v. Warley,* 245 U.S. 60, 38 S.Ct. 16, 62 L.Ed. 149 (1917), for example, this Court invalidated a Kentucky law forbidding Negroes from buying homes in white neighborhoods.

> "It is urged that this proposed segregation will promote the public peace by preventing race conflicts. Desirable as this is, and important as is the preservation of the public peace, this aim cannot be accomplished by laws or ordinances which deny rights created or protected by the Federal Constitution." *Id.,* at 81, 38 S.Ct., at 20.

Whatever problems racially-mixed households may pose for children in 1984 can no more support a denial of constitutional rights than could the stresses that residential integration was thought to entail in 1917. The effects of racial prejudice, however real, cannot justify a racial classification removing an infant child from the custody of its natural mother found to be an appropriate person to have such custody.

* * *

The judgment of the District Court of Appeal is reversed.

It is so ordered.

CASE QUESTIONS

1. Do you find the argument persuasive?
2. Was the court warranted in departing from its traditional hands-off policy with regard to domestic relations, as a matter reserved to the states?
3. What if race were merely one of several factors considered in placing a particular child (as opposed to the single factor or one of the factors routinely used)? A 1977 decision suggests this may be all right. *Drummond v. Fulton County Department of Family & Children's Services,* 563 F.2d 1200 (5th Cir. 1977), *cert. denied,* 437 U.S. 910 (1977).

Legal Bonds

Most jurisdictions substitute the adoptive parent for the natural parent for all legal purposes. This means that the adopting parent assumes a financial responsibility for the child and the natural parent is no longer responsible. This is true even though a stepparent adopts the child of a spouse who is the natural parent. A subsequent divorce does not relieve the adopting parent of responsibility. The child would inherit from an intestate adoptive parent but not an intestate natural parent. In fact, it is common to reissue a birth certificate with the surname of the adoptive family, without an indication of the adoption.

The states are not consistent in these rules. Some allow continued responsibility on the part of the natural parents. Some allow inheritance from blood relatives other than parents. Some do not include adopted children among the heirs of adoptive kin other than the parents.

QUERY

The reasoning in *Palmore v. Sidoti* indicates that custody could not be denied using race as the determinative factor when the justification was that the child would be subject to stigmatization for membership in a interracial family. Is this significantly different from the argument used by the NABSW that adoption of a black child by a white family would leave the child ill-equipped to deal with a racist environment?

CASE NO. 15-6 Blood Is Thicker than Law

The *Nunnally* case involves a Georgia statute that took exception to the general principle that adoption is the legal equivalent of a natural parent-child relationship.

NUNNALLY v. TRUST COMPANY BANK
244 Ga. 697, 261 S.E.2d 621 (1979)
Supreme Court of Georgia

JORDAN, Justice.

[Should adopted great-grandchildren take under a will left by their great-grandmother (Mrs. McKee), which refers to "children"? This is an attack on the Georgia statute, which changed the legal bonds on adoption only between the natural and adoptive parents.]

* * *

To begin, appellants do not attack the entire 1941 adoption statute. Rather, the offensive portion is as follows: ". . . *To all other persons* [besides natural and adoptive parents] *the adopted child shall stand as if no such act of adoption had been taken.*" Ga.L.1941, pp. 305-306.[1]

* * *

As the situation stood in 1945, then, the year of the death of Mrs. McKee, an adopted child could inherit from his or her adoptive parents and from a natural grandparent, aunt, etc., but not through the adoptive line from anyone except the adoptive parents, and not from the natural parents.

Appellants contend that within a class of similarly situated people, children within a family, the state has impermissibly drawn an invidious distinction between children adopted into the family and those born into it.

* * *

One aim of this statute is the state's interest in providing for the orderly disposition of property. Through its laws of intestate succession,

the state has established a method of descent based upon the presumed intention of the decedent. Distinctions based on preferences do exist in this area of law. It is presumed, by the state, that a person would wish for his or her property to pass within his or her bloodline, for example, and to children before grandchildren, and so forth. As long as these distinctions are rationally related to the state's interest in seeking the most orderly system possible for passing title to property from one person to another so that the state knows at all times exactly what is owned by whom, then the distinctions are constitutionally sound.

The right of an individual to inherit property through intestate succession is not a natural or inalienable right; rather, it is solely within the province of the state to prescribe for such succession as it deems necessary. The state must make choices. . . .

The state has used this concept of inheritance within the bloodline in drawing other valid distinctions. For example, if a person dies intestate survived by children, one of whom has predeceased the decedent, the spouse of that predeceased child is not allowed to take as the legal representative. The rationale for excluding a widowed daughter-in-law or son-in-law from the class of takers is very similar to the rationale for excluding adopted grandchildren. The deceased child took an affirmative act in bringing his or her spouse into the immediate family and between husband and wife, as between adopted child and adopting parent, inheritance rights do exist. However, beyond the immediate relationship of husband and wife, in terms of a daughter-in-law or son-in-law taking from the deceased spouse's ancestors, it is as if no such act of marriage ever took place. There is a distinction drawn between daughters-in-law and sons-in-law and natural children, even though proving the identity of a son-in-law, for example, presents no problem because of the ease in referring to the marriage license. However, the state assumes that one would rather have his or her property pass within the bloodline rather than have people with a bare legal relationship to them share. We would consider this assumption a rational means to dispose of property in an orderly fashion.

* * *

We have not forgotten that the subject matter of this controversy is a will, and the property passing from this testatrix is not by intestate succession. However, the law of the case directs that Section 11 be used to construe Mrs. McKee's intent in her silence, and that same section is the one used to guide administrators when no will is present, much less a silent one, as to the meaning of "children." . . .

The statute plays the decisive role in supplying the missing intent of the silent testatrix, "(T)his is true because the statute fixing our rules of inheritance must be construed in pari materia with our adoption statute. (Cit.)" Even though state action is involved we do not find an "invidious discrimination" in the statute such as would render it unconstitutional.

* * *

Judgment affirmed.

_____

1 That portion of the statute here under attack was amended in 1949 (after the death of the testatrix) to provide that an "adopted child shall be considered in all respects as if it were a child of natural bodily issue of petitioner or petitioners, and shall enjoy every right and privilege of a natural child of petitioner or petitioners; and shall be deemed a natural child of petitioner or petitioners to inherit under the laws of descent and distribution in the absence of a will and to take under the provisions of any instrument of testamentary gift, bequest, devise or legacy unless expressly excluded therefrom."

15.5 EQUITABLE ADOPTION

Some states have invented equitable devices to create a parent-child legal bond where no official legal relationship exists. The labels commonly applied to these situations are *equitable adoption* and *adoption by estoppel.* Equitable adoption seems most appropriate in instances in which a parentlike relationship existed, especially when an adoption process was promised or started but never completed prior to the death of the parent and the parent dies intestate. If the "child" would clearly be the natural recipient of part or all of the deceased's estate, some jurisdictions will create the relationship under equitable principles. Such an outcome is consistent with analogous devices used to create equitable marriages and divorces and serves the underlying policy of intestate succession, namely, that the law should distribute intestate property to those whom the deceased would have chosen if choice had been expressed.

Equitable estoppel has been applied particularly to the situation in which a husband allows or supports a wife's efforts at adoption but then divorces the wife. In appropriate circumstances, the court may find a duty to support and disallow defenses based on the absence of a legal parent-child relationship.

CASE NO. 15-7   Almost a Parent

This case should test your knowledge and your creativity. What rights should a lesbian parent have in children borne by her lover in the course of their relationship?

NANCY S. v. MICHELE G.
228 Cal. App. 3d 831, 279 Cal. Rptr. 212 (1991)
Court of Appeal, First District

STEIN, Associate Justice.

* * *

FACTS

In August of 1969, appellant and respondent began living together, and in November of that year they had a private "marriage" ceremony. Eventually they decided to have children by artificially inseminating respondent. In June of 1980, respondent gave birth to a daughter, K. Appellant was listed on the birth certificate as the father, and K. was given appellant's family name. On June 13, 1984, respondent gave birth to a son, S. Again appellant was listed as the father on the birth certificate, and S. was given appellant's family name. Both children refer to appellant and respondent as "Mom." Although the parties considered arranging for appellant to adopt the children, they never initiated formal adoption proceedings.

In January of 1985 appellant and respondent separated. They agreed that K. would live with appellant and that S. would live with respondent. They arranged visitation so that appellant would have K. five days a week and respondent would have S. five days a week, but the children would be together, either at appellant's or respondent's home, for four days a week.

After approximately three years, respondent wanted to change the custody arrangement so that each had custody of both children 50 percent of the time. Appellant opposed any change, and attempts to mediate the dispute failed.

* * *

ANALYSIS

* * *

A.   De Facto Parenthood

A de facto parent is "that person who, on a day-to-day basis, assumes the role of parent, seeking to fulfill both the child's physical needs and his psychological need for affection and care." Appellant alleged that she helped facilitate the conception and birth of both children and immediately after their birth assumed all the responsibilities of a parent. K. lived with appellant until the underlying dispute arose, and S. also lived with appellant until appellant and respondent separated, and thereafter S. visited with appellant on a regular basis. These facts may well entitle appellant to the status of a "de facto" parent. It does not, however, follow that as a "de facto" parent appellant has the same rights as a parent to seek custody and visitation over the objection of the children's natural mother. In *In re B.G., supra,* 11 Cal.3d 679, 114 Cal.Rptr. 444, 523 P.2d 244, the court acknowledged that the concept of "de facto" parenthood could apply to long-term foster parents for the purpose of permitting them to intervene in a dependency proceeding. The court went on to hold that, nonetheless, custody could not be awarded to the foster parents over the objections of the natural mother without a finding that parental custody would be detrimental to the children. The court also specifically stated that, "[w]e do not hold that a de facto parent is a 'parent' or 'guardian' as those terms are used in the Juvenile Court Law."

No cases support appellant's contention that if she could prove her status as a de facto parent, she would be entitled to seek custody of respondent's children according to the same standards applied in a dispute between two parents. To the contrary, the cases establish that nonparents, even if they qualify as "de facto parents," may be recognized in guardianship or dependency proceedings and may even obtain custody over children with whom they have established a de facto parent-child relationship, but that custody can be awarded to a de facto parent *only* if it is established by clear and convincing evidence that parental custody is detrimental to the children.

Appellant argues that, in this case, the "detriment" standard should not apply because appellant is not an "outsider" and does not seek to exclude the parent but wants to share custody. In *all* of the cases involving a "de facto" parent, the individual claiming such status necessarily is not an "outsider" and, like appellant, has undoubtedly developed deep psychological and emotional bonds with the child. Nonetheless, the courts and our Legislature have chosen to place paramount importance upon the relationship between the natural or adoptive parent and the child. . . .

B. In Loco Parentis

. . . In the context of torts, the concept of in loco parentis has been used to impose upon persons standing "in loco parentis" the same rights and obligations imposed by statutory and common law upon parents. . . . The concept of "in loco parentis," however, has never been applied in a custody dispute to give a nonparent the same rights as a parent, and we are unpersuaded that the concept should be so extended.

In *Perry v. Superior Court* (1980) 108 Cal.App.3d 480, 166 Cal.Rptr. 583, the court referred to the concept of in loco parentis in the context of a custody dispute. The trial court awarded the mother's husband of six years visitation rights to her child by a former marriage. The trial court found that the husband had performed the role of father to the child and the fact that there was no blood relationship was inconsequential because visitation was in the best interests of the child. The court of appeal reversed holding that the trial court had no authority to award custody or visitation unless the minor was a "child of the marriage." Noting that the result was "not particularly palatable," the court invited the Legislature to address the problem of visitation rights for stepparents. The Legislature responded by enacting Civil Code section 4351.5 in 1982. Although that section creates discretion to award a limited form of visitation rights to stepparents in a dissolution proceeding, the Legislature again acknowledged the importance of parental autonomy by cautioning that even an award of visitation to a stepparent "shall not conflict with any visitation or custodial right of a natural or adoptive parent who is not a party to the proceeding." (Civ.Code, § 4351.5, subd. (j).) . . .

C. Parenthood by Equitable Estoppel

Appellant argues that the court could apply the doctrine of equitable estoppel to prevent respondent from denying the existence of a parent-child relationship that she allegedly encouraged and supported for many years and which she now denies for the sole purpose of obtaining unfettered control over the custody of the children.

In California, equitable estoppel has been invoked for the purpose of imposing support obligations on a husband who has represented to his wife's children that he is their natural father and subsequently seeks to deny paternity for the purpose of avoiding support obligations. Equitable estoppel has never been invoked in California against a natural parent for the purpose of awarding custody and visitation to a nonparent. . . .

Other states, however, have begun to use the doctrine of equitable estoppel to prevent a wife from denying the paternity of her husband. . . . For example, in *In re Paternity of D.L.H.* (Ct.App.1987) 142 Wis.2d 606, 419 N.W.2d 283, the court held that a wife could be estopped to deny the paternity of her husband, even where human leukocyte antigen (HLA) tests had excluded the husband as the natural father. The husband knew, even before the child's birth, that he was not the biological father but promised to raise the child as his own. He had developed a strong relationship with the child and had paid support to the mother after the couple separated. The court held it was error to dismiss the husband from the paternity proceedings after the HLA tests excluded him as the natural father, and remanded to permit him to prove the elements of equitable estoppel. The court, however, specifically reserved the question whether, even if the wife were estopped to deny paternity, the husband would have the status of a parent in a custody dispute and could thereby invoke the standard of the best interests of the child. Even if the doctrine of equitable estoppel could be used against a wife and in favor of a husband to award custody as if the dispute were between two natural parents, we note that the use of the doctrine of equitable estoppel, in these out-of-state cases, is rooted in "[o]ne of the strongest presumptions in law [i.e.] that a child born to a married

woman is the legitimate child of her husband." No similar presumption applies in this case.

It is important not to confuse appellant's argument regarding equitable estoppel with the concept of an "equitable parent." The concept of an "equitable parent" has been recognized by the Michigan Court of Appeals in a divorce proceeding to permit a husband, who is not the biological father of a child born during the marriage, to obtain the status of a parent in a custody dispute with the natural mother, and to have the custody dispute settled as if it were between two natural parents, according to the child's best interests. The primary difference between the concept of an "equitable parent" and the equitable estoppel theory advanced by appellant is that the "equitable parent" theory is rooted in a statutory recognition of "equitable adoption" for purposes of inheritance and may require proof of an express or implied contract to adopt. At least one California court has already declined to adopt the concept of an "equitable parent" for the purpose of awarding joint custody to a stepfather over the objections of the child's natural mother despite the fact that California, like Michigan, recognizes the doctrine of "equitable adoption" for purposes of inheritance under Probate Code section 6408. The court stressed that given the "complex practical, social and constitutional ramifications" of expanding the class of persons entitled to assert parental rights, the decision was better left to the Legislature.

D.   Functional Definition of Parenthood

Finally, appellant urges us to adopt what she describes as a "functional" definition of parenthood in order to protect on-going relationships between children and those who function as their parents. In accordance with this new definition, the class of persons entitled to seek custody and visitation according to the same standards as a natural parent would include "anyone who maintains a functional parental relationship with a child when a legally recognized parent created that relationship with the intent that the relationship be parental in nature."

We agree with appellant that the absence of any legal formalization of her relationship to the children has resulted in a tragic situation.[7] As is always the case, it is the children who will suffer the most as a result of the inability of the adults, who they love and need, to reach an agreement. We do not, however, agree that the only way to avoid such an unfortunate situation is for the courts to adopt appellant's novel theory by which a nonparent can acquire the rights of a parent, and then face years of unraveling the complex practical, social, and constitutional ramifications of this expansion of the definition of parent.[8]

The judgment is affirmed.

---

[5] In *In re Marriage of Halpern, supra,* 133 Cal.App.3d 297, 184 Cal.Rptr. 740, relied upon by appellant, the court stated that even if the husband in a mariage dissolution, who was admittedly not the biological father of a child born to his wife during their marriage, had proved that he was a de facto parent, the presumption in favor of parental custody would still apply in a dispute over custody or visitation.

---

[7] This is not unique to same-sex domestic partners. Others often find they cannot maintain their close personal ties with children in the face of objection by their parents.

---

[8] Although the validity of an adoption in these circumstances is not before us, we note that Civil Code section 221 provides, in part, that "[a]ny unmarried minor child may be adopted by any adult person...." We see nothing in these provisions that would preclude a child from being jointly adopted by someone of the same sex as the natural parent.

15.6 DEPENDENCY PROCEEDINGS

In contrast to adoption proceedings, which are voluntary in nature, are dependency proceedings, in which the government steps in to question the parent-child relationship. These proceedings, as briefly outlined in this section, are based on Florida practice, but resemble practice in most states, if one allows for considerable variation in procedural detail.

Dependency proceedings involve an inquiry into the sufficiency of care provided by a person responsible for the welfare of a child. Typically the proceedings are initiated by an agent of the government, commonly by an agent of the Department of Health and Rehabilitative Services (HRS). Action is initiated because problems concerning the child's welfare have come to the attention of governmental authorities, frequently because of the child's misconduct. Thus, dependency hearings are often related to delinquency problems and involve the criminal law covering juveniles. This impinges on family law because the misconduct of a minor inevitably raises issues of adult supervision and care of a parental nature. Unlike adult miscreants, the juvenile offender is often viewed as a person at risk, whose welfare may be assumed by the state in the hope that intervention may divert the individual from a career of misconduct.

The grounds for finding a child dependent are established by abandonment, abuse, or neglect on the part of the person responsible for the child's care. An adjudication of dependency may also occur when a child has been put up for adoption with HRS or a private adoption agency. Abandonment is constituted by a failure of efforts to support and communicate with the child. Abuse occurs when a child is physically, mentally, or sexually injured by willful acts likely to cause significant impairment of the child's physical or emotional health. *Significant impairment* leaves room for discipline and punishment of both a physical and an emotional nature, the severity of which are insufficient to establish such impairment. Nevertheless, the court has considerable discretion to act in the best interests of the child, so a history of abuse on the part of a parent may be found to be sufficiently serious to remove as yet unimpaired children from that parent's care.

Neglect involves a deprivation of basic necessaries—food, shelter, clothing, health services—or a causation of significant impairment because of the conditions under which the child is allowed to live. A difficult issue in establishing neglect occurs when a child is denied medical treatment because of the religious beliefs of the parents. Although a court may order treatment, the parents may nevertheless be able to defend against a finding of dependency by arguing that their conduct was based on religious beliefs.

CASE NO. 15-8   Baby Jessica

DeBoer v. Schmidt presents a final test of the reader's understanding and perception of family law. Jessica DeBoer (or Anna Lee Schmidt) made the cover of *Time* magazine on July 19, 1993, in a celebrated case that seemed to simply put the rights of a nonmarital father above those of adopting parents who had raised Jessica nearly from birth to the age of 2½. As the excerpts here indicate, the case was a great deal more complicated than that. Two sets of parents competed for custody of this child and both fully exploited the means offered by the legal system in their quests for victory. This case is not merely one of adoption; it also raises basic issues of the rights of birth mothers and fathers. By the time the case got to the Michigan Supreme Court, the primary issue had become one of jurisdiction and the UCCJA. Numerous judges and justices were faced with a Solomon's choice to split the baby.

[IN RE BABY GIRL CLAUSEN]
DEBOER v. SCHMIDT
199 Mich. App. 10, ____ N.W.2d ____
(Mich. Ct. App. 1993)
Court of Appeals of Michigan

PER CURIAM.

[What follows was taken directly from the court's opinion, but the paragraphs were reformatted to facilitate the reader in following the very important chronology of events. Although not very personal, BGC (Baby Girl Clausen) has been retained to refer to Jessica/Anna Lee.

On February 8, 1991, Baby Girl Clausen (BGC) was born to Cara Clausen in Iowa.

On February 10, 1991, Clausen signed a release-of-custody form relinquishing her parental rights over BGC. Clausen, who was unmarried at the time of the birth (but who married Daniel Schmidt in April 1992), had named Scott Seefeldt as the father.

On February 14, 1991, Seefeldt executed a release-of-custody form.

On February 25, 1991, petitioners Roberta and Jan DeBoer, who are Michigan residents, filed a petition for adoption of BGC in juvenile court in Iowa. A hearing was held the same day. Cara Clausen received notice of, but did not attend, the hearing. At the hearing, the parental rights of Cara Clausen and Scott Seefeldt were terminated, and the petitioners were granted custody of BGC. The DeBoers returned to Michigan with BGC. The child has lived with the DeBoers in Michigan continuously since that time.

On March 6, 1991, Cara Clausen filed a request in the Iowa juvenile court to revoke her release of custody. In an affidavit accompanying the request, Clausen stated that she had lied when she named Seefeldt as the biological father of BGC and that the child's biological father was Daniel Schmidt.

On March 12, 1991, Schmidt filed an affidavit of paternity on March 12, 1991. At a hearing in juvenile court attended by Clausen and the DeBoers, the court dismissed Clausen's request to revoke her release of custody on the ground that it lacked subject matter jurisdiction because a petition for adoption had been filed. The court also dismissed Schmidt's attempt to claim custody. The DeBoers and BGC returned to Michigan.

On March 27, 1991, Schmidt filed a petition in the district court in Iowa, seeking to intervene in the adoption proceeding initiated by the DeBoers. He asserted that he had not given consent for the adoption. Doubting Clausen's truthfulness, the DeBoers denied that Schmidt was the natural father of the child. The court ordered blood tests. The DeBoers objected and, as a result, it was not until

September 1991 that the test results were available. They showed a 99.9 percent probability that Schmidt was the father of BGC, and a 0 percent probability that Seefeldt was the father.

On September 24, 1991, the DeBoers filed a petition in the Iowa district court to terminate Schmidt's parental rights. They alleged that Schmidt was an unfit parent because he had abandoned BGC and two other children, born several years earlier.

On November 4, 1991, the district court in Iowa conducted a bench trial with regard to the issues of paternity, termination of parental rights, and adoption.

On December 27, 1991, the district court found that Schmidt established by a preponderance of the evidence that he was the biological father of BGC; that the DeBoers failed to establish by clear and convincing evidence that Schmidt had abandoned the child or that his parental rights should be terminated; and that a best interests of the child analysis did not become material unless and until abandonment was established. On the basis of these findings, the court concluded that the termination proceeding was void with respect to Schmidt, and that the DeBoers' petition to adopt BGC must be denied. The court ordered that the DeBoers return physical custody of the child to Schmidt no later than January 12, 1992, at 6:00 p.m. The court retained jurisdiction under its general equitable powers to complete any matters necessary to protect the interests of BGC.

In the meantime, the Iowa Court of Appeals reversed the termination of Cara Clausen's parental rights and remanded the case to juvenile court for further proceedings. The Iowa Supreme Court granted further review of that decision.

On September 23, 1992, the Supreme Court of Iowa affirmed the decisions from below. The supreme court rejected the DeBoers' argument that a best interests of the child analysis governed the issue of termination in an adoption case, and found that because termination of parental rights was governed by statute, statutory grounds for termination must be established before reaching a determination of the child's best interests. The supreme court held that the district court correctly concluded that the DeBoers' petition for adoption should be dismissed.

On November 20, 1992, the Supreme Court denied the DeBoers' motion for reconsideration and remanded the case to the district court for issuance of an order changing physical custody of BGC from the DeBoers to Schmidt. The district court ordered the DeBoers to appear on December 3, 1992, with BGC. The DeBoers did not appear at the hearing; instead, their Iowa attorney informed the court that the DeBoers had received actual notice of the hearing, but had decided not to appear.

On December 3, 1992, the district court terminated the DeBoers' rights as temporary guardians and custodians of BGC, and, to the extent necessary, appointed Schmidt as temporary guardian and custodian until further order of the court. Schmidt was given authority to proceed by any legal means to enforce the order requiring the DeBoers to relinquish possession of the child.

On December 3, 1992, in Michigan, the same day the DeBoers' rights were terminated in Iowa, they filed a petition in Washtenaw Circuit Court pursuant to the Uniform Child Custody Jurisdiction Act (UCCJA). The petition sought modification of the Iowa order granting custody of BGC to Schmidt. The DeBoers argued that Michigan had jurisdiction under the UCCJA because BGC had resided in Michigan for all but approximately three weeks of her life, and Michigan was the home state of BGC as that term was defined by the UCCJA. The petition alleged that it would be in the best interests of BGC for Michigan to assume jurisdiction. On December 3, 1992, the Washtenaw Circuit Court entered an ex parte order entitled "preliminary injunction," which ordered Schmidt not to remove BGC from Washtenaw County.

On December 11, 1992, Schmidt filed a motion for summary disposition, to dissolve the preliminary injunction, and to recognize and enforce the Iowa judgment in the instant case.

On January 5, 1993, the Washtenaw Circuit Court held a hearing regarding Schmidt's motion. Schmidt argued that to grant the relief requested by the DeBoers (modification of the Iowa order), the Washtenaw Circuit Court would have to ignore (1) the constitutional right of a parent to develop a relationship with a child and (2) Cara Clausen's right under Iowa law to a 72-hour waiting period before parental rights can be released (Clausen had executed a form releasing her rights approximately 48 hours after BGC was born). Schmidt contended that, pursuant to *Bowie v. Arder,* 441 Mich. 23, 490 N.W.2d 568 (1992), the DeBoers lacked standing to initiate a custody dispute. The DeBoers argued that Michigan had jurisdiction under the UCCJA and that the court should consider the best interests of the child before making a decision. The DeBoers stated that they were seeking a decision that balanced the Iowa decision with the best interests of BGC, and contended that the child's best interests had not been considered in the Iowa proceedings.

On January 11, 1993, the Washtenaw Circuit Court issued an order denying Schmidt's motion for summary disposition, and directed that BGC was to remain with the DeBoers until further order.

On February 4, 1993, the Michigan Supreme Court remanded the case for consideration as on leave granted.

On January 29, 1993, the best-interests determination began in Washtenaw Circuit Court and continued for several days. During the course of the hearing, the parties learned that in Iowa, Cara Clausen's release of custody of BGC and waiver of parental rights had been set aside. In a decision rendered from the bench on February 12, 1993, the Washtenaw Circuit Court found that it was in the best interests of BGC for her to remain with the DeBoers. That decision is not at issue in the instant appeal.]

JURISDICTION

On appeal, Schmidt argues that the Washtenaw Circuit Court lacked jurisdiction to intervene in this case because the Iowa decision was not a judgment regarding custody but rather was a judgment regarding adoption. He contends that as a natural parent he has a constitutional right to custody of his child absent a determination that he is an unfit parent (a proposition with which the Iowa court agreed), and that no analysis, including a "best interests of the child" analysis, can override that right. *Stanley v. Illinois,* 405 U.S. 645, 92 S.Ct. 1208, 31 L.Ed.2d 551 (1972). Schmidt asserts that pursuant to the Full Faith and Credit Clause . . . the Washtenaw Circuit Court was obligated to recognize and enforce the valid judgment from Iowa. . . . Iowa has continued to

exercise jurisdiction throughout, even to holding the DeBoers in contempt of court.

We find that the Washtenaw Circuit Court lacked jurisdiction to intervene in this case. The UCCJA has been enacted by every state, including Michigan. Its primary purpose is to avoid jurisdictional competition between states by establishing uniform rules for deciding when states have jurisdiction to make child custody determinations. Michigan is precluded from exercising jurisdiction if a matter concerning custody is pending in another state at the time the petition to modify is filed in this state. . . . Although the issues concerning the dismissal of the DeBoers' adoption petition and the right to physical custody of BGC had been determined by the Iowa Supreme Court before December 3, 1992, further proceedings were scheduled in the case. . . . [T]he Washtenaw Circuit Court was precluded from intervening in this case, and was obligated to recognize and enforce the Iowa order of December 3, 1992.

We find that the DeBoers' contention that a Michigan court could modify the Iowa order because Iowa did not act substantially in conformity with the UCCJA by doing a "best interests of the child" analysis is without merit. The Iowa court dismissed the adoption petition and granted custody of BGC to Schmidt because he was the biological father of the child and because his parental rights had not been terminated. The Iowa court found that Iowa statutes and case law did not require the type of best interests analysis sought by the DeBoers in Michigan unless statutory grounds for termination had been established.

[The court also held that the DeBoers lacked standing to bring the case in the Michigan courts, because the Iowa court had "stripped the DeBoers of any legal claim to custody" and no statutory authority "gives standing to create a custody dispute to a third party who does not possess a substantive right to custody or is not a guardian. A right to legal custody cannot be based on the fact that a child resides or has resided with the third party."]

The Washtenaw Circuit Court's denial of Schmidt's motion for summary disposition and to dissolve the injunction is reversed. We find that the Iowa order of December 3, 1992, must be enforced, and that the custody of the child must be transferred to her father, Daniel Schmidt. The transfer of custody is stayed for twenty-one days from the date of the certification of this opinion to afford the parties an opportunity to appeal. This matter is remanded to the Washtenaw Circuit Court for proceedings consistent with this decision. We do not retain jurisdiction.

Reversed and remanded.

[On July 2, 1993, the Michigan Supreme Court, in a lengthy opinion, affirmed every aspect of this decision by a six-to-one vote. The US Supreme Court declined review of the case, and on August 2, 1993, the child was delivered to the Schmidts'.]

CASE QUESTIONS

1. Why is jurisdiction more important than the best interests of the child?
2. Did the DeBoers act in the best interests of the child? Did Cara Clausen?
3. Would you change the law? That is, was it the law or the parties who put Jessica in this position?

SUMMARY

Adoption severs the legal bonds between a child and its natural parent or parents. The law has developed a number of preferences with regard to adoption based on the relationship between the child and the potential adoptive parents prior to adoption. When the natural parents consent to the adoption, the only hurdle to adoption is the court's inquiry into the best interests of the child. When the natural parents do not consent, approval is difficult to obtain. Adoption through adoption agencies is usually more restrictive with regard to court approval, even requiring matching for religion in some states.

Legitimacy is often an issue in adoption, but even in the absence of the adoption question may pose special problems with regard to the legal bonds of parent and child. A modern phenomenon is the surrogacy contract, which has in recent years been the subject of legislative debate and resulting state statutes.

Adoption often focuses attention on the legal definition of the family and questions the validity of nontraditional relationship between the parents.

QUESTIONS

1. What is the order of preference for adoption among potential adoptive parents?
2. How is the legal relationship between a nonmarital father and his child different from that of a marital father?
3. What is the nature of surrogacy contracts? How are they different from other contracts?
4. What are the factors governing approval of adoptive parents with regard to religion and race?
5. What general effect does adoption have on the legal bonds between parent and child?
6. What is equitable adoption?
7. May persons having nontraditional family relationships adopt?
8. What is a de facto parent?

EXERCISES

Answer the questions according to the law of your state.

1. What constitutes abandonment or desertion of a child by its parents under adoption law? 35 A.L.R.2d 662.
2. What constitutes a sufficient parental consent to adoption? 24 A.L.R.2d 1127.
3. Does a natural parent have a right to withdraw consent to adopt? 74 A.L.R.3d 421.
4. Is a contract to pay birth expenses, conditioned on consent of the natural parents for adoption, an enforceable contract? 43 A.L.R.4th 935.
5. Must the spouse of an adopting parent consent to the adoption? 38 A.L.R.4th 768; 48 A.L.R.4th 860.
6. Can an illegitimate child bring an action to determine paternity? 19 A.L.R.4th 1082.
7. Under what circumstances may an adoption be annulled or vacated? 2 A.L.R.2d 887.
8. Are there any restrictions on adoption by single persons? By homosexuals? By unmarried couples? 2 A.L.R.4th 555.
9. What probative value is given to paternity based on blood testing and DNA testing? 43 A.L.R.4th 579; 37 A.L.R.4th 167; 84 A.L.R.4th 313.
10. What is the effect of paternity findings in subsequent divorce or annulment? 78 A.L.R.3d 846.

APPENDIX 15A

Uniform Adoption Act (1971)

§ 1. Definitions.

As used in this Act, unless the context otherwise requires,

(1) "child" means a son or daughter, whether by birth or by adoption;

(2) "Court" means the [here insert name of the court or branch] court of this State, and when the context requires means the court of any other state empowered to grant petitions for adoption;

(3) "minor" means [a male] [an individual] under the age of [18] [21] years [and a female under the age of 18 years];

(4) "adult" means an individual who is not a minor;

(5) "agency" means any person certified, licensed, or otherwise specially empowered by law or rule to place minors for adoption;

(6) "person" means an individual, corporation, government or governmental subdivision or agency, business trust, estate, trust, partnership or association, or any other legal entity.

§ 2. Who May Be Adopted.

Any individual may be adopted.[1]

§ 3. Who May Adopt.

The following individuals may adopt:

(1) a husband and wife together although one or both are minors;

(2) an unmarried adult;

(3) the unmarried father or mother of the individual to be adopted;

(4) a married individual without the other spouse joining as a petitioner,[2] if the individual to be adopted is not his spouse, and if

(i) the other spouse is a parent of the individual to be adopted and consents to the adoption;

(ii) the petitioner and the other spouse are legally separated; or

(iii) the failure of the other spouse to join in the petition or to consent to the adoption is excused by the Court by reason of prolonged unexplained absence, unavailability, incapacity, or circumstances constituting an unreasonable withholding of consent.

* * *

§ 5. Persons Required to Consent to Adoption.[3]

(a) Unless consent is not required under section 6, a petition to adopt a minor may be granted only if written consent to a particular adoption has been executed by:

(1) the mother of the minor;

(2) the father of the minor if the father was married to the mother at the time the minor was conceived or at any time thereafter, the minor is his child by adoption, or he has otherwise legitimated the minor according to the laws of [the place in which the adoption proceeding is brought] his consent is required under [the Uniform Legitimacy Act];

(3) any person lawfully entitled to custody of the minor or empowered to consent;

(4) the court having jurisdiction to determine custody of the minor, if the legal guardian or custodian of the person of the minor is not empowered to consent to the adoption;

(5) the minor, if more than [10] years of age, unless the Court in the best interest of the minor dispenses with the minor's consent; and

(6) the spouse of the minor to be adopted.

(b) A petition to adopt an adult may be granted only if written consent to adoption has been executed by the adult and the adult's spouse.

§ 6. Persons as to Whom Consent and Notice
Not Required.

(a) Consent to adoption is not required of:

(1) a parent who has deserted a child without
affording means of identification, or who has
abandoned a child;

(2) a parent of a child in the custody of another, if the parent for a period of at least one
year has failed significantly without justifiable
cause

(i) to communicate with the child or

(ii) to provide for the care and support of
the child as required by law or judicial decree;

(3) the father of a minor if the father's consent is not required by section 5(a)(2);

(4) a parent who has relinquished his right to
consent under section 19;

(5) a parent whose parental rights have been
terminated by order of court under section 19;

(6) a parent judicially declared incompetent
or mentally defective if the Court dispenses with
the parent's consent;

(7) any parent of the individual to be
adopted, if

(i) the individual is a minor [18] or more
years of age and the Court dispenses with the
consent of the parent or

(ii) the individual is an adult;

(8) any legal guardian or lawful custodian of
the individual to be adopted, other than a parent,
who has failed to respond in writing to a request
for consent for a period of [60] days or who, after examination of his written reasons for withholding consent, is found by the Court to be
withholding his consent unreasonably; or

(9) the spouse of the individual to be
adopted, if the failure of the spouse to consent to
the adoption is excused by the Court by reason of
prolonged unexplained absence, unavailability, incapacity, or circumstances constituting an unreasonable withholding of consent.

(b) Except as provided in section 11, notice of a
hearing on a petition for adoption need not be given to
a person whose consent is not required or to a person
whose consent or relinquishment has been filed with
the petition.

§ 7. How Consent is Executed.

(a) The required consent to adoption shall be executed at any time after the birth of the child and in the
manner following:

(1) if by the individual to be adopted, in the
presence of the court;

(2) if by an agency, by the executive head or
other authorized representative, in the presence of
a person authorized to take acknowledgments;

(3) if by any other person, in the presence
[of the Court or in the presence of a person
authorized to take acknowledgments];

(4) if by a court, by appropriate order or certificate.

(b) A consent which does not name or otherwise
identify the adopting parent is valid if the consent [is
executed in the presence of the Court and] contains a
statement by the person whose consent it is that the
person consenting voluntarily executed the consent irrespective of disclosure of the name or other identification of the adopting parent.

§ 8. Withdrawal of Consent.

(a) A consent to adoption cannot be withdrawn after the entry of a decree of adoption.

(b) A consent to adoption may be withdrawn prior
to the entry of a decree of adoption if the Court finds,
after notice and opportunity to be heard is afforded to
petitioner, the person seeking the withdrawal, and the
agency placing a child for adoption, that the withdrawal is in the best interest of the individual to be
adopted and the Court orders the withdrawal.

§ 9. Petition for Adoption.

(a) A petition for adoption shall be signed and
verified by the petitioner, filed with the clerk of the
Court, and state:

(1) the date and place of birth of the individual to be adopted, if known;

(2) the name to be used for the individual to
be adopted;

(3) the date [petitioner acquired custody of
the minor and] of placement of the minor and the
name of the person placing the minor;

(4) the full name, age, place and duration of
residence of the petitioner;

(5) the marital status of the petitioner, including the date and place of marriage, if
married;

(6) that the petitioner has facilities and resources, including those available under a subsidy
agreement, suitable to provide for the nurture and
care of the minor to be adopted, and that it is the
desire of the petitioner to establish the relationship of parent and child with the individual to be
adopted;

(7) a description and estimate of value of
any property of the individual to be adopted; and

(8) the name of any person whose consent to
the adoption is required, but who has not consented, and facts or circumstances which excuse
the lack of his consent normally required to the
adoption.

(b) A certified copy of the birth certificate or veri-
fication of birth record of the individual to be adopted,
if available, and the required consents and relinquish-
ments shall be filed with the clerk.

* * *

§ 14. Effect of Petition and Decree of Adoption.

(a) A final decree of adoption and an interlocutory decree of adoption which has become final, whether issued by a Court of this state or of any other place, have the following effect as to matters within the jurisdiction or before a court of this state:

(1) except with respect to a spouse of the petitioner and relatives of the spouse, to relieve the natural parents of the adopted individual of all parental rights and responsibilities, and to terminate all legal relationships between the adopted individual and his relatives, including his natural parents, so that the adopted individual thereafter is a stranger to his former relatives for all purposes including inheritance and the interpretation or construction of documents, statutes, and instruments, whether executed before or after the adoption is decreed, which do not expressly include the individual by name or by some designation not based on a parent and child or blood relationship; and

(2) to create the relationship of parent and child between petitioner and the adopted individual, as if the adopted individual were a legitimate blood descendant of the petitioner, for all purposes including inheritance and applicability of statutes, documents, and instruments, whether executed before or after the adoption is decreed, which do not expressly exclude an adopted individual from their operation or effect.

(b) Notwithstanding the provisions of subsection (a), if a parent of a child dies without the relationship of parent and child having been previously terminated and a spouse of the living parent thereafter adopts the child, the child's right of inheritance from or through the deceased parent is unaffected by the adoption.

(c) An interlocutory decree of adoption, while it is in force, has the same legal effect as a final decree of adoption. If an interlocutory decree of adoption is vacated, it shall be as though void from its issuance, and the rights, liabilities, and status of all affected persons which have not become vested shall be governed accordingly.

§ 15. Appeal and Validation of Adoption Decree.

(a) An appeal from any final order or decree rendered under this Act may be taken in the manner and time provided for appeal from a judgment in a civil action.

(b) Subject to the disposition of an appeal, upon the expiration of [one] year after an adoption decree is issued the decree cannot be questioned by any person including the petitioner, in any manner upon any ground, including fraud, misrepresentation, failure to give any required notice, or lack of jurisdiction of the parties or of the subject matter, unless, in the case of

the adoption of a minor the petitioner has not taken custody of the minor, or, in the case of the adoption of an adult, the adult had no knowledge of the decree within the [one] year period.

§ 16. Hearings and Records in Adoption Proceedings; Confidential Nature.

Notwithstanding any other law concerning public hearings and records,

(1) all hearings held in proceedings under this Act shall be held in closed Court without admittance of any person other than essential officers of the court, the parties, their witnesses, counsel, persons who have not previously consented to the adoption but are required to consent, and representatives of the agencies present to perform their official duties; and

(2) all papers and records pertaining to the adoption whether part of the permanent record of the court or of a file in [the Department of Welfare] or in an agency are subject to inspection only upon consent of the Court and all interested persons; or in exceptional cases, only upon an order of the Court for good cause shown; and

(3) except as authorized in writing by the adoptive parent, the adopted child, if [14] or more years of age, or upon order of the court for good cause shown in exceptional cases, no person is required to disclose the name or identity of either an adoptive parent or an adopted child.

§ 17. Recognition of Foreign Decree Affecting Adoption.

A decree of court terminating the relationship of parent and child or establishing the relationship by adoption issued pursuant to due process of law by a court of any other jurisdiction within or without the United States shall be recognized in this state and the rights and obligations of the parties as to matters within the jurisdiction of this state shall be determined as though the decree were issued by a court of this state.

§ 18. Application for New Birth Record.

Within 30 days after an adoption decree becomes final, the clerk of the court shall prepare an application for a birth record in the new name of the adopted individual and forward the application to the appropriate vital statistics office of the place, if known, where the adopted individual was born and forward a copy of the decree to the [Department of Welfare] of this state for statistical purposes.

§ 19. Relinquishment and Termination of Parent and Child Relationship.

(a) The rights of a parent with reference to a child, including parental right to control the child or to withhold consent to an adoption, may be relinquished and the relationship of parent and child terminated in or prior to an adoption proceeding as provided in this section.

(b) All rights of a parent with reference to a child, including the right to receive notice of a hearing on a petition for adoption, may be relinquished and the relationship of parent and child terminated by a writing, signed by the parent, regardless of the age of the parent,

(1) in the presence of a representative of an agency taking custody of the child, whether the agency is within or without the state or in the presence and with the approval of a judge of a court of record within or without this state in which the minor was present or in which the parent resided at the time it was signed, which relinquishment may be withdrawn within 10 days after it is signed or the child is born, whichever is later; and the relinquishment is invalid unless it states that the parent has this right of withdrawal; or

(2) in any other situation if the petitioner has had custody of the minor for [2] years, but only if notice of the adoption proceeding has been given to the parent and the court finds, after considering the circumstances of the relinquishment and the long continued custody by the petitioner, that the best interest of the child requires the granting of the adoption.

(c) In addition to any other proceeding provided by law, the relationship of parent and child may be terminated by a court order issued in connection with an adoption proceeding under this Act on any ground provided by other law for termination of the relationship, and in any event on the ground

(1) that the minor has been abandoned by the parent,

(2) that by reason of the misconduct, faults, or habits of the parent or the repeated and continuous neglect or refusal of the parent, the minor is without proper parental care and control, or subsistence, education, or other care or control necessary for his physical, mental, or emotional health or morals, or, by reason of physical or mental incapacity the parent is unable to provide necessary parental care for the minor, and the court finds that the conditions and causes of the behavior, neglect, or incapacity are irremediable or will not be remedied by the parent, and that by

reason thereof the minor is suffering or probably will suffer serious physical, mental, moral, or emotional harm, or

(3) that in the case of a parent not having custody of a minor, his consent is being unreasonably withheld contrary to the best interest of the minor.

(d) For the purpose of proceeding under this Act, a decree terminating all rights of a parent with reference to a child or the relationship of parent and child issued by a court of competent jurisdiction in this or any other state dispenses with the consent to adoption proceedings of a parent whose rights or parent and child relationship are terminated by the decree and with any required notice of an adoption proceeding other than as provided in this section.

(e) A petition for termination of the relationship of parent and child made in connection with an adoption proceeding may be made by:

(1) either parent if termination of the relationship is sought with respect to the other parent;

(2) the petitioner for adoption, the guardian of the person, the legal custodian of the child, or the individual standing in parental relationship to the child;

(3) an agency; or

(4) any other person having a legitimate interest in the matter.

(f) Before the petition is heard, notice of the hearing thereon and opportunity to be heard shall be given the parents of the child, the guardian of the person of the child, the person having legal custody of the child, and, in the discretion of the court, a person appointed to represent any party.

(g) Notwithstanding the provisions of subsection (b), a relinquishment of parental rights with respect to a child, executed under this section, may be withdrawn by the parent, and a decree of a court terminating the parent and child relationship under this section may be vacated by the Court upon motion of the parent, if the child is not on placement for adoption and the person having custody of the child consents in writing to the withdrawal or vacation of the decree.

* * *

§ 21. Short Title.

This Act may be cited as the Revised Uniform Adoption Act.

---

1 Many states have restrictions on adult adoptions.

2 Section 3(4) provides the special exceptions to adoption without the concurrence of the other spouse, the principal one being adoption of a stepchild (spouse's child).

3 Section 5 addresses the necessity of consent of the parents; Section 6 provides for exceptions.

APPENDIX 15B

Uniform Parentage Act (1973)

§ 1.   Parent and Child Relationship Defined.

As used in this Act, "parent and child relationship" means the legal relationship existing between a child and his natural or adoptive parents incident to which the law confers or imposes rights, privileges, duties, and obligations. It includes the mother and child relationship and the father and child relationship.

§ 2.   Relationship Not Dependent on Marriage.

The parent and child relationship extends equally to every child and to every parent, regardless of the marital status of the parents.

§ 3.   How Parent and Child Relationship Established.

The parent and child relationship between a child and

(1)   the natural mother may be established by proof of her having given birth to the child, or under this Act;

(2)   the natural father may be established under this Act;

(3)   an adoptive parent may be established by proof of adoption or under the Revised Uniform Adoption Act.

§ 4.   Presumption of Paternity.[1]

(a)   A man is presumed to be the natural father of a child if:

(1)   he and the child's natural mother are or have been married to each other and the child is born during the marriage, or within 300 days after the marriage is terminated by death, annulment, declaration of invalidity, or divorce, or after a decree of separation is entered by a court;

(2)   before the child's birth, he and the child's natural mother have attempted to marry each other by a marriage solemnized in apparent compliance with law, although the attempted marriage is or could be declared invalid, and,

(i)   if the attempted marriage could be declared invalid only by a court, the child is born during the attempted marriage, or within 300 days after its termination by death, annulment, declaration of invalidity, or divorce; or

(ii)   if the attempted marriage is invalid without a court order, the child is born within 300 days after the termination of cohabitation;

(3)   after the child's birth, he and the child's natural mother have married, or attempted to marry, each other by a marriage solemnized in apparent compliance with law, although the attempted marriage is or could be declared invalid, and

(i)   he has acknowledged his paternity of the child in writing filed with the appropriate court or Vital Statistics Bureau.

(ii)   with his consent, he is named as the child's father on the child's birth certificate, or

(iii)   he is obligated to support the child under a written voluntary promise or by court order;

(4)   while the child is under the age of majority, he receives the child into his home and openly holds out the child as his natural child; or

(5)   he acknowledges his paternity of the child in a writing filed with the [appropriate court or Vital Statistics Bureau], which shall promptly inform the mother of the filing of the acknowledgment, and she does not dispute the acknowledgment within a reasonable time after being informed thereof, in a writing filed with the appropriate court or Vital Statistics Bureau. If another man is presumed under this section to be the child's father, acknowledgment may be effected only with the written consent of the

presumed father or after the presumption has been rebutted.

(b) A presumption under this section may be rebutted in an appropriate action only by clear and convincing evidence. If two or more presumptions arise which conflict with each other, the presumption which on the facts is founded on the weightier considerations of policy and logic controls. The presumption is rebutted by a court decree establishing paternity of the child by another man.

§ 5. Artificial Insemination.[2]

(a) If, under the supervision of a licensed physician and with the consent of her husband, a wife is inseminated artificially with semen donated by a man not her husband, the husband is treated in law as if he were the natural father of a child thereby conceived. The husband's consent must be in writing and signed by him and his wife. The physician shall certify their signatures and the date of the insemination, and file the husband's consent with the [State Department of Health], where it shall be kept confidential and in a sealed file. However, the physician's failure to do so does not affect the father and child relationship. All papers and records pertaining to the insemination, whether part of the permanent record of a court or of a file held by the supervising physician or elsewhere, are subject to inspection only upon an order of the court for good cause shown.

(b) The donor of semen provided to a licensed physician for use in artificial insemination of a married woman other than the donor's wife is treated in law as if he were not the natural father of a child thereby conceived.[3]

§ 6. Determination of Father and Child Relationship; Who May Bring Action; When Action May Be Brought.

(a) A child, his natural mother, or a man presumed to be his father under Paragraph (1), (2), or (3) of Section 4(a), may bring an action

(1) at any time for the purpose of declaring the existence of the father and child relationship presumed under Paragraph (1), (2), or (3) of Section 4(a); or

(2) for the purpose of declaring the non-existence of the father and child relationship presumed under Paragraph (1), (2), or (3) of Section 4(a) only if the action is brought within a reasonable time after obtaining knowledge of relevant facts, but in no event later than [five] years after the child's birth. After the presumption has been rebutted, paternity of the child by another man may be determined in the same action, if he has been made a party.

(b) Any interested party may bring an action at any time for the purpose of determining the existence or non-existence of the father and child relationship presumed under Paragraph (4) or (5) of Section 4(a).

(c) An action to determine the existence of the father and child relationship with respect to a child who has no presumed father under Section 4 may be brought by the child, the mother or personal representative of the child, the [appropriate state agency], the personal representative or a parent of the mother if the mother has died, a man alleged or alleging himself to be the father, or the personal representative or a parent of the alleged father if the alleged father has died or is a minor.

(d) Regardless of its terms, an agreement, other than an agreement approved by the court in accordance with Section 13(b), between an alleged or presumed father and the mother or child, does not bar an action under this section.[4]

(e) If an action under this section is brought before the birth of the child, all proceedings shall be stayed until after the birth, except service of process and the taking of depositions to perpetuate testimony.

§ 7. Statute of Limitations.[5]

An action to determine the existence of the father and child relationship as to a child who has no presumed father under Section 4 may not be brought later than [three] years after the birth of the child, or later than [three] years after the effective date of this Act, whichever is later. However, an action brought by or on behalf of a child whose paternity has not been determined is not barred until [three] years after the child reaches the age of majority. Sections 6 and 7 do not extend the time within which a right of inheritance or a right to a succession may be asserted beyond the time provided by law relating to distribution and closing of decedents' estates or to the determination of heirship, or otherwise.

§ 8. Jurisdiction; Venue.

(a) [Without limiting the jurisdiction of any other court,] [The] [appropriate] court has jurisdiction of an action brought under this Act. [The action may be joined with an action for divorce, annulment, separate maintenance or support.]

(b) A person who has sexual intercourse in this State thereby submits to the jurisdiction of the courts of this State as to an action brought under this Act with respect to a child who may have been conceived by that act of intercourse.[6] In addition to any other method provided by [rule or] statute, including [cross reference to "long arm statute"], personal jurisdiction may be acquired by [personal service of summons outside this State or by registered mail with proof of actual receipt] service in accordance with [citation to "long arm statute"].

(c) The action may be brought in the county in which the child or the alleged father resides or is found or, if the father is deceased, in which proceedings for probate of his estate have been or could be commenced.

§ 9.   Parties.

The child shall be made a party to the action.[7] If he is a minor he shall be represented by his general guardian or a guardian ad litem appointed by the court. The child's mother or father may not represent the child as guardian or otherwise. The court may appoint the [appropriate state agency] as guardian ad litem for the child. The natural mother, each man presumed to be the father under Section 4, and each man alleged to be the natural father, shall be made parties or, if not subject to the jurisdiction of the court, shall be given notice of the action in a manner prescribed by the court and an opportunity to be heard. The court may align the parties.

§ 10.   Pre-Trial Proceedings.

(a)   As soon as practicable after an action to declare the existence or nonexistence of the father and child relationship has been brought, an informal hearing shall be held. [The court may order that the hearing be held before a referee.] The public shall be barred from the hearing. A record of the proceeding or any portion thereof shall be kept if any party requests, or the court orders. Rules of evidence need not be observed.

(b)   Upon refusal of any witness, including a party, to testify under oath or produce evidence, the court may order him to testify under oath and produce evidence concerning all relevant facts. If the refusal is upon the ground that his testimony or evidence might tend to incriminate him, the court may grant him immunity from all criminal liability on account of the testimony or evidence he is required to produce. An order granting immunity bars prosecution of the witness for any offense shown in whole or in part by testimony or evidence he is required to produce, except for perjury committed in his testimony. The refusal of a witness, who has been granted immunity, to obey an order to testify or produce evidence is a civil contempt of the court.

(c)   Testimony of a physician concerning the medical circumstances of the pregnancy and the condition and characteristics of the child upon birth is not privileged.

§ 11.   Blood Tests.

(a)   The court may, and upon request of a party shall, require the child, mother, or alleged father to submit to blood tests. The tests shall be performed by an expert qualified as an examiner of blood types, appointed by the court.

(b)   The court, upon reasonable request by a party, shall order that independent tests be performed by other experts qualified as examiner of blood types.

(c)   In all cases, the court shall determine the number and qualifications of the experts.

§ 12.   Evidence Relating to Paternity.[8]

Evidence relating to paternity may include:

(1)   evidence of sexual intercourse between the mother and alleged father at any possible time of conception;

(2)   an expert's opinion concerning the statistical probability of the alleged father's paternity based upon the duration of the mother's pregnancy;

(3)   blood test results, weighted in accordance with evidence, if available, of the statistical probability of the alleged father's paternity;

(4)   medical or anthropological evidence relating to the alleged father's paternity of the child based on tests performed by experts. If a man has been identified as a possible father of the child, the court may, and upon request of a party shall, require the child, the mother, and the man to submit to appropriate tests; and

(5)   all other evidence relevant to the issue of paternity of the child.

§ 13.   Pre-Trial Recommendations.

(a)   On the basis of the information produced at the pre-trial hearing, the judge [or referee] conducting the hearing shall evaluate the probability of determining the existence or non-existence of the father and child relationship in a trial and whether a judicial declaration of the relationship would be in the best interest of the child. On the basis of the evaluation, an appropriate recommendation for settlement shall be made to the parties, which may include any of the following:

(1)   that the action be dismissed with or without prejudice;

(2)   that the matter be compromised by an agreement among the alleged father, the mother, and the child, in which the father and child relationship is not determined but in which a defined economic obligation is undertaken by the alleged father in favor of the child and, if appropriate, in favor of the mother, subject to approval by the judge [or referee] conducting the hearing. In reviewing the obligation undertaken by the alleged father in a compromise agreement, the judge [or referee] conducting the hearing shall consider the best interest of the child, in the light of the factors enumerated in Section 15(e), discounted by the improbability, as it appears to him, of establishing the alleged father's paternity or nonpaternity of the child in a trial of the action. In the best interest of the child, the court may order that the alleged father's identity be kept confidential. In that case, the court may designate a person or agency to receive from the alleged father and disburse on behalf of the child all amounts paid by the alleged father in fulfillment of obligations imposed on him; and

(3) that the alleged father voluntarily acknowledge his paternity of the child.

(b) If the parties accept a recommendation made in accordance with Subsection (a), judgment shall be entered accordingly.

(c) If a party refuses to accept a recommendation made under Subsection (a) and blood tests have not been taken, the court shall require the parties to submit to blood tests, if practicable. Thereafter the judge [or referee] shall make an appropriate final recommendation. If a party refuses to accept the final recommendation, the action shall be set for trial.

(d) The guardian ad litem may accept or refuse to accept a recommendation under this Section.

(e) The informal hearing may be terminated and the action set for trial if the judge [or referee] conducting the hearing finds unlikely that all parties would accept a recommendation he might make under Subsection (a) or (c).

§ 14. Civil Action; Jury.

(a) An action under this Act is a civil action governed by the rules of civil procedure. The mother of the child and the alleged father are competent to testify and may be compelled to testify. Subsections (b) and (c) of Section 10 and Sections 11 and 12 apply.

(b) Testimony relating to sexual access to the mother by an unidentified man at any time or by an identified man at a time other than the probable time of conception of the child is inadmissible in evidence, unless offered by the mother.

(c) In an action against an alleged father, evidence offered by him with respect to a man who is not subject to the jurisdiction of the court concerning his sexual intercourse with the mother at or about the probable time of conception of the child is admissible in evidence only if he has undergone and made available to the court blood tests the results of which do not exclude the possibility of his paternity of the child. A man who is identified and is subject to the jurisdiction of the court shall be made a defendant in the action.

[(d) The trial shall be by the court without a jury.]

§ 15. Judgment or Order.[9]

(a) The judgment or order of the court determining the existence or nonexistence of the parent and child relationship is determinative for all purposes.

(b) If the judgment or order of the court is at variance with the child's birth certificate, the court shall order that [an amended birth registration be made] [a new birth certificate be issued] under Section 23.

(c) The judgment or order may contain any other provision directed against the appropriate party to the proceeding, concerning the duty of support, the custody and guardianship of the child, visitation privileges with the child, the furnishing of bond or other security for the payment of the judgment, or any other matter in the best interest of the child. The judgment or order may direct the father to pay the reasonable expenses of the mother's pregnancy and confinement.

(d) Support judgments or orders ordinarily shall be for periodic payments which may vary in amount. In the best interest of the child, a lump sum payment or the purchase of an annuity may be ordered in lieu of periodic payments of support. The court may limit the father's liability for past support of the child to the proportion of the expenses already incurred that the court deems just.

(e) In determining the amount to be paid by a parent for support of the child and the period during which the duty of support is owed, a court enforcing the obligation of support shall consider all relevant facts including

(1) the needs of the child;

(2) the standard of living and circumstances of the parents;

(3) the relative financial means of the parents;

(4) the earning ability of the parents;

(5) the need and capacity of the child for education, including higher education;

(6) the age of the child;

(7) the financial resources and the earning ability of the child;

(8) the responsibility of the parents for the support of others; and

(9) the value of services contributed by the custodial parent.

§ 16. Costs.

The court may order reasonable fees of counsel, experts, and the child's guardian ad litem, and other costs of the action and pre-trial proceedings, including blood tests, to be paid by the parties in proportions and at times determined by the court. The court may order the proportion of any indigent party to be paid by appropriate public authority.

§ 17. Enforcement of Judgment or Order.

(a) If existence of the father and child relationship is declared, or paternity or a duty of support has been acknowledged or adjudicated under this Act or under prior law, the obligation of the father may be enforced in the same or other proceedings by the mother, the child, the public authority that has furnished or may furnish the reasonable expenses of pregnancy, confinement, education, support, or funeral, or by any other person, including a private agency, to the extent he has furnished or is furnishing these expenses.

(b) The court may order support payments to be made to the mother, the clerk of the court, or a person, corporation, or agency designated to administer them for the benefit of the child under the supervision of the court.

(c)   Willful failure to obey the judgment or order of the court is a civil contempt of the court. All remedies for the enforcement of judgments apply.

§ 18.   Modification of Judgment or Order.

The court has continuing jurisdiction to modify or revoke a judgment or order

(1)   for future education and support, and

(2)   with respect to matters listed in Subsections (c) and (d) of Section 15 and Section 17(b), except that a court entering a judgment or order for the payment of a lump sum or the purchase of an annuity under Section 15(d) may specify that the judgment or order may not be modified or revoked.

§ 19.   Right to Counsel; Free Transcript on Appeal.

(a)   At the pre-trial hearing and in further proceedings, any party may be represented by counsel. The court shall appoint counsel for a party who is financially unable to obtain counsel.

(b)   If a party is financially unable to pay the cost of a transcript, the court shall furnish on request a transcript for purposes of appeal.

§ 20.   Hearings and Records; Confidentiality.

Notwithstanding any other law concerning public hearings and records, any hearing or trial held under this Act shall be held in closed court without admittance of any person other than those necessary to the action or proceeding. All papers and records, other than the final judgment, pertaining to the action or proceeding, whether part of the permanent record of the court or of a file in the [appropriate state agency] or elsewhere, are subject to inspection only upon consent of the court and all interested persons, or in exceptional cases only upon an order of the court for good cause shown.

§ 21.   Action to Declare Mother and Child Relationship.

Any interested party may bring an action to determine the existence or nonexistence of a mother and child relationship. Insofar as practicable, the provisions of this Act applicable to the father and child relationship apply.

§ 22.   Promise to Render Support.

(a)   Any promise in writing to furnish support for a child, growing out of a supposed or alleged father and child relationship, does not require consideration and is enforceable according to its terms, subject to Section 6(d).

(b)   In the best interest of the child or the mother, the court may, and upon the promisor's request shall, order the promise to be kept in confidence and designate a person or agency to receive and disburse on behalf of the child all amounts paid in performance of the promise.

§ 23.   Birth Records.

(a)   Upon order of a court of this State or upon request of a court of another state, the [registrar of births] shall prepare [an amended birth registration] [a new certificate of birth] consistent with the findings of the court and shall substitute the new certificate for the original certificate of birth.

(b)   The fact that the father and child relationship was declared after the child's birth shall not be ascertainable from the [amended birth registration] [new certificate] but the actual place and date of birth shall be shown.

(c)   The evidence upon which the [amended birth registration] [new certificate] was made and the original birth certificate shall be kept in a sealed and confidential file and be subject to inspection only upon consent of the court and all interested persons, or in exceptional cases only upon an order of the court for good cause shown.

§ 24.   When Notice of Adoption Proceeding Required.

If a mother relinquishes or proposes to relinquish for adoption a child who has (1) a presumed father under Section 4(a), (2) a father whose relationship to the child has been determined by a court, or (3) a father as to whom the child is a legitimate child under prior law of this State or under the law of another jurisdiction, the father shall be given notice of the adoption proceeding and have the rights provided under [the appropriate State statute] [the Revised Uniform Adoption Act], unless the father's relationship to the child has been previously terminated or determined by a court not to exist.

§ 25.   Proceeding to Terminate Parental Rights.[10]

(a)   If a mother relinquishes or proposes to relinquish for adoption a child who does not have (1) a presumed father under Section 4(a), (2) a father whose relationship to the child has been determined by a court, or (3) a father as to whom the child is a legitimate child under prior law of this State or under the law of another jurisdiction, or if a child otherwise becomes the subject of an adoption proceeding, the agency or person to whom the child has been or is to be relinquished, or the mother or the person having custody of the child, shall file a petition in the [_____] court to terminate the parental rights of the father, unless the father's relationship to the child has been previously terminated or determined by a court not to exist.

(b)   In an effort to identify the natural father, the court shall cause inquiry to be made of the mother and any other appropriate person. The inquiry shall include the following: whether the mother was married at the time of conception of the child or at any time thereafter; whether the mother was cohabiting with a man at the time of conception or birth of the child; whether the mother has received support payments or promises of support with respect to the child or in connection with her pregnancy; or whether any man has formally or informally acknowledged or declared his possible paternity of the child.

(c) If, after the inquiry, the natural father is identified to the satisfaction of the court, or if more than one man is identified as a possible father, each shall be given notice of the proceeding in accordance with Subsection (e). If any of them fails to appear or, if appearing, fails to claim custodial rights, his parental rights with reference to the child shall be terminated. If the natural father or a man representing himself to be the natural father, claims custodial rights, the court shall proceed to determine custodial rights.

(d) If, after the inquiry, the court is unable to identify the natural father or any possible natural father and no person has appeared claiming to be the natural father and claiming custodial rights, the court shall enter an order terminating the unknown natural father's parental rights with reference to the child. Subject to the disposition of an appeal upon the expiration of [six months] after an order terminating parental rights is issued under this subsection, the order cannot be questioned by any person, in any manner, or upon any ground, including fraud, misrepresentation, failure to give any required notice, or lack of jurisdiction of the parties or of the subject matter.

(e) Notice of the proceeding shall be given to every person identified as the natural father or a possible natural father [in the manner appropriate under rules of civil procedure for the service of process in a civil action in this state, or] in any manner the court directs. Proof of giving the notice shall be filed with the court before the petition is heard. [If no person has been identified as the natural father or a possible father, the court, on the basis of all information available, shall determine whether publication or public posting of notice of the proceeding is likely to lead to identification and, if so, shall order publication or public posting at times and in places and manner it deems appropriate.]

* * *

§ 27. Short Title.

This Act may be cited as the Uniform Parentage Act.

* * *

§ 30. Time of Taking Effect.

This Act shall take effect on _____.

---

1 A legal presumption requires that one fact or set of facts be assumed to be true, in this case a presumption that a particular man is the father of a child. Although this is a rebuttable presumption, it is often been declared in the cases as one of the strongest in the law.

2 Although the Act outlines a procedure for establishing paternity of the husband and the nonpaternity of the semen donor, it leaves gaps in determining paternity where the procedures are not followed.

3 Could this provision leave a child without a father?

4 Paragraphs (d) and (e) are aimed at protecting the child from actions by the parents determining paternity.

5 Section 7 attempts to balance rights of the respective parties, including the lack of legal status of a minor and the interests of leaving decedents' estates undisturbed.

6 It may be amusing to consider that one may be subject to a long-arm statute by the act of sexual intercourse.

7 Making a child a party to the case and providing for a guardian ad litem recognizes that the child's interests may not always be served by the parents.

8 Sections 11 and 12 demonstrate the reliance on blood tests in proving paternity. Statistically, blood tests present powerful conclusory evidence.

9 Sections 15-17 bear a strong resemblance to support requirements following divorce. It is to be expected that most states would have identical or analogous support requirements regardless of the marital status of the father, although the opposite was true historically.

10 This section addresses the problem of the unknown father in cases where the mother desires to terminate her relationship, as in adoption.

APPENDIX 15C

Uniform Status of Children of Assisted Conception Act (1988)

§ 1. Definitions.

In this [Act]:

(1) "Assisted conception" means a pregnancy resulting from

(i) fertilizing an egg of a woman with sperm of a man by means other than sexual intercourse or

(ii) implanting an embryo, but the term does not include the pregnancy of a wife resulting from fertilizing her egg with sperm of her husband.

(2) "Donor" means an individual [other than a surrogate] who produces egg or sperm used for assisted conception, whether or not a payment is made for the egg or sperm used, but does not include a woman who gives birth to a resulting child.

(3) "Intended parents" means a man and woman, married to each other, who enter into an agreement under this [Act] providing that they will be the parents of a child born to a surrogate through assisted conception using egg or sperm of one or both of the intended parents.

(4) "Surrogate" means an adult woman who enters into an agreement to bear a child conceived through assisted conception for intended parents.

§ 2. Maternity.

[Except as provided in Sections 5 through 9,] a woman who gives birth to a child is the child's mother.

§ 3. Assisted Conception by Married Woman.

[Except as provided in Sections 5 through 9,] the husband of a woman who bears a child through assisted conception is the father of the child, notwithstanding a declaration of invalidity or annulment of the marriage obtained after the assisted conception, unless within two years after learning of the child's birth he commences an action in which the mother and child are parties and in which it is determined that he did not consent to the assisted conception.

§ 4. Parental Status of Donors and Deceased Individuals.

[Except as otherwise provided in Sections 5 through 9:]

(a) A donor is not a parent of a child conceived through assisted conception.

(b) An individual who dies before implantation of an embryo, or before a child is conceived other than through sexual intercourse, using the individual's egg or sperm, is not a parent of the resulting child.

Alternative A [§ 5. Surrogacy Agreement.[1]

(a) A surrogate, her husband, if she is married, and intended parents may enter into a written agreement whereby the surrogate relinquishes all her rights and duties as a parent of a child to be conceived through assisted conception, and the intended parents may become the parents of the child pursuant to Section 8.

(b) If the agreement is not approved by the court under Section 6 before conception, the agreement is void and the surrogate is the mother of a resulting child and the surrogate's husband, if a party to the agreement, is the father of the child. If the surrogate's husband is not a party to the agreement or the surrogate is unmarried, paternity of the child is governed by [the Uniform Parentage Act].]

Alternative B [§ 5. Surrogate Agreements.[2]

An agreement in which a woman agrees to become a surrogate or to relinquish her rights and

458

duties as parent of a child thereafter conceived through assisted conception is void. However, she is the mother of a resulting child, and her husband, if a party to the agreement, is the father of the child. If her husband is not a party to the agreement or the surrogate is unmarried, paternity of the child is governed by [the Uniform Parentage Act].]

§ 6. Petition and Hearing for Approval of Surrogacy Agreement.[3]

(a) The intended parents and the surrogate may file a petition in the [appropriate court] to approve a surrogacy agreement if one of them is a resident of this State. The surrogate's husband, if she is married, must join in the petition. A copy of the agreement must be attached to the petition. The court shall name a [guardian ad litem] to represent the interests of a child to be conceived by the surrogate through assisted conception and [shall] [may] appoint counsel to represent the surrogate.

(b) The court shall hold a hearing on the petition and shall enter an order approving the surrogacy agreement, authorizing assisted conception for a period of 12 months after the date of the order, declaring the intended parents to be the parents of a child to be conceived through assisted conception pursuant to the agreement and discharging the guardian ad litem and attorney for the surrogate, upon finding that:

(1) the court has jurisdiction and all parties have submitted to its jurisdiction under subsection (e) and have agreed that the law of this State governs all matters arising under this [Act] and the agreement;

(2) the intended mother is unable to bear a child or is unable to do so without unreasonable risk to an unborn child or to the physical or mental health of the intended mother or child, and the finding is supported by medical evidence;

(3) the [relevant child-welfare agency] has made a home study of the intended parents and the surrogate and a copy of the report of the home study has been filed with the court;

(4) the intended parents, the surrogate, and the surrogate's husband, if she is married, meet the standards of fitness applicable to adoptive parents in this State;

(5) all parties have voluntarily entered into the agreement and understand its terms, nature, and meaning, and the effect of the proceeding;

(6) the surrogate has had at least one pregnancy and delivery and bearing another child will not pose an unreasonable risk to the unborn child or to the physical or mental health of the surrogate or the child, and this finding is supported by medical evidence;

(7) all parties have received counseling concerning the effect of the surrogacy by [a qualified health-care professional or social worker] and a report containing conclusions about the capacity of the parties to enter into and fulfill the agreement has been filed with the court;

(8) a report of the results of any medical or psychological examination or genetic screening agreed to by the parties or required by law has been filed with the court and made available to the parties;

(9) adequate provision has been made for all reasonable health-care costs associated with the surrogacy until the child's birth including responsibility for those costs if the agreement is terminated pursuant to Section 7; and

(10) the agreement will not be substantially detrimental to the interest of any of the affected individuals.

(c) Unless otherwise provided in the surrogacy agreement, all court costs, attorney's fees, and other costs and expenses associated with the proceeding must be assessed against the intended parents.

(d) Notwithstanding any other law concerning judicial proceedings or vital statistics, the court shall conduct all hearings and proceedings under this section in camera. The court shall keep all records of the proceedings confidential and subject to inspection under the same standards applicable to adoptions. At the request of any party, the court shall take steps necessary to ensure that the identities of the parties are not disclosed.

(e) The court conducting the proceedings has exclusive and continuing jurisdiction of all matters arising out of the surrogacy until a child born after entry of an order under this section is 180 days old.

§ 7. Termination of Surrogacy Agreement.

(a) After entry of an order under Section 6, but before the surrogate becomes pregnant through assisted conception, the court for cause, or the surrogate, her husband, or the intended parents may terminate the surrogacy agreement by giving written notice of termination to all other parties and filing notice of the termination with the court. Thereupon, the court shall vacate the order entered under Section 6.

(b) A surrogate who has provided an egg for the assisted conception pursuant to an agreement approved under Section 6 may terminate the agreement by filing written notice with the court within 180 days after the last insemination pursuant to the agreement. Upon finding, after notice to the parties to the agreement and hearing, that the surrogate has voluntarily terminated the agreement and understands the nature, meaning, and effect of the termination, the court shall vacate the order entered under Section 6.

(c) The surrogate is not liable to the intended parents for terminating the agreement pursuant to this section.

§ 8. Parentage Under Approved Surrogacy Agreement.[4]

(a) The following rules of parentage apply to surrogacy agreements approved under Section 6:

(1) Upon birth of a child to the surrogate, the intended parents are the parents of the child and the surrogate and her husband, if she is married, are not parents of the child unless the court vacates the order pursuant to Section 7(b).

(2) If, after notice of termination by the surrogate, the court vacates the order under Section 7(b) the surrogate is the mother of a resulting child, and her husband, if a party to the agreement, is the father. If the surrogate's husband is not a party to the agreement or the surrogate is unmarried, paternity of the child is governed by [the Uniform Parentage Act].

(b) Upon birth of the child, the intended parents shall file a written notice with the court that a child has been born to the surrogate within 300 days after assisted conception. Thereupon, the court shall enter an order directing the [Department of Vital Statistics] to issue a new birth certificate naming the intended parents as parents and to seal the original birth certificate in the records of the [Department of Vital Statistics].

§ 9. Surrogacy: Miscellaneous Provisions.

(a) A surrogacy agreement that is the basis of an order under Section 6 may provide for the payment of consideration.

(b) A surrogacy agreement may not limit the right of the surrogate to make decisions regarding her health care or that of the embryo or fetus.

(c) After the entry of an order under Section 6, marriage of the surrogate does not affect the validity of the order, and her husband's consent to the surrogacy agreement is not required, nor is he the father of a resulting child.

(d) A child born to a surrogate within 300 days after assisted conception pursuant to an order under Section 6 is presumed to result from the assisted conception. The presumption is conclusive as to all persons who have notice of the birth and who do not commence within 180 days after notice, an action to assert the contrary in which the child and the parties to the agreement are named as parties. The action must be commenced in the court that issued the order under Section 6.

(e) A health-care provider is not liable for recognizing the surrogate as the mother before receipt of a copy of the order entered under Section 6 or for recognizing the intended parents as parents after receipt of an order entered under Section 6.

§ 10. Parent and Child Relationship; Status of Child.

(a) A child whose status as a child is declared or negated by this [Act] is the child only of his or her parents as determined under this [Act].

(b) Unless superseded by later events forming or terminating a parent and child relationship, the status of parent and child declared or negated by this [Act] as to a given individual and a child born alive controls for purposes of:

(1) intestate succession;

(2) probate law exemptions, allowances, or other protections for children in a parent's estate; and

(3) determining eligibility of the child or its descendants to share in a donative transfer from any person as a member of a class determined by reference to the relationship.

* * *

§ 12. Short Title.

This [Act] may be cited as the Uniform Status of Children of Assisted Conception Act.

* * *

§ 14. Effective Date.

This [Act] shall take effect on _____. Its provisions are to be applied prospectively.

* * *

§ 16. Application to Existing Relationships.

This [Act] applies to surrogacy agreements entered into after its effective date.

---

1   Alternative A would be appropriate for states wishing to recognize and to regulate surrogacy arrangements.

2   Alternative B might be adopted by a state that does not recognize the validity of surrogacy contracts.

3   Section 6 suggests a significant level of state involvement in surrogacy contracts, in contrast to the attitude prior to the *Baby M* case.

4   Whether or not a state recognizing surrogacy contracts accepts state intrusion into the regulation of such contracts, the provisons in § 8 sorting out the legal status of the parents offer a solution to a continuing problem.

...dy Watkins and Wayne Norville an-
the engagement of their daughter
Watkins-Norville to Michael Curtis.
Marlene Curtis and Kevin Curtis of
. Shannon Watkins-Norville attended
a Polytechnic University of San Luis
graduating with a doctorate in Nu-
ysics. She lives in New York City,
k and works at New York University.
Curtis graduated from the Institute of
California with a degree in Engineer-
ives in Amherst, New York and works
or for the Department of Health and
Services. The two met at a physics
ce. They will be married at New York
ty. The wedding will be held in June.

and John Cage of Kansas City an-
the engagement of their daughter
Cage to Steven Fox, son of Barbara
nael Fox of Garland, Kansas. Patricia
ended Mason College of Hair and
Kansas City. She currently lives and
Kansas City. Steven Fox is a gradu-
oston University in Massachusetts. He
the District Attorney's office. The
be married May 1 in Kansas City.
They will honeymoon in Ireland.

erine Shaefer of Eagle Bluffs, an-
the engagement of her daughter
o Robert Patterson, son of Christine
c Patterson of Tustin, California.
haefer, a marketing consultant, is a

Harvard Law School. He currently works for
the legal department of Stanford University.
The two will be married at the Windmill Farm.
They plan to remain in California after a long
honeymoon in Jamaica.

WEDDINGS

Shari Ellis, daughter of Sophie and Zach Ellis
of Spring Valley, Virginia, and Brian Marino,
son of Lois and Adam Marino of Colorado
Springs, were married in Colorado Springs
May 12. The Reverend Billings officiated at
the Church. The bride wore a white silk and
lace gown. The dress had a ruffled semicathe-
dral train and a bustle with pink and white
roses. The groom wore a black and white tuxedo. The reception was held at the Hilton in
Colorado Springs. Th...
in Europe.

Zoe Mathison, daug...
Mathison of Bould...
Kearns, son of Const...
in Colorado Springs...
The Reverend Jane...
ceremony, held at th...
bride wore ivory, as...
ily, and was driven...
drawn carriage. The...
tuxedo, met the bride...
reception, held at the Broadmoor, was attended by hundreds. A popular local band entertained the crowd. The happy couple is
honeymooning in Egypt.

Yuka Fujishima, daughter of C.W. Fujishima
and R. Fujishima, was married to Kazuteru
Murakami, son of Reiko and Haruki Murakami, in Monterey, California on May 26.
The Reverend R. Stuart officiated at the ceremony, done first in traditional Japanese style.
The bride wore a stunning kimono, the groom
a classic hakama. The second, western-style
ceremony saw the bride in a white-beaded lace
sheath with a pink obi sash. The reception was
held at the Rastafarian Reggae Bar on Light-
house Avenue. The two are honeymooning in
San Francisco.

Helen Davis, daughter of Lindsay and Daniel
Davis, was married to Keith Bronson, son of
Marie and Greg Bronson, in Hacienda, New
Mexico, on May 15. Helen Davis, who is a
graduate of New Mexico State University, is
an advertising specialist working for the U.S.
Government. Keith Bronson, a graduate of
Massachusetts Institute of Technology, is a
systems administrator for International
Computers, Inc. in Monte Vista, New Mexico.

...tion was held on Mayor Carwile's grou...
The couple will honeymoon in Asia.

ANNIVERSARIES

Barbara and John Slater will celebrate
10th wedding anniversary by repeating
wedding vows in the presence of a few
friends. The couple will then board an o
liner bound for the South Pacific and enj
second honeymoon.

Mary and Bruce Martin celebrated their
wedding anniversary in Breckenridge, C
rado on June 11 in the presence of family
friends. The couple were married on the is
of Maui and have lived overseas throug
their marriage. After a long second ho
...
1941 in San Francisco, held the celebratio
Pali Lookout. Their three children, who
ranged the festivities, flew in from New
and Montreal. Distinguished guests from
over the world attended.

BIRTHS

Robert Christopher Halliwell, a boy,
pounds ten ounces and twenty-two inche
length, was born at 10:21 P.M. on June 2
Maria and James Halliwell. Both mother
son are doing well and will be returning
the hospital soon.

Julianna Leigh Kroft, a girl, seven pound
ounces and nineteen inches in length,
born at 8:35 P.M. on July 12, to Stephanie
Lee Kroft. Mother and daughter have alr
gone home to a joyous welcome from fa
and friends.

Caroline Chase Montgomery, a girl, s
pounds 10 ounces and twenty inches in len
was born at 5:28 A.M. on July 19, to Jan
and Brian M. Montgomery. Both mother
daughter are doing well and will be retur
home next week.

PART FOUR

Dicta Ultima

DICTA ULTIMA

Closing comments in a text on family law are difficult because no chapter on family law is truly closed. In every major area of family law, an important case is on appeal, or Congress or a state legislature is debating an issue of significance. Changes are so frequent that some law school texts come out with paperback supplements of 200 or 300 pages every other year between editions of the casebooks. Authors naturally fear that their text, cases, and comments will quickly become stale and outdated. While the present text was being written, the administrative branch of the United States switched from a Republican to a Democratic administration that began bent on social engineering, or so it seemed. The outgoing vice president campaigned on traditional "family values"; the incoming president immediately proposed lifting the ban on homosexuals in the military. Regardless of where one stands on these issues, it is apparent that the American family is the subject of constant controversy and change. What is noteworthy about this from the perspective of a text on family law is that the family is also in the forefront of political and legal change.

An underlying premise of this book is that the American republic has always included the family and the status of family members as an essential ingredient in political and legal change. Americans have always engaged in debate over directing social change through legal intervention into family life. At every stage, the proponents of new directions have met with resistance from those who would preserve the status quo.

Americans place great faith in the rule of law, even when criticizing the law and the legal system. That faith includes a strongly held belief that human conduct can be directed and controlled by law. This belief apparently extends to the regulation and control of intimate relations, despite the ever-recurring revolutions in family relations and sexual behavior. If social change continues at its present pace, legislation will inevitably follow quickly thereafter (as in *Baby M*), and the courts will necessarily follow legislation somewhat more remotely.

When family law is assessed in terms of practical results rather than novel cases decided in appellate courts, the picture is somewhat different.

Although laws may change quickly, values and prejudices are less susceptible to change. The vast majority of divorces are negotiated in lawyers' offices, subject to approval by judges who are likely to represent mainstream values; only affluent clients can afford to pay for law at the leading edge. An attorney must pursue a case taking into account the resources of the client and the predilections of the judge. The paralegal is a partner in this process.

The long and the short of it is that the law of domestic relations continues to have an exciting future. Unless we can legislate marital bliss and parental perfection, there will be plenty of work for lawyers, mediators, paralegals, and mental health professionals.

GLOSSARY

Asterisked entries are from Nolo's *Family Law Dictionary*.

*adoption   Adoption is a legal method of creating a parent-child relationship that is recognized for all purposes—including child support obligations, inheritance rights, and custody—as equivalent to the biological relationship. While in most cases adults adopt minors, it is possible in most states for one adult to adopt another. (Only Alabama, Arizona, Hawaii, Michigan, Nebraska, and Ohio prohibit adult adoptions.)

Adoptions are categorized by courts and social service agencies into three basic types: stepparent adoptions (the child is living with a natural parent who has remarried, and the new spouse wants to adopt); agency adoptions (the child is under the care of a charity or publicly funded agency and is put up for adoption); and private adoptions (nongovernment agencies or individuals arrange adoptions).

Regardless of type, adoptions can be granted only by a court and are allowed only when the court declares the adoption to be in the best interests of the child. To assist the court in making this determination, the state (or local) welfare department conducts an investigation into the home maintained by the prospective adopting parents. The court looks at:

- the occupations, earnings, and stability of the prospective parents;
- the medical, emotional, and physical needs of the child;
- religious and racial compatibility (religion and race need not be the same, but the court looks at the potential societal difficulties if they are not);
- whether the prospective parent has any criminal record of child abuse; and
- the age of the child.

In addition, most states require the consent of the person being adopted if she is over a certain age, usually about twelve. Most states give preference to married people in granting adoptions, although in many states anyone capable of being a good parent may adopt, including single people. In fact, to encourage adoption of hard-to-place children . . . , increased numbers of single people, including lesbians and gay men, are being allowed to adopt. A few states, however, including Florida and New Hampshire, expressly prohibit lesbians and gay men from adopting.

An adoption results in a termination of parental rights and responsibilities of the natural parents of the adopted child.

*adultery   Sexual intercourse by a married person with somebody other than his or her spouse is called adultery. In many states, adultery is technically a crime, but rarely is anyone prosecuted for it. In states which still permit fault divorce, adultery is virtually always a ground for granting a divorce. In states where marital misconduct affects the division of property and/or alimony, an adulterous spouse may be awarded less property or alimony (or ordered to pay) had there been no accusation.

*adversary system   The legal system in the United States is based on the philosophy that the true facts of a given situation—and hence justice—

464

will emerge if the parties to a court action act as adversaries rather than cooperative participants. The theory is that if each side vigorously advances its own version of the facts, an impartial third person or group of persons (judge or jury) will sift out the truth. Critics point out that this system depends on equality of representation (assuming the parties are proceeding through advocates). If one advocate is better than the other, or has more money to prepare the case, the truth may not emerge. The adversary system's use has been especially criticized in family law cases on the ground that it intensifies divisions within a family rather than ameliorates them. Because cooperation between former spouses is necessary if children are involved, the adversary system seems particularly inappropriate in these instances. Accordingly, many family law courts and practitioners are beginning to emphasize conciliation services and mediation techniques instead of traditional divorce litigation.

*agency adoption   Adoptions arranged by charities or publicly funded social services agencies are called agency adoptions (also called *county adoptions* or *public adoptions*). Agency adoptions take more court or welfare department involvement than do private adoptions. Agency adoptions usually occur when a child lives at an orphanage or in a foster home, or when a mother simply places an infant "up for adoption."

*alienation of affection   When a person intentionally "came between" a husband and wife, he was technically guilty of "alienation of affection." At one time, courts in all states but Louisiana allowed the injured spouse to sue the interloper for the harm done to the marriage. Most states have eliminated alienation of affection lawsuits. They still exist in a few states, however, including Hawaii, Kansas, Rhode Island, and Tennessee.

alienation of affections   A cause of action based on willful and malicious interference with the marriage relationship by a third party.

*alimony   Alimony is paid by one ex-spouse to the other for support.

alimony in gross   *See* lump-sum support.

*a mensa et thoro   A mensa et thoro is a Latin term meaning "from table and bed," which became used in English as "from bed and board." A

separation a mensa et thoro—that is, a separation from bed and board—is another term for a legal separation.

amicus curiae brief   In some instances, most commonly on appeal to a high court, interested persons or groups may petition the court to submit briefs as a "friend of the court" (*amicus curiae*), and this request is usually granted. Such briefs indicate that the dispute has ramifications extending beyond the parties themselves, as when certain groups are concerned that an unfavorable precedent might be set.

*annulment   Annulment is a court procedure that dissolves a marriage and treats it as though it never happened. In the past, when divorces were difficult to obtain because fault had to be proved (for example, until 1966, adultery was the only ground for divorce in New York), judges interpreted annulment statutes liberally in order to make annulments readily available. Today, however, when it is relatively easy to obtain a divorce in most states, annulments are rare. Where an annulment occurs after children have been born, those children are not considered illegitimate, even though the parents were "never married."

*antenuptial agreement   Before the couples marry, they make an agreement concerning certain aspects of their relationship, including how they will characterize their property during marriage, whether alimony will be paid in the event the couple later divorces, and other issues. A spouse, however, cannot agree to give up child support in the event of a divorce. These agreements are also called *prenuptial* or *premarital* agreements.

*artificial insemination   Artificial insemination is a procedure by which a woman is inseminated by a means other than sexual intercourse. If the semen came from her husband (homologous artificial insemination), the law considers this father-child relationship the same as any father-child relationship where the child is born during marriage. If the semen is from a man other than her husband, the procedure is termed "artificial insemination by donor" or "heterologous artificial insemination."

attorney/client privilege   Because of the need for full disclosure by clients, custom (and now law) dictate that such disclosures are privileged and may not be revealed by the attorney without the client's consent.

best interests of the child The overriding consideration (the *polestar*, as it is sometimes referred to) in determining issues of child custody.

*bigamy A person who knows he or she is already legally married and marries another person is guilty of the crime of bigamy in every state.

breach of contract Contract remedy that ordinarily seeks compensation for injury due to failure to perform.

breach of promise to marry A cause of action against someone who breaks off a marriage engagement. It was commonly used by women to collect damages for the loss of expected economic gain, namely, a life of luxury with a rich fiance.

*breach of promise to marry Under traditional common law, a broken engagement could be treated as a breach of promise to marry, which would support a lawsuit for money damages against the person who broke the engagement. Today, most states have done away with this type of lawsuit. It may be possible, however, for the giver of an engagement ring or other gift made in contemplation of marriage to get the gift back if the other person broke off the engagement and the couple understood that the ring or other gift was a precursor to marriage.

canon law The law of the church. Domestic relations were formerly a matter for the church (divorce was rare and adoption not allowed), which was governed by canon law, observed to this day by the Catholic Church.

*child support All states require natural parents and adoptive parents to support their children until the children reach the age of majority (and sometimes longer), are declared emancipated by a court, or until there is a termination of parental rights and responsibilities (as in the case where a child is adopted). In a divorce, this means that the noncustodial parent is often required to pay some kind of child support while the custodial parent is deemed to be meeting his or her support duty through the custody itself. For parents awarded joint custody, the support obligation of each is often based on the ratio of each parent's income to their combined incomes, and the percentage of time the child spends with each parent.

clean hands doctrine Doctrine providing that courts of equity do not hear claims brought by claimants who have acted improperly or in bad faith.

*cohabitation Cohabitation generally refers to when a man and a woman live together in an intimate sexual relationship without marrying. In some states, cohabitation by a person receiving alimony is grounds for termination of alimony. Also, in some states, a parent who cohabits may have difficulty obtaining custody of his or her children. Cohabitation is still a crime in some places, though rarely is anyone prosecuted for it. Some people describe a cohabitating couple's relationship as a *meretricious relationship*.

Coke Sir Edward Coke (pronounced "cook"), 1552-1634, rose to the exalted position of Chief Justice of the King's Bench, but is best known as the first complier of annotated law reports in his *Institutes*, which may well mark the beginning of modern Anglo-American law.

collateral attack An attack on a judgment or decree that uses a proceeding other than a direct challenge to the judgment or decree.

*common law marriage In Alabama, Colorado, Georgia, Idaho, Iowa, Kansas, Montana, Ohio, Oklahoma, Pennsylvania, Rhode Island, South Carolina, Texas, Utah, and Washington, D.C., couples can become legally married by living together for a long period of time and either holding themselves out to others as husband and wife or intending to be married. These are called common law marriages. Contrary to popular belief, however, even if two people cohabit for a certain number of years, if they don't intend to be married or don't hold themselves out as married, there is no common law marriage—even in those states which recognize common law marriages.

When a common law marriage does exist, the spouses are entitled to the same legal treatment received by other married couples, including the necessity of going through a formal divorce to end the marriage.

*community property Community property is a method of defining the ownership of property acquired (including earnings) during a marriage and the responsibility for debts incurred during the marriage and all property acquired with those earnings are considered community property. This includes wages, stock options, pensions and other employment compensation, family business profits, business good will, household goods, motor vehicles, bank accounts, life insurance policies, tax refunds, real property, art collections, copyrights and inventions. Additionally, all debts incurred during marriage, unless the creditor was specifically looking for payment from the separate property of one spouse, are community property debts.

The major exceptions to these rules are that gifts and inheritances specifically made to one spouse during marriage, personal injury awards received by one spouse during marriage, and the proceeds of a pension which had already vested (that is, the pensioner was legally entitled to receive it) before marriage are separate property.

Property purchased with the separate funds of a spouse remains that spouse's separate property. A business owned by one spouse before the marriage remains his or her separate property during the marriage, although a portion of the value of the business may be attributed to the community if it increased in value during the marriage or both spouses worked at it. Property purchased partially with separate funds and partially with community property funds is part community and part separate property.

condonation Forgiveness for marital fault, commonly adultery, based on the continuation or resumption of cohabitation by the married couple.

*condonation Condonation is someone's approval of another's activities. For example, a wife who does not object to her husband's adultery may be said to condone it. In states with fault divorce, condonation may constitute a defense to divorce. If the wife sues her husband for divorce, claiming he has committed adultery, the husband may argue as a defense that she condoned his behavior.

conflict of interest Whenever financial interests or personal relationships present any likelihood that an attorney might provide less than faithful representation to a client, a potential conflict of interest arises. Ethically, the attorney is responsible for taking appropriate action, usually declining to accept such employment.

consensual union One of many terms used to refer to a marriage-like union that lacks official or

recorded legal recognition. It is relatively stable and potentially permanent and often results in offspring.

*consortium Consortium is the relationship between husband and wife, which includes love, affection, fellowship, and sexual companionship. If a third party interferes with that relationship (for example, a neck injury disables the husband from having sexual intercourse), the spouse who loses elements of consortium can sue the third party on that ground. Although cohabiting and same-sex couples have argued that loss-of-consortium statutes should apply to their relationships as well, virtually no states have applied the law to them.

*contempt of court A judge who feels someone is improperly challenging or ignoring the court's authority has the power to declare the defiant person (called the "contemnor") in contempt of court.

Civil contempt occurs when the contemnor willfully disobeys a court order. (This is also called *indirect contempt* because it occurs outside the judge's immediate realm, and evidence must be presented to the judge to prove the contempt.) A civil contemnor, too, may be fined, jailed, or both; however, the fine or jailing is meant to coerce the contemnor into obeying the court, not to punish him or her, and the contemnor will be released from jail as soon as he or she complies with the court order. In divorce proceedings, civil contempt is one way the court enforces alimony, child support, and custody and visitation orders which have been ignored.

contingency fee In personal injury cases, attorneys often contract to provide legal services for a percentage of the final recovery. This is generally considered unethical in other areas of law, with the exception of some collections of debts.

county adoption *See* agency adoption.

criminal conversation A cause of action in tort for adultery, brought against the outsider to the marriage who has been engaged in adultery; brought by the injured (nonadulterous) spouse.

*criminal conversation Criminal conversation is a ground for a lawsuit brought by a husband for damages against a man who has seduced the husband's wife. This action is no longer available in most states.

*curtesy Under the traditional common law, a spouse was automatically entitled to inherit a portion of the other spouse's property. Curtesy was the portion of a wife's property that the husband was entitled to when the wife died, while dower was the portion of the husband's property that the wife was entitled to receive when he died. Curtesy and dower laws don't exist in community property states, and many other states abolished or modified the laws when they adopted equitable distribution rules.

*custodial parent The parent who has physical custody of a child is called the custodial parent. The other parent is termed the non-custodial parent. This is true even if the parents share legal custody. Some states now grant joint (physical) custody, where the parents share physical custody of their child (for example, alternate months or years, three days a week in one home and four in the other, or bird's nest custody). In joint custody arrangements, a parent is considered the custodial parent when he or she actually has the child.

*custody Custody includes both the legal authority to make decisions about the medical, educational, health, and welfare needs of a child (legal custody) and physical control over a child (physical custody). Traditionally, legal and physical custody were granted to the mother and visitation rights to the father. This arrangement is still the norm in many states. Some states, however, have joint custody laws which allow divorced parents to share physical custody, legal custody, or both. When only legal custody is shared, one parent is given physical custody and the other is given visitation rights. When physical custody is shared, usually so is legal custody. The primary standard used by courts when awarding custody is the best interests of the child.

dissolution of marriage Another name for divorce, which has in recent years been favored by several states.

divorce A legal proceeding that dissolves the legal bonds of marriage. Derived from two forms of divorce (*a mensa et thoro* and *a vinculo matrimonii*).

domestic relations Family law as a field. Textbooks and law school courses commonly use this terminology.

*dower Under traditional common law, a dower was the portion of a husband's property which he brought into the marriage or acquired during the marriage to which his wife was automatically entitled if he died leaving a child. Dower law barred a husband from selling, giving away, or disposing of, in his will, the portion his wife was entitled to, unless she consented.

*emancipated minor A minor demonstrating freedom from parental control or support is considered emancipated, or may be declared emancipated by a court. An emancipated minor is considered an adult for purposes such as entering into contracts (for employment, buying a car, etc.) and signing a will.

*equitable adoption In some states, when a close relationship like that of parent and child exists between a child and an unrelated adult, the courts recognize that an equitable adoption has occurred. Usually, the adult has agreed or intended to adopt the child but has not validly done so. The effect of calling the relationship an equitable adoption means that the adult must support the child and the child can inherit from the adult when the adult dies.

*equitable distribution Equitable distribution is a principle under which assets and earnings accumulated during marriage are divided equitably (fairly) at divorce. In theory, equitable means equal, or nearly so. In practice, however, equitable is often 2/3 to the higher wage earner, and 1/3 to the lower (or non) wage earner, unless the court believes it is fairer to award one or the other spouse more. In some equitable distribution states, if a spouse obtains a fault divorce, the "guilty" spouse may receive less than his or her share of the marital property upon divorce.

*equitable distribution states Washington, D.C., and the 40 states which require their courts to employ equitable distribution principles when dividing property at divorce are called the equitable distribution states. These are every state except Arizona, California, Idaho, Louisiana, Nevada, New Mexico, Texas, Washington (the community property states), Wisconsin (modified community property state), and Mississippi (common law property state).

*estoppel In certain situations, the law refuses to allow a person to deny facts when another person has relied on and acted in accordance with the facts. This is called estoppel.

family　The traditional family, defined as a husband, a wife, and their children, is under attack by those who have nontraditional relationships but want to enjoy the legal benefits of marriage and family. The ensuing debate threatens to last for many years.

fee tail　One of the estates in land that describe the extent of ownership in Anglo-American property law. The fee tail, created by language such as "to my eldest son and the heirs of his body," was designed to ensure that property would descend through bloodlines in each generation. This prevented the estate from being conveyed out of the family, but resulted in many estates becoming hopelessly "entailed" and ill-suited for changing circumstances.

fiduciary　Person who has a high duty of loyalty, trust, and fair dealing because of a special relationship with another.

fixed fee　Attorneys sometimes charge flat, or fixed, fees, which are specified amounts ordinarily paid in advance or in installments.

foreign　Used in law to refer to out-of-state jurisdiction as well as foreign countries.

*foster parent　Adults who take children into their homes when those children have been removed from their biological parents' home by a court are called foster parents. Foster parents are often entitled to receive payments from the state welfare department to assist them in supporting the children. Foster parents who parent disabled children may receive even higher payments. The payments usually terminate, however, if the foster parents adopt the children.

full faith and credit clause　"Full Faith and Credit shall be given in each State to the public Acts, Records, and judicial Proceedings of every other State." Art. IV, § 1, U.S. Constitution.

garnishment　A statuory procedure diverting payment of debts from a third party, typically an employer. For example, an ex-wife might be able to garnish her ex-husband's wages, so that parts of the payment go directly to her. Because the procedure is statutory, state statutes should be consulted.

guardian ad litem　Person appointed by the court to represent a minor or incompetent in a lawsuit.

*heart-balm lawsuits　Heart-balm lawsuits are those brought to soothe broken hearts and include lawsuits for alienation of affection, breach of promise to marry, criminal conversation, and seduction.

indirect contempt　*See* contempt of court.

*joint custody　Parents who don't live together have joint custody (also called *shared custody*) when they agree, or a court orders them, to share the decision-making responsibilities for, and/or physical control and custody of, their children. Joint custody can exist if the parents are divorced, separated, no longer cohabiting, or even if they never lived together. Joint custody may be joint legal custody (where the parents share in decision-making), joint physical custody (where the children spend a significant portion or half the time with each parent) or both. It is common for couples who share physical custody to also share legal custody.

　　Over 40 states have statutes which refer to joint custody. Seventeen states have written a preference for joint custody into their laws, which means that judges are supposed to award joint custody of children unless there are circumstances that make it not in the best interests of the child. Three states, by contrast, expressly disfavor joint custody awards, believing that parents who did not get along sufficiently to stay married will probably not cooperate in raising their children.

laches　The equitable equivalent of a statute of limitations. It may be used as a defense to an action in equity if the action has been unreasonably delayed to the prejudice of a party who has changed position during the delay.

*legal custody　Legal custody of a child is the right and obligation to make decisions about a child's upbringing. Decisions regarding schooling and medical and dental care, for example, are made by a parent with legal custody. In many states, courts now award joint legal custody to the parents, which means that the decision making is shared.

*legal separation   A legal separation results when the parties separate and a court rules on the division of property, alimony, child support, custody and visitation, but does not grant a divorce. This separation is also called a separation from bed and board. The money awarded for support of the spouse and children under these circumstances is often called *separate maintenance* (as opposed to alimony and child support).

Legal separation is usually a substitute for, and not a step toward, divorce. It often occurs when there is a religious objection to the divorce, or if a dependent spouse needs medical care and cannot afford it on his or her own.

legal technicians   Those who provide legal services as paralegals but independent of attorney supervision. They walk a narrow line bordering the unauthorized practice of law.

*lis pendens   Lis pendens means pending lawsuit. A lis pendens notice is a document filed in the public records of the county where particular real property is located stating that a pending lawsuit may affect the title to the property. Because nobody wants to buy real estate if its ownership is in dispute, a lis pendens notice effectively ties up the property until the case is resolved. Lis pendens notices are often filed in divorce actions when there is disagreement about selling or dividing the family home.

*lump-sum support   In a few states, a spouse may pay his or her total alimony (and occasionally child support) obligation at the time of the divorce by giving the other spouse a lump-sum payment equal to the total amount of the future monthly payments. This is also called *alimony in gross*.

malpractice suit   A negligence suit brought against someone for negligent provision of professional services. It differs from ordinary negligence suits in that the professional is held to a higher standard of care.

*marital deduction   When a person dies leaving property worth more than $600,000, the federal government requires that taxes be paid on the excess unless the property is left to a surviving spouse. In that case, under a federal estate tax deduction known as the marital deduction, no taxes need be paid.

marital property   Certain property acquired during a marriage, which is legally deemed marital property. Its principal significance concerns treatment and distribution upon divorce or death. Ownership and distribution vary from state to state.

*marital property   Most property accumulated by a married couple is called marital property. In community property states, marital property is called community property. The rules as to what constitutes marital property in non-community property states differ. Some states include all property and earnings during marriage. Others exclude gifts and inheritances from this general rule. Some states exclude certain types of property even if acquired during marriage, while others exclude improvements to property that existed before marriage.

marital settlement agreement   Called by different names; the usual manner by which divorcing parties contract to divide up their own property. Without such an agreement, the judge would be responsible for deciding who should get what.

*marriage   Marriage is the legal union of a man and a woman as husband and wife. Once two people become married to each other, their responsibilities and rights toward one another concerning property and support are defined by the laws of the state in which they live.

*marriage certificate   In order for people to be legally married, most states require that a couple undergo a wedding with a judge, justice of the peace, court clerk, or religious official (for example, priest, rabbi, or minister) and then file a marriage certificate with the proper authorities, usually the county clerk. (Usually, whoever performs the ceremony may file the marriage certificate for the couple.) The filing usually must be done within a few days (often five) after the ceremony.

*married women's property acts   Married women's property acts were 19th-century statutes enacted throughout the United States and England granting to married women, for the first time, the right to own property in their own names.

*mediation   Mediation is a non-adversarial process where a neutral person (a mediator) meets with disputing persons (often parties to a lawsuit or a threatened lawsuit) to help them settle the dispute. The mediator, however, does not have the power to impose a solution on the parties.

Mediation is often used to help a divorcing or divorced couple work out their differences concerning alimony, child support, custody, visitation, and division of property. Some lawyers and mental health professionals employ mediation as part of their practice. Eight states require mediation in custody and visitation disputes. Thirteen states encourage mediation; some states merely inform couples of the availability of mediation, while other states permit the judge to order mediation in certain circumstances. A few states have started using mediation to resolve financial issues as well.

meretricious relationship *See* cohabitation.

modification Agreement or orders with regard to custody and support may change at a later time by petitioning the court for modification.

*natural parent The term natural parent has different meanings in different contexts. With adoptions, it means the biological parents who conceive and give birth to a child, as opposed to the adoptive parents who raise the child.

In the context of artificial insemination, surrogacy, and in vitro fertilization, the natural parent is the one who provides the egg or sperm for conception, but not necessarily the one who carries the child to term or gives birth.

*necessaries Necessaries (also called necessities, necessities of life, or necessaries of life) are the articles needed to sustain life, such as food, clothing, medical care, and shelter. In all states, the law requires men to provide necessaries for their wives and children; in many states, women must provide them for their spouses and offspring. When it comes to enforcing this obligation, however, courts have been notoriously reluctant to intervene as long as the couple is living together. The barest provision of food and shelter has been found sufficient under the law.

In some states, debts incurred by a spouse for necessaries are considered to be joint debts of the spouses even if the couple is living apart but not yet divorced. This means that in most states, creditors may sue either spouse for debts incurred for necessaries by either spouse.

*no-fault divorce No-fault divorce describes any divorce where the spouse suing for divorce does not have to accuse the other of wrongdoing. Rather, the spouse can simply state that the couple no longer gets along, or that the couple has been living apart for a specified period.

Until recently, the only way a person could get a divorce was to prove that the other spouse was guilty of marital misconduct and was at fault for the marriage not working . . . . Today, all states allow divorces regardless of who is at "fault." In 12 states, including California, Michigan, Oregon, and Wisconsin, no-fault divorces have completely replaced fault divorces; in most states, however, both no-fault divorces and fault divorces can be obtained.

No-fault divorces are usually granted for reasons such as incompatibility, irreconcilable difference, or irretrievable or irremediable breakdown of the marriage. Also, some states allow incurable insanity as the basis for a no-fault divorce.

In 25 states, couples may obtain a no-fault divorce based on separation; the length of the separation required varies between six months and five years. In nine states which have separation-based divorces, separation is the only no-fault ground for divorce.

*non-custodial parent When one parent is awarded sole physical custody of a child, the other parent is referred to as the non-custodial parent. Non-custodial parents almost always have some sort of visitation arrangement with the child. Where the parents have joint physical custody (that is, the child spends near-equal amounts of time with each parent), each is considered the custodial parent when the child is with that parent.

*nunc pro tunc Nunc pro tunc literally means "now for then." Occasionally, a court or party to a divorce forgets to file the papers necessary to obtain the final decree (after the interlocutory judgment has been granted), and the result is that the divorce never becomes final. If the oversight presents a problem (for example, one party has already remarried, or there is a tax advantage to being divorced earlier), the court may agree to issue a nunc pro tunc order, which grants the final divorce retroactive to the earlier date.

*open adoption An open adoption is an adoption where the birth mother remains in contact with the adoptive parents and the child throughout the child's life. In traditional adoptions, birth and adoption records are sealed by court order, and the child and adoptive parents may never know the mother's identity.

*palimony Palimony isn't a legal term; it was coined by journalists to describe the division of property or alimony-like support given by one member of an unmarried couple to the other after they break up.

*Parental Kidnapping Prevention Act (PKPA) The Parental Kidnapping Prevention Act (28 U.S.C. § 1738A and 42 U.S.C. §§ 654, 663) is a federal statute enacted in 1980 to address childnapping by non-custodial parents and inconsistent child custody decisions made by state courts. The law provides for the maintenance of a federal parent locator service, penalties for kidnapping, and requires states to recognize and enforce the custody decisions of courts in other states, rather than make a second, and possibly inconsistent, decision.

*partition Partition means selling real property and dividing the proceeds among the joint owners. A partition action is a lawsuit brought by one owner of jointly owned real property to force its sale and split the proceeds in accordance with the state's property laws.

partition When a husband and a wife own property jointly in a form of co-ownership called *tenancy in the entireties*, a suit in partition, which would normally be available to co-owners, may not be brought. A tenancy by the entireties may only be terminated by death, divorce, or mutual conveyance by husband and wife.

*physical custody Physical custody is the right of a parent to have a child live with him or her. A parent to whom a court has granted physical custody is called the custodial parent. Some states recognize the concept of joint physical custody, where the child spends approximately half the time in each parent's home.

*post-marital agreement Contracts made between a husband and wife during their marriage are interchangeably called post-nuptial, marital, and post-marital agreements.

premarital agreement *See* antenuptial agreement.

prenuptial agreement *See* antenuptial agreement.

*presumption A fact assumed to be true under the law is called a presumption. (For example, a criminal defendant is presumed to be innocent until the prosecuting attorney proves beyond a reasonable doubt that he or she is guilty.) Presumptions are used to relieve a party from having to actually prove the truth of the fact being presumed. Once a presumption is relied on by one party, however, the other party is normally allowed to offer evidence to disprove (rebut) the presumption. (The presumption is known as a rebuttable presumption.) In essence, then, what a presumption really does is place the obligation of presenting evidence . . . concerning a particular fact on a particular party.

The law does not allow some presumptions to be disproved, no matter how strong the evidence to the contrary. These are called conclusive presumptions.

primogeniture The custom (and sometimes the law) requiring that titled estates descend to the eldest son.

*probate Probate is a legal proceeding in which a court oversees the distribution of property left when a person dies. The property is distributed according to the will, or, where there is no will, according to state intestate succession laws. Probate proceedings—even uncontested ones—are lengthy, because they involve determining all the assets and liabilities of the deceased, and paying debts, death taxes, lawyers, accountants, appraisers, and court fees.

*psychological parent An adult who is not legally responsible for the care, custody, and support of a child, but who has established a significant emotional bond with the child such that termination of the contact between them would be detrimental to the child, is referred to by the courts in some states as the child's psychological parent. A few courts give psychological parents visitation rights with the children.

public adoption *See* agency adoption.

*putative father A putative father is the man named the father of a child born to unwed parents, but for whom paternity has not yet been established. Many states apply a conclusive presumption that the husband is the father of any child conceived by or born to his wife during marriage. This may prevent a putative father from proving that he is the father, even where blood tests show a 99.85 percent likelihood of his paternity. Generally, these statutes permit only the husband or the wife to raise the issue of paternity and then only in rare situations.

*putative marriage   When two people reasonably and honestly think that they are married, but for some technical reason are not (for example, the clergyperson who married them was not capable of performing a marriage), the couple is said to have a putative (meaning "reputed" or "supposed") marriage. In virtually all situations, the law treats putative marriages the same as any valid marriage. A putative marriage need not be "formalized," though the couple may do so by repeating the marriage ceremony.

*putative spouse   A person who reasonably but erroneously thinks he or she is married is called a putative spouse. If one spouse believes the marriage is valid while the other knows it is not, the innocent or putative (meaning "reputed" or "supposed") spouse is entitled to the legal rights and privileges normally enjoyed by a regularly married spouse (for example, the right to alimony or property division). The guilty spouse (the one who knew the marriage was not valid) may not have these same rights.

*quasi-community property   Quasi means "like." Quasi-community property is a term used in only California and Arizona. It refers to the property accumulated by a married couple living in a noncommunity property state when the couple later moves to California or Arizona. (Property accumulated in another community property state during a marriage already is and remains community property when the couple moves to California or Arizona.)

recrimination   A defense used by one who is sued for divorce on the grounds of adultery, claiming that the other party also engaged in adultery. Under recrimination, if both partners to a marriage were adulterers, the divorce could be denied.

rehabilitative alimony   A modern form of alimony, ordinarily in the form of monthly payments of short duration.

res judicata   Literally means "the thing has been decided." An affirmative defense which argues that

the issues of a case that have been adjudicated may not be litigated again.

retainer   When used in connection with hiring an attorney, refers to an amount paid in advance to "retain" the attorney, i.e., make the attorney the agent of the client.

seduction   A cause of action based on a man's enticing a chaste woman into sexual intercourse without the use of force.

*separate maintenance   In some states, a spouse may obtain separate maintenance (alimony) from her husband while she lives apart from him, even though no divorce has been granted.

*separate property   In all states, a married person is permitted to treat certain types of earnings and assets as his or her separate property. This means that the property can be disposed of (sold, given away, left in a will) without the consent of the other spouse, and upon divorce the property is not divided under the state's property distribution laws, but rather is kept by the spouse who owns it. By contrast, most property accumulated during marriage is called marital property. Marital property in most states is divided equally or equitably (fairly) upon divorce.

In community property states, Arizona, California, Idaho, Louisiana, Nevada, New Mexico, Texas, and Washington, and in Wisconsin (a modified community property state), the following is considered separate property:

- property accumulated by a spouse before marriage;
- property accumulated during marriage with pre-marital earnings or with the proceeds of the sale of pre-marital property;
- gifts directed to only one spouse, whenever received;
- inheritances, whenever received; and
- property acquired after permanent separation.

In equitable distribution states (all the states not listed above except Mississippi), the laws usually define most earnings and property acquired during marriage as marital property. Some property is separate, however, including:

- property accumulated by a spouse before marriage;

- gifts directed to only one spouse, whenever received; and
- inheritances, whenever received.

In the common law property state (Mississippi), all property is the separate property of the acquiring spouse unless a document showing title to property indicates otherwise. This means that the court has no authority to divide that property on divorce.

*separation agreement   If a couple agrees to all the terms of a legal separation, or agrees to live apart for a lengthy period of time in contemplation of divorce, the parties often write and sign a separation agreement which settles the property, custody, alimony, and child support issues between them. The agreement should be presented to the court for approval if it is part of a legal separation. The agreement becomes part of the legal separation order and does away with the necessity of having a trial on the issues covered by the agreement. It serves the same purpose as a divorce agreement except that the couple does not obtain a divorce at that time. The term separation agreement is also used to refer to agreements made by couples living apart which are later incorporated into divorce agreements.

shared custody   *See* joint custody.

specific performance   Contract remedy that asks the court to order a party to the contract to perform its obligation(s) under the contract.

surrogate motherhood contracts   Contracts in which a woman agrees to carry a baby and, after birth, give it up to the contracting parties, usually a husband-and-wife couple. The baby is produced by artificial insemination with the husband's sperm or by implanting a fertilized ovum of the adopting mother. The famous *Baby M* case focused national attention on the problems with this sort of contract and led many states to enact strict laws governing them.

tenancy by the entirety   Form of co-ownership of property that can be held only by husband and wife. It has a right of survivorship (if one spouse dies, the other owns the property). States recognizing this ancient tenancy often encounter problems with creditors. This tenancy is destroyed by divorce or death but is not subject to a suit in partition, as are other forms of co-ownership.

*tenancy by the entirety   Tenancy by the entirety is a way married couples can hold title to property in some states. Tenancy by the entirety is very similar to joint tenancy; upon the death of one of the spouses, the property automatically passes to the surviving spouse, regardless of will provisions to the contrary. Unlike joint tenancy, however, one person cannot unilaterally sever the tenancy by the entirety.

*tender years doctrine   In the past, most states provided that custody of children of tender years (about five and under), had to be awarded to the mother when parents divorced. This rule has been rejected in most states, or relegated to the role of tie-breaker when both parents request custody, are fit to have custody, and the children are pre-school age. In many areas, the trend in this situation is toward joint custody.

trust   An agreement, recognized by the law, whereby property may be given by a donor to a trustee, who manages the property on behalf of a third party called a *beneficiary*. One early form of trust was a *separate estate*, which fathers often set up for their daughters so that the son-in-law would not control the property.

Uniform Marriage and Divorce Act (UMDA)

A product of the National Conference of Commissioners on Uniform State Laws. Like other uniform laws published by this body, the UMDA is unofficial unless and until adopted by a state legislature. Nevertheless, as a state proposal for family law, it represents an up-to-date view of the law of this area and is persuasive authority in cases where existing statutes and cases do not cover an issue confronting a court.

INDEX

NOTE: Italicized page numbers refer to non-text material. Italicized page numbers following the word "defined" refer to definitions placed in the margins of the pages referred.

A

A mensa et thoro. See Divorce *a mensa et thoro*
ABA. *See* American Bar Association
Abandonment, 53, 365, 419, 442
Ability to pay, 296, 309, 319
Abortion, 44, 45, 56, 76
Abuse of discretion, 253, 412
  custody awards, 354, 358
  defined, *253*
Adoption, 417–18
  adult, *451*
  approval factors, 429
    race, 429, 432–35
    religion, 4, 429–32
  blood relatives, 419
  child support and, 317
  effect, 435
  equitable, 437–41
  foster parents, 419
  history of, 54, 418
  legal, 419
  natural parents, 435, 442
    consent, 419, *451*
    termination of rights, 74, 418, 420
  parties to, 418–26
  restrictions, 57–58, 418, 435
  single parent, 4
  stepchild, 419, 435, *451*
  strangers, 420
  surrogacy contracts. *See* Surrogacy contracts
  unmarried fathers, 420

Adultery, 54, *197*, 354, 359
  as basis for divorce, 49, 50, 53, 196
Adversary system, 10, *11*
  role in divorce, 25, 53, 68
AFDC. *See* Aid to Families with Dependent Children
Affidavits. *See* Financial affidavits
Agency adoption, 420
Agreement to marry, 219
Aid to Families with Dependent Children (AFDC), 325
Albiston, Catherine R., 413
Alderson v. Alderson, 241–43
Alienation of affections, 47, 200, 201
  defined, *47*
Alimony, 50, 319. *See also* Spousal support
  ability to pay, 296, 309
  availability after annulment, 88, 100
  cohabitation and, 299, 302
  defined, 288–89
  discretion in award, 289–90
  enforcement, 308
  fault, 299
  historical reasons for, 252, 267, 288
  in gross, 289, 290
  lump sum, 289, 290, 292
  modification, 290, 292, 308–312, 364
  need for, 294–96, 299, 309

  pendente lite, 289
  periodic, 289
  permanent, 289, 297–98, 300
  rehabilitative, 101, 121, 289, 299, 300
    defined, *102*
  reimbursement, 304–307
  statutory guidelines for, 296–97
  taxation, 289, 294, 307–308, *309*
  temporary, 289
  termination upon remarriage, 101, 299–304
Alimony in gross. *See* Alimony
Alimony pendente lite. *See* Alimony
Allen, Woody, 2
Alternating custody. *See* Custody
Alternative lifestyles. *See* Family
American Bar Association (ABA), 23
Amicus curiae brief, 358
  defined, *359*
Anders v. Anders, 99
Annulment, 50, 53
  childbearing and, 96
  consequences of, 99–101
  defined, 85
  distinguished from divorce, 86–87
  existing defect criterion, 86
  history of, 86, 288
  retroactive invalidation, 88
Antenuptial agreements, 53
  effect, 121, 127

enforcement, 118, 120–22, *150*, 189
consent, 134
contemplation of divorce, 118
contract status, 121, 127, 153
disclosure, 131–34, *146*, *150*
drafting, 127–39
fairness, 128–31
legal acceptance, 118, 128, 139
need for, 123
promotion of divorce, 139–42
provisions generally, 120–22
requirements for validity, 118, 122, 127, 128
sample, 147–50
support, 142–43, *146*
voluntariness, 134
waiver of rights, 135–36, *150*
Appearance of impropriety, 33, 34
Arden v. State Bar of California, 29–31
Arnold, Roseanne Barr, *62*
Artificial insemination, 427
Assets. *See* Financial assets; Property
Attorney/client privilege, 24
defined, *25*
Attorneys
antenuptial agreement drafting, 127–39
biases, 11, 45
role in divorces, 10, 68, 69, 70, 71, 281–82
contract drafting, 159
supervision of paralegals, 11
Attorneys' fees, 25, 26, 32–33

B

Baby M, In re, *4*, *416*, 427–28, 462
Back v. Back, 93
Bankruptcy, *309*
Barbara A. v. John G., 35–36
Bear v. Reformed Mennonite Church, 201
Beck v. Beck, 382, 387–97
Bell v. Bell, 302
Bennett v. Jeffreys, 380
Berko, Malcolm, 321
Best interests of the child, 24, 54–55, 442
adoption standard, 429
defined, *25*
custody standard, *114*, 349, 351, 353–58, 369, 381

Betrothal, 47, 48, 197
Bigamous marriage, 88–89, 101, *113*, 231
Bigamy, 50
Bilowit v. Dolitsky, 87–88
Blackstone, William, 49, 50
Blood relationship. *See* Kindred, degrees of
Booth v. Booth, 280–81
Boswell v. Boswell, 219–20
Bradwell, Myra, 47
Brancoveanu v. Brancoveanu, 260–61
Brazina v. Brazina, 158
Breach of contract, 163
defined, *162*
Breach of promise to marry, 47, 197
defined, *47*
Brooks v. Brooks, *117*, 118–119
Brown v. Brown, 212
Business partnership. *See* Cohabitation; Marriage as partnership
Butler, In re Estate of, 231–33
Byers v. Mount Vernon Mills, Inc., 225
Byrne, In re, 136

C

Canon law, 46, 49, *86*, 226–27
defined, *47*
Canons of Ethics, 23
Capacity, *114*, 219, 222
Case handling, 15
Catalano v. Catalano, 7–8, 91–92, 221
Changed circumstances, 309–12
Child abuse, 64, 65–68, 74, 75, 442
Child custody. *See* Custody
Child-parent suit, 4, 74–75
Child support, 288, 294
ability to pay, 319
agreements re, 143, *146*, *163*
arrearages, 325–27
duty of, 316–19, 365
education, 320–23
enforcement, 15, 77, 123, 325–27
contempt of court, 159
interstate, 335–38
guidelines for, 327–34
schedules, 330–34
health care, 324

modification, 166, 309, 325, 364
need, 319
remarriage and, 324–25
taxation, 307
waiver of, 319
Children
legal representation of, 10, 350, *457*
as property, 54, 351
protection of, 10, 43, 54, 352
status and rights, 53–54, 74–75, 352
support. *See* Child support
Choice of law clauses, 122
Clean hands doctrine, 102, 310
defined, *102*
Client interviews, 12
Client relations, 34–36
Clinton, Bill, *314*
Clinton, Hillary Rodham, 75, *314*
Cohabitation, 237–39
alimony and, 299, 302
element of common law marriage, 219
property disputes, 237, 240–45
state policies, 243–44
Cohabitation agreements, 53, 237, 238, 240, 243, 244–45
Coke, Sir Edward, 50, *50*
Collateral attack, defined, *166*
Commingle, 262
defined, *262*
Common law, 46, 50, 203, 210
Common law marriage, *219*, *222*, *226*, 231
binding nature of, 218
conflict of laws, 221–26
equivalents of, 226
requirements, 219
states recognizing, *223*, 233
Common law states. *See* Equitable distribution states
Community property, 210, 240, 261–65
cohabitant's rights, 245
defined, 121
professional licenses, 275–76
Community property states, 227, 257, 261
map, *258*
treatment of property status, 269
Competence, 10
Conception, assisted, 73

Condonation, 53
  defined, *53*
Confidentiality, 24
Conflict of interests, 24–25
  communication with opposing
    party, 33
  defined, *25*
  simultaneous (multiple)
    representation, 25–32, 68
Conflict of laws, 221–26
Conscionability, *114*, 129
Consensual union, 218
  defined, *219*
Consent, *114*, 134. *See also*
  Adoption
Consideration, 154, 156
Consortium, 190
  defined, *193*
Constructive trust, 131
Consummation of marriage, 86,
  99
Contempt of court, 13, 159, 308,
  364
Contingency fee, 32
  defined, *33*
Contract, marriage as. *See*
  Marriage
Contracts, 134
  antenuptial. *See* Antenuptial
    agreements
  attorneys' fees. *See* Attorneys'
    fees
  cohabitation. *See* Cohabitation
    agreements
  modification, 163
  surrogacy. *See* Surrogacy
    contracts
  void versus voidable, 88
Contractual capacity, 86
Conway v. Dana, 316
Counseling, 71
County adoption. *See* Adoption
Court orders, 163
Courts of equity, 46, 50
Coverture, 210, 262
  defined, *262*
Criminal conversation, 47, 50,
  197, 198–200
  defined, *47*
Criminal law, 48
Cruelty, 53
Custody
  alternating, 353
  child's wishes, 354
  divided, 353

factors in decision, 350–51,
    355, 397–98
  parental misconduct, 359–62,
    373, 397
history of, 54, 351–52
joint, 352, 353, 382–97, 412–13
legal, 352
modification, 166, 361–63
mother favored, 54, 351,
    353–54, 397, *408*, 412
nonparents, 369–70
physical, 352
PKPA, 371–72
presumptions re, 359
siblings, 354
sole, 353, 413
split, 353
standards for decisions,
    353–54, 367, 381
types of, 352–53
UCCJA, 370–71, *371*
visitation, 54, 166, 363–64

D

David M. v. Margaret M., *349*,
    397, 398–411
Davis, Junior Lewis, 22
Davis, Mary Sue, 22
Dawley, In re Marriage of, 121
DeBoer v. Schmidt, 442–46
Degree, defined, 50
DeLorean v. DeLorean, 122, 127,
    131
Dependency proceedings, 441–42
Depositions, 14
Desertion, 50, 53
Dexter v. Dexter, 154–56
Disclosure. *See* Antenuptial
    agreements
Discovery, 14
Discretion, 252–55, 260, 282,
    399, 442
  abuse of. *See* Abuse of
    discretion
  alimony awards, 289–90
  custody awards, 354, 355, 381
  defined, *253*
  statutory limitation, 255–56,
    330–31
Dissipation, 280
Dissolution of marriage. *See*
  Divorce
  defined, *5*
Divided custody. *See* Custody
Divorce

annulment distinguished, 86–87
asset distribution. *See* Property
    rights
children and, 9–10
decree. *See* Divorce decree
defined, *5*
grounds for, 86, *113*
history of, 44, 46, 49–53
as legal matter, 4, 5–6
legislative, 50, 52
marital settlement agreement.
    See Marital settlement
    agreement
mediation, 68–71
no-fault. *See* No-fault divorce
noncompliance, 159
perceptions of, 266–67
promotion. *See* Antenuptial
    agreements
property settlements. *See*
    Property rights; Property
    settlement agreements
representation of both spouses,
    25, *257*
stress of, 10–11
time of effect, 88
Divorce a mensa et thoro, 49–50,
    53, 288
Divorce a vinculo matrimonii,
    49, 50, 53, 86, 288
Divorce decree, 159, 162–63
  appeal, 253
  modification, 163, 166–67
Domestic relations. *See* Family
  law
  defined, *9*
  questionnaire, 17–20
Donohue v. Getman, 325, 328–30
Dower, 267
*Drummond v. Fulton County
    Department of Family &
    Childrens Services*, 435
Duty to support. *See* Alimony;
    Child support

E

Educational costs, 64, 319,
    320–23
Emancipation, defined, *255*
Embryos, legal status of, 22
Equal protection, 288, 316, 350,
    351, 365, 429, 432
Equitable adoption. *See* Adoption
Equitable distribution, 252, 255,
    258, 262, 282

Equitable distribution states, 210, 257–65
  treatment of property status, 269
Equity considerations in family law cases, 6, 46, 102, 130, 218, 252
Essentials of marriage. *See* Marriage as contract
Estoppel, 231, 437
Ethical issues, 22, 23–39, 68
Ethics opinions, 27

F

Fadgen v. Lenkner, 198
Fahrer v. Fahrer, 300–302
Family
  defined, *4*, 4, 45, 72–73
  legal intervention in domestic matters, 3–4, 43–44, 72
  model, 9, 45, 47, 56, 75, 188
  nontraditional, 57, 72, 188, 189, 238
  as societal unit, 5, 200
Family-expense statutes, 196
Family law
  attorney's role, 11, 23, 63, 281–82
  constitutional questions, 72
  history of, 43–47
  judicial interpretation, 72
  legislation, 72
  practice of, 5, 11–13, 281–82
  scope and issues, 4–5, 9–10, 44, 46, 63–78, 381
Farrow, Mia, 2
Fault
  parental, 75, 349, 359–61
  spousal, 121, 203, 257, 260, 282, 297, 299, 310
Federal Parent Locator Service, 372
Fee tail, 54
  defined, *55*
Fees, attorney. *See* Attorneys' fees
Fiduciary, defined, *123*
Fiduciary relationship, 35, 127, 131–32
Filius nullius, *325*
Financial affidavits, 14, 170–74
Financial assets
  disclosure of, 276
  discovery of, 14, *269*
  valuation, 276–77, *307*
First Amendment, 429

Fitness, parental, 354
Fixed fee, 32
  defined, *33*
Florida Bar v. Furman, 13–14
Folber & Graham, 413
Foreign, 222
  defined, *222*
Fornication, 53
Foster parents, 419
Foster v. Alston, 380
Fourteenth Amendment, 57, 197, 288, 316, 350, 351, 365, 429
Francis, In re Marriage of, 304, 305–307
Fraud, 86, 94–99
Fraud on the court, 99
Fried v. Fried, 309
Full faith and credit clause, 222, 335, 370, 371
  defined, *222*
Fundermann v. Mickelson, 200
Furman, Rosemary, 13–14, 36

G

Garduno v. Garduno, 233–37
Garges, In re, 225
Garnishment, 308
  defined, *309*
Gates v. Foley, 190–92
Gender equality, 48, 55, 123, 136, 212, 252, 268
  alimony and, 288, 297
  child custody, 349, 350, 351, 365, 381
  child support duty, 316
Geyer, In re, 128, 136–39, 144
Glickman v. Collins, 157
Goldman, In re, 430–32
Goldstein, Freud, & Solnit, 412
Golub v. Golub, 275
Graham, Bob, 13, 14
Graham v. Graham, 317
Grant v. Superior Court, 225, 226
Gregory K., 74, 75
Grimaldi family, *84*
Guardian ad litem, 50, *384*, *457*
  defined, *351*

H

Hague Convention on the Civil Aspects of International Child Abduction, 372
Hawn, Goldie, 218
Healthcare costs, 64, 320, 324

Heartbalm lawsuits, 47–48, 196–200
Helms v. Franciscus, 380
Hewitt v. Hewitt, 243, 244
Hick ex rel. Feiock v. Feiock, 327
Hill v. Hill, 208–209
Home state, 371
Homemakers, 256, 258, 266
Homosexuals, 57
  adoption, 57–58
  marriage, 4, 63–64, 96, *113*, 189
Horner v. Graves, *190*
Hourly fees, 32–33

I

Illegitimacy. *See* Legitimacy
Immunity. *See* Interspousal immunity
Impotence, 96–99
  as ground for annulment, 86, 96, *114*
Incest, 64, 65–68
Incestuous marriages, 89, 101, *113*, *114*
Incompatibility, 53
Incorporation, 159–66
Indirect contempt. *See* Contempt of court
Infertility, 50
Inheritance, 435, 437
Insurance, *325*
Intentional infliction of emotional distress, 201
Interrogatories, 14
Interspousal immunity, 203–209
  defined, *203*
Interviews, 12
Intestate, 228
Invasion of privacy, 201

J

Jennison, Judith B., 413
Jersey Shore Medical Center-Fitkin Hospital v. Estate of Baum, 194–96
Johnston, Janet R., 413
Johnston v. Johnston, 163–66, 169
Joint custody. *See* Custody
Jones v. Daly, 240
Jordan v. Jordan, *86*, 94, 95
Judicial discretion. *See* Discretion
Jurisdiction, 370–71, 372

K

Karin T. v. Michael T., 58–59
Kinship, degrees of, 7, 50, 86
  void marriage, 89, 91
Kirchberg v. Feenstra, 210–11
Krause, Harry, 320, 326–27, 412
Krauss, Michael, *286*

L

Laches, 102
  defined, *102*
Latchkey children, 64
Law
  intervention in domestic
      affairs, 3, 5, 8, 77, 197
    adoption, 418
    child support, 70, 252,
        441–42
    divorce, 52, 53, 252–53, 255
    marriage contract, 117, 189
  relationship to behavior in
      society, 45, 189–90
Legal assistants. *See* Paralegals
Legal capacity. *See* Capacity
Legal competence, 10
Legal custody. *See* Custody
Legal separation. *See* Separation
Legal technicians, 13, 24
  defined, *25*
Legitimacy, 50, 218
  annulment and, 85, 99
  common law marriage, 219
  rights of offspring, 54, *113*
Leo, John, 78–79
Lepis v. Lepis, 309–10
Levie, In re Estate of, 228–30
License
  marriage. *See* Marriage license
  mediators, 70
Litigation, role in shaping law,
    252
Lively, Edwin and Virginia, 64,
    65
Livesay v. Hilley, 359, 362–63
Low v. Low, 292–93
Luepnitz, Deborah Anne, 413
Lump sum alimony. *See* Alimony
Lump-sum support. *See* Alimony
Lunden, Joan, 266, *286*
Lutgert v. Lutgert, 134–35
Lynch v. Lynch, 263–65

M

Maccoby, Eleanor E., 413
Magruder v. Magruder, 298

Mahan v. Mahan, 93–94
Maine, Sir Henry, 6, 92, 117
Maintenance, 289. *See* Alimony
Majority, age of, 10, 86
Malpractice suit, defined, 37
Maples, Marla, *250*, 266
Marital property, *150*
  defined, *5*, 256
  dissipation, 280
  distribution, 5
Marital settlement agreement, 45,
    156, 319
  child custody provisions, 352
  defined, *45*
Marriage
  annulment. *See* Annulment
  common law. *See* Common
      law marriage
  as contract. *See* Marriage as
      contract
  dissolution of. *See* Divorce
  history of, 46–47
  homosexuals. *See* Homosexuals
  legal obligations of spouses, 5
  legal regulation of, 4, 5
  legal protection of, 200–201
  as partnership. *See* Marriage as
      partnership
  putative. *See* Putative marriage
  reasons for, 46, 86–87, 96, 188
  status of relationship, 217–19
  validity, 218, 221–22, 226
  void. *See* Void marriage
  voidable. *See* Voidable
      marriage
Marriage as contract, 5, 8–9, 47,
    53, 188
  antenuptial contracts. *See*
      Antenuptial agreements
  essentials of, 87, 94
  postnuptial contracts. *See*
      Postnuptial agreements
  sham, 99
  validity, 86, 88, 154. *See also*
      Annulment; Divorce; Void
      marriage; Voidable
      marriage
Marriage as partnership, 9, 52,
    188, 209–13
  acceptance of model, 258
  spousal roles, 188–89, 210,
      212, 258
  weakness of model, 265, 268
Marriage counseling, 71
Marriage license, 217, 222

Marriage settlements, 56, 118
Married women's property acts,
    47, 55, 56, 203
Martin v. Farber, 130–31
Marvin, Lee, *216*, 240
Marvin, Michelle Triola, *216*, 240
Marvin v. Marvin, *216*, 240, 243,
    244, 246, 253–54
Mason v. Mason, 231
Massachusetts rule, 94
Mayer v. Mayer, 382–87
Maynard v. Hill, 8–9
McCarty v. McCarty, 268
McConkey v. McConkey, 100–101
McDowell v. McDowell, 269–71
McGowan v. McGowan, 274
McQuiddy v. McQiddy, 327
Mediation, 68–71
Mental incompetence, 90
Meretricious relationship. *See*
    Cohabitation
Merger, 159–66
M.H.B. v. H.T.B., 317–19
Military pension. *See* Pensions
Miller, In re, 212–13
Mnookin, Robert R., 413
Model Code of Professional
    Responsibility, 23
Model Rules of Professional
    Conduct, 24, 26, 34
Modification, 163
  alimony. *See* Alimony
  child custody. *See* Custody
  defined, *162*
Monogamy, 46
Motion to dismiss divorce
    complaint, *90*
Motion to vacate marital home,
    267
Moye v. Moye, 354, 355–58
Multiple representation. *See*
    Conflict of interests

N

Nancy S. v. Michele G., 438–41
National Association of Black
    Social Workers, 432
National Conference of
    Commissioners on Uniform
    State Laws, 258, 335, 418
Natural parent
  consent to adoption, 419–20,
      451
  custody rights, 364–68, 369,
      413, 427

termination of rights, 74, 420, 435

Necessaries, 33, 193, 196, 316, 319, 320

Need, 294–96, 309, 319

Neglect, 442

Neilson v. Neilson, 140–42, 257

No-fault divorce, 27, 45, 256
  child custody and, 54–55
  development of, 52, 53, 299
  goals of, 68

Noghrey, In re Marriage of, 140

Noncustodial parent. *See* Child support

Nunnally v. Trust Company Bank, 436–37

O

O'Brien v. O'Brien, 272–73, 275, 281, 304, 307

O'Connor Bros. Abalone Co. v. Brando, 302–304

Oedekoven v. Oedekoven, 160

Office of Child Support Enforcement, 325

Onassis, Aristotle, *116*

Onassis, Jacqueline Kennedy, *116*

O'Neil v. Schuckardt, 201–203

Orr v. Orr, 288

P

Painter v. Bannister, 369–70

Pajak v. Pajak, 124–26

Palimony, 240

Palmore v. Sidoti, 433–35, *435*

Paralegals
  attorney supervision, 11
  confidentiality and, 24
  role in divorce cases, 11, 64
  role in family law cases, 11–15
  romance with client, 35
  unauthorized practice of law, 13–14, 36–39

Parens patriae, 74, 75

Parental Kidnapping Prevention Act (PKPA), 371–72

Parental responsibility. *See* Custody

Parental rights, 5, 420
  termination, 74, 75, 441–42

Parenthood, 4, 73–74

Parillo v. Parillo, 359–61

Parkinson v. J.&S. Tool Co., 226

Partition, 88
  defined, *88*

Partnership model of marriage. *See* Marriage as partnership

Paternity, determining, *457*

Pensions
  cohabiting partners, 237
  military, 37, 268
  spousal right to, 223, 225, 226, 268–69
  valuation, 277

People v. Liberta, 48–49

Per verbi praesenti, *222*

Periodic alimony. *See* Alimony

Permanent alimony. *See* Alimony

Petition for modification, 308

Pfohl v. Pfohl, 295

Physical custody. *See* Custody

Piscopo v. Piscopo, 277–79

PKPA. *See* Parental Kidnapping Prevention Act

Pleadings, 13

Polestar, *25*, 353

Ponder v. Graham, 51–52

Posner v. Posner, 132

Post-marital agreements. *See* Postnuptial agreements

Postnuptial agreements
  as change to contract, 153–54
  child support provisions, *163*
  consideration, 154, 156
  defined, 157
  drafting, *167*
  property settlement agreement. *See* Property settlement agreements
  sample, 175–85
  separation agreement, 156, 157. *See also* Property settlement agreements
  types, 156–57
  validity, 157, 189

Posttrial tasks, 15

Powell v. Powell, 102

Premarital agreements. *See* Antenuptial agreements

Prenuptial agreements. *See* Antenuptial agreements

Presumptions
  custody, 353, 354, 359, 382
  legitimacy, 218
  marriage validity, 86, 88–89, 91, 218, 230–31, 233
  paternity, 73, *457*

Pretrial matters, 14

Primary caregiver rule, 349, 397–411, 412

Primogeniture, 54
  defined, *55*

Prince Charles, *186*

Princess Diana, *186*

Privacy rights, 56, 197, 201

Professional licenses, 4, 271–76, 304

Property
  change in nature, 269
  community. *See* Community property
  dissipation, 280
  distribution at divorce, 252, 255, 267
  identification, 262, 265
  marital. *See* Marital property
  pensions as, 268–69
  professional licenses, 271–76, 304
  separate. *See* Separate property
  state variations, 251
  valuation, 256, 276–79, 282

Property rights, 46
  cohabiting partners, 237
  distribution per agreement, 121, *150*
  married women, 47, 55

Property settlement agreements, 282, 299
  enforcement, 159
  incorporation in divorce decree, 162
  judicial acceptance, 118
  judicial approval, 159
  merger, *159*
  terms of divorce, 156, 159
  waivers, 308

Psychological parent, 354, *384*, 412

Public adoption. *See* Adoption

Public assistance, 142, 316, 325

Public policy, 45, 46, 71, 77, 158, *190*
  alimony, 288
  breach of promise to marry, 197
  child support, 316
  cohabitation, 244
  common law marriage, 222
  gender equality, 252
  nature and changes, 189–90
  postnuptial agreements, 156, 157, 308
  social values, 189–90

Pulitzer, Peter, *348*

Pulitzer, Roxanne, *348*

Putative marriage, 88, 226–30, 231, 233
Putative spouse, *114*

Q

Quilloin v. Walcott, 421–22

R

Rape, 48, 197
Ratification, 102
Read v. Read, 196
Reagan, Nancy Davis, *42*, 75
Reagan, Ronald, *42*
Reconciliation, 36, 71
Recrimination, 53
   defined, *53*
Rehabilitative alimony. *See* Alimony
Reimbursement alimony. *See* Alimony
Relation back, 219
Remarriage, 53, 86, *86*
   child support and, 324–25
   termination of alimony, 101
Renshaw v. Heckler, 222, 223–25, 226
Reproductive rights, 76–77
Repute, 219
Res judicata, defined, *166*
Retainer, 32
   defined, *33*
Revised Uniform Reciprocal Enforcement of Support Act (RURESA), 335, 341–46
Reynolds v. Reynolds, 94, 95
Riegler v. Riegler, 321–23, 339
Ripley v. Ewell, 192–93
Rivers, Joan, 245
Robinson, In re Marriage of, 290–92
Roe v. Wade, 45, 56
Romantic involvement with client, 34–36
Rosenberger Estate, 219
Rumbaugh v. Rumbaugh, 323
RURESA. *See* Revised Uniform Reciprocal Enforcement of Support Act
Russell, Kurt, 218
Ruth v. Fletcher, 423–26

S

S.A.V. v. K.G.V., 204–206
Schilling v. Bedford County Memorial Hospital, Inc., 193–94

Schwartz, Laura, 430
Seduction, 47, 197
   defined, *47*
Separate estates, 56
Separate maintenance, 288, 289
Separate property, *150*, 256, 261–62, 269
Separate property states. *See* Equitable distribution states
Separation, 53, *114*
   alimony and, 100
   intention to live apart, 157–58
Separation agreements. *See also* Property settlement agreements
   defined, 156, 157
   drafting, 162–63
   encouragement of divorce, 156–58
   merger and incorporation, 159–66
Sexual abuse of children, 65–68
Sexual harassment, 34–35
Sexual relations
   alimony and, 299
   legal rules regarding, 4, 44, 46–47
   refusal of, 96
Sexual services, compensation for, 238, 240, 243, 245
Sham marriage, 99
Shared custody. *See* Joint custody
Significant impairment, 442
Simultaneous representation. *See* Conflict of interests
Singer v. Hara, 188
Smith v. Lewis, 37–39
Social Security. *See* Pensions
Sole custody. *See* Custody
Sousa v. Freitas, 230
Specific performance, 163
   defined, *162*
Split custody. *See* Custody
Spousal immunity. *See* Interspousal immunity
Spousal support, 166, 193. *See also* Alimony; Antenuptial agreements
Spouses, 24–25, 203–209
Stanley v. Illinois, 420, 421
Stare decisis, defined, *193*
State ex rel. McDonnell v. McCutcheon, 336–38
State law conflicts, 221–26
State v. Clark, 196

State v. Winder, 36, 37
Status or contract, 6, 92, 117
Statute of Frauds, *123*, *146*
Statute of limitations, 102
Step relationships, 124, 317, 419–20
Sterility, 86, 96
Stewart v. Hampton, 89, 102
Stregack v. Moldofsky, 132–34
Strock v. Presnell, 201
Substitution of judgment, 253–54
   defined, *253*
Suggs' Estate, In re, 219, 220
Suggs v. Norris, 239, 240, 243
Support, defined, 288
Surrogacy contracts, 4, 426–28
   defined, *4*
   state treatment of, 427, *460*
Surviving spouse, 91, 121
Sweeney, In re Estate of, 160–62
Swift v. Swift, 167

T

T. v. M., 96–99
Taxation, 289, 294, 307–308
Temporary alimony. *See* Alimony
Temporary orders, 14
Tenancy by the entirety, defined, *94*
Tender years doctrine, 54, 349, 353–54, 397
Termination of marriage. *See* Annulment; Divorce
Thomas, Clarence, 34
Tort suits against spouse, 203–209
Tower, In re Marriage of, 253, 254–55
Townsend v. Townsend, 206
Transmutation, 269
Trial, 15
Trump, Donald, 129, *152*, *250*, 266
Trump, Ivana, 129, *152*, *250*, 266
Trust, 56, 118
   defined, *56*

U

UCCJA. *See* Uniform Child Custody Jurisdiction Act
UMDA. *See* Uniform Marriage and Divorce Act
UMPA. *See* Uniform Marital Property Act
Unauthorized practice of law, 13–14, 36–39

Uniform Adoption Act, *418*, 418, 448–51
Uniform Child Custody Jurisdiction Act (UCCJA), 370–71, *371*, 375–79
Uniform Marital Property Act (UMPA), 258
Uniform Marriage and Divorce Act (UMDA), *99*, 104–14, 167–69, 258
  alimony, 296–97
  child custody, 355, 361
  invalid marriages, 88
  legitimacy of children, 99–100
  putative marriage, 227
Uniform Parentage Act, 452–57
Uniform Premarital Agreement Act, 128, *129*, 142, 145–46
Uniform Putative and Unknown Fathers Act (1988), 80–82
Uniform Reciprocal Enforcement of Support Act (URESA), 335–38, *336*
Uniform Status of Children of Assisted Conception Act, 426, 458–60
Uniformed Services Former Spouse's Protection Act (USFSPA), 269

Unmarried fathers
  adoption, 420–22
  custody, 354, 365–68, 413
  duty of child support, 317, 335, 365
URESA. *See* Uniform Reciprocal Enforcement of Support Act
USFSPA. *See* Uniformed Services Former Spouse's Protection Act

V

Vaughn v. Hufnagel, 225–26
Visitation. *See* Custody
Void, defined, 85, 88
Void marriages, 49, 50, 53, 85
  effect of, 101
  types, 88–89, 94
Void versus voidable, 88, 101
Voidable, defined, 88
Voidable marriages, *114*
  effect of, 101
  failure to meet requirements, 94
  fraud as basis, 94–99
  parental consent, 94
Voluntariness, 134

W

Wadlington, 160

Waiver of rights, 135
Wallerstein, Judith S., 413
Warren v. State, 55
Waskin v. Waskin, 310–12
Watts v. Watts, 244
Welfare. *See* Public assistance
Weyrauch and Katz, 45, 412
Whitehead, Mary Beth, *416*
Widow's share. *See* Surviving spouse
Wills, 121, 228
Womack v. Eldridge, 426
Women's rights, 47, 49, 55–56, 75, 189, 203
  contracts, 123, 136
  lawsuits, 203, 206
  marriage, 192–93, 200–201
  reproduction, 76–77
Worden v. Worden, 365–68
Worker's compensation. *See* Pensions

Z

Zysk v. Zysk, 206–207